the
UNDERSIDE
of American History: Other Readings

Fourth Edition

Volume I: To 1877

Edited by
Thomas R. Frazier
The Bernard M. Baruch College of The City University of New York

Harcourt Brace Jovanovich, Inc.
New York   San Diego   Chicago   San Francisco   Atlanta
London   Sydney   Toronto

To the peacemakers

ILLUSTRATION CREDITS

  8–9: (top and bottom) Library of Congress
128–29: Library of Congress
220–21: (top) New York Public Library
        (bottom) New-York Historical Society
348–49: (top) Smithsonian Institution, Bureau of Ethnology
        (bottom) Association of American Railroads

Copyright © 1982, 1978, 1974, 1971 by Harcourt Brace Jovanovich, Inc.
All rights reserved. No part of this publication may be reproduced or
transmitted in any form or by any means, electronic or mechanical,
including photocopy, recording, or any information storage and retrieval
system, without permission in writing from the publisher.
ISBN: 0–15–592850–3
Library of Congress Catalog Card Number: 81–84023
Printed in the United States of America

Preface

The study of American history in colleges and universities has undergone a profound change in the past two decades. This change started when scholars began to examine the social and economic roots of the social upheaval of the 1960s. The picture of the American past as an idyllic and relatively peaceful development of the natural and human resources was shattered. In its place emerged a history of violence and turmoil in which race was pitted against race and class against class in a struggle for always-scarce resources and the status their possession confers.

Most history texts published in recent years have tried to take account of this change and have included material dealing with its emergent themes. Formats, however, and a focus on the "mainstream" of American history have constrained their presentation. The purpose of *The Underside of American History* has always been to supplement these more general academic works. The first three editions dealt with groups and themes that had traditionally been ignored or slighted in the existing textbooks—American Indians, blacks, women, working-class culture, East Asian immigrants, poor whites, the elderly, Mexican-Americans, children. This fourth edition, in which over half of the selections are new, continues the concerns of the first three but adds such topics as poverty and crime, revivalism, the female labor force, westward migration, labor violence, socialism, the peace movement, and undocumented workers. It points out that many of the problems of America today have their roots in the past and suggests that without resolution of the social and economic inequities of American life, conflict, stress, and repression will continue to characterize much of American society.

Selections are arranged in roughly chronological order: Volume I begins with the colonial period and continues through Reconstruction, and Volume II covers mainly the period between Reconstruction and the present. Each volume contains a general introduction presenting the major themes taken up in the readings. In addition, each selection is introduced by a brief headnote that places the selection in historical context and indicates its significance. Annotated bibliographies close each of the collection's major sections.

I gratefully acknowledge the advice and assistance of the following historians: Carol Ruth Berkin of Baruch College of the City University of New York, David Reimers of New York University, Robert Calhoon of the University of North Carolina at Greensboro, William H. Chafe of Duke University, Joseph Conlin of California State University at Chico, Nancy Cott of Yale University, Juan Gómez-Quiñones of the University of California at Los Angeles, John Murrin of Princeton University, Gary B. Nash of the University of California at Los Angeles, Daniel Walkowitz of New York University, and Sean Wilentz of Princeton University.

—THOMAS R. FRAZIER

Contents

The New **2** Nation

The Ante-Bellum **3** North and South

Westward 4 Expansion   *348*

Introduction

This introduction is intended to provide a broad overview of the often neglected aspects of American history treated in the following selections. In these pages, the traditional emphases have been abandoned. The stress in many cases is on the failings of the system; the focus here is not on the victors but on the victims. Other selections deal with material or episodes from the past that are left out of or given short shrift in the standard histories. The result, of course, is not a comprehensive or balanced view of our history, but an attempt to redress an existing imbalance. These notes and these readings, unless they are considered within a larger context, provide a distorted view of history. They are, however, an essential part of the whole story, and they must be taken into account in any attempt to reach a valid assessment of the American past.

It is natural that the study of the history of the United States should concentrate in the beginning on the English colonization of the North American continent. It was, after all, not the French or Spanish but the English who gained a secure foothold in this part of the New World by the middle of the seventeenth century, and it was their institutions that prevailed in shaping the new society.

When the English began settling the Eastern seaboard of what was to become the United States, they found it virtually free of European colonization from Maine through Georgia, with the exception of the Dutch settlements in New Netherland, around present-day New York. They were thus freed from the necessity of adapting to any established social or religious system. Moreover, chiefly because of the distance that separated the colonies from the mother country, they were very nearly free from English control. Left to their own devices, their first problem was that of surviving in the wilderness—a feat that they were able to accomplish with the help of the Indians who were already well established in the territory. Then, typically, came the problem of turning the vast natural resources of the New World to their profit. As the early colonists concentrated on building up their strength, they began to consider their Indian neighbors a threat to their progress.

The "Indian problem" provided the first major test of English policy in the New World, and the settlers, by all accounts, fell far short of what might be desired. Their way of dealing with these aliens in their new society was simply to displace them by any means at hand. The Indians struggled with all the skill at their disposal—often with French and Spanish support—to preserve their lives, their culture, and their land, but they were no match for the technologically more advanced Europeans, and their civilization ultimately came to an end under the onslaught of Western ideas and ambitions. The Indians who survived the initial confrontations with the colonists were forced to retreat southward and westward, and their sporadic attempts at organization and resistance proved futile.

During the early decades of the nineteenth century, the Indians again mounted a significant opposition to the dominant policy toward them. One group—the Five Civilized Tribes of the southeastern United States—tried to escape alien status by assimilating to the dominant way of life. Their offer was rejected, and they not only remained foreign but were forcibly moved outside the borders of the then existing states. Another group of Indians, in the old Northwest, sought to revitalize their culture through a revival of native religion which encouraged some measure of acculturation. The Indians were continually displaced until there was no more vacant land. They were then removed to reservations on undesirable property, most of it west of the Mississippi River.

A second major threat to the progress of the English in the New World was the chronic shortage of settlers to provide a labor base for economic development in the colonies. Here, two major sources of supply were found. First, poor whites from Europe—primarily from England in the seventeenth century—were brought to the New World as indentured servants. Under the popular "headright" system of land distribution, anyone who paid for a passage to the New World received fifty acres of land. Thus investors could send over settlers, and both would presumably profit from the transaction. The investors, whether or not they also emigrated to the New World, could acquire title to large estates and claim most of the profits from their cultivation. The servants worked for a specified number of years in return for their passage and, sometimes, a percentage of the profits. When their term of service expired, they became freemen with the right to participate in colonial government and to hold land without sharing profits or paying rents to absentee landlords.

During the first hundred and fifty years of settlement, the practice of indentured servitude was a major source of new population for the New World. Moreover, during most of the seventeenth century, indentured servants were the main labor force in the colonies. Some of these servants ultimately prospered in the New World. Others, upon achieving their independence, moved into the yeoman farmer class of the developing society and established small subsistence farms. Though they thus lived in freedom, they never really shared in the nation's wealth, and many of their descendants live in poverty to this day in the foothills of the Appalachian Mountains.

By the end of the seventeenth century, a second and vastly more profitable labor supply had opened up to the colonists—African slavery. The first Africans, involuntary immigrants and, with the Indians, perpetual aliens, were brought to North America in 1619, and Africans arrived in increasing numbers in the two centuries before the trade was officially banned in 1808. By 1790, when the first federal census was taken, black people made up 19.3 percent of the total population of the United States. Over fifty thousand Afro-Americans, scattered throughout the nation, were free, yet even they were not permitted to move into the mainstream of American life. A few blacks in Eastern cities led relatively comfortable lives and attained some measure of economic security, but most lived the lives of unskilled laborers and met racial discrimination on every hand. In the North, white craftsmen protested against the employment of blacks in the skilled trades, giving rise to a pattern of black exclusion from certain crafts that has continued to the present, with ruinous economic results for the black community.

Any consideration of the oppression suffered by blacks in this country, however, must focus first on plantation slavery in the South. From the beginning, the great majority of Afro-Americans were slaves in the South, employed in various occupations ranging from skilled craftsman to common field hand. By 1860 almost half of the four million slaves in North America were engaged in cotton production, an economic fact that seems to have had the deciding voice in the controversy over the continuation of slavery in the South. Relying almost exclusively on imported African labor, nineteenth-century white Southerners developed a thriving plantation economy. In the process, they developed a devastating system of chattel slavery—perhaps the most devastating in the modern world in terms of its long-range impact. Further, by identifying slavery with color, they set into motion a pattern of color discrimination that has had endless reverberations for North American society. Over the years, the African and his descendants, along with the Indians, have been the most oppressed segments of American society.

The life of a Southern slave was almost totally circumscribed by his master. He was deprived of education, was given little opportunity for self-improvement and advancement, and, in some cases, was even denied the security of family life and religion. The slaves fought the system by developing a subculture of their own, reaching back for what they could recover from their African past, borrowing some from the whites, and adding elements drawn from their own unique experience in the Americas. More visibly, they protested their condition by rebelling and conspiring to rebel, by running away, and by refusing in innumerable ways to cooperate with the system.

Nonetheless, the superior power and efficiency of the slave system effectively limited the experiences of most of the black bondsmen. When emancipation came at the conclusion of the Civil War, few of the freedmen were trained in the skills freedom would require, and since racial prejudice persisted among even their liberators, blacks were given little opportunity during Reconstruction to move into positions of economic independence. In 1877, when the Reconstruction period ended and federal troops were removed from the South, most of the freed blacks who remained had been forced back into positions of dependence on white society. The South's recovery from the war, like her earlier rise to economic stability, was achieved at the expense of the black man, who was relegated by law and custom to a position of agricultural serfdom.

A third initial challenge faced by the English in the New World was basically governmental. How was order to be established and upheld in the vast new territory opened up by colonization? The process was by no means as orderly as some accounts of colonial history suggest. The English system of representative government was adapted for use in some of the colonies, but others were ruled indirectly from England through governors or proprietors. When colonists throughout the country began to demand a high degree of self-government, conflict between governors and settlers became commonplace, and violence was often the issue. Indeed, violent struggles against the English authorities marked most attempts to establish order within the individual colonies. In addition, in almost every colony serious struggles took place between the settlers in the coastal areas and those of the interior, who vied over the distribution of power and benefits and, not least, the system of taxation.

The issue of colonial self-government ultimately led to the struggle for independence. The leaders in this fight were for the most part members of the political elites of the colonies and descendants of the English settlers. Independence won, it was they who met in Philadelphia in 1787 to shape the American nation.

Although the political genius of a number of the Founding Fathers cannot be questioned, there were grave deficiencies in the outline they drew up for the form of the new nation. Slavery, to take a prime example, was given permanent legal status in the Constitution of 1787, and in the same document Indians were recognized as a people apart from the mass of Americans. A less obvious but perhaps more serious flaw in the legacy of the Founding Fathers was a pattern of thinking not explicitly articulated. That is, many of their ideas seemed to proceed from the assumption that the people of the United States would share the same language, religion, customs, and political and economic institutions. The strain toward homogeneity that can be seen in the thought of the earliest American political theorists has been at the root of many of the nation's difficulties for the past two hundred years. For since the first surges of nationalism in the revolutionary era, American leaders have tended to regard any challenge to the political and economic status quo as an alien threat, as something foreign to and incompatible with the American way of life.

For the first century of the new nation's life, many of the so-called alien ideas came from real aliens—either from immigrants or from domestic aliens who were barred from citizenship, the Indians and the African slaves. Later, even challenges brought by the native-born were frequently considered to be alien-inspired and were suppressed in the name of patriotism. Political power remained largely in the hands of the descendants of the Protestant English settlers, and their traditions continued to set the patterns of political, economic, and cultural life in the United States. Although foreign emigration would continue and would even be promoted, the tacit assumption was that immigrants would conform to the dominant way of life. Those who could not or would not could expect to meet serious opposition.

The first political parties in this country appeared in the 1790s, when Madison and Jefferson sought to organize opposition to Alexander Hamilton, President Washington's strongest adviser. Members of the existing government took the name of Federalists, and their opponents called themselves Republicans. Party organization at state and local levels developed rapidly, and the party system in the United States was institutionalized within a few decades. Naturally, party strife was rampant from the beginning, and one of its first products was the passage of the flagrantly repressive Alien and Sedition Acts in 1978, an expression of early nativist sentiment as well as an attempt to stifle Republican opposition. These acts were hotly protested, and by the time they went out of effect in 1801, they had stirred up the first of many furious debates between nationalists and the advocates of states' rights.

Another threat to the dominance of the well-to-do Americans of English descent came from the poorer members of the same ethnic group. During the colonial period, harsh penal practices and traditional patterns of deference kept the poor "in their place." With the coming of independence, however, the poor, particularly in the growing cities, took the revolutionary ideology seriously and sought an increased role in the governance of the society. New methods of social control, including penal reform and political organization, were developed in an attempt to cope with this new challenge. A sharp competition for employment kept many of the "deserving" (i.e., deferential) poor quiescent, but the rebellious poor continued to plague those interested in maintaining an orderly (and hierarchically structured) society.

In the nineteenth century, immigration proceeded apace. After the 1840s, a massive influx of Irish and German Catholics began to threaten Protestant hegemony on the Eastern seaboard. Most of the new immigrants were unskilled and penniless, and they came too rapidly to be dispersed and in too great numbers to be assimilated. Public programs to help them get settled in homes and jobs were at first nonexistent. Many immigrants found themselves placed in prisons, juvenile homes, mental hospitals, and the like—institutions growing in number and intended to care for the socially "undesirable." Public systems of education, whatever the good intentions that lay behind them, attempted to drill the newcomers in the dominant way of life, and many immigrant groups, clinging to their traditions, resisted by setting up private school systems. Suspicion of anything foreign, fear that by sheer numbers the immigrants would dilute the dominant Anglo-Saxon strains of the American population, and virulent anti-Catholicism contributed to the rise of a nativist movement that stretched across almost a century before it finally subsided. In many cities of the Northeast, there were violent clashes between Protestants and Irish Catholics, provoked primarily by the refusal of the Catholics to accept Protestant indoctrination.

Along with religious conflicts came bitter competition for jobs in the Northeast. By mid-century the Industrial Revolution had overtaken the United States, and the machinery of production had become so efficient that for the first time in American history there was a surplus of unskilled labor. This provided factory owners, members of a rising industrialist class, with the opportunity to stretch hours and reduce wages in the search for greater profits. Wage reductions, in turn, often meant that women and children had to go to work in the mills and mines in order to bring family incomes up to survival level. The struggle of the unskilled worker and the urban factory operative, immigrant or native-born, is one of the major motifs of nineteenth- and twentieth-century American life. Workers were able to improve their conditions only when they presented organized resistance to the dominant economic policies through national trade unions, which were slow to evolve.

Up to this point in history, the dominant sector of Americans had been not only white, Protestant, and English, but also male. Indeed, few women in the Western world have had any direct power or influence over the direction of society until quite recently. In America, as elsewhere, women were schooled only in the domestic arts and social graces, were deprived of the right to vote, were denied participation in politics and public life, and were expected to find fulfillment by living in the shadow of a successful male. In the second quarter of the nineteenth century, however, caught up by the general movement for reform, American women began to challenge male dominance. A women's rights movement called attention to the society's prejudices against "the weaker sex," and women, despite stinging denunciations, began to take leading roles in the religious movements and communitarian social experiments of the day. The more radical women joined with radical male reformers in advocating complete reorganization of society and complete restructuring of religious life. Since many theories of male dominance were based on an analogy with the structure of traditional religion, in which God, the father, or Jesus, the male child, was the ruler of the church, many women felt it was especially in their interest to attack the traditional religion. Some became prophets and seers, and some went so far as to found new religious movements.

Even during this first period of awakening to women's rights, most women remained submissive, apparently content in their traditional roles. But as the leisure of the middle-class woman increased and as servants and machines took on many of her customary household duties, masses of women found themselves hard pressed to reconcile the roles society foisted on them with their own feelings and needs. At the same time, a growing factory and commercial system provided a new measure of independence for married and unmarried women alike, and the ranks of working women swelled.

By the 1850s, the size of the American nation had increased dramatically. National interest in geographical expansion soared, and, combined with the ideology of Manifest Destiny, led to the incorporation of the West Coast into the union. Before the completion of the transcontinental railroad, settlers seeking their fortunes in the West were forced to travel overland for the most part. This covered wagon migration, so famed in American popular culture, provided new opportunities for land speculation and exploitation for those dissatisfied with their lives in the Middle West.

Though one might have expected that the lonely struggle to pacify the wilderness—and the Indians—would lead to strong emphasis on individuality, the westward advance carried with it powerful pressure toward conformity with the Eastern establishment. Perhaps the insecurity of life on the Great Plains and in the Far West lay behind the extravagant attempts to impose on the various Western peoples a homogeneity similar to that which now prevailed in the East. In any case, geographical expansion became synonymous with the expansion of Anglo-Saxon culture and control.

Predictably, those who suffered most from the settlement and development of the West were the aliens. With the conclusion of the Mexican War in 1847, many thousands of persons of Spanish and mixed Spanish-Indian descent suddenly found themselves foreigners living within American territory. "Vigilante" justice all too often held sway in the remote and virtually lawless West, and the Chinese, chicanos, Indians, and other ethnic minorities were the most frequent victims of the summary justice dealt out by self-appointed citizen groups.

The years between the Mexican War and the Civil War were years of deepening sectional crisis, for with every new state admitted to the union, arguments over slavery grew more pointed and more intense. The westward advance continued as a backdrop to civil war and recovery. By the end of the Reconstruction period, the United States stretched from coast to coast, and Protestant-English influence over the whole area was secured. The dominant Americans would continue to strive vainly to convert all whites to their points of view. More successfully, they would continue to exclude all nonwhites from full participation in American life.

1

Colonial
America

Savage War

FRANCIS JENNINGS

When the Europeans landed on the North American continent at the turn of the sixteenth century, the area north of the Rio Grande was inhabited by an estimated ten to twelve million people. Although it was at first assumed that these people—mistakenly called Indians by Columbus—were members of one cultural group, it was soon clear that they were divided into a large number of separate nations, with many separate and distinctive cultural traditions.

In the sixteenth century most of the exploration and conquest in the New World was carried out by the Spanish and the Portuguese. These early adventurers were able to justify their activities by citing the authority of the Pope, who had divided the newly discovered (for Europeans) hemisphere between Spain and Portugal with the Line of Demarcation of 1493. The Pope had given the Catholic countries a mandate to take possession of the land and to convert the natives to Christianity. And, indeed, the conquistadors were almost always accompanied by missionaries who sought to convince the conquered populations that Catholic Christianity was the one true religion. During the period of conquest, much of the Indian population from New Mexico through South America added Christianity as an overlay to their traditional religions.

The situation was very different in the area colonized by the English, where major settlement was not begun until the seventeenth century. The English intended not merely to explore, conquer, and exploit the land but also to settle on it, and the presence of many Indian nations along the Eastern seaboard presented a formidable obstacle to their attempts to secure political control and exclusive ownership of the land. The English were able to make use of existing hostilities among various Indian groups by allying themselves with one group against another. The English did not avidly seek to convert the Indians to Protestant Christianity. To the contrary, on numerous occasions they used the "heathenism" of the Indians as an excuse

for betraying them, arguing that since heathens could not be expected to uphold treaties or agreements, such agreements were
invalid from the start.

  After centuries of scholarship that had as its main purpose the
justification of the colonists' seizing of Indian lands, we are now in
the midst of a new perspective, one that treats the Indian peoples not
as inferior but as different. Francis Jennings, director of The Center
for the History of the American Indian at the Newberry Library, has
published a work that has challenged many of the myths of the early
period of contact between Amerindian and Euroamerican. In the selection from this work reprinted below, he shows how the colonists tried
to attach the label "savage" to the Indian style of warfare, in partial
justification of their attempts to dispossess the Indians. Jennings'
reevaluation of this process, however, indicates that war is indeed hell,
but that any attempt to evaluate war as "civilized" or "savage" usually
depends on which side one is on.

Myth contrasts civilized war with savage war by accepting the former
as a rational, honorable, and often progressive activity while attributing
to the latter the qualities of irrationality, ferocity, and unredeemed retro-
gression. Savagery implies unchecked and perpetual violence. Because
war is defined as organized violence between politically distinct communities, some writers have questioned whether savage conflicts really
qualify for the dignity of the name of war. By whatever name, savage
conflicts are conceived to be irrational because they supposedly lack
point or objective beyond the satisfaction of sadistic appetites that civilization inhibits, and savages are ferocious through the force of these
appetites.

  These images are byproducts of the master myth of civilization
locked in battle with savagery. Civilized war is the kind *we* fight against
them (in this case, Indians), whereas savage war is the atrocious kind
that they fight against us. The contrast has been sustained by means of
biased definition on the one hand and tendentious description on the
other. Savage war has been dismissed as mere "vengeance" or "feud,"
and writers have made it seem incomparably more horrible than civilized

"Savage War." From *The Invasion of America: Indians, Colonialism, and the Cant
of Conquest* by Francis Jennings (Chapel Hill, N.C.: The University of North Carolina Press, 1975), pp. 146–70. Reprinted by permission of the publisher and the
Institute of Early American History and Culture.

  This [selection] is based on a paper read at the Fourth Conference on Algonquian
Studies, Sept. 26, 1971, at Big Moose, N.Y.; in revised form it was read again at the
Seventh Annual Bloomsburg State College History Conference, "War and Peace,"
May 2, 1974, Bloomsburg, Pa.

war by dwelling upon the gory details of personal combat, massacre, and torture on the Indian side while focusing attention diversely on the goals and strategy of wars on the European side.

Still another circumstance has contributed to the myth. Indian governments held jurisdiction over relatively small territories, and there were a great many of them. No supreme power existed to suppress conflicts; the tribes settled their differences themselves by negotiation or struggle. With so many possible combinations of interest groups, statistical odds dictated frequent intertribal conflicts. European governments, in comparison, extended over larger territories, and thus the possible number of international wars was statistically a good deal less. Furthermore, European society may have deferred some "organized" warfare, not by abolishing violence, but by internalizing much of it. Nearly all the violence of Indian society expressed itself intertribally in the form of war, but internal violence in the European states required a vast apparatus for its suppression, the means of which were also violent: Londoners could always find sadistic entertainment at Tyburn or the Tower, and the gaolers buried more prisoners than they discharged. There were also means of violent struggle between nation-states other than declared war; Sir Francis Drake sacked Spanish towns in time of peace, and pirates were ever present on all the seas. We tend to glorify these "sea dogs" instead of putting them on the same low level as Indian raiders, but the victims in both cases went through much the same experiences. If we focus entirely on internal order, the Indian village was a peaceful place compared to the European town. If we focus instead on relations between polities, the nation-states were under tighter controls than the tribes.[1] It seems to me that a proper comparison should include both internal and external relations and should examine the total level of violence in each society, its forms and motives, and the methods used to control and direct it. From this perspective aboriginal Indian society appears to have been far less violent than seventeenth-century European society. The wasting wars so prominent among Indians in historic times were a factor of adaptation to European civilization.

Indian tribes were internally more peaceful than European nations partly because of the kin-oriented sanctions pervading Indian villages, as distinct from the greater impersonality of European social relationships, and partly because Indian custom defined and punished fewer crimes than European law. If there is merit in the argument that psychological aggressions are the cause of social violence (and, like most psychological explanations, this one permits large flights of fancy), then the aggressive feelings of Indians were vented mostly upon persons outside the protection of kin obligation—that is to say, outside the clan and tribe. The same customary sanctions were notably tolerant of many sorts of behavior that Europeans classed as crime, especially regarding deviant sexual and religious conduct. There was no crime of fornication or "unnatural vice" among Indians, nor was there any heresy as that was defined

---

[1] [J. H.] Kennedy, *Jesuit and Savage in New France*, [Yale Historical Publications, Miscellany (L. New Haven, Conn., 1950)], 114–15, 130.

by European law.[2] All sex relations except rare cases of rape were personal matters outside the jurisdiction of sachem and council, and religious *belief* was totally personal. Although participation in rituals was expected, the punishment for withdrawal was limited to public obloquy; in extreme cases the offender might be bewitched or poisoned by the tribal powwow, but such acts were clandestine. Indians knew nothing of the whole class of offenses called by European lawyers "crimes without victims." When one considers the floggings, jailings, hangings, torture, and burnings inflicted by European states for the multitude of crimes that did not even exist in Indian society, one becomes painfully aware that an incalculably great proportion of European violence against persons was inflicted by the very agencies whose ostensible function was to reduce violence. In due course "civil society" would seek to tranquilize its communities by emulating savage toleration of human variety, but even today this has still only begun.

Of crimes common to both societies, murder requires special notice. It was conceived of differently by Indian and European and was therefore punished by different processes. In Europe murder was an offense against the state; among Indians it was an offense against the family of the victim. European law demanded the murderer's life as atonement to the state; Indian custom made his life forfeit to his victim's family. In Europe the state apprehended the murderer; among Indians it was the family's obligation to do so. European observers tagged the Indian custom "revenge" and blathered much about the savagery revealed by it. Yet, as compared to the state's relentlessness, the tribe provided an institution carefully and precisely designed to stanch the flow of blood. The obligation of blood for blood could be commuted into a payment of valuable goods by the murderer's own kinsfolk to the relatives of his victim.[3] This custom (which had been known centuries earlier in Anglo-Saxon England as *wergild*) was a widespread stabilizer of Indian societies, forestalling the development of obligatory revenge into exterminating feuds. Although the term *feud* has been used freely by the condemners of savage society, Marian W. Smith has been unable to find the phenomena properly denoted by it. "True feud," she remarks, "in its threat of con-

---

[2] Fornication and adultery comprised most of colonial New England's court load. Edmund Morgan, "The Puritans and Sex," *New England Quarterly*, XV (1942), 596.

[3] [Daniel] Gookin, "Historical Collections [of the Indians in New England . . ." (1674), in Massachusetts Historical Society, *Collections*, 1st Sermon, I (Boston, 1792)], 149; Elisabeth Tooker, *An Ethnography of the Huron Indians, 1615–1649*, Smithsonian Institution, Bureau of American Ethnology, Bulletin 190 (Washington, D.C., 1964), 28; "Penn to Free Society of Traders, 1683," [Albert Cook] Meyers, ed., *Narratives of Early Pennsylvania, [West New Jersey, and Delaware, 1630–1707, Original Narratives of Early American History* (New York, 1912)], 236; [George S.] Snyderman, *Behind the Tree of Peace: [A Sociological Analysis of Iroquois Warfare, Pennsylvania Archaeologist*, XVIII, Nos. 3–4 (1948)], 31; David H. Corkran, *The Creek Frontier, 1540–1783*, Civilization of the American Indian Series (Norman, Okla., 1967), 26.

tinued violence between particular groups, is surprisingly rare in the New World."[4]

Europeans understood the *wergild* custom and used it themselves in their dealings with Indians, but only unilaterally. Europeans would pay blood money to avert Indian revenge for the killing of an Indian, but Indians were not permitted to buy absolution for the killing of a European. In the latter case the Europeans demanded the person of the accused Indian for trial in a European court.[5] In the event of nonapprehension of the suspected culprit, mass retribution might be visited upon his village or tribe.[6] The savagery of revenge, therefore, was simply a semantic function of its identification with an Indian; European revenge was civilized justice.

When Indians stirred abroad they were safe in their own territory and in those of tribes with whom they were at peace. The hospitality trait so prominent in all the tribes guaranteed to the traveler not only security but also shelter, sustenance, and sometimes sexual entertainment, all free of charge. Europeans traveling through Indian territory received the same treatment.[7] But travelers in seventeenth-century Europe risked life and property on every highway and in many inns, and they paid for all they got.

The violence and horrors of civil war were rare among Indians, probably because they tolerated secession, while England underwent the Puritan Revolution and France the Catholic-Huguenot agonies, to say nothing of dynastic upheavals by the score. Nor were there class wars or riots in Indian society. Nor did aboriginal Indians experience drunken orgies with their attendant tumults until rum and brandy were poured into the villages from Europe. Thereafter, however, drunken rage became a recurring menace everywhere.

When all this has been said, there still remains the problem of conflict between the tribes. The traditional conception of savage war depicts

[4] Marian W. Smith, "American Indian Warfare," New York Academy of Sciences, *Transactions*, 2d Ser., XIII (June 1951), 352.

[5] [Bruce G.] Trigger, "Champlain Judged by His Indian Policy: [A Different View of Early Canadian History,"] *Anthropologica*, N.S., XIII (1971), 96–97; *A Relation of Maryland* (1635), in Clayton Colman Hall, ed., *Narratives of Early Maryland, 1633–1684*, Original Narratives of Early American History (New York, 1910), 88–90; minutes, Jan. 27, 1672, and Lovelace to Salisbury, Jan. 27, 1672, in Victor Hugo Paltsits, ed., *Minutes of the Executive Council of the Province of New York: Administration of Francis Lovelace, 1668–1673* (Albany, N.Y., 1910), I, 156–57, II, 756–57.

[6] John Smith, *Generall Historie of Virginia*, in [Edward] Arber and [A. G.] Bradley, eds., *Travels and Works [of Captain John Smith, President of Virginia, and Admiral of New England, 1580–1631*, II (Edinburgh, 1910)], 538–39.

[7] [Robert] Beverley, [*The History and Present State of Virginia* (1705), ed. Louis B. Wright (Chapel Hill, N.C., 1947)], 186–89; Corkran, *Creek Frontier*, 23–25; [Lewis Henry] Morgan, [*League of the Ho-De-No-Sau-Nee, Iroquois* (Rochester, N.Y., 1851)], 327–29; [Roger] Williams, [*A Key into the Language of America: Or, An Help to the Language of the Natives in that part of America, called*

it as so unrelenting and frightful as to be incapable of proper comparison with the purposeful and disciplined process of civilized war. No less an authority than A. L. Kroeber has attributed to the east coast Indians of North America a kind of "warfare that was insane, unending, continuously attritional, from our point of view." It was nightmarish— "so integrated into the whole fabric of Eastern culture, so dominantly emphasized within it, that escape from it was well-nigh impossible. Continuance in the system became self-preservatory. The group that tried to shift its values from war to peace was almost certainly doomed to early extinction."[8] This harsh indictment would carry more weight if its rhetoric were supported by either example or reference. The only example that comes to mind in support of Kroeber is the Lenape mission of the Moravian church in the mid-eighteenth century. The Indians of that mission took their Christianity seriously, became absolute pacifists, and were unresistingly massacred. But their experience does not quite illustrate Kroeber's point, for their killers were not other Indians but backcountry Euramerican thugs, also Christian after a fashion, who were rather less ready to attack the old-fashioned pagan sort of Indian that fought back.[9]

Kroeber's implication of heavy casualties in aboriginal warfare is contradicted by seventeenth-century reports of Europeans with attitudes as diverse as those of Roger Williams and Captain John Underhill. From his observation post among the warring Narragansett and Pequot Indians, Williams saw that their fighting was "farre lesse bloudy and devouring than the cruell Warres of Europe."[10] Underhill was contemptuous of what Williams approved. He sneered at the Indian warriors who called off a battle after inflicting only a few deaths, and he reported complacently the Narragansetts' protest against his English-style war that "slays too many men."[11]

Imagined dogmas about warriors' lethal accomplishments have led sober scholars into impossible contradictions. For instance, Harold E. Driver has remarked, on the one hand, that "the greed, cupidity, deceit, and utter disregard of Indian life on the part of most of the European conquerors surpassed anything of the kind that the Indian cultures had been able to produce on their own in their thousands of years of virtual independence from the Old World." But Driver has also written, in

---

New-England . . . (1643), ed. James Hammond Trumbull, in Narragansett Club, *Publications*, I (Providence, R.I., 1866)], chap. 11; [John] Heckewelder, [*An Account of the History, Manners, and Customs of the Indian Nations, Who Once Inhabited Pennsylvania and the Neighbouring States* (1818), ed. William C. Reichel, Historical Society of Pennsylvania, *Memoirs*, XII (Philadelphia, 1871)], 148–49.

[8] [A. L.] Kroeber, [*Cultural and Natural Areas of Native North America*, University of California Publications in American Archaeology and Ethnology, XXXVIII (Berkeley and Los Angeles, 1939)], 148.

[9] Edmund De Schweinitz, *The Life and Times of David Zeisberger* (Philadelphia, 1870), chap. 35.

[10] Williams, *Key*, ed. Trumbull, Narragansett Club, *Pubs.*, I, 204.

[11] John Underhill, *Newes from America; or, A New and Experimentall Discoverie of New England* . . . (London, 1638), 26, 42–43.

conformity to savagery mythology, that "no young man ever thought of getting married or of being accepted as an adult citizen until he had slain an enemy and brought back a scalp to prove it."[12] The mathematical implications of the latter statement are wondrous. To demonstrate what it would mean in practice, let us imagine a situation in which two villages are perpetually raiding each other as they would be obliged to do in order to qualify their males for manhood and matrimony. Assuming that the age of eighteen is the threshold of manhood, we find that all of the eighteen-year-old men of one village achieve the right to marry by killing off an equal number of males in the other village. The total population of both villages would thus be reduced annually by the total number of eighteen-year-old men (at least this is so if the eighteen-year-olds from the two villages avoided killing each other). This is the minimum implication of one coup per warrior. If some braves showed more than minimum enthusiasm and skill, the whole process would be speeded up accordingly. Such a process would lead inexorably, year by year, not just to a low level of population, but to total extinction. The thing is impossible, of course, and so is the dogma on which it is predicated. Clearly there were young men in Indian society who got married before they ever killed anyone, and the mathematics imply that a lot of old Indian men also died without having killed. What really made an Indian youth a citizen of his community was an initiation ritual, and the process has been observed and reported thousands of times. William Penn reported that young Delawares were permitted to marry "after having given some Proofs of their Manhood by a good return of Skins" and that almost all of them were wed before they reached nineteen years of age.[13] Among the Delawares, therefore, a man could marry when he could demonstrate the ability to support a family. How many Euramerican parents have drilled that notion into their offspring? That the young Indian could gain prestige and status by killing and scalping is undeniable, and that many youngsters itched for such fame is as plain as the enlistment of European mercenaries for pay and plunder. But universal generalizations should be grounded in some minimum quantity of evidence and common sense.

Suppose it be argued that the disastrous demographic implications just presented are fallacious because warriors might diffuse the population loss by taking scalps from women and children. Deductively such an objection might have merit if not for the inductive evidence available. Contact-era Europeans agreed that, with few exceptions that occurred in the confusion of battle, Indians killed only men.[14] The cultural im-

---

[12] Harold E. Driver, *Indians of North America* (Chicago, 1961), 370, 384.

[13] "Penn to Free Society of Traders, 1683," Myers, ed., *Narratives of Early Pennsylvania*, 231.

[14] [Gabriel] Sagard, [*The Long Journey to the Country of the Hurons (1632)*, ed. George M. Wrong, trans. H. H. Langton, Champlain Society Publications, XXV (Toronto, 1939)], 140; [Adriaen] Van der Donck, *A Description of the New Netherlands* (2d ed., 1656), trans. Jeremiah Johnson, in New-York Historical Society, *Collections*, 2d Ser., I (New York, 1841)], 211; John Smith, *Map of Vir-*

perative may have been a survival trait rather than pure sentiment, because one reason for sparing these noncombatants was to assimilate them into the victorious tribe, thus to enlarge and strengthen it.[15] Some tribes were observed to begin war for the specific purpose of augmenting their female population.[16] Whatever the motive, the merciful custom was universal in regard to women and children.

Treatment of captured men was more varied. Early southern accounts indicate that all male prisoners were put to death except the chiefs.[17] By the seventeenth century torture of men was practiced fairly extensively, although some doubt exists about how widespread this trait had been at an earlier time. An ameliorating custom decreed the sparing of a large proportion of male captives, however. Again, the custom may have arisen out of the dire pressures of population decline, in this case pinpointed on particular families. Women among the victors, who had lost a husband or kinsman, held unchallengeable individual right to "adopt" a prisoner in his place, and the man so chosen became immediately assimilated into the tribe as well as the family. (In our terminology he was naturalized as well as adopted.[18]) Perhaps the most famous example of the custom is Pocahontas's rescue of John Smith, although Smith rejected assimilation at the first opportunity to escape. Not every European captive followed Smith's example. It was a constant crying scandal that Europeans who were adopted by Indians frequently preferred to remain with their Indian "families" when offered an opportunity to return to their genetic kinsmen.[19]

The adoption custom grew in importance with the intensification of war during the macrocontact era. Of all the Indians, the Iroquois, who are generally agreed to have been the most militaristic and to have suf-

---

ginia, in [Philip] Barbour, ed., [*The Jamestown Voyages under the First Charter, 1606–1609*, Hakluyt Society Publications, 2d Ser., CXXXVI–CXXXVII, II (Cambridge, 1609)], 372; Heckewelder, *Account of the Indian Nations*, ed. Reichel, in Hist. Soc. Pa., *Memoirs*, XII, 337–39; David Pietersz. de Vries, *Short Historical and Journal notes Of several Voyages made in the four parts of the World, namely, Europe, Africa, Asia, and America* (1655), trans. Henry C. Murphy, in N.-Y. Hist. Soc., *Colls.*, 2d Ser., III (New York, 1857), 116.

[15] Snyderman, *Behind the Tree of Peace*, in Pa. *Archaeol.*, XVIII (1948), 13–15.

[16] John Smith, *Map of Virginia*, in Barbour, ed., *Jamestown Voyages*, II, 360.

[17] *Ibid.*, II, 361; [Marc] Lescarbot, [*The History of New France* (1618), trans. W. L. Grant, Introduction by H. P. Biogar, Champlain Society Publications, I, (Toronto, 1907–1914)], 88.

[18] Morgan, *League of the Iroquois*, 341–344; Snyderman, *Behind the Tree of Peace*, in Pa. *Archaeol.*, XVIII (1948), 18; Heckewelder, *Account of the Indian Nations*, ed. Reichel, in Hist. Soc. Pa., *Memoirs*, XII, 217–18; [Cadwallader] Colden, [*The History of the Five Indian Nations Dependent on the Province of New-York in America* (Ithaca, N.Y., 1958 [orig. publ. 1727–1747])], Pt. I, chap. 1, 8; [Woodbury] Lowery, [*The Spanish Settlements within the Present Limits of the United States, 1513–1561*, I (New York, 1959; orig. publ. New York, 1901–1905)], 37.

[19] [Philip L.] Barbour, [*Pocahontas and Her World* (Boston, 1970)], 23–25. I thank James Axtell for providing an advance copy of his article "The White Indians of Colonial America," *WMQ*, 3d Ser., XXXII (1975), 55–88. This is the first objective treatment, to my knowledge, of the European prisoners who refused repatriation.

fered the most debilitating casualties, seem to have practiced adoption more than any other tribe. At one time adoptees constituted two-thirds of the Iroquois Oneidas.[20] The Senecas adopted whole villages of Hurons after the breakup of the Huron "nation" under Iroquois attack,[21] and various Iroquois tribes struggled for possession of Susquehannocks after the latter's dispersal under attack from Maryland and Virginia.[22]

Still another Indian custom served (aboriginally) to reduce the deadliness of war. Indians refrained from the total war that involved systematic destruction of food and property—until its use by Europeans roused the Indians to reprisal.[23] In this respect, as in so many others, the English continued a tradition of long standing from their devastations in Ireland.[24] Burning villages and crops to reduce Irish tribesmen to subjection under Elizabeth I led naturally enough to using the same tactics against the tribesmen of Virginia.[25] A "relation" of 1629 tells how the Virginia colonists compelled a hostile Indian chief to seek peace, "being forc't to seek it by our continuall incursions upon him and them, by yearly cutting downe, and spoiling their corne."[26] The same practice was used everywhere in North America when Indian guerrilla tactics prevented Europeans from gaining victory by decisive battle.[27] According to Indian logic, such destruction doomed noncombatants as well as warriors to die of famine during a winter without provisions.

These remarks are not intended to suggest that Indians of precontact days were gentle pacifists whom the Europeans seduced to evil warlike ways. On the contrary, all evidence points to a genuinely endemic state of sporadic intertribal violence. Had this base not been present, Europeans could not so readily have achieved hegemony by playing off one tribe against another. But the dispersion of violence tells nothing of its intensity. What is especially at issue here is the significance of the data in comparison with the phenomena of war in European society. As the

---

[20] Letter of Jacques Bruyas, Jan. 21, 1668, [in Reuben Gold] Thwaites, ed., [*The Jesuit Relations and Allied Documents: Travels and Explorations of the Jesuit Missionaries in New France, 1610–1791*, LI (Cleveland, Ohio, 1896–1901)], 123.

[21] Letter of Jacques Fremin, n.d. ("Relation of 1669–1670"), *ibid.*, LIV, 81–83.

[22] [Francis] Jennings, ["Glory, Death, and Transfiguration: The Susquehannock Indians in the Seventeenth Century," American Philosophical Society, *Proceedings*, CXII (1968)], 40.

[23] Minutes, Aug. 26, 1645, [David] Pulsifer, ed., *Acts of [the Commissioners of the United Colonies of New England*, in Nathaniel B. Shurtleff and David Pulsifer, eds., *Records of the Colony of New Plymouth in New England*, I (Boston, 1859)], 44.

[24] For the practice of Richard II in the late 14th century, see [J. F.] Lydon, [*The Lordship of Ireland in the Middle Ages* (Toronto, 1972)], 234.

[25] *Encyclopaedia Britannica*, 11th ed., s.v. "Ireland (History from the Anglo-Norman Invasion)."

[26] Capt. William Perse, "Relation," Aug. 1629, C.O. 1/5, Pt. 1, fol. 69, [Public Record Office].

[27] E.g., the French foray against the Mohawks in 1666. [E. B.] O'Callaghan, ed., [*The Documentary History of the State of New-York*, I (Albany, N.Y., 1849–1851)], 70.

history of feudal Europe well exemplifies, endemic war does not necessarily imply, although it may be associated with, population decline. The fact is unlovely, but growth in human societies is demonstrably compatible with bellicosity, up to a critical level of mortality. We have no difficulty in perceiving this rule at work in, say, ancient Greece; yet we deny that the rule also applied to Amerindians when we attribute to them a savage kind of war that supposedly was incomparably more continuous, more widespread, more integral to cultural values, and more senseless in the long view than the dedicated vocation of backward but civilized Sparta—or of Athens, for that matter. To show the falsity of these absolute antitheses is a primary objective here. Indians could be and often were as stupid and vicious as Europeans, which is to say that they belonged to the same human species. They were never so much more devoted than Europeans to killing each other that their uniquely violent natures or cultures doomed their societies to perpetual stagnation.

To discover the nature of aboriginal Indian war requires a skeptical and analytical approach not only to European sources but to Indian sources as well. Like old tales in other cultures, Indian "traditions" were of several sorts: some preserved the memory of historical events, and others were invented to amuse or edify. Wendell S. Hadlock has shown how legends diffused rapidly, being adapted to the local settings of different tribes so that "a single occurrence in history has been told in varying ways so as to appear like many incidents."[28] Sometimes one may doubt whether the "single occurrence" ever did happen anywhere.

One genre of such legends, dealing with the "grasshopper war," has been interpreted by chroniclers in its multiple manifestations as literal fact demonstrating the terrible carnage that Indians would wreak over such trivial causes as a children's quarrel about possession of a grasshopper. That grasshopper hopped over a lot of territory. He spilled the same mythical blood by gallons from the Micmacs of Newfoundland to the Shawnees, Lenape, and Tuscaroras of western Pennsylvania. The story seems to have been in the same class as Aesop's fables. Whatever may have been its remote origins, it diffused so widely because of its didactic utility rather than its historical reality. Hadlock associated it with a table of similar stories that "are not so much an explanation of a war incident as philosophical explanations of tribal fission."[29]

To Frank G. Speck it was fiction, and Speck's interpretation implies bittersweet irony as to how the Indian myth was absorbed and transformed in the European myth of savagery: "In the 'grasshopper war' legend we have an example of the type of Algonkian moral teaching with which the ethnologist has long been familiar. Need the moralist point out that its clarified motive is to portray the consequences of grown-ups taking over the disputes of children, the curse of partisanship in disputes of a trivial nature, the abomination of giving way to emo-

---

[28] Wendell S. Hadlock, "War among the Northeastern Woodland Indians," *Am. Anthro.*, N.S., XLIX (1947), 217–18.

[29] Wendell S. Hadlock, "The Concept of Tribal Separation as Rationalized in Indian Folklore," *Pa. Archaeol.*, XVI (1946), 84–88.

tional impulses? The myth is a great composition for the lesson it carries extolling self-restraint and the virtues of deliberation before taking action that may lead to disastrous outcome."[30]

By the transforming power of the savagery myth, a fable denouncing war's irrationality was converted into evidence of the real existence of widespread irrational bellicosity. The Indian could not even preach against war without convicting himself of obsessive love for it. By the same logic Quakers would be the most militaristic of Euramericans.

Historical sources strongly suggest that aboriginal war among the hunting Indians of the cold north differed markedly from the wars carried on by the agricultural tribes farther south. During most of the year the hunters lived dispersed in family bands that were occupied full-time in making a living. Opportunity to organize concerted tribal wars existed briefly during the summer months when the bands congregated at tribal centers and had some leisure. Wars could then be organized, but they were sporadic, individualistic affairs.[31] A Jesuit observer condemned both the Indians' motives and scale of operations with a succinct phrase—"their war is nothing but a manhunt"—and narrated how a war party of thirty men dwindled to fifteen who returned home satisfied after they had taken the scalps of three unoffending members of a friendly tribe.[32] In Europe such waylaying would have been called brigandage rather than war.

Farming Indians operated on a larger scale and under the direction of tribal purposes and policies. Their more complex culture provided a variety of motives. Sometimes they fought to gain territory, although apparently not in the fashion of European empire building; when Indians fought for territory as such, they wanted to displace its occupants rather than to subject them. Lands thus made available might be occupied by the victors, left empty for use as hunting grounds, or kept as a protective buffer against distant enemies.[33]

Sometimes, it seems, agricultural Indians fought to achieve dominance —to make the defeated tribe confess the victor's preeminence. The symbol of such acknowledgment was the payment of tribute. Because the

---

[30] Frank G. Speck, "The Grasshopper War in Pennsylvania: An Indian Myth That Became History," *Pa. Archaeol.*, XII (1942), 34. See also C. E. Schaeffer, "The Grasshopper or Children's War—A Circumboreal Legend?" *ibid.*, XII (1942), 60–61; John Witthoft, "The Grasshopper War in Lenape Land," *ibid.*, XVI (1946), 91–94.

[31] Hadlock, "War among Northeastern Indians," *Am. Anthro.*, N.S., XLIX (1947), 211–14.

[32] Andre Richard, "Relation of 1661–1662," Thwaites, ed., *Jesuit Relations*, XLVII, 221–39.

[33] Occupation: Pequot displacement of Niantics. [Frederick Webb] Hodge, ed., *Handbook of [American Indians North of Mexico*, Smithsonian Institution, Bureau of American Ethnology, Bulletin 30, 2 vols. (Washington, D.C., 1907–1910)], s.v. "Pequot." Hunting grounds: Five Nations displacement of tribes around Lake Erie. Five Nations deed, July 19, 1701, *N.Y. Col. Docs.*, IV, 908. Buffer lands: Hadlock, "War among Northeastern Indians," *Am. Anthro.*, N.S., XLIX, (1947), 217.

tributary role has been much confused, it needs a moment of special attention. First, tribute should be distinguished from plunder. When the Niantics raided Long Island's Montauks for wampum in 1638, they were after loot.[34] When the Iroquois Five Nations—the Mohawks among them—required wampum from the Lenape of the Delaware Valley in the eighteenth century, they wanted ceremonial recognition of a confederate relationship in which the Iroquois were superior.[35] Several contrasts mark the difference. Loot was seized by a raiding party; tribute was presented by a diplomatic mission. Loot's value increased precisely in accordance with quantity; tribute's value was primarily symbolic, secondarily quantitative. The taking of loot was a one-sided transaction; the presentation of tribute was reciprocated by a counter presentation of wampum to confirm the tributary agreement.

The last difference was especially important, because tribute symbolized subordinate alliance rather than subjection and thus entailed obligation on the part of the superior tribe as well as the tributary. In essence the alliance entitled the tributary to freedom from molestation by its patron and to protection by the patron against attack by a third party. In return the tributary was expected to give ceremonial deference on all occasions, to allow free passage through its territory by members of the patron tribe, and to permit or encourage the recruitment of its own young men to join the patron's war parties. This sort of mutual obligation can be identified in the historic period, but it does not appear that all tributary relationships were the same; there seem to have been grades and degrees of obligation,[36] and the word *tribute* was also applied to payments of wampum or other valuable goods in the nature of a toll. For instance, English officials agreed to pay tribute to the Illinois tribes in 1764 for the privilege of unobstructed passage through the tribes' territory, and the Indians knew perfectly well that the English were not submitting or subjecting themselves by the payment.[37]

It may be said quite positively that a tributary tribe did not neces-

---

[34] [Benjamin F.] Thompson, [*The History of Long Island*, 2d ed., I (New York, 1843)], 89–90.

[35] Minutes, May 19, 1712, [in Samuel Hazard, ed., *Minutes of the Provincial Council of Pennsylvania* . . . , II (Harrisburg, Pa., 1838–1853)], 546; draft minutes of treaty, Sept. 15, 1718, Logan Papers, XI, 7, and Sassoonan's speech, Aug. 7, 1741, Records of the Provincial Council and Other Papers, boxed manuscripts, fol. 1740–1749, both in Hist. Soc. Pa., Philadelphia.

[36] Snyderman, *Behind the Tree of Peace*, in *Pa. Archaeol.*, XVIII (1948), 33; Anthony F. C. Wallace, *King of the Delawares: Teedyuscung, 1700–1763* (Philadelphia, 1949), 195–96, and his "Political Organization," *Southwest. Jour. of Anthro.*, XIII (1957), 308–09; Beverley, *History of Virginia*, ed. Wright, 174; [Regina] Flannery, [*An Analysis of Coastal Algonquian Culture*, Catholic University of America Anthropological Series, VII (Washington, D.C., 1939)], 117–18; [Francis] Jennings, ["The Constitutional Evolution of the Covenant Chain," American Philosophical Society, *Proceedings*, CXV (1971)], 90–94.

[37] Gen. Thomas Gage to Johnson, May 28, 1764, [James Sullivan, et. al., eds., *The Papers of Sir William Johnson*, IV (Albany, N.Y., 1921–1965)], 433–34; Johnson to Gage, June 9, 1764, *ibid.*, XI, 223.

sarily give up title to its lands when it presented tribute. After the defeat of the upper Hudson Mahicans by the Mohawks in 1628, the Mahicans offered tribute as a means of purchasing peace, but they also sold land to the Dutch without Mohawk objection, and after two years of tribute payment they "got drunk and lost the pouch [of wampum]." Mohawk sachem Joseph Brant, who told the story, commented that the Mohawks did not "take it hard" when payment ceased.[38] Four decades later, when the Executive Council of New York considered purchase of land from the "Wickerscreek" (Wecquaesgeek) tribe, the council had to consider whether the Wickerscreeks could deliver good title, "now they are beaten off" by the Mohawks. The Indians replied that the Mohawks would not "have any pretence to their Land, though being at Warre they would destroy their Persons, and take away their Beavers and Goods."[39]

The "sales" by dominant tribes like the Pequots and Iroquois of their rights in tributaries' territory were in the nature of quitclaims, without prejudice to the tributaries' retained rights of habitation and enjoyment. The Pequots quit their own claims to the Connecticut Valley and permitted Englishmen to settle there, but after the English evicted a tributary chief, the Pequots attacked in reprisal. When the Iroquois were bribed by Pennsylvanians in the eighteenth century to "quit" a claim they had never made to the Delaware Valley, the swindle ruptured their confederacy.[40]

The customary situation was summarized by General Thomas Gage in the course of his systematic correspondence on Indian affairs with Sir William Johnson. Gage's confidential letter also clarifies the English motives that often led to the muddying of the formal records. "It is asserted as a general Principle that the Six Nations having conquered such and such Nations, their Territorys belong to them, and the Six Nations being the Kings Subjects which by treaty they have acknowledged themselves to be, those Lands belong to the King. I believe it is for our Interest to lay down such principles especially when we were squabbling with the French about Territory, and they played us off in the same stile of their Indian Subjects, and the right of those Indians." Gage went on to define the Indian customs as he privately understood them. "I never heard that Indians made War for the sake of Territory like Europeans, but that Revenge, and an eager pursuit of Martial reputation were the Motives which prompted one Nation to make War upon another. If we are to search for truth and examine her to the Bottom, I dont imagine we shall find that any conquered Nation ever formaly ceded their Country to their Conquerors, or that the latter ever required

---

[38] Douglas W. Boyce, ed., "A Glimpse of Iroquois Culture History through the Eyes of Joseph Brant and John Norton," Am. Phil. Soc., *Procs.*, CXVII (1973), 290; Bruce G. Trigger, "The Mohawk-Mahican War (1624–28): The Establishment of a Pattern," *Canadian Historical Review*, LII (1971), 281.

[39] Minutes, Oct. 30, 1671, Paltsits, ed., *Minutes of Council of N.Y.*, I, 105.

[40] [Francis] Jennings, ["The Delaware Interregnum," *Pennsylvania Magazine of History and Biography*, LXXXIX (1965)], 174–98; [Anthony F. C.] Wallace, [*The Death and Rebirth of the Seneca* (New York, 1970)], 154.

it. I never could learn more, than that Nations have yielded, and acknowledged themselves subjected to others, and some ever have wore Badges
of Subjection."[41]

Gage's remark refers to the most frequently mentioned motive for
Indian war—behavior that is almost invariably termed *revenge*. Like
most effective propaganda language, the term has a referent in reality,
and also like most propaganda, it distorts that referent in the mere naming of it. Our English word implies an act of retaliation intended to inflict suffering upon an enemy and performed in part for the emotional
satisfaction that the avenger will achieve from contemplation of that
suffering. (Who has not hated the villainous Iago?) Revenge connotes
ferocity—personal, unrestrained by charity or mercy or any of the nobler impulses of humanity—in short, savagery. The actual phenomenon
in Indian society to which this name has been given did not conform to
these connotations. As it manifested itself intratribally, we have already
noticed revenge as an obligatory retaliation for murder, together with
the commutation custom by which the obligation might be discharged
in lieu of blood for blood.[42] *Intertribal* retaliation for wrongs done or
fancied (a real and omnipresent occurrence) was also bound up in motives and restraints imposed by custom and social purpose, including
commutation by payment between tribes as well as between families. As
Marian W. Smith has noted, such retaliations bear "a legalistic tinge.
They serve as mechanisms for righting the balance of sanctions in the
society, and the reprisal is seen as justified, in view of the fact that it
reestablishes the validity of customs which had been violated."[43]

Smith wrote in the formal language of the twentieth-century scholar.
A seventeenth-century Lenape Indian phrased the "justified reprisal"
idea—which in Europe might readily have been classed as "just war"—in
simpler language when he told a Pennsylvanian, "We are minded to live
at Peace: If we intend at any time to make War upon you, we will let
you know of it, and the Reasons why we make War with you; and if
you make us satisfaction for the Injury done us, for which the War is
intended, then we will not make War on you. And if you intend at any
time to make War on us, we would have you let us know of it, and the
Reasons for which you make War on us, and then if we do not make
satisfaction for the Injury done unto you, then you may make War on
us, otherwise you ought not to do it." To one looking back from the
twentieth century this sounds quaintly moralistic. In the era of total

---

[41] Gage to Johnson, Oct. 7, 1772, *Sir William Johnson Papers*, XII, 994–95.

[42] See the description by missionary Francesco Bressani (1653) who remarked, "it is
the public that gives satisfaction for the crimes of the individual, whether the
culprit be known or not. In fine, the crime alone is punished, and not the criminal;
and this, which elsewhere would appear an injustice, is among them a most ef-
ficacious means for preventing the spread of similar disorders." Thwaites, ed.,
Jesuit Relations, XXXVIII, 273–87, quote at p. 277.

[43] M. W. Smith, "American Indian Warfare," N.Y. Acad. Sciences, *Trans.*, 2d Ser.,
XIII (1951), 352. See also the discussion of revenge in Snyderman, *Behind the
Tree of Peace*, in *Pa. Archaeol.*, XVIII (1948); A. F. C. Wallace, *Death and Re-
birth of the Seneca*, 44–48; Heckewelder, *Account of the Indian Nations*, ed.

"preventive" war, what is one to make of "otherwise you ought not to do it"?[44]

Marian W. Smith identifies a "mourning-war" complex of traits correlating to the northern distribution of maize agriculture. By implication she makes it a development of the revenge trait, but her definition is brief and unenlightening: it is "an elaborate socio-religious complex relating individual 'emotion' to social reintegration through group activity and sanctioned homicide."[45] This seems more to describe what happens psychologically to a tribe after it has gone to war than to explain the reasons for its choosing to fight a particular foe at a certain time and place; further, it could as well apply to the nations of World War II as to aboriginal Indians.[46] Pursued to their logical assumptions, such psychological explanations of war, primitive or modern, take one ultimately to a neo-Calvinist faith in the innate depravity/bellicosity of man, a position both unwarranted by science and vicious in effect and, ultimately, a self-fulfilling prophecy that stultifies investigation of the empirical sources of war and thus guarantees war's perpetuation. We shall do better to stick with Smith's genuine insight into Indian war as a means of reestablishing the validity of violated customs; it raises questions that can be answered historically.

In sum, the motives for aboriginal war appear to have been few, and the casualties slight. Contact with Europeans added new motives and weapons and multiplied casualties. The trade and dominance wars of the macrocontact era were indeed beyond the sole control of aboriginal cultural and political institutions, because they were bicultural wars, the motives and promptings for which originated in colony and empire as well as in tribe. These wars were truly attritional for Indians—appallingly so—but they were the result of civilization's disruption of aboriginal society rather than the mere outgrowth of precontact Indian culture.

Most discussions of Indian war have probably concerned themselves less with the Indians' motives than with their manner of fighting. Every "frontier" history abounds with tales of grim figures skulking through the woods, striking from ambush, spreading havoc and desolation, and culminating their horrors with scalping, torture, and cannibalism. In many instances the tales are verifiable, and no attempt will be made here to palliate their horrors. But when atrocity is singled out as a quality exclusive to tribesmen (Indians or others), myth is being invoked against evidence—indeed against the sorrowful experience of our own twentieth

---

Reichel, in Hist. Soc. Pa., *Memoirs*, XII, 175–76; Tooker, *Ethnography of the Huron Indians*, 28; [John] Lawson, [*A New Voyage to Carolina* (1709), March of America Facsimile Series, No. 35 (Ann Arbor, Mich., 1966)], 199; Driver, *Indians of North America*, 354.

[44] Thomas Budd, *Good Order Established in Pennsilvania & New-Jersey in America* (1685), March of America Facsimile Series, No. 32 (Ann Arbor, Mich., 1966), 33.

[45] M. W. Smith, "American Indian Warfare," N.Y. Acad. Sciences, *Trans.*, 2d Ser., XIII (1951), 359.

[46] See W. W. Newcomb, Jr., "Toward an Understanding of War," in Gertrude E. Dole and Robert L. Carneiro, eds., *Essays in the Science of Culture in Honor of Leslie A. White* (New York, 1960), 322–24, and Newcomb, "A Reexamination of the Causes of Plains Warfare," *Am. Anthro.*, LII (1950), 328–29.

century and our own "highest" civilization of all time. The Indians of
the macrocontact era, and presumably their aboriginal ancestors also,
undoubtedly showed plenty of ferocity when aroused; what will be
argued here is that the records of European war of the same era display
the same quality in ample measure also. There were no Indians in Ireland
when Cromwell's armies made it a wilderness, nor were there Indians
with Wallenstein and Tilly during the Thirty Years' War in central
Europe. If savagery was ferocity, Europeans were at least as savage as
Indians.

Many of the aspects of so-called savage war were taught to Indians
by European example. As to torture, for example, a systematic examination of the documents of the early contact era, published by Nathaniel
Knowles in 1940, found no references to torturing by Indians of the
southeast coast region "until almost 200 years after white contact."
Knowles added, "It seems even more significant that there are no expressions by the early explorers and colonizers indicating any fear of such
treatment. The Europeans were only too willing in most cases to call
attention to the barbarity of the Indians and thus justify their need for
either salvation or extermination."[47] Among the northeastern Indians,
Knowles found that deliberate torture, as distinct from simple brutality
(i.e., unplanned and unorganized cruelty), had not been practiced in
aboriginal times except by the Iroquois, who associated it with the practice of ritual cannibalism. These usages seem to have been derived from
an ancient complex of customs connected with human sacrifice and
perhaps tracing back to similar practices in Mexico. Iroquois torture
secondarily served as a terrorist device to keep surrounding tribes in
fear, but its usefulness for this purpose declined as some neighbors
adopted the same trait in reprisal, much as the southern Indians had retaliated against such European tortures as burning at the stake.[48] After
describing the torture of an Iroquois prisoner by Samuel de Champlain's
allies, Marc Lescarbot remarked, "I have not read or heard tell that any
other savage tribe behaves thus to its enemies. But someone will reply

[47] Nathaniel Knowles, "The Torture of Captives by the Indians of Eastern North
America," Am. Phil. Soc., *Procs.*, LXXXII (1940), 202. This is a systematic study
fundamental to any study of torture in North America. Knowles remarked that
Ponce de Leon in 1613 had met a Florida Indian who understood the Spanish
language, "thus making it apparent that the atrocious cruelty of the Spanish for
some twenty years in the West Indies had become known to the inhabitants of
the mainland prior to the discovery of the continent by the whites" (p. 156).
Knowles cites the speculation of Lowery that the Floridians' resistance to the
Spaniards indicated "they had learned somewhat of the treatment they were to
expect at the hands of such conquerors." Lowery, *Spanish Settlements*, I, 144–45.
In 1642 the Canadian Jesuit martyr Father Isaac Jogues wrote, "*Never till now* had
the Indian [torture] scaffold beheld French or other Christian captives." [E. B.
O'Callaghan and Berthold Fernow, eds., *Documents Relative to the Colonial History
of the State of New York*, XIII (Albany, N.Y., 1856–1887], 581 (emphasis added).
[48] Knowles, "Torture," Am. Phil. Soc., *Procs.*, LXXXII (1940), 190–91, 213, 215;
Heckewelder, *Account of the Indian Nations*, ed. Reichel, in Hist. Soc. Pa.,
Memoirs, XII, 343.

that these did but repay the Iroquois who by similar deeds have given cause for this tragedy."[49] Lescarbot stated positively that "our sea-coast Indians" did not practice torture, and his modern translator added a note of confirmation.[50] Although some Indians practiced the ritual cannibalism that Europeans had sublimated many centuries earlier into symbolic acts of "communion," other Indians abominated man-eating as much as the Europeans themselves. Algonquian speakers used a contemptuous epithet meaning "man-eaters" to refer to their Iroquois neighbors: it took the forms of Mengwe, Mingo, Maqua, and finally, in English, Mohawk.[51]

Europeans and Indians differed in the publicity given to torture. Europeans burnt heretics and executed criminals in ingeniously agonizing ways, but much European torture was inflicted secretly for the utilitarian purpose of extracting confessions from suspects. Public or private, European torture was performed by specialists appointed by governmental authority, whereas torture among Indians was a spectacle for popular participation as well as observation. It seems reasonable to infer that comparably painful practices in the two societies were sharply distinguished in European minds by what was conceived as their relative lawfulness. Torture by commission of civil authority was merely execution of the law, often highly approved as a means of preserving order, but torture by a self-governing rabble was savagery. The *Encyclopaedia Britannica* has noted that the name of torture has been historically used "especially" for those modes of inflicting pain "employed in a legal aspect by the civilized nations of antiquity and of modern Europe."[52] In such a context the remark of seventeenth-century friar Louis Hennepin becomes ironic: "We are surprised at the cruelty of tyrants and hold them in horror: but that of the Iroquois is not less horrible."[53]

Plenty of sadism was evident in both cultures. Indians vented it directly upon the person of their victim, hacking and slashing at his body democratically with their own hands. Even old women would satisfy some horrid lust by thrusting firebrands at his genitals or chewing off the joints of his fingers. Their culture sanctioned what they did in the same way that local and regional cultures in nineteenth- and twentieth-century America sanctioned somewhat similar practices by white supremacists at lynching parties. In the more authoritarian seventeenth century the European populace in general was not allowed to participate except as spectators in the tortures prescribed for condemned per-

---

[49] Lescarbot, *History of New France*, trans. Grant, III, 13–15.

[50] *Ibid.*, III, 20–21.

[51] [Allen W.] Trelease, [*Indian Affairs in Colonial New York: The Seventeenth Century* (Ithaca, N.Y., 1960)], 41. But see a dissenting meaning for "Mohawk" given by Mohawk sachem Joseph Brant who held that it came from the Mahican word *munkwas*, meaning "fish dryed." Brant may have been a little sensitive on the subject. Boyce, ed., "Glimpse of Iroquois Culture History," Am. Phil. Soc., *Procs.*, CXVII (1973), 291.

[52] *Encyclopaedia Britannica*, 11th ed., s.v. "torture."

[53] Louis Hennepin, *A Description of Louisiana* (1683), trans. John Gilmary Shea, March of America Facsimile Series, No. 30 (Ann Arbor, Mich., 1966), 311–12.

sons. When we consider that crowds brought their lunch along to be enjoyed during such entertainments as disemboweling and slow immolation, we may wonder about the significance of the cultural difference. We have no way of knowing how many Europeans were prevented from soaking their own hands in blood only by the state's armed guards. Equally we have no way of knowing how many of the persons in an Indian village were active participants in the grim sport of torture, or how many just looked on. The diverse qualities of character that we recognize as distinguishing one European or Euramerican from another are ignored or denied among Indians. Savages are homogeneously cruel.

In America, Europeans sometimes turned captives over to allied Indians for torture in order to make hostility between two tribes irrevocable. Their own complicity was not felt keenly enough to shame the Europeans into silence; after having thus condemned a victim they would sometimes fastidiously deplore the sadistic appetites of the Indian torturers who were carrying out the Europeans' own desires.[54] One French officer, after "prudently" consigning an old Onondaga to the torture in 1696, considered that the *victim's* taunting defiance "will be found perhaps to flow rather from ferociousness, than true valour."[55]

One thing is not in doubt: as befitted its greater progress in technology, Europe had designed a variety of implements for the specific purpose of creating agony, not merely death, in human bodies. Their function was to make pain excruciating—a word that itself commemorates one of the pioneering inventions in that field and recalls its connection with European worship. Indians never achieved the advanced stage of civilization represented by the rack or the Iron Maiden. They simply adapted instruments of everyday utility to the purposes of pain. It may be worth a moment to reflect on the cultural traits imaged in the specialized torture technology of Europe. Something more than sudden emotional impulse will have to be taken into account.

I have an impression that about midway through the seventeenth century the outlook toward torture began to change in opposite directions among the two peoples. It seems to me from general reading that European attitudes toward mutilation of the human body began to turn negative. The old delight in hacking enemies' corpses in the public square and exposing their heads on palings went out of fashion—gradually and with conspicuous exceptions such as the displays made of sachem Philip and "squaw sachem" Weetamoo in "King Philip's War."[56] Slowly the

54 Heckewelder, *Account of the Indian Nations,* ed. Reichel, in Hist. Soc. Pa., *Memoirs,* XII, 343–44; [*Dictionary of Canadian Biography*], I (1966), s.v. "Buade de Frontenac et de Palluau, Louis de." Sir William Johnson followed the same practice but masked it under euphemisms. For example, he told Cadwallader Colden, Mar. 16, 1764, "I was obliged to *give* them People 5 Prisoners for their good behaviour." To General Gage, on the same day, Johnson wrote that the Indians had "kept" the five prisoners. *Sir William Johnson Papers,* IV, 365, 368–69 (emphasis added).

55 O'Callaghan, ed., *Doc. Hist. of N.-Y.,* I, 334.

56 [Samuel G.] Drake, *Biography and History of the Indians* [*of North America from its First Discovery* . . . , 11th ed. (Boston, 1856)], 189–90, 227.

use of torture for extracting information from political prisoners came under disapproval and ultimately under official ban. At the same time, torture was increasing among Indians as trade wars multiplied and European conflicts dragged Indian allies along. It is easy to understand why the Europeans, who were apparently trying to overcome their own worst traits, should have found relief and a sense of superior righteousness by rejecting torture and cruelty as things foreign to their own best impulses and therefore to civilization per se. No one dreamed at the time that the increase of torture by Indians could have come as the result of exposure to the uplifting influence of Europe, but the idea seems more credible nowadays after the revelations of German and Russian secret police practices, French policy in Algiers, Mississippi justice, and the ministrations of nice young American boys in Vietnam.

Every day brings revelations of secret tortures committed as deliberate instrumentation of governmental policy. Today's newspaper leads off an article with this paragraph: "Amnesty International, the organization dedicated to assisting political prisoners, has charged that torture as a systematic weapon of control is being used by almost half the world's governments and is spreading rapidly." The civilized world's response to this information is symbolized by the United Nations Educational, Scientific, and Cultural Organization. UNESCO withdrew from Amnesty International the offer of its facilities because the torture report implicated more than 60 of UNESCO's 125 member countries.[57] Clearly civilization is not a homogeneous whole, whatever it may otherwise be. Nor was it in the seventeenth century.

Apart from torture, some Europeans have domineered over Indians, when they could, with a reign of terror functioning through indiscriminate cruelty. In early Virginia the curtain was opened briefly on the reality behind self-serving and self-glorifying reports when Englishmen slew twelve Chickahominy Indians without cause and by treachery. Relatives of the victims retaliated against ten colonists and then fled into the woods. The rest of the villagers, abused by both sides, "much feared the English would be revenged on them"—a fear they had unquestionably been taught by the swaggering Virginians. Grand sachem Opechancanough "saved" the village from causeless slaughter, and incidentally revealed the motive behind the English menaces, by ceding the village to the colonists.[58] On a larger scale, after the much-provoked Virginia Indians rebelled in 1622, English writers fumed against the Indian massacre even as English soldiers multiplied their vengeance massacres beyond counting. Virginian Dr. John Pott became "the Poysner of the Savages thear" in some sort of episode so shocking that the earl of Warwick insisted it was "very unfitt" that Pott "should be imployed by the State in any business." But Pott became governor.[59]

---

[57] *New York Times*, Dec. 16, 1973: "64 Nations Charged in Report as Users of Torture."

[58] John Smith, *Generall Historie of Virginia*, in Arber and Bradley, eds., *Travels and Works of Smith*, II, 528, 538–39.

[59] See [Wesley Frank] Craven, "Indian Policy in Early Virginia," [*William and Mary*

Virginia was not exceptional. Puritan New England initiated its own reign of terror with the massacres of the Pequot conquest. David Pieterszoon de Vries has left us an unforgettable picture of how Dutch mercenaries acted, under orders of New Netherland's Governor Willem Kieft, to terrorize Indians into paying tribute.

> About midnight, I heard a great shrieking, and I ran to the ramparts of the fort, and looked over to Pavonia. Saw nothing but firing, and heard the shrieks of the Indians murdered in their sleep. . . . When it was day the soldiers returned to the fort, having massacred or murdered eighty Indians, and considering they had done a deed of Roman valour, in murdering so many in their sleep; where infants were torn from their mother's breasts, and hacked to pieces in the presence of the parents, and the pieces thrown into the fire and in the water, and other sucklings being bound to small boards, and then cut, stuck, and pierced, and miserably massacred in a manner to move a heart of stone. Some were thrown into the river, and when the fathers and mothers endeavoured to save them, the soldiers would not let them come on land, but made both parents and children drown—children from five to six years of age, and also some old and decrepit persons. Many fled from this scene, and concealed themselves in the neighbouring sedge, and when it was morning, came out to beg a piece of bread, and to be permitted to warm themselves; but they were murdered in cold blood and tossed into the water. Some came by our lands in the country with their hands, some with their legs cut off, and some holding their entrails in their arms, and others had such horrible cuts, and gashes, that worse than they were could never happen.

And the sequel: "As soon as the Indians understood that the Swannekens [Dutch] had so treated them, all the men whom they could surprise on the farm-lands, they killed; but we have never heard that they have ever permitted women or children to be killed."[60]

Indians have often been charged with senseless bloodlust in their fighting, even to the point of treacherously murdering people who had befriended them. The variety of friendship claimed for the victims of such murders should always be investigated in particular detail. The purported friend often turns out to be no more than someone who lived close to the Indians in order to exploit them more efficiently than he could from a distance—his "friendship" is proved by nothing more than his toleration of their persons—or one who warded off other exploiters in order to preserve his own monopoly. For reasons of space and proportion, the subject cannot be fully discussed here, but examples can be cited of real discrimination by Indians in favor of persons that they

---

Quarterly], 3d Ser., I (1944), 73; Warwick to Sec. Conway, Aug. 9, 1624, C.O. 1/3, 94; C.O. 1/5, Pt. 2, fol. 206, Public Record Office.
60 De Vries, *Voyages,* in N.-Y. Hist. Soc., *Colls.,* 2d Ser., III, 115–16.

recognized as friends. David de Vries, himself one such person, was able, after Kieft's massacre, to walk alone, unmenaced and unscathed, in the midst of the very Indians whose kinsfolk had been treated so cruelly.[61] The most startling example is to be found in eighteenth-century Pennsylvania, where the entire Religious Society of Friends, whose members were settled the length and breadth of the colony, was excepted from the raids of the Seven Years' War. In 1758 the Yearly Meeting held at Burlington for New Jersey and Pennsylvania recorded its "Thankfulness for the peculiar favour extended and continued to our Friends and Brethren in profession, none of whom have as we have yet heard been Slain nor carried into Captivity." In consideration of Indian willingness to reciprocate benevolence, the Yearly Meeting displayed an unusual form of racist thinking: it urged all Friends to show their gratitude practically by freeing their slaves.[62]

Indian war, like European war, changed with time and circumstance. The guerrilla raids of small war parties became more common after the introduction of firearms made massed attack suicidal. Firearms also reduced the value of stockades around villages even as they had destroyed the invulnerability of walled castles in Europe. The most militaristic of Indians, the Iroquois, adapted to fighting with guns by casting aside their encumbering wooden and leather body armor to gain greater mobility. The naked warrior of the savage stereotype became real enough, but among the Iroquois, at least, he was the product of acculturation rather than an aboriginal prototype.[63]

The influence of European contact on Indian warfare is quite plain. In New England, for instance, until the Pequot conquest, the tribes marched to war en masse, but the Pequots recognized that such tactics would be futile against English firepower. They therefore approached the Narragansetts to propose joint harassment of the English rather than confrontation. They would kill livestock, waylay travelers, and ambush isolated farmers. The Narragansetts rejected this proposal in favor of an English alliance and later fought a battle against the Mohegans with the traditional tactics of a large army; but when they were finally forced into open violence against the English in "King Philip's War," they adopted the Pequots' proposed guerrilla tactics, to New England's great distress. Cultural change in response to the contact situation was not one-sided, however. While Pequots and Narragansetts changed traditional tactics to cope with English colonials, the Englishmen were also modifying ancient military wisdom to meet the needs created by Indian guerrilla war. In James Axtell's words, "From these opponents the English gradually learned to fight 'Indian-style,' an ability that once again spelled

[61] *Ibid.,* 116–20.

[62] Minutes, 1758, Minutes of the Yearly Meeting Held at Burlington for New Jersey and Pennsylvania, Manuscripts, Bk. A3, 121, Department of Records, Philadelphia Yearly Meeting, Society of Friends, 302 Arch St., Philadelphia.

[63] Keith F. Otterbein, "Why the Iroquois Won: An Analysis of Iroquois Military Tactics," *Ethnohistory,* XI (1964), 57–59; Snyderman, *Behind the Tree of Peace,* in *Pa. Archaeol.,* XVIII (1948), 75–77.

the difference between their destruction and survival in the New World."[64]

Customs and practices changed from decade to decade, even in regard to the trait of scalping, which, while apparently Indian in origin, did not exist among many Indian tribes in the early seventeenth century. It seems to have been adopted in New England, for example, as a convenient way to collect provincial bounties for heads without having to lug about the awkward impedimenta attached to the scalps.[65]

Both Indians and Englishmen took heads as trophies and put them on show, and the practice of paying bounties for heads was well established among Englishmen. It had been conspicuous in the wars in Ireland in the thirteenth and fourteenth centuries.[66] In the sixteenth century Sir Humphrey Gilbert had terrorized the Irish by ordering that "the heddes of all those (of what sort soever thei were) which were killed in the daie, should be cutte off from their bodies and brought to the place where he incamped at night, and should there bee laied on the ground by eche side of the waie ledyng into his owne tente so that none could come into his tente for any cause but commonly he muste passe through a lane of heddes which he used *ad terrorem*. . . . [It brought] greate terrour to the people when thei sawe the heddes of their dedde fathers, brothers, children, kinsfolke, and freinds. . . ."[67]

As Europeans taught Indians many of the traits of "savage" war, so also their intrusion into Indian society created new situations to which the Indians responded by cultural change on their own initiative. The attritional warfare of the macrocontact era did indeed justify A. L. Kroeber's indictment of having become so integrated in the culture that escape from it had become impossible, but it was not the aboriginal culture that took such a grim toll. It was instead a culture in which European motives and objectives of war multiplied war's occasions and casualties. Four different kinds of war took place in the macrocontact era: European versus European, Indian versus Indian, intermixed allies versus other allies, and, rarely, European versus Indian. In all of them the influence of European political or economic institutions is apparent. Many of the Indian versus Indian combats were really European wars in which the Indians unconsciously played the role of expendable surrogates. The curbs and restraints of aboriginal custom held no power over Europeans, and particular tribes were in various states of dependency or "ambipendency" with regard to particular colonies. Continual European initiatives and pressures for war created a *macrocontact* system in which tribal bellicosity was indeed self-preservatory for particular

[64] [William] Bradford, *Of Plymouth Plantation*, [*1620–1647*, ed. Samuel Eliot Morison (New York, 1952)], 294–95, 330–31; James Axtell, "The Scholastic Philosophy of the Wilderness," *WMQ*, 3d Ser., XXIX (1972), 340.

[65] Hodge, ed., *Handbook of N. Am. Indians*, s.v. "scalping."

[66] Lydon, *Lordship of Ireland*, 195.

[67] [Nicholas P.] Canny, ["The Ideology of English Colonization: From Ireland to America," *William and Mary Quarterly*, 3d Ser., XXX (1973)], 582.

groups in particular circumstances, even though it worked general calamity upon the whole of Indian society.

There were no innate differences between Indians and Europeans in their capacity for war or their mode of conducting it. Their differences were matters of technology and politics.[68] Only a few generations before the invasion of America, Europeans had conducted war according to feudal rules very different from those of the nation-state but startlingly similar in many respects to the practices of Indian war. Admittedly Indian society was not class-stratified like feudal society, and the Indian warrior differed from the feudal knight by being an all-purpose man who turned his hand to peasant occupations between battles. Clearly, also, Indians did not build or besiege castles, or fight with metal weapons and armor. But let not reality disappear behind the knight's armor plate; there was a naked warrior within. From childhood he had received special training in the use of arms, and he spent much time in strenuous sports that would strengthen and condition his body for war. So did the Indian. Both were hunters, and in the hunt both maintained their skill in the use of weapons. Like the Indian the medieval knight hunted for food as well as for sport and training; and, as with the Indian's hunting territories, unauthorized persons were forbidden to hunt in the knight's domain.[69]

A special purification ritual admitted the European esquire into the status of warrior; so also for the Indian, although in his case the ritual was also an ordeal. Knight and warrior mobilized for war in similar ways: the knight responded, if he felt like it, to the call of a lord to whom he had commended himself as vassal; the warrior responded, if he felt like it, to the invitation of an admired chief. No warrior was conscripted against his will. In neither case was there a bureaucracy to recruit and organize a fighting force; such loyalty as existed was that of man to man and family to family. Naturally enough, such soldiers knew nothing of Prussian discipline. Knights and warriors were free men fighting in wars and battles of their own choosing, unlike the hireling standing armies of the nation-state, who accepted orders with their wages.

---

[68] The only extended discussion seems to be one without visible virtues: Henry Holbert Turney-High, *Primitive War: Its Practice and Concepts* (Columbia, S.C., 1949). This is an unreliable, superficial, Colonel Blimp sort of repetitive dogma and slippery semantics. The author repeatedly expresses his contempt of the social sciences and declares that any noncommissioned officer knows more than all the social scientists. He hastens to add that he was himself a commissioned officer.

[69] A. F. C. Wallace has erroneously extrapolated the American custom of freedom to hunt on unposted lands back into European times, and the error is repeated by Vaughan; but hunting in Europe was stringently limited to the nobility and to "stinted" limits of rights in commons for the lower orders. Wallace, "Political Organization," *Southwest. Jour. of Anthro.*, XIII (1957), 312, n. 7; [Alden T.] Vaughan, *New England Frontier: [Puritans and Indians, 1620–1675* (Boston, 1965)], 108; E. C. K. Gonner, *Common Land and Inclosure* (London, 1912), 14–16.

One of the most striking parallels between the customs of feudal knights and those of Indian warriors was a code of behavior that in Europe is called chivalry. The sparing of women and children in Indian warfare fits snugly into the doctrines of chivalry avowed by feudal knights (and even practiced by them when the women and children were of their own religion). The practice was abandoned by the more rational or efficient killing machines organized by the nation-states; chivalry belonged to the knights, and the knights belonged to the Middle Ages. Chivalry, in short, was barbarous.

Perhaps an opportunity exists here to use the parallel between America and Europe to learn more about Europe. A customary explanation of chivalry's rise has been that the sweet moan of minnesingers and troubadours softened the hearts and manners of the great hulks on horseback. This lacks persuasion. Indians had a different sort of explanation for their own variety of chivalry: they needed to rebuild their declining populations. Feudal Europe was a time of population uncertainty, and the damsels spared by gallant knights were prime breeding stock—a fact sometimes put to test by the knights. In this respect the Indians seem to have been the more chivalrous, for they were observed everywhere to refrain from sexual molestation of female prisoners; they took the women and girls, untouched, back to the captors' villages for assignment to families as wives and daughters.[70] The knight, however, though he served the public interest by preserving his prisoners' lives, served himself also by demanding ransom.

Knight and warrior both gave first allegiance to their kin. This reservation of loyalty from the monopoly demanded by the nation-state was the unforgivable sin that has roused nationalists to denounce the special barbarity of feudal Europe and the special savagery of Indian America. That all war is cruel, horrible, and socially insane is easy to demonstrate, but the nationalist dwells upon destiny, glory, crusades, and other such claptrap to pretend that his own kind of war is different from and better than the horrors perpetrated by savages. This is plainly false. The qualities of ferocity and atrocity are massively visible in the practices of European and American powers all over the world, quite recently in the assaults of the most advanced civilized states upon one another.

[70] Hodge, ed., *Handbook of N. Am. Indians*, s.v., "captives"; Heckewelder, *Account of the Indian Nations*, ed. Reichel, in Hist. Soc. Pa., *Memoirs*, XII, 339–40.

Time, Space, and the Evolution
of Afro-American Society

IRA BERLIN

By the end of the seventeenth century the English colonies in North America had turned to African slaves and their descendants to solve the problems arising from a chronic shortage of labor. The English adopted for their own use the Spanish system of African enslavement, which had begun early in the sixteenth century in the Caribbean. Indian slavery, too, had been widely practiced in Latin American, to the point of bringing the native Indian populations close to extinction. But in the North American colonies, although Indian captives were frequently enslaved in the early years of colonization, it appears that Indian slavery was never economically profitable. As a result, the African became *the* slave in the English colonies.

Slavery, in the sense of lifetime bondage, is an institution as old as human history. Almost every past civilization has had some system of involuntary service that may, with some accuracy, be called slavery. Throughout history, military conquest has been the most common means of enslavement. What distinguished North American slavery, however, was its racial character. By the beginning of the eighteenth century, any African in the English colonies was assumed to be a slave unless he could prove otherwise. Except in exceptional circumstances, not only the original African but his descendants forever were confined to slave status.

From the earliest days of settlement in North America, the historical record clearly shows that some blacks were free. What it does not show is the process by which African slavery became the widespread institution that it was by 1700. In fact, historians have argued as to whether slavery produced racial prejudice or racial prejudice produced slavery—a question that could have vital sgnificance for easing racial tensions in America today. If, for instance, slavery, as an absolute form of economic inequality, led to racial prejudice, then the elimination of economic inequality in the United States might contribute immensely to the elimination of racial prejudice. If, on the other hand, prejudice preceded slavery, then equal economic

opportunity might not be expected for blacks until the roots of racial
prejudice have been identified and removed.

    Historians are only now beginning to explore the nature of
slavery and slave life in the earliest days of English settlement in
North America. One of the persistent myths of that period is that
Africans imported to the New World were empty vessels culturally
and had to be taught by the English all those things they would be
required to do in their new life. While this myth is in the process of
being exploded, another problem remains. Most of the studies of
slavery treat the institution as though it were static—the same at all
times and in all places. The article reprinted below, by Ira Berlin, of
the University of Maryland, seriously challenges that position. Using a
comparative analysis of three different geographical sections of colonial America, he shows that over a period of time three distinct types
of Afro-American culture evolved according to the needs and usages
of the three areas. Many of the subsequent developments in Afro-
American history are more fully illuminated by virtue of this
approach.

Time and space are the usual boundaries of historical inquiry. The last
generation of slavery studies in the United States has largely ignored these
critical dimensions but has, instead, been preoccupied with defining the
nature of American slavery, especially as compared with racial bondage
elsewhere in the Americas. These studies have been extraordinarily valuable not only in revealing much about slave society but also in telling a
good deal about free society. They have been essential to the development of a new understanding of American life centered on social transformation: the emergence of bourgeois society in the North with an upward-striving middle class and an increasingly self-conscious working class
and the development of a plantocracy in the South with a segmented social
order and ideals of interdependence, stability, and hierarchy. But viewing
Southern slavery from the point of maturity, dissecting it into component
parts, comparing it to other slave societies, and juxtaposing it to free society have produced an essentially static vision of slave culture. This has
been especially evident in the studies of Afro-American life. From
Stanley M. Elkins's Sambo to John W. Blassingame's Nat-Sambo-Jack
typology, scholars of all persuasions have held time constant and ignored
the influence of place. Even the most comprehensive recent interpretation
of slave life, Eugene D. Genovese's *Roll, Jordan, Roll,* has been more

"Time, Space, and the Evolution of Afro-American Society" by Ira Berlin. From
the *American Historical Review,* LXXXV (February 1980), 44–78. Reprinted by
permission of the author.

concerned with explicating the dynamic of the patriarchal ideal in the making of Afro-American culture than in explaining its development in time and space. None of the histories written since World War II has equaled the temporal and spatial specificity of U. B. Phillips's *American Negro Slavery*.[1]

Recent interest in the beginnings of slavery on the mainland of British North America, however, has revealed a striking diversity in Afro-American life. During the seventeenth and eighteenth centuries, three distinct slave systems evolved: a Northern nonplantation system and two Southern plantation systems, one around Chesapeake Bay and the other in the Carolina and Georgia lowcountry. Slavery took shape differently in each with important consequences for the growth of black culture and society. The development of these slave societies depended upon the nature of the slave trade and the demographic configurations of blacks and whites as well as upon the diverse character of colonial economy. Thus, while cultural differences between newly arrived Africans and second and third generation Afro-Americans or creoles[2] everywhere provided the basis for social stratification within black society, African-creole differences emerged at different times with different force and even different mean-

[1] Stanley Elkins, *Slavery: A Problem in American Institutional and Intellectual Life* (Chicago, 1959); John W. Blassingame, *The Slave Community: Plantation Life in the Antebellum South* (New York, 1972); Eugene D. Genovese, *Roll, Jordon, Roll: The World the Slaves Made* (New York, 1974); and Ulrich B. Phillips, *American Negro Slavery* (New York, 1918). For a historical perspective on post–World War II scholarship on slavery, see David Brion Davis, "Slavery and the Post–World War II Historians," *Daedalus*, 103 (1947): 1–16; and, on the importance of temporal change. see Herbert G. Gutman, "Slave Culture and Slave Family and Kin Network: The Importance of Time," *South Atlantic Urban Studies*, 2 (1978): 73–88.

[2] I have used these terms synonymously. Both are mined with difficulties. "Afro-American" has recently come into common usage as a synonym for "black" and "Negro" in referring to people of African descent in the United States. Although "creole" generally refers to native-born peoples, it has also been applied to people of partly European, but mixed racial and national, origins in various European colonies. In the United States, "creole" has also been specifically applied to people of mixed but usually non-African origins in Louisiana. Staying within the bounds of the broadest definition of "creole" an the literal definition of "Afro-American," I have used both terms to refer to black people of native American birth.

Earlier versions of this essay were presented at the Conference on Comparative Perspectives on Slavery in the New World, held in New York, May 1976, at the Ninth World Congress of Sociology, held in Uppsala, Sweden, August 1978, and at the Symposium on the Slave Trade, held in Petersburg, Virginia, October 1979. In addition to the commentators at these conferences, I am grateful to Stanley Engerman, Eric Foner, Eugene D. Genovese, Herbert G. Gutman, Ronald Hoffman, Philip Morgan, Joseph P. Reidy, Leslie S. Rowland, and Armstead Robinson for their critical comments and suggestions. Much of the research for this essay was done while I was a fellow at the Davis Center for Historical Studies. I would especially like to thank the center's director, Lawrence Stone, for his support and intellectual camaraderie.

ing in the North, the Chesapeake region, and the lowcountry.[3] A careful examination of the diverse development of Afro-American culture in the colonial era yields important clues for an understanding of the full complexity of black society in the centuries that followed.

The nature of slavery and the demographic balance of whites and blacks during the seventeenth and first decades of the eighteenth centuries tended to incorporate Northern blacks into the emerging Euro-American culture, even as whites denied them a place in Northern society.[4] But changes in the character of the slave trading during the middle third of the eighteenth century gave new impetus to African culture and institutions in the Northern colonies. By the American Revolution, Afro-American culture had been integrated into the larger Euro-American one, but black people remained acutely conscious of their African inheritance and freely drew on it in shaping their lives.

Throughout the colonial years, blacks composed a small fraction of

[3] As used in this essay, the concept of acculturation or creolization does not mean the liquidation of a culture, only its transformation. African culture transported to the New World was not lost or destroyed but transformed. The transformation of Africans to Afro-Americans entailed the joining together of a variety of distinctive African cultures as well as the compounding of those cultures with various European and native American ones to create a new cultural type: the Afro-American. Scholars have only begun to study the making of Afro-American culture; therefore, any judgment about its nature and the process of its creation must be tentative and incomplete. I would emphasize that "Africans" and "creoles" as used here do not represent autonomous categories, if for no other reason than African and creole people were connected by ties of blood and kinship. Instead, these categories are used as two poles within a range of an historical experience that was varied and overlapping. The process of creolization was not always synchronized with generational change. Beginning with Melville J. Herskovits's *The Myth of the Negro Past* (New York, 1941), scholars have produced a wide-ranging theoretical literature on the question of cultural transformation of African people in the New World. For some that have been most useful for this essay, see Sidney W. Mintz and Richard Price, *An Anthropological Approach to the Caribbean Past* (Philadelphia, 1976); Melville J. Herskovits, "Problems, Method. and Theory in Afro-American Studies," *Phylon*, 7 (1946): 337–54; M. G. Smith, *The Plural Society in the British West Indies* (Berkeley and Los Angeles, 1965), and "The African Heritage in the Caribbean," in Vera Rubin, ed., *Caribbean Studies* (Seattle, 1960), 34–45; H. Orlando Patterson, "Slavery, Acculturation, and Social Change: The Jamaican Case," *British Journal of Sociology*, 17 (1966): 151–64; and Edward Brathwaite, *The Development of Creole Society in Jamaica, 1770–1820* (London, 1971), and "Caliban, Ariel, and Unprospero in the Conflict of Creolization: A Study of the Slave Revolt in Jamaica in 1831–32," in Vera Rubin and Arthur Tuden, eds., *Comparative Perspectives on Slavery in New World Plantation Societies*, Annals of the New York Academy of Sciences, no. 292 (New York, 1977), 41–62.

[4] In the discussion of the Chesapeake region and the lowcountry, scholars have employed the term "Anglo-American" to refer to the culture of white people. Because of the greater diversity of origins of white peoples in the Middle Colonies, the term "Euro-American" seems more applicable to white culture in the North.

the population of New England and the Middle Colonies. Only in New York and Rhode Island did they reach 15 percent of the population. In most Northern colonies the proportion was considerably smaller. At its height, the black population totaled 8 percent of the population of New Jersey and less than 4 percent in Massachusetts and Connecticut. But these colony-wide enumerations dilute the presence of blacks and underestimate the importance of slave labor. In some of the most productive agricultural regions and in the cities, blacks composed a larger share of the population, sometimes consituting as much as one-third of the whole and perhaps one-half of the work force.[5] Although many Northern whites never saw a black slave, others had daily, intimate contact with them. And, although some blacks found it difficult to join together with their former countrymen, others lived in close contact.

The vast majority of Northern blacks lived and worked in the countryside. A few labored in highly capitalized rural industries—tanneries, salt works, and iron furnaces—where they often composed the bulk of the work force, skilled and unskilled. Iron masters, the largest employers of industrial slaves, also were often the largest slaveholders in the North. Pennsylvania iron masters manifested their dependence on slave labor when, in 1727, they petitioned for a reduction in the tariff on slaves so they might keep their furnaces in operation. Bloomeries and forges in other colonies similarly relied on slave labor.[6] But in an overwhelmingly agrarian society only a small proportion of the slave population engaged in industrial labor.

Like most rural whites, most rural blacks toiled as agricultural workers. In southern New England, on Long Island, and in northern New Jersey, which contained the North's densest black populations, slaves tended stock and raised crops for export to the sugar islands. Farmers engaged in provisioning the West Indies with draft animals and foodstuffs were familiar with slavery and had easy access to slaves. Some, like the Barbadian émigrés in northern New Jersey, had migrated from the sugar islands. Others, particularly those around Narragansett Bay, styled themselves planters in the West Indian manner. They built great houses,

---

[5] For a collection of the relevant censuses, see William S. Rossiter, *A Century of Population Growth* (Washington, 1909), 149–84. Also see Robert V. Wells, *The Population of the British Colonies before 1776: A Survey of Census Data* (Princeton, 1975), 69–143, and Wells's correction of the 1731 enumeration, "The New York Census of 1731," *New York Historical Society Quarterly*, 57 (1973): 255–59. For estimates of the Northern black population predating these censuses, see U.S. Bureau of the Census, *Historical Statistics of the United States, Colonial Times to 1957* (Washington, 1960), 756.

[6] Edgar J. McManus, *Black Bondage in the North* (Syracuse, N.Y., 1973), 42–43; Charles S. Boyer, *Early Forges and Furnaces in New Jersey* (Philadelphia, 1963), 30–31, 149, 166, 194–99, 239; Frances D. Pingeon, "Slavery in New Jersey on the Eve of the Revolution," in Williams C. Wright, ed., *New Jersey in the American Revolution* (rev. ed., Trenton, N.J., 1974), 51–52, 57; Darold D. Wax, "The Demand for Slave Labor in Colonial Pennsylvania," *Pennsylvania History*, 34 (1967): 334–35; and William Binning, *Pennsylvania Iron Manufacture in the Eighteenth Century* (Harrisburg, Pa., 1931), 122–25.

bred race horses, and accumulated slaves, sometimes holding twenty or more bondsmen. But, whatever the aspirations of this commercial gentry, the provisioning trade could not support a plantation regime. Most slaves lived on farms (not plantations), worked at a variety of tasks, and never labored in large gangs. No one in the North suggested that agricultural labor could be done only by black people, a common assertion in the sugar islands and the Carolina lowcountry. In northern New England, the Hudson Valley, and Pennsylvania, the seasonal demands of cereal farming undermined the viability of slavery. For most wheat farmers, as Peter Kalm shrewdly observed, "a Negro or black slave requires too much money at one time," and they relied instead on white indentured servants and free workers to supplement their own labor. Throughout the North's bread basket, even those members of the gentry who could afford the larger capital investment and the concomitant risk that slave ownership entailed generally depended on the labor of indentured servants more than on that of slaves. Fully two-thirds of the bond servants held by the wealthiest farmers in Lancaster and Chester counties, Pennsylvania, were indentured whites rather than chattel blacks. These farmers tended to view their slaves more as status symbols than as agricultural workers. While slaves labored in the fields part of the year, as did nearly everyone, they also spent a large portion of their time working in and around their masters' houses as domestic servants, stable keepers, and gardeners. Significantly, the wills and inventories of Northern slaveholders listed their slaves with other high status objects like clocks and carriages rather than with land or agricultural implements.[7]

The distinct demands of Northern agriculture shaped black life in the countryside. Where the provisioning trade predominated, black men worked as stock minders and herdsmen while black women labored as dairy maids as well as domestics of various kinds. The large number of slaves demanded by the provisioning trade and the ready access to horses and mules it allowed placed black companionship within easy reach of most bondsmen. Such was not always true in the cereal region. Living scattered throughout the countryside on the largest farms and working in the house as often as in the field, blacks enjoyed neither the mobility

[7] Kalm, *Peter Kalm's Travels in North America*, ed. and trans. A. B. Benson, 1 (New York, 1937): 205, as quoted in Alan Tully, "Patterns of Slaveholding in Colonial Pennsylvania: Chester and Lancaster Counties, 1729-1758," *Journal of Social History*, 6 (1973): 286; Lorenzo J. Greene, *The Negro in Colonial New England* (New York, 1942), 103-12; McManus, *Black Bondage in the North*, 40-41; Pingeon, "Slavery in New Jersey," 51; William D. Miller, "The Narragansett Planters," *American Antiquarian Society Proceedings*, 43 (1933): 67-71; Tully, "Patterns of Slaveholding in Colonial Pennsylvania," 284-303; Steven B. Frankt, "Patterns of Slave-Holding in Somerset County, N.J.," seminar paper, 1967, in Special Collections, Rutgers University Library, New Brunswick, N.J.; Wax, "The Demand for Slave Labor in Colonial Pennsylvania," 332-40; and Jerome H. Woods, Jr., "The Negro in Early Pennsylvania: The Lancaster Experience, 1730-1790," in Elinor Miller and Eugene D. Genovese, eds., *Plantation, Town, and County: Essays on the Local History of American Slave Society* (Urbana, Ill., 1974), 447-48.

nor the autonomy of slaves employed in the provisioning trade. But, if the demands of Northern agriculture affected black life in different ways, almost all rural blacks lived and worked in close proximity to whites. Slaves quickly learned the rudiments of the English language, the Christian religion, the white man's ways. In the North, few rural blacks remained untouched by the larger forces of Euro-American life.

Northern slaves were also disproportionately urban. During the eighteenth century, a fifth to a quarter of the blacks in New York lived in New York City. Portsmouth and Boston contained fully a third of the blacks in New Hampshire and Massachusetts, and nearly half of Rhode Island's black population resided in Newport. Ownership of slaves was almost universal among the urban elite and commonplace among the middling classes as well. On the eve of the Revolution, nearly three-fourths of Boston's wealthiest quartile of propertyholders ranked in the slaveholding class. Fragmentary evidence from earlier in the century suggests that urban slave-ownership had been even more widespread but contracted with the growth of a free working class. Viewed from the top of colonial society, the observation of one visitor that there was "not a house in Boston" that did "not have one or two" slaves might be applied to every Northern city with but slight exaggeration.[8]

Urban slaves generally worked as house servants—cooking, cleaning, tending gardens and stables, and running errands. They lived in back rooms, lofts, closets, and, occasionally, makeshift alley shacks. Under these cramped conditions, few masters held more than one or two slaves. However they might cherish a large retinue of retainers, urban slaveholders rarely had the room to lodge them. Because of the general shortage of space, masters discouraged their slaves from establishing families in the cities. Women with reputations for fecundity found few buyers, and some slaveholders sold their domestics at the first sign of pregnancy. A New York master candidly announced the sale of his cook "because she breeds too fast for her owners to put up with such inconvenience," and others gave away children because they were an unwarranted expense. As a result, black women had few children, and their fertility ratio was generally lower than that of whites. The inability or unwillingness of urban masters to support large households placed a severe strain on black family life.[9] But it also encouraged masters to allow their slaves to live out,

---

[8] N. B. Shurtleff *et al.*, eds., *Rewards of the Governor and Company of Massachusetts Bay in New England (1628–1698)*, 1 (Boston, 1853): 79, as quoted in Carl Bridenbaugh, *Cities in the Wilderness, 1625–1742* (New York, 1938), 49; Rossiter, *A Century of Population Growth*, 149–84; Greene, *The Negro in Colonial New England*, 78, 81–82, 84–88, 92–93; Gary B. Nash, "Slaves and Slaveowners in Colonial Philadelphia," *William and Mary Quarterly*, 3d ser., 30 (1973): 226–52; and Thomas Archdeacon, *New York City, 1664–1710: Conquest and Change* (Ithaca, N.Y., 1976), 46–47.

[9] New York *Weekly Post-Boy*, May 17, 1756, as quoted in McManus, *Black Bondage in the North*, 38; Carl Bridenbaugh, *Cities in Revolt, 1743–1776* (New York, 1955), 88, 285–86, and *Cities in the Wilderness*, 163, 200–01; Nash, "Slaves and Slaveowners in Colonial Pennsylvania," 243–44; Archdeacon, *New York City*, 89–90; Rossiter, *A Century of Population Growth*, 170–80; Edgar J. McManus,

hire their own time, and thereby gain a measure of independence and freedom.

Slave hirelings along with those bondsmen owned by merchants, warehouse keepers, and ship chandlers kept Northern cities moving. Working outside their masters' houses, these bondsmen found employment as teamsters, wagoners, and stockmen on the docks and drays and in the warehouses and shops that composed the essential core of the mercantile economy. In addition, many slaves labored in the maritime trades not only as sailors on coasting vessels, but also in the rope walks, shipyards, and sail factories that supported the colonial maritime industry. Generally, the importance of these slaves to the growth of Northern cities increased during the eighteenth century. Urban slavery moved steadily away from the household to the docks, warehouses, and shops, as demonstrated by the growing disproportion of slave men in the urban North. Aside from those skills associated with the maritime trades, however, few slaves entered artisan work. Only a handful could be found in the carriage trades that enjoyed higher status and that offered greater opportunity for an independent livelihood and perhaps the chance to buy freedom.[10]

In the cities as in the countryside, blacks tended to live and work in close proximity to whites. Northern slaves not only gained first-hand knowledge of their masters' world, but they also rubbed elbows with lower-class whites in taverns, cock fights, and fairs where poor people of varying status mingled.[11] If urban life allowed slaves to meet more frequently and enjoy a larger degree of social autonomy than did slavery in the countryside, the cosmopolitan nature of cities speeded the transformation of Africans to Afro-Americans. Acculturation in the cities of the North was a matter of years, not generations.

For many blacks, the process of cultural transformation was well under way before they stepped off the boat. During the first century of American settlement, few blacks arrived in the North directly from Africa. Although American slavers generally originated in the North, few gave priority to Northern ports. The markets to the south were simply too large and too lucrative. Slaves dribbled into the Northern colonies from the West Indies or the mainland South singly, in twos and threes, or by the score but rarely by the boatload. Some came on special

---

A History of Slavery in New York (Syracuse, N.Y., 1966), 44–45, and *Black Bondage in the North*, 37–39; and Wells, *The Population in the British Colonies of America before 1776*, 116–23. The low ratio of women to children may have been the result of high child mortality as well as low fertility. In 1788, J. P. Brissot de Warville observed, "Married Negroes certainly have as many children as whites, but it has been observed that in the cities the death rate of Negro children is higher"; Brissot de Warville, *New Travels in the United States of America, 1788*, ed. Durand Echeverria (Cambridge, Mass., 1964), 232n.

[10] Nash, "Slaves and Slaveowners in Colonial Philadelphia," 248–52; Archdeacon, *New York City*, 89–90, esp. 89 n. 16; Greene, *The Negro in Colonial New England*, 111–18; and Bridenbaugh, *Cities in Revolt*, 88, 274, 285–86.

[11] Eric Foner, *Tom Paine and Revolutionary America* (New York, 1976), 48–56.

order from merchants or farmers with connections to the West Indian trade. Others arrived on consignment, since few Northern merchants specialized in selling slaves. Many of these were the unsalable "refuse" (as traders contemptuously called them) of larger shipments. Northern slaveholders generally disliked these scourings of the transatlantic trade who, the governor of Massachusetts observed, were "usually the worst servants they have"; they feared that the West Indian re-exports had records of recalcitrance and criminality as well as physical defects. In time, some masters may have come to prefer seasoned slaves because of their knowledge of English, familiarity with work routines, or resistance to New World diseases. But, whatever their preference, Northern colonies could not compete with the wealthier staple-producing colonies for prime African field hands. Before the 1740s, Africans appear to have arrived in the North only when a temporary glut made sale impossible in the West Indies and the mainland South. Even then they did not always remain in the North. When conditions in the plantation colonies changed, merchants reexported them for a quick profit. The absence of direct importation during the early years and the slow, random, haphazard entry of West Indian creoles shaped the development of black culture in the Northern colonies.[12] While the nature of the slave trade prevented the survival of tribal or even shipboard ties that figured so prominently in Afro-American life in the West Indies and the Lower South, it better prepared blacks to take advantage of the special circumstances of their captivity.

Newly arrived blacks, most already experienced in the New World and familiar with their proscribed status, turned Northern bondage to their advantage where they could. They quickly established a stable family life and, unlike newly imported Africans elsewhere on the continent, increased their numbers by natural means during the first generation. By 1708, the governor of Rhode Island observed that the colony's slaves were "supplied by the offspring of those they have already, which increase daily. . . ." The transplanted creoles also seized the opportunities provided by the complex Northern economy, the relatively close ties of master and slave, and, for many, the independence afforded by urban life. In New Amsterdam, for example, the diverse needs of the Dutch mercantile economy induced the West India Company, the largest slaveholder in the colony, to allow its slaves to live out and work on their own in return for a stipulated amount of labor and an annual tribute. "Half-free-

---

[12] W. N. Sainsbury *et al.*, eds., *Calendar of State Papers, Colonial Series, 1708–1709*, 110, as quoted in Greene, *The Negro in Colonial New England*, 35; McManus, *Black Bondage in the North*, 18–25, and *Slavery in New York*, 23–39; James G. Lydon, "New York and the Slave Trade, 1700 to 1774," *William and Mary Quarterly*, 3d ser., 35 (1978): 275–79, 381–90; Greene, *The Negro in Colonial New England*, 15–45; and Darold D. Wax, "Negro Imports into Pennsylvania, 1720–1766," *Pennsylvania History*, 32 (1965): 254–87, and "Preferences for Slaves in Colonial America," *Journal of Negro History*, 58 (1973): 374–76, 379–87. So many of the slaves entering the North were re-exports from other parts of the Americas that Philip D. Curtin has not included the North in his calculation of the African population transported to the New World; see *The Atlantic Slave Trade: A Census* (Madison, Wisc., 1969), 143.

dom," as this system came to be called, enlarged black opportunities and allowed for the development of a strong black community. When the West India Company refused to make these privileges hereditary, "half-free" slaves organized and protested, demanding that they be allowed to pass their rights to their children. Failing that, New Amsterdam slaves pressed their masters in other ways to elevate their children's status. Some, hearing rumors that baptism meant freedom, tried to gain church membership. A Dutch prelate complained that these blacks "wanted nothing else than to deliver their children from bodily slavery, without striving for piety and Christian virtues." Even after the conquering English abolished "half-freedom" and instituted a more rigorous system of racial servitude, blacks continued to use the leverage gained by their prominent role in the city's economy to set standards of treatment well above those in the plantation colonies. Into the eighteenth century, New York slaves informally enjoyed the rights of an earlier era, including the right to hold property of their own. "The Custome of this Country," bristled a frustrated New York master to a West Indian friend, "will not allow us to use our Negroes as you doe in Barbados."[13]

Throughout the North, the same factors that mitigated the harshest features of bondage in New York strengthened the position of slaves in dealing with their masters. Small holdings, close living conditions, and the absence of gang labor drew masters and slaves together. A visitor to Connecticut noted in disgust that slaveowners were "too Indulgent (especially the farmers) to their Slaves, suffering too great a familiarity from them, permitting them to sit at Table and eat with them (as they say to save time) and into the dish goes the black hoof as freely as the white hand." Slaves used knowledge gained at their masters' tables to press for additional privileges: the right to visit friends, live with their families, or hire their own time. One slaveholder reluctantly cancelled the sale of his slaves because of "an invariable indulgence here to permit Slaves of any kind of worth or Character who must change Masters, to choose those Masters," and he could not persuade his slaves "to leave their Country (if I may call it so), their acquaintances & friends."[14] Such indulgences originated not only in the ability of slaves to manipulate their masters to their own benefit, but also from the confidence of slaveholders in their

---

[13] Governor Samuel Cranston to the Board of Trade, December 5, 1708, in J. R. Bartlett, ed., *Records of the Colony of Rhode Island and Providence Plantations*, 4 (1860): 55, as quoted in Miller, "Narragansett Planters," 68 n. 2; and Cadwallader Colden to Mr. Jordan, March 26, 1717, in *Letters and Papers of Cadwallader Colden*, 1 (New York, 1917): 39, as quoted in Arthur Zilversmit, *The First Emancipation: The Abolition of Negro Slavery in the North* (Chicago, 1967), 22. Joyce D. Goodfriend, "Burghers and Blacks: The Evolution of a Slave Society at New Amsterdam," *New York History*, 59 (1978): 125–44; McManus, *Slavery in New York*, 2–22; and Gerald F. DeJong, "The Dutch Reformed Church and Negro Slavery in Colonial America," *Church History*, 40 (1971): 430.

[14] Sara Kemble Knight, as quoted in Ralph F. Weld, *Slavery in Connecticut* (New Haven, 1935), 8–9; John Watts, *Letterbook of John Watts*, New York Historical Society Collections, no. 61 (New York, 1938), 151; and McManus, *Black Bondage in the North, passim.*

own hegemony. Surety of white dominance, derived from white numerical superiority, complemented the blacks' understanding of how best to bend bondage to their own advantage and to maximize black opportunities within slavery.

During the middle decades of the eighteenth century, the nature of Northern slavery changed dramatically. Growing demand for labor, especially when European wars limited the supply of white indentured servants and when depression sent free workers west in search of new opportunities, increased the importance of slaves in the work force. Between 1732 and 1754, blacks composed fully a third of the immigrants (forced and voluntary) arriving in New York. The new importance of slave labor changed the nature of the slave trade. Merchants who previously took black slaves only on consignment now began to import them directly from Africa, often in large numbers. Before 1741, for example, 70 percent of the slaves arriving in New York originated in the West Indies and other mainland sources and only 30 percent came directly from Africa. After that date, the proportions were reversed. Specializing in the slave trade, African slavers carried many times more slaves than did West Indian traders. Whereas slaves had earlier arrived in small parcels rarely numbering more than a half-dozen, direct shipments from Africa at times now totaled over a hundred and, occasionally, several times that. Slaves increasingly replaced white indentured servants as the chief source of unfree labor not only in the areas that had produced for the provisioning trade, where their pre-eminence had been established earlier in the century, but in the cities as well. In the 1760s, when slave importation into Pennsylvania peaked, blacks composed more than three-quarters of Philadelphia's servant population.[15]

Northern whites generally viewed this new wave of slaves as substitutes for indentured labor. White indentured servants had come as young men without families, and slaves were now imported in much the same way. "For this market they must be young, the younger the better if not quite children," declared a New York merchant. "Males are best." As a result, the sex ratio of the black population, which earlier in the century had been roughly balanced, suddenly swung heavily in favor of men. In Massachusetts, black men outnumbered black women nearly two to one. Elsewhere sex ratios of 130 or more became commonplace.[16] Such sexual imbalance and the proscription of interracial marriage made it increasingly difficult for blacks to enjoy normal family lives. As the birth rate slipped, mortality rates soared, especially in the cities where newly arrived blacks

---

[15] Nash, "Slaves and Slaveowners in Colonial Philadelphia," 226–37; Lydon, "New York and the Slave Trade," 387–88; and Darold D. Wax, "Quaker Merchants and the Slave Trade in Colonial Pennsylvania," *Pennsylvania Magazine of History and Biography*, 86 (1962): 145, and "Negro Imports into Pennsylvania," 256–57, 280–87.

[16] Watts, *Letterbook of John Watts*, 31; McManus, *Black Bondage in the North*, 38–39; Wax, "Preferences for Slaves in Colonial America," 400–01; Rossiter, *A Century of Population Growth*, 149–84; and Greene, *The Negro in Colonial New England*, 93–96.

appeared to be concentrated. Since most slaves came without any previous exposure to New World diseases, the harsh Northern winters took an ever higher toll. Blacks died by the score; the crude death rate of Philadelphia and Boston blacks in the 1750s and 1760s was well over sixty per thousand, almost double that of whites.[17] In its demographic outline, Northern slavery at mid-century often bore a closer resemblance to the horrors of the West Indies during the height of a sugar boom than to the relatively benign bondage of the earlier years.

Whites easily recovered from this demographic disaster by again switching to European indentured servants and then to free labor as supplies became available, and, as the influx of slaves subsided, black life also regained its balance. But the transformation of Northern slavery had a lasting influence on the development of Afro-American culture. Although the Northern black population remained predominantly Afro-American after nearly a century of slow importation from the West Indies and steady natural increase, the direct entry of Africans into Northern society reoriented black culture.

Even before the redirection of the Northern slave trade, those few Africans in the Northern colonies often stood apart from the creole majority. While Afro-American slaves established precedents and customs, which they then drew upon to improve their condition, Africans tended to stake all to recapture the world they had lost. Significantly, Africans, many of whom did not yet speak English and still carried tribal names, composed the majority of the participants in the New York slave insurrection of 1712, even though most of the city's blacks were creoles.[18] The division between Africans and Afro-Americans became more visible as the number of Africans increased after mid-century. Not only did creoles and Africans evince different aspirations, but their life-chances— as reflected in their resistance to disease and their likelihood of establishing a family—also diverged sharply. Greater visibility may have sharpened differences between creoles and Africans, but Africans were too few in number to stand apart for long. Whatever conflicts different life-chances and beliefs created, whites paid such distinctions little heed in incorporating the African minority into their slaveholdings. The propensity of Northern whites to lump blacks together mitigated intraracial differences. Rather than permanently dividing blacks, the entry of Africans into Northern society gave a new direction to Afro-American culture.[19]

Newly arrived Africans reawakened Afro-Americans to their African past by providing direct knowledge of West African society. Creole

[17] Nash, "Slaves and Slaveowners in Colonial Philadelphia," 232–41, esp. n. 46.
[18] Kenneth Scott, "The Slave Insurrection in New York in 1712," *New York Historical Society Quarterly*, 45 (1961): 43–74, esp. 62–67.
[19] The shortage of African women and a sexual balance among Indians and, to a lesser extent, whites that favored women encouraged black men to marry Indian and, occasionally, white women, especially in New England; Winthrop D. Jordan, "American Chiaroscuro: The Status and Definition of Mulattoes in the British Colonies," *William and Mary Quarterly*, 3d ser., 19 (1962): 197–98, esp. n. 28.

blacks began to combine their African inheritance into their own evolving culture. In some measure, the easy confidence of Northern whites in their own dominance speeded the syncretization of African and creole culture by allowing blacks to act far more openly than slaves in the plantation colonies. Northern blacks incorporated African culture into their own Afro-American culture not only in the common-place and unconscious way that generally characterizes the transit of culture but also with a high degree of consciousness and deliberateness. They designated their churches "African," and they called themselves "Sons of Africa."[20] They adopted African forms to maximize their freedom, to choose their leaders, and, in general, to give shape to their lives. This new African influence was manifested most fully in Negro election day, a ritual festival of role reversal common throughout West Africa and celebrated openly by blacks in New England and a scattering of places in the Middle Colonies.

The celebration of Negro election day took a variety of forms, but everywhere it was a day of great merrymaking that drew blacks from all over the countryside. "All the various languages of Africa, mixed with broken and ludicrous English, filled the air, accompanied with the music of the fiddle, tambourine, the banjo, [and] drum," recalled an observer of the festival in Newport. Negro election day culminated with the selection of black kings, governors, and judges. These officials sometimes held symbolic power over the whole community and real power over the black community. While the black governors held court, adjudicating minor disputes, the blacks paraded and partied, dressed in their masters' clothes and mounted on their masters' horses. Such role reversal, like similar status inversions in Africa and elsewhere, confirmed rather than challenged the existing order, but it also gave blacks an opportunity to express themselves more fully than the narrow boundaries of slavery ordinarily allowed. Negro election day permitted a seeming release from bondage, and it also provided a mechanism for blacks to recognize and honor their own notables. Most important, it established a framework for the development of black politics. In the places where Negro election day survived into the nineteenth century, its politics shaped the politics within the black community and merged with partisan divisions of American society. Slaves elsewhere in the New World also celebrated this holiday, but whites in the plantation colonies found the implications of role reversal too frightening to allow even symbolically. Northern whites, on the other hand, not only aided election day materially but sometimes joined in themselves. Still, white cooperation was an important but not the crucial element in the rise of Negro election day. Its origin in the 1740s and 1750s suggests how the entry of Africans reoriented Afro-American culture at a formative point in its development.[21]

[20] For petitions by blacks, see Robert C. Twombly, "Black Resistance to Slavery in Massachusetts," in William L. O'Neill, ed., *Insights and Parallels* (Minneapolis, 1973), 13–16; and, for various association names, see Dorothy Porter, ed., *Early Negro Writings, 1760–1837* (Boston, 1971).

[21] Henry Bull, "Memoir of Rhode Island," Newport *Rhode-Island Republican*, April 19, 1837, as quoted in William D. Pierson, "Afro-American Culture in Eighteenth-

African acculturation in the Northern colonies at once incorporated blacks into American society and sharpened the memory of their African past and their desire to preserve it. While small numbers and close proximity to whites forced blacks to conform to the forms of the dominant Euro-American culture, the confidence of whites in their own hegemony allowed black slaves a good measure of autonomy. In this context it is not surprising that a black New England sea captain established the first back-to-Africa movement in mainland North America.[22]

Unlike African acculturation in the Northern colonies, the transformation of Africans into Afro-Americans in the Carolina and Georgia lowcountry was a slow, halting process whose effects resonated differently within black society. While creolization created a unified Afro-American population in the North, it left lowcountry blacks deeply divided. A minority lived and worked in close proximity to whites in the cities that lined the rice coast, fully conversant with the most cosmopolitan sector of lowland society. A portion of this urban elite, increasingly light-skinned, pressed for further incorporation into white society, confident they could compete as equals. The mass of black people, however, remained physically separated and psychologically estranged from the Anglo-American world and culturally closer to Africa than any other blacks on continental North America.

The sharp division was not immediately apparent. At first it seemed that African acculturation in the Lower South would follow the Northern pattern. The first blacks arrived in the lowcountry in small groups from the West Indies. Often they accompanied their owners and, like them, frequently immigrated in small family groups. Many had already spent considerable time on the sugar islands, and some had doubtless been born there. Most spoke English, understood European customs and manners, and, as their language skills and family ties suggest, had made the difficult adjustment to the conditions of black life in the New World.

As in the Northern colonies, whites dominated the population of the pioneer Carolina settlement. Until the end of the seventeenth century, they composed better than two-thirds of the settlers. During this period and into the first years of the eighteenth century, most white slaveholders engaged in mixed farming and stock raising for export to the West Indian islands where they had originated. Generally, they lived on small farms, held few slaves, and worked closely with their bond servants. Even when they hated and feared blacks and yearned for the prerogatives of West

---

Century New England" (Ph.D. dissertation, Indiana University, 1975), 181; Joseph P. Reidy, " 'Negro Election Day' and Black Community Life in New England, 1750–1860," *Marxist Perspectives*, 1 (1978): 102–17; Alice M. Earle, *Colonial Days in Old New York* (5th ed., New York, 1922); Woods, "The Negro in Early Pennsylvania," 451; and Pierson, "Afro-American Culture in Eighteenth-Century New England," 181–313.

[22] Peter Williams, *A Discourse, Deliverd in the Death of Capt. Paul Cuffee* (New York, 1817).

Indian slave masters, the demands of the primitive, labor-scarce economy frequently placed master and slave face-to-face on opposite sides of a sawbuck.[23] Such direct, equalitarian confrontations tempered white domination and curbed slavery's harshest features.

White dependence on blacks to defend their valuable lowland beachhead reinforced this "sawbuck equality." The threat of invasion by the Spanish and French to the south and Indians to the west hung ominously over the lowcountry during its formative years. To bolster colonial defenses, officials not only drafted slaves in time of war but also regularly enlisted them into the militia. In 1710 Thomas Nairne, a knowledgeable Carolina Indian agent, observed that "enrolled in our Militia [are] a considerable Number of active, able, Negro Slaves; and Law gives every one of those his freedom, who in Time of an Invasion kills an Enemy." Between the settlement of the Carolinas and the conclusion of the Yamasee War almost fifty years later, black soldiers helped fend off every military threat to the colony. Although only a handful of slaves won their freedom through military service, the continued presence of armed, militarily experienced slaves weighed heavily on whites. During the Yamasee War, when the governor of Virginia demanded one Negro woman in return for each Virginia soldier sent to defend South Carolina, the beleaguered Carolinians rejected the offer, observing that it was "impracticable to Send Negro Women in their Roomes by reason of the Discontent such Usage would have given their husbands to have their wives taken from them which might have occasioned a Revolt."[24]

The unsettled conditions that made the lowcountry vulnerable to external enemies strengthened the slave's hand in other ways. Confronted by an overbearing master or a particularly onerous assignment, many blacks took to the woods. Truancy was an easy alternative in the thinly settled, heavily forested lowcountry. Forest dangers generally sent truant slaves back to their owners, but the possibility of another flight induced slaveholders to accept them with few questions asked. Some bondsmen, however, took advantage of these circumstances to escape permanently. Maroon colonies existed throughout the lowland swamps and into the backcountry. Maroons lived a hard life, perhaps more difficult than slaves, and few blacks chose to join these outlaw bands. But the ease of escape

---

[23] Peter H. Wood, *Black Majority: Negroes in Colonial South Carolina from 1670 through the Stono Rebellion* (New York, 1974), 13–24, 94–97. The image is derived from an account of a French refugee living near the Santee River who reported in 1697 that "he worked many days with a Negro man at the Whip saw"; Alexander S. Salley, ed., "Journal of General Peter Horry," *South Carolina Historical Magazine*, 38 (1937): 51–52, as quoted in *ibid.*, 97.

[24] Memorial of Joseph Boone and Richard Beresford to the Lord Commissioners of Trade and Plantations, December 6, 1716, Public Record Office, London, as quoted in Clarence L. Ver Steeg, *Origins of a Southern Mosaic: Studies of Early Carolina and Georgia* (Athens, Ga., 1975), 106; Wood, *Black Majority: Negroes in Colonial South Carolina*, 124–30; Ver Steeg, *Origins of a Southern Mosaic*, 105–07; and Verner W. Crane, *The Southern Frontier, 1670–1732* (Durham, N.C., 1928), 162–81.

and the existence of a maroon alternative made masters chary about abusing their slaves.[25]

The transplanted African's intimate knowledge of the subtropical lowlands environment—especially when compared to the Englishman's dense ignorance—magnified white dependence on blacks and enlarged black opportunities within the slave regime. Since the geography, climate, and topography of the lowcountry more closely resembled the West African than the English countryside, African not European technology and agronomy often guided lowland development. From the first, whites depended on blacks to identify useful flora and fauna and to define the appropriate methods of production. Blacks, adapting African techniques to the circumstances of the Carolina wilderness, shaped the lowland cattle industry and played a central role in the introduction and development of the region's leading staple. In short, transplanted Englishmen learned as much or more from transplanted Africans as did the former Africans from them.[26] While whites eventually appropriated this knowledge and turned it against black people to rivet tighter the bonds of servitude, white dependence on African know-how operated during those first years to place blacks in managerial as well as menial positions and thereby permitted blacks to gain a larger share of the fruits of the new land than whites might otherwise allow. In such circumstances, white domination made itself felt, but both whites and blacks incorporated much of West African culture into their new way of life.

The structure of the fledgling lowland economy and the demands of stock raising, with deerskins as the dominant "crop" during the initial years of settlement, allowed blacks to stretch white military and economic dependence into generous grants of autonomy. On the small farms and isolated cowpens (hardly plantations by even the most latitudinous definition), rude frontier conditions permitted only perfunctory supervision and the most elementary division of labor. Most units were simply too small to employ overseers, single out specialists, or benefit from the economies of gang labor. White, red, and black laborers of varying legal status worked shoulder to shoulder, participating in the dullest drudgery as well as the most sophisticated undertakings. Rather than skilled artisans or prime field hands, most blacks could best be characterized as jacks-of-all-trades. Since cattle roamed freely through the woods until fattened for market, moreover, black cowboys—suggestively called "cattle chasers"—moved with equal freedom through the countryside, gaining full familarity with the terrain.[27] The autonomy of the isolated cowpen and the freedom

---

[25] John D. Duncan, "Servitude and Slavery in Colonial South Carolina, 1670–1776" (Ph.D. dissertation, Emory University, 1971), 587–601; and Herbert Aptheker, "Maroons within the Present Limits of the United States," *Journal of Negro History*, 24 (1939): 167–84.

[26] Wood, *Black Majority: Negroes in Colonial South Carolina*, 35–62, 119–30.

[27] *Ibid.*, 28–34; Converse D. Clowse, *Economic Beginnings of Colonial Carolina, 1670–1730* (Columbia, S.C., 1971), 61; Crane, *The Southern Frontier, 1670–1732*, 91, 120, 163, 184–85; Ver Steeg, *Origins of a Southern Mosaic*, 114–16; Gary S. Dunbar, "Colonial Carolina Cowpens," *Agricultural History*, 35 (1961): 125–30; and David L. Coon, "The Development of Market Agriculture in South

of movement stock raising allowed made a mockery of the total dominance that chattel bondage implied. Slaves set the pace of work, defined standards of workmanship, and divided labor among themselves, doubtless leaving a good measure of time for their own use. The insistence of many hard-pressed frontier slaveowners that their slaves raise their own provisions legitimated this autonomy. By law, slaves had Sunday to themselves. Time allowed for gardening, hunting, and fishing both affirmed slave independence and supplemented the slave diet. It also enabled some industrious blacks to produce a small surplus and to participate in the colony's internal economy, establishing an important precedent for black life in the lowcountry.[28]

Such independence burdened whites. They complained bitterly and frequently about blacks traveling unsupervised through the countryside, congregating in the woods, and visiting Charles Town to carouse, conspire, or worse. Yet knowledge of the countryside and a willingness to take the initiative in hunting down cattle or standing up to Spaniards were precisely the characteristics that whites valued in their slaves. They complained but they accepted. Indeed, to resolve internal disputes within their own community, whites sometimes promoted black participation in the affairs of the colony far beyond the bounds later permitted slaves or even black freemen. "For this last election," grumbled several petitioners in 1706, "Jews, Strangers, Sailors, Servants, Negroes, & almost every French Man in Craven & Berkly County came down to elect, & their votes were taken."[29] Such breaches of what became an iron law of Southern racial policy suggest how the circumstances of the pioneer lowcountry life shrank the social as well as the cultural distance between transplanted Africans and the mélange of European settlers. During the first generations of settlement, Afro-American and Anglo-American culture and society developed along parallel lines with a large degree of overlap.

If the distinction between white and black culture remained small in

---

Carolina, 1670–1785" (Ph.D. dissertation, University of Illinois, Urbana-Champaign, 1972), 113–14, 134–37. Georgia developed later than South Carolina; a description of an isolated cowpen in the Georgia countryside in 1765 may, therefore, suggest practices of an earlier era in South Carolina. See Harold E. Davis, *The Fledgling Province: Social and Cultural Life in Colonial Georgia, 1733–1776* (Chapel Hill, N.C., 1976), 67–68.

[28] Frank J. Klingberg, *An Appraisal of the Negro in Colonial South Carolina* (Washington, 1941), 6–7; Klaus G. Leowald, Beverly Starika, and Paul S. Taylor, trans. and eds., "Johann Martin Bolzius Answers a Questionnaire on Carolina and Georgia," *William and Mary Quarterly*, 3d ser., 14 (1957): 235–36, 256; Thomas Cooper and David J. McCord, comps., *The Statutes at Large of South Carolina*, 10 vols. (Columbia, S.C., 1836–41), 7: 404; and Wood, *Black Majority: Negroes in Colonial South Carolina*, 62. For black participation in the internal economy of the sugar islands, see Sidney W. Mintz, *Caribbean Transformations* (Chicago, 1974), esp. chap. 7.

[29] "The Representation and Address of Several Members of This Present Assembly," in William James Rivers, *A Sketch of the History of South Carolina* (Charleston, S.C., 1856), 459, as quoted in Ver Steeg, *Origins of a Southern Mosaic*, 38 (italics removed); and Wood, *Black Majority: Negroes in Colonial South Carolina*, 102–03.

the lowcountry, so too did differences within black society. The absence of direct importation of African slaves prevented the emergence of African-creole differences; and, since few blacks gained their liberty during those years, differences in status within the black community were almost nonexistent. The small radius of settlement and the ease of water transportation, moreover, placed most blacks within easy reach of Charles Town. A "city" of several dozen rude buildings where the colonial legislature met in a tavern could hardly have impressed slaves as radically different from their own primitive quarters. Town slaves, for their part, doubtless had first-hand familiarity with farm work as few masters could afford the luxury of placing their slaves in livery.[30]

Thus, during the first years of settlement, black life in the lowcountry, like black life in the North, evolved toward a unified Afro-American culture. Although their numbers combined with other circumstances to allow Carolina blacks a larger role in shaping their culture than that enjoyed by blacks in the North, there remained striking similarities in the early development of Afro-American life in both regions. During the last few years of the seventeenth century, however, changes in economy and society undermined these commonalities and set the development of lowcountry Afro-American life on a distinctive course.

The discovery of exportable staples, first naval stores and then rice and indigo, transformed the low country as surely as the sugar revolution transformed the West Indies. Under the pressure of the riches that staple production provided, planters banished the white yeomanry to the hinterland, consolidated small farms into large plantations, and carved new plantations out of the malaria-ridden swamps. Before long, black slaves began pouring into the region and, sometime during the first decade of the eighteenth century, white numerical superiority gave way to the lowcountry's distinguishing demographic characteristic: the black majority.

Black numerical dominance grew rapidly during the eighteenth century. By the 1720s, blacks outnumbered whites by more than two to one in South Carolina. In the heavily settled plantation parishes surrounding Charles Town, blacks enjoyed a three to one majority. That margin grew steadily until the disruptions of the Revolutionary era, but it again increased thereafter. Georgia, where metropolitan policies reined planter ambition, remained slaveless until mid-century. Once restrictions on slavery were removed, planters imported blacks in large numbers, giving lowland Georgia counties considerable black majorities.[31]

Direct importation of slaves from Africa provided the impetus to the growth of the black majority. Some West Indian Afro-Americans con-

[30] Wood, *Black Majority: Negroes in Colonial South Carolina*, 99–103, 157, 159.

[31] Peter H. Wood, "'More like a Negro Country': Demographic Patterns in Colonial South Carolina, 1670–1740," in Stanley L. Engerman and Eugene D. Genovese, eds., *Race and Slavery in the Western Hemisphere: Quantitative Studies* (Princeton, 1975), 131–45; Julian J. Petty, *The Growth and Distribution of Population in South Carolina* (Columbia, S.C., 1943), 15–58, 220–27; Bureau of the Census, *Historical Statistics of the United States*, 756; and *Returns of the Whole Number of Persons within the . . . United States [1790]* (Philadelphia, 1791).

tinued to enter the lowcountry, but they shrank to a small fraction of the whole.[32] As African importation increased, Charles Town took its place as the largest mainland slave mart and the center of the lowland slave trade. Almost all of the slaves in Carolina and later in Georgia—indeed, fully 40 percent of all pre-Revolutionary black arrivals in mainland North America—entered at Charles Town. The enormous number of slaves allowed slave masters a wide range of choices. Lowcountry planters developed preferences far beyond the usual demands for healthy adult and adolescent males and concerned themselves with the regional and tribal origins of their purchases. Some planters may have based their choices on long experience and a considered understanding of the physical and social character of various African nations. But, for the most part, these preferences were shallow ethnic stereotypes. Coromantees revolted; Angolans ran away; Iboes destroyed themselves. At other times, lowland planters apparently preferred just those slaves they did not get, perhaps because all Africans made unsatisfactory slaves and the unobtainable ones looked better at a distance. Although lowcountry slave masters desired Gambian people above all others, Angolans composed a far larger proportion of the African arrivals. But, however confused or mistaken in their beliefs, planters held them firmly and, in some measure, put them into practice. "Gold Coast and Gambia's are the best, next to them the Windward Coast are prefer'd to Angola's," observed a Charles Town merchant in describing the most salable mixture. "There must not be a Callabar amongst them."[33] Planter preferences informed lowcountry slave traders and, to a considerable degree, determined the tribal origins of lowland blacks.

Whatever their origins, rice cultivation shaped the destiny of African people arriving at Charles Town. Although the production of pitch and tar played a pivotal role in the early development of the staple-based economy in South Carolina, rice quickly became the dominant plantation crop. Rice cultivation evolved slowly during the late seventeenth and early eighteenth centuries as planters, aided by knowledgeable blacks, mastered the complex techniques necessary for commercial production. During the first half of the eighteenth century, rice culture was limited to the inland swamps, where slave-built dikes controlled the irrigation of low-lying rice fields. But by mid-century planters had discovered how to regulate the tidal floods to irrigate and drain their fields. Rice production moved to the tidal swamps that lined the region's many rivers and

---

[32] W. Robert Higgins, "Charleston: Terminus and Entrepôt of the Colonial Slave Trade," in Martin L. Kilson and Robert I. Rotberg, eds., *The African Diaspora* (Cambridge, Mass., 1976), 115.

[33] Wood, *Black Majority: Negroes in Colonial South Carolina*, xiv, and " 'More like a Negro Country,' " 149–54; Higgins, "Charleston: Terminus and Entrepôt of the Colonial Slave Trade," 187–27; Wax, "Preferences for Slaves in Colonial America," 388–99; Curtin, *The Atlantic Slave Trade*, 143, 156–57; and Henry Laurens, *The Papers of Henry Laurens*, ed. Philip M. Hamer, George C. Rogers, Jr., and David R. Chestnutt, 7 vols. (Columbia, S.C., 1970–), 1: 294–95. For a continuing discussion of slave preferences in the lowcountry, see Laurens, *Papers of Henry Laurens*, esp. vols. 1–3.

expanded greatly. By the beginning of the nineteenth century, the rice coast stretched from Cape Fear in North Carolina to the Satilla River in Georgia.[34] Throughout the lowcountry, rice was king.

The relatively mild slave regime of the pioneer years disappeared as rice cultivation expanded. Slaves increasingly lived in large units, and they worked in field gangs rather than at a variety of tasks. The strict requirements of rice production set the course of their work. And rice was a hard master. For a large portion of the year, slaves labored knee deep in brackish muck under the hot tropical sun; and, even after the fields were drained, the crops laid-by, and the grain threshed, there were canals to clear and dams to repair. By mid-century planters had also begun to grow indigo on the upland sections of their estates. Indigo complemented rice in its seasonal requirements, and it made even heavier labor demands.[35] The ready availability of African imports compounded the new harsh realities of plantation slavery by cheapening black life in the eyes of many masters. As long as the slave trade remained open, they skimped on food, clothing, and medical attention for their slaves, knowing full well that substitutes could be easily had. With the planters' reliance on male African imports, slaves found it increasingly difficult to establish and maintain a normal family life. Brutal working conditions, the disease-ridden lowland environment, and the open slave trade made for a deadly combination. Slave birth rates fell steadily during the middle years of the eighteenth century and mortality rates rose sharply. Between 1730 and 1760, deaths outnumbered births among blacks and only African importation allowed for continued population growth. Not until the eve of the Revolution did the black population begin again to reproduce naturally.[36]

As the lowcountry plantation system took shape, the great slave masters retreated to the cities of the region; their evacuation of the countryside was but another manifestation of the growing social and

---

[34] Clowse, *Economic Beginnings of Colonial South Carolina*, 122–33, 167–71, 220–21, 231–35, 256–58; Wood, *Black Majority: Negroes in Colonial South Carolina*, 35–62; Lewis C. Gray, *History of Agriculture in the Southern United States to 1860*, 2 vols. (Washington, 1933), 1: 277–89; James M. Clifton, "Golden Grains of White: Rice Planting on the Lower Cape Fear," *North Carolina Historical Review*, 50 (1973): 368–78; Douglas C. Wilms, "The Development of Rice Culture in 18th-Century Georgia," *Southeastern Geographer*, 12 (1972): 45–57; and Coon, "Market Agriculture in South Carolina," 126–27, 168–69, 178–86, 215–68. For the importance of naval stores in the transformation, see Ver Steeg, *Origins of a Southern Mosaic*, 117–32.

[35] For excellent descriptions of the process of rice growing and its changing technology, see David Doar, *Rice and Rice Planting in the Carolina Low Country* (Charleston, S.C., 1936), 7–41; and Gray, *Agriculture in the Southern United States*, 1: 290–97.

[36] Wood, "'More like a Negro Country,'" 153–64; and Philip D. Morgan, "Afro-American Cultural Change: The Case of Colonial South Carolina Slaves," paper presented at the annual meeting of the Organization of American Historians, held in New Orleans, April 1979, 3–6, esp. tables 1, 4, 7. In the 1760s, as blacks began to increase naturally, slaveholders began to show some concern for their slaves' family life; see Laurens, *Papers of Henry Laurens*, 4: 595–96, 625, 5: 370.

cultural distance between them and their slaves. The streets of Charles Town, and, later, of Beaufort, Georgetown, Savannah, Darien, and Wilmington sprouted great new mansions as planters fled the malarial lowlands and the black majority. By the 1740s, urban life in the lowcountry had become attractive enough that men who made their fortunes in rice and slaves no longer returned home to England in the West Indian tradition. Instead, through intermarriage and business connections, they began to weave their disparate social relations into a close-knit ruling class, whose self-consciousness and pride of place became legendary. Charles Town, as the capital of this new elite, grew rapidly. Between 1720 and 1740 its population doubled, and it nearly doubled again by the eve of the Revolution to stand at about twelve thousand. With its many fine houses, its great churches, its shops packed with luxury goods, Charles Town's prosperity bespoke the maturation of the lowland plantation system and the rise of the planter class.[37]

Planters, ensconced in their new urban mansions, their pockets lined with the riches rice produced, ruled their lowcountry domains through a long chain of command: stewards located in the smaller rice ports, overseers stationed near or on their plantations, and plantation-based black drivers. But their removal from the plantation did not breed the callous indifference of West Indian absenteeism. For one thing, they were no more than a day's boat ride away from their estates. Generally, they resided on their plantations during the non-malarial season. Their physical removal from the direct supervision of slave labor and the leisure their urban residences afforded appear to have sharpened their concern for "their people" and bred a paternalist ideology that at once legitimated their rule and informed all social relations.[38]

The lowcountry plantation system with its urban centers, its black majority, its dependence on "salt-water" slaves transformed black culture and society just as it reshaped the white world. The unified Afro-American culture and society that had evolved during the pioneer years disappeared as rice cultivation spread. In its place a sharp division developed between an increasingly urban creole and a plantation-based African population. The growth of plantation slavery not only set blacks further apart from whites, it also sharply divided blacks.

[37] George C. Rogers, Jr., *Charleston in the Age of the Pinckneys* (Norman, Okla., 1969); Carl Bridenbaugh, *Myths and Realities* (Baton Rouge, 1952), 59–60, 76–94, and *Cities in Revolt*, 216; and Frederick P. Bowes, *The Culture of Early Charleston* (Chapel Hill, S.C., 1942).

[38] Eugene D. Genovese has not made either regional or temporal distinctions in the development of Southern ideology but has leaned heavily on South Carolina for his understanding of Southern paternalism; see his *Roll, Jordan, Roll,* 1–113. For the interplay of quasi-absenteeism and planter ideology in the nineteenth century, see William W. Freehling, *Prelude to Civil War: The Nullification Controversy in South Carolina, 1813–1836* (New York, 1966), 65–70; and Michael P. Johnson, "Planters and Patriarchy: A Family History of Planter Ideology, Charleston, South Carolina," *Journal of Southern History* (forthcoming). The degree of absenteeism and its effect on social relations between planters and slaves has yet to be explored.

One branch of black society took shape within the bounds of the region's cities and towns. If planters lived removed from most slaves, they maintained close, intimate relations with some. The masters' great wealth, transient life, and seasonal urban residence placed them in close contact with house servants who kept their estates, boatmen who carried messages and supplies back and forth to their plantations, and urban artisans who made city life not only possible but comfortable. In addition, coastal cities needed large numbers of workers to transport and process the plantation staples, to serve the hundreds of ships that annually visited the lowcountry, and to satisfy the planters' newly acquired taste for luxury goods. Blacks did most of this work. Throughout the eighteenth century they composed more than half the population of Charles Town and other lowcountry ports. Probably nothing arrived or left these cities without some black handling it. Black artisans also played a large role in urban life. Master craftsmen employed them in every variety of work. A visitor to Charles Town found that even barbers "are supported in idleness & ease by their negroes . . . ; & in fact many of the mechaniks bear nothing more of their trade than the name." Although most black artisans labored along the waterfront as shipwrights, ropemakers, and coopers, lowcounty blacks —unlike blacks in Northern cities—also entered the higher trades, working as gold beaters, silversmiths, and cabinetmakers. In addition, black women gained control over much of the marketing in the lowcountry ports, mediating between slave-grown produce in the countryside and urban consumption. White tradesmen and journeymen periodically protested against slave competition, but planters, master craftsmen, and urban consumers who benefited from black labor and services easily brushed aside these objections.[39]

Mobile, often skilled, and occasionally literate, urban slaves understood the white world. They used their knowledge to improve their position within lowcountry society even while the condition of the mass of black people deteriorated in the wake of the rice revolution. Many urban creoles not only retained the independence of the earlier years but en-

---

[39] Joseph W. Barnwell, ed., "The Diary of Timothy Ford," *South Carolina Historical Magazine*, 13 (1914): 142; Alexander Hewatt, *An Historical Account of the Rise and Progress of the Colonies of South Carolina and Georgia*, 2 (London, 1779): 97; Alan Candler, ed., *The Colonial Records of the State of Georgia*, 18 (Atlanta, 1912): 277–82; Charles S. Henry, comp., *A Digest of All the Ordinances of Savannah* (Savannah, Ga., 1854), 94–97; Petition from Charleston Carpenters and Bricklayers, 1783, and Petition from Charleston Coopers, 1793, Legislative Papers, South Carolina Department of Archives and History, Columbia: Cooper and McCord, *Statutes at Large of South Carolina*, 2: 22–23, 7: 385–87, 9: 692–97; Donald R. Lennon and Ida B. Kellam, eds., *The Wilmington Town Book, 1743–1778* (Raleigh, N.C., 1973), 165–66; Petition from Newberne, 1785, North Carolina Legislative Papers, North Carolina State Archives, Raleigh; Carl Bridenbaugh, *Colonial Craftsmen* (New York, 1950) 139–41, and *Cities in Revolt*, 88–89, 244, 274, 285–86; Leila Sellers, *Charleston Business on the Eve of the American Revolution* (Chapel Hill, N.C., 1934), 99–108; Duncan, "Servitude and Slavery in Colonial South Carolina," 439–46; and Kenneth Coleman, *Colonial Georgia, A History* (New York, 1976), 229–30.

larged upon it. They hired their own time, earned wages from "over-work," kept market stalls, and sometimes even opened shops. Some lived apart from their masters and rented houses of their own, paying their owners a portion of their earnings in return for *de facto* freedom. Such liberty enabled a few black people to keep their families intact and perhaps even accumulate property for themselves. The small black communities that developed below the Bluff in Savannah and in Charles Town's Neck confirm the growing independence of urban creoles.[40]

The incongruous prosperity of urban bondsmen jarred whites. By hiring their own time, living apart from their masters, and controlling their own family life, these blacks forcibly and visibly claimed the white man's privileges. Perhaps no aspect of their behavior was as obvious and, hence, as galling as their elaborate dress. While plantation slaves—men and women —worked stripped to the waist wearing no more than loin cloths (thereby confirming the white man's image of savagery), urban slaves appropriated their masters' taste for fine clothes and often the clothes themselves. Low-country legislators enacted various sumptuary regulations to restrain the slaves' penchant for dressing above their station. The South Carolina Assembly once even considered prohibiting masters from giving their old clothes to their slaves. But hand-me-downs were clearly not the problem as long as slaves earned wages and had easy access to the urban market-place. Frustrated by the realities of urban slavery, lawmakers passed and repassed the old regulations to little effect. On the eve of the Revolution, a Charles Town Grand Jury continued to bemoan the fact that the "Law for preventing the excessive and costly Apparel of Negroes and other Slaves in this province (especially in *Charles Town*) [was] not being put into Force."[41]

Most of these privileged bondsmen appear to have been creoles with long experience in the New World. Although some Africans entered urban society, the language skills and the mastery of the complex inter-personal relations needed in the cities gave creoles a clear advantage over Africans in securing elevated positions within the growing urban enclaves. To be sure, their special status was far from "equal." No matter how essential their function or intimate their interaction, their relations with whites no longer smacked of the earlier "sawbuck equality." Instead, these relations might better be characterized as paternal, sometimes literally so.

[40] Candler, *Colonial Records of the State of Georgia*, 23–30, 252–62; Henry, *Ordinances of Savannah*, 95–97; Alexander Edwards, comp., *Ordinances of the City Council of Charleston* (Charleston, S.C., 1802), 65–68; Cooper and McCord, *Statutes at Large of South Carolina*, 7: 363, 380–81, 393; Lennon and Kellam, *The Wilmington Town Book*, xxx–xxxi, 165–68, 204–05; Duncan, "Servitude and Slavery in Colonial South Carolina," 467–69, 481–84; and Sellers, *Charleston Business on the Eve of the American Revolution*, 99–102, 106–08.

[41] *South Carolina Gazette*, May 24, 1773, as quoted in Duncan, "Servitude and Slavery in Colonial South Carolina," 234; Leowald, *et al.*, "Bolzius Answers a Questionnaire on Carolina and Georgia," 236; Cooper and McCord, *Statutes at Large of South Carolina*, 7: 396–412; and Duncan, "Servitude and Slavery in Colonial South Carolina," 233–37.

Increasingly during the eighteenth century, blacks gained privileged positions within lowcountry society as a result of intimate, usually sexual, relations with white slave masters. Like slaveholders everywhere, lowland planters assumed that sexual access to slave women was simply another of the master's prerogatives. Perhaps because their origin was West Indian or perhaps because their dual residence separated them from their white wives part of the year, white men established sexual liaisons with black women frequently and openly. Some white men and black women formed stable, long-lasting unions, legitimate in everything but law. More often than other slaveholders on continental British North America, lowcountry planters recognized and provided for their mulatto offspring, and, occasionally, extended legal freedom. South Carolina's small free Negro population, almost totally confined to Charles Town, was largely the product of such relations. Light-skinned people of color enjoyed special standing in the lowcountry ports, as they did in the West Indies, and whites occasionally looked the other way when such creoles passed into the dominant caste. But even when the planters did not grant legal freedom, they usually assured the elevated standing of their mulatto scions by training them for artisan trades or placing them in household positions. If the countryside was "blackened" by African imports, Charles Town and the other lowcountry ports exhibited a mélange of "colored" peoples.[42]

While one branch of black society stood so close to whites that its members sometimes disappeared into the white population, most plantation slaves remained alienated from the world of their masters, physically and culturally. Living in large units often numbering in the hundreds on plantations that they had carved out of the malarial swamps and working under the direction of black drivers, the black majority gained only fleeting knowledge of Anglo-American culture. What they knew did not encourage them to learn more. Instead, they strove to widen the distance between themselves and their captors. In doing so, they too built upon the large degree of autonomy black people had earlier enjoyed.

In the pioneer period, many masters required slaves to raise their own provisions. Slaves regularly kept small gardens and tended barnyard fowl to maintain themselves, and they often marketed their surplus. Blacks kept these prerogatives with the development of the plantation system.

[42] Winthrop D. Jordan, *White over Black: American Attitudes toward the Negro* (Chapel Hill, N.C., 1968), 144–50, 167–78, and "American Chiaroscuro: The Status and Definition of Mulattoes in the British Colonies," 186–200; Wood, *Black Majority: Negroes in Colonial South Carolina*, 100–03; and General Tax, Receipts and Payments, 1761–69, Records of the Public Treasurers of South Carolina, South Carolina Department of Archives and History, Columbia (I am grateful to Peter H. Wood for telling me about these records). A sample of manumissions taken from the South Carolina records between 1729 and 1776 indicates that two-thirds of the slaves freed were female and one-third of the slaves freed were mulattoes at a time when the slave population of South Carolina was disproportionately male and black; Duncan, "Servitude and Slavery in Colonial South Carolina," 395–98.

In fact, the growth of lowcountry towns, the increasing specialization in staple production, and the comparative absence of nonslaveholding whites enlarged the market for slave-grown produce. Planters, of course, disliked the independence truck gardening afforded plantation blacks and the tendency of slaves to confuse their owners' produce with their own, but the ease of water transportation and the absence of white supervision made it difficult to prevent.

To keep their slaves on the plantation, some planters traded directly with their bondsmen, bartering manufactured goods for slave produce. Henry Laurens, a planter who described himself as a "factor" for his slaves, exchanged some "very gay Wastcoats which some of the Negro Men may want" for grain at "10 Bushels per Wastcoat." Later, learning that a plantation under his supervision was short of provisions, he authorized the overseer "to purchase of your own Negroes all that you know Lawfully belongs to themselves at the lowest price they will sell it for." As Laurens's notation suggests, planters found benefits in slave participation in the lowcountry's internal economy, but the small profits gained by bartering with their bondsmen only strengthened the slaves' customary right to their garden and barnyard fowl. Early in the nineteenth century, when Charles C. Pinckney decided to produce his own provisions, he purchased breeding stock from his slaves. By the Civil War, lowland slaves controlled considerable personal property—flocks of ducks, pigs, milch cows, and occasionally horses—often the product of stock that had been in their families for generations.[43] For the most part, slave property holding remained small during the eighteenth century. But it helped insulate plantation blacks from the harsh conditions of primitive rice production and provided social distance from their masters' domination.

The task system, a mode of work organization peculiar to the lowcountry, further strengthened black autonomy. Under the task system, a slave's daily routine was sharply defined: so many rows of rice to be sowed, so much grain to be threshed, or so many lines of canal to be cleared. Such a precise definition of work suggests that city-bound planters found it almost impossible to keep their slaves in the fields from

---

[43] Laurens, *Papers of Henry Laurens*, 4: 616, 5: 20, 41; C. C. Pinckney, Plantation Journal, 1812, and George Lucas to Charles Pinckney, January 30, 1745/46, Manuscript Division, Library of Congress, Washington, D.C.; Entries in Memo Book "per self" and "Negro Esquire per self," Cameron Family Papers, Southern Historical Collection, University of North Carolina, Chapel Hill; Charles Town Grand Jury Presentment, January 1772, South Carolina Department of Archives and History; and Depositions from Liberty County, Georgia, Southern Claims Commission, Third Auditor, General Accounting Office, RG 217, National Archives, Washington, D.C. A similar division of labor between master and slave has been found in various nineteenth-century African slave societies. Whether these similar patterns have a common root or are the product of independent development is a subject for future research. See Paul O. Lovejoy, "The Characteristics of Plantations in the Nineteenth Century Sokoto Caliphate (Islamic West Africa)," *AHR*, 84 (1979): 1283–84. Also see footnote 19, above.

sunup to sundown. With little direct white supervision, slaves and their black foremen conspired to preserve a large portion of the day for their own use, while meeting their masters' minimum work requirements. Struggle over the definition of a task doubtless continued throughout the formative years of the lowcountry plantation system and after, but by the end of the century certain lines had been drawn. Slaves generally left the field sometime in the early afternoon, a practice that protected them from the harsh afternoon sun and allowed them time to tend their own gardens and stock.[44] Like participation in the lowcountry's internal economy, the task system provided slaves with a large measure of control over their own lives.

The autonomy generated by both the task system and truck gardening provided the material basis for lowland black culture. Within the confines of the overwhelmingly black countryside, African culture survived well. The continual arrival of Africans into the lowcountry renewed and refreshed slave knowledge of West African life. In such a setting blacks could hardly lose their past. The distinctive pattern of the lowland slave trade, moreover, heightened the impact of the newly arrived Africans on the evolution of black culture. While slaves dribbled into the North through a multiplicity of ports, they poured into the lowcountry through a single city. The large, unicentered slave trade and the large slaveholding units assured the survival not only of the common denominators of West African culture but also many of its particular tribal and national forms. Planter preferences or perhaps the chance ascendancy of one group sometimes allowed specific African cultures to reconstitute themselves within the plantation setting. To be sure, Africans changed in

[44] By the middle of the nineteenth century, the work required under the task system had been carefully defined. Indeed, for many lowcountry crops, the task had become so standardized that it was often used interchangeably as a unit of land (the amount necessary to grow a task of peas) or even a unit of time (the amount of time it took to plant a task of peas). Nevertheless, the struggle over the definition of the task did not end. Following emancipation, when planters attempted to eliminate the task system, freed people objected, often violently. In 1865, a Union soldier reported from Georgetown that the freedmen "have been accustomed to working by task, which has always given them leisure to cultivate land for themselves, tend their stock, and amuse themselves, and, therefore very correctly, I think, [believe] that with such a change in the march of labor all their privileges will go and their condition will be less to their taste than it was when they were slaves." Lt. Col. A. J. Willard to Capt. George H. Hooker, Georgetown, November 7, 1865, Letters Sent, vol. 156 DS, U.S. Army Commands, RG 393, pt. 2, National Archives, Washington, D.C. Also see Ulrich B. Phillips, ed., *Plantation and Frontier*, 1 (Cleveland, 1909): 115–19; and Frederick Law Olmsted, *The Cotton Kingdom*, ed. Arthur M. Schlesinger, 1 (New York, 1953): 190–94. The origins of the task system and the struggle over the definition of work in the eighteenth century has not yet been investigated, but, for the kinds of disputes that defined the measure of a task, see Josiah Smith to George Austin, July 22, 1773, Josiah Smith Letterbook, Southern Historical Collection, and Richard Hutson to Mr. Croll, "per Caser," August 22, 1767, Charles W. Hutson Papers, Southern Historical Collection, University of North Carolina, Chapel Hill.

the lowcountry. Even where blacks enjoyed numerical superiority and a considerable degree of autonomy, they could no more transport their culture unchanged than could their masters. But lowcountry blacks incorporated more of West African culture—as reflected in their language, religion, work patterns, and much else—into their new lives than did other black Americans. Throughout the eighteenth century and into the nineteenth, lowcountry blacks continued to work the land, name their children, and communicate through word and song in a manner that openly combined African traditions with the circumstances of plantation life.[45]

The new pattern of creolization that developed following the rice revolution smashed the emerging homogeneity of black life in the first years of settlement and left lowcountry blacks deeply divided. One branch of black culture evolved in close proximity to whites. Urban, often skilled, well-traveled, and increasingly American-born, creoles knew white society well, and they used their knowledge to better themselves. Some, clearly a well-connected minority, pressed for incorporation into the white world. They urged missionary groups to admit their children to school and later petitioned lawmakers to allow their testimony in court, carefully adding that they did not expect full equality with whites.[46] Plantation slaves shared few of the assimilationist aspirations of urban creoles. By their dress, language, and work routine, they lived in a world apart. Rather than demand incorporation into white society, they yearned only to be left alone. Within the quarter, aided by their numerical dominance, their plantation-based social hierarchy, and their continued contact with Africa, they developed their own distinctive culture, different not only from that of whites but also from the cosmopolitan world of their Afro-American brethren. To be sure, there were connections between the black majority and the urban creoles. Many—market women, jobbing artisans, and boatmen—moved easily between these two worlds, and most blacks undoubtedly learned something of the other world through chance encounters, occasional visits, and word of mouth.[47] Common white oppression continually shrank the social distance that the distinctive experience created, but by the eve of the Revolution, deep cultural differences separated those blacks who sought to improve their lives through incorporation into the white world and those who determined to disregard the white man's ways.

---

[45] Wood, *Black Majority: Negroes in Colonial South Carolina*, esp. chap. 6; Lorenzo D. Turner, *Africanisms in the Gullah Dialect* (Chicago, 1949); William R. Bascom, "Acculturation among the Gullah Negroes," *American Anthropologist*, 43 (1941): 43–50; Klingberg, *An Appraisal of the Negro in South Carolina;* and Hennig Cohen, "Slave Names in Colonial South Carolina," *American Speech*, 28 (1952): 102–07.

[46] Klingberg, *An Appraisal of the Negro in Colonial South Carolina*, 116–17; and Petition of John and William Morriss, 1791, and Petition from Camden Negroes, 1793, South Carolina Legislative Papers, South Carolina Department of Archives and History, Columbia.

[47] For one planter's attempt to keep boatmen from mixing with his plantation hands, see Laurens, *Papers of Henry Laurens*, 4: 319, 633; and Sellers, *Charleston Business on the Eve of the American Revolution*, 108.

If the movement from African to creole obliterated cultural differences among Northern blacks, creolization fractured black society in the low-country.

Cultural distinctions between Africans and Afro-Americans developed in the Chesapeake as well, although the dimension of differences between African and creole tended to be time rather than space. Unlike in the lowcountry, white planters did not promote the creation of a distinctive group whose origins, function, and physical appearance distinguished them from the mass of plantation slaves and offered them hope, however faint, of eventual incorporation into white society. And, compared to the North, African immigration into the Chesapeake came relatively early in the process of cultural transformation. As a result, African-creole differences disappeared with time and a single, unified Afro-American culture slowly emerged in the Chesapeake.

As in the lowcountry, little distinguished black and white laborers during the early years of settlement. Most of the first blacks brought into the Chesapeake region were West Indian creoles who bore English or Spanish surnames and carried records of baptism. Along the James, as along the Cooper, the demands of pioneer life at times operated to strengthen the slaves' bargaining position. Some blacks set the condition of their labor, secured their family life, participated in the region's internal economy, and occasionally bartered for their liberty. This, of course, did not save most black people from the brutal exploitation that almost all propertyless men and women faced as planters squeezed the last pound of profit from the tobacco economy. The blacks' treatment at the hands of planters differed little from that of white bound labor in large measure because it was difficult to treat people more brutally.[48] While the advantages of this peculiar brand of equality may have been lost on its beneficiaries, those blacks who were able to complete their terms of servitude quickly joined whites in the mad scramble for land, servants, and status.

Many did well. During the seventeenth century, black freemen could be found throughout the region owning land, holding servants, and occasionally attaining minor offices. Like whites, they accumulated property, sued their neighbors, and passed their estates to their children. In 1651, Anthony Johnson, the best known of these early Negro freemen, received a two-hundred-and-fifty-acre headright for importing five persons into Virginia. John Johnson, a neighbor and probably a relative, did even better, earning five hundred and fifty acres for bringing eleven persons into the colony. Both men owned substantial farms on the Eastern Shore, held servants, and left their heirs sizable estates. As established members of their communities, they enjoyed the rights of citizens. When a servant claiming his freedom fled Anthony Johnson's plantation and took refuge

---

[48] Edmund S. Morgan, *American Slavery, American Freedom: The Ordeal of Colonial Virginia* (New York, 1975), 108–79, 215–49; and Wesley Frank Craven, *White, Red, and Black: The Seventeenth-Century Virginian* (Charlottesville, Va., 1971), 75–99.

with a nearby white farmer, Johnson took his neighbor to court and won the return of his servant along with damages against the white man.[49]

The class rather than racial basis of early Chesapeake society enabled many black men to compete successfully for that scarcest of all New World commodities: the affection of white women. Bastardy lists indicate that white female servants ignored the strictures against what white lawmakers labeled "shameful" and "unnatural" acts and joined together with men of their own condition regardless of color. Fragmentary evidence from various parts of seventeenth-century Virginia reveals that approximately one-quarter to one-third of the bastard children born to white women were mulattoes. The commonplace nature of these interracial unions might have been the reason why one justice legally sanctified the marriage of Hester, an English servant woman, to James Tate, a black slave. Some successful, property-owning whites and blacks also intermarried. In Virginia's Northampton county, Francis Payne, a Negro freeman, married a white woman, who later remarried a white man after Payne's death. William Greensted, a white attorney who represented Elizabeth Key, a mulatto woman, in her successful suit for her freedom, later married her. In 1691, when the Virginia General Assembly finally ruled against the practice, some propertied whites found the legislation novel and obnoxious enough to muster a protest.[50]

By the middle of the seventeenth century, Negro freemen sharing and fulfilling the same ideals and aspirations that whites held were no anomaly in the Chesapeake region. An Eastern Shore tax list of 1668 counted nearly a third of black tithables free. If most blacks did not escape the tightening noose of enslavement, they continued to live and work under conditions not much different from white servants. Throughout the seventeenth and into the first decades of the eighteenth century, black and white servants ran away together, slept together, and, upon occasion, stood shoulder to shoulder against the weighty champions of established authority. Thus viewed from the first years of settlement—the relatively small number of blacks, their creole origins, and the initial success of some in establishing a place in society—black acculturation in the Chesapeake appeared to be following the nonplantation pattern of the Northern colonies and the pioneer lowcountry.[51]

[49] Ross M. Kimmel, "Free Blacks in Seventeenth-Century Maryland," *Maryland Historical Magazine*, 71 (1976): 19–25; John H. Russell, *The Free Negro in Virginia, 1619–1865* (Baltimore, 1913), 24–38, 88, 116, 119–20, 136–37; James H. Brewer, "Negro Property Owners in Seventeenth-Century Virginia," *William and Mary Quarterly*, 3d ser., 12 (1955): 575–80; and Susie M. Ames, *Studies of the Virginia Eastern Shore in the Seventeenth Century* (Richmond, Va., 1940), 99–108.

[50] Morgan, *American Slavery, American Freedom*, 329–37; Warren M. Billings, "The Cases of Fernando and Elizabeth Key: A Note on the Status of Blacks in the Seventeenth Century," *William and Mary Quarterly*, 3d ser., 30 (1973): 467–74; and Kimmel, "Free Blacks in Seventeenth-Century Maryland," 20–21.

[51] Edmund S. Morgan, "Slavery and Freedom: The American Paradox," *Journal of American History*, 59 (1972): 17–18; and T. H. Breen, "A Changing Labor Force and Race Relations in Virginia, 1660–1710," *Journal of Social History*, 7 (1973): 3–25. The confused, uncertain status of black people generally and of

The emergence of a planter class and its consolidation of power during a series of political crises in the middle years of the seventeenth century transformed black life in the Chesapeake and threatened this pattern of cultural change. Following the legalization of slavery in the 1660s, black slaves slowly but steadily replaced white indentured servants as the main source of plantation labor. By 1700, blacks made up more than half the agricultural work force in Virginia and, since the great planters could best afford to purchase slaves, blacks composed an even larger share of the workers on the largest estates. Increased reliance on slave labor quickly outstripped West Indian supplies. Beginning in the 1680s, Africans entered the region in increasingly large numbers. The proportion of blacks born in Africa grew steadily throughout the waning years of the seventeenth century, so that by the first decade of the eighteenth century, Africans composed some three-quarters of the region's blacks.[52] Unlike the low-country, African imports never threatened the Chesapeake's overall white numerical superiority, but by the beginning of the eighteenth century they dominated black society. Some eighty years after the first blacks arrived at Jamestown and some forty years after the legalization of slavery, African importation profoundly transformed black life.

Slave conditions deteriorated as their numbers increased. With an eye for a quick profit, planters in the Chesapeake imported males disproportionately. Generally men outnumbered women more than two to one on Chesapeake slavers. Wildly imbalanced sex ratios undermined black family life. Physically spent and emotionally drained by the rigors of the Middle Passage, African women had few children. Thus, as in the North and the Carolina lowlands, the black birth rate fell and mortality rate surged upward with the commencement of direct African importation.[53]

---

free blacks in particular during the seventeenth century also indicates the unwillingness, inability, or, more probably, lack of interest on the part of whites in firmly fixing the status of blacks. For the farrago of legislation governing free blacks, see Ira Berlin, *Slaves without Masters: The Free Negro in the Antebellum South* (New York, 1974), 7-9; and Jordan, *White over Black*, 136-78. The status of blacks, free or slave, has become something of a historical perennial, with scholars agreeing that before the 1660s at least some blacks were free and some were slave and the precise status of most is simply impossible to determine. For a review of the evidence, see Jordan, *White over Black*, chap. 2.

[52] Allan Kulikoff, "A 'Prolifick' People: Black Population Growth in the Chesapeake Colonies, 1700–1790," *Southern Studies*, 16 (1977): 391–96, 403–05, and "The Origins of Afro-American Society in Tidewater Maryland and Virginia, 1700 to 1790," *William and Mary Quarterly*, 3d ser., 35 (1978): 229–31; Russell R. Menard, "The Maryland Slave Population, 1658 to 1730: A Demographic Profile of Blacks in Four Counties," *ibid.*, 32 (1975): 30–32; and Craven, *White, Red, and Black*, 89–103. Herbert S. Klein has maintained that West Indian re-exports remained the majority into the first two decades of the eighteenth century; see his "Slaves and Shipping in Eighteenth-Century Virginia," *Journal of Interdisciplinary History*, 5 (1975): 384–85.

[53] Kulikoff, "A 'Prolifick' People: Black Population Growth," 392–406; Menard, "The Maryland Slave Population," 30–35, 38–49; and Craven, *White, Red, and Black*, 98–101.

The hard facts of life and death in the Chesapeake region distinguished creoles and Africans at the beginning of the eighteenth century. The demands of the tobacco economy enlarged these differences in several ways. Generally, planters placed little trust in newly arrived Africans with their strange tongues and alien customs. While they assigned creoles to artisanal duties on their plantations and to service within their households, they sent Africans to the distant, upland quarters where the slaves did the dull, backbreaking work of clearing the land and tending tobacco. The small size of these specialized upcountry units, their isolation from the mainstream of Chesapeake life, and their rude frontier conditions made these largely male compounds lonely, unhealthy places that narrowed men's vision. The dynamics of creole life, however, broadened black understanding of life in the New World. Traveling freely through the countryside as artisans, watermen, and domestic servants, creoles gained in confidence as they mastered the terrain, perfected their English, and learned about Christianity and other cultural modes that whites equated with civilization. Knowledge of the white world enabled black creoles to manipulate their masters to their own advantage. If Afro-Americans became increasingly knowledgeable about their circumstances and confident of their ability to deal with them, Africans remained provincials, limited by the narrow alternatives of plantation life.[54]

As in the lowcountry and the Northern colonies, Africans in the Chesapeake strove to escape whites, while creoles used their knowledge of white society for their own benefit. These cultural differences, which were reflected in all aspects of black life, can be seen most clearly in the diverse patterns of resistance. Africans ran away toward the back country and isolated swamps. They generally moved in groups that included women and children, despite the hazards such groups entailed for a successful escape. Their purpose was to recreate the only society they knew free from white domination. In 1727, Governor William Gooch of Virginia reported that about a dozen slaves had left a new plantation near the falls of the James River. They headed west and settled near Lexington, built houses, and planted a crop before being retaken. But Afro-Americans ran away alone, usually with the hope of escaping into American society. Moving toward the areas of heaviest settlement, they found refuge in the thick network of black kinship that covered the countryside and sold their labor to white yeomen with few questions asked. While the possibility of passing as free remained small in the years before the Revolution, the creoles' obvious confidence in their ability to integrate themselves into American society stands in stark contrast to that of Africans, who sought first to flee it.[55]

---

[54] Gerald W. Mullin, *Flight and Rebellion: Slave Resistance in Eighteenth-Century Virginia* (New York, 1972), esp. chaps. 2–3; Menard, "The Maryland Slave Population," 32–54; and Kulikoff, "Origins of Afro-American Society in Tidewater Maryland and Virginia," 236–49.

[55] Mullin, *Flight and Rebellion: Slave Resistance in Eighteenth-Century Virginia*, 34–110, esp. table 3 (pp. 108–09); and Kulikoff, "Origins of Afro-American Society in Tidewater Maryland and Virginia," 253–54.

As reflected in the mode of resistance, place of residence, occupation, and much else, Africans and creoles developed distinctive patterns of behavior and belief. To a degree, whites recognized these differences. They stigmatized Africans as "outlandish" and noted how creoles "affect our language, habits, and customs." They played on African-creole differences to divide blacks from each other, and they utilized creole skills to maximize the benefits of slave labor. But this recognition did not elevate creoles over Africans in any lasting way. Over the course of the century following legal enslavement, it had precisely the opposite effect. Chesapeake planters consolidated their class position by asserting white racial unity. In this context, the entry of large numbers of African—as opposed to creole—blacks into the region enlarged racial differences and helped secure planter domination. Thus, as reliance on black labor increased, the opportunities for any black—no matter how fluent in English or conversant with the countryside—to escape bondage and join the scramble for land, servants, and status diminished steadily.

By the middle of the eighteenth century, the size and character of the free Negro population had been significantly altered. Instead of a large minority of the black population, Negro freemen now composed just a small proportion of all blacks, probably not more than 5 percent. Many were cripples and old folks whom planters discarded when they could no longer wring a profit from their labor. While most were of mixed racial origins, few of these free mulattoes of the Chesapeake, in contrast to those of the lowcountry, traced their ancestry to the planter class. Instead, they descended from white servants, frequently women. These impoverished people had little status to offer their children. Indeed, planter-inspired legislation further compromised their liberty by requiring that the offspring of white women and black men serve their mother's master for thirty-one years. Those who survived the term could scarcely hope for the opportunities an earlier generation of Negro freemen had enjoyed.[56] The transformation of the free Negro caste in the century between 1660 and 1760 measured the change in Chesapeake society as its organizing principle changed from class to race.

The free Negro's decline reveals how the racial imperatives of Chesapeake society operated to lump all black people together, free and slave, creole and African. In the Chesapeake, planters dared not grant creoles special status at the expense of Africans. Since the Africans would shortly be creoles and since creoles shared so much with whites, distinctions among blacks threatened the racial division that underlay planter domination. In the lowcountry, where geography, economy, and language separated white and black, those few blacks who spoke, dressed, acted, and

---

[56] Hugh Jones, *The Present State of Virginia* (1724), ed. Richard L. Morton (Chapel Hill, N.C., 1956), 75; Berlin, *Slaves without Masters*, 3–6; Donald L. Horowitz, "Color Differentiation in the American Systems of Slavery," *Journal of Interdisciplinary History*, 3 (1973): 526–30; and George M. Fredrickson, "Toward a Social Interpretation of the Development of American Racism," in Nathan I. Huggins et al., eds., *Key Issues in the Afro-American Experience*, 1 (New York, 1971): 246–47.

looked like whites might be allowed some white prerogatives. But, if low-country planters could argue that no white man could do the work required to grow rice commercially, no one in the Chesapeake could reasonably deny that whites could grow tobacco. The fundamental unity of Chesapeake life and the long-term instability of African-creole differences pushed blacks together in the white mind and in fact.

During the middle years of the eighteenth century, changes in the Chesapeake economy and society further diminished differences within black society and created a unified Afro-American culture. The success of the tobacco economy enlarged the area of settlement and allowed planters to increase their holdings. The most successful planters, anxious to protect themselves from the rigors of the world marketplace, strove for plantation self-sufficiency. The great estates of the Chesapeake became self-contained enterprises with slaves taking positions as artisans, tradesmen, wagoners, and, sometimes, managers; the plantation was "like a Town," as a tutor on Robert Carter's estate observed, "but most of the Inhabitants are black." The increased sophistication of the Chesapeake economy propelled many more blacks into artisanal positions and the larger units of production, tighter pattern of settlement, and the greater mobility allowed by the growing network of roads ended the deadening isolation of the upcountry quarter. Bondsmen increasingly lived in large groups, and those who did not could generally find black companionship within a few miles' walk. Finally, better food, clothing, and shelter and, perhaps, the development of immunities to New World diseases enabled blacks to live longer, healthier lives.[57]

As part of their drive for self-sufficiency, Chesapeake slaveholders encouraged the development of an indigenous slave population. Spurred by the proven ability of Africans to survive and reproduce and pressed in the international slave market by the superior resources of West Indian sugar magnates and lowland rice growers, Chesapeake planters strove to correct the sexual imbalance within the black population, perhaps by importing a large proportion of women or lessening the burden of female slaves. Blacks quickly took advantage of this new circumstance and placed their family life on a firmer footing. Husbands and wives petitioned their owners to allow them to reside together on the same quarter and saw to it that their families were fed, beyond their masters' rations. Planters, for their part, were usually receptive to slaves' demands for a secure family life, both because it reflected their own values and because they profited mightily from the addition of slave children. Thomas Jefferson frankly considered "a woman who brings a child every two years as more profit-

---

[57] Philip V. Fithian, *The Journal and Letters of Philip Vickers Fithian, 1773-1774*, ed. Hunter D. Farish (Williamsburg, Va., 1943), 73; Mullin, *Flight and Rebellion: Slave Resistance in Eighteenth-Century Virginia*, 19-32; Kulikoff, "Origins of Afro-American Society in Tidewater Maryland and Virginia," 240-42, 246-49; Louis Morton, *Robert Carter of Nomini Hall: A Virginia Tobacco Planter of the Eighteenth Century* (Charlottesville, Va., 1941); Michael Greenberg, "William Byrd II and the World of the Market," *Southern Studies*, 16 (1977): 429-56; and, especially, Landon Carter, *The Diary of Colonel Landon Carter of Sabine Hall, 1752-1778*, ed. Jack P. Greene, 2 vols. (Charlottesville, Va., 1966), *passim*.

able than the best man on the farm [for] what she produces is an addition
to capital, while his labor disappears in mere consumption." Under these
circumstances, the black population increased rapidly. Planters relied less
and less on African importation and, by the 1740s, most of the growth
of the black population came from natural increase. Within a generation,
African importation was, for all practical purposes, no longer a significant
source of slave labor. In the early 1770s, the period of the greatest importation into the lowcountry, only five hundred of the five thousand
slaves added annually to the black population of Virginia derived directly
from Africa.[58]

The establishment of the family marked the re-emergence of Afro-
American culture in the Chesapeake. Although Africans continued to
enter the region, albeit at a slower pace, the nature of the slave trade
minimized their impact on the development of black society in the region.
Unlike those in the lowcountry, newly arrived Africans could rarely hope
to remain together. Rather than funnel their cargo through a single port,
Chesapeake slavers peddled it in small lots at the many tobacco landings
that lined the bay's extensive perimeter. Planters rarely bought more than
a few slaves at a time, and larger purchasers, usually the great planter-
merchants, often acted as jobbers, quickly reselling these slaves to backcountry freeholders.[59] The resulting fragmentation sent newly arrived
Africans in all directions and prevented the maintenance of tribal or
shipboard ties. Chesapeake slaveholders cared little about the origins of

[58] Allan Kulikoff, "The Beginnings of the Afro-American Family in Maryland," in
Aubrey C. Land *et al.*, eds., *Law, Society, and Politics in Early Maryland* (Baltimore, 1977), 177–96, "A 'Prolifick' People: Black Population Growth," 401–03,
405–14, and "Origins of Afro-American Society in Tidewater Maryland and Virginia," 246–53; Daniel Dulany to Robert Carter, December 18, 1768, Colonial
Papers, Maryland Historical Society, Baltimore; Robert Carter to John Pound,
March 16, 1779, to Fleet Cox, January 2, 1788, and to George Newman, December
29, 1789, typescript, Robert Carter Papers, Duke University, Durham, N.C.;
John C. Fitzpatrick, ed., *The Writings of George Washington*, 39 vols. (Washington, 1931–44), 2: 526, 29: 154, 398; and Edwin M. Betts, ed., *Thomas Jefferson's
Farm Book* (New York, 1953), pt. 2: 46, 12–13, 21, 24–26, 42–46. Planters also
found a relationship between family stability and social stability. A Maryland
planter instructed his overseer about a returned fugitive: "While his wife continues at home, I suppose there will be no danger of his making a second attempt
to get off. You may let him know, that his pardon depends upon his good future behavior, that if he behaves well, and endeavours to make amends for his
past behavior I will when I return purchase his wife if her master will sell her
at a reasonable price." Letter of John Hanson, January 29, 1782, John Hanson
Papers, Maryland Historical Society, Baltimore.

[59] Mullin, *Flight and Rebellion: Slave Resistance in Eighteenth-Century Virginia*,
14–16; Kulikoff, "Origins of Afro-American Society in Tidewater Maryland and
Virginia," 230–35; Darold D. Wax, "Black Immigrants: The Slave Trade in Colonial Maryland," *Maryland Magazine of History*, 73 (1978): 30–45; and Winthrop D. Jordan, "Planter and Slave Identity Formation: Some Problems in the
Comparative Approach," in Rubin and Tuden, *Comparative Perspectives on
Slavery in New World Plantation Societies*, 38.

their slaves. In their eyes, newly arrived Africans were not Iboes, Coro-mantees, or Angolans, but "new Negroes." While the unicentered slave trade sustained and strengthened African culture in the lowcountry, the Chesapeake slave trade facilitated the absorption of Africans into the evolving creole society.

Differences between creoles and Africans did not disappear with the creation of a self-sustaining Afro-American population. The creoles' advantages—language skills, familiarity with the countryside, artisanal standing, and knowledge of the plantation routine—continued to propel them into positions of authority within the slave hierarchy. In some ways, the growing complexity of the Chesapeake economy widened the distance between Africans and creoles, at least at first. Most of the skilled and managerial positions within the region's expanding iron industry went to creole blacks as did the artisanal work in flour mills and weaving houses. On some plantations, moreover, artisan and house status became lodged in particular families with parents passing privileged positions on to their children. Increasingly, skilled slaves entered the market economy by selling their own time and earning money from "overwork," thereby gaining a large measure of freedom. For the most part, Africans remained on rude, backwoods plantations tending the broad-leaf weed. Since creole slaves sold at a premium price and most great planters had already estab-lished self-sustaining slave forces, small planters purchased nearly all of the newly arrived Africans after mid-century. These upward-striving men generally owned the least developed, most distant farms. Their labor requirements remained primitive compared to the sophisticated division of labor on the self-contained plantation-towns.[60]

Over the long term, however, economic changes sped the integration of Africans into Afro-American society. Under the pressure of a world-wide food shortage, Chesapeake planters turned from the production of tobacco to that of food-stuff, especially wheat. The demands of wheat cultivation transformed the nature of labor in the region. Whereas tobacco farming required season-long labor, wheat farming employed workers steadily only during planting and harvesting. The remainder of the year, laborers had little to do with the crop. At the same time, however, wheat required a larger and more skilled labor force to transport the grain to market and to store it, mill it, and reship it as flour, bread, or bulk grain. Economic changes encouraged masters to teach their slaves skills and to hire them out during the slack season. At first, these opportunities went mostly to creoles, but as the wheat economy grew, spurring urbanization and manufacturing, the demands for artisans and hirelings outstripped the

[60] Kulikoff, "The Beginnings of the Afro-American Family in Maryland," 185–86; Jordan, *White over Black*, 405 n. 7; Mullin, *Flight and Rebellion: Slave Resis-tance in Eighteenth-Century Virginia*, 83–139; "Description of Servants, 1772," Northampton Furnace, Ridgely Account Books, Maryland Historical Society, Baltimore; and Ronald L. Lewis, *Coal, Iron, and Slaves: Industrial Slavery in Maryland and Virginia, 1715–1865* (Westport, Conn., 1979), 82–84, 162–63.

creole population.[61] An increasing number of Africans were placed in positions previously reserved for creoles. The process of cultural transformation that earlier in the eighteenth century had taken a generation or more was considerably shorter at mid-century. Africans became Afro-Americans with increasing rapidity as the century wore on, eliminating the differences within black society that African importation had created.

Chesapeake blacks enjoyed considerably less autonomy than their lowcountry counterparts. Resident planters, small units of production, and the presence of large numbers of whites meant that most blacks lived and worked in close proximity to whites. While lowcountry planters fled to coastal cities for a large part of the year, the resident planter was a fixture of Chesapeake life. Small freeholders labored alongside slaves, and great planters prided themselves on regulating all aspects of their far-flung estates through a combination of direct personal supervision and plantation-based overseers. The latter were usually white, drawn from the region's white majority. Those few blacks who achieved managerial positions, moreover, enjoyed considerably less authority than lowland drivers. The presence of numerous nonslaveholding whites circumscribed black opportunities in other ways as well. While Chesapeake slaves commonly kept gardens and flocks of barnyard animals, white competitors limited their market and created a variety of social tensions. If lowcountry masters sometimes encouraged their slaves to produce nonstaple garden crops, whites in the Chesapeake—slaveholders and nonslaveholders alike—complained that blacks stole more than they raised and worked to curb the practice. Thus, at every turn, economy and society conspired to constrain black autonomy.

The requirements of tobacco cultivation reinforced the planters' concern about daily work routine. Whereas the task system insulated lowcountry blacks against white intervention and maximized black control over their work, the constant attention demanded by tobacco impelled Chesapeake planters to oversee the tedious process of cultivating, topping, worming, suckering, and curing tobacco. The desire of Chesa-

---

[61] Carville Earle and Ronald Hoffman, "The Urban South: The First Two Centuries," *Perspectives in American History*, 10 (1976): 26–76; Mullin, *Flight and Rebellion: Slave Resistance in Eighteenth-Century Virginia*, 87–88, 124–27; and Gray, *Agriculture in the Southern United States*, 2: 602–17. Although the best study of slave hiring in the Chesapeake region focuses on the post-Revolution years, the forces promoting slave hire after the war suggest that the practice predates the Revolution. See Sarah S. Hughes, "Slaves for Hire: The Allocation of Black Labor in Elizabeth City County, Virginia, 1782 to 1810," *William and Mary Quarterly*, 3d ser., 35 (1978): 260–86. Also see Robert Carter to Warner Lewis, October 16, 1773, and October 20, 1774, to Mrs. Corbin, September 27, 1775, to Griffin Garland, September 29, 1775, and to John Ballantine, July 7, 1777, Carter Papers, typescript, Duke University, Durham, N.C. Allan Kulikoff has estimated that the proportion of blacks working as agricultural laborers dropped from 90 to 82 percent between 1733 and 1776; see his "Tobacco and Slaves: Population, Economy, and Society in Eighteenth-Century Prince George's County, Maryland" (Ph.D. dissertation, Brandeis University, 1976), 235–39.

peake masters to control their slaves went beyond the supervision of labor. Believing that slaves depended on them "for every necessity of life," they intervened in the most intimate aspects of black life. "I hope you will take care that the Negroes both men and women I sent you up last always go by the names we gave them," Robert "King" Carter reminded his steward. "I am sure we repeated them so often . . . that everyone knew their names & would readily answer to them." Chesapeake planters sought to shape domestic relations, cure physical maladies, and form personalities. However miserably they failed to ensure black domestic tranquility and reform slave drunkards, paternalism at close quarters in the Chesapeake had a far more potent influence on black life than the distant paternalism that developed in the lowcountry. Chesapeake blacks developed no distinct language and rarely utilized African day names for their children.[62] Afro-American culture in the Chesapeake evolved parallel with Anglo-American culture and with a considerable measure of congruence.

The diverse development of Afro-American culture during the seventeenth and eighteenth-centuries reveals the importance of time and place in the study of American slavery. Black people in colonial America shared many things: a common African lineage, a common racial oppressor, a common desire to create the richest life possible for themselves and their posterity in the most difficult of circumstances. But these commonalities took different shape and meaning within the diverse circumstances of the North American mainland. The nature of the slave trade, the various demographic configurations of whites and blacks, and the demands of particular staples—to name some of the factors influencing the development of slave society—created at least three distinctive patterns of Afro-American life. Perhaps a finer analysis will reveal still others.

This diversity did not end with the American Revolution. While African-creole differences slowly disappeared as the centerpole of black society with the closing of the slave trade and the steady growth of an Afro-American population, other sources of cohesion and division came

---

[62] Robert Carter to Robert Jones, Robert "King" Carter Letterbooks, Alderman Library, University of Virginia, Charlottesville (I am grateful to Emory Evans for alerting me to this letter); and Robert Carter to William Carr, March 15, 1785, Carter Papers, typescript, Duke University, Durham, N.C. Also see Carter, _Diary of Colonel Landon Carter of Sabine Hall, passim;_ Robert Carter to his various stewards and overseers (Rubin Sanford, Clement Brooke, Newyear Branson), Carter Papers, typescript, Duke University, Durham, N.C.; Fitzpatrick, _The Writings of George Washington,_ esp. vols. 32–34; Depositions of James Holland, William Ferguson, and Charles Gardiner, August 23, 1793, Lloyd Family Papers, Maryland Historical Society, Baltimore; and Betts, _Thomas Jefferson's Farm Book,_ pt. 2: 16. For the striking difference in naming patterns of Chesapeake and lowcountry bondsmen, compare the slave lists in the Charles Carroll Account Book, Maryland Hall of Records, Annapolis, and the Charles C. Pinckney Plantation Journal, Manuscript Division, Library of Congress, Washington, D.C.

to the fore.[63] Differences between freemen and bondsmen, urban and rural folk, skilled and unskilled workers, and browns and blacks united and divided black people, and made black society every bit as variable and diverse during the nineteenth century as in the eighteenth. Indeed the diversity of black life increased substantially during the antebellum years as political changes abolished slavery in some places and strengthened it in others, as demographic changes set in motion by the Great Migration across the Lower South took effect, as the introduction of new crops enlarged the South's repertoire of staples, and as the kaleidoscopic movement of the world market sent the American economy in all directions.

If slave society during the colonial era can be comprehended only through a careful delineation of temporal and spatial differences among Northern, Chesapeake, and lowcountry colonies, a similar division will be necessary for a full understanding of black life in nineteenth-century America. The actions of black people during the American Revolution, the Civil War, and the long years of bondage between these two cataclysmic events cannot be understood merely as a function of the dynamics of slavery or the possibilities of liberty, but must be viewed within the specific social circumstances and cultural traditions of black people. These varied from time to time and from place to place. Thus no matter how complete recent studies of black life appear, they are limited to the extent that they provide a static and singular vision of a dynamic and complex society.

[63] For the importance of African-creole differences in understanding black reactions to the revolutionary crises of the last quarter of the eighteenth century, see Michael Mullin, "British Caribbean and North American Slaves in an Era of War and Revolution, 1775–1807," in Jeffrey J. Crow and Larry E. Tise, eds., *The Southern Experience in the American Revolution* (Chapel Hill, N.C., 1978), 235–67.

White
Servitude

RICHARD HOFSTADTER

Though African slavery was to become the most important form of unfree labor in North America in the eighteenth and nineteenth centuries, during the first hundred years of English colonization the labor force was primarily made up of indentured servants from England— men, women, and children who sold themselves into temporary bondage in return for passage to the New World. It is estimated that from one-half to three-fourths of the immigrants to the English colonies in the seventeenth century fit into this category.

In view of the many hazards faced by New World settlers, the reluctance of prosperous tradesmen or skilled craftsmen to journey from Europe to North America is understandable. The three thousand miles that separated it from England, the strangeness of the land, and the danger of conflict with the Indians made the attraction of the New World slight for those with any degree of comfort in the old. Apart from a few daring speculators, most of the prosperous immigrants were men seeking religious freedom. Most of these immigrants settled in New England and Pennsylvania.

There was, however, a great demand for new population in America. Laborers were needed to grow food for the colonists and to develop commerce. Moreover, additional manpower was needed to defend the settlements against increasingly hostile Indians as well as against the French and the Spanish.

Fortunately for the development of the colonies, several conditions made labor available. First, there was a growing surplus of population in England. Farmland, which had hitherto been divided into individually owned strips and farmed communally, was increasingly consolidated into large tracts of land, thereby forcing the English peasants either to become tenant farmers or to look for new means of livelihood. Industrialization, which might have absorbed these landless peasants, was more than a century away, and city life held little promise for them. Many turned to indentured servitude in the colonies as a solution to their problems, to the relief of both England and

America. Other servants came to the colonies as a result of the civil wars in the British Isles during the seventeenth century. James I, Oliver Cromwell, and the later Stuart kings sent Scottish and Irish prisoners to the colonies—chiefly to the West Indies but also to the North American mainland.

In the following selection, the late Richard Hofstadter describes still other sources of the dependent labor class that grew up in the New World. He also demolishes the myth that these servants, when freed, moved for the most part into the yeoman farmer class.

Except during brief periods of recession, the shortage of labor in the colonies and then in the United States continued until the enormous mid-nineteenth-century influx of poor Irish and German immigrants. Skilled labor was always scarcer, and craftsmen were among the most favored of immigrants.

1

The transportation to the English colonies of human labor, a very profitable but also a very perishable form of merchandise, was one of the big businesses of the eighteenth century. Most of this labor was unfree. There was, of course, a sizable corps of free hired laborers in the colonies, often enjoying wages two or three times those prevalent in the mother country. But never at any time in the colonial period was there a sufficient supply of voluntary labor, paying its own transportation and arriving masterless and free of debt, to meet the insatiable demands of the colonial economy. The solution, found long before the massive influx of black slaves, was a combined force of merchants, ship captains, immigrant brokers, and a variety of hard-boiled recruiting agents who joined in bringing substantial cargoes of whites who voluntarily or involuntarily paid for their passage by undergoing a terminable period of bondage. This quest for labor, touched off early in the seventeenth century by the circulars of the London Company of Virginia, continued by William Penn in the 1680's and after, and climaxed by the blandishments of various English and continental recruiting agents of the eighteenth century, marked one of the first concerted and sustained advertising campaigns in the history of the modern world.

If we leave out of account the substantial Puritan migration of 1630–40, not less than half, and perhaps considerably more, of all the white immigrants to the colonies were indentured servants, redemptioners,

"White Servitude." From *America at 1750: A Social Portrait* by Richard Hofstadter. Copyright © 1971 by Beatrice K. Hofstadter, Executrix of the Estate of Richard Hofstadter. Reprinted by permission of Alfred A. Knopf, Inc.

or convicts. Certainly a good many more than half of all persons who went to the colonies south of New England were servants in bondage to planters, farmers, speculators, and proprietors.[1] The tobacco economy of Virginia and Maryland was founded upon the labor of gangs of indentured servants, who were substantially replaced by slaves only during the course of the eighteenth century. "The planters' fortunes here," wrote the governor of Maryland in 1755, "consist in the number of their servants (who are purchased at high rates) much as the estates of an English farmer do in the multitude of cattle." Everywhere indentured servants were used, and almost everywhere outside New England they were vital to the economy. The labor of the colonies, said Benjamin Franklin in 1759, "is performed chiefly by indentured servants brought from Great Britain, Ireland, and Germany, because the high price it bears cannot be performed in any other way."[2]

Indentured servitude had its roots in the widespread poverty and human dislocation of seventeenth-century England. Still a largely backward economy with a great part of its population permanently unemployed, England was moving toward more modern methods in industry and agriculture; yet in the short run some of the improvements greatly added to the unemployed. Drifting men and women gathered in the cities, notably London, where they constituted a large mass of casual workers, lumpenproletarians, and criminals. The mass of the poverty-stricken was so large that Gregory King, the pioneer statistician, estimated in 1696 that more than half the population—cottagers and paupers, laborers and outservants—were earning less than they spent. They diminished the wealth of the realm, he argued, since their annual expenses exceeded income and had to be made up by the poor rates, which ate up one-half of the revenue of the Crown.[3] In the early seventeenth century, this situation made people believe the country was overpopulated and emigration to the colonies was welcomed; but in the latter part of the century, and in the next, the overpopulation theory gave way to the desire to hoard a satisfactory labor surplus. Yet the strong outflow of population did not by any means cease. From the large body of poor drifters, many of them diseased, feckless, or given to crime, came a great part of the labor supply of the rich sugar islands and the American mainland. From the London of Pepys and then of Hogarth, as well as from many lesser ports and inland towns, the English poor, lured, seduced, or forced into the emigrant stream, kept coming to America for the better part of two centuries. It is safe to guess that few of them, and indeed few persons from the other sources of emigration, knew very much about what they were doing when they committed themselves to life in America.

Yet the poor were well aware that they lived in a heartless world. One of the horrendous figures in the folklore of lower-class London in

---

[1] Abbott E. Smith, *Colonists in Bondage* (1947), 3–4; Richard B. Morris, *Government and Labor in Colonial America* (1946), 315–16.

[2] Smith, 27; M. W. Jernegan, *Laboring and Dependent Classes in Colonial America* (1931), 55; see also K. F. Geiser, *Redemptioners and Indentured Servants in . . . Pennsylvania* (1901), 24–5.

[3] Christopher Hill, *The Century of Revolution* (1961), 206.

the seventeenth and eighteenth centuries was the "spirit"—the recruiting agent who waylaid, kidnapped, or induced adults to get aboard ship for America. The spirits, who worked for respectable merchants, were known to lure children with sweets, to seize upon the weak or the gin-sodden and take them aboard ship, and to bedazzle the credulous or weak-minded by fabulous promises of an easy life in the New World. Often their victims were taken roughly in hand and, pending departure, held in imprisonment either on shipboard or in low-grade hostels or brothels. To escaped criminals and other fugitives who wanted help in getting out of the country, the spirits could appear as ministering angels. Although efforts were made to regulate or check their activities, and they diminished in importance in the eighteenth century, it remains true that a certain small part of the white colonial population of America was brought by force, and a much larger portion came in response to deceit and misrepresentation on the part of the spirits.

With the beginnings of substantial emigration from the Continent in the eighteenth century the same sort of concerted business of recruitment arose in Holland, the Rhenish provinces of Germany, and Switzerland. In Rotterdam and Amsterdam the lucrative business of gathering and transshipping emigrants was soon concentrated in the hands of a dozen prominent English and Dutch firms. As competition mounted, the shippers began to employ agents to greet the prospective emigrants at the harbor and vie in talking up the comforts of their ships. Hence the recruiting agents known as *Neülander*—newlanders—emerged. These newlanders, who were paid by the head for the passengers they recruited, soon branched out of the Dutch ports and the surrounding countryside and moved up the Rhine and the Neckar, traveling from one province to another, from town to town and tavern to tavern, all the way to the Swiss cantons, often passing themselves off as rich men returned from the easy and prosperous life of America in order to persuade others to try to repeat their good fortune. These confidence men—"soul sellers" as they were sometimes called—became the continental counterparts of the English spirits, profiteers in the fate of the peasantry and townspeople of the Rhineland. Many of the potential emigrants stirred up by the promises of the newlanders were people of small property who expected, by selling some part of their land or stock or furnishings, to be able to pay in full for their passage to America and to arrive as freemen. What the passage would take out of them in blood and tears, not to speak of cash, was carefully hidden from them. They gathered in patient numbers at Amsterdam and Rotterdam often quite innocent of the reality of what had already become for thousands of Englishmen one of the terrors of the age—the Atlantic crossing.

2

In 1750 Gottlieb Mittelberger, a simple organist and music master in the Duchy of Württemberg, was commissioned to bring an organ to a German congregation in New Providence, Pennsylvania, and his journey inspired him to write a memorable account of an Atlantic crossing. From Heilbronn, where he picked up his organ, Mittelberger went the well-traveled route along the Neckar and the Rhine to Rotterdam, whence he sailed to a stopover at Cowes in England, and then to Philadelphia. About four hundred passengers were crowded onto the ship, mainly German and Swiss redemptioners, men pledged to work off their passage charges. The trip from his home district to Rotterdam took seven weeks, the voyage from Rotterdam to Philadelphia fifteen weeks, the entire journey from May to October.

What moved Mittelberger, no literary man, to write of his experiences was first his indignation against the lies and misrepresentations used by the newlanders to lure his fellow Germans to America, and then the hideous shock of the crossing. The voyage proved excruciating and there is no reason to think it particularly unusual. The long trip down the Rhine, with constant stops at the three dozen customs houses between Heilbronn and Holland, began to consume the limited funds of the travelers, and it was followed by an expensive stop of several weeks in Holland. Then there was the voyage at sea, with the passengers packed like herring and cramped in the standard bedsteads measuring two feet by six. "During the journey," wrote Mittelberger, "the ship is full of pitiful signs of distress—smells, fumes, horrors, vomiting, various kinds of sea sickness, fever, dysentery, headaches, heat, constipation, boils, scurvy, cancer, mouth-rot, and similar afflictions, all of them caused by the age and the highly salted state of the food, especially of the meat, as well as by the very bad and filthy water, which brings about the miserable destruction and death of many. Add to all that shortage of food, hunger, thirst, frost, heat, dampness, fear, misery, vexation, and lamentation as well as other troubles. Thus, for example, there are so many lice, especially on the sick people, that they have to be scraped off the bodies. All this misery reached its climax when in addition to everything else one must suffer through two or three days and nights of storm, with everyone convinced that the ship with all aboard is bound to sink. In such misery all the people on board pray and cry pitifully together."[4]

Even those who endured the voyage in good health, Mittelberger reported, fell out of temper and turned on each other with reproaches. They cheated and stole. "But most of all they cry out against the thieves of human beings! Many groan and exclaim: 'Oh! If only I were back at home, even lying in my pig-sty!' Or they call out: 'Ah, dear God, if I only once again had a piece of good bread or a good fresh drop of water.'" It went hardest with women in childbirth and their offspring: "Very few escape with their lives; and mother and child, as soon as they have died, are thrown into the water. On board our ship, on a day on which we had a great storm, a woman about to give birth and unable to deliver under the circumstances, was pushed through one of the portholes into the sea because her corpse was far back in the stern and could not be brought forward to the deck." Children under seven, he thought

---

[4] For the voyage, Mittelberger, *Journey to Pennsylvania* (edn. 1960), ed. and trans. by Oscar Handlin and John Clive, 10–7.

(though the port records show him wrong here), seldom survived, especially those who had not already had measles and smallpox, and their parents were condemned to watch them die and be tossed overboard. The sick members of families infected the healthy, and in the end all might be lying moribund. He believed disease was so prevalent because warm food was served only three times a week, and of that very little, very bad, very dirty, and supplemented by water that was often "very black, thick with dirt, and full of worms . . . towards the end of the voyage we had to eat the ship's biscuit, which had already been spoiled for a long time, even though no single piece was there more than the size of a thaler that was not full of red worms and spiders' nests."

The first sight of land gave heart to the passengers, who came crawling out of the hatches to get a glimpse of it. But then for many a final disappointment lay in wait: only those who could complete the payment of their fare could disembark. The others were kept on board until they were bought, some of them sickening within sight of land and, as they sickened, losing the chance of being bought on good terms. On landing some families were broken, when despairing parents indentured their children to masters other than their own.

Not even passengers of means who paid their way, moved more or less freely about ship, occupied cabins or small dormitories, and had superior rations could take an Atlantic crossing lightly. In addition to the hazards of winds too feeble or too violent, of pirates, shipwrecks, or hostile navies, there were under the best of circumstances the dangers of sickness. Travelers in either direction frequently died of smallpox or other diseases on board or soon after arrival. Anglican colonials often complained of the high mortality rate among their young would-be clergymen crossing to England to be ordained. The Dutch Reformed preacher Theodorus Frelinghuysen lost three of his five sons on their way to be ordained in Amsterdam. The evangelist George Whitefield on his first crossing to the colonies in 1738 saw a majority of the soldiers on board afflicted with fever and spent much of his time "for many days and nights, visiting between twenty and thirty sick persons, crawling between decks upon his knees, administering medicines and cordials" and giving comfort. On this voyage the captain's Negro servant died, was wrapped in a hammock and tossed into the sea. In the end all but a handful of the passengers took the fever, including Whitefield, who survived treatment by bleeding and emetics. The ship on which he returned a few months later was afflicted by a "contrary wind," drifted for over a week to the point at which crew and passengers were uncertain where they were, and took so long to arrive at Ireland that water rations, which had been cut to a pint a day, were just about to run out.[5]

When paying passengers were exposed to such afflictions, how much worse must have been the sufferings of the servants and redemptioners packed into the holds, frequently at a density that violated the laws, and without adequate ventilation. Food provisions were calculated to last

[5] Quoted in Luke Tyerman, *The Life of the Rev. George Whitefield* (1876), I, 124–5, 144–5.

fourteen weeks, which was normally sufficient, but the rations deteriorated rapidly, especially in summer. Water turned stale, butter turned rancid, and beef rotted. If Mittelberger's voyage ranked among the worst, Atlantic crossings were frequently at or near the worst, and many more disastrous ventures were recorded.[6] With bad luck, provisions could give out. The *Love and Unity* left Rotterdam for Philadelphia in May 1731 with more than 150 Palatines and a year later landed with 34, after having put in toward the end at Martha's Vineyard for water and food. On the way rations became so low that water, rats, and mice were being *sold*, and the storage chests of the dead and dying were broken open and plundered by the captain and crew. A ship called the *Good Intent*—the names of eighteenth century vessels often reek with irony—arrived off the American coast in the winter of 1751 but found herself unable to make port because of the weather; she was able to put in to harbor in the West Indies only after twenty-four weeks at sea. Nearly all of the passengers had died long before. The *Sea Flower*, which left Belfast with 106 passengers in 1741, was at sea sixteen weeks, and lost 46 passengers from starvation. When help arrived, six of the corpses had been cannibalized.

It is true that given adequate ventilation, a stock of lemon juice and vegetables, and good luck with the winds, decent sanitary arrangements were possible. The philanthropic Georgia Trustees, who were concerned about the health of their colonists, "put on board turnips, carrots, potatoes, and onions, which were given out with the salt meat, and contributed greatly to prevent the scurvy." Out of some fifteen hundred people who had gone to Georgia at the public expense, it was claimed in 1741, not more than six had died in transit. A traveler to Jamaica in 1739 reported that the servants on his ship "had lived so easily and well during the voyage, that they looked healthful, clean and fresh, and for this reason were soon sold," yet he saw another vessel arrive not long afterward with "a multitude of poor starved creatures, that seemed so many skeletons: misery appeared in their looks, and one might read the effects of sea-tyranny by their wild and dejected countenances."[7]

3

The situation in which the indentured servant or the redemptioner found himself upon his arrival depended in large measure upon his physical condition. There would be a last-minute effort to clean up and appear presentable, and in some ports the healthy were separated from the sick, once colonial officials adopted quarantine measures. Boston, the most vigilant of the ports, had long kept a pesthouse on an island in the harbor and fined captains who disregarded the regulations. "As Christians and men," the governor of Pennsylvania urged in 1738, "we are obliged to make a charitable provision for the sick stranger, and not by confining

---

[6] See Geiser, chapter v; F. R. Diffenderfer, *German Immigration into Pennsylvania . . .* (1900), chapter v, esp. 63–7.

[7] Smith, 217–8.

him to a ship, inhumanly expose him to fresh miseries when he hopes that his sufferings are soon to be mitigated."[8] Pennsylvania then designated Province Island for quarantine and built a pesthouse to harbor sick immigrants. In 1750 and again in 1765 it passed laws to bar overcrowding on ships. Laws passed by Virginia and Maryland in the 1760's providing for the quarantine of convict ships were frowned upon in London, and Virginia's law was disallowed.

Buyers came on shipboard to take their pick of the salably healthy immigrants, beginning a long process of examination and inspection with the muscles and the teeth, and ending with a conversational search for the required qualities of intelligence, civility, and docility. At Philadelphia buyers might be trying to find Germans and eschew the Scotch-Irish, who were reputed to be contumacious and work resistant and disposed to run away. Some buyers were "soul drivers" who bought packs of immigrants and brutally herded them on foot into the interior where they were offered along the way to ready purchasers. On the ships and at the docks there were final scenes of despair and frenzy as servants searched for lost articles of indenture, or lamented the disappearance of baggage, unexpected overcharges, the necessity of accepting indentures longer than their debts fairly required, the separation of families.

The final crisis of arrival was the process we would call acclimatization, in the eighteenth century known as "seasoning." Particularly difficult in the tropical islands, seasoning also took a heavy toll in the Southern colonies of the mainland. People from cities and from the mild English climate found the summer hard going in any colony from Maryland southward, especially on plantations where indentured servants were put to arduous field labor by owners whose goal it was to get a maximum yield of labor in the four or five years contracted for. Fevers, malaria, and dysentery carried many off, especially in their first years of service. Seasoning was thought to be more or less at an end after one year in the new climate, and servants who had been wholly or partly seasoned were at a premium.

During the voyage, thoughtful servants might have recalled, quite a number of persons had battened on their needs—the spirit or the newlander, the toll collectors and the parasites of the seaports, the ship captain or merchant; now there was the master. Any traffic that gave sustenance to so many profiteers might well rest on a rather intense system of exploitation. A merchant who would spend from six to ten pounds to transport and provision an indentured servant might sell him on arrival—the price varied with age, skill, and physical condition—for fifteen to twenty pounds, although the profits also had to cover losses from sickness and death en route. The typical servant had, in effect, sold his total working powers for four or five years or more in return for his passage plus a promise of minimal maintenance. After the initially small capital outlay, the master simply had to support him from day to day as his services were rendered, support which was reckoned to cost about thirteen or fourteen pounds a year. In Maryland, where exploitation was as intense as any-

[8] Diffenderfer, 82.

where, the annual net yield, even from unskilled labor, was reckoned at around fifty pounds sterling.[9] The chief temptation to the master was to drive the servant beyond his powers in the effort to get as much as possible out of him during limited years of service. The chief risk was that the servant might die early in service before his purchase price had been redeemed by his work. That he might run away was a secondary risk, though one against which the master had considerable protection. Still, hard as white servitude bore on servants, it was nevertheless not always a happy arrangement for owners, especially for those with little capital and little margin for error: shiftless and disagreeable servants, as well as successful runaways, were common enough to introduce a significant element of risk into this form of labor.

Indentured servants lived under a wide variety of conditions, which appear to have softened somewhat during the eighteenth century. Good or bad luck, the disposition of the master, the length of the term of work, the size of the plantation or farm, the robustness or frailty of the worker— all these had a part in determining the fate of each individual. Servants in households or on small farms might be in the not uncomfortable situation of familiar domestic laborers. Tradesmen who were trying to teach special skills to their workers, or householders who wanted satisfactory domestic service, might be tolerable masters. The most unenviable situation was that of servants on Southern plantations, living alongside—but never with —Negro slaves, both groups doing much the same work, often under the supervision of a relentless overseer. One has to imagine the situation of a member of the English urban pauper class, unaccustomed to rural or to any sustained labor, thrust into a hot climate in which heavy field labor— including, worst of all, the backbreaking task of clearing new land of rocks, trees, and shrubs—was his daily lot. Even as late as 1770 William Eddis, the English surveyor of customs at Annapolis, thought that the Maryland Negroes were better off than "the Europeans, over whom the rigid planter exercises an inflexible severity." The Negroes, Eddis thought, were a lifelong property, so were treated with a certain care, but the whites were "strained to the utmost to perform their allotted labour; and, from a prepossession in many cases too justly founded, they were supposed to be receiving only the just reward which is due to repeated offenses. There are doubtless many exceptions to this observation, yet, generally speaking, they groan beneath a worse than Egyptian bondage." Yet in Virginia, as the blacks arrived in greater numbers, white laborers seemed to have become a privileged stratum, assigned to lighter work and more skilled tasks.[10]

The status and reputation of Southern indentured laborers were no doubt kept lower than elsewhere because there were a considerable number of transported convicts among them. Colonies to the north were not completely free of convict transportees, but the plantation system regu-

---

[9] Raphael Semmes, *Crime and Punishment in Early Maryland* (1938), 80, 278; *cf.* Samuel McKee, Jr., *Labor in Colonial New York* (1935), 111.

[10] William Eddis, *Letters from America* (1777), 69–70; J. C. Ballagh, *White Servitude in the Colony of Virginia* (1895), 89–92.

larly put honest unfortunates alongside hardened criminals and lumped them all together as rogues who deserved no better than what was meted out to them. Among the by-products of English social change of the seventeenth and eighteenth centuries was a very substantial pool of criminal talents. The laws devised to suppress the criminal population were so harsh—scores of crimes were defined as felonies and hanging was a standard punishment for many trivial offenses—that England would have been launched upon mass hangings far beyond the point of acceptability had it not been for two devices that let many accused off the penalties prescribed for felons. One was the benefit of clergy—a practice inherited from the Middle Ages and continued until the early nineteenth century—which permitted a convicted felon to "call for the book" and prove his literacy. On the ancient assumption that those who could read were clerics and thus exempt from severe punishments by the secular state, the relatively privileged class of literate felons could be permitted to escape with the conventional branding on the thumb.

A second practice, the predecessor of convict transportation, was to secure royal pardons for ordinary offenders deemed by the judges to be worthy of some indulgence. Until the end of the French wars in 1713 it was customary to send them into the army, but in peacetime England did not know what to do with felons and drifters. In 1717 Parliament passed an act which in effect made royal clemency contingent upon transportation to the colonies for a term of labor; in consequence the large-scale shipping of convicts began which continued to the time of the American Revolution. To America at large, including the island colonies, around thirty thousand felons were transported in the eighteenth century, of whom probably more than two-thirds reached Virginia and Maryland, where they were readily snapped up by the poorer planters.[11]

The whole procedure, though clearly intended to be a humane and useful alternative to wholesale hangings, was dreadfully feared by convicts, who may have guessed, quite rightly, that whoever bought their services would try to get the most out of them during their seven-year terms (fourteen years in the case of transmuted death penalties) of hard labor. In transit felons probably were fed somewhat better than they were used to, but usually they were kept below deck and in chains during the entire voyage, and on the average perhaps one in six or seven would die on the way. "All the states of horror I ever had an idea of," wrote a visitor to a convict ship, "are much short of what I saw this poor man in; chained to a board in a hole not above sixteen feet long, more than fifty with him; a collar and padlock about his neck, and chained to five of the most dreadful creatures I ever looked on."[12] Mortality could run very high: on one ship, the *Honour*, which arrived in Annapolis in 1720, twenty of the sixty-one convicts had died. Merchants transporting felons on government contracts pleaded for subsidies to cover losses that hit them so hard.

[11] See Smith, 116–9; *cf.* Lawrence H. Gipson, *The British Empire before the American Revolution*, II (1936), 69, 79.
[12] Smith, 125.

While some planters rushed to the seaports to find convicts for their field labor supply, others were disturbed by the effect they expected criminals would have on the character of the population. These hazardous importations caused most anxiety in the colonies that received masses of transported felons. Pennsylvania subjected the importation of convicts to constant statutory harassment after 1722. Virginia at mid-century seems to have thought herself in the midst of a crime wave. The Virginia *Gazette* complained in 1751: "When we see our papers fill'd continually with accounts of the most audacious robberies, the most cruel murders, and infinite other villainies perpetrated by convicts transported from Europe, what melancholy, what terrible reflections it must occasion! What will become of our posterity? These are some of thy favours Britain. Thou art called our Mother Country; but what good mother ever sent thieves and villains to accompany her children; to corrupt some with their infectious vices and murder the rest? What father ever endeavour'd to spread a plague in his family? . . . In what can Britain show a more sovereign contempt for us than by emptying their jails into our settlements; unless they would likewise empty their jakes [privies] on our tables!"[13] The concluding metaphor seems to have come quite naturally to the colonials: Franklin also used it, although he is better remembered for his suggestion that the Americans trade their rattlesnakes for the convicts.[14] But all laws rejecting transported convicts were disallowed in England by the Board of Trade and the Privy Council, while subterfuge measures designed to impede or harass the trade were looked at with suspicion.

4

The system of indenture was an adaptation, with some distinctively harsh features, of the old institution of apprenticeship. In fact, a few native-born colonials, usually to discharge a debt or answer for a crime but sometimes to learn a trade, entered into indentures not altogether unlike those undertaken by immigrants. In law an indenture was a contract in which the servant promised faithful service for a specified period of time in return for his housing and keep and, at the end of his term of work, that small sum of things, known as "freedom dues," which his master promised him upon their parting. The typical term was four or five years, although it might run anywhere from one or two years to seven. Longer terms were commonly specified for children, and were calculated to bring them to freedom at or just past the time they reached majority. Most indentures followed a standard pattern: as early as 1636 printed forms were available, needing only a few details to be filled out by the contracting parties. Often an emigrant's original indenture was made out to a merchant or a ship's captain and was sold with its holder to an employer on arrival. Indentures became negotiable instruments in the colo-

---

[13] Ibid., 130.
[14] Cheesman A. Herrick, *White Servitude in Pennsylvania* (1926), 131–2.

nies, servants bound under their terms being used to settle debts, even gambling debts. In theory the contract protected the servant from indefinite exploitation, but in practice it had quite limited powers. It was a document vulnerable to loss, theft, or destruction, and when one considers both the fecklessness and inexperience of most indentured servants and the lack of privacy under which they lived, it is little wonder that their contracts often disappeared.

During the eighteenth century, however, circumstances began to alter the prevailing system of indentures and to lessen its severities, particularly when a special class of bonded servants, the redemptioners, became numerous. The redemptioner appeared at the beginning of the century, coming largely from the Continent, often emigrating with a family and with a supply of tools and furnishings. The passengers who traveled with Mittelberger were mostly redemptioners. Indentured servants were simply a part of a ship's cargo, but redemptioners were low-grade, partially paid-up passengers. The redemptioner embarked without an indenture, sometimes having paid part of the money for his own and his family's passage, and arranged with the shipping merchant to complete payment within a short time after landing. Once here, he might try to find relatives or friends to make up his deficit; failure to pay in full meant that he would be sold to the highest bidder to redeem whatever part of his fare was unpaid. The length of his servitude would depend upon the amount to be redeemed. It could be as short as one or two years, although four years seems to have been much more common. Redemptioners would try to go into service as a whole family group. Although redemptioners were often swindled because of their lack of English and were overcharged for interest, insurance, and the transportation of their baggage, it was less profitable to carry them than indentured servants. Still, merchants were eager to fill their ships as full as possible with a ballast of redemptioners.[15]

All bonded servants, indentured and redemptionist, were chattels of their masters, but the terminability of their contracts and the presence of certain legal rights stood between them and slavery. A servant could be freely bought and sold, except in Pennsylvania and New York where laws required the consent of a court before assigning a servant for a year or more. His labor could be rented out; he could be inherited on the terms laid down in his master's will. Yet he could own property, although he was forbidden to engage in trade. He could also sue and be sued, but he could not vote. It was expected that he would be subject to corporal punishment by his master for various offenses, and whipping was common; but a master risked losing his servant on the order of a court for a merciless or disfiguring beating. The right of a servant to petition the courts against abuse was more than a negligible protection. Penniless servants were, of course, at a disadvantage in courts manned by representatives of the master class: in effect they were appealing to the community pride, compassion, or decency of the magistrates, and the sense that there were certain things that ought not be done to a white Christian. Yet the

---

[15] Smith, 41.

frequency of complaints by servants makes it clear that the prerogative of appeal was widely used, and the frequency of judgments rendered for servants shows that it was not used in vain. No colony recognized the validity of agreements between master and servant made *during* servitude unless both parties appeared before a magistrate and registered their consent. Statutes regulated the terms of servitude in cases in which no papers of indenture existed.

For many thousands of servants their term of indentured servitude was a period of enforced celibacy. Marriage without the consent of the master was illegal, and the crimes of fornication and bastardy figure importantly in the records of bound servitude—not surprisingly, when we realize how many of the servant population were between the ages of eighteen and thirty. The sexuality of redemptioners, since they commonly came in families, was a much less serious problem for them and their masters. Among indentured servants as a whole, however, there were many more men than women. The situation of maidservants was full of both opportunities and hazards. Their services were considerably prized, and a clever or comely woman, as mistress or wife, might escape from the dreariest exactions of servitude. Still, women were also vulnerable to sexual abuse, and the penalties for simply following their own inclinations were high. Masters were unwilling to undergo the loss of time, the expense of rearing a child, or the impairment of health or risk of death in childbirth, and thus were unlikely to give consent to marriage. But the laws contrived to give masters the chance to turn such events to their own account. For fornication and bastardy there were ceremonial whippings, usually of twenty-one lashes; more to the point, sentences of from one to two or three years of extra service were exacted, an overgenerous compensation for the loss of perhaps no more than a few weeks of work. From Pennsylvania southward, Richard B. Morris has concluded, the master was often enriched far beyond his actual losses. Where a manservant fathered a child, he could be required to do whatever extra service was necessary to provide for its maintenance. Merely for contracting unsanctioned marriages, servants could be put to a year's extra service. If a maidservant identified her master as the father of her child, he could be punished for adultery, and she removed from him and resold. A keen disrelish for miscegenation provided an additional term of punishment: for bearing a mulatto bastard a woman might get heavy whipping and seven years of extra service. Despite such restraints, there were a substantial number of illegitimate births, mulatto and otherwise.

However, the commonest crime committed by servants, not surprisingly, was running away—not an easy thing to get away with, since in the colonies everyone had to carry a pass, in effect an identity card, and stiff penalties ranging from fines and personal damages to corporal punishment were imposed upon persons harboring fugitives. Runaways were regularly advertised in the newspapers, rewards were offered, and both sheriffs and the general public were enlisted to secure their return. Returned they often were, and subjected to what were regarded as suitable penalties; captured servants who were unclaimed were resold at public auction. On the whole, and especially in Pennsylvania and colonies to the south, the laws turned the punishment of the recovered runaway into an advantage for the master. The standard penalty in the North, not always rigorously enforced, was extra service of twice the time the master had lost, though whipping was also common. In Pennsylvania, a five-to-one penalty was fixed and commonly enforced, while in Maryland, the harshest of all the colonies, a ten-to-one penalty was authorized by a law of 1661 and very often enforced to the letter. A habitual runaway, or one who succeeded in getting away for weeks, could win himself a dreary extension of servitude. There was one horrendous case of a maidservant in Anne Arundel County, Maryland, who ran off habitually for short terms, and whose master quietly kept a record, true or false, of her absences. Finally taking her to court, the master rendered an account of 133 accumulated days of absence. Since it was impossible for her to deny her frequent absences, she had no shadow of an answer, and was booked for 1,330 days of extra service.[16] Hers was an unusual but not a singular case: there are recorded penalties of 1,530 days, 2,000 days, and even one of 12,130 days, which the master handsomely commuted to an even five years.[17] Virginia assessed double time, or more if "proportionable to the damages" which could be high in tobacco-harvesting time, plus an additional punishment, more commonly inflicted in the seventeenth than the eighteenth century, of corporal punishment. On the eve of the Revolution, Negro slavery had largely replaced indentures in the tidewater plantations but indentures were still important on the accessible and inviting edges of settlement, and there runaways became a critical problem. In South Carolina, where fear of insurrection had been a dominant motive, a law of 1691 had authorized a week's extra service for a day of absence, and for absences that ran as long as a week, a year for a week—a fifty-two-to-one ratio that made Maryland seem relaxed. In 1744 the week-for-a-day ratio was still kept, but the maximum penalty was set at a year's service. Whipping was also routine.

The problem of preventing and punishing runaways was complicated by what was held to be the "pirating" of labor by competing employers —and it became necessary to establish a whole series of penalties for enticing or distracting indentured labor. Plainly, if neighbors could entice bound laborers from their owners for occasional or even permanent service by offering money or promising better treatment, a rudimentary subterranean labor market would begin to replace servitude, and property in servants would become increasingly hazardous. Pirating was not taken lightly in the law, and enticers of labor were subject to personal damage suits as well as to criminal prosecution, with sentences ranging from whipping or sitting in the stocks to fines. The penalties were so heavy in the tobacco colonies that law-abiding planters might even hesitate to feed or shelter a servant who had apparently been deserted by his master. Indeed, innkeepers in these colonies were often fined simply for entertaining or selling liquor to servants. Suits for damages for brief enticements were hardly worth the trouble in the case of servants whose work was valued at a few pence a day. But in New York a skilled cabinetmaker

[16] Ibid., 268–9.
[17] Morris, 452.

and chair carver indentured in 1761 was lured away by a competitor at frequent intervals, and a few years later his master won a smashing judgment of £128.[18]

Plots hatched by several servants to run away together occurred mostly in the plantation colonies, and the few recorded servant uprisings were entirely limited to those colonies. Virginia had been forced from its very earliest years to take stringent steps against mutinous plots, and severe punishments for such behavior were recorded. Most servant plots occurred in the seventeenth century: a contemplated uprising was nipped in the bud in York County in 1661; apparently led by some left-wing offshoots of the Great Rebellion, servants plotted an insurrection in Gloucester County in 1663, and four leaders were condemned and executed; some discontented servants apparently joined Bacon's Rebellion in the 1670s. In the 1680s the planters became newly apprehensive of discontent among the servants "owing to their great necessities and want of clothes," and it was feared they would rise up and plunder the storehouses and ships; in 1682 there were plant-cutting riots in which servants and laborers, as well as some planters, took part.

By the eighteenth century, either because of the relaxed security of the indenture system or the increasing effectiveness of the authorities, disturbances were infrequent, although in 1707 a gang of runaways planned to seize military stores, burn Annapolis, steal a ship, and set up as pirates, but were stopped. Again in 1721 a band of convict servants conspired unsuccessfully to seize military stores at Annapolis. An insurrection of some consequence did actually break out among white servants under the British regime in East Florida during the summer of 1768, when three hundred Italians and Greeks in that very heterogeneous colony revolted against hard work and stern treatment, seized the arms and ammunition in the storehouse, and prepared to set sail from a ship at anchor in the river at New Smyrna. They were intercepted by a government vessel and promptly surrendered. Three leaders were convicted of piracy, one of whom was pardoned on condition that he execute his two comrades. Discontent and dissension, reaching into the local elite, were still rife in Florida at the time of the Revolution.[19]

A serious threat to the interests of masters, one which gives testimony to the onerousness of servitude, was the possibility of military enlistment. In New England, where there were not many servants, military service was obligatory and seems to have posed no major temptation to escape servitude, but in Pennsylvania and the tobacco colonies, where servants were numerous and essential, the competing demand by the army for manpower in the intercolonial war of the 1740s, and, even more, in the French and Indian War of the 1750s, aroused great anxiety among the masters. In the 1740s, more than a third of the Pennsylvania enlistments were from men in the servant class whose masters were compensated at the colony's expense; in Maryland, during the French and Indian War, Governor Horatio Sharpe reported not only that "servants immediately flocked in to enlist, convicts not excepted," but also that recruits among

---

[18] Ibid., 416–29, esp. 421–3.
[19] On insurrections, see ibid., 169–81.

freemen were extremely scarce, and in Virginia George Washington urged that servants be allowed to enlist in the Virginia volunteers lest they seize the alternative and join the regular army.[20] The resistance of the Pennsylvania Assembly to enlistments during the 1750s became provocatively stubborn and in Maryland there was armed resistance and rioting against recruitment. Parliament, whose interest it was to increase the army, passed a measure in 1756 authorizing officers to enlist indentured servants regardless of restraining colonial laws or practices. The best that masters could hope for was compensation from their colony's legislature, a practice that was repeated in Pennsylvania in 1763, or suing the recruiting officer for civil damages. During the Revolution, the Continental Congress and some of the states encouraged the enlistment of servants, but Pennsylvania and Maryland exempted them from military service. When despite this recruiting officers in Pennsylvania continued to enlist servants, a group of Cumberland County masters complained with magnificent gall that apprentices and servants "are the property of their masters and mistresses, and every mode of depriving such masters and mistresses of their property is a violation of the rights of mankind. . . ."[21] A good number of servants ran off to the British forces, especially in Virginia, but neither the wars nor the Revolution ended the practice of servitude, which declined but did not die until the nineteenth century.

5

Numerous as are the court records of penalties which lengthened service, most servants did not run afoul of the law; their periods of servitude did at last come to an end, entitling them to collect "freedom dues" if they could, and to start in life for themselves. Freedom dues were usually specified by law, but little seems to be known about their payment. Virginia and North Carolina laws of the 1740s required £3 in money, and North Carolina added an adequate suit of clothes. The Crown provided 50 acres of land, free of quitrent for ten years, in South Carolina. A Pennsylvania law of 1700 specified two complete suits of clothes, one of which was to be new, one new ax, one grubbing hoe, and one weeding hoe. Massachusetts long before in the seventeenth century had provided in biblical fashion that servants after seven years' labor should "not be sent away empty," but what this maxim was actually worth to servants is difficult to say. Like the dues of ordinary apprentices, freedom dues may have functioned most importantly as a kind of inducement to servants to carry out in good faith the concluding months and weeks of servitude. Where the labor of a servant was particularly valuable, his master might strengthen that inducement by a cash payment considerably beyond what had been promised.[22]

[20] Ibid., 284n, 286; E. I. McCormac, *White Servitude in Maryland* (1904), 90.
[21] Morris, 292; on the enlistment problem generally, see ibid., 278–94; Geiser, 94–101; Smith, 278–84; McCormac, 82–91.
[22] McKee, 95–6.

What was the economic situation of the servant after completing his servitude? It varied, no doubt, from colony to colony, and with the availability of lands. In the mainland colonies, it appears to have been assumed that an ex-servant was to be equipped for work as a free hired man with enough clothes and tools or money to give him a small start. It was assumed that wages for a freeman were high enough to enable him to earn an adequate competence or to provide himself with a plot of land within a fairly short time. Some ex-servants no doubt went westward and took up new lands. "The inhabitants of our frontiers," wrote Governor Alexander Spotswood of Virginia in 1717, "are composed generally of such as have been transported hither as servants, and being out of their time, settle themselves where land is to be taken up that will produce the necessaries of life with little labour."[23] But it is quite likely that Spotswood erred considerably on the side of optimism. For example, in Maryland, where a freed servant in the seventeenth century was entitled to 50 acres of land upon showing his certificate of freedom at the office of the land office secretary, the records show that relatively few became farmers, though many assumed their land rights and sold them for cash. Abbott E. Smith, in one of the most authoritative studies of colonial servitude, estimates that only one out of ten indentured servants (not including redemptioners) became a substantial farmer and another became an artisan or an overseer in reasonably comfortable circumstances. The other eight, he suggests, either died during servitude, returned to England when it was over, or drifted off to become the "poor whites" of the villages and rural areas. There is reason to think that in most places servants who had completed a term of bondage and had a history of local residence met the prevailing parochial, almost tribal qualifications for poor relief, and were accepted as public charges.[24] Redemptioners, Smith remarks, did a good deal better, but the scrappy evidence that has thus far been found does not yet allow much precision. Sir Henry Moore, governor of New York, thought them so anxious to own land that they made great sacrifices to do so: "As soon as the time stipulated in their indentures is expired, they immediately quit their masters, and get a small tract of land, in settling which for the first three or four years they lead miserable lives, and in the most abject poverty; but all this is patiently borne and submitted to with the greatest cheerfulness, the satisfaction of being land holders smooths every difficulty, and makes them prefer this manner of living to that comfortable subsistence which they could procure for themselves and their families by working at the trades in which they were brought up."[25] An Englishman who traveled in America in the opening years of the nineteenth century noticed "many families, particularly in Pennsylvania, of great respectability both in our society and amongst others, who had themselves come over to this country as redemptioners; or were children of such."[26]

As for the indentured servants, the dismal estimate that only two out of ten may have reached positions of moderate comfort is an attempt to

---

[23] Smith, 297.
[24] See ibid., 251–2.
[25] McKee, 112–3.
[26] Geiser, 108–9.

generalize the whole two centuries of the experience of English servitude, taking the seventeenth century when the system was brutal and opportunities were few with the eighteenth, when it became less severe.[27] In the early years more servants returned to England, and mortality was also higher. But it will not do simply to assume that freed servants, especially those from the tobacco fields, were in any mental or physical condition to start vigorous new lives, or that long and ripe years of productivity lay ahead for them. If we consider the whole span of time over which English indentured servitude prevailed, its heavy toll in work and death is the reality that stands out.

The Horatio Alger mythology has long since been torn to bits by students of American social mobility, and it will surprise no one to learn that the chance of emergence from indentured servitude to a position of wealth or renown was statistically negligible. A few cases to the contrary are treasured by historians, handed down from one to another like heirlooms—but most of them deal with Northern servants who came with education or skills. The two most illustrious colonial names with servitude in their family histories are Benjamin Franklin and the eminent Maryland lawyer Daniel Dulany. Franklin's maternal grandfather, Peter Folger of Nantucket, a man of many trades from teacher and surveyor to town and court clerk and interpreter between whites and Indians, had bought a maidservant for £20 and later married her. Dulany, who came from a substantial Irish family, arrived in 1703 with two older brothers; the brothers melted into the anonymity that usually awaited indentured arrivals, but Daniel was picked up by a lawyer who was pleased to buy a literate servant with some university training to act as his clerk and help with his plantation accounts. The closest thing to a modest, American-scale family dynasty to come out of servitude was that of the New England Sullivans. John Sullivan and Margery Browne both came to Maine as indentured servants in the 1720's. After Sullivan earned his freedom he became a teacher, bought Margery out of servitude, and married her. Their son John became a lawyer, a Revolutionary patriot, one of Washington's leading generals, and governor of New Hampshire. His younger brother, James, also a lawyer, became a congressman from Massachusetts and in time governor of the state. In the third generation, John's son, George, became a Federalist congressman and the attorney general of New Hampshire; James's son, William, pursued a successful legal career in Boston, played a prominent role in state politics, and was chosen to be one of the three delegates to take the manifesto of the Hartford Convention to Washington. John Lamb, a leader of the Sons of Liberty and later an officer in the Revolution, was the son of Anthony Lamb who had followed an improbable career: an apprentice instrument maker in London, Anthony became involved with a notorious burglar who ended on the gallows at Tyburn; as a first offender, Lamb was sentenced to be transported, served out an indenture in Virginia, moved to New York, and became a reputable instrument maker and a teacher of mathematics, surveying, and navigation. Charles Thomson, one of six children orphaned

[27] See Smith, 288–9, on later conditions.

by the death of their father on shipboard in 1739, began his American life as an indentured servant and became a teacher in Philadelphia, a merchant, a Revolutionary patriot, and Secretary of the Continental Congress. Matthew Thornton, whose parents came to Maine in the Scotch-Irish emigration of 1718, began life under indenture, became a physician, a patriot leader in New Hampshire, and a signer of the Declaration of Independence. Matthew Lyon, who won notoriety as a peppery Republican congressman from Vermont and as a victim of the Sedition Act, emigrated from Ireland in 1765 and paid off his passage by three years of indentured service on farms in Connecticut before he bought his own farm in Vermont. And there were others, brands snatched from the burning, triumphs of good fortune or strong character over the probabilities.

6

Thoreau, brooding over the human condition in the relatively idyllic precincts of Concord and Walden Pond, was convinced that the mass of men lead lives of quiet desperation. His conviction quickens to life again when we contemplate the human costs of what historians sometimes lightly refer to as the American experiment. It is true that thousands came to the colonies in search of freedom or plenty and with a reasonably good chance of finding them, and that the colonies harbored a force of free white workers whose wages and conditions might well have been the envy of their European counterparts. Yet these fortunate men were considerably outnumbered by persons, white or black, who came to America in one kind of servitude or another. It is also true that for some servants, especially for those who already had a skill, a little cash, or some intelligence or education or gentility, servitude in America might prove not a great deal worse than an ordinary apprenticeship, despite the special tribulations and hazards it inflicted. But when one thinks of the great majority of those who came during the long span of time between the first settlements and the disappearance of white servitude in the early nineteenth century—bearing in mind the poverty and the ravaged lives which they left in Europe, the cruel filter of the Atlantic crossing, the high mortality of the crossing and the seasoning, and the many years of arduous toil that lay between the beginning of servitude and the final realization of tolerable comfort—one is deeply impressed by the measure to which the sadness that is natural to life was overwhelmed in the condition of servitude by the stark miseries that seem all too natural to the history of the poor. For a great many the journey across the Atlantic proved in the end to have been only an epitome of their journey through life. And yet there must have seemed to be little at risk because there was so little at stake. They had so often left a scene of turbulance, crime, exploitation, and misery that there could not have been much hope in most of them; and as they lay in their narrow bedsteads listening to the wash of the rank bilge water below them, sometimes racked with fever or lying in their own vomit, few could have expected very much from American life, and those who did were too often disappointed. But with white servants we have only begun to taste the anguish of the early American experience.

The Small Circle of Domestic Concerns

MARY BETH NORTON

When the British began settling their American colonies, they brought with them few women. The early settlements in Virginia were speculative ventures in which gentlemen intended to turn a quick profit and return home. Colonists farther to the north, and later settlers in the southern regions, did intend to stay. Nevertheless, women remained in short supply. The rigors of frontier life and the dangers of continuous childbirth without proper hygienic or medical care made the female mortality rate extremely high. Indeed, it was not unusual for a hardy male settler to outlive three or four wives.

This scarcity of women accounts in large part for the relative independence granted them in both law and custom in the early period. Women could insist on certain rights and privileges as conditions of marriage. Although under British common law a woman lost her legal rights as an individual when she married, the colonies allowed some wives to sign contracts, to own property, and to operate businesses in certain cases.

This breach of the common law was made not only to secure women in the home, but also because the nascent society was reluctant to follow a course that might reduce some individuals to poverty and thus make them dependent on the community for subsistence. By granting women certain legal rights, usually exercised by them as widows, the society protected itself from what might have become an economic burden.

It must not be assumed that, because some women were able to act independently, all women had an elevated status. As Mary Beth Norton, of Cornell University, has shown in her detailed study of women in the late colonial and revolutionary periods, women's sphere was carefully circumscribed throughout these years. Although some scholars have suggested that women's status went into a decline in the nineteenth century after a period of greater equality during the colonial era, Norton demonstrates that women's status during both periods was low.

In the selection reprinted below, Norton describes the domestic sphere that was seen as the appropriate location for women's activities in the late colonial and revolutionary eras. She distinguishes between the work and roles of women in the city and country, between the activities of white and black women, of well-to-do and poor women, but in doing so, she notes the universality of women's domestic experience.

The household, the basic unit of eighteenth-century American society, had a universally understood hierarchical structure. At the top was the man, the lord of the fireside; next came the mistress, his wife and helpmate; following her, the children, who were expected to assist the parent of their own sex; and finally, any servants or slaves, with the former taking precedence over the latter. Each family was represented in the outside world by its male head, who cast its single vote in elections and fulfilled its obligations to the community through service in the militia or public office. Within the home, the man controlled the finances, oversaw the upbringing of the children, and exercised a nominal supervision over household affairs. Married men understandably referred to all their dependents collectively as "my family," thereby expressing the proprietary attitude they so obviously felt.[1]

The mistress of the household, as befitted her inferior position, consistently employed the less proprietary phrase "our family." Yet she, and not her husband, directed the household's day-to-day activities. Her role was domestic and private, in contrast to his public, supervisory functions. As the Marylander Samuel Purviance told his teenaged daughter Betsy in 1787, "the great Province of a Woman" was "Economy and Frugality in the management of [a] Family." Even if the household were wealthy, he stressed, "the meanest Affairs, are all and ought to be Objects of a womans

---

[1] The literature on the colonial family is vast. Useful starting places are David Rothman, "A Note on the Study of the Colonial Family," *WMQ*, 3rd ser., XXIII (1966), 627–634; and Rudy Ray Seward, "The Colonial Family in America: Toward a Socio-Historical Restoration of its Structure," *JMF*, XXXV (1973), 58–70. For an example of "my family," see Franklin B. Dexter, ed., *The Literary Diary of Ezra Stiles, D.D., LL.D.* (New York, 1901), I, 25.

"The Small Circle of Domestic Concerns." From *Liberty's Daughters: The Revolutionary Experience of American Women, 1750–1800* by Mary Beth Norton, pp. 3–39. Copyright © 1980 by Mary Beth Norton. Reprinted by permission of Little, Brown and Co.

cares." Purviance and his contemporaries would have concurred with the position taken in an article in Caleb Bingham's *The American Preceptor*, a textbook widely used in the early republic: "[N]eedle work, the care of domestic affairs, and a serious and retired life, is the proper function of women, and for this they were designed by Providence."[2]

Of course, such statements applied only to whites, for no eighteenth-century white American would have contended that enslaved black women should work solely at domestic tasks. But the labor of female slaves too was affected by their sexual identity, for they were often assigned jobs that differed from those of male slaves, even though such tasks were not exclusively domestic. Appropriately, then, an analysis of black and white women's experiences in eighteenth-century America must begin with an examination of their household responsibilities.

I

"I have a great and longing desire to be very notable," wrote a Virginia bride in 1801, declaring her allegiance to the ideal of early American white womanhood. In this context, the adjective "notable" connoted a woman's ability to manage her household affairs skillfully and smoothly. Thus the prominent clergyman Ezra Stiles asked that his daughter be educated in such a way as to "lay a founda[tion] of a notable Woman," and a Rhode Islander wrote of a young relative that she "Sets out to be a Notable house Wife." When the Virginian Fanny Tucker Coalter exuberantly told her husband, John, "I'm the picture of bustling notability," he could have had no doubt about her meaning.[3]

The characteristics of the notable wife were best described by Governor William Livingston of New Jersey in his essay entitled "Our Grand-Mothers," which was printed posthumously in two American magazines in the early 1790s. Decrying his female contemporaries' apparent abandonment of traditional values, Livingston presented a romanticized picture of the colonial women of the past. Such wives "placed their renown" in promoting the welfare of their families, Livingston asserted. "They were strangers to dissipation; . . . their own habitation was their delight." They not only practiced economy, thereby saving their husbands' earnings, but they also "augmented their treasure, by their industry." Most important, "they maintained good order and harmony in

[2] Samuel Purviance to Betsy Purviance, [c. 1787], Purviance-Courtenay Papers, DU; Caleb Bingham, *The American Preceptor*, 42nd ed. (Boston, 1811), 104. For "our family," see, e.g., Thomas Eliot Andrews, ed., "The Diary of Elizabeth (Porter) Phelps," *NEHGR*, CXIX (1965), 219.

[3] Ann Page to Elizabeth Randolph, Nov. 6, 1801, William B. Randolph Papers, box 1, LCMD; Dexter, ed., *Literary Diary of Ezra Stiles*, I, 577; William G. Roelker, ed., *Benjamin Franklin and Catharine Ray Green Their Correspondence 1755–1790* (Philadelphia, 1949), 105; Fanny Coalter to John Coalter, March 9, 1804, Brown-Coalter-Tucker Papers, box 2, EGS.

their empire" and "enjoyed happiness in their chimney corners," passing on these same qualities to the daughters they carefully raised to be like themselves. Their homes, in short, were "the source of their pleasure; and the foundation of their glory."[4]

Although other accounts of the attributes of notable housewives were couched in less sentimental form, their message was the same. Ministers preaching funeral sermons for women often took as their text Proverbs 31, with its description of the virtuous woman who "looketh well to the Ways of her Household and eateth not the Bread of Idleness." So too drafters of obituaries and memorial statements emphasized the sterling housewifely talents of the women they eulogized. Such a model of female perfection did not allow a woman an independent existence: ideally, she would maintain no identity separate from that of her male-defined family and her household responsibilities. A man like James Kent, the distinguished New York lawyer, could smugly describe himself as "the independent . . . *Lord of my own fireside*," while women, as William Livingston had declared, were expected to tend the hearth and find "happiness in their chimney corners."[5]

These contrasting images of autonomy and subordination were translated into reality in mid-eighteenth-century American household organization. Although the mistress directed the daily life of the household, her position within the home was secondary to that of her husband. She was expected to follow his orders, and he assumed control over the family finances. In 1750, the anonymous author of *Reflections on Courtship and Marriage*, a pamphlet long erroneously attributed to Benjamin Franklin, told men that it "would be but just and prudent to inform and consult a wife" before making "very important" decisions about monetary matters, but evidence drawn from a variety of sources indicates that few colonial husbands followed this advice. Instead, they appear to have kept the reins of financial management firmly in their own hands, rarely if ever informing their wives about even the basic details of monetary transactions.[6]

The most comprehensive evidence of this phenomenon comes from an analysis of the claims for lost property submitted by 468 white loyalist refugee women after the Revolution. The claims procedure as established by Parliament and carried out by a commission appointed for the purpose required that American loyalists prepare detailed written statements

---

[4] William Livingston, "Our Grand-Mothers," *American Museum*, IX (March 1791, 143–144; also printed in *Massachusetts Magazine*, IV (Jan. 1792), 14–15.

[5] James Kent, "Chronological Memoranda," May 1, 1799, James Kent Papers, LCMD. For a typical eulogy, see Roelker, ed., *Franklin-Greene Correspondence*, 138. Lonna Malmsheimer, "Daughters of Zion: New England Roots of American Feminism," *New England Quarterly*, L (1977), 491–492, discusses the widespread use of Proverbs 31 in funeral sermons for women.

[6] *A Series of Letters on Courtship and Marriage* . . . (Elizabethtown, N.J., 1796), 54–57, esp. 56. The following three paragraphs summarize the findings reported in Mary Beth Norton, "Eighteenth-Century American Women in Peace and War: The Case of the Loyalists," *WMQ*, 3d ser., XXXIII (1976), 386–398.

of their losses of property and testify orally about those statements. Because each claimant wanted to receive the maximum possible return on her claim, there was no reason for her to withhold any information from the commission or to feign ignorance of a particular item of property that had belonged to her family. As a result, claims prepared by female refugees, the vast majority of them widows of loyalist men, accurately depict the dimensions of the world in which they had lived prior to the war. If they had participated in economic decision making, the claims documents would demonstrate that fact by revealing their knowledge of their families' financial status. But instead the claims uniformly disclose loyalist women's insulation from the external affairs of the household and their confinement to a wholly domestic realm.

The evidence of women's ignorance of financial affairs takes a variety of forms in the claims records. Rural wives often were unable to place a precise value on tools, lands, or harvested grain, even if they knew a farm's total acreage or the size of the harvest. Urban women frequently did not know their husbands' exact income or the cost of the houses in which they lived. The typical wealthy female was not aware of her husband's net worth because she did not know the amount of his outstanding debts or what was owed to him, and poor women occasionally failed to list any value at all for their meager possessions. Women of all descriptions, moreover, shared an ignorance of legal language and an unfamiliarity with the details of transactions concerning property with which they were not personally acquainted. The sole exceptions to this rule were a few widows who had already served several years as executrices of the family estates; some wives of innkeepers, grocers, or other shopkeepers who had assisted their husbands in business; and a small number of single women who had supported themselves through their own efforts.

Loyalist husbands, then, did not normally discuss economic decisions with their wives. The women lacked exactly that information which their husbands alone could have supplied, for they were able to describe only those parts of the property with which they came into regular contact. That the practice in these loyalist homes was not atypical is shown when one looks at patriot families as well.

American wives and widows alike repeatedly noted their lack of information about their husbands' business dealings. "I don't know anything of his affairs," a Virginian resident in London wrote in 1757; "whether his income will admit of our living in the manner we do, I am a stranger to." Elizabeth Sandwith Drinker, a Philadelphia Quaker, commented years later, "I am not acquainted with the extent of my husband's great variety of engagements," quoting an apposite poem that began, "I stay much at home, and my business I mind."[7] To such married women, their spouses' financial affairs were not of immediate import. But widows, by contrast, had to cope with the consequences of their ignorance. On his

[7] John J. Smith, ed., *Letters of Doctor Richard Hill and His Children* (Philadelphia, 1854), 141; Elizabeth Drinker, Diary, Dec. 12, 1795, HSP. See also, e.g., B. Crannell to Catherine Livingston, Sept. 3, 1785, Gilbert Livingston Papers, NYPL.

deathbed, a New England cleric surprised his wife with the news that she would have "many debts to pay that [she] knew nothing about," and her subsequent experience was replicated many times over—by the Marylander whose husband left no records to guide her administration of his estate, by the Virginian who had to tell her husband's employer that he had evidently neglected to maintain proper rent rolls, by the New Yorker who admitted to her son-in-law that she had known "very little" of her spouse's affairs before his death.[8]

It might seem extraordinary that colonial men failed to recognize the potential benefits—to their children and their estates, if not to themselves—of keeping their wives informed about family finances. Yet the responsibility was not theirs alone. Married women rarely appear to have sought economic information from their husbands, whether in anticipation of eventual widowhood or simply out of a desire to understand the family's financial circumstances.[9] On the contrary, women's statements reveal a complete acceptance of the division of their world into two separate, sexually defined spheres.

"Nature & Custom seems to have destined us for the more endearing & private & the Man for the more active & busy Walks of Life," remarked Elizabeth Willing Powel, a leader of Philadelphia society, in 1784. A similar sense of the character of the difference between male and female realms shone through the 1768 observation of a fellow Philadephian of Mrs. Powel, the teenager Peggy Emlen, who described the men she saw hurrying about the city streets: they "all seem people of a great deal of business and importance, as for me I am not much of either." Men shared this same notion of the dichotomy between male public activity and female private passivity. In 1745, an essayist warned women that they were best "confined within the narrow Limits of Domestick Offices," for "when they stray beyond them, they move excentrically, and consequently without grace." A New Englander twelve years later worried that women might want "to obtain the other's Sphere of Action, & become Men," but he reassured himself that "they will again return to the wonted Paths of true Politeness, & shine most in the proper Sphere of domestick Life."[10]

---

[8] Jane Robbins to Hannah Gilman, Sept. 1799, Gilman Papers, MHS; Margaret Smith to Samuel Galloway, Sept. 22, 1762, Galloway-Maxcy-Markoe Papers, V, LCMD; Ann Peyton to [Battaile Muse], March 25, 1783, Battaile Muse Papers, DU; Catherine Livingston to [Smith Thompson], Dec. 25, Gilbert Livingston Papers.

[9] John Adams recorded an incident in which his mother asked for such information, but his father refused to give it (Lyman H. Butterfield et al., eds., *Diary and Autobiography of John Adams* [Cambridge, Mass., 1961], I, 65).

[10] Elizabeth Powel to Mrs. Page, [1784], Powel Collection, Miscellany, HSP; Peggy Emlen to Sally Logan, Sept. 3rd day morning, [no yr.], Marjorie P. M. Brown Collection, box 1, HSP; "Animadversions on the Affectation of ill-suited Characters among the Female Sex," *American Magazine and Historical Chronicle*, II (1745), 303; [Samuel Quincy] to [Robert Treat Paine], Feb. 2, 1756, Robert Treat Paine Papers, MHS.

If women were accordingly out of place in the world beyond the household, so men were not entirely at home in the female realm of domestic affairs. The family property may have been "his" in wives' terminology, but at the same time the household furnishings were "hers" in the minds of their spouses. Wartime letters from American husbands confirm the separation of male and female spheres, more because of what they do not contain than as a result of what they do. When couples were separated by the Revolutionary War, men for the most part neglected to instruct their wives about the ordinary details of domestic life. Since they initially sent explicit directions about financial affairs, their failure to concern themselves with household management would seem to indicate that they had been accustomed to leave that realm entirely to their wives. Only if they had not previously issued orders on domestic subjects would they have failed to include such directives in their correspondence.[11]

The evidence, then, suggests that female whites shared a universal domestic experience that differentiated their world from that of men. Their lives were to a large extent defined by their familial responsibilities, but the precise character of those obligations varied according to the nature of the household in which they resided. Although demographic historians have concentrated upon determining the size of colonial households, from the standpoint of an American woman, size—within a normal range—mattered less than composition. It meant a great deal to a housewife whether she had daughters who could assist her, whether her household contained a helpful servant or a demanding elderly relative, or whether she had to contend with a resident mother-in-law for control of her own domestic affairs.[12]

But ultimately of greater significance were differences in the wealth and location of colonial households. The chief factors that defined a white woman's domestic role arose from the family's economic status, which determined whether there would be servants or slaves, and from the household's location in a rural or urban setting. With a similarity of household roles as a basis, one can divide eighteenth-century women into four groups: poor and middling white farm women, north and south; white urban women of all social ranks; wealthy southerners who lived on plantations; and the female blacks held in bondage by those same wealthy southerners.

[11] For "his" estates, see, e.g., "Letters from Mrs. Ralph Izard to Mrs. William Lee," *VMHB*, VIII (1900), 24; for "her" furnishings, John Jones to Polly Jones, Oct. 3, 1779, Seaborn Jones Sr. Papers, DU, and Norton, "Eighteenth-Century American Women," *WMQ*, 3rd ser., XXXIII (1976), 396–397. One of the few men who regularly discussed ordinary household matters during the Revolution was William Palfrey of Massachusetts; see his letters, *passim*, HL.

[12] Household size is discussed in Robert V. Wells, *The Population of the British Colonies in America before 1776: A Survey of Census Data* (Princeton, N.J., 1975), 297–333. Problems caused by household composition are evident in [Sarah Nourse] to [James Nourse], Aug. 17, 1783, Nourse Family Papers (no. 3490a), box 1, ALUV; and Abigail Greenleaf to Robert T. Paine, Dec. 10, 1756, Paine Papers.

II

A majority of white women in eighteenth-century America resided in poor or middling farm households, and so it is reasonable to begin a discussion of female domestic work patterns with an assessment of their experience. Their heavy responsibilities are revealed most vividly in accounts left by two city families who moved to rural areas, for farm women were so accustomed to their burdensome obligations that they rarely remarked upon them.

Christopher Marshall and his wife abandoned Philadelphia when the British occupied the city in the fall of 1777, shifting their large family to Lancaster, Pennsylvania. There Marshall marveled at his wife's accomplishments, at how "from early in the morning till late at night, she is constantly employed in the affairs of the family." She not only did the cooking, baking, washing, and ironing, all of which had been handled by servants in their Philadelphia home, but she also milked cows, made cider and cheese, and dried apples. The members of the Palmer family of Germantown, Massachusetts, had a comparable experience when they moved in 1790 to Framingham, about twenty miles west of Boston. Mary Palmer, who was then fifteen and the oldest daughter in the home, later recalled that her father had had difficulty in adjusting to the change in his womenfolk's roles. "It took years to wean him from the idea that we must be ladies," she wrote, "although he knew that we must give up all such pretensions." Mary herself thrived in the new environment. "Kind neighbors" taught her mother how to make butter and cheese, and the girls "assisted in the laborious part, keeping churn, pans, cheesehoops and strainers nice and sweet." Afer she married Royall Tyler and set up housekeeping in Brattleboro, Vermont, Mary continued to practice the skills of rural housewifery she had gained as a teenager. Between managing her dairy in the summer and supervising spinning and weaving in the winter, not to mention raising five children, she observed, "I never realized what it was to have time hang heavy."[13]

Mary Palmer's recollections disclose the seasonal nature of much of farm women's labor. Such annual rhythms and the underlying, invariable weekly routine are revealed in the work records kept by farm wives like Sarah Snell Bryant, of Cummington, Massachusetts, and Mary Cooper, of Oyster Bay, Long Island. Each week Mrs. Bryant devoted one day to washing, another to ironing, and a third at least partly to baking. On the other days she sewed, spun, and wove. In the spring she planted her garden; in the early summer she hived her bees; in the fall she made cider and dried apples; and in mid-December came hog-killing time. Mary Cooper recorded the same seasonal round of work, adding to it spring housecleaning, a midsummer cherry harvest, and a long stretch of soap-

---

[13] William Duane, ed., *Extracts from the Diary of Christopher Marshall . . . 1774–1781* (Albany, N.Y., 1877), 157–158; Frederick Tupper and Helen Tyler Brown, eds., *Grandmother Tyler's Book, The Recollections of Mary Palmer Tyler 1775–1866* (New York, 1925), 142–143, 140, 296 (hereafter cited as Tyler, *Book*).

making, boiling "souse," rendering fat, and making candles that followed the hog butchering in December. In late 1769, after two weeks of such work, she described herself as "full of freting discontent dirty and miserabel both yesterday and today."[14]

Unlike the laconic Mrs. Bryant, who simply noted the work she had completed each day, Mrs. Cooper frequently commented on the fatiguing nature of her life. "It has been a tiresome day it is now Bed time and I have not had won minutts rest," she wrote in November 1768. One Sunday some months later she remarked, "I hoped for some rest but I am forst to get dinner and slave hard all day long." On those rare occasions when everyone else in the household was away, Mary Cooper understandably breathed a sigh of relief. "I have the Blessing to be quite alone without any Body greate or Small," she noted in late October 1768, and five years later another such day brought thanks for "some quiate moments which I have not had in weeks."[15]

Perhaps one of the reasons why Mrs. Cooper seemed so overworked was her obsession with cleanliness. Since travelers in rural America commented frequently upon the dirt they encountered in farmhouses and isolated taverns, it seems clear either that cleanliness was not highly valued or that farm wives, fully occupied with other tasks, simply had no time to worry about sweeping floors, airing bedding, or putting things away. Mary Cooper's experience suggests that the latter explanation was more likely. Often describing herself as "dirty and distrest," she faithfully recorded her constant battle against filth. "We are cleaning the house and I am tired almost to death," she wrote in December 1768; the following spring, after seven straight days of cleaning, she complained, "O it has been a week of greate toile and no Comfort or piece to Body or mind." Another time she noted with satisfaction, "I have got some clean cloths on thro mercy some little done to clean the house," and again, "Up very late But I have got my Cloths Ironed."[16] Obviously, if a farm woman was not willing to invest almost superhuman effort in the enterprise, keeping her household clean was an impossible task.

Mary Cooper's diary is unique in that it conveys explicitly what is only implicit in other farm wives' journals: a sense of drudgery and boredom. Sarah Snell Bryant would record that she had engaged in the same tasks for days on end, but she never noted her reaction to the repetition. This sameness was the quality that differentiated farm women's work from that performed by their husbands. No less physically demanding

---

[14] Sarah Snell Bryant, Diary, 1795, *passim*, HL; Mary Cooper, Diary, Dec. 14, 1769, and *passim*, NYPL. For another discussion of northern women's work patterns, see Nancy F. Cott, *The Bonds of Womanhood: "Woman's Sphere" in New England 1780–1835* (New Haven, Ct., 1977), chapter 1.

[15] Cooper diary, November 20, 1768; Feb. 12, 1769; Oct. 23, 1768; Sept. 18, 1773.

[16] Cooper Diary, Dec. [23?], 1768; May 20, 1769; Dec. 15, 1769; April 22, 1769. For some travelers' comments on dirty rural houses, see Francis Baily, *Journal of a Tour in Unsettled Parts of North America in 1796 & 1797*, ed. Jack D. L. Holmes (Carbondale and Edwardsville, Ill., 1969), 45–46; and Max Farrand, ed., *A Journey to Ohio in 1810 as Recorded in the Journal of Margaret Van Horn Dwight* (New Haven, Ct., 1914), 7–8.

or difficult, men's tasks varied considerably from day to day and month to month. At most—during planting or harvest time, for example—men would spend two or three weeks at one job. But then they would move on to another. For a farmer, in other words, the basic cycle was yearly; for his wife, it was daily and weekly, with additional obligations superimposed seasonally. Moreover, men were able to break their work routine by making frequent trips to town or the local mill on business, or by going hunting or fishing, whereas their wives, especially if they had small children, were tied to the home.[17]

Rural youngsters of both sexes were expected to assist their parents. "Their children are all brought up in industry, and have their time fully employed in performing the necessary duties of the house and farm," remarked a foreign visitor to a western Pennsylvania homestead in 1796. His inclusion of both sons and daughters was entirely accurate, for although historians have tended to emphasize the value of boys' labor to their fathers, extensive evidence suggests that girls were just as important as aides to their mothers. The fifteen-year-old Elizabeth Fuller, of Princeton, Massachusetts, for example, recorded occasionally baking pies, making candles, scouring floors, mincing meat for sausages, making cheese, and doing laundry, in addition to her primary assignments, spinning and weaving. Nabby and Betsy Foote, sisters who lived in Colchester, Connecticut, likewise noted helping their mother with housework, again in conjunction with their major chores of sewing, spinning, and weaving. When the parents of Ruth Henshaw, of Leicester, Massachusetts, called her home in mid-July 1789 after she had been visiting a relative for four days, saying, she recounted, that they "could not Subsist with out me any longer," they were only expressing what is evident in all these diaries: the labor of daughters, like that of wives, was crucial to the success of a farm household.[18]

Brissot de Warville, an astute foreign traveler, recognized both the value of women's work and the clearly defined gender role distinctions visible in rural life in his observations upon a fellow Frenchman's Pennsylvania farm in 1788. It is a "great disadvantage," Brissot remarked, that "he does not have any poultry or pigeons and makes no cheese; nor does he have any spinning done or collect goose feathers." The reason: he was a bachelor, and "these domestic farm industries . . . can be carried on well only by women."[19] Brissot's friend had two women indentured servants, so he did not lack female labor as such; what was missing was a wife or daughters to supervise the servants. Significantly, neither he nor Brissot seems to have considered the possibility that he could himself keep

---

[17] See, e.g., Matthew Patten, *The Diary of Matthew Patten of Bedford, N.H.* (Concord, N.H., 1903), *passim*.

[18] Baily, *Journal of a Tour*, 44; Elizabeth Fuller, Diary, 1790–1792, printed in Frances E. Blake, *History of the Town of Princeton . . . 1759–1915* (Princeton, Mass., 1915), I, 303–304, 316–318, 321; Nabby and Betsy Foote, Diaries, *passim*, CHS; Ruth Henshaw, Diary, July 14, 1789, AAS.

[19] J. P. Brissot de Warville, *New Travels in the United States of America 1788*, ed. Durand Echeverria and trans. Mara Soceanu Vamos and Durand Echeverria (Cambridge, Mass., 1964), 208.

poultry or learn enough about cheesemaking to direct the servants. That was clearly "woman's work," and if there was no woman present, such work was not done, no matter how pressing the need or how great the resulting loss of potential income.

Yet in some frontier areas the gender role divisions so apparent in more settled regions did blur, although they did not break down entirely. Farmers' wives and daughters occasionally worked in the fields, especially at harvest time. Travelers from the East were unaccustomed to the sight of white female fieldworkers and wrote about it at length. In 1778, for example, a doctor from Dorchester, Massachusetts, told his wife in some amazement that he had seen Pennsylvania German women "at work abroad on the Farm mowing, Hoeing, Loading Dung into a Cart." A New Hampshire farmer, by contrast, matter-of-factly recorded in his diary his use of female relatives and neighbors for field work. In that same colony in the early 1760s the pendulum swung the other way, and men helped with women's work. In the winters, recalled one woman many years later, "the boys did as much Knitting as the Girls, and the men and boys also did the milking to spare the women."[20]

Backcountry women had to cope with a far more rough-and-ready existence than did their counterparts to the east and south. The log cabins in which many of them lived were crudely built and largely open to the elements. Even the few amenities that brightened the lives of their poor contemporaries in areas of denser settlement were denied them; the Reverend Charles Woodmason, an Anglican missionary in western South Carolina, commented in 1768 that "in many Places they have nought but a Gourd to drink out off Not a Plate Knife or Spoon, a Glass, Cup, or any thing—It is well if they can get some Body Linen, and some have not even that." Later in the century, one woman on the Ohio frontier, lacking a churn, was reduced to making butter by stirring cream with her hand in an ordinary pail. Under such circumstances, simple subsistence would require most of a woman's energies.[21]

How, then, did frontier women react to these primitive conditions? At least one group of pioneer men termed their wives "the greatest of Heroines," suggesting that they bore such hardships without complaint, but other evidence indicates that some women, especially those raised in genteel households, did not adapt readily to their new lives. Many, like a Pennsylvanian, must have vetoed their husbands' plans to move west because of an unwillingness to exchange a civilized life for a residence in "what she deems a Wilderness." Others must have resembled the Shenandoah Valley woman, a mother of eight, who descended into invalidism

---

[20] Dr. Samuel Adams to Sally Adams, Aug. 5, 1778, Sol Feinstone Collection, microfilm, no. 29, reel 1, LCMD; Patten, *Diary*, 6, 16, 19, 22, and *passim;* Lucy Watson, "Account of New Settlers, 1762–1766" (written 1825), HSP.

[21] Richard J. Hooker, ed., *The Carolina Backcountry on the Eve of the Revolution. The Journal and Other Writings of Charles Woodmason, Anglican Itinerant* (Chapel Hill, N.C., 1953), 39 (see also 13, 16–17, 33); Clement L. Martzolff, ed., "Reminiscences of a Pioneer [Thomas Rogers]," *Ohio State Archaeological and Historical Publications,* XIX (1910), 209.

shortly after her husband moved her and their children to what their son described as a "valuable Farm but with a small indifferent house . . . & almost intirely in woods."[22] Perhaps, like a female traveler in the west, the Virginian "felt oppress'd with so much wood towering above . . . in every direction and such a continuance of it." This was not a unique reaction: a Scottish immigrant, faced with his wife's similar response to the first sight of their new home, comforted her by promising, "[W]e would get all these trees cut down . . . [so] that we would see from house to house."[23]

At least in this case the husband knew of his wife's discontent and reacted to it. In other instances, the lack of communication between spouses resulting from their divergent roles appears to have been heightened on the frontier, as wives deliberately concealed their unhappiness from their husbands, revealing their true feelings only to female relatives. Mary Hooper Spence, who described herself as having been beset by "misfortunes" ever since the day of her marriage, lived with her husband on the "dreary & cold" island of St. Johns (now Prince Edward Island) in the 1770s. In letters to her mother in Boston she repeatedly told of her loneliness and depression, of how she found a primitive, isolated existence "hard to bear." By contrast, her husband characterized their life as "happy" and reported to a relative that they were "comfortably" settled. Likewise, Mrs. Joseph Gilman, said by her husband to be pleased with living in the new settlement of Marietta, Ohio, in 1789, later recounted that on many occasions while milking their cows she would think of her New England home, "sob and cry as loud as a child, and then wipe her tears and appear before her husband as cheerful as if she had nothing to give her pain."[24]

To point out the apparent dissatisfaction of many frontier women with their lives in the wilderness is not to say that they and others did not cope successfully with the trials they encountered. To cite just one example: Mrs. Hutchens, a Mississippi woman whose husband was kidnapped and whose slaves were stolen, pulled her family together in the face of adversity almost by sheer force of will alone. Her son subsequently recalled that she had told her children they could survive if they were willing to work. Accordingly, she and her three sons cultivated the fields while her daughters did the housework, spun cotton, and wove the

[22] Cuthbert Harrison to Leven Powell, June 22, 1785, Leven Powell Papers, box 2, EGS; Edward Burd to Joseph Shippen, June 24, 1777, Joseph Shippen Papers, in Peter Force Collection, series 8D, no. 163, LCMD; John Coalter, Autobiography to 1787, Brown-Coalter-Tucker Papers, box 1.

[23] Elizabeth House Trist, Journal, spring 1784 (typescript), SHC/UNC; Robert Witherspoon, Family Memoirs, Anderson-Thornwell Papers, SHC/UNC. Annette Kolodny has sensitively analyzed female attitudes toward the American landscape in an essay in the forthcoming volume *Language in Women's Lives*, ed. Ruth Borker, Nelly Furman, and Sally McConnell-Ginet.

[24] Mary Spence to Mary Hooper, June 22, 1770, Aug. 20, 1773, and George Hooper to same, April 2, 1772, all in James M. Robbins Papers, III, MHS; Mary Emery to a brother, Jan. 14, 1852 (typescript), and Joseph Gilman to Nicholas Gilman, Feb. 23, 1790, both in Gilman Papers.

fabric for their clothing. By the time her husband returned seven years later, she had prospered sufficiently to be able to replace all the slaves taken by the robbers.[25]

The fact that Mrs. Hutchens put her daughters to work spinning and weaving is significant, for no household task was more time-consuming or more symbolic of the female role than spinning. It was, furthermore, a task quintessentially performed by young, single women; hence, the use of the word "spinster" to mean an unmarried female and the phrase "the distaff side" to refer to women in general. Farm wives, and especially their daughters, spent a large proportion of their time, particularly in the winter months, bending over a flax wheel or loom, or walking beside a great wheel, spinning wool. No examination of the domestic sphere can be complete without detailed attention to this aspect of household work.

Before 1765 and the subsequent rise in home manufacturing caused by colonial boycotts of British goods, spinning and weaving as ordinary chores were largely confined to rural areas of the northern and middle colonies and the backcountry South. Planters and even middling farmers who lived along the southeastern coast and city residents throughout America could usually purchase English cloth more cheaply than they could manufacture it at home, and so they bought fabric rather than asking their wives, daughters, or female slaves to spend the requisite amount of time to produce it. But rural women outside the plantation South spent much of their lives spinning. They began as girls, helping their mothers; they continued after their marriages, until their own daughters were old enough to remove most of the burden from their shoulders; and they often returned to it in old age or widowhood, as a means of supporting themselves or making use of their time. Not all farm women learned weaving, a skill open to men as well, but spinning was a nearly universal occupation among them.[26]

Rural girls understood at an early age that spinning was "a very proper accomplishment for a farmers daughter," as the New Jersey Quaker Susanna Dillwyn put it in 1790. Susanna's niece Hannah Cox began trying to spin on an "old wheel which was in the house" when she was only seven, so her mother bought her a little new wheel, upon which Hannah soon learned to spin "very prettily." Similarly, the tutor on Robert Carter's Virginia plantation observed that his small pupils would tie "a String to a Chair & then run buzzing back to imitate the Girls spinning." Such playful fascination with the process of cloth production later turned for many girls into monotonous daily labor at wheels or looms during the months between December and May. The normal output of an experienced spinner who carded the wool herself was four skeins a day, or six if an assistant carded for her. Teenaged girls like Elizabeth Fuller, who were less practiced than their mothers, produced on the

---

[25] John Hutchens, Autobiography, 6–7, Breckinridge Family Papers, SHC/UNC.
[26] On cloth production in the colonies, see Rolla M. Tryon, *Household Manufactures in the United States 1640–1860* (Chicago, 1917), 17–20, 75–99, 202–213; and Arthur H. Cole, *The American Wool Manufacture* (Cambridge, Mass., 1926), I, 5–29.

average two or three skeins a day. After a long stint of spinning tow (short coarse linen fibers) in January and February 1792, Elizabeth exploded in her diary, "I should think I might have spun up all the Swingling Tow in America by this time." Later that same year, she switched to weaving, at last completing her annual allotment on June 1. In three months she had woven 176 yards of cloth, she recorded, happily inscribing in her journal, "Welcome sweet Liberty, once more to me. How have I longed to meet again with thee."[27]

But clothwork, which could be a lonely and confining occupation, as Elizabeth Fuller learned, could also be an occasion for socializing. Rural girls sometimes attended "spinning frolics" or quilting bees, many of which lasted for several days and ended with dancing.[28] Even more frequently farm women "changed work," trading skills with others experienced in different tasks. Mary Palmer recalled that after her family moved to Framingham her mother would change work with other women in the area, "knitting and sewing for them while they would weave cotton and flax into cloth" for her, since as a city dweller she had never learned that skill. In a similar way Ruth Henshaw and her mother repaid Lydia Hawkins, who warped their loom for them, by helping her quilt or making her a pair of stays. Ruth regularly exchanged chores with girls of her own age as well; in December 1789, for example, she noted, "Sally here Spining Changing works with Me," while ten days later she was at Sally's house, carding for her.[29]

From such trading of labor farm women could easily move on to work for pay. By 1775 Betsy and Nabby Foote had taken that step. Nabby, like Lydia Hawkins of Leicester, specialized in warping webs and making loom harnesses; her sister Betsy worked in all phases of cloth production, carding wool, hatcheling flax, and spinning, as well as doing sewing and mending for neighbors. In the rural North and South alike white women spun, wove, and sold butter, cheese, and soap to their neighbors, participating on a small scale in the market economy long before the establishment of textile factories in New England and the consequent introduction of widespread wage labor for young northern women.[30]

[27] Susanna Dillwyn to William Dillwyn, Jan. 28, 1790, Dillwyn Papers, box 1, LCP/ HSP; Hunter Dickinson Farish, ed., *Journal & Letters of Philip Vickers Fithian 1773–1774: A Plantation Tutor of the Old Dominion* (Williamsburg, Va., 1957), 189; Fuller diary, in Blake, *History of Princeton*, I, 311–315, esp. 313, 315. The estimate of a spinner's output is from Tryon, *Household Manufactures*, 118n; it is borne out by the entries in Bryant diary, Feb.–April, 1797, *passim*.

[28] Spinning frolics and quilting bees are mentioned in, e.g., Cooper diary, Feb. 3, March 17, and Nov. 14, 1769; and Henshaw diary, Sept. 15, 1789; Sept. 14, Oct. 27, Nov. 4, 1790.

[29] Tyler, *Book*, 141; Henshaw diary, Dec. 21, Dec. 31, 1789. For the Henshaws' relationship with Lydia Hawkins, see *ibid.*, April 2, May 17, Sept. 3, Nov. 12, 1790; April 22, July 19, 22, 1791.

[30] Nabby Foote diary, August 1775; Betsy Foote diary, Jan.–May 1775, *passim*. See also Elizabeth Hook, Account Book, EI. Patten, *Diary*, 18, 21, 30, 34, 35, 42 shows purchases from his female neighbors, as does Robert Carter, Daybook XIII, 1775–1776, *passim*, Robert Carter Papers, DU.

Given the significance of spinning in women's lives, it is not surprising that American men and women made that occupation the major symbol of femininity. William Livingston had declared that "country girls . . . ought to be at their spinning-wheels," and when Benjamin Franklin sought a wedding present for his sister Jane, he decided on a spinning wheel instead of a tea table, concluding that "the character of a good housewife was far preferable to that of being only a pretty gentlewoman."[31]

Compelling evidence of the link between spinning and the female role in the eighteenth-century American mind comes from the observations of two visitors to Indian villages. Confronted by societies in which women did not spin but instead cultivated crops while their husbands hunted and fished, both the whites perceived Indian sex roles as improper and sought to correct them by introducing the feminine task of spinning. Benjamin Hawkins, United States agent for the Creek tribe, admired the industrious Creek women and encouraged them to learn to spin and weave. This step, he believed, would lead to a realignment of sex roles along proper lines, because the women would be freed from dependence upon their hunter husbands for clothing, and they would also no longer have time to work on the crops. The men in turn would therefore be "obliged to handle the ax & the plough, and assist the women in the laborious task of the fields." A similar scheme was promoted by the Quaker woman Anne Emlen Mifflin, who traveled in the Seneca country as a missionary in 1803. Men should work in agriculture, she told her Indian audience, so that women would be able to learn spinning and dairy management, which were "branches suited to our sex," as opposed to "drudging alone in the labors of the field."[32]

As Mifflin's comment shows, women, too, found spinning a necessary component of femininity, a fact best illustrated by reference to Elizabeth Graeme Fergusson's poem "The Contemplative Spinner." In 1792, Mrs. Fergusson, one of the leaders of intellectual life in republican Philadelphia, composed a poem in which she compared her spinning wheel to a wheel of fortune, leading her to a series of observations on life, death, and religion. But the wheel did more: it also reminded her of other women, linking her inextricably to "a train of Female Hands/Chearful uniting in Industrious Bands." And so, she wrote:

> *In such Reflections I oft passed the Night,*
> *When by my Papas solitary Light*
> *My Wheel I turnd, and thought how others toild*
> *To earn a morsel for a famishd Child.*[33]

[31] Livingston, "Our Grand-Mothers," *Amer. Museum*, IX (1791), 143; Carl Van Doren, ed., *The Letters of Benjamin Franklin & Jane Mecom* (Princeton, N.J., 1950), 35.

[32] Benjamin Hawkins, *Letters of Benjamin Hawkins 1796–1806*, Collections of the GHS, IX (Savannah, 1916), 478 (also 21–22, 57); Anne Mifflin, Journal of Visit to Senecas, October 1803, 28, Logan-Fisher-Fox Papers, box 2A, HSP.

[33] Elizabeth Graeme Fergusson, "The Contemplative (or Sentimental) Spinner," in volume labeled "Selections 1797–1799," Elizabeth Graeme Fergusson Papers, HSP.

To Elizabeth Graeme Fergusson, spinning symbolized her tie to the female sisterhood, just as to Benjamin Hawkins and other eighteenth-century men that occupation above all somehow appertained to femininity. It is consequently ironic that the one factor that differentiated the lives of urban women most sharply from those of their rural counterparts was the fact that they did not have to engage in cloth production. Women who had access to stores saw no point in spending hour after tedious hour at the wheel or loom. Not, at least, until doing so came to have political significance in the late 1760s, as Americans increasingly tried to end their dependence on British manufactured goods.

III

Although urban women did not have to spin and weave, the absence of that time-consuming occupation did not turn their lives into leisured ones. Too often historians have been misled by the lack of lengthy work entries in urban women's diaries, concluding therefrom that city "ladies" contributed little or nothing to the family welfare. Admittedly, white urban women of even moderate means worked shorter hours and at less physically demanding tasks than did their rural counterparts, but this did not mean that their households ran themselves. Women still had the responsibility for food preparation, which often included cultivating a garden and raising poultry. The wives of artisans and shopkeepers also occasionally assisted their husbands in business. Furthermore, their homes were held to higher standards of cleanliness—by themselves and by their female friends—than were the homes of farm women like Mary Cooper. Even if they could afford to hire servants, they frequently complained that supervising their assistants took almost as much time and effort as doing the work themselves.

Middling and well-to-do urban women who described their daily routines in letters or diaries disclosed a uniform pattern of mornings devoted to household work, a late dinner at about two o'clock, and an afternoon of visiting friends, riding, or perhaps reading quietly at home. Although some women arose as late as eight o'clock (which one female Bostonian termed "a lazy hour"), others, including Abigail Adams, recorded that they habitually rose at five. A Pennsylvanian summed up the common practice in a poem:

> *Like a notable house wife* I rise with the sun
> *Then bustle about till the business is done,*
> *Consult with the Cook, and* attend to the spiting [*sic*]
> *Then quietly seat myself down to my* kniting—
> *Should a neighbour step in we* talk of the weather
> *Retail all the* news *and the* scandle *together,* . . .

The tea things removed *our party disperses,*
And of course puts an end to my very fine verses.[34]

The chores that city women performed in the mornings resembled those of farm wives. Their diaries noted hours devoted to washing and ironing, cooking and baking, sewing and knitting. Like that of their rural counterparts, their labor was affected by the seasons, although less consistently so: in the autumn they preserved fruit and stored vegetables, and early in the winter they salted beef and pork and made sausage. Yet there were differences. Most notably, urban dwellers made daily trips to large markets, where they bought most of their meat, vegetables, cheese, and butter. Rebecca Stoddert, a Marylander who had moved to Philadelphia, marveled that her neighbors quickly killed chickens they had purchased without "think[ing] of fatting them up," a practice she deplored as wasteful and shortsighted.[35]

Although urban women were not burdened with the major stock-tending and clothmaking chores that devolved upon farm wives, some of the time thus saved was devoted to cleaning their homes. Many of the travelers in rural areas most horrified by dirty farmhouses and taverns were themselves urban women, who had adopted standards of cleanliness for their homes, clothes, and beds that were utterly alien to farm wives. Certainly no rural woman except Mary Cooper would have written a journal entry resembling that of a Philadelphian in 1781: "As we were whitewashing & cleaning house this day I seemed anxious, I fear over anxious to have every thing clean, & in order." Another Philadelphia resident, the Quaker Sally Logan Fisher, seems to have painted, whitewashed, or wallpapered her house each spring, even though she remarked in April 1785 that it was "troublesome work indeed, the pleasure afterwards of being nice, hardly pays for the trouble." Other wives in small towns similarly recorded their commitment to keeping their homes neat and clean.[36]

[34] E. H. Wister to [Betsy] Wister, Aug. 15, 1808, Bache Family Papers, APSL. The "lazy hour" phrase comes from Lucy Knox to Henry Knox, Aug. 23, 1777, Henry Knox Papers, microfilm, reel 4, no. 43, MHS. One of the best sources for urban women's work patterns is Sally Logan Fisher's diary, HSP; her comment on ordinarily rising at five o'clock comes on Aug. 9, 1785. See Abigail Adams's description of her daily routine in Stewart Mitchell, ed., *New Letters of Abigail Adams 1788–1801* (Boston, 1947), 91 (hereafter cited as Adams, *New Letters*).

[35] Rebecca Stoddert to Elizabeth Gantt, Sept. 15, 1799, Rebecca Stoddert Papers, Miscellaneous Manuscripts, LCMD. Excellent descriptions of city markets are contained in Kenneth and Anna Roberts, eds. and trans., *Moreau de St. Mery's American Journey 1793–1798* (Garden City, N.Y., 1947), 154–155, 316–317; and Alfred J. Morrison, ed. and trans., *Travels in the Confederation (1783–1784). From the German of Johann David Schoepf* (Philadelphia, 1911), I, 112–113; II, 189–190.

[36] Hannah Bringhurst, "A Spiritual Diary from the 25th of 3d Mo. 1781, to the 19th of 9th Mo. inclusive," 38, HSP; Fisher diary, April 18, 1785. For urban women's reactions to dirty farmhouses, see Margaret Dwight's comments (n. 16) and those in Trist journal, Dec. 30, 1783, Jan. 1, 8, 1784.

Cleaning, though, was perhaps the only occupation at which city dwellers of moderate means expended more energy than women living in agricultural regions. One of the benefits of residing in a city or a good-sized town was the availability of a pool of female workers who could be hired at relatively low rates. If a woman decided that she could not afford even a minimal payment, she could take a girl into her home as a sort of apprentice in housewifery, compensating her solely with room, board, and others. . . .

The mistresses of such homes felt caught in a dilemma. On the one hand, servants were impertinent, lazy, untrustworthy, careless, and slovenly (to list just a few of their complaints), but on the other hand it was impossible to run a household without some help. The women who offered themselves for hire were usually either single girls or elderly widows; only in rare cases can one identify white females who spent their entire lives as servants.[37] Instead, girls worked as maids, cooks, or laundresses for a few years before marriage, often for a series of employers. From the diaries and letters of mistresses of urban households one gains the impression of a floating population of "young Giddy Headed Girls" who did largely as they pleased, knowing that with the endemic American shortage of labor they could always find another position. Few seem to have stayed in the same household for more than a few months, or a year at most, before moving on to another post. For example, in just the five years from 1794 to 1799, Deborah Norris Logan, Sally Logan Fisher's sister-in-law, employed at least ten different female servants in fairly rapid succession. Among them were two widows, some immigrants from Ireland and Germany, a pair of sisters, and several girls.[38]

Deborah Logan had no daughters to assist her in the home, but even if she had, she, like other urban mothers, would not have expected them to contribute as much work to the household as did their rural counterparts. City daughters from well-to-do homes were the only eighteenth-century American women who can accurately be described as leisured. The causes of their relative lack of employment have already been indicated: first, the work of an urban household was less demanding than that of a farm, so that mothers and perhaps one or two servants could do all that was necessary; and, second, city girls did not have to produce the cloth supply for the family. Accordingly, they could live at a relaxed pace, sleeping late, learning music and dancing, spending hours with male and female friends, and reading the latest novels.[39]

[37] Abigail Adams's complaints about servants are especially detailed; see Adams, *New Letters*, 33, 47–48, 68–69, 76, 91. The career of a long-term white female servant is traced in Lucy Searle, "Memoir of Mrs. Sarah Atkins," *EIHC*, LXXXV (1949), 155.

[38] The quotation is from Adrian Bancker to Evert Bancker, June 23, 1774, Bancker Family Papers, NYHS. See the letters of Deborah Logan to Mary Norris, Loudoun Papers, box 42, *passim*, HSP. Elizabeth deHart Bleecker [McDonald], Diary, *passim*, NYPL, also mentions large numbers of youthful servants.

[39] Descriptions of the daily routines of urban girls are contained in Ethel Armes, ed., *Nancy Shippen Her Journal Book* (Philadelphia, 1935), 220–221; Susanna

This is not to say, as some historians have argued, that these young women were entirely idle and decorative, for they did extensive amounts of sewing for their families. Girls began to sew at an early age—Hannah, Sally Logan Fisher's daughter, was only eight when she made her first shirt—and they thereafter devoted many hours each day to their needles. Most of their tasks were mundane: mending and altering clothes; making shirts for their fathers and brothers; and stitching apparently innumerable aprons, caps, and shifts for themselves, their mothers, and their aunts. Such "common sewing" won a girl "no great Credit," the New Englander Pamela Dwight Sedgwick admitted in 1789, but at the same time, she pointed out to her daughter, "[I]t will be thought unpardonable negligence . . . not to doe it very nicely." Sometimes girls would work samplers or make lace, but even the wealthiest among them occasionally felt apologetic for spending a considerable amount of their time on decorative stitchery. Betsy DeLancey, a daughter of the prominent New York family, defended such evidently frivolous employment to her sister Anne in 1768 by referring to Proverbs: "I must be industrious and make myself fine with my own Hands, and who can blame me for spending some of my time in that manner when it is part of the virtuous Womans Character in the Bible."[40]

In poor households, daughters' sewing skills could contribute significantly to family income, as may be demonstrated by reference to the Banckers of New York City. Christopher Bancker was an alcoholic, and his wife Polly tried to support the family by working as a seamstress. Yet she alone could not "du the whole," as she wrote in 1791, and so her two oldest daughters, Peggy and Betsy, also sought employment as seamstresses. Even with the girls' help the family experienced severe economic difficulties, yet the combined income of wife and daughters, coupled with charity proffered by reluctant relatives, kept the Banckers out of the poor house. Peggy and Betsy—and, by implication, other urban girls as well—thus proved to be economic assets to their families in a way that sons were not. The best that could be done with the two oldest Bancker boys was to send them out of the household to learn trades, so that they would no longer be a drag on family resources. Not until they had served apprenticeships of several years, with the expenses being borne by relatives, could they make positive contributions to the support of their parents and siblings. But their sisters had been "apprenticed" to their mother, and so they had developed salable skills at an early age. The other side of the coin was the fact that the Bancker boys' advanced training eventually

---

Dillwyn to William Dillwyn, March 13–23, 1787, Dillwyn Papers; and Jane Lansing to Maria Van Schaick, Oct. 8, 1804, Lansing Family Papers, I, 69, Gansevoort-Lansing Collection, NYPL.

[40] Fisher diary, Dec. 27, 1785; Pamela Sedgwick to Elizabeth Mayhew, Aug. 21, 1789, Sedgwick Papers III, MHS; Betsy DeLancey to Anne DeLancey, [c. 1768], DeLancey "Reminiscences," DeLancey Family Papers, MCNY. See also Alice M. Earle, ed., *Diary of Anna Green Winslow, A Boston School Girl of 1771* (Boston, 1894), *passim*, esp. 40, 47.

paid off in higher wages, whereas the girls had little hope of ever improving their position, except through a good marriage.[41]

Because sewing was readily portable, and because they lived so close to each other, well-to-do urban girls frequently gathered to work in sizable groups. While one of their number read, usually from a popular novel, the others would pass the afternoon or evening in sewing. Like farm girls, they created an opportunity for socializing out of the necessity for work, but as a result of their proximity they were able to meet more often, more regularly, and in greater numbers. One sewing group called itself the "Progressive Society" and confined its reading to edifying tracts. "Our design is to ameliorate, by every probable method, the morals, opinions, manners and language of each other," one of the members wrote, explaining why they excluded cardplaying, gossip, and men from their meetings.[42]

In addition to sewing, city girls, like their rural counterparts, were taught what one of them termed "the mysteries of housewifery" by conscientious mothers. Sally Logan Fisher began to instruct her daughter Hannah in "Family affairs" when she was just ten, so that she would become "a good Housewife & an active Mistress of a Family." Daughters did some cooking, baking, and cleaning, helped to care for younger siblings, and on occasion took charge of the household. Sometimes they acquired this responsibility only when their mothers became ill, but in other cases adults deliberately adopted it as a training device. Abigail Adams, who believed it "an indispensable requisite, that every American wife, should herself know, how to order, and regulate her family," commented approvingly in 1788 that her son-in-law William Stephens Smith's four sisters were "well educated for wives as well as daughters" because "their Mamma had used them to the care of her Family by Turns. Each take it a week at a Time."[43]

The words chosen by Mrs. Adams and Mrs. Fisher revealed a key difference in the domestic roles of urban and rural girls. Farm daughters learned to perform household tasks because their family's current well-being required their active involvement in daily work, whereas city girls acquired domestic skills primarily so that they could eventually become good wives and mothers. The distinction was crucial. Urban daughters participated sporadically in household tasks as a preparation for their own futures, but farm girls worked regularly at such chores as a direct contri-

---

[41] The saga of the Banckers may be traced in Bancker Papers, 1790–1800, *passim*, esp. letters of Polly or Christopher Bancker to Evert Bancker, Feb. 3, 1791; April 16, July 1, Oct. 17, 1794.

[42] Such work groups are described in Armes, èd., *Shippen Journal*, 185, and Susan I. Lesley, *Recollections of My Mother* (Boston, 1886), 40. The quotation comes from Constantia [Judith Sargent Murray], *The Gleaner. A Miscellaneous Production* (Boston, 1798), III, 307.

[43] William Maxwell, comp., "My Mother: Memoirs of Mrs. Helen Read," *Lower Norfolk County Virginia Antiquary*, II (1897–1898), 26; Fisher diary, Sept. 27, 1788; Abigail Adams to Elizabeth Peabody, June 6, 1809, Shaw Family Papers, box 1, LMCD; Adams, *New Letters*, 5–6.

bution to their family's immediate welfare.[44] The difference points up the overall contrast between the lives of urban and rural white women. In both city and farm, women made vital contributions to the success and survival of the household, but in rural areas those contributions were both more direct and more time-consuming.

IV

Wealthy southern women were directly responsible for even fewer household tasks than northerners with comparable means. But northerners who moved south soon realized the falsity of an initial impression that "a mrs of a family in Carolina had nothing to doe but be waited on as their was so many negros." Anna Bowen, a young Rhode Island woman who first went to South Carolina to visit a married sister and subsequently married a planter herself, told another sister in 1790 about the problems of running a large household. Required to "think incessantly of a thousand articles of daily supply," she sometimes did not know "which way to turn," Bowen admitted, but, she added confidently, "I shall learn in time."[45]

The daily schedules of mistresses of large plantations resembled those of wealthy urban women in the North, with the exception of the fact that social visits were confined to one or two afternoons a week because of the distance beween plantations. The mornings were devoted to household affairs, although white southerners spent their time supervising the work of slaves instead of doing such chores themselves. The day began, sometimes before breakfast, with what one southern man termed "Grand Rounds from the Kitchen to the Larder, then to the Poultry Yard & so on by the Garret & Store Room home to the Parlour." After she had ascertained that the daily tasks were proceeding as planned, the mistress of the household could spend some time reading or playing music before joining her husband for dinner in early to mid-afternoon. Afterward, she would normally turn to needlework until evening, and then again to reading and writing.[46]

The supervision of what were the largest households on the North American continent involved plantation mistresses in varied activities, almost always in the role of director rather than performer. What were small-scale operations on northern farms—running a dairy, raising poultry,

---

[44] Cf. Bleecker diary, *passim*, with the farm girls' diaries cited in n. 18 above. A city woman expresses regret for not having taught her granddaughter enough about housewifery in Smith, ed., *Hill Letters*, 445.

[45] Elizabeth Smith to James Murray, Feb. 7, 1762, Robbins Papers, I; Anna [Bowen] to Lydia Clark, May 31, 1790, John Innes Clark Papers, RIHS.

[46] Thomas Pinckney to Harriott Horry, Feb. 22, 1779, Pinckney Family Papers, ser. 1, box 8, LCMD. For other descriptions of the daily routine of plantation mistresses, see Ann Kinloch, Diary, April 1799, Langdon Cheves Collection, SCHS; and Elise Pinckney, ed., *The Letterbook of Eliza Lucas Pinckney 1739-1762* (Chapel Hill, N.C., 1972), 7, 34–35.

tending a garden—were magnified many times on southern plantations, but they remained within the female sphere. Chores that northern women could do in a day, such as laundry, took nearly one week of every two on at least one South Carolina plantation. Food management, easily accomplished in small northern urban families with access to markets, occupied a significant amount of time and required much forethought on large plantations, where each year's harvest had to feed perhaps one hundred or more people for months. White women, it is true, did not usually make the decisions about how many hogs to kill or how many barrels of corn to set aside for food and seed, but they did manage the distribution of food once it had been stored, not to mention the supervision of its initial preservation. Furthermore, they coordinated the manufacture of the slaves' clothing, spending many hours cutting out garments or superintending that work, in addition to making, altering, and mending their families' clothes.[47]

Such women invariably aroused the admiration of observers, who regularly commended their "industry and ingenuity," their "very able and active manner," or their character as "worthy economists" and "good managers."[48] Surviving correspondence indicates that the praise could be completely deserved. A prime example is provided by the Marylander Hannah Buchanan, who in August 1809 returned alone to Woburn plantation while her husband remained in Baltimore on business. She reported to him in anger that the white couple they had left in charge did not have "the smallest idea of the proper economy of a Farm." Among the abuses she discovered were a misassignment of slave women to nonessential tasks, a lack of planning for the slaves' winter clothing, and extremely poor handling of food supplies, including such errors as allowing the slaves to have wheat flour, consuming all the pork, and having no vegetables at all. "This is miserable management," she declared, and set herself to correct the situation. A month later the work on winter clothes was coming along "Wonderfully," and she was filled with ideas on how to prepare and distribute the food more efficiently. Although she expressed a desire to rejoin her husband in the city, she proposed, "[L]et me direct next year and you will spend less believe me and the people will live much better."[49]

Appropriately, then, the primary task of girls from wealthy southern

---

[47] An excellent sense of the work patterns of plantation mistresses may be obtained by consulting Sarah Nourse, Diary, 1781–1783, Nourse-Morris Papers (no. 3490b), ALUV; Anna Bowen Mitchell to Eliza [Bowen], April 1, 1793, Clark Papers; and Farish, ed., *Fithian Journal, passim,* esp. 38, 44–45, 63, 75, 79 (for the work of Ann Tasker Carter).

[48] John Brown Cutting to Thomas Pinckney, Dec. 19, 1794, Pinckney Family Papers, ser. 3, box 6; Harry Toulmin, *The Western Country in 1793: Reports on Kentucky and Virginia,* ed. Marion Tinling and Godfrey Davies (San Marino, Calif., 1948), 28; Farish, ed., *Fithian Journal,* 194; Lucy Armistead to Maria Armistead, Feb. 16, 1788, Armistead-Cocke Papers, EGS. I have pluralized the last two quotations.

[49] Hannah Buchanan to Thomas Buchanan, Aug. 13, Sept. 11, Sept. 12, 1809, Hooker Collection, SLRC.

families was to gain expertise in running large estates. Like their northern counterparts, they did some cooking and baking and a fair amount of sewing, but their household roles differed from those of both farm and city girls. Whereas one New England father told his daughter, "[L]earn to work as fast as you can to make Shirts etc & assist your Mother," Thomas Jefferson advised his younger daughter, Maria, who was usually called Polly, that she should know how to "manage the kitchen, the dairy, the garden, and other appendages of the hous[e]hold." Teenaged girls like Eleanor Parke (Nelly) Custis accordingly served as "deputy House-keeper" to the mistress of the family, who in her case was her grand-mother Martha Washington.[50] If this training was successful, parents could look with pleasure upon the accomplishments of such excellent managers as Martha Jefferson Randolph, who assured her father in 1791 that at Monticello under her direction "there is as little wasted as possible," or Harriott Pinckney Horry, whose fond mother, Eliza Lucas Pinckney, had herself managed three South Carolina plantations in the 1740s while she was still a teenager. "I am glad your little wife looks well to the ways of [her] hou[se]," Mrs. Pinckney told her new son-in-law within a month of his marriage, especially remarking upon her daughter's ability to run a "perfectly neat" dairy.[51]

In the end, being a good plantation mistress involved very different skills from those of the usual notable housewife of northern communities. Most importantly, the well-to-do southern white woman had to know how to command and direct the activities of others, often a great many others, not just the one or two servants common to northern households. It was less essential for a wealthy female southerner to know how to ac-complish tasks herself than it was for her to know how to order blacks to perform them, and to ensure that her orders were carried out. Thus when the Virginian Elizabeth Foote Washington, who feared that she would not survive until her baby daughter reached maturity, decided to leave her a book of household advice, she devoted most of its pages to hints on the management of slaves. A mistress should behave with "steadiness," she advised; she should show the servants that she would not be "impos'd upon." The most important goal was to maintain "peace & quietness" in the household, and to this end a mistress should be careful not to com-plain about the slaves to her husband or her friends. Such a practice

50 Jonathan Jackson to [Hannah Jackson], Feb. 1785, Lee Family Papers, MHS; Edwin Morris Betts and James Adam Bear, Jr., eds., *The Family Letters of Thomas Jefferson* (Columbia, Mo., 1966), 84; Eleanor Parke Custis to Elizabeth Bordley, March 18, 1797, Lewis-Gibson Letters (typescript), I, 31, HSP. The best source for the work of southern daughters is William Bottorff and Roy Flannagan, eds., "The Diary of Frances Baylor Hill of 'Hillsborough' King and Queen County Virginia (1797)," *EAL*, II, no. 3 (winter, 1967), 4–53.

51 Betts and Bear, eds., *Jefferson Family Letters*, 68; Eliza Lucas Pinckney to Daniel Horry, March 7, 1768, Mrs. Francis B. Stewart Collection, SHC/UNC. Contrast these to complaints about daughters in Jack P. Greene, ed., *The Diary of Colonel Landon Carter of Sabine Hall, 1752–1778* (Charlottesville, Va., 1965), I, 553; II, 809.

would make the servants grateful and perhaps encourage their industry, she wrote.[52]

As it happened, both the daughters born to Mrs. Washington died in infancy, and so her detailed delineation of the way to handle house servants was not passed on as she had hoped. But other white southern girls early assumed the habit of command. A telling incident involved Anne, the daughter of James Iredell, the North Carolina attorney and eventual associate justice of the Supreme Court. At the early age of four, she showed how well she had learned her lessons by "strutting about in the yard after Susanna (whom she had ordered to do something) with her work in her hand & an Air of as much importance as if she had been Mistress of the family."[53]

The story of Anne Iredell's behavior inevitably forces one to confront a difficult question: how did Susanna, a mature black woman, react to being ordered about by a white child? Or, to broaden the issue, what sort of lives were led by the black women who, with their husbands and children, constituted the vast majority of the population on southern plantations? Many female slaves resided on small farms and presumably worked in both field and house, but the discussion here will concentrate upon larger plantations, for it was in such households that most black women lived, since the relatively small proportion of white families who possessed slaves tended to own large numbers of them.[54]

Significantly, the size of these plantations allowed the specialization of domestic labor. White northern farm wives had to be, in effect, jills-of-all-trades, whereas planters often assigned slave women more or less permanently to particular tasks. A wide variety of jobs were open to black women, jobs that demanded as much skill as those performed by such male artisans as blacksmiths and carpenters. The slave list prepared by Thomas Middleton for his Goose Creek, South Carolina, plantation in 1784 included a dairymaid, a nurse, two laundresses, two seamstresses, and three general house servants. On other plantations women were also employed as cooks, spinners and weavers (after the mid-1760s), midwives, and tenders of poultry and livestock.[55]

Female blacks frequently worked at the same job for a number of years, but they were not necessarily restricted to it for a lifetime, although practices varied from plantation to plantation. Thomas Jefferson used children of both sexes under ten as infant nurses; from the ages of

---

[52] Elizabeth Foote Washington, Journal, summer 1784, spring 1789, Washington Family Papers, box 2, LCMD.

[53] Helen Blair to James Iredell, April 20, 1789, James Iredell Sr. and Jr. Papers, DU.

[54] See Wells, *Population of British Colonies*, 310–311. on the concentration of slaves in proportionately few households. The findings reported in Sarah S. Hughes, "Slaves for Hire: The Allocation of Black Labor in Elizabeth City County, Virginia, 1782 to 1810," *WMQ*, 3rd ser., XXXV (1978), 260–286, suggest that the experiences of black women on smaller farms and plantations were probably quite different from those outlined here.

[55] Detailed lists of women's occupations are in Thomas Middleton, Goose Creek Plantation Book, Nov. 5, 1784, Middleton Papers, SHC/UNC; and Robert Carter, Deed of Emancipation, Aug. 1, 1791, Carter Papers.

ten to sixteen he assigned girls to spinning and boys to nailmaking; and then either put them into the fields or had them learn a skilled occupation. Even as adults their jobs might be changed: when Jefferson went to France as ambassador in 1784, his "fine house wench" Dinah, then twenty-three, began to work in the fields, continuing at that assignment at least until 1792. The descriptions of slaves bought or sold on other plantations likewise showed women accustomed to different occupations. Colonel Fitzgerald's Nell, aged thirty-four, was "a stout able field wench & an exceeding good Washer & Ironer"; her daughter Sophy, eighteen, was a "Stout Wench & used to both field & [hou]se Work."⁵⁶

All field work was not the same, of course, and women who labored "in the crop" performed a variety of functions. Evidence of work assignments from both the Jefferson and Washington plantations shows that there were some field jobs reserved for men, most notably cradling wheat and cutting and hauling timber for fences, but that women sometimes built fences. Women plowed, hoed and grubbed the land, spread manure, sowed, harrowed, and at harvest time threshed wheat or husked corn. At Landon Carter's Sabine Hall plantation in Virginia two women, Grace and Maryan, each headed a small gang of female fieldworkers.⁵⁷

On outlying quarters, most women were agricultural laborers, with the occasional exception of a cook or a children's nurse. But female slaves raised at the home plantation could sometimes attain a high level of skill at conventionally "feminine" occupations. White masters and mistresses frequently praised the accomplishments of their cooks, seamstresses, and housekeepers. In a typical passage, Alice DeLancey Izard, a wealthy South Carolinian returning home after a long absence, commended her dairy-maid Chloe because she found "the Dairy in excellent order, & plentifully supplied with Milk, & Butter," further observing that Chloe "has made little Chloe very useful in her line."⁵⁸

Mrs. Izard thereby called attention to the transmission of skills among generations of female blacks. Thomas Jefferson's censuses of his plantations demonstrate that women who were house servants tended to have daughters who also worked in the house, and the inventory of a Pinckney family plantation in 1812 similarly included a mother-daughter midwife team. Indeed, midwifery, which was most likely an occupation passed on from woman to woman rather than one taught deliberately by a master, was one of the most essential skills on any plantation. Slave midwives were often called upon to deliver white children as well as black,

---

⁵⁶ Edwin M. Betts, ed., *Thomas Jefferson's Farm Book* (Princeton, N.J., 1953), facsimile, 77, pt. 2, 14; List of Negroes Purchased from Col. Fitzgerald, n.d., Muse Papers.

⁵⁷ Betts, ed., *Jefferson Farm Book*, facsimile, 46, 58; Plantation Work Journal, Nov. 1786–April 1787, George Washington Papers, box 28, LCMD; Greene, ed., *Carter Diary*, I, 568; II, 1137.

⁵⁸ Alice Izard to Ralph Izard, Dec. 11, 1794, Ralph Izard Papers, SCL. See also Maxwell, comp., "Read Memoirs," *Lower Norfolk Cnty Va. Antiq.*, I (1895–1896), 97; and Hugh Nelson to Battaile Muse, April 12, 1779, Muse Papers. The Muse Papers contain many inventories showing the work assignments of slaves on small quarters.

and masters recognized the special demands of their profession. In 1766, the midwife at Landon Carter's Fork Quarter, who was also the poultry tender, left her post to deliver a baby, an act resulting in the death of four turkeys. Even the petulant Carter realized that her midwifery duties came first, and so he did not punish her.[59]

In this case, a conflict arose between the midwife's divergent duties within her master's household. More commonly, slave women must have had to contend with contradictory demands placed upon them by their plantation tasks and the needs of their own husbands and children. Only a few aspects of the domestic lives led by black women within their own families can be traced in the records of white planters, for masters and mistresses did not, on the whole, concern themselves with the ways in which female slaves organized their homes. Yet occasional comments by slaveowners suggest that black women carefully made the most of what little they had and were even able to exercise some entrepreneurial initiative on occasion. Slave families occasionally maintained their own garden plots and supplemented their meager food and clothing allowances through theft or guile. Further, black women established themselves as the "general Chicken Merchants" in the plantation South. Whites often bought fowls from their female slaves instead of raising chickens themselves, as a means, Thomas Jefferson once explained, of "drawing a line between what is theirs & mine."[60]

That some black women had a very strong sense indeed of what was "theirs" was demonstrated on Nomini Hall plantation in the summer of 1781. Robert Carter had authorized two white overseers to begin making salt, and in order to accomplish that task they commandeered an iron pot from its two female owners. Joan and Patty, the aggrieved slaves, awaited their chance and then removed the pot from the saltworks. After the whites repossessed it, the women dispatched Patty's husband, Jesse, to complain to Carter about the treatment they had received. Carter sided with the women, agreeing that their pot had been taken in an "arbitrary" manner, and he ordered it returned to them.[61]

One could argue that Joan and Patty were emboldened to act as they did because they anticipated that Carter, a well-meaning master who eventually emancipated his slaves, would sympathize with their position. But bondwomen less favorably circumstanced also repeatedly displayed a desire to control as much of their lives as was possible under the conditions of servitude. Robert Carter's relative Landon was quick to anger, impatient with his servants and children. He frequently had recalcitrant

[59] Betts, ed., *Jefferson Farm Book*, facsimile, *passim*; Charles Cotesworth Pinckney, Jr., Plantation Book, 1812, Pinckney Family Papers, ser. 2, vol. 1; Greene, ed., *Carter Diary*, I, 306. For other comments on slave midwives, see Robert Carter, Letterbooks IV, 117, and VII, 20, Carter Papers.

[60] James Mercer to Battaile Muse, April 8, 1779, Muse Papers; Betts, ed., *Jefferson Farm Book*, 16. See Farish, ed., *Fithian Journal*, 96, 140, 203; Anna Mitchell to Lydia Clark, April 13, 1793, Clark Papers; and Greene, ed., *Carter Diary*, I, 484; II, 602, 1095–1096.

[61] Robert Carter to Thomas Olive, July 24, 1781, to James Clarke, July 28, 1781, Letterbook IV, 93, 95, Carter Papers.

slaves whipped, a tactic to which Robert rarely resorted, yet the women at Sabine Hall were no less insubordinate than those at Nomini. If Robert Carter's "Young & Stout" Jenny deliberately had fits "upon her being reprimanded," Landon Carter's Sarah pretended to be pregnant for a full eleven months so that she could avoid work, and Criss sent her children to milk his cows in the middle of the night in retaliation for a whipping. Similarly ingenious was James Mercer's Sall, who in August 1777 convinced her master that she had consumption and persuaded him to send her to the mountain quarter where her parents lived. That summer he ordered that she should be well fed and allowed to ride six or seven miles on horseback each day until she recovered her health, but by the following year, Mercer had concluded she was faking and directed that "she must turn out at all events unless attended with a fever."[62]

The same willful spirit asserted itself when masters and mistresses attempted to move female slaves from their accustomed homes to other locations. A North Carolina woman who was visiting Boston wanted to have her servant Dorinda sent north to join her, but learned from a relative that Dorinda "would by no means go to Boston or, from Cape Fear." Some years later a Pennsylvanian who had sent a slave woman to Cuba to be sold learned that she had managed to convince the white woman accompanying her that she should be returned to her Philadelphia home, because she was "Very Unhappy and always Crying." And "Miss Charlotte," an East Florida black, demonstrated her autonomy by her reaction to a dispute over who owned her. One of the two whites involved reported that she lived with neither of them, but instead "goes about from house to house," saying "now she's a free woman."[63]

Charlotte, Sall, Dorinda, and the others gained at least a little freedom of movement for themselves, but they were still enslaved in the end. All their victories were minor ones, for they could have only limited impact upon the conditions of their bondage. White women were subject to white men, but black women had to subordinate themselves to all whites, men, women, and children alike. The whites demanded always that their needs come first, before those of black women's own families. Female slaves' work lives were thus complicated by conflicting obligations that inflicted burdens upon them far beyond those borne by most whites.

V

White Americans did not expect their slaves to gain satisfaction from their work, for all that masters and mistresses required of their bond

---

[62] Robert Carter to Clement Brooke, Nov. 11, 1776, Letterbook III, no. 2, 76, 78, Carter Papers; Greene, ed., *Carter Diary*, I, 371–372; James Mercer to Battaile Muse, July 10, Aug. 25, 1777, June 13, 1778, Muse Papers.

[63] Thomas Clark to Dolly Forbes, Aug. 10, 1768, Robbins Papers, I; Thomas Cullen to Oliver Pollock, July 2, 29, 1783, Oliver Pollock Papers, in Force Collection, ser. 8D, no. 145, vol. 2, LSMD; Dolly Forbes to Elizabeth Smith, Sept. 8, 1769, Robbins Papers, II. On slave women's reluctance to move even from quarter to quarter, see J. H. Norton to Battaile Muse, April 21, May 11, 1782, Muse Papers.

servants was proper behavior and a full day's labor. But white women, as already indicated, were supposed to find "happiness in their chimney corners," to return to William Livingston's striking phrase. Men certainly believed that women should enjoy their domestic role. As a Georgian told his married sister in 1796, "I am sure that those cares which duty requires to your husband, and your child—must fill up every moment of time—and leave you nothing but those sensations of pleasure—which invariably flow—from a consciousness of having left no duty unperformed." Women too anticipated happiness from achieving the goal of notable housewifery. "Domestick oeconomy . . . is the female dignity, & praise," declared Abigail Adams's younger sister, Elizabeth Smith, in the late 1760s, and a Virginian observed to a friend nearly forty years later that she had "always been taught, that within the sphere of domestic life, Woman's chief glory & happiness ought to consist."[64]

The expectation, then, was clear: domesticity was not only a white American woman's inevitable destiny, but it was also supposed to be the source of her sense of pride and satisfaction. Regardless of the exact shape of her household role—whether she was a rural or an urban wife, or the mistress of a southern plantation—she should find fulfillment in it, and she should take pleasure in performing the duties required of her as mistress of the home.

Unsurprisingly, women rarely found the ideal as attractive in reality as it was in theory. But the reasons for their dissatisfaction with the restrictions of notable housewifery, which required them to be consistently self-effacing and constantly employed at domestic tasks, are both illuminating and unanticipated.

First, it must be noted that Mary Cooper was alone among her contemporaries in emphasizing the difficult, fatiguing nature of housework as the primary source of her complaints. Only she wrote of "the continnel cross of my famaly," only she filled her diary with accounts of weariness and endless drudgery.[65] Women's unhappiness with their domestic lives, in other words, stemmed not from the fact that the work was tiring and demanding. Their husbands' labor was also difficult, and in eighteenth-century America there were few models of a leisured existence for either men or women to emulate. Rather, women's expressed dissatisfaction with their household role derived from its basic nature, and from the way it contrasted with their husbands' work.

As has been seen, farmers' lives were much more varied than those of their wives, not only because they rarely repeated the same chore day after day in immediate succession, but also because they had more breaks from the laboring routine. The same was true of southern planters and of urban husbands, regardless of their occupation. The diaries of planters, professional men, and artisans alike demonstrate that their weeks were punctuated by travel, their days enlivened not only by visits with

---

[64] William Scarborough to Eliza Gillett, May 15, 1796, Georgia Society of Colonial Dames Collection, GHS; Elizabeth Smith to Isaac Smith, Jr., Aug. [torn], Shaw Papers, box 1; Ann Page to Elizabeth Adams, [c. 1803], Randolph Papers.
[65] Cooper diary, Aug. 21, 1769.

friends—which their wives also enjoyed—but also by a variety of business activities that took them on numerous errands. It was an unusual week, for example, when Thomas Hazard, a Rhode Island blacksmith, worked in his shop every day without any sort of respite from his labors, or when Ebenezer Parkman, a New England clergyman, did not call on parishioners, confer with neighbors about politics, or meet with other ministers.[66]

Against the backdrop of their husbands' diverse experiences, the invariable daily and weekly routines of housewifery seemed dull and uninteresting to eighteenth-century women, especially those who lived in urban areas, where the housework was less varied and their spouses' opportunities for socializing simultaneously greater. "The same cares and the same wants are constantly returning in domestic Life to take up my Time and attention," Pamela Dwight Sedgwick told her husband, Theodore, the Massachusetts Federalist, in words that reappeared in other womens' assessments of their lives. "A continual sameness reigns throughout the Year," wrote Christian Barnes, the wife of a Marlborough, Massachusetts, merchant, and Mary Orne Tucker, a Haverhill lawyer's wife, noted in her diary that she did not record her domestic tasks in detail because "each succeeding day with very little variety would present a compleat history of the last."[67]

New England city dwellers were not the only women who made such observations about the unchanging character of their experiences. The transplanted Rhode Islander Anna Bowen Mitchell reported from her new South Carolina home in 1793, "[T]he detail of one day . . . would be the detail of the last six months of my life," while hastening to add that her days were not "insipid," but rather filled with "heart-soothing tranquility." A Virginia planter's wife was more blunt about her situation in 1785, describing herself and her friends as "almost in a State of vegitation" because of their necessary attention to the "innumerable wants" of their large households.[68]

She thus touched upon yet another source of housewives' discontent with their lot: the fact that their all-encompassing domestic responsibilities left them little time to themselves. In 1755, a New England woman remarked longingly to a correspondent, "[T]he little scraps of time that can be rescued from Business or Company, are the greatest cordials to my tired Spirits that I meet with." Thirty years later Pamela Sedgwick echoed her sentiments, telling her unmarried friend Betsy Mayhew, "[W]e that have connected ourselves in the famely way, find the small circle of domestic concerns engross almost all our attention." Sally Logan

[66] Cf. Caroline Hazard, ed., *Nailer Tom's Diary* (Boston, 1930), and Harriett Forbes, ed., *The Diary of Rev. Ebenezer Parkman, of Westborough, Mass.* (Westborough, Mass., 1899), with, e.g., Fisher diary.

[67] Pamela Sedgwick to Theodore Sedgwick, Jan. 24, 1791, Sedgwick Papers III, MHS; Christian Barnes to Elizabeth Inman, Dec. 3, 1773, Christian Barnes Letterbook, LCMD; Mary Orne Tucker, Diary, May 4, 1802, EI.

[68] Anna Mitchell to Lydia Clark, April 13, 1793, Clark Papers; Armes, ed., *Shippen Journal*, 236 (see also 221).

Fisher too commented, "[I] find so much to do in the Family that I have not all the time for retirement and improvement of my own mind in the best things that I wish," revealingly referring to her domestic duties as "these hindering things." Again, such complaints were not confined to northerners. A young Virginia wife observed in 1769 that "Domestick Business . . . even deprives thought of its Native freedom" by restricting the mind "to one particular subject without suffering it to entertain itself with the contemplation of any thing New or improving." A wry female poet made the same point in verse: "Ah yes! 'tis true, upon my Life! / No *Muse* was ever yet a *Wife*," she wrote, explaining that "Muses . . . in *poultry yards* were never seen," nor were they required "from Books and Poety to Turn / To mark *the Labours of the Churn*."⁶⁹

The point of all these remarks was the same, despite their divergent geographical and chronological origins. White American women recognized not only that their domestic obligations were never-ending, but also that their necessary concentration upon those obligations deprived them of the opportunity to contemplate "any thing New and improving." So Elizabeth Smith Shaw told her oldest sister, Mary Cranch, in 1781, several years after her marriage to the clergyman John Shaw, "[I]f Ideas present themselves to my Mind, it is too much like the good seed sown among Thorns, they are soon erased, & swallowed up by the Cares of the World, the wants, & noise of my Family, & Children." Abigail Adams in particular regretted her beloved younger sister's preoccupation with domestic concerns during her second marriage, to another clergyman, who boarded a number of students. In February 1800 she told Elizabeth (then Mrs. Stephen Peabody) that her "brilliant" talents were "encumbered" and "obstructed" by her household chores, lamenting "that the fire of imagination should be checked, that the effusions of genious should be stifled, through want of leisure to display them." Abigail's characterization of the impact of domestic responsibilities on her sister's life bore little resemblance to William Livingston's glorification of those same activities: "The mind which is necessarily imprisoned in its own little tenement: and fully occupied by keeping it in repair: has no time to rove abroad for improvement," she observed. "The Book of knowledge is closely clasped against those who must fullfil there [*sic*] daily task of manual labour."⁷⁰

Even with their expressed dissatisfaction at the endless, unchanging nature of housework, one might theorize that late eighteenth-century American women could nevertheless have found their domestic lives meaningful if they and their husbands had highly valued their contribu-

---

⁶⁹ Mary Palmer to Abigail Greenleaf, Oct. 12, 1755, Paine Papers; Pamela Sedgwick to Elizabeth Mayhew, Feb. 6, 1785, Sedgwick Papers III; Fisher diary, Jan. 14, 1793; Mary Jones to Fanny Bland, May 10, 1769, Tucker-Coleman Papers, microfilm, reel 1, EGS; Margaret Lowther Page, "To Miss J—— L———," in her Journal and Letters, EGS. The original reads: "From Books and Poetry must turn."

⁷⁰ Elizabeth Shaw to [Mary Cranch], April 6, 1781; Abigail Adams to Elizabeth S. Peabody, Feb. 4, 1800, both in Shaw Papers, box 1. A boarder's memoir of Elizabeth Peabody is Samuel Gilman, *Contributions to Literature* (Boston, 1856), 220–230. I owe this reference to Lyman H. Butterfield.

tions to the family well-being. But such was not the case. Women revealed their assessments of the importance of their work in the adjectives they used to describe it: "my Narrow sphere," my "humble duties," "my little Domestick affairs."[71]

Always the words belittled their domestic role, thereby indicating its low status in contemporary eyes. Modern historians can accurately point to the essential economic function of women within a colonial household, but the facts evident from hindsight bear little relationship to eighteenth-century subjective attitudes. In spite of the paeans to notable womanhood, the role of the household mistress in the family's welfare was understood only on the most basic level. Such minimal recognition did not translate itself into an awareness that women contributed to the wider society. Instead, just as a woman's activities were supposed to be confined to the domestic sphere, so, too, was any judgment of her importance. Americans realized that a successful household needed a competent mistress, but they failed to endow that mistress with an independent social standing or to grant to her domestic work the value it deserved. Notable housewifery was conceived to be an end in itself, rather than as a means to a greater or more meaningful goal. As such, it was an inadequate prop for feminine self-esteem.

Accordingly, it comes as no surprise to learn that women generally wrote of their household work without joy or satisfaction. They spoke only of "the discharge of the necessary duties of life," of "perform[ing] the duties that are annex'd to my Station." Even the South Carolinian Martha Laurens Ramsay, described by her husband, David, as a model wife, regarded her "self denying duties" as "a part of the curse denounced upon Eve," as a penalty to be endured, instead of as a fulfilling experience. The usage was universal and the message unmistakable: their tasks, with rare exceptions, were "duties," not pleasures. The only Americans who wrote consistently of the joys of housewifery and notable womanhood were men like William Livingston. In contrast, Christian Barnes found the household a prison that offered no intellectual stimulation, describing it as a place where women were "Chain'd down to domestic Dutys" that "Stagnate[d] the Blood and Stupefie[d] the Senses."[72]

Yet still women did not question the overall dimensions of the ideal domestic role. Sometimes, to be sure, they inquired about its details, as

---

[71] Eunice Paine to Thomas Paine, June 30, 1753, Paine Papers; Tucker diary, May 1, 1802; Rebecca Foster to Dwight Foster, June 7, 1791, Dwight Foster Papers, box 24, AAS. On the universality of this devaluation of women's work, see Margaret Mead, *Male and Female: A Study of Sexes in a Changing World* (New York, 1949), 159–160.

[72] Elizabeth DeLancey to Anne DeLancey, Dec. 20, 1760, "DeLancey Reminiscences," DeLancey Papers; Elizabeth Meredith to David Meredith, July 12, 1795, Meredith Papers, box 4, HSP; David Ramsay, *Memoirs of the Life of Martha Laurens Ramsey*, 3rd ed. (Boston, 1812), 44; Christian Barnes to Elizabeth Smith, Nov. 24, 1770, Barnes Letterbook. For a unique—and significantly later—expression of pleasure about domestic duties, see Deborah N. Logan, "Biographical Sketches of Life & Character of Dr. George Logan," 1821, Logan Papers, LXI, 161–162, HSP.

when Esther Edwards Burr, Jonathan Edwards's daughter, and her close friend Sarah Prince carried on a learned discussion about the precise meaning of the parts of Proverbs 31 that outlined the virtuous woman's daily routine. But ultimately they saw no alternative to domesticity. Many were simply resigned to the inevitable, for they had few options. Certainly some expressed the philosophy that "the height of happiness is Contentment" with one's lot, that although their life had "no great veriety . . . custom has made it agreable . . . and to desire more would be ungreatfull."[73] More probable, though, is the fact that the household duties women found unsatisfying were intertwined in their own minds with responsibilities from which they gained a great deal of pleasure. Their role as mistress of the household, in the end, constituted but a third of their troika of domestic duties. They were wives and mothers as well as housekeepers, and these components of domesticity gave them the emotional and psychological rewards they did not receive from running their households efficiently.

[73] C[atherine] R[ead] to Betsy [Ludlow], Sept. 16, [1790?], Read Family Papers, SCL; Simon P. Gratz, "Some Material for a Biography of Mrs. Elizabeth Fergusson, Née Graeme," *PMHB*, XXXIX (1915), 277. For the Burr-Prince discussion, see Esther Edwards Burr, Journal-Letters, Nov. 24, 1754 [Dec. 1, 12], YL.

Suggestions for Further Reading

Gary Nash provides an excellent introduction to the various cultures in the colonies in *Red, White and Black: The Peoples of Early America** (Prentice-Hall, 1974). For Virginia, see Wesley Frank Craven, *White, Red, and Black: The Seventeenth Century Virginian** (University Press of Virginia, 1971).

Good introductions to American Indian life are Alvin M. Josephy, Jr., *The Indian Heritage of America** (Knopf, 1968); Peter Farb, *Man's Rise to Civilization as Shown by the Indians of North America from Primeval Times to the Coming of the Industrial State** (Dutton, 1968); Angie Debo, *A History of the Indians in The United States* (University of Oklahoma Press, 1970); and Wilcomb E. Washburn, *The Indian in America** (Harper and Row, 1975). Relations between Indians and whites throughout American history are treated in Francis Paul Prucha, *A Bibliographical Guide to the History of Indian-White Relations in the United States** (University of Chicago Press, 1977); William T. Hagan, *American Indians** (University of Chicago Press, 1961); Roy Harvey Pearce, *The Savages of America: A Study of the Indian and the Idea of Civilization** (Johns Hopkins Press, 1953); and two works by Wilcomb E. Washburn, *Red Man's Land/ White Man's Law: A Study of the Past and Present Status of the American Indian* (Scribner, 1971) and *The Indian and the White Man** (Doubleday, 1964), a collection of documents. Special problems are confronted in Alfred W. Crosby, Jr., *The Columbian Exchange: Biological and Cultural Consequences of 1492** (Greenwood Press, 1972); William M. Denevan, *The Native Population of the Americas in 1492* (University of Wisconsin Press, 1976); and Wilbur R. Jacobs, *Dispossessing the American Indian: Indians and Whites on the Colonial Frontier** (Scribner, 1972). Important recent studies include Bernard Sheehan, *Savagism and Civility: Indians and Englishmen in Colonial Virginia** (Cambridge University Press, 1980) and James Axtell, *The Indian Peoples of Early America: A Documentary History of the Sexes** (Oxford University Press, 1981).

American slavery is placed in the context of world history in David B. Davis' works, *The Problem of Slavery in Western Culture** (Cornell University Press, 1966) and *The Problem of Slavery in the Age of Revolution, 1770–1823** (Cornell University Press, 1975). On the origin of slavery in the United States, see Winthrop D. Jordan, *White Over Black: American Attitudes Toward the Negro, 1550–1812** (University of North Carolina Press, 1968) and Edmund S. Morgan, *American Slavery, American Freedom: The Ordeal of Colonial Virginia** (Norton, 1975). The basic primary source on the slave trade is Elizabeth Donnan, ed., *Documents Illustrative of the Slave Trade to America*, 4 vols. (Carnegie Institution, 1930–1935). Philip D. Curtin's book *The Atlantic Slave*

* Available in paperback edition.

Trade: A Census* (University of Wisconsin Press, 1969) is a provocative study of the numbers of slaves imported to the various parts of the New World. A good secondary treatment of the trade is Daniel P. Mannix and Malcolm Cowley, *Black Cargoes: A History of the Atlantic Slave Trade, 1518–1865** (Viking, 1962). On slavery in the individual colonies, see Lorenzo Greene, *The Negro in Colonial New England** (Colonial University Press, 1942); Thaddeus Tate, Jr., *The Negro in Eighteenth-Century Williamsburg** (University of Virginia Press, 1965); Gerald W. Mullin, *Flight and Rebellion: Slave Resistance in Eighteenth Century Virginia** (Oxford University Press, 1972); and Peter H. Wood, *Black Majority: Negroes in Colonial South Carolina from 1670 through the Stono Rebellion** (Knopf, 1974). An important study of free blacks in the early colonies is *"Myne Owne Ground": Race and Freedom on Virginia's Eastern Shore, 1640–1676* (Oxford University Press, 1980), by T. H. Breen and Stephen Innes.

The standard works on white servants and laborers in the colonies are Abbot E. Smith, *Colonists in Bondage: White Servitude and Convict Labor in America, 1607–1776** (University of North Carolina Press, 1947) and Richard B. Morris, *Government and Labor in Early America** (Columbia University Press, 1946). Warren B. Smith examines the situation in a single state with *White Servitude in Colonial South Carolina** (University of South Carolina Press, 1961). John Barth's novel *The Sot-Weed Factor** (Doubleday, 1960) gives a hilarious, bawdy, and generally correct picture of life in colonial Maryland, in the process conveying a good deal of information about white servitude.

Works which provide an overview of the history of women in America are Mary Ryan, *Womanhood in America: From Colonial Times to the Present** (New Viewpoints, 1975); Jean E. Friedman and William G. Shade, eds., *Our Sisters: Women in American Life and Thought** (Allyn and Bacon, 1973); and Carol Ruth Berkin and Mary Beth Norton, eds., *The Women of America: Original Essays and Documents** (Houghton-Mifflin, 1978). For an older but still valuable study of Southern women, see Julia Cherry Spruill, *Women's Life and Work in the Southern Colonies** (University of North Carolina Press, 1938). Most studies of family life in the colonies provided insight into the role of women. See, for example, Edmund S. Morgan, *The Puritan Family** (Harper and Row, 1966); John Demos, *A Little Commonwealth: Family Life in Plymouth Colony** (Oxford University Press, 1970); and Philip J. Greven, Jr., *Four Generations: Population, Land, and Family in Colonial Andover, Massachusetts** (Cornell University Press, 1970). For a study of women in the early period, see Lyle Koehler, *A Search for Power: The "Weaker Sex" in Seventeenth-Century New England* (University of Illinois Press, 1980). Linda K. Kerber, in *Women of the Republic: Intellect and Ideology in Revolutionary America** (University of North Carolina Press, 1980), traces the role of women in the new nation.

2

The New Nation

Crime and Punishment in Philadelphia

JOHN K. ALEXANDER

Poverty has been seen as a problem in this country since colonial times. Although poor people have always been evident in civilized society, somehow poverty was considered out of place in the New World settlements. The new societies in America were founded, in part, to escape the evils of the old world, one of which was the increasing visibility of the independent poor.

Some of the *dependent* poor in early America, on the other hand, were seen as useful. They worked as the servants, apprentices, and common, seasonal labor of the more prosperous of the early settlers. This dependent class of people was considered necessary to the functioning of society. Those poor people who fell into poverty as a result of ill health, death, or misfortune, however, were not welcome in colonial society. They were often expelled from colonial settlements or imprisoned in jails or almhouses as a result of their economic condition. These measures led to the creation of a rootless, drifting body of poor people, who sought whatever relief they could in whatever ways they could. Needless to say, one form of relief some sought was in petty and not so petty criminality. As a result, poverty and crime soon became linked in the minds of more prosperous citizens.

As the villages of the early colonial period grew to be the cities of the late eighteenth century, many poor people settled on the outskirts of these municipalities. The problem of poverty then became an urban problem, one of the issues city dwellers had to face. But, as long as the poor maintained their traditional attitudes of deference toward their "betters," the situation could be kept under control, and the problem was seen as manageable.

With the coming of American independence, however, many of the poor began to change their attitudes. Increasingly, they believed that their economic condition should not keep them in a position of inferiority in the new nation. As the suffrage was extended under the influence of egalitarian ideas, the newly independent poor felt that they had as much right to participate in the affairs of the new nation as did the older elite. This created a new problem for the leaders of the society. Suddenly the poor seemed more visible. And they were clamoring for rights, the rights they had been told they could claim simply by virtue of being citizens of the new nation.

Those who were accustomed to governing the towns and cities of America were faced with a dilemma. In order to maintain their control over society, either they had to eliminate poverty through reform, or they had to subject the poor to more rigid and effective controls.

In his study of the Philadelphia poor during the last half of the eighteenth century, John K. Alexander, of the University of Cincinnati, describes the attempts of the Philadelphia elite to assert control over the growing number of independent poor of the city. In the chapter from his book that is reprinted below, Alexander describes the attempts to treat crime as an outgrowth of the problem of poverty and describes the attempted reforms of the criminal justice system that could lead to a better resolution of this problem of poverty.

These attempts failed, of course, and the "problem" of poverty became more severe as the poor increasingly refused to pattern themselves according to the desires of the dominant class. It is possible to say that the situation has changed only slightly from that day to this. One of the most often criticized aspects of modern urban living is the threat of violent crime, and the people who are considered to be threatening in our cities today are those same undeferential poor who so worried the leaders of late eighteenth-century Philadelphia.

I n the colonial period, Philadelphians, knowing that social disorder often accompanied urban living, worked to suppress the forces seen as supporting disorder, vice, and crime. However, they evidenced little concern about why crime occurred or who committed it. During the revolutionary era, Philadelphians began examining the issues of social disorder, crime, and punishment far more closely than ever before. Embracing Enlightenment humanitarianism, some reformers maintained that the system of justice must be rendered more evenhanded and humane.[1] These reformers could, in the postwar years, rejoice when debtors and the innocent poor

[1] [Merle] Curti, [The] Growth [of American Thought, 3rd ed. (New York, 1964)], pp. 163–65.

"Crime and Punishment in Philadelphia." Reprinted from *Render Them Submissive: Responses to Poverty in Philadelphia, 1760–1800* by John K. Alexander. Copyright © 1980 by the University of Massachusetts Press.

were no longer routinely tossed into a miserable existence in jail. Enlightenment ideals did not, however, dominate the new analysis of crime and punishment that flourished in the revolutionary city. Considering the nature and supposed perpetrators of crime, many inhabitants concluded that the poor increasingly threatened social order and stability. They did not argue that the dignity of mankind and the ideal of social progress made reform of the social justice system necessary. Rather, emphasizing themes presented in the moral crusade, . . . they stressed that ways had to be found to control or reform the potentially dangerous poor, lest vice and crime plague the city. Only after these views were forcefully presented to the legislature in the mid-1780s did the legislature move to revise the penal code. And the reviewers reflected the views and concerns articulated in the moral crusade both by trying to make criminals emulate the industrious poor and by trying to stop the evil of idleness associated with imprisonment for debt.

Philadelphians of the prewar era believed that tippling houses presented a special source of concern. As early as 1744, the city government cried out against the vast number of such houses, arguing that they lowered the city's moral tone. The problem persisted. In 1764 a legislative committee observed that "public Houses and Dram-shops have increased to an enormous Degree, to the great Corruption of Morals in the Populace." In the decade before the war, the mayor's court of Philadelphia worked diligently to stamp out disorderly houses and to control the number of taverns. The effect of these actions is not clear, but even if the court improved the situation, that improvement covered only the area between Vine and South streets. The mayor's court jurisdiction did not extend to the suburbs, and as "A Citizen" asserted in 1772: "The environs of this city very much abound" with "abominable [tavern] houses." By the eve of the Revolution, Philadelphians still sought an effective way to control taverns and disorderly houses.[2]

Philadelphia produced better results in providing the colonial equivalent of a police force. Beginning in 1749, the wardens of Philadelphia could hire night watchmen to stop social disorder and prevent crime by capturing nightwalkers, malefactors, rogues, vagabonds, and disorderly persons who disturbed the public peace. According to Carl Bridenbaugh, the night watch that developed soon set the colonial standard. By 1772 the watch patrolled seventeen separate beats from 10:00 P.M. to 4:00 A.M. in summer and from 9:00 P.M. to 6:00 A.M. in winter. During the day, over twenty constables performed similar duties to maintain the peace.[3] As with the mayor's court, the power of the watch ended at Vine and South streets, and the environs therefore lacked a police force. Still, by the eve

[2] [Leonard W.] Labaree and [William B.] Willcox, eds., *The Papers of Benjamin Franklin*, [23 vols. to date (New Haven, Conn., 1959)], 3: 10, 11; *Penn. Archives*, 8th ser., 7: 5592; HSP, "Mayor's Court Docquets From October Sessions 1766 to January 1771 Inclusive," passim; "A Citizen," *Penn. Packet*, 26 Oct. 1772.

[3] *Penn. Statutes*, 8: 99; [J. Thomas] Scharf and [Thompson] Westcott, *History [of Philadelphia, 1609–1884*, 3 vols. (Philadelphia, 1884)], 1: 265; Carl Bridenbaugh, *Cities in Revolt*, rev. ed. (New York, 1971), pp. 108–10, 297.

of the Revolution, the city proper had developed what was for the times a reasonably effective police system.

In the decade and a half before the Revolution, residents of Philadelphia made surprisingly few observations on crime in the city. James Hamilton, deputy governor of the province, suggested in 1761 that the poor perpetrated most crimes by asserting that legal fees would not maintain the attorney general, since the people prosecuted were, "in general, the most indigent of Mankind, and consequently unable to pay." Records proving or refuting Hamilton's claim have not survived, but a fragmentary piece of evidence from 1766 supports his contention. In that year, ten men escaped from the city jail. Included in that breakout were two laborers, two persons with no occupation listed, and one each of the following: joiner, shipwright, tailor, sailor, shoemaker, rope maker. At least five of the eight escapees with listed occupations were, if typical of their occupational groups, probably numbered among the poor.[4] Save for such general comments and bits of evidence, the questions of who committed crime and why escaped systematic analysis in prerevolutionary Philadelphia.

Persons convicted of criminal acts during the period 1760–76, whether poor or not, faced harsh penalties. By 1760, Pennsylvania followed the English practice of emphasizing corporal punishment, including the death penalty, rather than imprisonment. Diverse crimes, including rape, highway robbery, arson, counterfeiting, and burglary, carried the death penalty. A person convicted of a capital felony for which the laws of Great Britain allowed benefit of clergy could use that rule and be branded rather than executed. In addition to being branded, such a criminal might, at the court's discretion, be incarcerated at hard labor for from six months to two years. If convicted a second time on a similar count, the criminal faced the death penalty. Simple larceny was punishable by a sliding scale of retribution. In all cases, the convicted thief had to restore the goods or pay their full value to the rightful owner. In addition, the criminal was to pay the government the following amounts: for the first such conviction, the value of the goods taken; for the second, twice the value of the goods taken; for the third, three times the value of the stolen goods. Until these sums were paid, the thief underwent confinement. Further, public whipping with stripes well laid on their bare backs awaited all convicted larcenists. First offenders received not more than twenty-one stripes; a second conviction drew twenty-one to forty lashes; and the third offense brought thirty-nine to fifty stripes. At the discretion of the court, third-time offenders could also be imprisoned and there set at work and "corrected" for a period of one to four years.[5]

As in England, the intent of this criminal code was the prevention of

[4] *Penn. Archives*, 8th ser., 6: 5266. The listing of criminals is in *Penn. Journal*, 18 Dec. 1766; on the economic position of the occupations, see [Jackson Turner] Main, [*The*] *Social Structure* [*of Revolutionary America* (Princeton, N.J., 1965)], pp. 72–81.

[5] The basic law, passed in 1718, is in *Penn. Statutes*, 3: 199–214; see also Harry E. Barnes, *The Evolution of Penology in Pennsylvania: A Study in American Social History* (1927; reprinted ed., Montclair, N.J., 1968), pp. 28, 37, 52–53.

crime by means of the threat of death or other corporal punishment. Imprisonment constituted a mere supplement to this system, which featured punishment rather than reformation of criminals. Thus, the jails of colonial Philadelphia housed few convicted criminals.[6] This does not mean that the jails were thinly populated during these years—far from it. Because imprisonment for debt existed throughout the prerevolutionary period, many poor persons found themselves in jail.

During the colonial era, the predicament of indebted Philadelphians who could not pay their creditors was indeed bleak. The basic law on insolvent debtors and imprisonment for debt, passed in 1730, established a complex and expensive procedure for gaining freedom once imprisoned for debt.[7] The legislature realized this fact by saying that the procedure required to gain freedom would work a very great hardship upon a poor prisoner confined for a small debt. To avoid this potential problem, persons in debt for not more than forty shillings, besides the cost of the suit, could petition for release. In addition, such poor persons could retain clothes, bedding, and tools to a value of twenty shillings for a single person and fifty shillings for a married person.

This law had two major flaws. The government made no provision for providing imprisoned debtors with *any* necessities of life—save the prison roof over their heads. Thus, persons in jail because they could not pay their debts, which could be quite small, were expected to pay for their own food, clothing, and fuel. Nor did the law allow court and prison fees to be included in the cancellation of debts totaling less than forty shillings. Given these regulations, many poor persons languished in the debtors' prison for long periods.[8]

The difficulty of getting out of jail once imprisoned for debt significantly increased a year later. The legislature, believing that some persons used the law for insolvent debtors to avoid paying bills they could afford to pay, materially altered the law. Henceforth, childless persons in debt for less than twenty pounds could not take advantage of the provisions of the 1730 act. Instead, they must surrender all their material goods. If the value of these did not cover their debts, the residue had to be paid by servitude if the creditor demanded it. Single persons under the age of fifty-three could not be forced to serve more than seven years; married men under the age of forty-six could not be made to serve more than five years. Within these limits, the court decided upon the length of servitude required. A person owing less than forty shillings could be freed by the order of two magistrates if he was willing to pay his debt by servitude. This 1731 act remained in force until at least 1765 and quite possibly after that.[9]

The poor were thus caught in a web of legal entanglements. If they

[6] Barnes, *Evolution of Penology*, p. 71.

[7] *Penn. Statutes*, 4: 171–83 passim.

[8] Ibid., 7: 347; 13: 257.

[9] See ibid., 4: 211–15, for law and quotations; cf. 2: 249–51. A 1765 law may have repealed the earlier limitation, but the law was not unquestionably repealed until 1798. See ibid., 16: 98–99; cf. 6: 459–60.

owed less than forty shillings, they could escape prison by serving a period of servitude worth the debts they could not pay. That provision certainly was not onerous. But people owing forty shillings to twenty pounds faced a potentially lengthy period of servitude to cancel their debts. A person jailed for a debt of more than twenty pounds was hard pressed to use the legal procedures to free himself.

In 1765 the legislature attempted to ease the burden of imprisoned debtors by decreeing that creditors must pay for the maintenance of imprisoned debtors, or they would be freed. Such maintenance was not to exceed five shillings a week for a single person and seven shillings and sixpence for a person with children. However, this act did not eliminate the jail fees and court costs that could keep a poor person in jail, and, as the legislature noted in 1770, the law decreeing that creditors must pay for maintenance was not fully effective.[10]

Despite the efforts of the legislature to reform the laws, many persons imprisoned for debt in Philadelphia between 1760 and 1776 found it hard to subsist, since they had to pay for food, clothing, and fuel. Fortunately for the debtors, a wide variety of private actions, sometimes undertaken at the request of poor debtors, helped them subsist; but such aid was given only sporadically.[11] Realizing "the miserable situation of numbers confined in pail (particularly during the inclemency of the winter)," a group of Philadelphians banded together in February 1776 to form the Philadelphia Society for Assisting Distressed Prisoners. Members of the society began by assessing themselves ten shillings each and by establishing a group of managers to administer whatever relief they thought necessary. This organization apparently functioned well for about nineteenth months but dissolved when the British occupied Philadelphia in 1778.[12]

In the decade and a half before the Revolution, then, Philadelphia's government combated social disorder and crime by maintaining a watch and by trying to reduce the number of disorderly houses and regulate the number of taverns. The ventures for controlling taverns appear to have been less successful than the endeavors to create an effective watch system. Philadelphians of this period expended little effort in analyzing why crimes were committed, but they apparently believed that a large number of criminals were poor, as probably was the case. The criminal code of the day sought to prevent crime through fear of death or other corporal punishment rather than through reforming offenders. Persons who could not pay their debts faced imprisonment. There were attempts to reform the system of imprisonment for debt, but few meaningful improvements materialized before the Revolution.

By 1800, the situation was, in most respects, quite different. And the

[10] Ibid., 6: 392–93; 7: 347.

[11] *Penn. Chron.*, 25 Dec. 1769, 29 Jan. 1770; *Penn. Gaz.*, 10 Mar. 1763; "P. B.," ibid., 21 Dec. 1774.

[12] *Penn Eve. Post*, 3 Feb. and 12 Mar. 1776; HSP, Philadelphia Society for Alleviating the Miseries of Public Prisons: Minutes, 1787–93, 13 July 1789 (hereinafter HSP, Soc. for Alleviating Miseries, 1787–93). . . .

American Revolution helped produce significant changes in the perception and handling of social disorder, crime, and punishment. As in politics, the Constitution of 1776 proved a vital instrument for bringing about such change, especially in the criminal code and in the system of imprisonment for debt.

The Constitution of 1776 pointed the way to reform of the system of imprisonment for debt by directing the legislature to enact laws enabling an honest debtor who delivered his real and personal property to his creditors to remain free. Despite repeated revision of the laws on insolvent debtors, the Constitution's suggestion was still not implemented by 1787. The prerevolutionary problems persisted, as even people who owed only small debts continued to suffer confinement for long periods. Persons found innocent of criminal charges but unable to pay the costs of prosecution were still clamped into jail as debtors, and they had to pay all the costs of their maintenance. The number of people who faced these problems was indeed large.[13] For the period 1780–90, when criminals were more likely than in colonial days to be incarcerated, the number of debtors in the city and county jail of Philadelphia actually outnumbered criminals, 4,061 to 3,999.[14]

Not all people imprisoned for debt in the postrevolutionary period were poor. Some swindlers went into debt purposely to obtain and transfer goods, and then used the insolvent debtors act to gain freedom.[15] However, the number of people following this course could not have been a significant portion of the imprisoned debtors. Further, according to "A Citizen of Philadelphia," writing in 1787, those who owed fifteen pounds to fifty thousands pounds had, besides the statutes for freeing insolvent debtors, "fifty different ways of escaping the horrors" of jail. "Consult its archives," he flatly asserted, "and you will find it is the poor, the ignorant, and the most miserable who are most found upon its records." "Justice in Mercy" agreed and offered precise data for 1785 to prove the point. Citing the reports of the head jailer, "Justice" noted that about one-half of the 151 prisoners then confined were debtors. Of that half, not more than 15 could support themselves, and the other 60 were "so *miserably poor*, that they must *perish* with *hunger* and *cold*, unless fed and cloathed by the charitable inhabitants of the city!" Such assistance was, however, at best a stopgap measure.[16]

The continuing problems of persons imprisoned for debt led in 1787 to the creation of the Philadelphia Society for Alleviating the Miseries of Public Prisons. This group, like the earlier prison society, assessed its members 10 shillings a year and elected a committee to visit the prison

---

[13] Thayer, *Pennsylvania Politics*, p. 222; "Charitable," *Penn. Mer.*, 4 Feb. 1785, 22 Jan. 1787. *Penn. Statutes*, 4: 183, gives a guide to the various acts passed after 1776.

[14] *Fed. Gaz.*, 8 Oct. 1790. These are the only general returns of the total number of prisoners I have found.

[15] *Penn. Eve. Her.*, 23 Apr. 1785; "Honestus," ibid., 3 May 1786.

[16] "A Citizen," *Penn. Packet*, 30 Aug. 1787; "Justice in Mercy," *Penn. Gaz.*, 7 Dec. 1785. Cf. "Citizens," *Indep. Gaz.*, 29 Nov. 1783; ibid., 16 Nov. 1786.

each week. The committee was to distribute relief, watch over the morals of the prisoners, and report any abuses they discovered to the officers of government authorized to redress them. In addition, four physicians from the society would visit prisons as needed to give advice on matters of health.[17]

The society immediately began helping prisoners in all of the city's houses of confinement. It arranged for a man to stay at the jail at all times to receive food offered as benevolent donations. Old clothes were advertised for, collected, and given to those most in need. Wood and soup were distributed on an irregular basis until February 1789, when it was decided that soup would be delivered weekly during the winter season. The society also petitioned the Assembly and the city to correct various evils.[18] It is not clear if the society was directly responsible for the major reform bill of 1792, but in that year the legislature acknowledged its duty to aid those confined for debt in Philadelphia who were so poor that they could not procure food, fuel, or clothing. It was, said the legislature, "inconsistent with humanity to suffer them to want the common necessaries of life." Correspondingly, inspectors of jails, as well as county justices of the peace, were to begin inspecting the debtors' prison. Fuel and blankets would be distributed at county expense to all who could not afford them. The creditor whose complaint had put the person in prison was to supply seven cents per day so that the inspectors could buy food for the prisoner. If the creditor proved unwilling to provide the required sum, the debtor would go free.[19]

This improvement in the living conditions of debtors marked a significant victory for the society. But it was only half the battle. The original prison relief society founded in 1776 had decried the fact that many whose labor might be useful to society had to endure imprisonment because they could not pay fees. This charge was well founded: Pennsylvania law required that even a person found innocent must pay court costs. Despite repeated attacks on this practice, it still existed when the Society for Alleviating the Miseries of Public Prisons was formed.[20] To combat the problem, the society announced in 1787 that it would work for the release of "proper objects" held in jail only for fees. It soon found itself inundated with petitions. Elizabeth Donnovan, signing with her mark, proclaimed that she lived "in the greatest distress" in "this place of dreadfull distress, the Work House, . . . for my fees which I shall never be able to pay while kept in here, being a poor old Woman unable to earn even a subsistence for myself, notwithstanding the heard [sic] hearted

---

17 "Constitution" and "Observations," *Indep. Gaz.*, 19 Mar. 1787. HSP, Soc. for Alleviating Miseries: files, "Report of the Aceting Committee," . . . 4 Aug. 1788. . . .

18 *Penn. Journal*, 24 Nov. 1787; HSP, Soc. for Alleviating Miseries: files, committee meetings of 16 Jan., 6 and 26 Feb. and 3 and 13 Mar. 1789; HSP, Soc. for Alleviating Miseries, 1787–93, 18 Oct. and 21 Dec. 1790; HSP, "Minutes of the Corporation [of Philadelphia, 1789–93]," 1 Dec. 1789.

19 *Penn. Statutes*, 14: 267–69 (quotation from p. 267).

20 *Penn. Eve. Post*, 24 Feb. 1776; "An old Man," *Indep. Gaz.*, 2 Nov. 1782; "Jail fees," *Penn. Eve. Her.*, 4 Nov. 1786; *Penn. Packet*, 25 Sept. 1786; HSP, petition of Thomas Wise dated 13 Nov. 1784, filed under Soc. Misc. Coll., Box 3A-B.

Keeper will not discharge me until I pay for my Bread & his fees." William Leslie pleaded: "No Man can be more unjustly kept here [in jail] than I am—I was tried last City Court for a Larceny, and acquited . . . , & have been confined about 9 weeks, every [sic] since my Trial for My Court Charges, which I can never pay if kept here."[21]

In addition to the innocent but poor, the debtors' prison also housed many held merely for nonpayment of insignificant debts. One investigation of the prison in 1786 revealed that seven prisoners owed debts totaling not quite as many pounds.[22] The society, also having pledged to help free "proper objects" held for such small debts, after investigating the reputation and character of the various petitioners, began paying the fees and trifling debts of many of them. From January to July 1788, the society secured the release of at least fifty-two prisoners by paying fees or debts. In all of these cases, save one, the cost per person was four shillings and sixpence (sixty cents), which was a jail fee. In 1789 the legislature admitted that the practice of long confinement for small debts, fines, or forfeitures still existed for persons incapable of making satisfaction. Arguing that this punishment "tends to the distress of their families as well as to the public injury by the burdens created and idle habits contracted thereby," the legislators took action. Henceforth, any person owning less than five pounds in debts, fines, or forfeitures would be freed after having served thirty days.[23] Here was a major change and a major reform, called forth as much by a growing desire to control the evil influence of idleness as it was by a humanitarian concern for the plight of the poor. However, this law did nothing to eliminate the problem of jail fees.

In December of 1790, the society petitioned the legislature and requested that the jail fees of people incarcerated for debt be dropped, seeing that these persons frequently faced many months of confinement because they could not pay fees. The petition also urged that the keeper of the debtors' apartment be made a salaried officer, since his fees, even if collectable, would not equal a living wage. In September 1791, the legislature moved to remedy these problems. Now the costs of indictments thrown out for lack of evidence would be paid by the city or county, and persons found innocent of alleged crime would not pay costs. Anyone held only for costs could use the various acts for the relief of insolvent debtors to obtain freedom. Finally, if the court imposing costs believed

[21] "Observations," *Indep. Gaz.*, 19 May 1787; HSP, Soc. for Alleviating Miseries; files, petitions of Eliz Donnovan (13 Feb. 1788), and William Leslie (14 Aug. 1787). Cf. ibid., George Duffield to John Olden, 8 May 1788, and associated petitions.

[22] *Penn. Packet*, 25 Sept. 1786.

[23] On checking reputations see HSP, Soc. for Alleviating Miseries, 1787-93, 13(?) Jan. and 6 and 20 Feb. 1789; HSP, Soc. for Alleviating Miseries: files, George Duffield to John Olden, 8 May 1788, Thomas Cutubert(?) to George Duffield, 3 May 1788, Thomas Welch to President and Supreme Executive Council, 2 May 1788. On the general action see ibid., "Fees assumed for the Following Prisoners" and "The Prison Society—To John Reynolds [ca. July 1788]"; and *Penn. Statutes*, 13: 257-58. Cf. *Penn. Gaz.*, 16 Nov. 1785.

that the person could not pay, he was to be discharged. Six months later, the legislature made the keeper of the debtors' prison a salaried officer.[24]

The society was so pleased with the actions of the governmental inspectors and the April 1792 law ordering that debtors be provided with the necessities of life that it decided to curtail its activities in July 1792. Henceforth, the meetings of the society would be less frequent, and the cost of joining the society was reduced to seven shillings and sixpence a year.[25]

Despite the society's substantial achievements, its victory was not complete. People could still be confined for small debts. The *Philadelphia Gazette*, complaining that 287 persons were locked in prison for such debts in 1793, maintained: "Let fraud be punished when proved, as a crime, but let the state no more be the collector of tavern debts, or the arbiter of tipling house disputes." The *Gazette* further urged that no one be imprisoned for a debt of less than forty shillings. But, in 1795, it was still possible for a gentlewoman to pay a debt of twenty-four shillings and thereby secure the release of a person who had been in prison for several weeks.[26]

Nor could all innocent people automatically avoid jail. Calling forth the image of the noted Enlightenment reformer, "Beccaria" charged in 1796 that "scarce a session of any of our inferior courts of *justice* passes over, without many people being thrown into prison for no crime at all, unless we should rank poverty under this head." "Many poor wretches," he thundered, "are suffering all the miseries of a jail for no other crime than—POVERTY!" Citing a list of legal fees that could be charged, he argued that such fees sent innocent but poor people to jail, and he offered specific examples to prove this assertion. Such complaints apparently had validity, for, in 1797, the legislature noted that a person indicted and then acquitted by a petit jury frequently had to pay for the prosecution. Calling this an injustice and a punishment to the innocent, the legislature ordered counties to pay all the trial costs of persons found innocent.[27]

"Beccaria" also attacked the procedure that allowed those held only for costs to use the laws for insolvent debtors. He correctly noted that, to use the insolvency laws, a person had to attend a quarterly court. The person could, therefore, if unable to pay costs, be jailed for up to three months. Despite "Beccaria's" plea, the situation remained. This and other charges of improper treatment of imprisoned debtors continued to be voiced, but imprisonment for debt had not been completely eliminated by 1800.[28] Still, in the postwar period, the gross abuses associated with im-

[24] HSP, Soc. for Alleviating Miseries, 1787–93, 21 Dec. 1790; *Penn. Statutes*, 14: 136–37, 268.

[25] HSP, Soc. for Alleviating Miseries, 1787–93, 9 July 1792.

[26] *Phila. Gaz.*, 13 Jan. 1794; *Am. Daily Adv.*, 22 Mar. 1796.

[27] Quotations from *New World*, 2 Nov. 1796. See also issues of 16 Nov. and 10 Dec. 1796; and *Penn. Statutes*, 15: 501.

[28] "Beccaria," *New World*, 16 Nov. 1796; letter of Daniel Thomas, *Aurora*, 3 Mar. 1794; PCA, "Minutes of Board of Inspectors [of Philadelphia Jail] from May 1794 to August 1801," 19 May 1795, 19 Dec. 1797; "Prison," *Gaz. of U.S.*, 1 Feb. 1800; Barnes, *Evolution of Penology*, pp. 114–15.

prisonment for debt were greatly reformed. The charges of the Constitution of 1776 had been taken up. Although the desire, associated with the moral crusade, to attack idleness was a vital force for bringing about reform, at least in the area of imprisonment for debt, Philadelphia's poor did feel the transforming hand as an instrument of improvement.

The reform spirit and concern for the poor that marked the work of the Philadelphia Society for Alleviating the Miseries of Public Prisons was evidenced even more forcefully in attacks upon trading justices. The magistrates with whom the poor most likely dealt derived their income from fixed fees for services rendered. Such a magistrate might, in dealing with the unwary and uninformed, charge higher fees than the laws specified or multiply the legal papers issued. Persons employing such practices gained the name of trading justices.

Complaints that legal officers gouged the people by overcharging on fees existed before the war. In January 1767 the legislature, after considering petitions from persons imprisoned for debt, established a committee of grievances to hear the complaints of those who believed they had been aggrieved by any public officer taking exorbitant fees.[29] Still, "A Federalist," writing in 1788, claimed that before the Revolution there had been only one trading justice and that the abuse was thus a limited one before the 1780s.[30] If public complaints are an accurate index, this writer was correct in claiming that few abuses existed before and during the war. But from 1785 to 1789 the actions of trading justices became a pressing issue; essays and comments on the unethical practices of magistrates appeared in the press with great regularity.[31]

Philadelphians who attacked the practice of retailing justice in the year 1785 clearly raised a legitimate grievance. In October, Alexander Carlisle, high constable for the city and county, was found guilty of extorting fees and fired.[32] Once he departed, complaints of trading justices subsided for half a year. When the issue again surfaced, it involved questions about the type of person who should be a magistrate. "A Wellwisher to the Community" spoke for numerous Philadelphians when he warned that some of the candidates for justice of the peace "are canvasing for themselves; of these latter gentlemen beware! they will grind the faces of the poor to support their imaginary dignity." Such essayists wanted only men of established wealth and reputation as justices of the peace.[33] It is therefore possible that some Philadelphians attempted to raise the specter of trading justices to keep as many positions of power as possible in the hands of the wealthy.

Although some citizens speaking against the retailing of justice prob-

---

[29] *Penn. Gaz.*, 5 Feb. 1767; *Penn. Archives*, 8th ser., 7: 5968.

[30] *Penn. Mer.*, 11 Mar. 1788; cf. "Amicus," ibid., 10 June 1788.

[31] Of items dealing with trading justice activity, those cited in n. 29 to this chapter are the only ones I discovered dated before 1785; over fifty such items appeared in the years 1785–89.

[32] *Freeman's Journal*, 2 Nov. 1785.

[33] Quotations from *Indep. Gaz.*, 6 May 1786. See also "Astrea," ibid., 21 May 1787; "Casca. No. IV," ibid., 28 Apr. 1789; "Monus," ibid., 1 May 1789; and "Zenophon," *Penn. Mer.*, 26 June 1788.

ably did so for political reasons, many others attacked trading justices simply because they were evil.[34] Some urged publishing lists of fees so that the people would at least not be overcharged by magistrates, and a few essayists did publish fee schedules. Other reformers sensibly urged that putting magistrates on a fixed salary would stop trading.[35] Also, an attempt was made to establish a subscription fund and a lawyer's association to help the poor in dealing with the law. Such actions seemed necessary to prevent the retailers of law from acquiring fortunes by gouging their fellow inhabitants. The fact was that "the poor, whose labor is scarcely sufficient to support them, cannot be supposed able to obtain redress in the courts by law. Every extortion from them is sunk in oblivion for want of power to bring forward their complaints."[36] These actions and comments show that attacks on trading justices were more than political ploys, and it does appear that trading justices vigorously practiced their trade in the late 1780s.

Philadelphians who spoke out against the retailers of justice realized that any city inhabitant might be victimized. As "Civis" said, Philadelphia magistrates too often were "rapacious wolves, who look on all classes of their fellow-citizens as their common prey." But the rich and powerful were hardly the wolves' favorite target. They much preferred to prey upon the poor, since such actions "pass un[n]oticed." Clearly, "the common people," the "poor and friendless," were most likely to fall into "the clutches" of those "monsters," the trading justices.[37]

When Philadelphia was reincorporated in 1789, the direct election of justices of the peace stopped. Instead, the aldermen of the city served as justices of the peace. Although this revised system did not stop all complaints about trading justices, it appears that the worst abuses, which affected primarily the poor, abated in the 1790s.[38] But again, for a large portion of the period under study, the poor had ample reason to fear the power of the law. It was not just trading justices; it was not just going to prison if innocent but unable to pay court costs; it was also lacking the resources to have recourse to the courts. Certainly, during the years 1785 to 1789, the poor of Philadelphia were subjected to the arbitrary power and criminality of at least some of the the city's legal officers. Ironically, in this same period, more prosperous Philadelphians came to believe that

---

[34] Some of the people who supported reincorporation argued that that action would do away with trading justices. But such comments did not, it appears, form a major part of the effort to attain reincorporation. See "Civis," *Fed. Gaz.,* 3 Mar. 1789; "Philo-Roscius," *Indep. Gaz.,* 16 Jan. 1789; and *Penn. Gaz.,* 4 Feb. 1789.

[35] "Volucius," *Penn. Mer.,* 1 July 1788; "A Citizen," ibid., 3 July 1788; "Aristides," *Indep. Gaz.,* 17 Sept. 1785; *Penn. Eve. Her.,* 27 July 1785; "A. B., *Penn. Packet,* 9 Sept. 1785.

[36] "A Citizen" and "A Friend," *Indep. Gaz.,* 14 June 1787; "A Hint," ibid., 22 Aug. 1787; "A Young Lawyer," ibid., 23 Aug. 1787; *Penn. Eve. Her.,* 10 Mar. 1787. It appears that neither the subscription fund nor the lawyers' association came into being.

[37] "Civis," *Fed. Gaz.,* 3 Mar. 1789; "A Friend," *Indep. Gaz.,* 14 June 1787.

[38] *Penn. Statutes,* 13: 201; 14: 329; "A Citizen," *Indep. Gaz.,* 3 July 1790; "Observer," ibid., 14 Aug. 1790.

the disorder and potential criminality of the poor had reached dangerous new heights.

During the war years, Philadelphians, as they had done in colonial days, occasionally voiced concern about social disorder and crime.[39] In the fall of 1785, such passing references gave way to an anguished outpouring that decried the degree of vice and crime flourishing in the area. The *Pennsylvania Packet* sadly found that it could sketch "*The Picture of an insignificant Fellow.*" He "gets drunk every day, and revels at bagnios every night. He joins in mobs, beats down the watchmen, breaks open doors, takes off knockers, and disturbs the quiet of honest people." "Honestus" agreed, proclaiming it "next to impossible in the crouds of vice, to preserve the morals of children, not under the immediate eye of faithful guardians."[40]

The grand jury of the city, at its quarter sessions held in October 1785, drew a yet more foreboding picture. In a memorial to the legislature, the grand jury recorded its concern over the great and increasing degree of vice and immorality in the city. Contrivances for gaming did great injury to the morals of many, and the uncommonly high number of bills for assault, larceny, keeping tippling houses, and the like offered "melancholy proofs of the depravity of morals which too greatly prevails." Moreover, there was reason to believe that many of the criminals were poor, because the city faced a constant influx of vagabonds, "who, encouraged to hope for a more plentiful harvest of plunder in this metropolis, resort here, where they may also be better concealed in their villanies, by wretches as abandoned as themselves." Asserting that such vagabond types dread hard labor more than a thousand stripes, the grand jury maintained that many such people had probably been driven to Philadelphia because the city of New York had abandoned whipping criminals and had substituted hard labor while chained to wheelbarrows. Although the grand jury did not call for a similar mode of punishment in Philadelphia, the general import of this point was surely understood by the legislature.[41]

"A Native of Philadelphia," writing in mid-November, agreed that the situation had gotten out of hand. Youths were frequently being seduced by the vicious allure of the billiard table and the brothel. The list of criminals apprehended in the city was, in size and content, simply too unpleasant to be described. Even given the corrupting effect of any large city, he continued, Philadelphia had to be considered the harbor and refuge of numerous criminals, since the number of offenders annually convicted in the city and suburbs probably equaled half the number sentenced in the rest of the state. In addition, he added, at least half as many more criminals probably eluded capture. A group of Philadelphians who petitioned the legislature in late December concurred by bemoaning the

---

[39] *Penn. Packet,* 5 July 1783 offers one example; such comments were, however, quite rare in the war years.

[40] Ibid., 20 Aug. 1785; "Honestus," ibid., 3 Sept. 1785.

[41] "The Memorial," *Indep. Gaz.,* 12 Nov. 1785, was designed to support the move for reincorporation and so may have painted a particularly bleak picture.

great increase of vice, immorality, and crime. Something *had* to be done, they argued, to strike at the causes of these evils, which this group felt could chiefly be found in the numerous houses devoted to gaming, drunkenness, receipt of stolen goods, and concealment of criminals.[42]

This outpouring of concern and anguish was probably not lost on the state's legislators when they began considering a bill to alter the nature of the criminal code. But, according to the legislature, the new code that became law in September 1786 was prompted by two other considerations. The legislature first cited the Pennsylvania Constitution of 1776 as a basis for action by observing that it had directed the legislature to reform the penal code. As the lawmakers noted, the Constitution indicated that punishments should be made more proportional to the crimes and that visible punishment of long duration at hard labor should, where appropriate, be used to deter crime more effectually. The second reason offered in support of a change in the penal code asserted that the old punishments sprang from the wrong philosophy. Indeed, the prewar emphasis on death and other corporal punishments did not answer the principal goals of society, which were "to correct and reform the offenders, and to produce such strong impression upon the minds of others as to deter them from committing the like offenses." Furthermore, "it is the wish of every good government to reclaim rather than to destroy." Here then was a major social change produced by the revolutionary Constitution and by an increasing belief that a better method of controlling crime had to be found.

The new penal code severely limited the use of the death penalty and corporal punishment. Now, persons convicted of robbery, burglary, or sodomy or buggery, or convicted as accessories to such crimes, had to forfeit to the state all the lands, tenements, goods and chattels they owned. Having been reduced to poverty, these criminals faced jail sentences of not more than ten years. Persons convicted of a simple larceny where the value of the stolen goods was less than twenty shillings were to restore the goods or the full value of goods, pay a like amount to the state, and undergo imprisonment for not more than one year. The same penalties held for a simple larceny where the value of the goods taken was twenty shillings or more, save that the maximum period of servitude was three years. Other crimes previously punished by branding, mutilation of the ears, whipping, or imprisonment for life now brought fines and incarceration for up to two years.

The legislature firmly believed that continued hard labor, publicly and disgracefully imposed, would "correct and reform" criminals. Accordingly, prisoners were to work in the streets while chained to wheelbarrows. To guarantee that criminals did labor, for every day of work missed without good cause, two days would be added to the sentence. For their efforts, the prisoners received shelter and coarse, wholesome food provided at public expense. To insure that criminals would be shamed, their uniforms were made of rough materials, bearing on the outer garment some visible mark designating the nature of their crime,

---

[42] Ibid., 17 Nov. 1785; "Petition," *Penn. Packet*, 30 Dec. 1785.

and males were to have their hair and beards close shaven every week. In this way, escape would be made more difficult and the prisoners could be marked for public censure. Thus, shame, hard work, and fear of long sentences would supposedly combine to deter crime and reform criminals.

This legislation also aimed to reduce criminality by distinguishing between the different classes of offenders. The lawmakers, in terms similar to those of the moral crusade, maintained that many young offenders committed crimes "from habits of idleness and intemperance and from want of pious education." Persons not "so hardened as to be void of shame or beyond the hope of being reclaimed" needed help. To save "the remaining seeds of virtue and goodness in the young and unwary," it would be best to separate them from old and hardened offenders.

This 1786 criminal code held out special hope for those who modeled themselves after the industrious poor lionized in the moral crusade. If prisoners "laboured faithfully . . . and evidenced a patient submission," they could be pardoned without serving their full sentence. This policy was inaugurated "to encourage those offenders in whom the love of virtue and the shame of vice is not wholly extinguished to set about a sincere and actual repentance and reformation of life and conduct." The Assembly expressed its hope that such prisoners, once freed, would become useful members of society.[43]

From 1786 until 1790, when it was significantly altered, this act helped draw Philadelphians into an extended analysis of the new penal system and also of criminality in general. Parts of the act, such as that section separating youthful offenders from hardened criminals, drew praise. But the wheelbarrow section of the law seems to have produced havoc. Apparently, numerous Philadelphians offered alms and sympathy, rather than shame, to prisoners working in the streets. And having criminals do work that honest laboring people could do evoked the wrath of many of the city's laboring persons. Worse yet, when out of doors, prisoners proved hard to control and, it was claimed, often escaped.[44] In July 1789 the *Universal Magazine* of London offered a biting analysis of the problem by asserting that wheelbarrow convicts escaped in such large numbers that no person dared to venture upon the streets after eight in the evening unless the night watch was nearby. The danger was such that the Supreme Executive Council was forced to have militiamen patrol the streets. This fear of wheelbarrow men may have been excessive, but Philadelphians had good reason to be concerned about crime: it appears that criminal activity was quite high between 1786 and 1790.[45]

As the level of criminal activity and the attack upon the wheelbar-

---

[43] *Penn. Statutes*, 12: 280–90 passim; see also 13: 244, 254.

[44] *Penn. Eve. Her.*, 18 Sept. 1787; *Penn. Journal*, 4 Apr. and 23 May 1787; *Indep. Gaz.*, 31 Mar. 1787; "Dennis K———y," ibid., 10 July 1787; Mease, *Picture*, pp. 160–61.

[45] *Universal Magazine of Knowledge and Pleasure* 85 (July 1789): 17. Numerous essays claimed that criminality was increasing, and it appears from the number of criminals in the city jail for 1787–96 that 1786 and 1787 were years of higher criminality than the period following 1791. See Samuel Harard, ed., *Register of Pennsylvania . . .*, 16 vols. (Philadelphia, 1828–36), 1: 206.

row law increased, Philadelphians engaged in a more extensive public discussion than ever before of what caused crime and who perpetrated it. Most analysts suggested a lack of moral strength as the cause. Some perceived this weakness as inevitable, since "Vices, like diseases, are often hereditary. The property of the one is to infect the manners, as the other poisons the springs of life." Whether inherited or not, as this group saw it, habits of "indolence and dissipation" led people to rob even when work was available. "Idleness . . . will be found the source of every vice, and consequently the cause of every crime." Others who focused on moral weakness considered it unnecessary to look beyond the tippling houses: spirituous liquors led persons to perpetrate crimes that rendered their confinement necessary for the safety and repose of society. Philadelphians holding this view rejoiced in 1789 when the number of taverns in the city was significantly reduced. They argued that this reduction laid the foundation "for a *restoration* of sobriety, industry and morality among the lower orders of the people." Closing a number of taverns, it was maintained, protected society "from midnight plunderers and strolling vagrants, by striking at the very root of vice." Some commentators believed that all these weaknesses worked in combination, since the principal cause of vice and crime supposedly were "spirituous liquors, a love of ease or laziness, and a fondness for loose and idle companions."[46]

A second group of people writing in the 1780–90 period maintained that the poor were especially prone to fall into crime, but only if they could not find work. The *Independent Gazetteer*, in urging creation of a city manufacturing enterprise, asserted that this step would "make our poor more sober and moral by employing them in honest industry instead of fixing them on loose and idle habits, or temp[t]ing them by want of bread to pilfering and still greater crimes." Dr. Enoch Edwards, who joined with other Philadelphians in promoting agriculture and domestic manufacturing, held that only by providing the poor with constant employment could one bring "security to government": when the poor "are depressed for want of employment, they become idle, lazy, indolent and necessitous—and it is from the starved part of every community, that we may look for danger; their idleness gives time to invent, and their necessities push them forward, with a courage sharpened by despair, to perpetuate acts of the most daring criminality."[47] The *Evening Herald* voiced a similar position but placed special emphasis on the plight of immigrants. A society to help industrious immigrants find employment was needed, lest bad fortune and an insufficient knowledge of America cause these new arrivals to become a discouraged, "useless, and perhaps dangerous acquisition." In describing the alarming increase of robberies occurring in Philadelphia in the fall of 1787, the *Herald* maintained that the crime wave stemmed from the new penal code, which punished criminals by hard labor rather than by inflicting corporal punishment. This new law proved ineffective because, "so far from being considered as a punish-

---

[46] "Vice," *Penn. Eve. Her.*, 26 May 1787; ibid., 27 June 1787; "Oration," *Penn. Gaz.*, 1 Oct. 1788; *Fed. Gaz.*, 24 June 1789 (emphasis added), 20 Mar. 1790.

[47] *Indep. Gaz.*, 14 Aug. 1787; "Address," *Fed. Gaz.*, 20 Mar. 1789.

ment, it is viewed with desire by many poor wretches who are in want of work and subsistence."[48]

"The American Moralist," in the spring of 1789, agreed that the poor could be forced into crime, but he apparently did not blame them. Noting that some people who were not in need committed crime, he asked, "What may not be expected from him, who is pushed forward into sin by the impulse of poverty, who lives in continual want of what he sees wasted by thousands in negligent extravagance, and who[se] pain is every moment aggravated by the contempt of those whom nature has subjected to the same necessities with himself, and who are only his superiors by that wealth which they know not how to possess with moderation and decency?" He answered his own question with the comment, "How strongly may such a man be tempted to declare war upon the prosperous and the great!"[49]

These analysts, despite their differing opinions about the causes of crime, agreed that the poor were the people most likely to commit criminal acts. If the extant sources, which cover the years 1794–1800, accurately reflect the situation in the last decade and a half of the century, this view was firmly rooted in fact. Joseph Gale, editor of *Gale's Independent Gazetteer*, observed in January 1797 that "the most afflictive and accumulated distress" in Philadelphia existed "amongst the *Irish Emigrants* and the *French Negroes;* and it may not perhaps, be unworthy of public attention," he commented, "to enquire how these people are generally supported, and whether many acts of depredation, and many scenes of horror which have occurred in this and neighboring States, may not, in some degree, be traced to the extreme poverty of this distressed class of people. . . ."[50] Gale was strikingly perceptive. In the preceding year, people born in Ireland accounted for 38.9 percent of all the convictions in the mayor's court.[51] Blacks represented at least another 28.2 percent of those found guilty. Slightly more than 70 percent of all people convicted in the mayor's court in 1796 were born outside the United States. Nor was 1796 an abnormal year. Of the persons convicted in the mayor's court from 1794 to 1800, 31.8 percent were blacks and 31.7 percent were born in Ireland. As we have seen, the vast majority of blacks in the city were poor, and, as Joseph Gale and others noted, Irish immigrants were very likely to be numbered among the poor. Considering just these two groups, it seems clear that those people convicted in the mayor's court came predominantly from Philadelphia's "other half."[52]

The occupations of the criminals convicted between 1794 and 1800 also attest to their poverty. Of the convicts whose occupations were

---

[48] 7 July and 18 Sept. 1787.

[49] *Fed. Gaz.*, 13 June 1789.

[50] 3 Jan. 1797.

[51] Because Southwark and the Northern Liberties were not parts of incorporated Philadelphia, any crimes committed in those areas would not have been tried in the mayor's court.

[52] . . . Using a list of convictions may somewhat overstate the degree of crime by the poorer element, for it is quite possible that more prosperous inhabitants, if they engaged in crime, may have avoided conviction.

noted, 27 percent were laborers. The next highest group, mariners, accounted for only 7.9 percent of the total. Equally significant, the mayor's court convicted few people whose occupations indicated possibly high income.[53]

The nature and extent of the criminal activities of these convicts also point to their poverty. Although the court tried a wide variety of crimes, the great majority of convictions, over 80 percent, were for robbery. Some fairly spectacular robberies occurred. Three blacks from Cape Francis stole $500, and another three men stole $160 in paper currency and $160 worth of silver; Joseph Wyatt, a silversmith working with an accomplice, embezzled five hundred ounces of silver from the U.S. Mint.[54] Slightly more typical was the theft of watches and other small items of high value that could be pawned. However, in a great number of cases, the items taken indicate that a pressing need for clothing pushed people into crime. Oliver O'Hara, Joe Martin, and John Baston stole one pair of boots or shoes each. James Fisher, John Thomas, and Hugh McDowell each pilfered five or fewer pairs of stockings. John McNeil, who could not work during his confinement because of a lump on the right shoulder, shoplifted a coat. Esther Green, John Williams, and Thomas Divine each took one piece of cloth. Others apparently needed food. Richard Butler absconded with a salmon, and Joseph, a black man, snatched two loaves of sugar. William Beemery(?) purloined two shillings and sixpence worth of mutton. James Barry tried to meet both his food and his clothing needs at one time when he filched two baskets of poultry and some clothing.[55]

However examined, the detailed records from the mayor's court confirm that Philadelphians convicted of criminal acts were likely to be poor. This was not, of course, a new phenomenon produced by the Revolution. What was new was the effort in the years 1786–90 to understand why such poor people became criminals.

The Philadelphians who denounced the wheelbarrow law and maintained that crime sprang from the worst evils associated with idle, vicious poverty had to be pleased with the revisions of the penal code enacted in the spring of 1790. The legislature, conceding that the practice of having criminals work in the streets had proven a debacle, said that convicts would now labor only in houses of correction. The legislature also expressed its hope that "the addition of unremitted solitude to laborious employment . . . will contribute as much to reform as to deter" crime. To insure that all prisoners did labor, the law required that they work eight hours a day from November to January and ten hours a day from February to October, Sundays excepted.

[53] . . . For an example that shows the same pattern, see p. xx above.

[54] . . . On the individual crimes see PCA, Sentence Docket, 2 Dec. 1794–February 1804, pp. 3, 14 (hereinafter PCA, Sentence Docket); and PCA, Philadelphia County Inspectors of the Jail and Penitentiary House Prisoners for Trial Docket, 1798–1802, p. 40 (hereinafter PCA, Trial Docket, 1798–1802).

[55] PCA, Philadelphia County Inspectors of the Jail and Penitentiary House Prisoners for Trial Docket, 1790–97, pp. 21, 258, 260, 276, 285, 315, 349, 392, 430; PCA, Trial Docket, 1798–1802, pp. 5, 38, 66, 103, 269; PCA, Sentence Docket, p. 100.

This new penal code repealed the 1786 law and thus eliminated the possibility of an early release for those who worked hard and behaved well. The 1790 code did, however, offer a new incentive to criminals willing to labor with diligence "as an evidence of reformation." If the labor of the convict, after the costs of maintenance and work materials were subtracted, produced a surplus, the convict received one half of that sum. This law also gave special attention to segregating prisoners in the Philadelphia jail. Cells, six by eight feet square and nine feet high, were to be built in the yard and separated from the common yard by walls high enough to prevent all external communication. These cells would house "the more hardened and attrocious offenders." This action reaffirmed the legislators' efforts to reclaim persons who still had "remaining seeds of virtue and goodness."

The Philadelphians who had since 1785 vigorously railed against the increase of vagabonds and social disorder in the streets could also applaud this new act because it gave the legal officers of Philadelphia strong powers to keep undesirables from infesting the streets. Henceforth, any vagrant or idle and disorderly person, once convicted, faced a jail sentence at hard labor of up to thirty days. The city had gained the power to sweep the vulgar riffraff off the streets.[56]

Five years later, the legislature voiced approval of this major change in the penal code by saying that the act, as slightly modified, had evidently diminished the number of crimes and been highly beneficial in reforming offenders. Philadelphians agreed.[57] But despite such applause, residents of the city in the 1790s remained deeply concerned about the evils of vice and social disorder; some believed that governmental action, even with the new penal code, did not effectively suppress these evils. Correspondingly, a new social institution—the citizen association that aimed to attack and control vice, social disorder, and crime—came into being.[58] The Association in Southwark for Suppressing Vice and Immorality, the first such Philadelphia agency, apparently began functioning in 1790. It sought to close gaming houses and every other house "of bad character." The *Federal Gazette* praised this effort and called for more such groups to protect the rising generation and to save it from "destruction." The paper also suggested that such organizations could work to educate youths "in habits of virtue and industry."[59]

Concern for the morality of the youth of the city played a vital role in the creation of the second association to combat vice. In 1791 three of the city's newspapers printed and reprinted articles denouncing the "brigades" of "low idle boys" who roamed the streets looking for mischief to do.[60] The antisocial actions of youths reached such heights that in

[56] *Penn. Statutes*, 12: 511–28 passim.

[57] Ibid., 15: 355–57; see also pp. 174–81.

[58] Other major cities had had such organizations before the Revolution. See Bridenbaugh, *Cities in Revolt*, pp. 124, 319.

[59] 16 Nov. 1790; "To the orderly," *Aurora*, 24 Aug. 1795, implies that the 1790 association no longer existed.

[60] *Penn. Gaz.*, 10 Sept. 1791.

June 1795, Matthew Clarkson, the mayor of Philadelphia, published an essay calling for *"the better government of youth."* Citing the "disorderly practices of ungoverned boys" in the streets, the mayor claimed that "our youth are becoming generally corrupt." He urged all parents to govern carefully the activities and moral training of their children on the grounds that the worst and most daring crimes could usually be traced to youthful mischiefs. Although Clarkson spoke of the corruption of youth in general, he emphasized the "present . . . loud and general complaints of the insubordination of apprentice youth, as well as servants of other descriptions."[61] The special attention Clarkson gave children from the lower strata of Philadelphia society is revealing; it suggests that he may well have believed that the children of the poor were the ones most likely to engage in youthful mischiefs leading to adult crime.[62]

Mayor Clarkson's presentation struck a responsive chord among residents of Southwark, who held that "virtue and good government are the ornament and stability of Society, while vice and disorder procure its misery and destruction." Believing this and spurred by Clarkson's address, the group formed the "Association of the district of Southwark, for the suppression of vice and immorality" in August of 1795. Their goal, broadly stated, was to aid the civil officers in bringing disorderly persons to punishment and to halt the spread of immoral and vicious practices. The haunts of drunkenness and debauchery, violence in the streets, and Sabbath lawbreaking would all come under their watchful eye. Association members indicated whom they believed most likely to need regulation and assistance by pledging that the group would "endeavor to afford advice to the stranger and distressed, to procure employment for the destitute and to join in the establishment of free schools for the children of the poor, for apprentices and orphans in which they may be taught to read and become acquainted with the principles of morality."[63]

Possibly following the lead of the Southwark association, citizens in Philadelphia in late 1797 or early 1798 established their own Society for the Suppression of Vice and Immorality. But, at least in the view of William Cobbett, the ultraconservative newspaper owner, the problems of stopping social disorder seemed overwhelming. While wishing the society well, he feared that the successful suppression of vice and immorality was impossible "where the abominable vices of *whoring, drunkenness, swindling, fraud,* and *daring impiety* abound to the extent they do in this city."[64]

Records do not reveal how effective the associations were. But it is essential to note that they began functioning in the 1790s in response to a perceived increase in immorality, especially immorality among the poor.

---

61 *An Address to the citizens of Philadelphia, respecting the better government of youth* (Philadelphia, 1795), passim; see also "Philadelphus," *Penn. Eve. Her.,* 10 Aug. 1785.

62 Cf. pp. 155–57 above.

63 "To the orderly," *Aurora,* 24 Aug. 1795.

64 HSP, petitions "To the Senate and House . . ." dated at Philadelphia in December 1798, filed under Y12 7324 f 24; *Porcupine's Gaz.,* 16 Jan. 1798.

As we shall see, their work was augmented by that of private poor relief groups, which often made moral reform of the poor an integral part of their activities. But all such efforts together were not, at times, strident enough for some citizens, whose anger over vice and immorality led to extralegal actions. In early August of 1800, a quarrel occurred between two men who had met in the China Factory, a house of ill fame in Southwark. As a result of the fight, one of the combatants died. According to the *Daily Advertiser*, a group assembled on the night of August 12 and proceeded to demolish houses of prostitution in Southwark. The work reportedly went on, without interruption, until the fourteenth. The results: "Scarce any thing but the chimnies of six houses, are now left standing." The police made "but few and feeble (if any) efforts" to stop this "Riot." The *Advertiser* added that such efforts would have been useless and voiced tacit approval of the "tumult and destruction," saying that the buildings in question had long been "the subject of regret by all well-disposed Citizens of Southwark." Clearly, "the eagerness with which this opportunity was seized for their destruction, is sufficient proof of the detestation in which their infamous occupants was [*sic*] held by the public."[65] This "riot" was apparently an atypical event for Philadelphia, but it illustrates a basic point: in the postwar years, Philadelphians became increasingly disturbed by the supposed vice and immorality that seemed to abound, especially among the poor. And Philadelphians worked as never before to find ways to attack vice and immorality.

A comparison of prewar with postwar Philadelphia suggests that the American Revolution produced significant changes in how social disorder, crime, and punishment were perceived and acted upon. Of course, some things did not change. It appears that, throughout the period 1760–1800, the convicted criminals of Philadelphia were likely to be poor. And while the gross abuses of trading justices that occurred from 1785 to 1789 were halted, throughout the period 1760–1800 the poor apparently found it more difficult than did the affluent to utilize fully and benefit from the legal system. Still, the changes that did occur were quite impressive. In the prewar years, one could be imprisoned for very small debts. Even if found innocent of criminal charges, the poor might land in jail because they lacked the money to pay court costs or jail fees, and persons imprisoned for debt were, nonetheless, required to pay for their food, clothing, and fuel. Spurred by the call of the Constitution of 1776, by persons espousing Enlightenment ideals of prison reform, and by a fear of idleness, the state government had by 1800 instituted major changes: (1) food and other necessities were provided for imprisoned debtors; (2) persons acquitted of criminal charges no longer faced imprisonment because they could not pay court costs; (3) the number of people confined for small debts declined significantly. Imprisonment for debt still existed in the Philadelphia of 1800, but the changes just outlined marked a major reform effort.

Reform ideals, as well as a growing concern for controlling crime, were also instrumental in helping to produce the dramatic postwar altera-

[65] *Am. Daily Adv.*, 23 Aug. 1800.

tion of the criminal code. By the dawn of the nineteenth century, only murder in the first degree carried a death penality; for all other crimes, corporal punishment had been outlawed. Thus, the prewar efforts to prevent crime by fear of death and other corporal punishment gave way to an emphasis upon rehabilitation of criminals, which utilized (1) the attempt to reform criminals by confining them at hard labor and (2) physical separation of criminals into different classes to protect young offenders from older, hardened criminal types. All of these changes illustrate that the American Revolution helped produce transformations in the area of criminal justice that affected the poor.

Although the directives of the Constitution of 1776 were instrumental in bringing about alterations in imprisonment for debt and in the criminal code, it must be noted that the major reforms just outlined occurred in the period 1785–1800. Why was so little done from 1776 to 1785? Why was so much done from 1785 to 1800? One plausible explanation is that, during the war years, the pressing need of winning independence deflected people and government from undertaking the reforms they wished to pursue. There is merit in this argument. But it is only part of the answer. The mid-1780s were, as we have and shall see again, important because they marked a new awareness by Philadelphians of the poor and more especially of the seeming danger the poor posed for society. It was in the period 1785 and following that Philadelphians began to distinguish more precisely between the "industrious" and the "idle" poor. It was in this period that Philadelphians put greater emphasis on the fact that "idle" poverty constituted "vicious" and "vulgar" poverty. It was in 1785 that Philadelphians began to analyze the nature of social disorder and crime to a far greater extent than before, coming to the conclusion that the poor often caused social disorder and were likely, because of supposed moral weakness, to engage in crime. The fear of and anxiety about such social disorder and crime led to a social innovation. By the 1790s, groups of citizens became convinced that the efforts of governmental agencies could not stop what was perceived as the rise in vice, immorality, and crime, and they responded by creating private associations to suppress these evils.

Thus, the increasing effort to transform the city's system of criminal justice stemmed from more than the philosophical desire for reform usually associated with the Enlightenment ideals flourishing in revolutionary America; it was rooted as well in an increasing fear of the potential for vice and criminality among the poor. Philadelphians evidenced a marked concern for training or forcing the poor in general to conform to the ideals of industrious poverty only when it appeared that the poor as a group posed an imminent danger to the peace, order, and stability of society. The general perception that special exertions were required to control the poor did not reach major proportions until the 1780s. But the city officials charged with administering public assistance to the city's needy faced what they believed was a crisis as early as the 1760s. Their efforts to resolve this crisis produced major changes even before the Revolution and fomented a long bitter debate over the proper goals for the city's public poor relief system.

Pentecost in Rochester

PAUL E. JOHNSON

When historians discuss the religious history of the American colonies and new nation, they tend to stress two related elements: Puritan-
ism and the Great Awakening of the mid-eighteenth century. Puritans
and their successors who led the Awakening left voluminous written
records of themselves, which tend to overshadow accounts of the
influence of various other religious movements in our culture. In
addition, historians often mention in passing the development of
theories and practical methods for working out a separation of
church and state, a unique phenomenon in Western civilization. In
this connection, Roger Williams' halting efforts at establishing religious
tolerance in Rhode Island colony and the intellectual rigors of the
Deists among the Founding Fathers are prominent.

By 1800, however, the Puritan tradition began to give way as
New England Congregationalism went through the throes of the
Unitarian schism, and Calvinist theology was fast being replaced by
the more humane doctrines of Arminianism, seen primarily in the
work of the Methodists. It now seems clear that the most critical
period of American religious development and the one which has had
the most lasting impact on the lives of religious Americans was the
period known as the Second Great Awakening.

The best-known aspect of this movement is that connected with
religious camp meetings on the southern and western frontier, beginning at the turn of the nineteenth century. It seems that the old-
world churches had brought to the new world certain traditions that
turned out to be inappropriate in the rapidly spreading new nation.
The tradition of high culture, with an emphasis on education and
public decorum, found a narrow foothold on the eastern seaboard,
but then it languished there. As settlers moved to the interior, high
culture did not follow. In the pioneer's lonely and risky life, tradition
was not as important as sociability and eternal security. The camp
meetings provided the former, and Arminian theology, with its stress
on the availability of salvation to all, served the latter needs.

153

The older churches of the eastern seaboard were unable to cope with the revival phenomenon and left this task, for the most part, to the newly developing evangelical denominations, particularly the Methodists and the Baptist churches. Both of these groups encouraged the growth of new congregations on the southern and western frontiers through such devices as the acceptance of an uneducated clergy, a measure opposed by the older churches. The Methodists also made wide use of the circuit rider—a clergyman, usually untrained but God-called, who would travel from one backwoods settlement to another preaching and ministering to the religious needs of the frontier people. Even though both Baptist and Methodist denominations went through traumatic divisions over the slavery issue, they became the largest Protestant denominations in the United States by mid-nineteenth century and have remained the largest up to the present.

The Second Great Awakening in the South had a northern counterpart. Without the peculiarly denominational character of the southern revivals, those in the North were equally enthusiastic. In the early nineteenth century, Western New York State was so swept by religious revivals of all sorts that it came to be called the "burned-over" district. In a brilliant study of religious revival in Rochester, New York, Paul E. Johnson, of Yale University, seeks to explain the impact of evangelist Charles Finney's preaching in that city. In doing a detailed analysis of the social changes taking place in Rochester, Johnson is able to show that the breakup of the traditional household was a major factor in preparing the middle-class population for religious revival. In the selection from his book reprinted below, the author notes that many of those converted during the period were men who were losing their roles as patriarchal leaders of households and society and were seeking, through the medium of religion, to reorder their world in such a way that the social order they favored would prevail. They hoped, through religious sanctions, to restore "the natural relations between beings," thereby maintaining sobriety and eliminating sin from the Christian society.

Charles Grandison Finney came to Rochester in September 1830. For six
months he preached in Presbyterian churches nearly every night and three
times on Sunday, and his audience included members of every sect. During the day he prayed with individuals and led an almost continuous series
of prayer meetings. Soon there were simultaneous meetings in churches
and homes throughout the village. Pious women went door-to-door praying for troubled souls. The high school stopped classes and prayed. Business closed their doors early and prayed with their families. "You could
not go upon the streets," recalled one convert, "and hear any conversation, except upon religion."[1] By early spring the churches faced the world
with a militance and unity that had been unthinkable only months before, and with a boundless and urgent sense of their ability to change society. In the words of its closest student, ". . . no more impressive revival has occurred in American history."[2]

NEW MEASURES

First, a word on the evangelical plan of salvation. Man is innately evil
and can overcome his corrupt nature only through faith in Christ the redeemer—that much is common to Christianity in all forms. Institutional
and theological differences among Christians trace ultimately to varying
means of attaining that faith. The Reformation abolished sacred beings,
places, and institutions that had eased the path between the natural and
supernatural worlds. Without ritual, without priest-magicians, without
divine immanence in an institutional church, Protestants face God across
infinite lonely space. They bridge that space through prayer—through
the state of absolute selflessness and submission known generally as transcendence. The experience of transcending oneself and this world through
prayer is for Protestants direct experience of the Holy Ghost, and it con-
stitutes assurance of salvation, sanctification, and new life.

Prayer, then, is the one means by which a Protestant establishes his
relation with God and his assurances that he is one of God's people. Prayer
is a personal relationship between God and man, and the decision whether
that relationship is established belongs to God. No Protestants dispute
that. But they have argued endlessly on man's ability to influence the decision. The evangelical position was phrased (and it was understood by
its detractors) as an increase in human ability so great that prayer and in-

[1] Robert L. Stanton to Charles Finney, January 12, 1872, Finney Papers.
[2] [Whitney R.] Cross, [*The*] *Burned-Over District:* [*A Social and Intellectual History of Enthusiastic Religion in Western New York, 1800–1850* (Ithaca, N.Y.,
1950)], 155. The most complete narrative of the Rochester revival is in Robert S.
Fletcher, *A History of Oberlin College from Its Founding through the Civil War*
(Oberlin, 1943), 1:17–24.

dividual salvation were ultimately voluntary. Hurried notes to Charles Finney's Rochester sermons insisted: "It should in all cases be required now to repent, now to give themselves up to God, now to say and feel Lord here I am take me, it's all I can do. And when the sinner can do that . . . his conversion is attained."[3] "The truth," he explained, "is employed to influence men, prayer to move God . . . I do not mean that God's mind is changed by prayer . . . But prayer produces such a change *in us* as renders it consistent for him to do otherwise."[4] To hyper-Calvinists who protested that this filled helpless man with false confidence, Finney shouted, "What is that but telling them to hold on to their rebellion against God? . . . as though God was to blame for not converting them."[5] The only thing preventing individual conversion was the individual himself.

This reevaluation of human ability caught the evangelicals in a dilemma. But it was a dilemma they had already solved in practice. Finney and his friends insisted that God granted new life in answer to faithful prayer. But the ability to pray with faith was itself experimental proof of conversion. By definition, the unregenerate could not pray. For Finney there was a clear and obvious way out, a way that he and Rochester Protestants witnessed hundreds of times during the revival winter: "Nothing is more calculated to beget a spirit of prayer, than to unite in social prayer with one who has the spirit himself."[6] That simple mechanism is at the heart of evangelical Protestantism.

Conversion had always ended in prayer and humiliation before God. But ministers had explained the terms of salvation and left terrified sinners

---

[3] Bradford King Diary, November 11, 1830 (notes to a Finney sermon).

[4] Charles G. Finney, *Lectures on Revivals of Religion*, ed. William G. McLoughlin (Cambridge 1960), 52.

[5] Bradford King Diary, November 9, 1830. Finney's published sermons and his *Lectures on Revivals* were attempts to justify his methods and their theological implications to academic seminarians. The plan of salvation as it was understood in the churches was often confused, but tended in the same direction as Finney's more academic formulations. In 1825 the founding congregation at Brick Presbyterian Church in Rochester affirmed their faith that "the only reason why men do not embrace the Gospel is a voluntary opposition to God and holiness. And that the nature of this opposition is such, that none will believe in Christ, but as faith is wrought in their hearts by the influence of the Holy Ghost." This was pure Finney, but they went on to affirm "that God did from Eternity choose some of our sinful race to everlasting life, through sanctification of the spirit unto obedience and belief of the truth, so that repentence, faith and obedience are not the cause but the effect of election." In the summer following the Finney revival, the trustees threw out these articles and wrote new ones. While reaffirming a strong belief in original sin, they stated that "we believe God, in infinite goodness, has provided a savior for lost man, who is Jesus Christ and that in consequence of his atonement, righteousness, and intercession, all who will repent of their sins and believe in him, will be saved from hell, and received to eternal glory," then reminded themselves that "none can believe until they are renewed by the Holy Ghost." (Brick Church Session Minutes, December 1825 and June 1831.)

[6] Finney, *Lectures on Revivals*, 125.

to wrestle with it alone. Prayer was transacted in private between a man and his God, and most middle-class Protestants were uncomfortable with public displays of humiliation. As late as 1829, Rochester Presbyterians had scandalized the village when they began to kneel rather than stand at prayer.[7] More than their theological implications, Finney's revival techniques aroused controversy because they transformed conversion from a private to a public and intensely social event. The door-to-door canvass, the intensification of family devotions, prayer meetings that lasted till dawn, the open humiliation of sinners on the anxious bench: all of these transformed prayer and conversion from private communion into spectacular public events.

What gave these events their peculiar force was the immediatist corollary to voluntary conversion. The Reverend Whitehouse of St. Luke's Church (yes, the Episcopalians too) explained it in quiet terms:

> Appeals are addressed to the heart and the appeals are in reference to the present time. And each time the unconverted sinner leaves the house of God without having closed with the terms of the Gospel he rejects the offer of mercy. Had some future time been specified as that in which we were to make a decision we might listen time after time to the invitations and reject them. But it is expressly said today and now is the accepted time.[8]

Initially, these pressures fell on the already converted. It was the prayers of Christians that led others to Christ, and it was their failure to pray that sent untold millions into hell. Lay evangelicals seldom explained the terms of salvation in the language of a Reverend Whitehouse—or even of a Charles Finney. But with the fate of their children and neighbors at stake, they carried their awful responsibility to the point of emotional terrorism. Finney tells the story of a woman who prayed while her son-in-law attended an anxious meeting. He came home converted, and she thanked God and fell dead on the spot.[9] Everard Peck reported the death of his wife to an unregenerate father-in-law, and told the old man that his dead daughter's last wish was to see him converted.[10] "We are either marching towards heaven or towards hell," wrote one convert to his sister. "How is it with you?"[11]

The new measures brought sinners into intense and public contact with praying Christians. Conversion hinged not on private prayer, arbitrary grace, or intellectual choice, but on purposive encounters between people. The secret of the Rochester revival and of the attendant transformation of society lay ultimately in the strategy of those encounters.

[7] *Observer*, January 8, 1830.

[8] Diary of Nathaniel Thrift Rochester, September 4, 1836 (notes to a sermon), University of Rochester. This lecture was delivered during the revival of 1836, but Whitehouse had been minister to St. Luke's Church since 1829.

[9] Finney, *Lectures on Revivals*, 68.

[10] Everard Peck to Samuel Porter, January 1, 1831, Porter Papers.

[11] Ferdinand D. W. Ward to Henrietta Ward, May 21, 1831, Freeman Clarke Papers, University of Rochester.

While Finney led morning prayer meetings, pious women visited families. Reputedly they went door-to-door. But the visits were far from random. Visitors paid special attention to the homes of sinners who had Christian wives, and they arrived in the morning hours when husbands were at work. Finney himself found time to pray with Melania Smith, wife of a young physician. The doctor was anxious for his soul, but sickness in the village kept him busy and he was both unable to pray and unwilling to try. But his wife prayed and tormented him constantly, reminding him of "the woe which is denounced against the families which call not on the Name of the Lord."[12] Soon his pride broke and he joined her as a member of Brick Presbyterian Church. Finney's wife, Lydia, made a bolder intrusion into the home of James Buchan, a merchant-tailor and a Roman Catholic whose wife, Caroline, was a Presbyterian. Buchan, with what must have been enormous self-restraint, apologized for having been out of the house, thanked Finney for the tract, and invited him and his wife to tea.[13] (It is not known whether Finney accepted the invitation, but this was one bit of family meddling which may have back-fired. In 1833 Caroline Buchan withdrew from the Presbyterian Church and converted to Catholicism.) In hundreds of cases the strategy of family visits worked. As the first converts fell, the *Observer* announced with satisfaction that the largest group among them was "young heads of families."[14]

Revival enthusiasm began with the rededication of church members and spread to the people closest to them. Inevitably, much of it flowed through family channels. Finney claimed Samuel D. Porter, for instance, as a personal conquest. But clearly he had help. Porter was an infidel, but his sister in Connecticut and his brother-in-law Everard Peck were committed evangelicals. Porter came under a barrage of family exhortation, and in January Peck wrote home that "Samuel is indulging a trembling hope . . ." He remained the object of family prayer for eight more months before hope turned into assurance. Then he joined his sister and brother-in-law in praying for the soul of their freethinking father.[15] The realtor Bradford King left another record of evangelism within and between related households. After weeks of social prayer and private agony, he awoke and heard himself singing, "*I am going to the Kingdom will you come along with me?*" He testified at meeting the next day, but did not gain assurance until he returned home and for the first time prayed with his family. He rose and "decided that as for me & my house we would serve the Lord." Immediately King turned newfound powers on his brother's house in nearby Bloomfield. After two months of visiting and prayer he announced, "We had a little pentecost at brothers . . . all

---

[12] Melania Smith to Charles Finney, January 10, 1831, Finney Papers.

[13] James Buchan to Charles Finney, November 16, 1830, Finney Papers. For further comments on the strategy of family visits, see Cross, *Burned-Over District*, 176.

[14] *Observer*, November 12, 1830.

[15] Jane Porter to Samuel D. Porter, December 17, 1830; Everard Peck to Samuel Porter, January 11, 1831; S. D. Porter to Samuel Porter, January 31, 1832, Porter Papers.

were praising and glorifying God in one United Voice."[16] The revival made an evangelist of every convert, and most turned their power on family members.

Charles Finney's revival was based on group prayer. It was a simple, urgent activity that created new hearts in hundreds of men and women, and it generated—indeed it relied upon—a sense of absolute trust and common purpose among participants. The strengthening of family ties that attended the revival cannot be overestimated. But it was in prayer meetings and evening services that evangelism spilled outside old social channels, laying the basis for a transformed and united Protestant community.

Bradford King had no patience for "Old Church Hipocrites who think more of their particular denomination than Christ Church,"[17] and his sentiments were rooted in an astonishing resolution of old difficulties. Presbyterians stopped fighting during the first few days, and peace soon extended to the other denominations. Before the first month was out, Finney marveled that "Christians of every denomination generally seemed to make common cause, and went to work with a will, to pull sinners out of the fire."[18] The most unexpected portent came in October, when the weight of a crowded gallery spread the walls and damaged the building at First Church. Vestrymen at St. Paul's—most of them former Masons and bitter enemies of the Presbyterians—let that homeless congregation into their church.[19] But it was in prayer meetings and formal services that the collective regeneration of a fragmented churchgoing community took place, for it was there that "Christians of different denominations are seen mingled together in the sanctuary on the Sabbath, and bowing at the same altar in the social prayer meeting."[20]

---

[16] Bradford King Diary, undated account of conversion in October 1830, and entries for December 9, 1830, January 22, 1831, and February 1, 1831. Emphasis in original.

[17] Bradford King Diary, December 18, 1830.

[18] [Charles G.] Finney, *Autobiography* [*of Charles G. Finney* (New York, 1876)], 291–92.

[19] H. Pomeroy Brewster, "The Magic of a Voice: Rochester Revivals of Rev. Charles G. Finney," RHS *Publications* 4 (1925), 281; [Charles M.] Robinson, *First Church Chronicles* [*1815–1915* (Rochester, N.Y., 1915)], 78.

[20] *Observer*, October 15, 1830. Every congregation took in large numbers of new members while Finney was in Rochester. It started among Finney's own Presbyterians, but their gains were matched in every church but the Methodist. Initially, Finney came to Rochester at the invitation of Third Presbyterian Church. That congregation added 159 new members between December and March, roughly doubling in size. Baptists, who shared the Presbyterians' New England Calvinist inheritance, also doubled their numbers. But Finney's message transcended cultural and theological traditions. At the end of 1831, vestrymen at St. Luke's counted their total communicants. A full 49.4 percent were new within the preceding year. At First Baptist the comparable figure was a near-identical 50.2 percent. See St. Luke's Church, Parish Register (a year-by-year tabulation of the membership in the 1830s is included at the end of the volume); *Minutes of the Anniversary of the Monroe Baptist Association* (Rochester, annually after 1828); and Rev. Andrew Gillies to Orlo J. Price, October 4, 1932, Local History Division, Rochester Public Library. Similar figures for other

Crowded prayer meetings were held almost every night from September until early March, and each of them was managed carefully. When everyone was seated the leader read a short verse dealing with the object of prayer. Satisfied that everyone understood and could participate, he called on those closest to the spirit. These prayed aloud, and within minutes all worldly thoughts were chased from the room. (Finney knew that the chemistry of prayer worked only when everyone shared in it, and he discouraged attendance by scoffers, cranks, and the merely curious.) Soon sinners grew anxious; some of them broke into tears, and Christians came close to pray with them. Then followed the emotional displays that timid ministers had feared, but which they accepted without a whimper during the revival winter. In October Artemissia Perkins prayed with her fiancé in Brick Church. Suddenly her voice rose above the others, and over and over she prayed, "Blessed be the Name of Jesus," while her future husband, her neighbors, and people who never again could be strangers watched and participated in the awesome work.[21] It was in hundreds of encounters such as this that the revival shattered old divisions and laid the foundation for moral community among persons who had been strangers or enemies. "I know this is all algebra to those who have never felt it," Finney explained. "But to those who have experienced the agony of wrestling, prevailing prayer, for the conversion of a soul, you may depend on it, that soul . . . appears as dear as a child is to the mother who brought it forth with pain."[22]

At formal services this mechanism took on massive proportions.[23] During services Christians gathered in other churches and nearby homes to pray for the evangelist's success. Sometimes crowds of people who could not find seats in the house prayed outside in the snow. Downstairs the session room was packed, and every break in the lecture was punctuated by the rise and fall of prayer.

Inside, every seat was filled. People knelt in the aisles and doorways. Finney reserved seats near the pulpit for anxious sinners—not random volunteers, but prominent citizens who had spoken with him privately. None sat on the anxious bench who was not almost certain to fall. Separated from the regenerate and from hardened sinners, their conversions became grand public spectacles. In the pulpit, Finney preached with enormous power, but with none of the excesses some people expected. He had dropped a promising legal career to enter the ministry, and his preaching demonstrated formidable courtroom skills, not cheap theatrics. True, he took examples from everyday experience and spoke in folksy, colloquial

---

churches are unavailable. Their records list incoming members, but fail to name people who either died or left the church. Thus there is no means of determining the year-by-year size of most congregations. . . .

[21] Bradford King Diary, October 1830.

[22] Finney, *Lectures on Revivals*, 69. Cf. 124–39.

[23] The following two paragraphs are pieced together from Finney, *Autobiography*, 288–89; *Observer*, February 17, 1831, and March 3, 1831; Bradford King Diary, December 28, 1830; [Henry B.] Stanton, *Random Recollections* [(New York, 1887)], 41–42. On all the new measures, see Cross, *Burned-Over District*, 173–84.

terms. (With what may have been characteristic modesty, he reminded his listeners that Jesus had done the same.) Most of his lectures lasted an hour, but it was not uncommon for a packed church to listen twice that long "without the movement of a foot." When he gestured at the room, people ducked as if he were throwing things. In describing the fall of sinners he pointed to the ceiling, and as he let his finger drop people in the rear seats stood to watch the final entry into hell. Finney spoke directly to the anxious bench in front of him, and at the close of the lecture he demanded immediate repentance and prayer. Some of Rochester's first citizens humbled themselves on the anxious bench, sweating their way into heaven surrounded by praying neighbors. It was the most spectacular of the evangelist's techniques, and the most unabashedly communal.

NEW CHRISTIANS

Charles Finney's revival created a community of militant evangelicals that would remake society and politics in Rochester. The work of that community will fill the remainder of this book. But now it is time to keep promises made in the Introduction, to attempt a systematic explanation of Finney's triumph at Rochester. The pages that follow isolate the individuals who joined churches while Finney was in town, then locate experiences that they shared and that explain why they and not others were ripe for conversion in 1830–31. Insofar as the revival can be traced to its social origins, I shall consider it traceable to those experiences.

Finney claimed to have converted "the great mass of the most influential people" in Rochester.[24] The *Observer* agreed that new church members included most of the town's "men of wealth, talents, and influence —those who move in the highest circles of society,"[25] and church records reinforce those claims. Table 1 compares the occupational status of Finney's male converts with that of men who joined churches in the years 1825–29. (Pre-revival figures are limited to the four years surrounding the tax list of 1827. Occupations of Finney converts are derived from the 1830 assessment rolls. Thus each occupation in the table is measured within two years of the time of conversion.)

Both in the 1820s and in the revival of 1830–31, new church members came disproportionately from among businessmen, professionals, and master workmen. During the Finney revival conversions multiplied dramatically within every group. But the center of enthusiasm shifted from the stores and offices to the workshops. Indeed it is the sharp increase in conversions among master craftsmen that accounts for slight declines in every other group. Whatever the problems that prepared the ground for Finney's triumph, they were experienced most strongly by master workmen.

Table 2 begins the attempt to infer just what those problems were. The table isolates specific occupations within the business community and

[24] Finney, *Autobiography*, 298.
[25] *Observer*, November 12, 1830.

TABLE 1.

Occupations of the new male admittants to
Rochester Protestant churches in the late 1820s, and in the
revival of 1830–31 (percentages)

	YEAR OF ADMISSION	
	1825–29 (N = 85)	1830–31 (N = 170)
businessman-professional	22	19
shopkeeper-petty proprietor	14	11
master craftsman	16	26
clerical employee	12	10
journeyman craftsman	24	22
laborer-semiskilled	13	12

NOTE: The 1825–29 figures are derived from the tax list and directory of 1827. Figures for the years 1830–31 are derived from the 1830 tax list and the directories of 1827 and/or 1834. To ensure that these men were in Rochester when the tax list was compiled, inclusion is limited to those who appear in the 1827 directory or the 1830 census.

calculates the percentage of church members within them in 1827 and again in 1834. Increases were most spectacular among master craftsmen and manufacturers, but there were significant variations within that group. Master builders and shoemakers had made dramatic breaks with the traditional organization of work, and with customary relations between masters and journeymen. The proportions of church members among them increased 70 percent and 73 percent, respectively. Proprietors of the small indoor workshops participated in the revival, but their increase was a less

TABLE 2.

Percent Protestant church members among selected
proprietors, 1827–34

	1827	1834	PERCENT CHANGE
merchant (N = 73, 63)	23	33	+30
hotelkeeper (N = 14, 30)*	21	13	−38
doctor (N = 21, 28)	29	54	+46
lawyer (N = 23, 31)	22	58	+62
grocer (N = 80, 59)	9	31	+71
forwarding merchant (N = 7, 18)	14	50	+72
master builder (N = 14, 13)†	21	69	+70
master shoemaker (N = 15, 15)†	20	73	+73
small-shop proprietor (N = 20, 37)†	30	62	+52

* Includes tavernkeepers and innkeepers.
† Includes only those identified as masters through newspaper advertisements and antiquarian sources.

impressive 51 percent. Change in the operations they controlled came more slowly. They hired relatively few journeymen, and they continued into the 1830s to incorporate many of those men into their homes.

Among white-collar proprietors, lawyers, forwarding merchants, and grocers made the greatest gains: 62 percent, 72 percent, and 71 percent, respectively. Rochester was the principal shipping point on the Erie Canal, and most boats operating on the canal belonged to Rochester forwarders. It was their boat crews who were reputedly the rowdiest men in an unruly society, and it was the forwarders who had been the chief target of the Sabbatarian crusade. Grocers were another white-collar group with peculiarly close ties to the working class. The principal retailers of liquor, they were closely regulated by the village trustees. In 1832 the trustees not only doubled the price of grocery licenses but began looking into the moral qualifications of applicants.[26] The increased religiosity among grocers (as well as the decline in the total number of men in that occupation) reflects that fact. Reformers had branded forwarders and grocers the supporters both of the most dangerous men in society and of their most dangerous habits. While they had resisted attacks on their livelihood, grocers and boat owners could not but agree to their complicity in the collapse of old social forms. Most of them remained outside the churches. But a startlingly increased minority joined with master workmen and cast their lots with Jesus.

With these occupations removed, the revival among white-collar proprietors was weak. Doctors and merchants had only tenuous links with the new working class, and little personal responsibility for the collapse of the late 1820s. Increases among them were 46 percent and 30 percent, respectively. Hotelkeepers in particular were divorced from contact with workingmen, for they were dependent for their livelihoods on the more well-to-do canal travelers. Church membership among hotelkeepers actually declined 38 percent during the revival years. (The one remaining occupation—the law—was a special case: the increase was 62 percent. No doubt part of the explanation lies in Finney himself, who was a former attorney and took special pride in the conversion of lawyers. But perhaps more important is the fact that many lawyers were politicians, and in the 1830s resistance to the churches was political suicide.)

With few exceptions, then, Charles Finney's revival was strongest among entrepreneurs who bore direct responsibility for disordered relations between classes. And they were indeed responsible. The problem of social class arose in towns and cities all over the northern United States after 1820. It would be easy to dismiss it as a stage of urban-industrial growth, a product of forces that were impersonal and inevitable. In some ways it was. But at the beginning the new relationship between master and wage earner was created by masters who preferred money and privacy to the company of their workmen and the performance of old patriarchal duties. Available evidence suggests that it was precisely those masters who filled Finney's meetings.

[26] [Blake] McKelvey, [*Rochester: The Water-Power City, 1812–1854* (Cambridge, Mass., 1954)], p. 179.

TABLE 3.
Composition of households headed by proprietors in
1827, by religious status of householders

HOUSEHOLDER		PERCENT WHICH INCLUDED		
	N	KIN	BOARDERS	EMPLOYEES
church member in 1829	81	15	14	41
revival convert	89	8	7	33
non-church member	151	13	17	43

Perhaps more than any other act, the removal of workmen from the homes of employers created an autonomous working class. Table 3 compares households headed in 1827 by proprietors who joined churches during the revival with those headed by non-church members and by men who belonged to churches before the revival. Finney's converts kept fewer workmen in their families than did other proprietors, suggesting either that they had removed many of those men or that they had never allowed them into their homes. Table 4 traces households that included "extra" adult men in 1827 over the next three years. The table is compiled from the 1830 census. That document names heads of households and identifies others by age and sex. By counting males over the age of sixteen (the age at which men were included in the 1827 directory, and thus in Table 3), we may trace the broadest outlines of household change in the years immediately preceding the revival. Most proprietors thinned their families between 1827 and 1830. But while old church members and those who stayed outside the churches removed one in four adult men, converts cut their number by more than half.[27] Thus the analyses of occupations and of household structure point clearly to one conclusion: Finney's converts were entrepreneurs who had made more than their share of the choices that created a free-labor economy and a class-bounded society in Rochester.

The transformation began in the workshops, but it was not contained there. For in removing workmen the converts altered their own positions

---

[27] My interpretation of these figures may be questioned, for it is not possible to control them for the age of household heads. Of those whose birth dates are known, the median age of Finney's converts was thirty years. It is possible that their households included few employees only because they were beginning in business and did not as yet employ many men. Tax assessments and newspaper advertisements, however, suggest that they operated substantial businesses. More important are the figures in Table 4. If the relative absence of wage earners in convert-headed households was indeed due to the youth of household heads, then we would expect a relative increase in the number of men in their families as time went on. But they removed men from their homes faster than other (presumably older) entrepreneurs. While the youth of Finney's converts has doubtless distorted the figures in Table 3 (it helps to account for the relative absence of sons over the age of sixteen, for example), I think that the figures on co-residing employees reflect the business practices and social attitudes of Finney's converts, and not their ages.

TABLE 4.
Changes in the composition of households headed by
proprietors ,1827–30, by religious status of householders

	NUMBER OF MALES OVER 16 YEARS		
HOUSEHOLDER*	1827	1830	PERCENT CHANGE
church member in 1829	67	48	—24
revival convert	74	31	—58
non-church member	113	80	—29

* Includes only householders who appear in both the 1827 directory and the 1830 census.

within families. The relative absence of even boarders and distant kin in their homes suggests a concern with domestic privacy. And within those families housewives assumed new kinds of moral authority. The organization of prayer meetings, the pattern of family visits, and bits of evidence from church records suggests that hundreds of conversions culminated when husbands prayed with their wives. Women formed majorities of the membership of every church at every point in time. But in every church, men increased their proportion of the communicants during revivals, indicating that revivals were family experiences and that women were converting their men.[28] In 1830–31 fully 65 percent of male converts were related to prior members of their churches (computed from surnames within congregations). Traditionalists considered Finney's practice of having women and men pray together the most dangerous of the new measures, for it implied new kinds of equality between the sexes. Indeed some harried husbands recognized the revival as subversive of their authority over their wives. A man calling himself Anticlericus complained of Finney's visit to his home:

> He *stuffed* my wife with tracts, and alarmed her fears, and nothing short of meetings, night and day, could atone for the many fold sins my poor, simple spouse had committed, and at the same time, she made the miraculous discovery, that she had been "unevenly

[28] This statement is based on the percentages of women among the new communicants in four congregations in the pre- and post-revival years. These are the only four churches whose records both include women members and span the 1820s and 1830s. Figures for peak revival years are in italics.

	1815–29	1830–31	1832–38
First Presbyterian (N = 395, 214, 365)	69.9	58.9	69.0
Second Presbyterian (N = 150, 218, 619)	60.7	63.8	54.7
St. Luke's Episcopal (N = 158, 133, 276)	72.2	66.2	69.6
St. Paul's Episcopal (N = 6, 63, 138)	(50.0)	77.8	71.7

Graphs demonstrating the annual numbers of new members in these churches are presented in Johnson, "A Shopkeeper's Millennium," 196–201.

yoked." From this unhappy period, peace, quiet, and happiness have fled from my dwelling, never, I fear, to return.[29]

The evangelicals assigned crucial religious duties to wives and mothers. In performing those duties, women rose out of old subordinate roles and extended their moral authority within families. Finney's male converts were driven to religion because they had abdicated their roles as eighteenth-century heads of households. In the course of the revival, their wives helped to transform them into nineteenth-century husbands.[30]

Charles Finney's revival enlarged every Protestant church, broke down sectarian boundaries, and mobilized a religious community that had at its disposal enormous economic power. Motives which determined the use of that power derived from the revival, and they were frankly millenarian.

As Rochester Protestants looked beyond their community in 1831, they saw something awesome. For news of Finney's revival had helped touch off a wave of religious enthusiasm throughout much of the northern United States. The revival moved west into Ohio and Michigan, east into Utica, Albany, and the market towns of inland New England. Even Philadelphia and New York City felt its power.[31] Vermont's congregational churches grew by 29 percent in 1831. During the same twelve months the churches of Connecticut swelled by over a third.[32] After scanning reports from western New York, the Presbyterian General Assembly announced in wonder that "the work has been so general and thorough, that the whole customs of society have changed."[33] Never before had so many Americans experienced religion in so short a time. Lyman Beecher, who watched the excitement from Boston, declared that the revival of

---

[29] *Liberal Advocate*, September 29, 1832. For clerical worries about the role that Finney was assigning to women, see Charles C. Cole, Jr., "The New Lebanon Convention," *New York History* 31 (October 1950), 385–97; Cross, *Burned-Over District*, 177–78.

[30] On the creation of a distinct women's sphere among the middle class and the centrality of religion to that sphere, see [Nancy F.] Cott, *The Bonds of Womanhood: ["Woman's Sphere" in New England, 1780–1830* (New Haven, 1977)]; Mary P. Ryan, "A Woman's Awakening: Revivalistic Religion in Utica, New York, 1800–1835" (unpublished paper, 1976); Ann Douglas Wood, *The Feminization of American Culture* (New York, 1976); Barbara Welter, "The Feminization of American Religion, 1800–1860," in Mary Hartman and Lois W. Banner, eds., *Clio's Consciousness Raised: New Perspectives on the History of Women* (New York, 1974), 137–57; and Carroll Smith Rosenberg, *Religion and the Rise of the American City: The New York City Mission Movement, 1812–1870* (Ithaca, 1971), esp. 97–124.

[31] Plotted from the *Observer*, 1830–31.

[32] Samuel W. Dike, "A Study of New England Revivals," *American Journal of Sociology* 15 (November 1909), 375.

[33] Cited in James A. Hotchkin, *A History of the Purchase and Settlement of Western New York . . . and of the Presbyterian Church in that Section* (New York, 1848), 160.

1831 was the greatest revival of religion that the world had ever seen.[34]

Rochester Protestants saw conversions multiply and heard of powerful revivals throughout Yankee Christendom. They saw divisions among themselves melt away, and they began to sense that the pre-millennial unanimity was at hand—and that they and people like them were bringing it about. They had converted their families and neighbors through prayer. Through ceaseless effort they could use the same power to convert the world. It was Finney himself who told them that "if they were united all over the world the Millennium might be brought about in three months."[35] He did not mean that Christ was coming to Rochester. The immediate and gory millennium predicted in Revelation had no place in evangelical thinking. Utopia would be realized on earth, and it would be made by God with the active and united collaboration of His people. It was not the physical reign of Christ that Finney predicted but the reign of Christianity. The millennium would be accomplished when sober, godly men—men whose every step was guided by a living faith in Jesus—exercised power in this world. Clearly, the revival of 1831 was a turning point in the long struggle to establish that state of affairs. American Protestants knew that, and John Humphrey Noyes later recalled that "in 1831, the whole orthodox church was in a state of ebullition in regard to the Millennium."[36] Rochester evangelicals stood at the center of that excitement.

After 1831 the goal of revivals was the christianization of the world. With that at stake, membership in a Protestant church entailed new kinds of personal commitment. Newcomers to Brick Presbyterian Church in the 1820s had agreed to obey the laws of God and of the church, to treat fellow members as brothers, and "to live as an humble Christian." Each new convert was told that "renouncing all ungodliness and every worldly lust, you give up your all, soul and body, to be the Lord's, promising to walk before him in holiness and love all the days of your life."[37] Not easy requirements, certainly, but in essence personal and passive. With the

---

[34] Finney, *Autobiography*, 301. For accounts of the revival of 1831 outside Rochester, see Cross, *Burned-Over District*, 252–54; Roy H. Nichols, *Presbyterianism in New York State: A History of the Synod and its Predecessors* (Philadelphia, 1963), 101–3; Charles R. Keller, *The Second Great Awakening in Connecticut* (New Haven, 1942), 38–49; David M. Ludlum, *Social Ferment in Vermont, 1791–1850* (Montpelier, 1948); [Bernard] Weisberger, *They Gathered at the River* [*The Story of the Great Revivalists and Their Impact upon Religion in America* (Boston, 1958)], 130; Dike, "New England Revivals"; and [William G.] McLoughlin, *Modern Revivalism: [Charles Grandison Finney to Billy Graham* (New York, 1959)], 57.

[35] Bradford King Diary, December 18, 1830.

[36] Cited in Ernest R. Sandeen, *The Roots of Fundamentalism: British and American Millenarianism, 1800–1930* (Chicago, 1970), 49. My brief discussion of these ideas relies heavily on [H. Richard] Niebuhr, *The Kingdom of God in America* [(New York, 1937)], Cross, *Burned-Over District*, and Ernest Lee Tuveson, *Redeemer Nation: The Idea of America's Millennial Role* (Chicago, 1968).

[37] Brick Church Session Minutes, December 1825.

Finney revival, the ingrown piety of the 1820s turned outward and aggressive. In 1831 Brick Church rewrote its covenant, and every member signed this evangelical manifesto:

> We [note that the singular "you" has disappeared] do now, in the presence of the Eternal God, and these witnesses, covenant to be the Lord's. *We promise to renounce all the ways of sin, and to make it the business of our life to do good and promote the declarative glory of our heavenly Father.* We promise steadily and devoutly to attend upon the institutions and ordinances of Christ as administered in this church, and to submit ourselves to its direction and discipline, until our present relation shall be regularly dissolved. We promise to be kind and affectionate to all the members of this church, to be tender of their character, and to endeavor to the utmost of our ability, to promote their growth in grace. *We promise to make it the great business of our life to glorify God and build up the Redeemer's Kingdom in this fallen world,* and constantly to endeavor to present our bodies a living sacrifice, holy and acceptable to Him.[38]

In that final passage, the congregation affirmed that its actions—both individually and in concert—were finally meaningful only in relation to the Coming Kingdom. Everything they did tended either to bring it closer or push it farther away.

Guiding the new activism was a revolution in ideas about human ability. The Reverend William James of Brick Church had insisted in 1828 that most men were innately sinful. Christians could not change them, but only govern their excesses through *"a system of moral regulations, founded upon the natural relations between moral beings, and having for its immediate end the happiness of the community."*[39] We have seen, however, that certain of those "natural relations" were in disarray, and that the businessmen and master workmen who were expected to govern within them were the most active participants in the revival. Evangelical theology absolved them of responsibility by teaching that virtue and order were products not of external authority but of choices made by morally responsible individuals. Nowhere, perhaps, was this put more simply than in the Sunday schools. In the 1820s children had been taught to read and then forced to memorize huge parts of the Bible. (Thirteen-year-old Jane Wilson won a prize in 1823 when she committed a numbing 1,650 verses to memory.)[40] After 1831 Sunday-school scholars stopped memorizing the Bible. The object now was to have them study a few verses a week and to come to an understanding of them, and thus to prepare themselves for conversion and for "an active

---

[38] *Ibid.*, June 1831 (my emphases).

[39] William James, *The Debt of Nations to Christianity. A Discourse Delivered in Rochester, June 8, 1828* (Rochester, 1828), 11 and *passim*. Italics in original.

[40] Gerald B. F. Hallock, *A Living Church: The First Hundred Years of the Brick Church in Rochester* (Rochester, 1925), 124–25.

and useful Christian life."[41] Unregenerate persons were no longer to be disciplined by immutable authority and through fixed social relationships. They were free and redeemable moral agents, accountable for their actions, capable of accepting or rejecting God's promise. It was the duty of Christian gentlemen not to govern them and accept responsibility for their actions but to educate them and change their hearts.

William Wisner, pastor at Brick Church during these years, catalogued developments that were "indispensably necessary to the bringing of millennial glory." First, of course, was more revivals. Second, and tied directly to the first, was the return of God's people to the uncompromising personal standards of the primitive Christians and Protestant martyrs.[42] For the public and private behavior of converts advertised what God had done for them. If a Christian drank or broke the Sabbath or cheated his customers or engaged in frivolous conversation, he weakened not only his own reputation but the awesome cause he represented. While Christian women were admonished to discourage flattery and idle talk and to bring every conversation onto the great subject, troubled businessmen were actually seen returning money to families they had cheated.[43] Isaac Lyon, half-owner of the Rochester Woolen Mills, was seen riding a canal boat on Sunday in the fall of 1833. Immediately he was before the trustees of his church. Lyon was pardoned after writing a confession into the minutes and reading it to the full congregation. He confessed that he had broken the eighth commandment. But more serious, he admitted, was that his sin was witnessed by others who knew his standing in the church and in the community, and for whom the behavior of Isaac Lyon reflected directly on the evangelical cause. He had shamed Christ in public and given His enemies cause to celebrate.[44]

Finney's revival had, however, centered among persons whose honesty and personal morals were beyond question before they converted. Personal piety and circumspect public behavior were at bottom means

---

[41] [Henry] O'Reilley, *Settlement of the West: [Sketches of Rochester* (Rochester, 1838)]*, 295. For similar developments in Sunday-school curricula in 1831, see Judith M. Wellman, "The Burned-Over District Revisited: Religion and Reform in Ithaca, Paris, and Mexico, New York" (Ph.D. dissertation, University of Virginia, 1975), esp. 243. That the ideas of individual accountability and moral free agency were central to the revivals of the 1830s has been spelled out most clearly by students of the antislavery movement. See especially Lewis Perry, *Radical Abolitionism: Anarchy and the Government of God in Antislavery Thought* (Ithaca, 1973); and David Brion Davis, "The Emergence of Immediatism in British and American Antislavery Thought," *Mississippi Valley Historical Review* 49 (September 1962), 209–30.

[42] William Wisner, *A Narrative of the State of Religion in the Second Presbyterian Church in Rochester, Monroe County, N.Y. From the First Sabbath in May, 1831, to the First Sabbath in May, 1883* (Rochester, 1833), 3.

[43] *Observer*, February 10, 1831; Mary Gill to Charles Finney, January 18, 1831, Finney Papers; F. D. W. Ward to Henrietta Ward, January 6, 1833, Clarke Papers; Finney, *Lectures on Revivals*, 111; Bradford King Diary, November 28, 1830, and November 13, 1830.

[44] Brick Church Session Minutes, September 8, 1833, and September 14, 1833.

toward the furtherance of revivals. At the moment of rebirth, the question came to each of them: "Lord, what wilt thou have me do?" The answer was obvious: unite with other Christians and convert the world. The world, however, contained bad habits, people, and institutions that inhibited revivals and whose removal must precede the millennium. Among church members who had lived in Rochester in the late 1820s, the right course of action was clear. With one hand they evangelized among their own unchurched poor. With the other they waged an absolutist and savage war on strong drink.

On New Year's Eve of the revival winter, Finney's co-worker Theodore Weld delivered a four-hour temperance lecture at First Presbyterian Church. Weld began by describing a huge open pit at his right hand, and thousands of the victims of drink at his left. First he isolated the most hopeless—the runaway fathers, paupers, criminals, and maniacs—and marched them into the grave. He moved higher and higher into society, until only a few well-dressed tipplers remained outside the grave. Not even these were spared. While the audience rose to its feet the most temperate drinkers, along with their wives and helpless children, were swallowed up and lost. Weld turned to the crowd and demanded that they not only abstain from drinking and encourage the reform of others but that they unite to stamp it out. They must not drink or sell liquor, rent to a grogshop, sell grain to distillers, or patronize merchants who continued to trade in ardent spirits. They must, in short, utterly disengage from the traffic in liquor and use whatever power they had to make others do the same. A packed house stood silent.[45]

The Reverend Penney rose from his seat beside the Methodist and Baptist preachers and demanded that vendors in the audience stop selling liquor immediately. Eight or ten did so on the spot, and the wholesale grocers retired to hold a meeting of their own. The next day Elijah and Albert Smith, Baptists who owned the largest grocery and provisions warehouse in the city, rolled their stock of whiskey out onto the sidewalk. While cheering Christians and awestruck sinners looked on, they smashed the barrels and let thousands of gallons of liquid poison run out onto Exchange Street.[46]

Within a week, Everard Peck wrote home that "the principal merchants who have traded largely in ardent spirits are about abandoning this unholy traffic & we almost hope to see this deadly poison expelled from our village."[47] The performance of the Smith brothers was being repeated throughout Rochester. Sometimes wealthy converts walked into groceries, bought up all the liquor, and threw it away. A few grocers with a fine taste for symbolism poured their whiskey into the Canal. Even grocers who stayed outside the churches found that whiskey on their shelves was bad for business. The firm of Rossiter and Knox announced that it was discontinuing the sale of whiskey, but "not thinking

---

[45] There is a summary of Weld's lecture in the *Rochester Gem*, April 16, 1831. See also the *Observer*, January 7, 1831.

[46] *Observer*, January 13, 1831.

[47] Everard Peck to Samuel Porter, January 11, 1831, Porter Papers.

it a duty to 'feed the Erie Canal' with their property, offer to sell at cost their whole stock of liquors . . ."[48] Those who resisted were refused advertising space in some newspapers,[49] and in denying the power of a united evangelical community they toyed with economic ruin. S. P. Needham held out for three years, but in 1834 he announced that he planned to liquidate his stock of groceries, provisions, and liquors and leave Rochester. "Church Dominancy," he explained, "has such influence over this community that no honest man can do his own business in his own way . . ."[50]

Almost immediately, Weld's absolutist temperance pledge became a condition of conversion—the most visible symbol of individual rebirth.[51] The teetotal pledge was only the most forceful indication of church members' willingness to use whatever power they had to coerce others into being good, or at least to deny them the means of being bad. While whiskey ran into the gutters, two other symbols of the riotous twenties disappeared. John and Joseph Christopher, both of them new Episcopalians, bought the theater next door to their hotel, closed it, and had it reopened as a livery stable. The Presbyterian Sprague brothers bought the circus building and turned it into a soap factory. Increasingly, the wicked had no place to go.[52]

These were open and forceful attacks on the leisure activities of the new working class, something very much like class violence. But Christians waged war on sin, not workingmen. Alcohol, the circus, the theater, and other workingmen's entertainments were evil because they wasted men's time and clouded their minds and thus blocked the millennium. Evangelicals fought these evils in order to prepare society for new revivals. It was missionary work, little more. And in the winter following Finney's departure, it began to bear fruit.

[48] *Daily Advertiser*, March 19, 1831.
[49] *Observer*, October 29, 1830.
[50] *Daily Advertiser*, January 1, 1834.
[51] Cross, *Burned-Over District*, 211–14.
[52] Brewster, "Magic of a Voice," 281.

The Treatment

of

Delinquent Children

JOSEPH M. HAWES

A continuous problem of human society is the conflict between the adult and the young. Going back to the beginnings of human history we find references in literature to the disrespect that children and young people showed toward their elders. While this conflict is pervasive on all socioeconomic levels, societies have always been particularly disturbed by the recalcitrance of the youthful poor, and it is out of that segment of society that the "juvenile delinquent" first emerged.

In early American history the government assumed that the middle-class family would take the responsibility for the antisocial behavior of its children. When the family could not control its children, the government might take those children from their homes and place them in another, which was supposed to have greater control. Often recalcitrant children were placed in apprenticeships with notably tough masters who had developed reputations for breaking even the most willful youths.

Colonial Virginia, in an attempt to increase its population, requested that the authorities in London send several hundred young vagrants to the colony. London obliged readily, eager to rid her streets of young troublemakers. These young people were then indentured and put to work on the plantations of the New World, where it was assumed their undesirable habits would be curbed. They were not, so London's problem became Virginia's.

Massachusetts Bay, always the extremist on moral matters, passed a law stating: "If any child, or children, above sixteen years old, and of sufficient understanding, shall CURSE or SMITE their natural FATHER, or MOTHER, he or they shall be putt to death" unless that behavior had been deliberately provoked. While this law was never applied, it indicates the seriousness with which the authorities viewed the problem of youthful disrespect.

When a foster home or apprenticeship seemed inadequate for rehabilitating a young person, he might be placed in the common jails where all classes and categories of "criminals" were herded together in large rooms that became the breeding grounds for more overtly criminal behavior.

When the prison reform movement of the late eighteenth century began to change the conditions of prison life, it was not unexpected that a movement began to try to deal with youthful offenders in an altogether different way. The selection reprinted below, by Joseph M. Hawes, of Kansas State University, describes one of the first of such attempts. These reformers dealt with the urban poor youth, not so much hardened criminals as footloose and undisciplined pauperized children. The juvenile delinquency problem of our own time is concerned with these same poor children and the attempts to deal with it today are no more successful and only a little less inhumane than those made one hundred and fifty years ago.

In the fall of 1822 two men met in one of New York City's parks. They were James W. Gerard, a young lawyer, and Isaac Collins, a Quaker, and both were members of the Society for the Prevention of Pauperism. Every year this Society presented a public report to suggest ways of carrying out its purposes. Usually, one man, with the assistance of two others "for form's sake," wrote this report. Gerard was talking to Collins about the street children of New York because he was going to write the report for 1822 on "the reformation of juvenile delinquents." Collins, whose father was a Philadelphia printer, became interested in the treatment of juvenile delinquents after reading the annual report of an English institution for young offenders. Gerard had become interested in juvenile crime as a result of the very first case he tried, that of a fourteen-year-old boy accused of stealing a bird. The young lawyer won acquittal for his client by arguing that prison would corrupt the boy. The case so interested Gerard that he began to investigate the facilities for detaining prisoners in New York. He also decided to join the Society for the Prevention of Pauperism.

Gerard presented his report at a public meeting held in the ballroom of the City Hotel in February, 1823. "Those who are in the habit of attending our criminal courts, as jurors or otherwise," Gerard said,

> must be convinced of the very great increase of juvenile delinquency within these few years past, and of the necessity of im-

"The New York House of Refuge: The First Institution for Juvenile Delinquents in the United States" (Editor's title: "The Treatment of Delinquent Children"). From *Children in Urban Society: Juvenile Delinquency in Nineteenth-Century America* by Joseph M. Hawes, pp. 27–60. Copyright © 1971 by Oxford University Press, Inc. Reprinted by permission.

mediate measures to arrest so great an evil. . . . Those whose
walks are limited to the fairer parts of our city know nothing of
the habits, the propensities and criminal courses, of a large population in its remote and obscure parts. . . . it is with pain we state
that, in five or six years past, and until the last few months, the
number of youth under fourteen years of age, charged with offenses
against the law, has doubled; and that the same boys are again and
again brought up for examination, some of whom are committed,
and some tried; and that imprisonment by its frequency renders
them hardened and fearless.

This was hardly surprising, Gerard said, if one knew the conditions of
the prisons and the Bridewell. (A Bridewell then had about the same
functions as a county jail in twentieth-century America.) At the Bridewell
persons awaiting trial because they could not afford to pay bail were all
packed into one large room, "the young and the old . . . promiscuously
crowded together. . . . Boys who have been charged with picking
pockets, stealing watches, and the like crimes," Gerard continued, "have
declared before the police when [asked] how they came to such things,
that they learned the art from the experienced offenders they met in
[the] Bridewell. . . ."
   Every year one to two hundred children between the ages of seven
and fourteen appeared in the criminal courts of New York City. Some
were homeless and most of them were "the children of poor and abandoned parents" whose "debased character and vicious habits" caused them
to be "brought up in perfect ignorance and idleness, and what is worse in
street begging and pilfering." Gerard concluded with a recommendation
that a "house of refuge" for young convicts be established where juvenile
delinquents might be reformed. "Unless the heart is corrupt indeed, and
sunk deep in guilt," Gerard said, "the youth would undergo a change of
feeling and character, and he would look on crime with greater abhor-
rence, because he himself had been a criminal."[1] Gerard's report led to the
creation of the first separate institution for juvenile delinquents in the
United States, the New York House of Refuge.

II

   Even before the end of the second decade of the nineteenth century,
the City of New York was well on its way to becoming the largest and

---

[1] Isaac Collins to James W. Gerard, March 4, 1850, in New York House of Refuge,
Thirtieth Annual Report (1855), p. 73; Gerard to Collins, March 6, 1850, *ibid.*, p.
75; "Reminiscences of James W. Gerard, Esq.," in *Proceedings of the First Con-
vention of Managers and Superintendents of Houses of Refuge and Schools of
Reform in the United States of America, Held in the City of New York, on the
Twelfth, Thirteenth and Fourteenth Days of May, 1857* (New York: Wynkoop,
Hallenbeck & Thomas, 1857), pp. 75–78; "Extracts from the Annual Report of the
Society for the Prevention of Pauperism in the City of New York for the Year,
1822," *ibid.*, pp. 79–82.

most prosperous city in the United States. But as the city increased in wealth and size, some of its most prominent citizens worried about the depressing conditions of the city's poor.[2] The nationally known chemistry teacher, John Griscom, his neighbor, Thomas Eddy, and a set of like-minded friends began meeting to discuss what they called "the perishing and dangerous classes," the impoverished and criminal elements among the city's population. Somehow, it did not seem right that an American city should have the same kind of discouraging problems which beset the cities of the Old World. The informal gatherings at Griscom's house set the stage for the creation of a formal organization to do something about the problems of the lowest classes of society.

On December 16, 1817, Griscom's friends and other philanthropic citizens formed the Society for the Prevention of Pauperism in the City of New York. They elected a veteran of the Revolutionary War, General Matthew Clarkson, as chairman and appointed a committee to draw up a constitution, to study the "causes" of pauperism and continual and hereditary poverty, and to suggest remedies. The Society met again in February of the following year to hear the committee report on the causes of pauperism. The committee listed "juvenile delinquency" as one of the major causes of pauperism. To alleviate the threat of youthful crime the committee suggested that child convicts be confined in a building separate from the regular prison for adult criminals. For the next three years the Society for the Prevention of Pauperism continued to recommend the complete separation of youthful offenders from older convicts in prisons and jails.[3]

In the meantime John Griscom had gone to Europe to visit the Continent's charitable institutions, particularly those devoted to children. One of the most important of the institutions Griscom saw was that maintained by the Philanthropic Society at Hoxton, England. The Society had been organized in London in 1788 as a means of preventing the children of convicts from growing up in idleness and crime. In 1804 the directors moved their Society's operation to Hoxton and began accepting other children, especially juvenile offenders, who seemed likely to grow up into a criminal life. Griscom noted that "it is the peculiar distinction of this society, to seek for children in the nurseries of vice and iniquity, in order to draw them away from further contamination, and to bring them up to the useful purposes of life." The Society received both boys and girls, although it kept them separated "by a high wall which prevents all intercourse." The chemistry teacher from New York thought that the boys received "a sufficient share of school learning," and described the various trades which master workmen taught the boys: printing, bookbinding,

[2] Constance McLaughlin Green, *American Cities in the Growth of the Nation* (London: Univ. of London, Athlone Pr., 1957), p. 9.

[3] Bradford Kenny Peirce, *A Half-Century with Juvenile Delinquents, or The House of Refuge and its Times* (New York: D. Appleton and Co., 1869), pp. 32–42; Grace Abbott, *The Child and the State*, 2 vols. (Chicago: Univ. of Chicago Pr., 1938), II, 345–46; Samuel L. Knapp, *The Life of Thomas Eddy; Comprising an Extensive Correspondence with many of the most Distinguished Philanthropists and Philosophers of this and other Countries* (New York: Connel and Cooke, 1834), p. 23.

shoemaking, tailoring, rope-making, and twine spinning. The girls learned domestic skills, "so as to qualify . . . for useful and respectable service." In passing through the workshops of this beneficent institution, "where industry and skill were apparent," Griscom concluded, "it was cheering to find that so many wretched children were 'snatched as fire brands' from criminality and ruin, and restored to the prospects of respectable and honourable life."[4]

On the Continent Griscom was especially impressed by "Hofwyl," an institution in Switzerland devoted to "problem" children. M. Philip Emanuel Fellenberg had founded this complex of schools only a few years earlier. Fellenberg and Heinrich Pestalozzi, one of the seminal minds in the history of education, had worked together in an effort to teach the orphans, the homeless, and the delinquent children of Switzerland how to make a living for themselves. In 1774, Pestalozzi, who had been brooding about the failures of the institutions society had developed to aid the poor—orphan asylums, poor-houses, prisons, and the like—brought a group of vagrant children to his farm at Neuhof. He treated the children as if they were members of his own family, worked with them in the fields, and tried to give them the rudiments of an education. But Pestalozzi was a poor manager and, despite a number of appeals to the public for funds, was forced to abandon the project in 1780. In one of his appeals he had written: "I have for a long time thought it probable that, under favorable circumstances, young children might be able to earn their own living without undue labor, provided that enough capital were advanced to organize an establishment, in which they would not only live, but at the same time receive a certain elementary education." Pestalozzi tried in vain to attract the necessary finances to promote his ideas until Fellenberg invited him early in the nineteenth century to help at the experimental establishment at Hofwyl, Fellenberg's estate. In 1807 Fellenberg had founded the "Literary Institution" for the sons of the nobility and upper classes. The next year he founded the "Agricultural Institution," or "Poor School" for the children of the common people. Pestalozzi's gentle and abstract ways led to conflict with the stricter and more businesslike Fellenberg and they soon parted, but the teacher of the poor school, Joseph Vehrly, conducted his school on Pestalozzi's principles.[5]

Soon after he arrived at Hofwyl, Griscom had a brief interview with Fellenberg, who discussed the principles of his institution and his own particular philosophy of education. Briefly he explained that Hofwyl's

[4] Edouard Ducpetiaux, *Des Progrès et de l'état actuel de la réform pénitentiaire et des institutions préventives, aux Etats-Unis, en France, en Suisse, en Angleterre et en Belgique* (Bruxelles: Hauman, Cattari and Co., 1838), p. 323; Henry Barnard, *Reformatory Education; Papers on Preventative, Correctional, and Reformatory Institutions in Different Countries . . .* , 3 vols. (Hartford, Conn.: F. C. Brownell, 1857), III, 295; John Griscom, *A Year in Europe: Comprising a Journal of Observations in England, France, Switzerland, the North of Italy and Holland, In 1818 and 1819*, 2 vols. (New York: Collins and Co., 1823), I, 121–23.

[5] Charles A. Bennett, *A History of Manual and Industrial Education up to 1870* (Peoria, Ill.: Manual Arts Press, 1926), pp. 111, 112, 131–35; Barnard, *Reformatory Education*, pp. 34–35, 55.

two schools were designed to give the two extreme classes of society a better understanding of each other. The rich, observing the poor, would learn to respect their industry and skill; the poor would regard the rich as benefactors by experiencing their kindly influence. All of this would be accomplished without any mingling of the classes, since the two schools—though conducted in close proximity—were separate.

The school for the poor boys particularly impressed Griscom. "Their teacher [Vehrly]," he wrote, "is a young man of very extraordinary qualifications. . . . He lives with them, eats, sleeps, and works with them, dresses as they do, and makes himself their friend and companion, as well as their instructor." Vehrly had clearly borrowed his principles from Pestalozzi: "Much pains are taken to impress on the minds of the pupils, a deep sense of the importance of time, and of habits of industry," Griscom recalled, "and from the reports that have been published by commissioners appointed to examine the establishments, it is evident that the most favourable results had attended these endeavors." Vehrly taught his young charges traditional and vocational matter. He concentrated on agriculture, and each boy had his own plot to cultivate. Those who wished could also learn a trade in one of the several workshops on the grounds. Both Vehrly and Fellenberg were "strongly imbued with a sense of religious obligation, and unremittingly attentive to awaken those sentiments in the minds of the pupils." The New York philanthropist was so impressed with what he had seen at Hofwyl that he recommended that the United States adopt a similar approach: "The greatest recommendation of the Pestalozzian and Fellenberg plan of education is the moral charm which is diffused throughout all its operations." Griscom knew that many of Fellenberg's notions—especially those of his upper-class school—were alien to American traditions, but he argued that poor schools like the one Vehrly taught "would soon impart to a large and populous district . . . a moral tone of incalculable importance to its highest interests and welfare." If white children could not be induced to attend such a school, he suggested that the school accept Negro children. "Such an experiment, with persons of this description, would be highly interesting," he added, for "it would put to flight the ridiculous theory of those who contend for an organic inferiority on the part of the blacks." Finally, he noted that to succeed such an institution needed a man of unusual talents to run it—a man like Vehrly.[6]

When Griscom returned to New York, he found that the Society for the Prevention of Pauperism was still discussing the causes of pauperism, although the members of the Society found their attention turning increasingly to the question of juvenile delinquency. To them a juvenile delinquent was a young person (under twenty-one) who had broken the the law, or who wandered about the streets, neither in school nor at work and who obviously lacked a "good" home and family. Such a criminal or vagrant youth would probably lack the skills of a trade and would be illiterate as well. Most such children would certainly grow up to be paupers or criminals, persons which the community would have to

[6] Griscom, *A Year in Europe*, pp. 384–400.

maintain with charity or tax money. By the second decade of the nineteenth century this dependent class had grown large enough to disturb the
prosperous middle-class members of the Society for the Prevention of
Pauperism. The members reasoned that adult paupers and criminals had
been delinquents in their youth and that the best way to eliminate pauperism was to reform juvenile delinquents. The Society's *Annual Report*
for 1819 discussed conditions in the New York penitentiary—particularly
the fact that there were many children confined there—and asked: "Shall
we send convicts in the morning of life, while the youthful mind is ardent
and open to vivid and durable impressions, to this unhallowed abode, to be
taught in all the requisites that will enable them to come forth when
their terms of imprisonment expire, more prepared to invade the peace
of cities and communities?" No, the report concluded, "to say that this
is not a great source of pauperism and nursery of crime and outrage, is
denying the fairest deductions of reason."[7]

Meanwhile, the problem of wayward and criminal children had been
taken up by other groups and individuals in New York. In 1803 Edward
Livingston, the Mayor of the city who later became one of the country's
leading penal reformers, attempted to form a society to help young ex-
convicts, but he was unable to find enough people interested to initiate
his project. On August 14, 1809, the Common Council of New York City
designated the Almshouse as "an asylum for lost children." But the Almshouse and the penitentiary seemed inappropriate places for children, and
in March, 1812, the Council reported that it had received "a communication of John Stanton on the subject of erecting an asylum for the protection of profligate orphans of the city." "Stanton" in this case was undoubtedly the Reverend John Standford, chaplain of the Almshouse, who
asked the Council to "make an attempt to rescue from indolence, vice,
and danger, the hundreds of vagrant children and youth, who day and
night infest our streets." He recommended the creation of "an asylum for
vagrant youth," but beyond noting the receipt of his letter, the Council
took no action on his request.[8]

Seven years later, in June, 1819, Mayor Cadwallader Colden, Jr.,
who was also a member of the Society for the Prevention of Pauperism,
and the Recorder, Peter Augustus Jay, went on an inspection tour of the
city's charitable institutions and reported their findings to the board in
charge of the prison and the Bridewell. They complained about the mixing of young and old convicts in the penal institutions and noted that
young criminals posed a difficult problem. "The members of the board,
who are judges of the Criminal Court," the Mayor and the Recorder said,
"must often have felt how difficult it is, satisfactorily to dispose of these

[7] Quoted in Abbott, *Child and State,* II, 346.

[8] Peirce, *Half-Century,* pp. 32–42; Abbott, *Child and State,* II, 345–46. The actions
of the New York City Common Council relevant to the creation of the New York
House of Refuge may be found in New York, Common Council of the City of New
York, *Minutes of the Common Council of New York* (New York: Published by
the City of New York, 1917), V, 641; VII, 65; X, 467–68, 556, 747; XI, 722. See also
New York Spectator, Jan. 23, 1824; and Charles G. Sommers, *Memoir of the Rev.
John Stanford, D.D.* (New York: Swards, Stanford and Co., 1835), pp. 272–77.

young culprits." If the judge turned them loose, they would soon be back on another charge, but if the judge sentenced them to prison, they would mingle with older convicts and be encouraged in a life of crime. "The jury, as well as the Court," the report continued, "feel a reluctance to convict and condemn them when it is believed that the infliction of punishment, by confinement in the Penitentiary, will tend to harden them in vice." In their conclusion Colden and Jay argued that if the boys could be effectively isolated from the other convicts and then taught a trade, "imprisonment would sometimes produce reformation."

In September of the same year, two more members of the Common Council, the Alderman for the Second Ward and his assistant, visited the Almshouse, the Bridewell, and the penitentiary, and found that conditions had slightly improved. The children were now kept separate from the older convicts, and "considerable attention" was devoted to teaching them "the common branches of education." But the Council members complained that the children were not learning a trade.

In February, 1820, the Grand Jury included among the presentments which it forwarded to the Common Council the recommendation that "all persons under 15 years of age who may be committed to Bridewell be confined in a separate apartment to preclude intercourse with persons of mature age." The following year, in June, the Reverend John Standford sent the Council another letter, again suggesting that it establish "an asylum for vagrant youth." The Council referred the letter to the Mayor and the Commissioners of the Almshouse, who endorsed the chaplain's recommendation and indicated that they had already ordered the boys in the penitentiary charged with vagrancy transferred to the Almshouse. Shortly after this step, the Commissioners of the Almshouse decided to take the remainder of the boys in the penitentiary into the Almshouse, even though more than half of the boys moved there originally had escaped. The boys could stay only for the summer, however, since the building usually filled up with adults during the winter months.

By the spring of 1823 several different efforts to create a separate institution for wayward and criminal children in New York had coalesced into a movement. The Mayor and Almshouse Commissioners had endorsed the Reverend John Standford's suggestion to establish an asylum for vagrant youth, and in June the members of the Society for the Prevention of Pauperism, probably in response to the paper James Gerard had given in February, established a committee "to prepare a report on the subject of establishing a House of Refuge, or prison for the reformation of juvenile delinquents." Among the committee members were John Griscom, Isaac Collins, and Gerard. As the committee prepared its report, Griscom's account of his travels in Europe appeared and probably helped to publicize the movement on behalf of an institution for juvenile delinquents.[9]

The Society called a public meeting in the ballroom of the City

[9] Society for the Prevention of Pauperism in the City of New York, *Report on the Expediency of Erecting an Institution for the Reformation of Juvenile Delinquents* (New York: Mahlon Day, 1823), title page; Peirce, *Half-Century,* pp. 45–48.

Hotel in December, 1823, and John Griscom read the committee's report. "It will be admitted by every person conversant with human nature, and with the great objects of political association," Griscom said, "that there are few judicial considerations of greater importance than the wise adaptation of punishment to crime." Then Griscom stressed the idea that punishment deters criminals and thereby protects property. One of the purposes of this public meeting, then, was to find new, better, and possibly cheaper ways of defending society against the threat of crime—including juvenile crime.[10]

Griscom went on to charge that most penitentiaries had not lived up to their original promise, because their officers now lacked "the same intelligent and disinterested zeal" which their founders had possessed. The greatest deficiency in the penitentiaries was inadequate classification, the separation of prisoners by offenses and ages. Consequently, convicts "of all ages and degrees of guilt" found themselves thrown together and the penitentiaries were fast becoming "schools and colleges of crime." Perhaps, Griscom continued, the old system of "whipping posts, pillories, and croppings" would be better. In some states, however, there were penal institutions, "where classification is an object of careful attention." These were penitentiaries "directed with a constant reference to the moral faculties" and "clothed in the spirit which seeks to restore, in order that it may safely forgive." Thus, Griscom argued, governments should recognize that "those who are guilty of crime should receive the chastisement due to their offenses," and that "no pains should be spared to remove the causes of offense, and to diminish, as far as possible, the sources of temptation and corruption." Such an approach was particularly appropriate for juvenile delinquents—"a class whose increasing numbers, and deplorable situation in this city, loudly call for the more effective interposition of its police, and the benevolent interference of our citizens in general."

Following Gerard's earlier report, Griscom turned to a discussion of the byways of the city where one could see "the ragged and uncleanly appearance, the vile language, and the idle and miserable habits of great numbers of children, most of whom were of school age or capable of some useful employment." Many of these children had no parents, and many had parents who were "too poor or too degenerate" to provide their children with the clothing necessary to go to school or to work. It was no surprise that many of these children turned to vagrancy and crime:

> Accustomed, in many instances, to witness at home, nothing in the way of an example, but what is degrading; early taught to observe intemperance, and to hear obscene and profane language without disgust; obliged to beg, and even encouraged to acts of dishonesty, to satisfy the wants induced by the indolence of their parents— what can be expected, but that such children will, in due time, become responsible to the laws for crimes, which have thus, in a man-

[10] Society for the Prevention of Pauperism, *Report on Expediency*, pp. 3–36; *New York Spectator*, Dec. 25, 1823, Jan. 23, 1824.

ner, been forced upon them? Can it be consistent with real justice, that delinquents of this character, should be consigned to the infamy and severity of punishments, which must inevitably tend to perfect the work of degradation, to sink them still deeper in corruption, to deprive them of their remaining sensibility to the shame of exposure, and establish them in all the hardihood of daring and desperate villainy?

To gain further evidence, the members of the committee had asked both the District Attorney and the keeper of the Bridewell about the treatment of juvenile offenders. The District Attorney gave them a list of "more than 450 persons" under twenty-five who had been sentenced either to the Bridewell or the penitentiary. "A very considerable number" of them were between nine and sixteen years old. These were vagrants; none of them had been charged with a specific offense. The list included "children who profess to have no home, or whose parents have turned them out of doors and take no care of them." The committee believed that children in such circumstances would "eventually have recourse to petty thefts." If they were girls, they would "descend to practices of infamy, in order to save themselves from the pinching assaults of cold and hunger." The members of the committee decided to visit the Bridewell themselves. There the keeper told them that the old and young spent a part of every day together, "because the prison is so constructed that it will not admit of keeping them otherwise." Two-thirds of the young people in the Bridewell had been there before. "It may well be submitted to the judgment of a discerning public," they wrote, "whether an exposure of a few days to such company and fare as here represented, is not sufficient to suppress, in youthful minds, all virtuous emotions." Having noted these facts, they concluded that it was "highly expedient" that a "house of refuge" for juvenile delinquents be established near the City of New York "as soon as practicable."

According to the committee, a house of refuge would be "an asylum in which boys under a certain age, who become subject to the notice of the Police, either as vagrants, or homeless, or charged with petty crimes, may be received, [and where they may be] judiciously classed according to their degrees of depravity or innocence, [and then] put to work at such employments as will tend to encourage industry and ingenuity." The committee also proposed to teach the boys "reading, writing, and arithmetic, and . . . the nature of their moral and religious obligations." The primary purpose of the treatment of the boys was "to afford a prompt and energetic corrective of their vicious propensities and hold out every possible inducement to reformation and good conduct."

The proposed house of refuge would also have a department for girls "either too young to have acquired habits of fixed depravity, or those whose lives have in general been virtuous, but who, having yielded to the seductive influence of corrupt associates, have suddenly to endure the bitterness of lost reputation, and are cast forlorn and destitute upon a cold and unfeeling public." The committee realized that this was a controversial proposal, but indicated that they thought a girls' department would be an "advantage to the institution." They also pointed out that "similar institutions in Europe" included departments for girls. The committee thought that the institution maintained by the Philanthropic Society near London appeared "to come nearest in its general system to that which we would recommend."

Griscom finished the report and turned the platform over to Mayor Colden. The assembly, probably at the committee's suggestion, then passed a series of resolutions. The first endorsed the creation of a house of refuge, and the second urged "that a society be now formed under the appelation of the 'Society for the Reformation of Juvenile Delinquents.' " Successive resolutions named the board of managers and the treasurer of the new society and outlined rules for membership. Once these resolutions passed, Peter Augustus Jay, the City Recorder, James W. Gerard, and others gave brief speeches in support of the proposed house of refuge. They touched themes which were now familiar: that prison corrupted young people who were sent there, that there were as many as four hundred boys under sixteen arrested annually, and that such an arrest almost always meant the beginning of another criminal career. The speakers also said that society now made it practically impossible for a criminal to reform, and claimed that the house of refuge might save as many as two hundred children a year from crime and infamy. At the conclusion of the meeting the officers of the new Society collected over $800 and announced that they would canvass the entire city for funds.

Shortly after this meeting the Reverend Mr. Standford wrote to the Common Council for the third time about the city's vagrant youth. He reminded the Council of his interest in an asylum for them and concluded: "If I may be permitted to name a permanent spot for such an establishment, it is the premises now occupied as the U.S. Arsenal, at the fork of the Bloomingdale Road. . . . In my estimation, it could not be appropriated to a more useful purpose, or prove more honourable to the city."

In February the newly formed Society for the Reformation of Juvenile Delinquents sent a memorial to the Common Council stating that they were "desirous of establishing an institution which shall serve at once as a refuge for neglected or depraved children . . . and praying the aid of the corporation in donations of lands or otherwise." The Council referred the request to a special committee, which wholeheartedly endorsed the proposal: "The committee believes that such an institution, properly regulated and conducted, would not only tend to improve the condition of society by lessening the commission of crime, and the number of convicts sent to our prisons, but would have a tendency to diminish the expences [*sic*] of the city incurred on that account." The Common Council arranged to have the land on which the Arsenal was located returned to the city's jurisdiction. The city then gave the land to the Society, and the Society paid the federal government $2000 for the buildings and the wall.[11]

---

[11] *Minutes of Common Council*, XIII, 538, 578–81; "Daybook No. 1," New York House of Refuge Records, Manuscript Collections, Carnegie Library, Syracuse University. Hereafter, these records will be cited as NYHR.

The Society now sought state financial aid and sent a memorial to the New York legislature in Albany. John Griscom's report, read at the City Hotel in December, formed the main part of the memorial. The managers of the Society explained that they had obtained land and buildings for the proposed house of refuge, but they did not have enough money to keep the project going. While the members of the new Society waited to learn if the legislature would appropriate money for their institution, the Secretary of State for New York, J. V. N. Yates, in a report on pauperism in the state, noted that a great many paupers were children under fourteen, who might "at no distant day form a fruitful nursery for crime unless prevented by the watchful superintendence of the legislature."[12]

Meanwhile, a select committee of the legislature met to draft a bill to charter the New York House of Refuge and place it under state supervision. The bill passed without a negative vote on March 29, 1824. The question of state financial aid remained unsettled, however, and the Society for the Reformation of Juvenile Delinquents asked the Common Council of New York to endorse a request for the proceeds of a tax on public amusements in the City of New York. The Common Council agreed and sent a memorial of their own to Albany along with the request from the Society. But the state granted no money to the House of Refuge in 1824, and it was not until 1829 that the Society received a substantial and steady income from public funds.[13]

III

The act incorporating the Society for the Reformation of Juvenile Delinquents in the City of New York outlined the procedures for membership in the Society and made the Board of Managers responsible for the operation of the House of Refuge. Thus, America's first institution for juvenile delinquents was a "mixed" institution. That is, a private philanthropic group established and operated it, but the state had chartered it and provided for the conditions of its operation. The act of incorporation also contained the first statutory definition of juvenile delinquency in the United States. It authorized the Managers "to receive and take into the house of refuge to be established by them, all such children who shall be taken up or committed as vagrants, or convicted of criminal offenses" if a judge thought they were "proper objects." The Managers could also "place the said children committed to their care, during the minority of such children at such employments, and cause them to be instructed in such branches of useful knowledge, as shall be suitable to their years and capacities." The Managers had the power to bind out children (with their consent) as apprentices until they reached legal maturity. The children remained under the control of the Managers

---

[12] *New York Spectator*, Feb. 3, March 30, 1824; New York Legislature, Senate, *Journal* (1824) App. A., p. 96.

[13] *New York Spectator*, March 30, 1824; *Minutes of Common Council*, XIII, 648; Abbott, *Child and State*, II, 351.

until the boys were twenty-one and the girls were eighteen, or until the
officials at the House of Refuge decided that they were "reformed" and
agreed to their discharge. Thus, the New York House of Refuge began
the use of the indeterminate sentence long before penal reformers advocated it in the late nineteenth century as a necessary innovation in American penology.[14]

The House of Refuge began its operations in the old arsenal building
on January 1, 1825, with six boys and three girls. By the end of the
first year, a total of seventy-three children had come to the Refuge,
fifty-four boys and nineteen girls, and fifty-six remained in the institution.
Of the seventeen children who left during the first year, nine had been
indentured as apprentices or servants, four had been discharged, and four
boys had "absconded."[15]

Most of the children who came to the House of Refuge that first
year and most of the ones who came later were "very ignorant." Even
those few who had learned to read "had acquired no relish for intellectual
improvement. Their habits, as it [sic] respects skill and useful industry,
were still more deplorable." Particularly surprising was the fact that the
girls could not perform any of the standard feminine tasks; they could
not cook, sew, or iron. For the first year the boys spent most of their
time cleaning up the grounds and helping to erect a new building and
make the wall higher. When they were not busy with their newly learned
domestic tasks, the girls planted grass. Once the maintenance tasks were
finished, the boys began to learn shoemaking and tailoring, and the girls
found themselves doing all of the mending and laundry for the institution.

The schedule, which the superintendent had worked out, allowed
two hours a day, one in the morning and one in the evening, for formal
instruction. The curriculum included spelling, reading, writing, and cy-
phering (arithmetic). To some extent the inmates taught themselves, since
the Lancastrian or monitorial system was used. Apparently, the combination of labor and instruction and the system of discipline at the House of
Refuge were effective. The *Annual Report* for the first year noted that
"of the whole number in the house, the superintendent reports that [only]
eleven are still restless and refractory." Four of the boys had run away, but
the Managers and the superintendent were apparently satisfied with the
other children, who had been in the House of Refuge at one time or
another in 1825.[16]

Methods of discipline varied; the superintendent sometimes put the
"subjects" on a ball and chain. He also used handcuffs, leg irons, and the
"barrel." On January 28, 1825, Superintendent Curtis noted in his daily
journal that six subjects, two of whom were girls, had been talking during
a meal. He "took each of them to the barrel which supports them while

---

[14] New York, *Laws of 1824*, c 126.

[15] "Case Histories No. 1," NYHR.

[16] Society for the Reformation of Juvenile Delinquents in the City of New York,
First Annual Report (1825) in New York, Legislature, House, *Documents Relative
to a House of Refuge* (New York: Mahlon Day, 1832), pp. 38, 42–49; hereafter the
Society is cited as SRJD.

the feet are tied on one side and the hands on the other. . . . With the pantaloons down [this device] gives a convenient surface for the operation of the 6 line cat." On that same day a boy wearing handcuffs made himself a key. The superintendent "put him in prison," locked his leg iron to the wall, and instructed the staff to feed him on bread and water. In spite of these restraints, however, the boy broke out of "prison," but the police soon recaptured him. Curtis refused to have this boy back at the House of Refuge, and so he went to the penitentiary. Corporal punishment was not confined to boys. On March 13, 1825, the superintendent put leg irons on a girl who "does not obey the orders of coming when called, and neglects her work for playing in the yard." Curtis also gave one "sullen, ill-natured and disobedient" girl "a dose of salts"—apparently aloes, a purgative. She came to the House of Refuge in March, 1825, and was "very trying." She did not "transgress in things of importance" but she was "artful and sly" and told "many equivocating stories." Her conduct exasperated Superintendent Curtis and he "gave her a ball and chain and confined her to the house." She escaped twice; once the police recaptured her, and once she returned on her own. She went out as a servant, but voluntarily returned to the House of Refuge. Another indenture took the girl to her majority, but on December 26, 1829, the superintendent wrote that "she is said to be on the town."[17]

The situation at the Refuge made some of these punishments necessary. The walls presented no real barrier, and the superintendent had to appoint some of the boys as guards. There were, consequently, a number of escapes. On October 4, 1825, Superintendent Curtis noted in the daily journal that "this evening has been spent in making confessions on the repeated attempts of escaping." As a result,

> great freedom of speach [sic] and frankness appeared to our entire satisfaction, all the movements and plans as well as the persons who have manifested a desire to go has [sic] been fully exposed. . . . It tells us that the insecurity which we have daily felt on this subject has been well grounded; and that there is no security with our present encumbrances.

The fact that the magazine of the old arsenal still contained powder also added to the superintendent's worries. In addition many of the inmates in the House of Refuge were boys over sixteen, for legally any boy under twenty-one could be sent there. In September, 1826, the superintendent complained about the "large notorious & hardened villains" who came to the Refuge. "I fear," he said, "that our extended wish to do good will in consequence of introducing these ill bred hardened boys among the first and young offenders, will prove a curse rather than a blessing." Since the old arsenal building was clearly inadequate, the Acting Committee (which functioned as a board of trustees for the House of Refuge) decided to erect a new building which would provide "greater security."

---

[17] "Daily Journal, No. 1," NYHR, Jan. 28, March 13, 1825; "Case Histories No. 1," NYHR.

In April, 1825, the Committee resolved to add workshops and small utility buildings to their construction plans and decided that the new main building should contain "cells and accommodations for a number of delinq'nts not exceeding one hundred." In that same month the United States Army sent a man to remove the powder from the magazine, which somewhat reduced the "insecurity."[18]

To pay for the new building the managers of the Society appealed to the public for more money. In May, 1825, they issued an *Address to Annual Subscribers* in which they claimed that "already the number of vagrant children who beg and steal in our streets is perceptibly diminished." There were thirty-five boys and eleven girls in the House of Refuge at that time "in a situation where there is no temptation to vice . . . and, where, instead of being left to prey on the public, they will be fitted to become valuable members of society." To continue this important work the managers felt compelled "to erect . . . an additional stone building with separate dormitories for each child, on a plan somewhat resembling the State Prison at Auburn. . . ." To be sure that their contributions were worthwhile "subscribers and the public" were invited "to call at the House of Refuge, and see that idleness has become changed to industry, filth and rags to cleanliness and comfortable appearance, [and] boisterous impudence to quiet submission. . . ."

The Acting Committee directed the superintendent to employ a foreman and four to six masons to erect the building with the assistance of the boys. The masons and the boys finished the new cell-house in April, 1826. It was a two-story stone building with barred windows and heavy doors. Inside were small "dormitories"—three feet, three inches wide—for each boy. The new building did make it more difficult to escape and brought about the complete separation of the male and female departments. "We find ourselves in possession and enjoyment of all the long wished advantages of the new building," Superintendent Curtis wrote, "and we also find (as we may allways [*sic*] expect) that our anticipations are not realised." The boys now had to do their own cooking, and for a time they proved less adept than the girls.[19]

From the first the House of Refuge attracted a stream of visitors, distinguished and otherwise. Soon after the Refuge opened, a father appeared and demanded the return of his son. Only after he had secured a writ of habeas corpus did the superintendent permit the man to take his boy. In May, 1826, Governor De Witt Clinton of New York, the Governor of Ohio, the Mayor of New York, "and various other dignitaries and their wives" came to the House of Refuge and left apparently "well-pleased." In July three men from Pennsylvania came to study the House of Refuge because they were planning to establish a similar institution in Philadelphia. "They left us highly gratified," the superintendent noted in

---

[18] "Minutes of the Acting Committee, No. 1," NYHR, April 30, 1825; "Daily Journal, No. 1," NYHR, Oct. 4, 1825, Sept. 22, 1826.

[19] "Minutes of the Acting Committee, No. 1," NYHR, May 10, May 21, 1825; "Daily Journal No. 1," NYHR, April 14, 1825, [March ?] 1826; For a sketch of the new building see SRJD, *Fifth Annual Report* (1830), frontispiece.

the daily journal, "with a determined resolution to advance the same good cause they had witnessed. . . ." A week later, the sister of a former inmate came by to see some of her old friends. She was wanted by the police, however, and the superintendent arranged to have her detained. Such guests must have appeared frequently for on July 26, 1826, Superintendent N. C. Hart (Joseph Curtis had resigned on July 11, 1826) noted in the daily journal that "it is found that now and then improper persons get into our yard on visiting days. I have given direction to the gatekeeper not to permit any to enter (even on visiting days) Unless they are very respectable looking persons. . . ."[20]

On Sundays many of the Managers drove out to the House of Refuge to attend the worship services. Two of the most regular visitors were John Griscom and Isaac Collins, both of whom figured prominently in the founding of the refuge. Griscom sometimes talked to the boys about science. On August 13, 1826, for example, he spoke on "the creation of man and matter," and on New Year's Day, 1827, he illustrated his talk with a magic lantern. Collins gave some books for the library. Among the titles were *Essays on Virtue*, the *Life of Captain Cook*, a *Report* of the British and Foreign School Society, *Robinson Crusoe*, and *Wonderful Escapes*.[21]

At the end of the second year, in the *Annual Report* the Managers explained the theories which guided the efforts to reform juvenile delinquents at the House of Refuge. "The young offender," they said, "should, if possible, be subdued by kindness. His heart should first be addressed, and the language of confidence, though undeserved, be used towards him." They added that the young inmate should be taught that "his keepers were his best friends and that the object of his confinement was his reform and ultimate good. If he is made to believe that he is still of some use and value, he will soon endeavor to act up to the character which is set upon him." This kind of discipline, the managers argued, "will be willing, cheerful and lasting." The remarkably gentle—and from the lights of modern psychology, appropriate—methods espoused by the Managers of the New York House of Refuge came from a nineteenth-century theory about children and the development of their personalities. As the Managers explained, men of the early nineteenth century believed that "the minds of children, naturally pliant, can, by early instruction, be formed and moulded to our wishes. An inclination can there be given to them, as readily to virtuous as to vicious pursuits." Not only can the plastic minds of children be turned to vice or virtue, but earlier inclinations can be altered if the child is not too old: "The seeds of vice, which bad advisers may have planted, if skill is exercised, can yet be extracted . . . and on the mind which appeared barren and unfruitful may yet be engrafted those principles of virtue which shall do much to retrieve the errors of the past, and afford a promise of goodness and usefulness for the future."

[20] "Daily Journal, No. 1," NYHR, April 25, 1825, May 26, July 11, July 12, July 19, July 28, 1826.
[21] *Ibid.*, Aug. 8, 1825, Aug. 13, 1826, Jan. 1, 1827.

The Managers also reminded their readers that "these little vagrants, whose depredations provoke and call down upon them our indignation are yet but children, who have gone astray for want of that very care and vigilance we exercise towards our own." They were nonetheless, misbehaving children, whose actions had to be condemned. Furthermore, "a regard for our property and the good of society, requires that they should be stopped, reproved and punished. . . . But," the Managers continued, "they are not to be destroyed. The public must in some measure take the place of those who ought to have been their natural guardians and protectors." Here the Managers of the New York House of Refuge anticipated one of the key concepts of the Illinois Juvenile Court Act of 1899—the idea that the public (in the Illinois law it was the state) has a collective responsibility to and for society's misbehaving children. Ironically, this provision of the Illinois law was hailed as a great innovation in the legal treatment of delinquent children.[22]

In order to carry out their theories, the officials at the New York House of Refuge adopted rules which prescribed continuous activity for the inmates during their waking hours. They were to be employed "every day in the year, except Sundays, at such labor, business, or employment as from time to time [would] be designated by the Acting Committee." Other rules indicated that all the children wore "coarse but comfortable apparel of the cheapest and most durable kind," which was made on the premises. Inmates who refused to work or who used profane or indecent language, or who fought with their fellow delinquents, would be punished. Punishments included deprivation of play periods, being sent to bed without supper, and bread and water. In more serious cases, the officials might force the recalcitrant boy or girl to drink a bitter herb tea which caused them to sweat profusely, or they might put the offender in solitary confinement. In extreme cases, corporal punishment or iron fetters might be used. The rules provided that corporal punishment could only be inflicted in the presence of the superintendent (or the matron in the case of misbehaving girls). The rules also indicated that "the females shall eat their meals and lodge in a separate building from the males, with whom they shall have no intercourse or communication, except at family or public worship."[23]

Scarcely a week passed without some sort of incident. On September 5, 1826, one of the worst troublemakers in the girls' department returned of her own accord after having escaped. She and the school teacher got into an argument, and he began whipping her. According to Superintendent Hart,

> She commenced swearing most bitterly, tore his shirt considerable
> & made battle with her fists—having a pen knife secreted about her,
> she succeeded in opening it with her mouth, & made several attempts to stab him in his breast—to no purpose, but finally got it in

[22] SRJD, *Second Annual Report* (1826), in *Documents Relative to a House of Refuge,* p. 80.
[23] *Documents Relative to a House of Refuge,* pp. 106–8.

the flesh of his arm and ripped a gash at least 1½ inches long and very deep.

The superintendent put the girl in irons. In December, 1826, two boys escaped through the attic of the male cell house, and an officer went to town to look for them. He found one of the boys "in a small rum hole in Anthony St. with girls and other company of ill fame." The boy drew out a knife, while one of the patrons of the establishment shouted "Stick him [!] Stick him [!]." The boy cut the officer severely on the arm and on the neck "near the jugular vein." When the police had returned this boy to the House of Refuge, the superintendent punished him "with a cowskin up on his bare back" and then put him in solitary confinement "without a book to divert his mind" on a bread and water diet. The boy remained in solitary for three days, after which the superintendent put him in a cell in the upper tier. The boy then attempted another escape:

> [He] tied three sheets & a cord together—broke through the plas-
> tered wall into the garret—again fastened the cord to the same
> place where he had been successful in making his escape but a few
> evenings since—but alas! no sooner than he had . . . [placed] his
> weight upon the cord thus fastened, it broke & he fell about 30 feet
> upon frozen ground & stones—broke his foot badly—pitched upon
> his face cut a hole over his eye to the skull bone & fractured it,
> broke his nose & drove the bones so deep as to endanger his life—
> cut his lip through nearly up to his nose. Thus he rolls in agony.

To prevent similar escape attempts the officers moved the older boys to the first tier and put the younger boys in their place.[24]

The House of Refuge, following the penal theories of men like Thomas Eddy, also instituted a rudimentary classification system. When they entered, the officials placed the inmates in one of four grades, ranging from "those who are vicious, bad and wicked" in class four to "the best behaved and most orderly boys and girls; those that do not swear, lie, or use profane, obscene or indecent language or conversation," in class one. Every Sunday, the superintendent, his assistant, and the teacher reclassified the children according to their behavior. The upper classes enjoyed extra recreation, and the lower classes found themselves on a reduced diet and suffered from the loss of other privileges. The system of treatment at the New York House of Refuge, rudimentary as it was, is another example of an improvement in penal practice made in a juvenile institution which would later be hailed as an "innovation" in adult reformatories.

A typical day in the Refuge illustrates this system. A bell would ring at sunrise to arouse the sleeping children. They had fifteen minutes to dress, make their beds, and straighten up their cells; then they assembled in the corridors and marched off to the washrooms. After washing, the inmates lined up for a personal inspection. They were at best a motley

---

[24] "Daily Journal, No. 1," NYHR, Sept. 5, Dec. 18, Dec. 21, Dec. 24, 1826.

group. Their clothing had been cut from "a coarse, cheap material" to six standard sizes. In 1848 Elijah Devoe, formerly an assistant superintendent, recalled that they had "collectively a slovenly and untidy appearance." From inspection the children went to morning prayers, after which they went to school for an hour and a half. Then they sat down to a breakfast which usually consisted of bread, molasses, and rye coffee. After breakfast, the inmates trooped off to their various workshops, where they worked until noon. Washing up again and the noon meal occupied the next hour, after which the children returned to work. During this afternoon work period the children could gain extra recreation time if they finished their assigned tasks early. The work period ended at five o'clock; then there was a half-hour for supper and another hour and a half of school. Following the evening school session, there were evening prayers; the inmates then marched back to their cells, turned in, and followed a rule of silence for the night.[25]

The labor of the children in the House of Refuge was let out to contractors, who then paid the institution for the value of the work done by the children. While the contractors taught the children the skills necessary to perform their tasks, the officials of the House of Refuge maintained discipline. The girls worked mostly at sewing; and the boys made cane bottoms for chairs, various kinds of brushes, shoes, and boxes for soap and candles. The contractors represented an outside presence in the House of Refuge and an unending source of difficulty. On July 22, 1826, for example, two girls claimed that the shoemaker took them "into his dwelling & there perpetrated that heinous crime of seduction." An investigation quickly followed and on August 6, Superintendent Hart wrote that the shoemaker had "closed his business with us." On October 16, 1827, Hart noted in the daily journal that the parents of some of the boys in the House of Refuge had complained that their sons were not learning a trade since the shoemaker had set up an assembly line, assigning a separate task to each boy. "The remarks are in considerable degree true," Hart wrote, "& how the difficulty is to be obviated I cannot tell." It would take nearly half a century to eliminate the contract system.[26]

When the officials at the New York House of Refuge concluded that a boy or girl had sufficiently reformed to be trusted outside the institution itself, they often bound them out as apprentices. Some of the boys signed on as sailors in whaling ships, a practice which the managers endorsed heartily in the *Fifth Annual Report* because such a boy would find himself under "wholesome restraint and discipline" and would have the examples of "moral, industrious, and religious companions." Most of the boys, however, were apprenticed to farmers, including some in the West—a practice which anticipated the placing out system of Charles

[25] SRJD, *Sixth Annual Report* (1831), in *Documents Relative to a House of Refuge,* pp. 219–52; Elijah Devoe, *The Refuge System, or, Prison Discipline Applied to Juvenile Delinquents* (New York: J. R. M'Gown, 1848), pp. 36, 46, 56; SRJD, *Seventh Annual Report* (1832), in *Documents Relative to a House of Refuge,* pp. 253–302.
[26] "Daily Journal, No. 1," NYHR, July 22, Aug. 6, 1826, Oct. 16, 1827.

Loring Brace and the Children's Aid Society. Generally, the girls became servants in families not too distant from the House of Refuge. Boys were indentured until they were twenty-one, girls until they reached eighteen. To explain the purposes and methods of the New York House of Refuge, the superintendent sent a form letter to the masters of the apprentices, which warned against the overuse of corporal punishment and reminded the masters that "it has not been concealed from you, that this child has been a delinquent." The superintendent also addressed a form letter to the apprentice. "We should not have consented to part with you at this time," it began, "had not your conduct given us reason to hope, that the religious and moral instruction you have received since you have been under our care, have disposed you to lead an honest, industrious, and sober life." The letter to the apprentice also cautioned him against bad company, especially his former associates.[27]

IV

In 1820 a committee of the Massachusetts legislature began investigating the causes of poverty. In 1821 the committee recommended that the system of alms-giving then practiced throughout Massachusetts be abandoned and that cities and towns build work houses or houses of industry. As a result of this report, the town fathers of Boston launched an investigation of poverty in their city. They found the Boston Almshouse to be in deplorable condition. Crowded together were the poor who could not work, the able-bodied who were given make-work such as picking oakum, and those convicted of minor offenses such as drunkenness. The Boston investigators recommended the erection of a work house or industry for the able-bodied poor and a house of correction for minor offenders. By the summer of 1823 these new institutions were in use, but the south wing of the House of Correction remained empty. As in New York, hundreds of undisciplined and apparently homeless children roamed the streets of Boston. Their disturbing presence—the prosperous people of Boston also saw these waifs as a threat to society—and the creation of the New York House of Refuge stimulated the town fathers of Boston to do something about juvenile delinquency. Early in 1826 a committee of the City Council recommended that the unused wing of the House of Correction be converted to "a house of reformation for juvenile offenders."[28]

In March of 1826 the legislature passed an act authorizing the Boston City Council to use the House of Correction or any other building as an institution for juvenile offenders. This statute also gave the Commonwealth of Massachusetts a definition of juvenile delinquency. Like the

---

[27] SRJD, *Fourth Annual Report* (1829), in *Documents Relative to a House of Refuge*, pp. 179–80; SRJD, *Fifth Annual Report* (1830); Homer Folks, *Care of Destitute, Neglected, and Delinquent Children* (New York: Macmillan, 1902), p. 203.

[28] Josiah Quincy, *A Municipal History of the Town and City of Boston, during Two Centuries* (1630–1830) (Boston: Little and Brown, 1852), pp. 35–106.

act passed two years before in New York, the Massachusetts law defined juvenile delinquents as "all such children who shall be convicted of criminal offenses, or taken up and committed under and by virtue of an act of this Commonwealth, 'for suppressing and punishing of rogues, vagabonds, common beggars, and other idle, disorderly and lewd persons.'" In addition, the Massachusetts General Court also provided that the house of reformation could receive "all children who live an idle or dissolute life, whose parents are dead, or if living, from drunkenness, or other vices, neglect to provide any suitable employment, or exercise any salutary control over said children." The Massachusetts law was the first legislative recognition of the idea of preventing juvenile delinquency.[29]

The early years of the Boston House of Reformation were difficult. Ordinary citizens and members of the Boston City Council disagreed about its design, and, as Mayor Josiah Quincy indicated in his *Municipal History of Boston*, "the expenditures were immediate and considerable; the advantages distant and problematical." Many Bostonians felt that the institution should have been supported by the state instead of the city. Mayor Quincy also complained about parents who tried to have their sons removed from the institution and about "tender-hearted philanthropists, who regarded the length and nature of the restraint as severe, notwithstanding [the fact that] the boys were committed by a court of justice for serious offenses." The new institution was very fortunate, however, in the selection of its second superintendent, the Reverend E. M. P. Wells. According to Mayor Quincy, "Strictness without severity, love without indulgence, were the elements of his system of management." Quincy was not alone in his praise of Wells. In 1832 two French noblemen, Alexis de Tocqueville and Gustave Beaumont, came to the United States on an official mission for the French government to study American prison systems. They inspected several American prisons and the houses of refuge at New York and Philadelphia, and naturally they came to Boston and visited the House of Reformation. They were particularly impressed by Superintendent Wells and his administration of the Boston institution. "It is possible to find superintendents who are fit for the Philadelphia system," they wrote, "but we cannot hope to meet often with such men as Mr. Wells."[30]

What distinguished the House of Reformation in Boston from the New York House of Refuge and the House of Refuge established in Philadelphia in 1828 was its system of discipline. As Tocqueville and Beaumont noted, "the Boston discipline belongs to a species of ideas much more elevated than that established in New York and Philadelphia"; but it was difficult to practice because it was "entirely of a moral character." The Boston House of Reformation used a classification system based on the conduct of the inmates, but unlike the New York House of Refuge

---

[29] Massachusetts, "Laws of 1826," in *Private and Special Statutes of the Commonwealth of Massachusetts from May, 1822 to March, 1830* (Boston: Dutton and Wentworth, State Printers, 1837), c 182.

[30] Quincy, *Municipal History*, pp. 106–7; Alexis de Tocqueville and Gustave Beaumont, *On the Penitentiary System in the United States*, ed. by Thorstein Sellin (Carbondale, Ill.: Southern Illinois Univ. Pr., 1964), p. 121.

it required each child to evaluate his own conduct, and a jury composed of children in the institution tried cases of serious misconduct. In the House of Reformation there were six grades of conduct—three good ones and three bad ones. Each of the good grades carried with it certain privileges; boys in the highest grade could go outside the bounds of the House of Reformation by themselves. Conversely, each of the bad grades carried a degree of privation; boys in the two lowest grades were not allowed to speak unless it was absolutely necessary. Before the boys could participate in this system of discipline, they went through a period of probation. A new arrival met with the superintendent who interviewed him to determine his moral condition. Then, if the new inmate had been found guilty of a serious offense, he was placed in solitary confinement for two weeks so that he could reflect on his vices. Superintendent Wells then told him why he was in the Boston House of Reformation and explained the system of discipline. If the boy rebelled against the officials during his probationary period, they whipped him. Only at this first stage did the superintendent permit corporal punishment. At the end of the probationary period, the superintendent assigned the child one of the bad grades and encouraged him to move up.[31]

While the Society for the Prevention of Pauperism in the City of New York began concentrating on the problem of youthful offenders in its city, the Society for Alleviating the Miseries of Public Prisons met in Philadelphia and appointed a committee to investigate the conditions of vagrant children in the prisons of the city. At that time, juvenile vagrants and young offenders in Philadelphia were placed in the Walnut Street jail along with adult criminals. In May, 1824, the committee recommended that the Guardians of the Poor provide a suitable place for the reception of juvenile vagrants. In the meantime the Society had appointed another committee to consider what should be done about juvenile offenders. This committee recommended the creation of a House of Refuge for discharged prisoners, but soon after they filed their report "an association of females" petitioned the Society to create a House of Refuge for Juvenile Offenders. So the committee investigated again and decided that such an institution was desirable but beyond the means of the Society for Alleviating the Miseries of Public Prisons. The Society then called a public meeting in February, 1826, to find additional support for the proposed House of Refuge. The assembly adopted a resolution calling for the creation of such an institution for juvenile offenders and appointed a committee to draw up "articles of association" for that purpose and to ask the legislature for "such powers in law, as may be necessary to carry the designs of the association into full effect when it may be organized." The legislature readily acceded to the request and passed an act of incorporation for the Philadelphia House of Refuge in March, 1826. This act, like those statutes creating the New York House of Refuge and the Boston House of Reformation, provided that the Managers of the Philadelphia House of Refuge could receive "such children who shall be taken up as vagrants, or

---

[31] Tocqueville and Beaumont, *On the Penitentiary System*, pp. 119–21; "The House of Reformation," *New England Magazine*, III (Nov. 1832), 386–87.

duly convicted of criminal offenses," but it also gave the managers the authority to receive children "who shall be taken up . . . upon any criminal charge." Thus, by law, children suspected of crime could be placed in the Philadelphia institution.[32]

To accomplish their goals the Managers of the Philadelphia House of Refuge expected to rely on a combination of strict discipline, a classification similar to that used at the House of Reformation in Boston, work at a useful occupation, education, and moral instruction. The first step in such a program was "to raise the delinquent in his own estimation . . . to change his whole course of thought: to awake his latent pride and sensibility: to direct his ambition to useful and honorable pursuits: and thus to conduct him unconsciously as it were to the practical charms and advantages of a virtuous life." The managers expected to retain control over delinquents who entered the House of Refuge until they reached a majority, but the managers hoped to place the children out as apprentices well before they reached the upper age limit.[33]

V

The public image of an institution, derived in part from the reports of well-publicized visitors and investigations and also from the institution's own annual reports, is rarely a complete picture of its daily life. In a book that amounted to a polemic against the New York House of Refuge, Elijah Devoe, a discharged assistant superintendent, contended that the New York institution had deliberately falsified its public face. He charged that officials had altered the records to give a higher rate of reformation and that the day-by-day practices in the institution were far more cruel than any outsider realized. The routine was "a stern, brutal, coercive government and discipline, entirely the opposite of that paternal establishment so amiable and ingeniously pictured in the 'annual reports.' " Devoe also indicated that the rule prohibiting corporal punishment unless in the presence of the superintendent was a dead letter: "Corporal punishments are usually inflicted with the cat or a ratan. The latter instrument is applied in a great variety of places, such as the palm and back of the hands, top and bottom of the feet, and lastly, but not rarely or sparingly, to the posteriors over the clothes, and also on the naked skin." Ratans were readily available and "liable to be used everywhere and at all times of the day." In addition, Devoe deplored the mixing of "hardened culprits over fifteen years" of age with "small, younger, and less corrupt children." The older boys were just as likely to corrupt the younger ones as hardened adult criminals were to corrupt juveniles in prison; it was therefore an injustice that "boys under a certain age, who become subject to the notice of our police, either as vagrants or houseless, should be thrust into

[32] Negley K. Teeters, *They Were in Prison; A History of the Pennsylvania Prison Society, 1787–1937* (Philadelphia: John C. Winston Co., 1937), pp. 161–68; Pennsylvania, *Laws of 1826–27,* c XLVII.

[33] Philadelphia House of Refuge, *An Address from the Managers of the House of Refuge to their fellow Citizens* (Philadelphia: D. & S. Neall, 1826), pp. 9–12.

the society of confirmed thieves, burglars, and robbers, and subjected to the same discipline and punishments."[34]

Devoe's account, which was the work of an unhappy former employee, nonetheless provides an "inside view" of an early nineteenth-century juvenile institution. It seems probable that the annual reports of these institutions, which were made in response to state law and which represented to some extent arguments for state appropriations, presented only the most favorable aspects of houses of refuge and ignored the day-to-day activities which deviated from the high ideals set by the managers. In some respects, however, the view of juvenile institutions presented in their annual reports is more valuable than the "inside story," because the annual reports gave the public its only look at juvenile institutions. Thus, they are a rudimentary index to what nineteenth-century Americans knew about institutions for juvenile delinquents.

The creation of special institutions for juvenile offenders in the second decade of the nineteenth century indicated a growing awareness on the part of American city-dwellers of the problem of juvenile delinquency, and the new institutions also represented a modification in the application of criminal laws to young people. Under the common law as Blackstone explained it, children under seven were presumed to be unable to distinguish between right and wrong. Between the ages of seven and fourteen, "though an infant shall be *prima facie* adjudged to be *doli incapax* [not mentally competent]; yet if it appear to the court and jury that he was *doli capax*, and could discern between good and evil, he may be convicted and suffer death." That this understanding of the common law was generally adopted in the United States may be illustrated by a case involving a twelve-year-old Negro boy in New Jersey in 1828. The boy had been found guilty of the murder of a sixty-year-old woman by a lower court, and the case had been appealed to the New Jersey Supreme Court on the grounds that the boy was too young to be found guilty of such an offense. The Supreme Court upheld the verdict of the lower court, finding that the judge had correctly charged the jury with the relevant points of law in the case. The lower court judge had told the jury that "with respect to the ability of persons of his age, to commit crimes of this nature, the law is, that under the age of seven, they are deemed incapable of it. Between seven and fourteen, if there be no proof of capacity, arising out of this case, or by testimony of witnesses, the presumption is in their favor; a presumption however, growing weaker and more easily overcome, the nearer they approach to fourteen." The judge went on to explain that a twelve-year-old boy in New Jersey at that time probably possessed "sufficient capacity" to commit murder. Finally he told the jury: "you call to mind the evidence on this subject; and if you are satisfied that he was able, in a good degree, to distinguish between right and wrong; to know the nature of the crime with which he is charged; and that it was *deserving* of *severe* punishment, his infancy will furnish no obstacle, on the score of incapacity, to his conviction."[35]

---

[34] Devoe, *Refuge System*, pp. 11, 28–29, 50–51.
[35] Sir William Blackstone, *Commentaries on the Laws of England*, 4 vols. (Dublin: John Exshaw *et al.*, 1773), IV 23; *State v Guild*, 5 Halstead 163 (New Jersey

None of the statutes which established the houses of refuge in New York, Boston, and Philadelphia changed the basic premises of the common law, but in effect they raised the age below which a child could expect to receive some kind of preferential treatment from the law. The sentiment behind the creation of the new institutions for juvenile delinquents recognized that children—even children over fourteen—required different treatment from adults. The new laws, although they did not mention any ages except those for the end of minority, created institutions which would provide that treatment. The laws also provided a legal definition of juvenile delinquency. A juvenile delinquent was a child who broke the law, or who was in danger of breaking the law, and the community hoped to keep him from becoming an adult criminal by providing reformatory treatment in a house of refuge.

The creation of the House of Refuge, a unique institution in the United States, posed some new legal problems, which soon led to court action. In the case of *Commonwealth* v *M'Keagy*, heard before the Court of Common Pleas in Philadelphia in 1831, the issue was a plea for a writ of habeas corpus on behalf of one Lewis L. Joseph, who had been convicted on evidence supplied by his father of being "an idle and disorderly person" and sent to the Philadelphia House of Refuge. After reciting the relevant sections of the statute establishing the Philadelphia House of Refuge, the court noted that "great power is given to the managers of this institution, a power which could only be justified under the most pressing public exigencies, and whose continuance should depend only on the most prudent and guarded exercise of it." Particularly unusual, according to the court, was the power given to any magistrate or justice of the peace, "on a charge of vagrancy or crime . . . to take a child from its parent and consign it to the control of any human being, no matter how elevated or pure." The overseers of the poor generally had the power to provide for orphans and dependent children and even to bind them out as apprentices until they reached their majority. "Why is it that in some shape, and if necessary, in a more decided shape," the court asked, "the public cannot assume similar guardianship of children whose poverty had degenerated into vagrancy?" The court agreed that the House of Refuge indeed did have the power to receive and control children whose vagrancy fell within the categories the court had outlined. However, the court continued, "it is when the law is attempted to be applied to subjects who are not vagrants in the just and legal acceptation of the term"; when "preservation becomes mixed with a punitory character, that doubts are started and difficulties arise, which often and necessarily involve the most solemn questions of individual and constitutional rights."

Having thus stated its position, the court proceeded to find that Lewis Joseph was not a vagrant. His father, who had committed him, was not a pauper, and the boy, while he had misbehaved, was not a fit subject for the House of Refuge. The Superintendent of the House of Refuge had

---

State Law Reporter). Although the fact that the defendant was black may have affected the original decision, the appeal did establish a precedent for the application of the English Common Law to infants in American courts.

told the judge that the boy had been very well behaved there and had been very receptive to discipline. As the court said, "it is manifest, that gentle but firm discipline was all that was necessary to root out from his mind the luxuriant weeds produced by weak indulgence, bestowed by an erring parent of a sportive and volatile disposition." In opposing the petition for a writ of habeas corpus the lawyer for the House of Refuge had argued that the boy's father had transferred his parental authority to the managers of that institution, which now acted *in loco parentis.* But the court rejected this view, saying that the House of Refuge could only receive vagrant and criminal children; it was not "a place to correct refractory children." Accordingly, the court ordered Lewis L. Joseph released from the Philadelphia House of Refuge.[36]

In a later case, *Ex parte Crouse,* which the Pennsylvania Supreme Court heard in 1839, a similar petition for a writ of habeas corpus challenged the constitutionality of the statute which created the Philadelphia House of Refuge. The petition had been filed on behalf of Mary Ann Crouse by her father. "The House of Refuge is not a prison, but a school," the court said in opening its argument. The use of the House of Refuge "as a prison for juvenile convicts who would also be committed to a common gaol" is clearly constitutional, but in the case of juveniles admitted as vagrants or potential criminals, the constitutionality was open to some question. The main purpose of the House of Refuge was clearly reformation and not punishment; education was one of its principal activities. If a child's parents did not, for one reason or another, provide it with adequate education, the state by virtue of its power of *parens patriae* could provide the child with the necessary education. Such was Mary Ann Crouse's case: "The infant has been snatched from a course which must have ended in confirmed depravity; and not only is the restraint of her person lawful, but it would be an act of extreme cruelty to release her from it."[37]

These two cases illustrate that the House of Refuge was a legal institution with certain well-defined powers. Primarily, it was an institution designed to reform youthful criminals, but it also functioned to prevent crime by accepting young vagrants who were potential juvenile criminals. Once a house of refuge received a child, the managers had a wide latitude of authority over him. In effect, they had the same powers over their charges that a natural parent had over his own children. Thus the state, by chartering a private or municipal association to take the place of inadequate or missing parents, had taken a bold step in the direction of providing for the welfare of its children. In addition, such a step appeared almost too attractive to resist. When houses of refuge first appeared, they seemed to have a good chance of preventing or drastically reducing the rate of adult crime. They not only gave the community something to do with juvenile offenders and vagrant children, they promised to cut future welfare and prison costs. When they insisted that the inmates of houses of

---

[36] *Commonwealth* v *M'Keagy,* 1 Ashmead (1831), 248 (Pennsylvania State Law Reporter).

[37] *Ex parte Crouse* 4 Wharton (1839), 9 (Pennsylvania State Law Reporter).

refuge be taught a useful trade, the managers shrewdly responded to a community prejudice which not only condemned idleness as a sin but also linked it with serious crime. By teaching juvenile offenders how to work then, houses of refuge were exorcising sin and providing for the future security of life and property. The creation of the New York House of Refuge and similar institutions in Boston and Philadelphia marked the beginning of nineteenth-century America's concern for wayward children. It also marked the beginning of the process of separating juvenile delinquents from adult criminals—a process that would not be complete until the creation of the juvenile court in 1899. But the house of refuge had one essential weakness as an institution—it was a charity, which, although chartered by the state, private citizens operated. The involvement of private citizens had been necessary to launch the first institutions for juvenile delinquents, but once their worth had been proved, many philanthropists felt that the reformation of juvenile offenders was a duty for which the state should take full responsibility.

Indian Removal

MICHAEL PAUL ROGIN

Much has been written about the removal of the Cherokee Indian nation from Georgia, partly because this episode furnishes a dramatic illustration of conflict between the executive and judicial branches of the government, as represented by President Andrew Jackson and Chief Justice John Marshall. But the attempts to remove the Creeks, Choctaws, Chickasaws, and Seminoles from the South have been less widely noted, although they offer valuable insights into conflicts between red and white culture in the United States, as well as into the government's method of handling Indian affairs.

What makes the removal of the Five Civilized Tribes of the South particularly ironic is that, more than most other Indian nations, they sought to accommodate themselves to the culture of the white man. By tradition, those Indians were village agriculturalists rather than hunting nomads, so it was relatively easy for them to adjust to white ways. Many of them embraced white culture completely, drawing up constitutions, accepting the white man's religion and style of dress, and even owning Afro-American slaves. Only the Seminoles maintained a warrior tradition; the other nations settled down to farm their rich lands, feeling secure under the eighteenth-century treaties. By denying their own cultural traditions, the Indians eliminated much of the ostensible basis for white antipathy. Yet they stood in the way of the advancing white frontier, and methods of removing them were found. The "legal" basis for their ultimate dispossession was a result of a cultural difference that remained between them and the European settlers—a difference in the idea of land ownership.

When the English colonists first arrived in the New World, they brought with them the recently developed Anglo-Saxon notion of private land ownership. Many of the white settlers had themselves been driven off land in the Old World during the eighteenth century as a result of the consolidation of communally held lands into large, single-owner estates. But, they still believed in the notion of permanent and exclusive ownership of land by individuals. In contrast, the Indians understood possession of the land as a matter of use rather than ownership. Since the New World seemed to contain plenty of land for all, the Indians originally greeted the white settlers hospitably. Yet, as the years passed and white settlers occupied more and more land, barring the Indians from their claims, the implications of exclusive ownership became clear, and hostilities followed.

In the nineteenth century, in the Southeast, the federal and state governments cooperated to convince Indian nations to divide communally owned lands among individual Indians, who were then persuaded, sometimes fraudulently, to sell their property to speculators. The growth of large-scale cotton culture in the Deep South was a major factor in the ultimate removal of the Indians from their home ground.

When this method failed to eliminate many of the southeastern Indians, the federal government took more direct action. According to Michael Paul Rogin, of the University of California at Berkeley, the author of the selection reprinted below, the dominant rationale for the government's policy was paternalistic. The federal government, with the president as "Great White Father," had to act in ways that would be beneficial to its red children (the Indians). Therefore, acting in the children's best interests, the fatherly authorities forceably removed them from danger. While Rogin's thesis has been criticized, his description of the removal process and the resistance some Indians offered to this strategy graphically portrays the genocidal results of the government's actions.

Of the five southern Indian tribes, only the Seminoles made a determined physical resistance to removal. In part, these several thousand Florida Indians shared grievances with other tribes that did not go to war. Their removal treaties, for example, were probably fraudulent. The first, signed in 1832 under dubious conditions, provided that several Seminole chiefs examine the proposed western country before removal was confirmed. It was not clear whether the chiefs alone or the tribe as a whole had the power to agree to removal. J. F. Schermerhorn, shortly to negotiate the Cherokee treaty of New Echota, accompanied the chiefs west; there they signed a removal treaty. Seminole bands in Florida protested against this treaty; Jackson and other government officials in Florida threatened to remove them forcibly if they did not abide by it. Florida Indian agent Wiley Thompson "rebuke[d] the Indian chiefs as if they were wrong-headed schoolboys" and stripped those who opposed removal of their titles. He

"Indian Removal." From *Fathers and Children: Andrew Jackson and the Subjugation of the American Indian* by Michael Paul Rogin, pp. 236–48. Copyright © 1975 by Michael Paul Rogin. Reprinted by permission of Alfred A. Knopf, Inc.

placed the influential warrior Osceola in irons for opposing removal, and released him only after Osceola and his followers signed an agreement to move west. "These children of the forest," General Clinch explained to Cass, "are from peculiar circumstances and long habits suspicious of the white man." But, continued Clinch, "the manly and straightforward course pursued toward them by Genl. Thompson appears to have gained their confidence." Thompson's intimate relationship with Osceola, alternating between protectiveness and punitiveness, typified relations which often developed between Indians and government agents. Osceola killed Thompson at the outbreak of the war.[1]

Like members of the other southern tribes, hungry Seminoles committed depredations in the 1830s. There was factional conflict among bands opposing and favoring removal, as well as conflict between Indians and whites. Late in 1835, after Osceola's band killed a chief who favored removal, federal troops marched against the tribe. The Seminoles ambushed a boat coming up the Apalachicola River, killing soldiers and their families, and the Second Seminole War had begun.[2]

Fraudulent treaties, government attacks on the tribal structure, and interracial and intratribal conflict were not peculiar to the Seminoles, and cannot by themselves account for the war. Two factors were unique to the tribe. The first was a history of hostility to and independence of American authority. Tribal villages had long enjoyed freedom under weak Spanish rule. Jackson invaded Seminole country in 1814 and 1818, and the tribe was augmented by the migrations of hostile Creeks to Florida at the end of the First Creek War. The Seminoles were moved to south central Florida in the 1820s. Then Jackson insisted, over the bitter protests of the tribe, that it would have to live under the authority of the Creeks in the west. Seminole independence always angered Jackson. He justified his Florida invasions in part on the grounds that the Seminoles were merely a division of the Creeks. He urged in 1821 that the Seminoles be sent back to the Creeks. They ought now to join, in Benton's words, "the mother tribe, in the west."

Actually there was severe conflict between the two tribes, particularly once the Seminoles were joined by red sticks who had fought on the losing side of the Creek civil war. Creeks fought with Jackson against the Seminoles in 1818. Jackson's removal plan was thus part of his continuing vendetta against the tribe. By August 1835 the Seminoles were

[1] [John K.] Mahon, [*History of the Second Seminole War, 1835–1942* (Gainesville, Fla., 1967)], pp. 74–79, 82–85, 89–99; Edwin C. McReynolds, *The Seminoles* (Norman, Okla., 1957), pp. 140–45; Representative Horace Everett, *Register of Debates*, X (1883–34), 4144–59; [Grant] Foreman, *Indian Removal* [(Norman, Okla., 1932)], pp. 321–23; Harris, "Abstract," Feb. 9, 1836, Thompson to Cass, Dec. 28, 1834, April 24, 1835, to General George Gibson, June 3, 1835, Harris to Thompson, May 20, 1835, Clinch to Cass, Aug. 24, 1835, Cass to Clinch, Oct. 22, 1835, to Thompson, Oct. 28, 1835, ASPMA [U.S. Congress, *American State Papers, Military Affairs*, 7 vols. (Washington, D.C., 1832–61)], VI, 60, 70, 73–76, 494, 552.

[2] Mahon, pp. 94–101; Everett, *Register of Debates,* X, 4154; Joseph W. Harris to Gibson, Dec. 30, 1835, ASPMA, VI, 561–63.

reconciled to removal if they could retain tribal independence in the west; the administration refused.[3]

The Seminoles had an additional reason to resist amalgamation with the Creeks. They feared the Creeks would appropriate the escaped slaves, free blacks, and Indian slaves who lived freely as part of the Seminole tribe. The Creeks demanded Seminole Negroes to obtain their share of $250,000 appropriated by Congress under an 1821 Creek treaty. This sum was to pay Georgia's claim for slaves stolen by the Creeks prior to 1802 and taken to Florida, and whatever offspring such slaves had produced. The War Department was sympathetic to the Creek claim, which was being pushed by the small group of western Creeks friendly to Georgia who had illegally ceded tribal land in Georgia and moved west. The removed Seminoles were to be placed under the authority of this Creek faction. The western Creeks sent a white lawyer into Seminole country to appropriate Negroes. He was to receive a share of the profits from his undertaking and sell slaves to white claimants and traders.[4]

The presence of these Seminole Negroes was the most important distinguishing feature of the tribe. Seminole Negroes had the greatest reason to fear removal. They were not only in danger from the Creeks; they also made the tribe a target of white slaveholders. The blacks feared, with good reason, that they would be seized by slave-catchers when the Seminoles gathered for removal. Southern speculators and Florida planters wanted to appropriate the Negroes before the tribe went west. Raiders had already attacked Indian reserves along the Apalachicola River and stolen Negroes belonging to Indian planters. Apalachicola Indians attempting to move west with their slaves were pursued by white claimants and stripped of property and Negroes.[5]

Jackson's protégé Richard Keith Call, a leading Florida politician and speculator, urged Jackson to grant permission to a group of speculators to purchase Negroes in Seminole country. Call explained, "If the Indians are permitted to convert them into specie, one great obstacle in the way of removal may be overcome." Jackson agreed, "directing the agent to see they obtain a fair price for them." Commissioner Harris explained

---

[3] Mahon, pp. 1–70; Mark F. Boyd, "The Seminole War: Its Background and Onset," *Florida Historical Quarterly*, XXX (July 1951), 52–53; Cass to Gibson, Jan. 30, 1832, Eaton to Cass, March 8, 1835, Clinch to Cass, April 24, 1835, Seminole council to Cass, Aug. 19, 1835, Jackson to Seminoles, Feb. 16, 1835, ASPMA, VI, 472, 492–95, 524; Jackson to Calhoun, Sept. 2, 1821, Sept. 17, 1821, "Treaty with the Florida Indians," Feb. 2, 826, ASPIA [U.S. Congress, *American State Papers, Indian Affairs*, 2 vols. (Washington, D.C., 1834)], II, 414, 614–44; Everett, *Register of Debates*, X, 4147–48; Senator Thomas Hart Benton, U.S. Congress, *The Congressional Globe*, VI (1837–38), Appendix, 353; McReynolds, pp. 83–84.

[4] Everett, *Register of Debates*, X, 4147–48; Representative Joshua Giddings, *Congressional Globe*, IX (1840–41), Appendix, 347; "Causes of Hostilities of the Creek and Seminole Indians in Florida," ASPMA, VI, 450–71.

[5] Kenneth Wiggins Porter, "Negroes and the Seminole War 1835–1842," *Journal of Southern History*, XXX (Nov. 1964), 427–31; Boyd, p. 37; McReynolds, pp. 133–34; Giddings, *Congressional Globe*, IX (1840–41), Appendix, 348; Thompson to William P. Duval, Jan. 20, 1834, ASPMA, VI, 451–52.

to objecting Florida Indian agent Wiley Thompson that "their resources will be augmented, and they will not, upon their arrival west, have in their possession a species of property which . . . would excite the cupidity of the Creeks, and be wrested from them by their superior numbers and strength." True, the Negroes would be enslaved, wrote Harris, but "it is not to be presumed the condition of these slaves will be worse than that of others in the same section of the country." Thompson, however, objected that the change in the Negroes' condition would be "oppressively great," that no Indians wanted to sell Negroes, that speculators would use improper means to obtain them, and that the entrance of white slave-dealers would retard rather than further removal. Jackson retracted his permission, but it was too late to reassure the blacks.[6]

Seminole Negroes, their freedom endangered, prepared to resist removal. They received covert support from Florida free blacks and slaves, who helped supply ammunition for the tribe. Seminoles attacked Florida plantations at the outset of the war, and threatened St. Augustine in south central Florida. Some field slaves joined the uprising. General Philip Jesup, assuming command of the American troops, wrote the Secretary of War, "This, you may be assured, is a negro, not an Indian war; and if it be not speedily put down, the south will feel the effects of it on their slave population." Benton, obliquely recognizing the importance of slavery, blamed the war on the abolitionists.[7]

The administration, meeting the wishes of Florida planters, insisted it would not end the war on terms permitting Seminole Negroes to go west. Cass ordered General Winfield Scott at the outbreak of the war to "allow no terms to the Indians until every living slave in their possession, belonging to a white man, is given up." Decades-old white claims were recognized, including title to the then unborn children of escaped or captured slaves. Indians, moreover, rarely had proof they owned slaves they had actually purchased. Cass' order thus endangered the freedom of most Seminole Negroes, not merely of slaves who had escaped once the war began. To underline its interest in the Negroes, the War Department enlisted Creek warriors against the Seminoles, promising them that a bounty for captured Negroes would be paid from the Seminole annuity.[8]

General Jesup negotiated an end to the war in March 1837 which permitted Seminole Negroes to go west. Under Florida pressure, he reneged. He signed a secret agreement with some Seminole chiefs in which

[6] Richard K. Call to Jackson, March 22, 1835, Thompson to Harris, April 27, 1835, June 17, 1835, Harris to Thompson, May 22, 1835, Jackson endorsement on Thompson to Harris, June 6, 1835, ASPMA, VI, 464, 480–81, 512, 533, 478; Herring to Call, March 26, 1835, Harris to Thompson, July 11, 1835, OIALS [Office of Indian Affairs, Letters Sent]; McReynolds, pp. 150–52.

[7] Porter, pp. 433–34; Mahon, pp. 101–03; Jesup to Secretary of War Benjamin F. Butler, Dec. 9, 1836, ASPMA, VII, 821; Senator Thomas Hart Benton, *Register of Debates*, XII (1835–36), 821.

[8] R. Jones to Cass, Feb. 9, 1836, Cass to General Winfield Scott, Jan. 21, 1836, Jesup to Butler, Feb. 17, 1837, to Jones, March 26, 1837, to Secretary of War Joel R. Poinsett, Sept. 22, 1837, ASPMA, VI, 57–58, 62, VII, 832, 834, 882; McReynolds, pp. 185–86; Porter, pp. 438–39; Mahon, pp. 200–04.

they agreed to turn Negroes over to white claimants. He reversed an order prohibiting slave-catchers from entering Seminole country and appropriating blacks who had gathered in camps to await removal. Negroes and Indians fled these camps, and the war continued.[9]

Many Seminole Negroes and slaves who had joined the war were dead or captured by 1837. Most of the rest responded to Jesup's renewed promise they could go west in safety. But the lawyer for the Creeks and other slave-traders tried, with administration support, to capture and sell these Negroes. Secretary of War Joel Poinsett and Commissioner of Indian Affairs C. A. Harris sought to obtain the Negroes for speculators in Creek lands. James C. Watson, a leading participant in the Creek land frauds, took Poinsett's advice and made large purchases of claims on the Seminole Negroes. Watson's brother-in-law followed the Negroes west, but the army, to Harris' dismay, thwarted his efforts to appropriate them. Finally, in 1841, the new administration determined that the 1832 Seminole treaty settled all white claims on Seminole Negroes originating prior to 1832.[10]

The august *Niles' Register* hoped, at the outbreak of the Second Seminole War, "that the miserable creatures will be speedily swept from the face of the earth." But the tribe scored early victories over American troops and forced whites to abandon most of the territory south of St. Augustine. The American army was plagued throughout 1836 by disease, insufficient numbers, rivalry among its commanders, difficulties in supplying troops in the Florida interior, and a tropical terrain uniquely suited to Indian guerrilla warfare. Jackson had faced all these problems but the last in the Creek War and overcome them. Now he gave Call, whom he looked upon as a son, an opportunity to do the same. Call had no more luck than his predecessors. He ran out of supplies, was forced to retreat, and was then incapacitated by ill health. Jackson had triumphed over these adversities; Call was dismissed in an angry letter.[11]

There were enough troops in Florida, Jackson insisted, "as might eat Powell [Osceola] and his few." Army failures made the conflict "a disgraceful war to the american character," Jackson wrote after he left office. As the war dragged on, he resorted to the language and proposals of his own earlier Florida campaigns. He complained that General Scott's "combined operations, without knowing where the Indian women were, was like a combined operation to encompass a wolf in the hamocks without knowing first where her den and whelps were." To the Secretary of War he suggested search-and-destroy missions against hidden Indian villages. American commanders should have found "where their women are" and "captured or destroyed them."[12]

[9] Porter, pp. 438–39; Mahon, pp. 202–04.

[10] Porter, pp. 445–47; Mahon, pp. 205–06, 251–52; McReynolds, pp. 211–12; Harris to Nathaniel Collins, May 9, 1838, to George C. Reynolds, July 6, 1838, OIALS.

[11] Mahon, pp. 122, 135–93; Butler to Call, Nov. 4, 1836, ASPMA, VI, 992. . . .

[12] Jackson to James Gadsden, Nov. 1836, to Poinsett, Dec. 13, 1837, Oct. 1, 1837, "Memorandum," April 1837, AJC [John Spencer Bassett, ed., Correspondence of Andrew Jackson, 6 vols. (Washington, D.C., 1926–33)], V, 434, 521–22, 512–13, 468.

Seminole resistance did not merely provoke such proposals from Jackson. It led General Jesup and his successors to violate flags of truce, capture Indians invited to negotiate, hold them as hostages, threaten them with execution if they did not bring in their followers, employ blood-hounds against the tribe, and kill cattle that American troops did not need in order to deprive the Indians of food. The barbarous treachery of the Seminoles justified these measures, Jackson and Benton insisted. In Benton's words, "A bit of white linen, stripped, perhaps, from the body of a murdered child, or its murdered mother, was no longer to cover the insidious visits of spies and enemies. A firm and manly course was taken."[13]

Jesup captured the majority of the tribe by 1838; the remaining Indians fought bitterly for four more years. They raided white settlements for food and supplies, but promised to stop fighting if they could stay in Florida. In 1842, their ranks further reduced by death and capture, the few hundred remaining Seminoles were permitted to do so.

Violent rage marked Jackson's pre-presidential Indian relations; it surfaced again among Jacksonians during the Indian wars of the 1830s. War and primitive verbal violence were not typical, however, of Jackson's presidential Indian policy. The vast majority of Indians were removed without war. The administration met their intensified, prolonged suffering with a steady impoverishment of affect.

The southern tribes experienced intense hardships in their original homes after 1828, but the long journeys west were worst of all. Tens of thousands were clothed inadequately and marched through freezing south-western winters. Those who made the trip in the summer suffered from extreme heat and drought. Indians were fed inadequate and contaminated rations, including rancid meat, spoiled flour, and bad drinking water. In some cases food offered them was years old and had already been declared unfit to eat. They were crowded together on old, unseaworthy boats—the worst single accident killed 311 Creeks—and separated from their remaining possessions by emigrating agents, local citizens, and sheriffs prosecuting alleged debt claims. They traveled through areas in which cholera was raging. Weakened by the exhausting journey and bad food, tens of thousands caught fevers, measles, and cholera; thousands died from disease and exposure on the removal journeys alone. War, disease, accident, starvation, depredations, murder, whiskey, and other causes of death from the extension of state laws through removal and resettlement had killed by 1844 one-quarter to one-third of the southern Indians.[14]

The insistence on removal and the deadlines enforced on the tribes insured much of this suffering. Government methods also made matters worse. Contractors hired to provision Indians made money at their expense. They increased their profits by supplying bad food and unsafe

[13] Mahon, pp. 205–311; Jackson to Poinsett, Aug. 27, 1837, AJC, V, 506–08; Benton, *Congressional Globe*, VI, Appendix, 353–56.

[14] [James] Mooney, ["Myths of the Cherokees," *Bureau of American Ethnology, Annual Report*, XIX (1897–98), Part I], pp. 131–32; Foreman, *Indian Removal*, pp. 44–104, 152–90, 253–63, 273–312. . . .

boats. Jackson assigned the entire responsibility for Creek removal to contractors. In Cass' words, "The President, on full consideration, has determined to make an experiment to remove the Creek Indians by contract." The contractors would be paid $20 per head for the number of Indians they emigrated. Cass hired the very speculators who had defrauded the Creeks, and who now saw an opportunity to make more money off the tribe. These men desired removal, Cass apparently reasoned, and they would have the incentive to accomplish it.

The Creeks objected from the outset to removal by the speculators. Cass told Hogan not to "yield to the idle whims of the Indians, and indulge them in unnecessary preferences, which amount in fact merely to a wish that certain individuals, rather than others, should be concerned in their removal." Jackson had once sworn that "a pure government" would "make no concession" to "such men," but a contractual relationship was not a concession. Contracts, in a liberal society, created reciprocal obligations. Contractors had been paid to take responsibility for removal off the shoulders of the government.[15]

The army also played a role in removal. The contractors were retained after the Second Creek War broke out, but they were joined by the army. It identified 2,500 Creeks as hostile, and removed the warriors among them in chains. Soldiers scouted Cherokee country to round up Creeks who had fled there during the war; they also collected longtime Creek residents among the Cherokees, married or otherwise connected to that tribe.[16]

Two years later, in the spring of 1838, the army rounded up 15,000 Cherokees who had refused to remove in the time allotted under the New Echota treaty. They were seized as they worked in their farms and fields, separated from their possessions, and taken to military detention camps. They remained in captivity for months while hundreds died from inadequate and unaccustomed rations. The debilitation of others contributed to deaths during the removal march.

Eaton had promised during the debates on the Indian-removal bill, "Nothing of a compulsory nature to effect the removal of this unfortunate race of people has ever been thought of by the President, although it has been so asserted." The treaty of New Echota, the government now

---

[15] Cass to Hogan, Feb. 24, 1836, Sanford to Hogan, April 3, 1835, Hogan to Gibson, Nov. 6, 1835, ASPMA, VI, 779, 738, 745–46; Harris to Page, Jan. 24, 1837, April 26, 1837, to J. C. Watson, May 8, 1837, OIALS. Sanford was subsequently appointed Indian agent for the Creeks in the west. (Cf. Harris to Sanford, March 15, 1837, OIALS.)

Indian removal by contract is reminiscent of the late-eighteenth-century vendue method of caring for dependent children. Child paupers were sold to the lowest bidders at public auctions; the townships paid the bidders to maintain the children. Cf. Susan Grinel, "The Development of Child Welfare Institutions," unpublished paper, University of California at Berkeley, 1972, pp. 27–29.

[16] Foreman, *Indian Removal*, pp. 152–53; Harris to Page, Dec. 22, 1836, OIALS. This operation was suspended a year later. Harris to Lieutenant Edward Deas, Oct. 14, 1837, OIALS.

claimed, had committed the tribe; if Indians were not mature enough to fulfill their promises, the government would have to force them.[17]

Creek removal combined military with market pressures. Emigration was stalled after the Creek War; county officials arrested many principal men of the tribe for alleged debts, in an effort to strip the Creeks of their remaining possessions. The Creeks asked the government for an advance payment of their 1837 annuity to pay these debts. General Jesup, who had put down the Creek uprising and was on his way to Florida, insisted that to obtain the annuity several hundred Creek warriors would have to fight the Seminoles. Their families, sent west without them, were deprived of their help during removal and resettlement.[18]

Another group of several hundred Creek warriors was recruited to fight voluntarily in Florida. The government wished to avoid "sacrificing our own troops to the unhealthful climate in the sickly season of the year." It detained the warriors' families in Alabama camps and promised to feed and protect them. General Jesup kept these Creek warriors, over their objections, several months past the expiration of their terms of enlistment. He explained that he would otherwise have incurred the expense of hiring militia. But Georgia and Alabama wanted the Indians out of the south. Companies of county militia invaded the Indian camps, stole stock and possessions, raped women, manhandled and mistreated the Indians in other ways, and insisted they be removed from Alabama. Commissioner Harris responded to reports of these events by initiating the removal of the Indians. The government, "guardian and protector" of the Indians, was required by "the change in the state of things" to transport them west immediately. The Creek warriors were finally permitted to leave Florida, discharged, as Secretary of War Poinsett explained to Congress, because of the expense of maintaining their families.[19]

The War Department, violating its original agreement with the Creeks, did not wait for the warriors' return before removing their families. It gathered them at Pass Christian, near Mobile, where disease, exposure, and starvation claimed 177 deaths in the party of 3,500 between March 7 and July 31, 1837. Harris regretted this suffering "as sincerely as any man can," but doubted that "anything further can be done by

---

[17] Foreman, *Indian Removal*, pp. 276–90; Mooney, pp. 131–32; [Lewis] Cass, "Removal [of the Indians," *North American Review*, XXXI (Jan. 1830)], p. 120.

[18] Foreman, *Indian Removal*, pp. 161–62; Cass to Jesup, July 11, 1836, ASPMA, VI, 1047.

[19] Foreman, *Indian Removal*, pp. 180–83; Cass to Hogan, April 12, 1836, Poinsett to Jesup, March 27, 1837, Harris to Page, Feb. 17, 1837, OIALS; Jesup to Poinsett, April 11, 1837, George C. Reynolds to Major Wilson, March 31, 1837, Lieutenant T. J. Sloan to [unknown], March 31, 1837, Joel S. Poinsett, "Annual Report of the Secretary of War," Dec. 5, 1837, ASPMA, VII, 867–70, 572. The Commissioner of Indian Affairs wanted to make sure that none of the hostile Creeks still loose in Alabama would benefit from the arrangements made for the friendly Creeks. Any Creeks outside the detention camps, he instructed the army officers in Alabama, should be treated as hostiles; the government sent the friendly Creeks out to hunt them down. Cf. Harris to Page, Jan. 30, 1837, OIALS.

this office." In fact that same day he did do something further. He was concerned that the contractors would demand more money to transport Creek possessions. Creeks "had collected a much larger amount of baggage than the company, by their contract, are bound to transport," he wrote, and "the Indians are unwilling to dispose of any part of it, or to leave any part behind." He ordered the emigrating officer not to transport any "evidentally superfluous" possessions purchased from "whim or caprice," and to prevent any such purchases in the future.[20]

The worse the Indian suffering and death, as Creek removal suggests, the more disassociated the reaction of Washington officials. Indian Office records reveal monumental concern for the details of organizing removal, and monumental indifference to the suffering and death it caused. Overriding all other matters was concern for the costs of removal. Reports of suffering and death were met with demands for economy.

The Choctaws were the first tribe to be removed; the disorganized, disease-ridden removal of the first group of Choctaws, with its share of deaths, foreshadowed the fate of the other southern Indians. The War Department, however, was most concerned because the costs of removal far exceeded government expectations. The government reorganized removal, fed the Indians more cheaply and with spoiled food, forced them to walk rather than ride, reduced its costs, and increased the number of Indian dead.[21]

Creek removal caused the deaths of thousands of Indians, but that was not the government's concern. One of the Columbus speculators who had emigrated the Creeks wanted the contract to emigrate the Cherokees. Commissioner Harris listed the considerations which should govern the award, "1st, economy—2nd, the comfort, safety, and accommodation of the Emigrants, and 3rd the moral influence which the measure will probably have upon the Cherokees." Van Buren finally permitted "Ross and the others," "viewed in the light of contracters," to organize their own removal, although Jackson protested from the Hermitage that the "contract" was much too "extravagant." By the time the superintendent of Creek removal was ordered to close up Cherokee emigration, thousands of Creeks and Cherokees had died on the journey west. Commissioner Crawford's instructions made no references to these deaths. He insisted instead that the emigrating agent "avoid the loose and irregular manner of transacting business which occurred in the Creek removal." He sought to stop General Nathaniel Smith from feeding and clothing Cherokees who had escaped the military roundup and remained in the North Carolina mountains.[22]

[20] Foreman, *Indian Removal*, pp. 184–87; Harris to Hogan, Aug. 5, 1837, to Page, Aug. 5, 1837, OIALS.

[21] [Arthur H.] DeRosier, Jr., [*The Removal of the Choctaw Indians* (Knoxville, Tenn., 1970)], pp. 148–62.

[22] Harris to General Nathaniel Smith, April 26, 1838, to Deas, Sept. 21, 1837, to Smith, Sept. 5, 1838, Crawford to Page, Nov. 14, 1838, OIALS; Jackson to Felix Grundy, Aug. 23, 1838, *American Historical Magazine and Tennessee Historical Society Quarterly*, V (April 1900), 140; Crawford to Smith, Jan. 17, 1839, Feb. 11, 1839, OIALS.

As Indians died, the government demanded "economy" and sought to correct "the loose and irregular manner of transacting business." It sought, in Call's words, "to convert them into specie." It offered money for homes, money for land, and money incentives for removal. When Hogan exposed the Creek frauds, speculators were sure it was only because they had not found his price. Georgia insisted that Ross refused to sign a removal treaty because the government would not bribe him. Whites consistently converted what Van Buren called the "debt we owe to this unhappy race" into money.[23]

Dying Indians betrayed whites. They threatened to force them to encounter the consequences of their own policies and desires. To quote John Ross again, "the perpetrator of a wrong never forgives his victims." Whites responded to Indian deaths by deadening their own experience. Indians were turned into things—a small reserve remaining in Ohio after removal was a "blank spot," "a mote in the eye of the state"—and could be manipulated and rearranged at will. Money was the perfect representation of dead, interchangeable matter. It could not symbolize human suffering and human reproach. A money equivalent could be found for Indian attachments; they had no intrinsic, unexchangeable value. Indian love would give way to money; it could be bought. The "debt we owe to this unhappy race," converted into specie, could be paid.[24]

Indians, children of nature, had an uncontrolled instinctual life. It caused them, in the white view, first to kill and then to die. Indians lived in a relationship of basic trust with nature, but that relationship did not help them survive. Indians dead and suffering were out of control; demands for economy expressed anxiety about the loss of control in an area in which administrators could more safely experience it. Money, the solid product of self-reliance, replaced unreliable nature. Bureaucratic removal offered an enclosed realm, divorced from the human, natural world. Interchangeable entries on bureaucratic ledgers, Indians were not particular, specific, humans whose suffering could be pitied. The government would not save Indians; it would try to save money.[25]

Money, debt, and control were pervasive themes in Jacksonian democracy. . . . We turn now from defenses against death within the bureaucratic structure to the return of death in the world. Death cast its shadow over the entire removal experience; it deeply affected perceptions of the westward journey itself.

Savagery, proponents of Indian removal claimed, could maintain itself only by fleeing westward. Providence decreed that "the hunting tribes must retreat before the advance of civilization, or perish under the shade

---

23 Sanford and Co. to Gibson, May 14, 1836, ASPMA, VI, 763; Lumpkin to Jackson, May 20, 1835, AJC, V, 350; Representative George Towns, *Congressional Globe*, VI (1837–38), 366. Call and Van Buren are first quoted above, pp. 4 and 237.

24 Senator William Allen, *Congressional Globe*, XI (1841–42), Appendix, 688. Cf. Joel Kovel, *White Racism: A Psychohistory* (N.Y., 1970), pp. 110–17, 164–65.

25 On the petrification of experience, cf. [R. D.] Laing, [*The*] *Divided Self* [(Middlesex, Eng., 1965)], pp. 46–52, 112–13.

of the white man's settlements." "Mature consideration," said Jackson in his Seventh Annual Message, revealed that Indians "can not live in contact with a civilized community and prosper." White settlers would be excluded from the western lands; if the tribes chose to remain uncivilized, "they are upon the skirts of the great prairies" and could hunt the buffalo which roamed there. Entirely extruded from civilization, primitive experience could maintain itself. Alleged tribal willingness to go west had indicated to some writers that childhood would not resist maturity. "They are on the outside of us, and in a place which will ever remain on the outside," the Senate Committee on Indian Affairs declared as Indian removal came to an end.[26]

But politicians who argued that isolating the savages would protect them also called for the march of civilization across the continent. Jefferson proposed the northern Louisiana territory as a home for the eastern tribes; at the same time he forsaw Indians retreating westward to the Pacific as the tide of white civilization advanced. "When we shall be full on this side [of the Mississippi]," he wrote, "we may lay off a range of States on the western bank from the head to the mouth and so, range after range, advancing compactly as we multiply." Cherokee agent R. J. Meigs, an early advocate of removal, explained,

> A disposition to migrate seems to pervade the whole eastern part of the United States; we invite that emigration here; obstacles ought to be removed. The tendency is as uniform as the law of gravitation. It can no more be restrained *until the shores of the Pacfic Ocean make it impossible to go further.*

One Cherokee, said Meigs, suggested that land given the Indians not be bounded on the west. The Indians could then continue westward; they could flee, as the post Civil War chromolithograph *American Progress* . . . would picture it, before the advancing whites.[27] Temporarily the west would place Indians "far beyond the reach of the oppression—and, I was about to say, the example of the white man."[28] Permanently, only death would. Savage integrity could ultimately maintain itself only in death.

Childhood experience could not be integrated into adult life; living it

---

[26] Joel R. Poinsett, quoted in Arthur A. Ekirch, *The Idea of Progress in America, 1815–1860* (N.Y., 1944), pp. 43–44; Andrew Jackson, "Seventh Annual Message," Dec. 7, 1835, [in James D.] Richardson, [ed., *Messages and Papers of the Presidents* (N.Y., 1917)] III, 171–72; [Mary E.] Young, [*Redskins, Ruffleshirts, and Rednecks* (Norman, Okla., 1961)], pp. 47–51; Roy Harvey Pearce, *Savagism and Civilization* (Baltimore, Md., 1965 [first published as *The Savages of America;* Baltimore, Md., 1953]), pp. 173–74; A. Grenfell Price, *White Settlers and Native Peoples* (Melbourne, Aust., 1949), p. 16.

[27] DeRosier, p. 27; A. W. Putnam, *History of Middle Tennessee* (Nashville, Tenn., 1859), pp. 589–90; R. J. Meigs to Secretary of War William Crawford, Nov. 8, 1816, ASPIA, II, 115.

[28] Tennessee Representative John Bell, quoted by Representative Henry Storrs, *Register of Debates*, VI (1829–30), 994.

served as a reminder of what had been lost and rejected in the process of growing up. American nostalgia for childhood and the past reflected the failure of revered ideals actually to guide behavior, and the longing for what one's desires had killed. Like the dead twins in the frontier Tennessee poem, only dead Indians could safely be mourned. The white father was not merely helpless to prevent death; he identified with it, longed for it, and carried it out.

Indian removal carried out violence against symbolic childhood. The fantasies of its perpetrators also expressed longings for death itself. Americans wedded to competitive advancement in the world shared an arcadian dream life. The rural home would release them from worldly cares and return them to a state of primitive security. Such longings, however, did not protect whites from mobility "to better their condition," as Jackson put it, any more than they protected Indians. Jackson had longed to retire to his Hermitage refuge for thirty-five years. The heavenly father's eternal home offered the only permanent rest.

Removal promised the Indians, in Cass' words, "the probability of an adequate and final reward." It would transport them—the words are Jackson's on the death of John Coffee's mother—to "happier climes than these." Death was the western tribal utopia. Géza Róheim writes,

> [I]n the other world we have the land of wish fulfillment, the place where our infantile omnipotence of thoughts reigns supreme, and where we can be rid of all the pain and trouble that is inherent in the environment[.] The paradise once familiar to us all in our infancy, we have learned through bitter experience cannot exist in this world. Hence we use its shattered material to rebuild it at the very moment when we stand in greatest need of consolation, at the moment of death.[29]

Indians, the removal ideology asserted, were plagued by competitive forces which they and the government were powerless to resist. Removed Indians would benefit from "paternal care and guardianship." Their land would be "forever secured and guaranteed to them." "If a paternal authority is exercised over the aboriginal colonies" west of the Mississippi, wrote Cass, "we may hope so see that improvement in their conditions for which we have so long and vainly labored."[30]

A benevolent father would have total power in the west; he could free Indians from violent and competitive relations with their white brothers, and protect his red children. Jackson tried to convince the

---

[29] Cass, "Annual Report of the Secretary of War," Nov. 21, 1831, ASPMA, IV, 714; Jackson to Coffee, Feb. 28, 1804, AJC, I, 82–83; Géza Róheim, *The Panic of the Gods* (N.Y., 1972), p. 161. For European traditions which viewed the west as a land of eternal life and happiness, of apocalypse and the end of history, and their influence in America, cf. Loren Baritz, "The Idea of the West," *American Historical Review*, LXVI (Dec. 1961), 618–41.

[30] Benjamin F. Butler, "Annual Report of the Secretary of War," Dec. 3, 1836, ASPMA, VI, 814; Jackson, "Seventh Annual Message," Richardson, III, 171–72; Cass, "Removal," p. 121.

Creeks of this in the message he sent them three days after his inauguration. He told the tribe, "Your bad men have made my heart sicken, and bleed by the murder of one of my white children in Georgia. Our peaceful mother earth has been stained by the blood of the white man, and calls for the punishment of his murderers." In the west such conflicts would not arise. "Where you are now your white brothers have always claimed the land. The land beyond the Mississippi belongs to the President, and to none else; and he will give it to you forever. . . . You will be subject to your own laws, and the care of your father, the President." Jackson returned to the theme of refuge in his Farewell Address. "The philanthropist will rejoice," he said, "that the remnant of that ill fated race has at length been placed beyond the reach of injury and oppression, and that the paternal care of the General Government will hereafter watch over them and protect them."[31]

The Creeks recognized the utopian character of these promises. As early as the 1820s whites west of the Mississippi had successfully demanded land promised the southern Indians. One Creek delegation pointed out to Jackson that Alabama had recently been a remote frontier territory inhabited, like the western land offered the tribe, by Indians protected by the United States. Now whites were not only crowding Alabama Indians; they were also moving into the western territory. Their great father Jackson, they said, might protect them for a time, but he was old and a successor might not be bound by his promises.[32]

Jackson was old indeed. He suffered, as he said in his Farewell Address just before turning to the Indian question, from "advanced age and a broken frame." His promises of western utopia resembled his thoughts of death. Overton had gone beyond the reach of injury and oppression too, where his enemies could no longer hurt him. Emily Donelson also had an adequate and final reward; "she has changed a world of woe, for a world of eternal happiness." Elisabeth Coffee "has gone to the realms of bliss free from all the troubles of this wicked world." The old man, benignly surveying the destruction of the children of nature, was reconciling himself to death.[33]

Indian deaths transcended individual will and merged with the providential movement of history. America had begun with a radical assertion of the power of men to control their fate. But the country progressed through the destruction of another set of men, and responsibility for that destruction could not be faced. "The extinction of the Indians," wrote Cass, "has taken place by the unavoidable operation of natural causes, and as the natural consequences of the vicinity of white settlements." White men were placed by "Providence" on the "skirts of a boundless forest."

[31] Jackson to Creeks, March 23, 1829, OIALS; Jackson, "Farewell Address," March 4, 1837, Richardson, III, 294.

[32] Creeks to Jackson, June 13, 1835, OIA Creek file.

[33] Jackson, "Farewell Address," Richardson, III, 293; Jackson to Lewis, April 29, 1833, LP [The W. B. Lewis Papers, New York Public Library, New York]; Jackson to Andrew J. Donelson, Dec. 31, 1836, to Andrew Jackson Hutchings, Jan. 26, 1838, AJC, V, 442–43, 533.

Subduing it by industry, they advanced and multiplied by providential decree. They had superiority in arts, arms, and intelligence. How, then, could whites be blamed for the Indian plight? "Their misfortunes have been the consequence of a state of things which could not be controlled by them or us." Cass drew practical lessons from his theory of history. If the Creeks chose to stay in Alabama and "finally melt away before our people and institutions, the result must be attributed to causes, which we can neither stay nor control."[34]

As southern Indians actually began to die in large numbers, policy-makers denied not simply responsibility but reality itself. The worse the events, the less they could be admitted into consciousness. During the last large-scale Indian removal, 4,500 Cherokees died. President Van Buren and Secretary of War Poinsett ignored the deaths. They congratulated themselves instead that removal was at an end, and that they had finally permitted Chief Ross to lead the bulk of his tribe west. As Poinsett described the process,

> The generous and enlightened policy . . . was ably and judiciously carried into effect by the General appointed. . . . The reluctance of the Indians to relinquish the land of their birth . . . was entirely overcome. . . . Humanity, no less than sound policy, dictated this course toward these children of the forest.

The Commissioner of Indian Affairs amplified:

> A retrospect of the last eight months, in reference to this numerous and more than ordinarily enlightened tribe, cannot fail to be refreshing to well-constituted minds. . . . A large mass of men have been conciliated, the hazard of an effusion of blood has been put by, good feeling has been preserved, and we have quietly and gently transported 18,000 friends to the west bank of the Mississippi.

In Van Buren's words, "The wise, humane, and undeviating policy of the government in this the most difficult of all our relations foreign or domestic, has at length been justified to the world in its near approach to a happy and certain consummation."[35]

Instead of facing actual deaths, white policy-makers imagined Indian destruction as an abstracted and generalized process removed from human control and human reality. To face responsibility for specific killing might have led to efforts to stop it; avoiding individual deaths turned Indian removal into a theory of genocide. In Jackson's words,

---

[34] [Lewis] Cass, "On the State of the Indians," [*North American Review*, XVI (Jan. 1823)], p. 34; Cass, "Removal," pp. 107, 120–21.

[35] Foreman, *Indian Removal*, p. 312n; Joel R. Poinsett, "Annual Report of the Secretary of War," Nov. 28, 1838, T. H. Crawford, "Annual Report of the Commissioner of Indian Affairs," Nov. 25, 1838, U.S. Serial Set, *Executive Documents*, CCCXLIV, 101, 412; President Martin Van Buren, "Second Annual Message," Dec. 3, 1838, Richardson, III, 497.

Humanity has often wept over the fate of the aborigines of this
country, and Philanthropy has been busily engaged in devising
means to avert it, but its progress has never for a moment been
arrested, and one by one have many powerful tribes disappeared
from the earth. To follow to the land the last of his race and to
tread on the graves of extinct nations excites melancholy reflections.
But true philanthropy reconciles the mind to these vicissitudes, as
it does to the extinction of one generation to make room for another.[36]

Weeping over Indian deaths was immature. History rescued a man
from melancholy; he could tread on Indian graves in peace. "Independance
of mind and action," to recall Jackson's advice to his nephew, could not
be borne. Instead a man like Jackson had to justify himself as a "real tool
in the hands of" "his creator," "wielded, like a mere attamaton, sometimes, without knowing it, to the worst of purposes."[37] To be a man
meant to participate, separated from the actual experience, in a genocide.

[36] Jackson, "Second Annual Message," Richardson, II, 520–21.
[37] Jackson to Andrew Jackson Donelson, Nov. 21, 1819, AJC, II, 441. . . .

Suggestions for Further Reading

The development of working-class life in American cities is described in Gary B. Nash, *The Urban Crucible: Social Change, Political Consciousness, and the Origins of the American Revolution* (Harvard University Press, 1979). Continuing studies of Philadelphia workers are Allen F. Davis and Mark H. Haller (eds.), *The Peoples of Philadelphia: Ethnic Groups and Lower-Class Life, 1790–1940** (Temple University Press, 1973) and Bruce Laurie, *Working People of Philadelphia, 1800–1850* (Temple University Press, 1980). For a history of crime and punishment in the United States, see Samuel E. Walker, *Popular Justice: A History of American Criminal Justice** (Oxford University Press, 1980).

An exhaustive survey of American religion is found in Sidney E. Ahlstrom, *A Religious History of the American People** (Yale University Press, 1972). Revivalism in American life is analyzed by William G. McLoughlin in *Revivals, Awakenings, and Reform: An Essay on Religion and Social Change in America** (University of Chicago Press, 1978). The Second Great Awakening in the South is dealt with in John B. Boles, *The Great Revival, 1787–1805: The Origins of the Southern Evangelical Mind* (University of Kentucky Press, 1972) and Dickson D. Bruce, *And They All Sang Hallelujah: Plain-Folk Camp-Meeting Religion, 1800–1845* (University of Tennessee Press, 1974). Richard Carwardine places the revival in comparative perspective in *Trans-Atlantic Revivalism: Popular Evangelism in Britain and America, 1790–1865* (Greenwood Press, 1978). An important older study of the Northern revival is by Timothy L. Smith, *Revivalism and Social Reform** (Harper and Row, 1957).

A magnificent collection of primary sources is gathered in Robert H. Bremner, *et al.* (eds.), *Children and Youth in America: A Documentary History** (2 vols.; Harvard University Press, 1970–71). Three surveys of juvenile delinquency are Anthony M. Platt, *The Child Savers: The Invention of Delinquency** (University of Chicago Press, 1969); Robert M. Mennel, *Thorns and Thistles: Juvenile Delinquents in the United States, 1825–1940* (University Press of New England, 1973); and Stephen L. Schlossman, *Love and the American Delinquent: The Theory and Practice of "Progressive" Juvenile Justice, 1825–1920* (University of Chicago Press, 1977). For the background of poverty, see Raymond A. Mohl, *Poverty in New York, 1783–1825* (Oxford University Press, 1971). The development of a variety of institutions during this period is described in David J. Rothman, *The Discovery of the Asylum** (Little, Brown, 1971).

For the Indian policy of the federal government in the early years of the new nation, see Reginald Horsman, *Expansion and American Indian Policy, 1783–1812* (Michigan State University

---

* Available in paperback edition.

Press, 1967) and F. P. Prucha, *American Indian Policy in the Formative Years** (Harvard University Press, 1962). A special study of Indians during the revolutionary era is by Barbara Graymont, *The Iroquois in the American Revolution** (Syracuse University Press, 1972). Attempts at acculturation are described in Robert F. Berkhofer, Jr., *Salvation and the Savage: An Analysis of Protestant Missions and American Indian Response 1787–1862** (Atheneum, 1972).

The literature on Indian removal from the Southeast is voluminous. Good starting points are Dale Van Every's *Disinherited: The Lost Birthright of the American Indian** (Morrow, 1966) and the collection of documents edited by Louis Filler and Allan Guttman, *Removal of the Cherokee Nation: Manifest Destiny or National Dishonor** (Heath, 1962). Robert S. Cotterill discusses the life of the Indians before their dispossession in *The Southern Indians: The Story of the Civilized Tribes Before Removal* (University of Oklahoma Press, 1954). Grant Foreman tells the sad tale of removal in *Indian Removal: The Emigration of the Five Civilized Tribes of Indians** (2d ed.: University of Oklahoma Press, 1953). Angie Debo takes a close look at two of the Five Civilized Tribes in *The Road to Disappearance: A History of the Creek Indians* (University of Oklahoma Press, 1941) and *The Rise and Fall of the Choctaw Republic** (University of Oklahoma Press, 1961). See also Michael Rogin, *Fathers and Children: Andrew Jackson and the Subjugation of the American Indian** (Knopf, 1975).

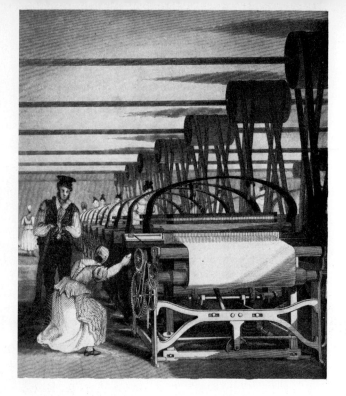

3
The Ante-Bellum
North and South

Rioting

in Its

Jacksonian Setting

DAVID GRIMSTED

From the Stamp Act revolts of 1765 to the ghetto uprisings of the
1960s, mob violence has been a powerful influence in American history. Although the specific intent of the mobs has varied, the process
by which they formed has tended to be much the same, and the
uprisings have generally had certain characteristics in common.

First, mobs rarely see the purpose of their action as illegal, although on occasion they see it as supralegal—that is, as carrying the
enforcement of the law beyond its stated limits. A lynch mob, for
example, may be unwilling to wait for or to trust the court system to
reach what they consider a just verdict; thus the mob may see itself
as the executor of proper justice. Similarly, the vigilante groups that
administered dubious justice in the old West joined together in posses
allegedly to enforce the law.

Generally, mobs tend to rally around some real or imagined
grievance that they have reason to believe the recognized authorities
will not deal with properly. This is especially apt to be the situation
when the ultimate authorities are far away or unsympathetic to local
conditions, as in Colonial America, the old West, or the pre–Civil War
South; when authorities are nearby and repressive, as in urban
ghettoes; or when local authorities side with citizen groups in opposition to higher authorities, as in Colonial America or the South during
the school desegregation crisis of the late 1950s and early 1960s.

Mob action is rarely directed against the **idea** of authority or
order, but rather against some particular condition that the authority
has either caused or allowed to exist. Studies of mob action in
Europe in the eighteenth and nineteenth centuries as well as studies
of more recent riots in the United States have shown that the targets
of mob violence are limited and selective. This has been the case in
the twentieth-century ghetto revolts in Northern cities, for instance, in
which attacks have been primarily on property and few deaths have
occurred at the hands of the rioters.

In the article that follows, David Grimsted, of the University of Maryland, discusses rioting during the Jacksonian era, when democratic ideas were in ferment and the nation was struggling to find the proper balance between individual freedom and the requirements of social order. The riots studied here do not fit neatly into the paradigm mentioned above because the government on all levels was testing the nature and limits of its authority and was reluctant to use excessive force against the citizens who were expressing their grievances, particularly when the victims of mobs were weak or unpopular.

"Americans have always been a beneviolent people." As the Romantics argued the kinship of madness and genius, so it is difficult clearly to segregate student inspiration from imbecility. And if not the student who wrote the comment in that eternal source of peculiar wisdom, last year's exam books, perhaps Providence acting through the student spoke suggestively, especially considering the root of the word: if *bene-volo* means to will good, "beneviolent" would suggest the willing of good in notably vigorous form. And here perhaps lies a clue to some of the paradoxes of both the origin and significance of social violence in its American contexts.[1]

Social violence has obvious roots in both the psychology of its participants and their socioeconomic situation, and analysts of crowd behavior understandably have concentrated their examinations around such causes. Yet the extent, nature, and direction of mob violence depend equally on shared cultural assumptions about the nature of power and law,

---

[1] As recent popular books have stressed the peculiar violence of American society, more scholarly ones have suggested the limits as well as the extent of disruptiveness in the United States. Irving J. Sloan, *Our Violent Past* (New York, 1970); David Abrahamsen, *Our Violent Society* (New York, 1970); Ovid Demaris, *America the Violent* (New York, 1970); Hugh Davis Graham and Ted Robert Gurr, eds., *The History of Violence in America* (New York, 1969); Richard Hofstadter, introd. to Hofstadter and Michael Wallace, eds., *Violence in America: A Documentary History* (New York, 1970).

"Rioting in Its Jacksonian Setting," by David Grimsted. From *American Historical Review*, LXXVII (April, 1972), 361–97. Reprinted by permission of the author.
An earlier version of this paper was read at the joint session of the American Studies Association and the Southern Historical Association at the annual meeting of the Southern Historical Association, November 13, 1970, in Louisville. This study has been supported in part by fellowships from the National Endowment for the Humanities and the Charles Warren Center for Studies in American History and summer grants from the Social Science Research Council, the American Council of Learned Societies, and the University of Maryland.

and the relation of the individual and the group to them.[2] For the Jacksonian period, the diversity of type and circumstance of riot offers presumptive evidence that social violence owed less to local and particular grievances than to widely held assumptions and attitudes about the relation of the individual to social control. Only a cause that was "general in its operation," wrote a Baltimore newspaper, could explain the variously directed outbursts of social violence in the mid-1830s.[3]

Historians of eighteenth-century America have shown that mobs in that period functioned more as an accepted part of the political structure than an attack on it, largely because authorities unofficially recognized their legitimacy so long as they acted within certain bounds.[4] This reflected in part English preference for granting the lower classes occasional informal sway to giving them any established influence on government and in part colonial willingness to use the mob to make imperial authorities heed local interests. With the achievement of independence both of these justifications of the mob were undercut. Power was no longer imperially centered, nor were there large groups of white males denied a measure of political influence through established channels. Royall Tyler's play, *The Contrast*, written partly as a Federalist political document in 1787, marked the change clearly. Tyler, who had been active in putting down Shays's Rebellion, has his likably naive American democrat, Jonathan, admit that he was talked out of siding with Shays only by the natural aristocrat, Colonel Manly, who explained to him, "It was a burning shame for the true blue Bunker Hill sons of liberty, who had fought Governor Hutchinson, Lord North, and the Devil to have any hand in kicking up a cursed dust against the government which we had, every mother's son of us, a hand in making."[5] The strong though unvindictive action of the authorities toward Shays's and Fries's and the Whisky rebellions—even the fact that these incidents were labeled "rebellions"—made clear that the eighteenth-century role of the riotous crowd had ended.

---

[2] Ted Robert Gurr, who has constructed the most complex and satisfactory sociological model for violence, argues that ideological sanctions for violence are important, but in "a secondary, rationalizing" way. Because "relative deprivation" is his key concept, Gurr claims that social tensions develop first, and from these grow intellectual sanctions for violence. One could argue equally well that deprivation relative to something or other is always with us, and violence depends more on ideological or cultural channeling. *Why Men Rebel* (Princeton, 1970), 13–15, 155–231.

[3] Baltimore *Republican*, Aug. 20, 1835.

[4] Pauline Maier, "Popular Uprisings and Civil Authority in Eighteenth-Century America," *William and Mary Quarterly*, ser. 3, vol. 27 (1970): 3–35; Maier, "The Charleston Mob and the Evolution of Popular Politics in Revolutionary South Carolina, 1765–1784," *Perspectives in American History*, 4 (1970): 173–96; Gordon Wood, "A Note on Mobs in the American Revolution," *William and Mary Quarterly*, ser. 3, vol. 23 (1966): 635–42; William Ander Smith, "Anglo-American Society and the Mob, 1740–1775" (Ph.D. dissertation, Claremont Graduate School, 1965).

[5] Royall Tyler, *The Contrast* (Boston, 1920), 55–56.

The United States in the first quarter of the nineteenth century was relatively free of internal group violence, but in the 1830s riot once again became frequent. Between 1828 and 1833 there were some twenty incidents of riot, in 1834 at least sixteen riots took place, and in 1835 the number increased to thirty-seven, most of them concentrated in the summer and fall of that year.[6] The Philadelphia *National Gazette* echoed the sentiments of many when it wrote in August 1835, "The horrible fact is staring us in the face, that, whenever the fury or the cupidity of the mob is excited, they can gratify their lawless appetites almost with impunity; and it is wonderful with all the evidence of the facts that have been furnished in such abundance, to behold the degree of supineness that exists."[7] Never again in the antebellum period was rioting this concentrated, but it remained a regular social phenomenon to be accepted with a degree of "supineness." Some of these incidents were in result minor—for example, the anti-Garrison mob, which resulted in one torn coat and one broken sign—but property damage was often extensive, and numerous lives were lost. By 1835 at least 61 people had been killed in riot; by 1840 that figure goes above 125, and the worst destructiveness was yet to come. Certainly over one thousand people were killed in antebellum riots, and the draft riots of 1863 added probably another thousand to that roll.[8] Even when the riots were comparatively undestructive, they revealed major tensions in the society: ethnic hatreds; religious animosities; class tensions; racial prejudice; economic grievances; moral fears over drinking, gaming, and prostitution; political struggles; the albatross of slavery.

That these incidents had been largely forgotten until the last few years tells us something, as current violence experts have said, about the way Americans have accentuated the positive in their past. More important, it reflects the way in which American democracy has been able to absorb quantities of violence in its structure without fundamentally shaking it.[9] Historians have neglected the topic in large part because people so quickly forgot about the incidents. At times between 1834 and 1837 there was in some men's minds a sense of real possibility of social disintegration, but even during these years there was always a quick return to placidity after the outbreaks. And as resort to violence proved not a steadily spreading disease but a kind of periodic social virus, unpleasant perhaps but also unthreatening to the social organism, fearful responses became shorter and more ritualistic. For a day or two after a riot some papers explored the specific situation and the general problem; a week later, unless a trial or coroner's inquest reawoke interest, it would be pub-

---

[6] Incidents of riot were compiled from secondary sources, particularly local histories, from a complete reading of *Niles' Register* and the *National Intelligencer*, and from scattered reading in other newspapers, journals, and manuscripts.

[7] Philadelphia *National Gazette*, Aug. 11, 1835.

[8] Accounts about the number of deaths in particular incidents are frequently vague, unconvincing, or contradictory, but these figures are minimal, except possibly for the New York Draft Riot.

[9] Richard E. Rubenstein, *Rebels in Eden* (Boston, 1970); Hugh Davis Graham, "The Paradox of American Violence: A Historical Approach," *Annals of the American Academy of Political and Social Science*, 391 (1970): 75–82.

licly forgotten. Riot had regained its eighteenth-century status as a frequent and tacitly accepted if not approved mode of behavior.

Acquiescence in riot owed much to the fact that rioting was not basically an attack on the social system itself. Francis Grund, the Jacksonian publicist, wrote that lynch law, a term often used interchangeably with riot in these years, "is not properly speaking an opposition to the established laws of the country . . . , but rather . . . a supplement to them—as a species of *common law*."[10] A working definition of riot would be those incidents where a number of people group together to enforce their will immediately, by threatening or perpetrating injury to people or property outside of legal procedures but without intending to challenge the general structure of society. Such a definition, in its psychological and social basis, distinguishes riot in a rough way from revolutionary violence, which aims at the destruction of the existing political structure; or insurrection, the uprising of people essentially excluded from political participation; or group criminality, where people act in defiance rather than alleged support of accepted communal standards; or acts of civil disobedience, which involve lawbreaking to dramatize a cause but without threatening injury or destruction; or acts of disruption or symbolic violence such as burning in effigy where no real threat is involved. Such a definition of riot would include some types of social violence—like lynchings or vigilance committees in areas where there were existing legal structures —often given other labels. Here, aside from some very quasi-judicial procedure, the main difference from riot was the unusual inactivity of the constituted power.[11]

Defenders of specific riots in the period talked of the action not as revolution or even illegality but as an enforcement of justice within the bonds of society—an immediate redressing of moral wrongs or a removal of social dangers that for various reasons could not be handled by ordinary legal process. Justifications of riots and vigilance committees often invoked the precedents of 1776 in their defense, but such invocations invariably implied no intention to destroy society, suggesting instead that existing society entailed the right of popular correction of social abuses in instances when the legal system was unable or unwilling to act. In the United States the "right of revolution" justified not overthrowing the government but considerable group violence within its structure.[12]

---

[10] Francis Grund, *The Americans in Their Moral, Social and Political Relations* (Boston, 1837), 180.

[11] Some other things have been suggested to distinguish riotous violence from vigilance committees: that they were composed of respectable citizens, that they were extralegal rather than antilegal organizations, and that they did not act "spontaneously" as rioters did. In truth the composition of some riotous mobs—especially those against abolitionists or Mormons—rivaled in respectability that of vigilance organizations. Both groups saw their actions as extralegal, and both acted usually with some preparation but with much responsiveness to chance developments and moods.

[12] Eugene Dumez, introd. to Alexandre Barde, *Histoire des Comités de Vigilance aux Attakapas* (Saint-Jean-Baptiste, La., 1861), iii, 36–37; Leonard L. Richards, *Gentlemen of Property and Standing: Anti-Abolition Mobs in Jacksonian America* (New

Observers realized that the traditional justifications of riot in colonial America or in Europe were absent, and they puzzled over explanations of why rioting re-established itself in the United States. In pondering the "disorganizing, anarchical spirit" of 1835, the editor of the Boston *Evening Journal* claimed, "There are strong reasons why the laws should be implicitly obeyed in this country for they are but the echo of public opinion. . . . Our laws are not made as in many countries abroad, by the few for the suppression of the many, but by the many for the advantage of the whole." Governor James F. Thomas of Maryland put the case most succinctly:

> In governments not formed in the principles of republicanism . . . these popular commotions may sometimes be palliated or excused. . . . But in a country like ours where the people are acknowledged to be supreme, and are in fact in the constant practical exercise of absolute sovereignty there can be no apology, there is no extenuation or excuse for such commotions, and their occurrence stains the character of the government and wounds deeply the cause of equal government.[13]

The irony in these observations was that the reason for denying the old justification of riot—the institutionally clear power of the individual to influence the state—had become central to the new. The ideological tenets and political emotions of the age of Jackson, focusing on the centrality and sovereignty of the individual, both encouraged riotous response to certain situations and made it difficult to put riot down when it broke out. Jacksonian political notions were in no sense new, but the intensity, the immediacy, indeed the simplicity with which they were held gave them a fresh cast and social significance.

American political theory had long stressed the centrality in the social structure of the individual rather than the state: here the state was to have little power, no more than was needed to safeguard, or if broadly construed, to promote the individual's pursuit of happiness and search for fulfillment. Authority was subdivided among federal, state, and local groups; it was checked and balanced on each level and bound by constitutional, natural, and democratic controls to prevent tyranny over the individual. "In contrast to Europe, where society is everything and the individual nothing, and where society crushes without pity all who stand in its way," wrote one of the ablest defenders of early vigilante groups, "in America the individual is all and society nothing. There an admirable system of laws protects the feeble, the poor, the accused; there especially is the jury favorable to the defense; and finally, there all aspects of the

---

York, 1970), 69, 97–98; Richard Maxwell Brown, "The American Vigilante Tradition," in Graham and Gurr, *History of Violence*, 181.

[13] Boston *Evening Journal*, Aug. 7, 1835; Governor Thomas's message, Dec. 30, 1835, quoted in the Baltimore *Republican*, Jan. 4, 1836; see also the Baltimore *Republican*, Aug. 10, 1835; and Francis Wyse, *America, Its Realities and Resources* (London, 1846), 1: 199–200.

law are subordinated to individual right, which is the basis and essence of the republic."[14] Democratic government was not only to reflect the will of the people but also was not to interfere with the proper private will of the individual.

Historians have generally seen the Jacksonian period as marking the fruition of the nation's democracy—a notion upheld even as the evidence mounts that most of the legal changes toward democracy occurred earlier and that the major techniques of the second party system had been pre-figured in the first.[15] The answer may lie in seeing democracy less as a legal and technical system than as a psychological construct: Everyman's sense of his equality of right to participate and of his ability to decide. Democracy in this psychological sense reaffirms the importance of Jack-son on the political scene: his lack of formal education, his intuitive strength, his belief that anyone had the ability to handle government jobs, his transformation of the presidency from that of guide for the people to a personalized representative of the Democracy, all helped create a sense of power justly residing in the hands of each man rather than in the state and a sense of the need for democratic citizens to pursue the right com-paratively free from mere procedural trammels and from deference to their social and intellectual betters.

Andrew Jackson himself deplored the rioting that accelerated during his second administration. In at least three instances he sent federal troops to quell riots, and at the height of rioting in 1835 he wrote Amos Ken-dall, "This spirit of mob-law is becoming too common and must be checked or, ere long, it will become as great an evil as servile war, and the innocent will be much exposed." Yet in this same letter he showed his willingness to circumvent laws that he thought were protecting the guilty. He approved of Kendall's decision to let postmasters withhold abolitionist literature from the mail if they chose on the grounds that, in Kendall's words, citizens owed "an obligation to the laws but a higher one to the communities in which we live." Jackson thought Kendall had perhaps not gone far enough and suggested that postmasters be ordered to deliver abolitionist mail only at the receiver's request and that the names of all those accepting the material be published to "put them in coventry."[16]

---

[14] Dumez, introd., iv. Dumez concluded that the great advantages of the American system had their reverse in the difficulties of punishing wrong doers, especially among "un peuple né d'hier."

[15] Richard P. McCormick, "New Perspectives on Jacksonian Politics," *AHR*, 65 (1959–60): 288–301; McCormick, *The Second American Party System: Party Formation in the Jacksonian Era* (Chapel Hill, 1966), 19–31; William Nisbet Chambers and Walter Dean Burnham, eds., *The American Party Systems: Stages of Political Development* (New York, 1967).

[16] Andrew Jackson to Amos Kendall, Aug. 9, 1835, Andrew Jackson Papers, Library of Congress; Amos Kendall to Alfred Huger, Charleston postmaster, Aug. 4, 1835, printed in the Washington *Globe*, Aug. 12, 1835. Richard Maxwell Brown suggests Jackson once advised settlers to punish a man by lynch law; actually Jackson said only that he had no right to pardon a man convicted by an informal jury in Iowa territory prior to the extension of United States law to the area and urged that pardon be sought from the informal authority. "Legal and Be-

Jackson's personality and actions rather than his ideas made him seem, more than any other American political figure, the anarchic hero, a man who when he decided something went ahead untouched by popular clamor in favor of the national bank, or judicial decisions supporting the Cherokees, or mere legal technicalities regarding bank deposits. The Whigs felt real fear at the implications of King Andrew's highhandedness, but their attempts to make political capital out of it foundered on popular acceptance of Jackson's own sense of his role: that he was the disinterested spokesman of the people and the Democracy and as such his actions could not abridge but only perfect democratic procedure.

Jackson fitted perfectly the popular American image of the man who need not follow accepted procedures because of the rectitude of his own character, which insured proper action in a world neatly segregated between the innocent and the guilty, the righteous and the monstrous. Jackson's popularity was rooted in his embodiment of the deepest American political myth: that man standing above the law was to be not a threat to society but its fulfillment. "Trust thyself. Every heart vibrates to that iron string," wrote Emerson in his exhortation to his countrymen to be truly self-reliant and hence to become truly representative men. And James Fenimore Cooper, intending to write a story glorifying the ways of his patrician father, created a subsidiary character who stole the novel and the affections of American and world readers. Natty Bumppo came into being as the representative of natural justice in contrast to the legal justice of the good Judge Temple, and Cooper intended to preach of the sad need for the latter to prevail. But the author himself, much less his democratic audience, had small enthusiasm for the formal dogma that Natty ought to be punished for illegally shooting a deer in a community where the respectable citizens killed maple trees for sugar and slaughtered passenger pigeons and fish for fun—legally, of course. And after Natty comes Henry David Thoreau and Huck Finn and William S. Hart and Gary Cooper and Humphrey Bogart and John Wayne and the Hemingway heroes—all men whose stature comes from their standing outside of society and the law in order to live by an individual code, which peculiarly does not threaten the social good but offers its best protection. "Self-interest rightly understood" was the term Americans used to suggest that there was no disjunction between individualism and social responsibility but rather perfect union, Alexis de Tocqueville reported—with great skepticism about how well this worked in fact.[17]

The anarchistic implications of these tenets of Jacksonian democracy influenced but never seriously undermined that social force which most

havioral Perspectives on American Vigilantism," *Perspectives in American History*, 5 (1971): 121–25.

[17] Ralph Waldo Emerson, "Self-Reliance," in *Complete Works* (London, 1873), 1: 19; James Fenimore Cooper, *The Pioneers* (New York, 1823), chs. 20–36; Alexis de Tocqueville, *Democracy in America*, ed. Phillips Bradley (New York, 1957), 2: 129–35.

affected the lives of citizens, the legal system. Foreign observers agreed that the United States in the 1830s and 1840s was characterized less by anarchy than by a strong conformity to accepted standards and a general adherence to laws with little external pressure.[18] Yet there were paradoxes here too: in the willingness of Americans to disregard law on particular occasions with no sense of striking at society itself, their frequent scorn of the legal process to which they had such frequent recourse, and their vehement dislike for lawyers, the "necessary evil" to which the populace nevertheless consistently gave political power.[19]

Richard Rush wrote in 1815 that "here law is everything," and he explained that this was so because of "an alliance between an active and restless spirit of freedom and the comfortable conditions of all classes." This contentious sense of liberty and the widespread ownership and transfer of property described by Rush have generally been seen as the main impetus to law in American society. But these essentially stand as symbols for a larger truth: that as people move from a traditional society their relations must be controlled less by inherited patterns and more by formalized law. Roscoe Pound's seeing the origin of law in "codified tradition" is clearly correct, but equally important is the fact that it need be codified only when or in those areas where tradition itself is no longer strong enough to hold sway in disputes.[20] In the United States both abundant resources and democratic traditions allowed the benefits of the new bourgeois order to be widely shared, and it also served, as did the nation's conglomerate population, to disintegrate traditional mores quickly. Tocqueville's study of the United States revealed to him essentially how democracy tended to destroy the traditional trammels, or human bonds, of aristocracy—the historical family, the permanent community, the established church, the inherited profession and social class—both to free man and to isolate him. Man in America, except for the network of voluntary associations with which he protected himself and the mass in general with which he identi-

---

18 Michael Chevalier, *Society, Manners and Politics in the United States: Letters on North America* (New York, 1961), 321–29; Harriet Martineau, *Society in America* (Paris, 1837), 1: 83–93; 2: 103–16; Tocqueville, *Democracy in America*, 1: 269–78; Grund, *Americans*, 155–80.

19 Thomas Low Nichols, *Forty Years of American Life, 1821–1861* (New York, 1937), 223–24; James Willard Hurst, *The Growth of American Law* (Boston, 1950), 3–15, 249–55, 276–85; Perry Miller, *The Life of the Mind in America from the Revolution to the Civil War* (New York, 1965), 99–116. Richard E. Ellis explores the political ramifications of antilegalism in an earlier period in *The Jeffersonian Crisis: Courts and Politics in the Young Republic* (New York, 1971). Americans' mixed feelings toward the law, although felt with a certain democratic acuteness, were of course part of man's larger ambiguous hostility to authority. The connections between this hostility and social violence are intriguingly explored in Jacob Bronowski, *The Face of Violence* (New York, 1955), and Elias Canetti, *Crowds and Power* (New York, 1963).

20 Richard Rush, *American Jurisprudence* (Washington, 1815), 7–10; Roscoe Pound, *Introduction to the Philosophy of Law* (New York, 1945), 4–7. The relationship between "made" and "implicit" law is ably explored in Lon L. Fuller, *Anatomy of the Law* (New York, 1968), 43–119.

fied, was man alone. Because of the identification with the mass, public
opinion was an effective police force ensuring general compliance with
accepted standards. But in subtler and especially commercial areas of human dealing, there were neither accepted familial, communal, religious,
nor traditional authorities to settle disputes. A bourgeois society, as
America fairly was by 1830, must elevate law both because of what it is
creating and what it has to destroy.

Americans knew they needed law and even in frontier areas tended
quickly to set up legal systems and generally to respect them. The *Spirit
of the Times* reported, "One of the first wants of our new settlements is
a regular administration of justice, for the privilege of litigation, so far as
being considered, as a witty writer has termed it, an expensive luxury, is
by our free and enlightened citizens regarded as one of the prime necessaries of life."[21] Chaotic or ridiculous instances occurred in frontier law,
but these were the exceptions rather than the rule and were cherished in
American folklore and memory because they corroborated the illusion of
freedom from oppressive technicalities.[22] The heavy dependence of Americans on law stimulated a need to remember circumventions of it because
the very use of the system denied the personal independence that was the
American ideal.

Covert public dislike for the legal system commonly took the form of
scorn of lawyers, the intellectual elite upon whom litigious Americans depended most directly.[23] Timothy Walker's defense of the profession in his
Introduction to American Law, long a textbook in American law schools,
canvassed the common charges against lawyers. People complained of the
undue complexity of the law, but Walker professionally exulted in it.
"Whatever . . . may be my feelings as a man and as a citizen, as a lawyer, I am bound to rejoice in those difficulties which render our profession

---

[21] *Spirit of the Times*, 10 (Jan. 9, 1841): 543; James Willard Hurst, *The Law and
Conditions of Freedom in the Nineteenth Century United States* (Madison, 1856),
3–32; Robert R. Dykstra, *The Cattle Towns* (New York, 1968), 112–48; Elizabeth
Gaspar Brown, "The Bar on the Frontier: Wayne County, 1796–1836," *American
Journal of Legal History*, 14 (1970): 136–56. Daniel Boorstin has argued that
settlement in the United States featured community preceding legal system, but
his evidence points to a different conclusion: Americans manufactured temporary
legal structures whenever they ventured beyond the pale of the established system
because they were not communities but simply groups of individuals held together
by temporarily common objectives. *The Americans: The National Experience*
(New York, 1965), 65–87.

[22] Anton-Hermann Chroust, *The Rise of the Legal Profession in America* (Norman,
1965), 2: 92–128. Joseph G. Baldwin, himself a Southwest lawyer between 1836
and 1854, chronicled during these years both the amusing exceptions and the
stability of general rules of frontier legal development in *The Flush Times of
Alabama and Mississippi*, ed. William A. Owens (New York, 1957), 34–51, 163–82.

[23] For various kinds of popular objections to lawyers, see the *Working Man's Advocate*, Dec. 19, 1829; *Niles' Register*, 37 (Nov. 7, 1829): 169; Cincinnati *Chronicle*,
Aug. 5, 1837; *North American Review*, 51 (July 1840): 234; Harriet Beecher
Stowe, *Dred, A Tale of the Great Dismal Swamp* (Boston, 1856), 1: 20–21; 2:
99–110; Gerard W. Gawalt, "Sources of Anti-Lawyer Sentiment in Massachusetts,
1740–1840," *American Journal of Legal History*, 14 (1970): 283–307.

so arduous, so exclusive, so indispensable." Walker added "respectable" to his list of traits resulting from legal technicality, but he might better have included "profitable." The lawyer's function, Walker continued, was "to vindicate rights and redress wrongs," but in the next sentence he added, "The guilty and the innocent, the upright and the dishonest, the wronging and the wronged, the knave and the dupe, alike consult him, and with the same unreserved confidence." That guilty, dishonest, wronging knaves could place "unreserved confidence" in lawyers might for some confirm the idea that the profession delighted in chicanery and hired "out their conscience as well as their skill, to any client who will pay the fee." Of those charges, Walker told young law students, "I, for one, am willing to admit their truth to some extent. . . . We also take refuge behind the principle that supply corresponds to demand. If there were no dishonest or knavish clients there would be no dishonest or knavish lawyers. Our profession, therefore, does but adapt itself to the community." This adaptability, the moral ambiguity and sophistry, the seemingly purposeless complexity, the expensiveness charged to lawyers were all in truth a part of the legal system they represented. The attempts of legislators to make every man his own lawyer were as telling of social desires as they were futile.[24]

Vice Unmasked, a book written in 1830 by P. W. Grayson, presents most coherently the intellectual structure of uneasiness with the law that ran through Jacksonian life. Little is known about Grayson except what he himself reveals in the book: that his criticism of lawyers is knowledgeable, he himself having been one before he repented. When the book was published, Grayson apparently had connections with the New York Workingmen's party; George Henry Evans published his book, and the *Working Man's Advocate* advertised it and reprinted a review of it from the *Daily Sentinel*, which judged *Vice Unmasked* an important study if "a little enthusiastic perhaps."[25]

Grayson was unenthusiastic about law because he considered it the greatest obstacle to the realization of the promise of American life. That promise for Grayson, as for many Americans, had been to free man's potential by lifting from him the weight of the superstitions and repressive institutions of the past. The American government was the beginning of improvement, but progress was still slight, as the injustices and inequalities and unhappiness of America amply showed. What had gone wrong? Grayson's answer was simple: the United States had ended repressive government but had left untouched a legal system that impeded man's freedom and hence tarnished his natural integrity. Grayson fervently summarized the complaints against lawyers: they were a class of men who had a vested interest in fomenting and prolonging disputes; who were es-

---

[24] Timothy Walker, *An Introduction to American Law, Designed as a First Book for Students* (2d ed.; Boston, 1844), 15–19.

[25] P. W. Grayson, *Vice Unmasked, An Essay: Being a Consideration of the Influence of Law on the Moral Essence of Man* (New York, 1830); *Working Man's Advocate*, Mar. 6, 1830. The paper reported that Grayson had at one time been a member of the Kentucky state legislature from Louisville.

sentially social prostitutes willing to take any position that the highest bidder for their talents desired; who eschewed any concern for pursuing truth in order to pursue their client's interest; and who exulted in the complexities of their profession because these prevented honest men from acting in their own interests. Yet Grayson's prime target was not lawyers but the system that encouraged their moral degradation. The law itself was a jumble of old formulas inherited from feudal times, rarely suited to modern instances, and always more helpful in telling the cunning man how much he could get away with than in setting positive standards of human conduct. And whatever was done to improve it only changed its façade; one passed bankruptcy laws to protect the poor debtor, but the speculative stockjobber made use of them to defraud his honest creditors. Weaving together Thomas Paine's and a transcendental vision of man's potential, Grayson centered his indictment on the effects of law on the "moral essence of man," the way it debased man's sense of self and social responsibility by turning him from his high moral potential to a tricksy tailoring of conduct to avoid legal prosecution. In short, law was generally a tool of the cleverly vicious, a snare for the simply virtuous, and a burden on everyone, crippling human decency and progress.

Practically, Americans were not about to accept Grayson's program that law should deal only with instances of gross physical attack and in all other areas let man "seek, by the light of his own conscience, in the joyous genial climate of his own free spirit, for all the rules of his conduct." But Grayson's thinking paralleled that of many other Jacksonians.[26] Indeed his major premise was perfectly correct: from a tough-minded point of view, law, as Oliver Wendell Holmes, Jr. argued later on, has much less to do with man's highest responsibilities than it does with telling bad men just how much they can get away with; in any legal system decisions must be based as much on technical requirements as on the unfettered pursuit of justice. "Law and right," wrote John Quincy Adams, "we know but too well by the experience of mankind, in all ages, including our own, are not convertible terms."[27] Such was the paradox of legal development: the desire to be free from individual power and whim impelled rational man to set up a judicial structure that inevitably impeded almost as much as it promoted perfect justice. And so mankind's favorite myths of justice once again enthroned personal wisdom: the judgment of Solomon, Louis IX under the oaks, Cervantes' Sancho Panza, and any number of wise men ensuring the triumph of right in fairy tales or melodramas.[28]

[26] Grayson, *Vice Unmasked*, 168. For other pleas for near-legal anarchism see the speech of 1837 by John M. Hunt quoted in Fitzwilliam Byrdsall, *The History of the Loco Foco or Equal Rights Party* (New York, 1842), 149–50; and the *Democratic Review*, 6 (Dec. 1839): 466–72 and 18 (Jan. 1846): 26–30.

[27] Oliver Wendell Holmes, Jr., *Collected Legal Papers* (New York, 1952), 169–74; John Quincy Adams, "On the Opium War" (1841), *Massachusetts Historical Society Proceedings*, 43 (1910): 304. Roscoe Pound describes the inevitable judicial tension between doing justice in the immediate case and establishing desirable precedents for future ones. *The Formative Era of American Law* (New York, 1938), 119–24.

[28] The plays of the early nineteenth century, fairly accurate reflectors of popular

Both popular animus to the law and its importance in the lives of citizens helped to make the Jacksonian period, in Pound's phrase, "the formative era" of American law. The militant majoritarianism of Jacksonian rhetoric also spurred the efforts of conservatives to strengthen what seemed to be the only brake on untrammeled popular will. Francis Bowen wrote, "Here, nothing stands between the individual citizen and *his* sovereign—the majority of the people —but the majesty of the law and the independence of the courts." Conservatives like Joseph Story, Lemuel Shaw, Timothy Walker, and a host of lesser figures were so successful in increasing legal learning, dignity, and responsiveness to social needs that legal antipathy was never able to become programmatic. Even the codification issue, which drew on many of Grayson's ideas in "practical" form, was neutralized by conservative judicial skill and flexibility.[29] Such efforts ensured that Jacksonian America became increasingly a government of laws not men, but democratic man was not entirely happy about it.

Within the legal structure, popular wariness about law appeared in the leniency with which juries tended to view offenders for whose crimes there were extenuating circumstances.[30] Such legal actions, if technically irregular, often provided a kind of rough equity that the law could not formally incorporate. For instance, a St. Louis jury acquitted an actress who had stabbed her faithless lover to death in the theater one night. The argument that the man had a bad heart that might have given way before the knife got there was something of a blow to technical justice, but who knows if eternal justice would have been better served by a conviction? And one sympathizes with the California judge who concluded his charge to a jury: "Well, gentlemen, that's the law, but I don't really think it's God Almighty's justice, and I guess you may just as well find for the defendant."[31] Democratic man admitted that a legal system was needed,

---

ideals, often used the motif of justice ensured by personal wisdom. The first popular melodrama in the United States, William Dunlap's translation of Louis Charles Caigniez's *The Voice of Nature* in 1803, was an updating of the Solomon and true motherhood story; and Royall Tyler, at one time chief justice of the Vermont Supreme Court, wrote plays glorifying the judicial wisdom of both Solomon and Sancho Panza. *Four Plays,* ed. Arthur W. Peach and George F. Newbrough (Princeton, 1941). The most successful American comedy of the 1840s showed a simple farmer distributing justice in the end to avoid mere legal solution for criminal acts. Anna Cora Mowatt, *Fashion; or Life in New York* (London, 1850), act 5.

29 Francis Bowen, "The Independence of the Judiciary," *North American Review,* 57 (Oct. 1843): 420; William W. Story, *Life and Letters of Joseph Story* (Boston, 1851), 1: 448; 2: 241–51, 570–600; Leonard W. Levy, *The Law of the Commonwealth and Chief Justice Shaw: The Evolution of American Law* (New York, 1967), 303–36.

30 Dumez, introd., iii–vi. Francis Bowen chided James Fenimore Cooper for his novelistic attack on the jury system, *The Ways of the Hour,* on the grounds that the central argument of the book was mistaken: American juries did not tend to convict unfairly but were notorious for their leniency even when evidence of guilt was substantial. "Cooper's *Ways of the Hour: The Trial by Jury,*" *North American Review,* 71 (July 1850): 121–35.

31 Noah M. Ludlow, *Dramatic Life as I Found It* (St. Louis, 1880), 550; Sol Smith, *Theatrical Management in the South and West for Thirty Years* (New York,

but he had an active responsibility to see that it did not contradict the will of God Almighty, as interpreted by himself, of course.

This refusal to accept the sanctity of the law had its most disruptive manifestations in the long series of riots in the Jacksonian period. These were very diverse in origin and goal, but patterns do emerge about the structure of rioting, its social and psychological results, the type of person who rioted, and the problems of riot control in the period. A consideration of two incidents and of an ethnic category of riot suggests something of the nature of social violence in Jacksonian America and its implications for riot theory in general. The Bank Riot in Baltimore and the Snow Riot in Washington, D.C., took place within a week of each other in early August 1835. The Baltimore riot was highly unusual in that the mob attacked their social and economic superiors; partly for this reason information on it is unusually abundant. The Washington riot is more typical both in its direction and in the sketchiness of the material available on it. Together the two constitute an introduction to Jacksonian social violence.

Both riots took place in a climate of national near-hysteria. Instances of riot and lynching around the country filled the Baltimore and Washington newspapers throughout July and August. The same day that major rioting broke out in Baltimore, its leading periodical, *Niles' Register*, began with "a great mass of curious and important matter" showing that "the state of society is awful. Brute force has superseded the law, at many places, and violence become the 'order of the day.' The time predicted seems rapidly approaching when the mob shall rule." Niles blamed both lawless mobs and "fanatics who . . . have set their presses at work to spread desolation and death through the whole south" for the trouble.[32] The most obvious precipitant of these "various excitements" was the growing effectiveness of abolition organization in the North and the sending of abolitionist literature southward. The South responded with fear and fury, claiming that these movements would create slave insurrection. The South threatened economic boycott against the North, and Northern commercial centers responded with huge public meetings condemning abolitionism and declaring that the North had no proper business even discussing slavery. Such declarations of sentiment failed to satisfy the South, which demanded "works" not "words"—specifically laws prohibiting the discussion of slavery and legal or illegal action to silence those promoting abolition. Laws curtailing freedom of speech or mobs seemed the only possible response to appease extreme Southern feeling.[33]

1868), 165, 192; George Templeton Strong, *Diary*, ed. Allan Nevins and Milton Halsey Thomas (New York, 1952), 2: 81.

[32] *Niles' Register*, 48 (Aug. 8, 1835): 397. A survey of shocked reaction to mobs from newspapers around the country appears in the *National Intelligencer*, Aug. 14, 1835.

[33] *Niles' Register* between July and November gives a vivid picture of this controversy, complete with the proceedings of the various meetings and a rich selection of editorial comment from all sections and parties. Until mid-September sentiment was almost wholly antiabolitionist, but this changed as the implications of Southern

The political situation of the nation further heated these passions. Martin Van Buren, running for the presidency as Jackson's chosen successor, was politically vulnerable in the South, while the leading opposition candidate, Jacksonian renegade Hugh Lawson White of Tennessee, had great strength there among both Jacksonians and Whigs. Since the South promised to be the central battleground for supremacy, the Whig and Democrat partisan press competed in rabid attacks upon the abolitionists. In many instances the press and leading politicians promoted proslavery mob action;[34] more commonly they condoned them with open expressions of approval or quiet toleration. No Baltimore or Washington newspaper directly encouraged these particular riots, but even nonpartisan papers edited by men deeply disturbed by riot tended to print without comment incidents of proslavery violence or to deplore them while laying major blame on "those unprincipled incendiaries," the abolitionists who were their victims.[35] Well over half of the riots in July and August of 1835 had no immediate connection with abolition, but they all sprang from a social climate with an extraordinary tolerance for riot. Circumstances allowed only a very few newspapers or public figures to take a strong stand against the best known of popular outbursts.

The Baltimore riot was an attack on those connected with the failure to settle the affairs of the Bank of Maryland, which had ceased operation

---

demands became clear and the Northern nonparty press became truculent against Southern extremism. Niles himself marks the shift. On September 19 he wrote that Southern willingness "to have *mob-law*—or accept of *regulations* that monarchs would 'turn pale' to think of" was a remedy considerably "worse than the disease" of abolitionism. 49 (Sept. 19, 1835): 33.

[34] The clearest case of politically instigated riot was the antiabolitionist mob in Utica in late October 1835. Van Buren, embarrassed by the comparatively mild New York City resolutions damning abolitionists, had his friends organize an Albany meeting, which passed stronger pro-Southern resolutions than those of any other city. The administration Richmond *Enquirer* praised them as "free from all qualification and equivocation—no idle denunciations of the *evils of slavery*—no pompous assertions of the *right of discussion*," but the Richmond *Whig* pointed out that they wanted only "the recognition of the power of the legislature to suppress the fanatics, and the recommendation to do so," and without this they were meaningless. Niles reported much Southern pressure on Van Buren to add legislative proposals to the resolves, and omission of these proposals was, for Niles, conclusive proof that nothing legally would be done. *Niles' Register*, 49 (Oct. 3, 1835): 75. About three weeks later, Samuel Beardsley, a Jacksonian congressman, led a mob that drove the New York Anti-Slavery Society out of Utica and sacked a press that embarrassed the Democratic party by being both antislavery and pro–Van Buren. Administration papers immediately touted this as proof of the purity of Van Buren's Southern feelings, and hinted that Beardsley would be appointed governor of New York if Van Buren were elected and could find a place in Washington for Governer William Marcy. Marcy stayed in New York after Van Buren's victory, but quickly appointed Beardsley the state's attorney-general. Another Democratic governer appointed him to the New York Supreme Court, and he became chief justice briefly in 1845.

[35] Georgetown *Metropolitan*, Aug. 12, 1835; Washington *Mirror*, Aug. 1, 1835; Baltimore *Gazette*, Aug. 3, 1835; *Niles' Register*, 49 (Oct. 31, 1835): 149.

almost a year and a half earlier. "Considerable numbers of people, 'good, bad, and indifferent' " congregated in Monument Square during the clear and pleasantly cool evenings between August 5 and 7.[36] The general topic of conversation was the action of the trustees and the "secret partners" of the bank, and the mood was one of frustration and anger at the prolonged legal obstacles to settlement. On Friday afternoon Mayor Jesse Hunt called a public meeting, which pledged itself to keep the peace and try to discover the source of the inflammatory handbills posted on walls, but which also requested that the bank's books be immediately opened for public investigation. A crowd of ten thousand gathered on Friday night, but, aside from minor rock throwing, the peace was kept. On Saturday the trustees announced that the bank's books were impounded by the Harford County Court, and the mayor organized a citizens' guard armed with two-foot long poplar sticks. That evening the guard managed to keep the mob from their main objective, the home of the leading "partner," Reverdy Johnson, but were unable to prevent the sacking of the house of another "partner." When the crowd bombarded the guard with stones and brickbats and wounded several guards seriously, some of the guard's leaders demanded the right to use guns, and the mayor reluctantly consented. At least five people were killed, and some ten or twenty were wounded by shooting. Sunday morning the mayor announced that the firing had been done "against my will and advice," and the leaders of the citizens' guard decided that prudence dictated leaving town. The mob was left unopposed. That evening and night hundreds systematically sacked and damaged the homes of the mayor and of four men connected with the bank and did minor damage to property of certain leaders of the citizens' guard, while thousands watched.[37] At about noon Monday, eighty-three-year-old Samuel Smith drove through the streets in a carriage flying an American flag to a large meeting where he effectively organized the citizens into an armed force to handle any further troubles. The destruction, which was still going on, immediately ceased, and the citizen patrols that guarded the city for well over a week met no opposition.[38]

Federal troops were dispatched to Fort McHenry near Baltimore shortly after Smith and his fellow citizens had the situation under control, but most troops were quickly withdrawn to Washington, D.C., to over-awe a riot that flourished between August 12 and 14 and sputtered on for several days thereafter. This riot resulted primarily in an attack on the property of free blacks. The mob congregated on Tuesday when it be-

---

[36] William Bartlett to Edward Stabler, Aug. 12, 1835, printed in *Maryland Historical Magazine*, 9 (1914): 157. The weather reports are in Henry Thompson's diary, in the Maryland Historical Society, Baltimore.

[37] This account is constructed from newspaper descriptions in the Baltimore *American*, *Republican*, and *Gazette*, from accounts in other papers reprinted from the Baltimore *Chronicle* and *Patriot*, and the testimony taken by the Maryland General Assembly on the riots, published in 1836. There are no major discrepancies about the facts of the incident and no probing considerations of its structure.

[38] When James Gordon returned to Baltimore a week after the riot, he reported the "military arrangement of cannon and soldiers" looked "more warlike" than anything he had ever seen. Diary, Aug. 17, 1835. Maryland Historical Society.

came known that abolitionist literature had been found in a trunk owned by Reuben Crandall, who was staying in Georgetown and was the brother of Prudence Crandall, already well known as a victim of riot when she had attempted to teach black girls in her school in Canterbury, Connecticut.[39] Crandall was quickly arrested and arraigned in jail to prevent his falling into the hands of the mob, who then turned their attention to a restaurant, the Epicurean House, which was run by a mulatto, Beverly Snow. Before the mob arrived, Snow had wisely disappeared; after a fruitless search for antislavery writings, and some more successful drinking, the mob left. The next day they returned to "get Snow," but again he escaped. A search of the homes of other free Negroes resulted in finding some abolition newspapers in the house of James Hutton, who was hustled to jail to protect him from the mob. The crowd, after staging a public meeting the proceedings of which no newspaper reported, returned to Snow's to destroy his property, "not forgetting to crack a bottle of hock, 'now and then.'" That night, and intermittently during the next week, the crowd burned or stoned several black-owned buildings.[40]

Such is the skeletal history of the two events. A closer examination of these two riots shows much not only about their own structure but about the nature of rioting in the Jacksonian period. The central question, of course, concerns what motivates riot. Seventy-five years ago Gustave Le Bon began the sociological study of crowd behavior with a discussion that can hardly be taken seriously today but that still informs much thinking about the problem. Man acting singly, Le Bon argued, acts rationally, but acting in groups—he lumps together such things as parliamentary bodies and riotous mobs—they revert to instinctual behavior; "bestial," "primitive," "childlike," "feminine" were Le Bon's favorite adjectives for it. Le Bon's explanatory devices are largely funny; the most irrational of crowds, Latin ones, he tells us, are so because they are "the most feminine of all." Yet his ideas have remained provocative because behavior within mobs suggests disruption more than continuity in the character of the participants, and aspects of his description are still convincing, particularly his emphasis on the emotive volatility, psychological release and anonymity, and the sense of total and totally justified power that comes from being part of a riotous crowd.[41]

---

[39] *The Trial of Reuben Crandall Charged with Publishing and Circulating Seditious and Incendiary Papers* (Washington, 1836).

[40] The Washington papers all reported the riot, but were very reticent about the destruction, particularly in the month following its supposed settlement. They agreed in what they reported. Duff Green's *U.S. Telegraph*, August 13, and Francis Blair's *Globe*, August 19, expressed some regret that Crandall was not hung, but the other papers—the *National Intelligencer*, Washington *Sun*, *Mirror*, Georgetown *Metropolitan* and Alexandria *Gazette*—regretted the rioting without condemning the rioters.

[41] Gustave Le Bon, *The Crowd: A Study of the Popular Mind*, ed. Robert K. Merton (New York, 1960), 35–59. A pervasive problem in the book is that Le Bon treats three groups as identical—mobs, for which his description is most valuable;

Sociologists have long raised questions about Le Bon's arguments, especially his emphasis on the irrationality of crowd behavior.[42] Historians, particularly Eric Hobsbawm and George Rudé, first directly attacked the irrationality hypothesis in regard to riotous violence and suggested that rioters tend to act not irrationally but in ways made understandable by their social situation and related integrally to their social needs and desires.[43] Certainly Rudé and Hobsbawm win the argument if rationality means simply an understandable response to a social situation that made people discontented. Such a criterion, however, excludes irrationality by definition, for no action can be wholly unrelated to man's unhappiness stemming from objective social experience; the lunatic who thinks he is Napoleon obviously does so because this illusion fulfills certain needs caused by real deprivations and traumas in his social history.[44]

Jacksonian riots do not readily fall into categories of either "irrational" or "socially purposive" behavior. The mobs in Baltimore and Washington were not particularly wanton or vicious. In both cases the action taken was sensibly directed toward the social source of riotous anger—the financial manipulations of some rich men in one case and the pretensions to social dignity of blacks in the other. The Baltimore mob was particularly fastidious. They refused to sack houses of intended victims when they were informed that they were still officially owned by the contractor or were the property of the would-be victim's mother; they put out fires in houses that they were busy demolishing so adjoining property would not be endangered; they reprimanded some people for

---

a mass society, about which his comments are inferior to Tocqueville's in complexity and suggestiveness; and decision-making bodies such as juries and parliaments, for which his analysis is at best quaint.

[42] A good survey of the sociological theories of crowd behavior is Stanley Milgram and Hans Toch, "Collective Behavior: Crowds and Social Movements," in Gardner Lindzey and Elliot Aronson, eds., *Handbook of Social Psychology* (2d ed.; New York, 1968), 4: 542–84.

[43] Eric J. Hobsbawm, "The Machine Breakers," *Past and Present*, no. 1 (1952): 57–70; Hobsbawm, *Primitive Rebels: Studies in Archaic Forms of Social Movements in the Nineteenth and Twentieth Centuries* (Manchester, 1959); George Rudé, *The Crowd in the French Revolution* (Oxford, 1959); Rudé, *The Crowd in History: A Study of Popular Disturbances in France and England, 1730–1848* (New York, 1964); Hobsbawm and Rudé, *Captain Swing* (New York, 1968). Rudé in his two books both defends his crowds' general social purposiveness and also argues that the crowds that followed—those after the French Revolution in the first book (pp. 209, 238–39) and in the "industrial" age that had fully arrived by 1848 in the second (pp. 218–34, 266–68)—were purged of certain backward qualities through the development of "a stable social-ideological content" (p. 234). The opposite may be the case: as popular movements developed ideological content and as Western governments opened channels of influence to a broader segment of their population, significant social protest took less violent and destructive forms, and riotous mobs became commonly more backward looking or self-indulgent.

[44] R. D. Laing, in his *Politics of Experience* (New York, 1967), suggests that insanity is often reasonable response to social inconsistencies in an existential reworking of the Romantic preference for madness to bourgeois normality.

stealing rather than destroying property; and they voted by a slim majority not to burn a lumber yard because it threatened an adjacent one. (The minority had argued that it could be safely burned if the fire trucks were called out to keep the flames in bounds.) Their chief victims were rationally chosen: four men—Reverdy Johnson, John Glenn, Evan T. Ellicott, and Hugh McElderry—who had been "secret partners" in the Bank of Maryland and who had avoided settlement of the bank's affairs through legal prosecution of its former president and his relatives; John B. Morris, one of the trustees of the bank since its failure, who had steadily supported the nonsettlement policy; and Mayor Hunt, who was blamed for the firing into the crowd on Saturday. None was guilty of indictable offenses, and Hunt and Morris had not obviously profited from the situation, although the latter had lent himself to the delay and to the publication of a very inaccurate report of the bank's situation under the influence of his legal counsel, Reverdy Johnson. This unconscionable postponement worked a great hardship on the unusual number of people of modest means—"widows and orphans, small dealers and thrifty persons, mechanics and others"—who were the bank's creditors, while its debtors, including the partners, profiteered shamelessly.[45] Given the complexity of the affairs of the Bank of Maryland, and judging by the mob's choice of victims, the Baltimore mob was not only but financially astute.[46] Less is known about the specific mob actions in Washington, but there is evidence of similar restraint and selectivity. When told that the building and many of the furnishings of Snow's restaurant were actually owned by others, the mob confined itself to destroying the sign and a few things of minor value. And the property they attacked—black businesses, schools, churches, and homes—were those things most contributive to the free Negroes' sense of status and dignity, however tenuous, in the community.[47]

Yet are selectivity and aspects of moderation incompatible with the

[45] *Niles' Register*, 46 (Mar. 29, 1834): 65. The bank had attracted small investors by offering interest on short term deposits. A letter of a retired sea captain, Thomas Williams, gives a vivid sense of the suffering the bank's prolonged trusteeship caused its unfortunate creditors. Baltimore *Republican*, Mar. 19, 1836.

[46] The conflicting accounts of the affairs of the Bank of Maryland were presented in two pamphlets by its former president, Evan Poultney, and in two replies by Reverdy Johnson and John Glenn, the second reply appearing a few days prior to the riot. Poultney argued that he and five other men had secretly controlled the bank, that there were sufficient funds to meet, or almost meet, all debts, and that the legal cases against him and his brothers were all ruses. Poultney's story was borne out by the bank's books, the results of the criminal cases, and the final settlement of the trust over four years after the bank's failure, when the full amount of debts was paid plus a ten cent dividend per dollar. This almost all went to speculators who had bought the credits at about a quarter of their value. The best accounts of these financial manipulations are a long letter from George Gibbs to the Union Bank of Tennessee, July 1834, in the Jonathan Meredith Papers, Library of Congress, and Thomas Ellicott's self-serving but generally accurate, *The Bank of Maryland Conspiracy* (Philadelphia, 1839).

[47] The Washington papers talked most of the burning of a house of prostitution to suggest the riot had a moral tone; presumably it was owned or run by blacks.

idea that a riotous crowd unleashes elements of emotion that in important ways distort reality and allow individuals to act in a manner at variance with their usual behavior? The ablest defender of the Baltimore mob stressed its restraint and the justice of its social position: "fraud produced violence," and the people "operated upon the republican maxim 'resistance to tyrants is obedience to God.'" But he also stressed the emotive quality of the crowd situation. When the mob in Monument Square became active "every countenance was flushed with the spirit of destruction —reason had thrown down the reins and ungovernable fury had taken them up," and the retreat of the city guard led to Sunday's "anarchical desolation and mournful paralysis of reason."[48] The handbills, which were sent through the mails and posted on the walls of Baltimore during the week preceding the riot, reveal this tying of highly irrational emotionalism to very real grievances:

> Arm! Arm! . . .—my Countrymen—Citizens of this Republic, and of this City, will you suffer your firesides to be molested—will you suffer your beds to be poluted—will you suffer your pockets to be riffled and your wives and children beggared. . . . Then arouse, and rally around the free and unbiass'd judge Lynch who will be placed upon the seat of justice and the people enmasse will be the members of the Bar, and these lions of the law shall be made to know that the people will rise in their majesty and redress their own grievances. . . . Have not the whole Bar and the judges linked in a combination together, and brow-beaten these very people out of their just rights, with a full determination to swindle and rob the industrious and poor part of the community out of their hard earnings. . . . Designing lawyers and lazy greedy peculators . . . , these smiling villains nearly all of them are building palaces and riding in their carriages with the very money taken from the poor laborer, orphans and honest hard working mechanics. . . . Want staring your poor heart broken wives in the face—your little children clinging around their mother, crying mother, mother a piece of bread—I say mother bread—O! mother give me some bread,—while these protected villains are roling in luxury and ease, laughing to scorn the people they have just robbed. These very villains stroll the streets with a bold and impudent assurance and pass for honest men—not satisfied with robbing you of your money, but treat you as Vassals to their noble lordships—to gratify their Venery desires hire pimps and procuresses to go polute your wives and prostitute your daughters—Gracious God! —is this our fair famed Baltimore—is our moral city come to this. . . . We have a remedy, my fellow citizens—Judge Lynch will be notified that he is at our head, and will take his place upon the bench—his maxims are Virtue, honesty, and good decent behavior —his remedies are simple, Tar and Feathers, effigys, gallowses and extermination from our much injured city—the victims that fall

---

[48] "Junius" to the Baltimore *Republican* Jan. 4, Feb. 26, Mar. 5, 31, 1836.

under this new law, I hope will be Johnson, Morris, Glenn, Mc-
Elderry, Freeman and that dirty fellow Bossier etc., etc., etc.—
Let the warhoop be given . . . Liberty, Equality, Justice or
Death!!![49]

Here a generalized social fury melted justified anger and real economic
hardship into an amalgam of major democratic grievances and fears: resentment at the deviousness and elitism of the law; a hatred of the powerful, the pretentious, the learned, the rich; uncertainties about economic
status and the moral stability of the family. All these fears could be
welded together and expressed because they resulted not from any intrinsic flaws in society but from the machinations of specific villains—in
this case five men and three etceteras. When Judge Lynch had those
people "exterminated from the city," supposedly Baltimore and the
United States could return to their "fair fame" and purity.

The talk in the circular of "Venery desires" shows how the anger of
the mob also united wholly separate incidents. The inclusion of "Bossier"
in the list of intended victims makes clear that the author joined a recent
Baltimore scandal with the long-brewing Bank of Maryland controversy.
Over a week before the riot, Joseph Bossière was assaulted by an irate
guardian who found his ward in Bossière's house. Rumor had it that
Bossière had seduced her and that the directress of the exclusive school
where the girl boarded had acted as procuress. The moralistic anger over
this incident, totally unconnected with the bank controversy, nonetheless
merged with it in the minds of the rioters. The mob attacked the house
where Bossière was staying, and to save it he gave himself up to the
crowd; what was done to him was not reported.[50]

In the Washington riot a similar event that had occurred about a
week prior to the disturbance influenced the emotion of the mob. The
slave of a prominent Washington widow entered her bedroom at night
with an ax and drunkenly threatened to kill her. Newspapers soon had
him spouting "abolitionist jargon" as he made the attack, and the conservative *National Intelligencer* labeled the story "The First Fruits."

[49] Handbill, in vertical file, Maryland Historical Society. Other handbills are in the
David M. Perine Papers, Maryland Historical Society, and one is copied in William
Bartlett's letter in the *Maryland Historical Magazine*, 9 (1914): 161–62. The
"Freeman" mentioned in the circular was W. H. Freeman, another Baltimore
banker, to whom the Union Bank of Tennessee sold its credits of some $275,000
on the Bank of Maryland for $60,000. Freeman owed the bank $50,000, so for an
additional $10,000 he bought over $200,000 worth of credits. The mob leaders must
have learned of the transaction even before the Baltimore *Gazette* announced on
August 8 that the claims of the Union Bank of Tennessee had been "satisfactorily
adjusted." John Bass to Jonathan Meredith, July 30, 1835; A. Van Wyck to Jonathan
Meredith, Nov. 6, 1835, Meredith Papers; "One of the Mob" to Brantz Mayer,
Aug. 12, 1835, Brantz Mayer Papers, Maryland Historical Society.

[50] Bossière's statement about his treatment during the riot appeared in the Baltimore
Gazette, Aug. 21, 1835, and in the Baltimore *American*, Sept. 16, 1835. Reports of
extreme excitement over the alleged seduction appeared in the Baltimore *Republican*, July 24, 1835, and in the Georgetown *Metropolitan*, Aug. 1, 1835.

While the widow, convinced that the slave had simply been drunk, hid him in her home and tried to sell him to safety, the press flaunted the incident as proof of coming terrors if abolitionists were not muzzled.[51] Hence Crandall's supposed activities could be seen as part of a plot threatening widows with violent death, and the attack on Negroes could then go forth in the guise of saving society from servile war. The purity of the family motif was also strangely tied to the attack on Snow. When no abolitionist literature was found in his restaurant, the official charge against him became that he had insulted the honor of mechanics' wives and daughters.[52]

In addition to a triggering generalized moral fury, another emotional set characterized Jacksonian riots. Once action began, anger was replaced by joy and release if the mob was not seriously opposed. The few reports of the Washington mob suggest great good humor, almost Bacchanalia, as the crowd destroyed, partly by drinking, the contents of Snow's Epicurean House. The reports of the Baltimore riot trials give a vivid sense of their saturnalian quality. Several rioters were convicted largely because they had lustily bragged about their riot exploits. James Spencer, furious against Mayor Hunt because Spencer had had his "knuckles shot off" on Saturday, amused the crowd as he broke Hunt's dinnerware on the street: "Gentlemen, who wants to go to a tea party, but stop I'll go and get the plates." Particular care and delight was taken in burning Reverdy Johnson's law library. The mob emptied Johnson's and Glenn's wine cellars and referred to the wine they abundantly drank as "American blood," perhaps suggesting that it was squeezed from their townsmen's labors as well as evoking old rituals of saturnalia, in which the continuance of patterns of authority was made acceptable by their brief ritual cessation. One rioter on Monday, before order was restored, went around saying "damned if he wasn't Mayor of the city" and appointing various friends to official positions. Such precise parallels to saturnalia's mock king were doubtless rare, but the mood often suggested the joy that comes from the destruction of official authority and its brief bestowal on self. Fifes and drums played and crowds of thousands watched the destruction, laughing and cheering on the rioters.[53] The moral or social issues that gave mobs life always circumscribed their action, but such restraints coexisted with a high degree of emotive fury and joy in power

[51] Mrs. William Thornton, diary, Aug. 5–8, 1835, Library of Congress; *National Intelligencer*, Aug. 8, 1835. The slave was sentenced to death, but Mrs. Thornton's ceaseless lobbying for him among her influential friends gained him a pardon from Jackson. See her diary, July 6–7, 1836.

[52] Snow begged for a hearing from a jail in Fredericksburg where he had gone for protective custody; the *National Intelligencer* published it, but apologized abjectly when a "respectable citizen" wrote a diatribe against the paper's so honoring one of Snow's "insolent class." "Let all blacks become subordinates and laborers," concluded the citizen, or leave Washington. Aug. 27, 28, 1835.

[53] Hester Wilkins to her sister Mrs. John Glenn, Aug. 11, 1835, John Glenn Papers, Maryland Historical Society. The quotations are all taken from the riot trials in the Baltimore City Court, published in the Baltimore *Gazette* between late November 1835 and the end of January 1836.

that transfigured social reality. Total self-righteousness, well or ill founded, joined with the unity and anonymity of the crowd to allow a saturnalia where social man's usual restraints could be shucked.

A bank clerk, witnessing a riot in 1843, was surprised that so little was done to protect the black victims:

> But the mob of Cincinnati must have their annual festival—their Carnival, just as at stated periods, the ancient Romans enjoyed the Saturnalia, and our city dignitaries must run no risk of forfeiting their "sweet voices" at the next charter election by any unceremonious interference with their "gentle violence"—their practical demonstrations of sovereignty.[54]

The cross-examination of a Baltimore defense witness is telling. Asked if he had been in Morris's house, the reporter recorded the witness as saying, "Not sure—thinks he went in—don't know if he went upstairs, if he did he might have been insane—drank two or three glasses from a decanter—was 'pretty warm.'" Had he been at Hunt's? "Might have been in the house, didn't know—thinks he was sober—was a 'little warm,' might have been insane—a great many passions make a man insane beside liquor—excited to see so much property destroyed."[55]

Most Jacksonian rioters were neither the "dregs of society," as Reverdy Johnson called the Baltimore mob, nor so much of a social elite as Richard M. Brown and Leonard Richards have found composing vigilante or antiabolition mobs.[56] Of the twelve people convicted of riot in

---

[54] James W. Taylor, "A Choice Nook of Memory": The Diary of a Cincinnati Law Clerk, 1840–42, ed. James Taylor Dunn (Columbus, 1950), 40. Ralph W. Conant suggests the idea of riot as saturnalia, but treats it as a largely benign phenomenon. "Rioting, Insurrection and Civil Disobedience," American Scholar, 37 (1968): 425–26. Jacob Bronowski's stress on the vicious possibilities of saturnalia makes the comparison truer. Face of Violence, 18–19.

[55] Testimony of Mr. Blakely, a carpenter, in the third mob case, Baltimore Gazette, Dec. 12, 1835.

[56] Reverdy Johnson, Memorial to the Legislature of Maryland (Annapolis, 1836), 8; Brown, "American Vigilante Tradition," 167–71; Richards, Gentlemen of Property and Standing, 131–55. The mobs Brown and Richards ably discuss were more "respectable" than most, but perhaps not generally so "upper class" as they suggest. Richards, for example, bases his key samples on the names of people who attended meetings that resolved basically that violence would occur if abolitionist editor James Birney stayed in Cincinnati or if the New York Slavery Society tried to meet in Utica. Such resolutions could be supported by a wide spectrum of citizens, from those who favored a mob to those who wished to avoid trouble, to those genuinely concerned for the safety of those threatened. That their action as it turned out supported the mob is clear, but that they intended it to do so is dubious. Participants in such meetings did not necessarily countenance riot, much less participate in it. In Cincinnati many citizens must have had in mind Birney's experience in Danville, Kentucky, where a similar public meeting had caused him to leave peaceably.

Baltimore, eight can be identified as to profession: three carpenters, two pavers, one blacksmith, one hatter, and one laborer. Of the ten people acquitted, four clearly did some rioting; two of these were carpenters, one a merchant, and one probably a farmer. Testimony revealed the names of nine other rioters, only two of whom were professionally identified, both as carpenters. Thus half of the fourteen rioters identified by job were carpenters and eleven (or 78.6 per cent) were "mechanics," that is workingmen with a particular skill.[57] No ages were given, but in about one-third of the cases the rioter's youth was mentioned. The evidence is sketchy but corresponds with the usually even less certain data on other riots. Rioters were predominantly lower-middle-class people with a skill or some property and some position in the community; the majority also tended to be young, in their late teens or twenties, and to have ties with the Jacksonian equivalent of the modern urban gang, the fire companies.

In Washington twenty-some persons were arrested, but the press mentioned only two names: John Laub, a ship carpenter from the Navy Yard, and a "Mr. Sweeting, of Philadelphia," possibly of the same vocation. The diary of Andrew Shiner, a black worker at the Navy Yard, offers the most helpful clues about who participated. A large group of out-of-town workers had been hired to refurbish the frigate *Columbia*. Late in July one mechanic was caught stealing copper, and the commander of the Navy Yard, Commodore Isaac Hull, ordered that workers be barred from eating in the storeroom. Considering this order an assault on their honor, the workers went on strike and ten days later eased their offended dignity and relieved their enforced leisure by terrorizing blacks. At some points the mechanics considered attacking the Navy Yard, but prudence and the fortifications kept the riot racial.[58] The strike explains how mechanics could spend Tuesday afternoon and all day Wednesday working at riot. The clearest evidence that the rioters were of this class grew from a meeting of "very respectable" mechanics called specifically to disavow such ties. The formal resolutions expressed resentment that mechanics should be thought involved with the riot and asked for the removal of federal troops from the streets, but several volunteer amendments, all adopted, revealed more than the meeting's sponsors wished. "Riotous" was changed to "excited," a resolution calling the presence of troops "an insult to freemen" was added, and finally the commander of the troops was damned "for stigmatizing those citizens of Washington who assembled . . . to inflict summary punishment on B. Snow as 'a set of ragamuffins.' " Little wonder that the Jacksonian journal, the *Globe*,

[57] Job identifications were made from the trial records and *Matchett's Baltimore Directory* (Baltimore, 1835–36). The possibilities of mistake are, of course, rife; the only Peter Harman listed for Baltimore in 1835 was a Lutheran or German Reformed minister, while the riotous Peter Harman was best known as a fireboy among whose favorite phrases were "damned" and "son of a bitch." The evidence against the only convicted laborer was very dubious as to his rioting, although he certainly took home a part of one of John Glenn's carpets.

[58] Andrew Shiner, diary, 1813–65, ff. 58–61, Library of Congress; Isaac Hull, *Papers of Isaac Hull, Commodore United States Navy*, ed. Gardner Weld Allen (Boston, 1929), 68–77.

an active sponsor of the meeting, had reservations about "the mode adopted to repel" those "unfounded" charges that mechanics had countenanced the riot.[59]

The question of leadership of Jacksonian riots is even harder to answer. In the Snow Riot no evidence remains of leadership, although John Laub was labeled a "ring leader." Those arrested in Baltimore were also called ringleaders, but their trials made clear that only two of them might have been influential even in a secondary way. Yet certainly someone wrote the hundreds of handbills inciting to riot, and witnesses testified that the mob had clear leadership from time to time. The identity of "Red Jacket," "Black Hawk," and "the Man in the Speckled Hat"—names given to alleged leaders—is unknown; perhaps people thought they were leaders only because of their notable costumes.[60] The riot testimony suggests that Leon Dyer was active in the crowd; he was not tried because of testimony that he helped prevent destruction at McElderry's. His doing this is not incompatible with being a leader; Benjamin Lynch, one of the convicted, reportedly said during the riot, "Gentlemen, we have gone far enough, if we go further we shall lose the sympathies of the people." Dyer, at any rate, was reported to have said, "I have got the party and can send them where I please," and to have bought drinks for the mob who worked destruction on the McElderry and Ellicott homes. A citizen of Baltimore much later identified "Red Jacket" as "Samuel M. . . , a cooper in Franklin street." This was Samuel Mass, a Jacksonian politician who had been president of the Maryland Executive Council the year before. Mass was arrested for leading a meeting, two days after the riot, of Tenth Ward Citizens who deplored the violence but also warned Reverdy Johnson that he would be deservedly driven out of Baltimore should he have the impudence to return.[61] Dyer and Mass were leaders of the plebian wing of the Jacksonians; when Roger B. Taney went to Annapolis to urge an indemnity for the victims of the riot, Baltimore's Democratic representatives pointedly avoided calling on him, causing Taney to lament that they, like Baltimore's Jacksonian editor, should countenance the

---

[59] *Globe*, Aug. 19, 1835.

[60] Witnesses identified Samuel Reed as a leader because he "acted like a madman" and Peter Harman as one because he wore a brass plate on his hat and a curtain ring around his neck. Baltimore *Gazette*, Dec. 28, 31, 1835.

[61] Dyer's name was that most frequently brought up in the trials; the testimony suggests he both directed the mob and modified its destructiveness at points. Dyer was born in Germany in 1807 and came with his parents to Baltimore in 1812. His father was the first president of Baltimore's Hebrew Congregation and one of the first beef packers in the United States. First identified in the *Baltimore Directory* of 1842 as a butcher, Leon Dyer was, because of his popularity, appointed acting mayor in the wake of Baltimore's Bread Riot of 1837. See Isidore Blum, *The Jews of Baltimore: An Historical Summary of Their Progress and Status from the Early Days to the Year 1910* (Baltimore, 1910), 9–10. Archibald Hawkins identified Mass as "Red Jacket" in perhaps the best of the historical accounts of the riot. He is the only historian to mention the Bossière affair, and his correctness about this encourages confidence that his identification of Mass may be right. *The Life and Times of the Honorable Elijah Stansbury* (Baltimore, 1874), 90–118.

political leadership of Leon Dyer and his sort.[62] The riot occurred because people were generally convinced of the exploitation by the bank's "partners" of the bank's creditors, but possibly the leaders and the most active rioters were lower-middle-class Jacksonians who found in the incident the perfect illustration of Jacksonian rhetoric about the people versus the monied interests, which they took considerably more to heart than did party leaders. When Henry Brown heard in the country that the people were rising up against the "monied aristocrats," he rushed to town, getting there in time to help sack at least John B. Morris's house. When an acquaintance chided Brown because Morris was "the poor man's friend," Brown said had he known that, he would not have hurt Morris's home, but went on railing against the "damned aristocrats."[63]

This political situation would explain how Moses Davis, a town drunk, presumably, from the joking newspaper references to him as a "very *spirited* man," got one-fourth of the vote for mayor, to replace Hunt, who resigned. Davis' opponent was the law-and-order candidate, Samuel Smith, who was endorsed by the town's entire power structure from both parties. It would also explain why the vote declined one-third from the previous election despite strenuous attempts to get out the electorate for Smith to salvage "Baltimore's fair reputation." Benjamin C. Howard, one of the city's Democratic congressmen standing for re-election, ostentatiously avoided voting for Smith, despite his friendship for and earlier support of the riot victims. And the political situation would explain the unusual degree of emotive sincerity one senses in this riot's inflammatory handbills.[64]

It is difficult to see much social purposiveness in Jacksonian riots. In Baltimore the riot resulted largely in reaction. The next legislature passed a law making local communities financially responsible for riot damage and an indemnity bill paying the victims of riot fully for their losses out of Baltimore's harbor funds. As the attorneys and leaders of the creditors —who desperately tried to prevent the riot—feared, the incident aided the exploiters by transforming the question of choosing between Johnson and Co. and the creditors to that of supporting Johnson and Co. or the mob. The victimization largely ensured the restored social position of Johnson, Glenn, E. T. Ellicott, and McElderry. None were elected to popular office, but all remained prominent and respected. Reverdy Johnson steered his election to the United States Senate as adroitly through the state legisla-

---

[62] Roger B. Taney to James Mason Campbell, Mar. 6, 1836, Benjamin C. Howard Papers, Maryland Historical Society. Taney, who had promised to protect the partners' reputation in return for their earlier support, swung enough Democratic votes to the Indemnity Bill to ensure its passage, partly by getting a statement of support for it from Jackson himself. Taney to David M. Perine, May 28, June 2, June 20, July 10, 1834, Perine Papers; Samuel Tyler, *Memoir of Roger B. Taney* (Baltimore, 1872), 244–45.

[63] Baltimore *Gazette*, Dec. 14, 1835. The case illustrated the willingness of American juries to neglect legalism. The jury, after several hours deliberation, requested to ask the leading witness one question: was Brown *"very* drunk?" The judge said that should have nothing to do with their decision, but added that if they had reasonable doubt of his guilt they should acquit him, which they immediately did.

[64] Baltimore *Gazette*, Sept. 9, 1835; Baltimore *Republican*, Sept. 9, 1835; Roger B. Taney to James Mason Campbell, Sept. 25, 1835, Howard Papers.

ture as he had his Indemnity Bill and became attorney-general of the
United States under Zachary Taylor.[65] But even had the riot succeeded
in ruining or driving out its victims, it would in no way have promoted
the relief of those people who lost heavily through the long-continuing
trusteeship. The Washington rioters were more successful. Beverly Snow
never returned to his nation's capital, no one even considered indemnify-
ing blacks for their losses, and the city council made gestures toward
meeting the rioters' demands for more stringent restrictions on free
Negroes. The moral is one that runs through Jacksonian riots. Mobs often
succeeded in their immediate goals but were in the long run counterpro-
ductive when directed against groups or institutions that had some social
power. Mormons, Catholics, and abolitionists were all injured by riots,
but more fundamentally drew much of their strength from these persecu-
tions. Riots generally succeeded only when directed against the socially
defenseless, particularly blacks.[66]

   The American Irish riots illustrate the problem in interpreting Jacksonian mobs as socially purposive. Certainly the Irish had much to be
unhappy about, both before and after their coming to the United States.
There was some prejudice against them, they had comparatively low-
paying jobs, their housing was bad, and they had to send their children
to schools tinged with Protestantism. And so Irish rioting could be seen
as the just social response of an oppressed group. But as one looks more
closely, these riots seem less against the injustices of the system than over
traditional religious and clan rivalries and against groups less socially
influential than they. Many of the so-called Irish labor riots on the canals,
railroads, and aqueducts generally turn out to have been imported clan
battles between groups of Irish Catholics from different areas of the old
country.[67] In an instance where they attacked management, records suggest that they were angrier about the foreman's Presbyterianism than his
economic exploitation.[68] It is significant that the Irish participated in riots
much more often in New York and Philadelphia where they were quickly
welcomed into the political system than they did in Boston where they

[65] Bernard C. Steiner, *The Life of Reverdy Johnson* (Baltimore, 1914). The creditors'
   attorneys urged the avoidance of violence so that their legal case would not be
   endangered, and one of them, William P. Preston, wrote a personal note to Mayor
   Hunt on August 9, 1835, urging strong action to prevent riot. William P. Preston
   Papers, Maryland Historical Society.
[66] There are two exceptions: the antirent riots of upstate New York encouraged a
   political solution to an outdated system of land tenure, and the mobs in some
   areas of the North did rescue a few blacks and help create sympathy for the
   slave's plight, especially after the Fugitive Slave Law of 1850.
[67] Especially the Chesapeake and Ohio Canal riots of June 1834 and August 1839;
   the riot on the Baltimore and Washington Railroad, June 1834; the riots on the
   Croton Water Works in New York, 1840–41; and the riot on the Erie Railroad
   near Port Jervis, New York, 1849. Sir George C. Lewis described tellingly how
   patterns of Irish rioting developed in response to English injustice, but came to be
   directed, largely per force, against the safer target of other groups of Irish. *On
   Local Disturbances in Ireland; and on the Irish Church Question* (London, 1836).
[68] The Washington and Baltimore Railroad Riot in November 1834; see *Niles' Register*, 47 (Dec. 20, 1834): 272.

were given no political jobs prior to the Civil War. The Philadelphia riot case is illuminating. Philadelphia's first important postrevolutionary riot occurred in 1825 when a serious brawl broke out between Irish Catholics and Protestants just after they disembarked from the ship that brought them from Ireland; six years later a group of Irish Catholics attacked a parade of Orangemen celebrating the Battle of the Boyne, and a general brawl ensued.[69] In 1829 the first of a series of eight Philadelphia riots against blacks and abolitionists occurred in which Irish names bulk large among those arrested, though they were obviously abetted by many home-grown rioters, especially in the antiabolition affrays. And the various antebellum railroad, weaver, nativist, fireboy, and antiprostitution riots seem to have had roots in the same ethnic animosities.[70]

Had the oppressed Irish risen over their social hardships against the power structure, Rudé's conclusions about the crowd in history might apply to Jacksonian America, where, instead, riots featured Irish Catholics fighting Irish Protestants, Corkonions attacking Fardowners, and Irishmen harrassing blacks and their supporters. Indeed favorite targets in some antiblack riots were Negro orphan asylums, homes for perhaps the most hapless of American citizens.[71] The sad truth about the Jacksonian riots was that, though the performers had real grievances and fears, action was generally taken only when there was large promise of safety: by groups in situations and places where they had fairly broad political and social influence and against individuals and groups less popular than they.[72]

[69] David Paul Brown, *Speech Before the Mayor's Court of Philadelphia, September 17, 1825, on the Subject of Riot and Assault and Battery* (Philadelphia, 1858); *A Full and Accurate Report of the Trial for Riot Before the Mayor's Court of Philadelphia on the 13th of October, 1831, Arising out of a Protestant Procession on the 12th of July in Which the Contending Parties Were Protestants and Roman Catholics* (Philadelphia, 1831).

[70] The many nativist riots, commonly seen as part of a "Protestant crusade" against Catholicism, had roots in much more complicated ethnic, religious, and social animosities in urban Jacksonian America. An able exploration of these many strands is William Baughin, "Nativism in Cincinnati Before 1860" (master's thesis, University of Cincinnati, 1950).

[71] The Philadelphia Abolitionist Riot, May 1838; the New York Draft Riot, July 1863. The orphanage attacks allowed release of social anger not only against that group the rioters were determined to keep as social inferiors, but also against their philanthropic social "betters," who endowed the institutions and whom it would have been dangerous to attack directly.

[72] Jacksonian riots could be fitted to the schemas social scientists have worked out for explaining civil disturbances, but this owes perhaps more to the flexibility of various models than their explanatory usefulness. "Social disequilibrium," the "expectation gap," the "J-curve of rising and declining satisfactions," and "relative deprivation" are sufficiently vague to be discoverable wherever sought. Chalmers Johnson, *Revolutionary Change* (Boston, 1966), 59–87, 119–34; Ivo K. Feierabend, Rosalind L. Feierabend, and Betty A. Nesvold, "Social Change and Political Violence: Cross National Patterns," and James C. Davies, "The J-Curve of Rising and Declining Satisfactions as a Cause of Some Great Revolutions and a Contained Rebellion," both in Graham and Gurr, *History of Violence*, 632–730; Gurr, *Why Men Rebel*, 3–91, 317–59. Jacksonian riots clustered in periods of general prosperity, the mid-1830s, 1840s, and 1850s.

Jeremiah Hughes's analysis of both the source and social effects of Jacksonian rioting was well taken:

A radical error in democratic ethics begins to develope itself. The people have been told so often that all power, government, and authority of right belong to them and that they in fact are the only sovereigns here, that it is not to be wondered at that they occasionally mistake the true limit of that sovereignty, and undertake to exercise despotic powers. Who dare control the *People, a Free People?* Don't they make the government itself, and can't they rule it as they please? Such to a great extent is the political education of the day. . . . Governments are instituted mainly for the protection of the weak from the power of the strong. But for this they would not be endured. The majority are always powerful—they require no protection. To restrain an undue exercise of power against the weak is one great motive for which government is instituted.[73]

Hughes's concern about the weak, about minorities, is very much to the point. Victims, more than rioters, were the oppressed, the unpopular, the unprotected.

The psychological effects of rioting are even harder to gauge than its social results. Mobs when unopposed clearly enjoyed themselves; two Baltimore rioters said that they got their $100 and $500 worth of enjoyment—presumably sums lost to the bank—out of their night's work. The amorphousness of bourgeois-democratic society and the constant Jacksonian stress on power belonging to the people made attractive the sense of group identity and invincibility that came from being part of what John Quincy Adams called "the mobility." A song recorded by a Campbellite minister and temperance lecturer who led the Hancock County anti-Mormon mob in Illinois caught some of the "togetherness" of the riotous crowd: "Hancock is a beautiful place/The Antis all are brothers./And when one has a pumpkin pie/He shares it with the others."[74] Democracy's mythic heroes stand outside of society; most of the people who idolize them are enmeshed in it and, if Tocqueville and others are right, have strong desires to merge entirely with the mass.[75] The psychological appeal of riot in democratic society is that the situation gives a sense of acting by a higher code, of pursuing justice and possessing power free from any structural restraint, and at the same time allowing a complete absorption in the mass so that the individual will and the social will appear to be one. To riot is to be Natty Bumppo in crowd, to be Randolph Scott en masse—and this is a kind of apotheosis for democratic man, fulfilling the official doctrine that power belongs to him and allowing

[73] *Niles' Register*, 66 (July 27, 1844): 344–45.
[74] John Quincy Adams, *Memoirs* (Philadelphia, 1876), 9: 252; Thomas Brockman to Andrew Johnston, Jan. 1, 1847, in the Mormon Collection, Chicago Historical Society.
[75] Tocqueville, *Democracy in America*, 2: 109–13, 334–39; Erich Fromm, *Escape from Freedom* (New York, 1965), 17–38, 157–230; Hannah Arendt, *The Origins of Totalitarianism* (New York, 1958), 305–39.

him to escape the real system that attempts to share influence by making everyone powerless.[76] The most famous rioter of the Jacksonian period was also the prime developer of the popular Western story.[77] The permanent value of such mental satisfactions is less certain. Psychologically as well as socially, perhaps, people who associated themselves with groups victimized gained most from riot, if their groups were not permanently oppressed by it.[78]

The problem of riot control in the Jacksonian period centered in a democratic sense of the limitations on the state's right to use strong physical force against the people. Five people died in Baltimore because the guard did get reluctant permission to fire, although many citizens felt that all trouble would have vanished if the guard had been properly armed in the first place and that fact had been made known. Total peace returned when Smith organized his heavily armed patrols, but by this time the use of force was supplemented by a revulsion of feeling against the mob, particularly when it was learned that a large list of additional victims had been designated.[79] On the first day after the Washington riot began, the militia was seemingly instructed to try to awe the mob but not to interfere very actively if assaults were confined to black property. When Jackson returned to the city his strategy became one of conciliating the rioters while keeping enough troops around to prevent serious damage. Andrew Shiner was obviously repeating gossip but described Jackson's method accurately.

[76] Hannah Arendt's distinction between power based on concerted popular acquiescence and violence based on instrumental force is pertinent here, although perhaps a more telling contrast is between power, the essence of which Bertrand de Jouvenal defines as the ability "to command and to be obeyed," and influence, which is the abilty to dictate action only through an ongoing process of convincing or manipulating others to agree with a particular policy. Arendt, *On Violence* (New York, 1970), 35–56; Jouvenal, *On Power: The Nature and History of Its Growth* (Boston, 1948), 96. Louis Hartz suggests the vacuousness of the Jacksonian stress on "the will of the people" because the idea promised a direct power that inevitably created distaste for the realities of the political system meant to embody it. *Economic Policy and Democratic Thought: Pennsylvania 1776–1860* (Cambridge, Mass., 1948), 23–33, 309–20.

[77] E. Z. C. Judson was convicted of instigating the Astor Place Riot of 1849 in New York and was indicted for his part in a St. Louis election riot of 1852. As "Ned Buntline," he also was the leading developer of the dime novel. Jay Monaghan, *The Great Rascal: The Life and Times of Ned Buntline* (New York, 1952).

[78] Helpful studies of the psychological sources and effects of violence are Hans Toch, *Violent Men: An Inquiry into the Psychology of Violence* (Chicago, 1969); Silvan S. Tomkins, "The Psychology of Commitment: The Constructive Role of Violence and Suffering for the Individual and for His Society," in Martin B. Duberman, ed., *The Anti-Slavery Vanguard: New Essays on the Abolitionist* (Princeton, 1965), 270–98.

[79] Joint Committee of the Maryland General Assembly on the Baltimore Riots, *The Report of and Testimony Taken Before the Joint Committee of the Senate and House of Delegates of Maryland* (Annapolis, 1836); Baltimore *American*, Aug. 12, 1835; "Junius" in the Baltimore *Republican*, Mar. 5, 1836.

> When this great excitement commenced the Hon. Major General
> Andrew Jackson that wher president . . . wher absent from the
> City and when it got in it height the general arrived home and
> after he arrived home he sent a message to those gentelmen Me-
> chanics to know what was the matter with them and if they were
> anny thing he could do for them in an IIon. way to promote their
> happiness he would do it.

When they complained of Negro actions, Jackson assured them "by the
eternal god in this city" he would personally see that the blacks were
punished if the mechanics had any disclosures to make about illegal activities, but he made clear "by the eternal god the law must be preserved
at the Risk of Hasards." Minor sporadic incidents occurred later, but in a
couple of weeks Washington "was as quiet as a church and the laws
wher all respected."[80]

Outside of Washington, the multileveled character of American government kept riot control largely a local problem to be coped with by
local officials. Such people, even more than Jackson, were often understandably sympathetic to their fellow citizen-voters or at least hesitant
to attack any large group of them. Hence there was much truth to the
frequent assertion that a greater show of determination on the part of
authorities would have proved effective in stopping trouble. Some observers considered even a real show of determination an inadequate response to threatened violence. Roger Taney complained that the Baltimore bank mob ought to have been met by a "firm and free" use of guns
at once, and Wendell Phillips accused the Boston mayor of being derelict
in his duty for not having "ten men shot and sent to deserved graves"
in the Garrison mob—this in a riot where the mayor acted with vigor
and personal courage and where the total estimated damage was fifteen
dollars.[81] Even gross dereliction of duty was perhaps better than Phillips's
emotive and moralistic approach, which could only feed the paranoiac
self-righteousness rioters, actual and potential, possess. The heaviest loss
of life tended to occur in two riotous situations: when authorities wholly
acquiesced in a mob's destructive tendencies—as was the case with the
Mormons in Missouri, with some groups of gentiles later in Mormon-
controlled Utah, and in alleged abolitionist and slave conspiracies in the
South; or when force was used to keep a mob from their ends. Elijah
Lovejoy would not have been killed if he had let his press be removed
from Alton as he had from St. Louis. No one died at the Ursuline Convent, which the mob burned unopposed; twenty were victims of the
military when the mob was not allowed to fire a Philadelphia Catholic
church. How weigh the five bodies in Baltimore against the property of
the bank partners or that of men whose crime was answering a public

---

[80] Shiner, diary, 60–61 ff. At least some damage to black property occurred as late as
mid-September, although the major Washington papers did not mention it. Baltimore *Gazette*, Sept. 15, 1835; *Niles' Register*, 49 (Sept. 19, 1835): 33.

[81] Frank Otto Gatell, "Roger B. Taney, the Bank of Maryland and a Whiff of
Grapeshot," *Maryland Historical Magazine*, 59 (1964): 262–67; Theodore Lyman
III, ed. *Papers Relating to the Garrison Mob* (Cambridge, Mass., 1870), 7.

call to aid in keeping the peace? How put Beverly Snow's small property and dignity in the balance with the lives that it might have cost to protect them? In some cases even human life may be less important than using force, if absolutely necessary, to allow unpopular faiths to be followed, unpopular people to be protected, unpopular ideas to be heard.

The clearest result of Jacksonian rioting was the development of professional police and fire companies in large cities.[82] In the wake of the Baltimore riots there was a strong recognition of the lack of organized civil authority to cope with such problems. The only "republican solution" seemed to be organization of volunteer peace-keeping forces because a professional "army" to ensure order among the people was certainly a mark of despotism. City guards were formed in each Baltimore ward, and gout-ridden Henry Thompson headed a corps of City Horse Guards, but such organizations, without the stimulus of any very urgent business, quickly waned. At the same time, Sir Robert Peel's organization of the London police suggested that a professional police force need not be despotic and pointed to the solution that Americans would accept in the 1840s and 1850s.[83] Riots, along with the increasing problem of crime, made clear in urban areas at least that the old voluntary principle could no longer handle social control among a people growing, and growing apart in economic status and ethnic diversity. American democracy, very reluctantly, came to accept that order and freedom required not only a legal system, but professionals specifically responsible for upholding it and forcing its dictates on recalcitrant fellow citizens. If Andrew Jackson was a political symbol for the mythic anarchic American ensuring the triumph of a higher code by his own strength and integrity in a world neatly divided between virtuous men and monstrous enemies, Abraham Lincoln came to represent the sadder side of the democratic psyche: the need to assert man's potential for freedom through accepting cruel responsibilities for using force in a world where the morality of all men was a mixed bag and where both sides prayed to the same God. Lincoln in his famous law-and-order speech of 1837 used recent riots to argue that only in unswerving respect for the law lay real protection from vicious disintegration and despotism. He and his nation in the Civil War proved their willingness to insist on their conception of law even if it had to be imposed by military force.[84] In his *Battle-Pieces*, Herman Melville, the

---

[82] Roger Lane, *Policing the City: Boston 1822–1885* (Cambridge, Mass., 1967), 26–38; James F. Richardson, *The New York Police, Colonial Times to 1901* (New York, 1970), 28–30; Sam Bass Warner, *The Private City: Philadelphia in Three Periods of Its Growth* (Philadelphia, 1968), 125–57; Andrew H. Neilly, "The Violent Volunteers: A History of the Volunteer Fire Department of Philadelphia, 1736–1831" (Ph.D. dissertation, University of Pennsylvania, 1960).

[83] Baltimore *Gazette*, Sept. 13, 19, 1835; Baltimore *American*, Aug. 27, Sept. 12, 1835; Thompson, diary, Sept.–Oct. 1835.

[84] Abraham Lincoln, "Address Before the Young Men's Lyceum of Springfield, January 27, 1838," in *Collected Works*, ed. Roy P. Basler (New Brunswick, 1953), 1: 110–12; Harry Jaffa, *The Crisis of the House Divided: An Interpretation of the Lincoln-Douglas Debates* (New York, 1959), 183–232.

American who had most developed the theme of the heroically destructive potential of self-reliant individualism, noted how the Civil War marked society's tacit acceptance of his grimmer vision of man's fate—especially in a poem commenting on New York City's Draft Riot of 1863 where for the first time a professional police force was used not to control but to conquer "the Atheist roar of riot":

> Hail to the low dull rumble, dull and dead,
> And ponderous drag that shakes the wall.
> Wise Draco comes, deep in the midnight roll
> Of black artillery; he comes, though late;
> In code corroborating Calvin's creed
> And cynic tyrannies of honest kings;
> He comes, nor parlies; and the Town, redeemed,
> Gives thanks devout; nor, being thankful, heeds
> The grimy slur on the Republic's faith implied,
> Which holds that Man is naturally good,
> And—more—is Nature's Roman, never to be scourged.[85]

Still unshaken in their democratic convictions, Americans admitted in their prosecution of the Civil War and their growing resistance to rioters that the nation was in practice willing to temper the democratic myth of social responsibility through freedom with some of Draco's stern legalism and Calvin's harsh estimate of man's character and destiny. With a willingness, if you will, to use law not only to release human energy but to check and control it.

The Jacksonian experience suggests that riot is not antithetical to, or abnormal in, a democracy but the result of very basic tendencies and tensions within it. Because of these the riot situation poses in stark form many of the deepest dilemmas a democracy faces. To react harshly is to threaten groups who act within its bounds and in accord with some of its basic precepts; to react tolerantly is inevitably to make the state an accomplice in whatever is done. Riot crystallizes the paradox of vital democracy that must live in the shadow of twin totalitarianisms—that of total submission of all to the state's power and that of the tyranny of favored groups or individuals because of the state's weakness. And to avoid the ascendancy of either totalitarianism requires that democratic man live uneasily and creatively with the dangerous proclivities, potential and sometimes realized, in both his legalistic and anarchic myths.

[85] Herman Melville, "The Housetop," in *The Battle-Pieces*, ed. Hennig Cohen (New York, 1963), 89–90. The change in attitude toward the power of the state paralleled other intellectual shifts, some of which are traced in George M. Frederickson, *The Inner Civil War: Northern Intellectuals and the Crisis of the Union* (New York, 1965), in R. Jackson Wilson, *In Quest of Community* (New York, 1968), and in Hurst, *Law and the Conditions of Freedom*.

The Lowell Work Force, 1836,
and the Social Origins of
Women Workers

THOMAS DUBLIN

The decades before the Civil War resounded with the cry of reform. Hardly any institution in American life escaped the scrutiny of some groups determined to change it. There were campaigns for the abolition of slavery, for penal reform, for better care of the insane, for temperance, for communal living, for industrial socialism, and for many other schemes to improve the status quo. Not the least of these was a campaign for women's rights led by such impressive figures as Elizabeth Cady Stanton, Frances Wright, and the Grimke sisters.

Women had always been a valuable commodity in colonial America. In seventeenth-century Virginia, wives were actually sold by the Virginia Company, which transported young women from England and exchanged them for one hundred and fifty pounds of good tobacco. Women continued to be in short supply in the colonies, as the rigors of frontier life and the dangers of continuous child-bearing made the female mortality rate—along with that of infants—extremely high.

With the coming of the War for Independence, women began to look for some benefits for themselves to be derived from the egalitarian ethos of the time. However, they were to be disappointed as the attempts to enlarge women's sphere beyond the home seemed doomed to fail.

As long as American society was primarily agricultural, there was a fairly clear-cut distinction between the functions of men and women. Most of the woman's time was taken up with housework and child-rearing. When she had time, she joined the men in the fields, where there was always plenty of work for all.

With urban society, however, came challenges to the traditional division of labor between the sexes. Urban industrialization greatly affected the young women who went to work in the new factories. These women were found primarily in the textile factories of New

England. Aside from the young women who entered domestic service —a line of work that raised no challenge to the traditional sexual differentiation in the society—the women who went to work in the textile mills made up the largest number of independent, unmarried white women in the nation.

Thomas Dublin, of the University of California at San Diego, has studied the first generation of young women who left home to seek their fortunes in the nation's factories. His detailed case study of the Lowell mills provides us with a thorough analysis of the reasons the young women went to work in the mills, where they came from, and, to the extent possible, their experience's impact on them. In the selection from his work reprinted below, Dublin provides us with an understanding of the social forces that led the young women to seek factory work. He indicates that their experiences there led them to be more assertive than had been their mothers back on the farms. In this way, many of these female millworkers and their offspring provided a sympathetic audience for new ideas that were developing about women's place in society.

A ccording to the conventional view, women in the early Lowell mills were young, single women attracted from the surrounding New England countryside. They entered and left the mills frequently, working for repeated short stretches in the years before marriage. While in Lowell they resided in company boardinghouses, erected by the textile corporations and managed by boardinghouse keepers. These are time-honored generalizations, enunciated initially by contemporary observers and corroborated by the research of subsequent historians.[1]

This description is basically correct and uncontroversial, but it does

[1] [Henry A.] Miles. *Lowell As It Was [and As It Is* (Lowell: Powers and Bagley, 1845)], pp. 162–94; Mass. House Document No. 50 (1845), in [John R.] Commons et al., eds., *A Documentary History of American Industrial Society* [(Cleveland: Arthur H. Clark, 1910)], 8:133–51. For subsequent historians' accounts see [Caroline F.] Ware, [*The*] *Early New England Cotton Manufacture: [A Study in Industrial Beginnings* (New York: Russell and Russell, 1966)], ch. 8; [Hannah] Josephson, [*The*] *Golden Threads: [New England's Mill Girls and Magnates* (New York: Duell, Sloan, and Pearce, 1949)], ch. 4; [Robert G.] Layer, *Earnings of Cotton Mill Operatives*, pp. 70–71. [Robert G.] Layer, "Wages, Earnings, and Output [of Four Cotton Textile Companies in New England, 1825–1860" (Ph.D. dissertation, Harvard University, 1952)], table 27, p. 226ff.

"The Lowell Work Force, 1836, and the Social Origins of Women Workers." From *Women at Work: The Transformation of Work and Community in Lowell, Massachusetts, 1826-1860* by Thomas Dublin, pp. 23–57. Copyright © 1979 by Columbia University Press. Reprinted by permission.

not take the analysis of the early work force in the Lowell mills far enough. In the first place, it is possible to quantify these generalizations more carefully, determining the actual proportions of men and women, native-born and immigrant, children and adults, and boardinghouse residents and family members in the overall work force. Determination of these proportions for the mid-1830s provides a base line for later discussion of the transformation of the Lowell labor system in succeeding decades.

In the second place, it is possible to extend this framework beyond the confines of Lowell by tracing workers back to the rural families and communities from which they came. Such tracing illuminates the social origins, and also the motivations, of women workers in the early mills, besides placing the mill experience within the broader life cycle of rural women. Taken together, these approaches establish the human context of life and work in early Lowell and point to the broader significance of the experience in the lives of women workers.

The lives of two women show in microscopic detail the interacting themes that the quantitative evidence demonstrates for Lowell women as a whole. The diary of Mary Hall and the autobiography of Harriet Hanson Robinson offer rare glimpses into the personal lives and attitudes of women in the early mills. Let us begin the analysis, then, with brief sketches of these two women.

Mary Hall first came to Lowell in September 1831 at the age of 23. The diary she kept during this period reveals an unsettledness common among mill operatives at this time. Over the next six years, Mary Hall worked short stretches in the mills, ranging from four to eleven months at a time, for three different firms in Lowell. Interspersed with her work were numerous visits back home to Concord, New Hampshire, including one stay at home that lasted a year and a half. During the Lowell years, she remained in close touch with her family. Frequent letters helped sustain the bond; her father and brothers visited repeatedly; a sister and two cousins also worked in the mills, and another sister and an uncle lived in Lowell. Finally, Mary Hall's residence in Lowell extended well beyond her six years in the mills. In 1838 she married Albert Capen, a railroad worker, and the couple continued to reside in Lowell at least until 1855. In all, she lived in Lowell for more than two decades.[2]

Why did Mary Hall go to Lowell in the first place? Though her diary reveals little in the way of personal feelings, company payrolls may provide part of the answer. Mary Hall made good wages in the mills. As a weaver at the Lawrence Company, she earned $115 during an eight-month period in 1834, and in 11 months in 1836 and 1837 her wages totaled more than $150.[3] Over the course of her mill career, Hall averaged

---

[2] Mary Hall Diary, *passim*, NHHS [New Hampshire Historical Society]; New Hampshire Bureau of Vital Statistics, marriage of Mary Hall to Albert G. Capen, June 5, 1838; Lowell *City Directory*, 1834–1855.

[3] Lawrence Co., vols. GA-1, GA-2, GA-3, BL. Hall worked in the Lower Weaving Room and her wages are recorded with that room in the monthly payroll series.

about $3.25 per week. Given a weekly charge of $1.25 for room and board in company boardinghouses over most of this period, these earnings must have enabled Hall to support herself quite well. The economic and social independence which her wages provided must have been important to Mary Hall, a 29-year-old, single woman in her final year of employment in the mills.

Harriet Hanson Robinson did not keep a diary during her years in the mills, but her autobiography, *Loom and Spindle,* published in 1898 when she was 73 years old, provides a rich source for the social historian. Harriet came to Lowell as a child when her widowed mother took a boardinghouse at the Lawrence Corporation. At first she attended school and helped her mother with household chores, but in 1834, at the age of 10, she began working as a doffer, or bobbin girl, in a spinning room in the Lawrence mills. Though a child she took an active part in a strike in 1836, and her reminiscences provide a vivid, firsthand account of the affair. Her career also affords evidence of the occupational mobility common for women in the early mills. After working several years she moved up to tend a spinning frame, where she earned regular adult wages. Still later, she learned drawing in, one of the more skilled and better-paid occupations open to women. Her mill career came to an end in 1848, when at the age of 24 she married a young newspaper editor, William Robinson.[4]

These sketches of the lives of Mary Hall Capen and Harriet Hanson Robinson are much more complete than those that can be reconstructed for most mill operatives. But even if other surviving accounts were equally full, it would be risky to generalize about the makeup of the early mill work force or the social origins of women workers solely on the basis of letters, diaries, and reminiscences. The two dozen literary accounts that are available to us are indeed valuable, but they remain simply the stories of twenty or so women out of the tens of thousands who worked in the Lowell mills in these years. Luckily for the historian, however, other sources are available. The Lowell textile firms were pioneers in the development of business accounting procedures in the decades before the Civil War, and they kept remarkably complete payroll records. These sources enable the historian to reconstruct the mill work force in the mid-1830s and to trace a sample of workers back to their native homes in rural New England. Analysis of these systematic business records provides a strong foundation for generalizations about the makeup of the early mill work force and the social origins of operatives. When supplemented by a consideration of the beliefs and attitudes of women as expressed in surviving literary accounts, they illuminate the place and significance of the mill experience in the lives of women workers.

The richest available evidence on the composition of the mill work force in the mid-1830s is contained in the labor records of the Hamilton Manufacturing Company of Lowell.[5] Hamilton records enable one to

---

[4] Harriet Hanson Robinson, *Loom and Spindle; [or Life Among the Early Mill Girls* (New York: Crowell, 1898)], chs. 2–4, 8.

[5] The actual choice of which Lowell firm to study is limited by the fact that payrolls are extant for only the Hamilton and Lawrence companies. The earlier

TABLE 1.
Ethnic Makeup of the Hamilton Company
Work Force, July 1836

NATIVITY	MALES	FEMALES	OVERALL
United States	93.9%	96.6%	96.3%
Ireland	2.0	2.4	2.3
England	2.0	0.3	0.5
Canada	2.0	0.8	0.9
Total cases	98	765	863
Missing cases[a]	51	116	167

NOTE: Columns may not add up to 100.0% due to rounding.
[a] Missing cases include individuals unlinked in company register books, and individuals successfully linked but for whom the clerk failed to record nativity. . . .

determine the sex, nativity, place of residence, literacy, occupation, wage rates, and overall earnings of mill employees. The records must be sampled, however, as the survival of almost complete payroll records over the period 1830–1860 means that there are on the order of 400,000 individual monthly payroll entries. Thus the single payroll months of July 1836, August 1850, and June 1860 were chosen for detailed study. . . .

The work force of the Hamilton Company in July 1836 was overwhelmingly female.[6] More than 85 percent—881 of 1030—of those employed in the company's three mills were women. Less than 4 percent of the work force were foreign-born.[7] As table 1 indicates, the proportion of immigrants among men, 6.1 percent, was considerably greater than the corresponding figure among women. The overall total of immigrants was very small; the Irish, numbering 20 in all, comprised the largest single group.[8]

---

starting point for the Hamilton payroll series, 1826 compared to 1833, coupled with the existence of separate register volumes providing the nativity and residence of workers, led to the selection of the Hamilton Company. . . .

[6] The work force consisted of employees in the company's three mills at this time, in the repair shop, in the millyard, and on the firm's night watch force.

[7] Layer, *Earnings of Cotton Mill Operatives*, pp. 70–71, presents almost identical figures for the ethnic makeup of the Hamilton work force at this date although utilizing somewhat different techniques to analyze company registers. He computes the ethnic composition of the work force by drawing samples of entrants as recorded in registers between 1830 and 1876. His figures thus indicate the makeup of those entering the mills in a given period, not of those actually working at a single point in time.

[8] . . . A discussion of potential bias in the findings reported here . . . [has been] made to estimate bias due to the incompleteness of linkage between payrolls and register volumes. That this problem is worth consideration should be evident from

Another factor unifying the female work force was its homogeneity in terms of age. Of females 10 years of age or older who were resident in Hamilton Company boardinghouses in 1830 and 1840, more than 80 percent were between 15 and 30 years of age.[9] Company records suggest that only about 3 percent of Hamilton workers were children under 15 years old. Thus children were a small and not very significant part of the work force of the early Lowell mills. Women in their teens and twenties dominated the work force of the Hamilton Company in these years.[10]

---

the fact that table 1 indicates that 167 of 1030 workers—more than 16 percent—could not be traced in register volumes. For men, this proportion reached fully a third.

[9] Age analysis based on examination of the enumerations for Hamilton Company boardinghouses in the manuscript censuses for Lowell in 1830 and 1840. Linkage of Hamilton rental records and the census located 49 of 50 Hamilton tenants in 1830 and 48 of 50 in 1840. In the computation children under 10 and all males in the households were excluded from consideration. The overall female age distribution, summarized [here], is given in table N.1.

TABLE N.1.
Estimate of Age Distribution of Female Operatives at
the Hamilton Company, 1830 and 1840

AGE (IN YEARS)	1830	1840
10–14	2.8%	3.9%
15–19	32.9	28.2
20–29	51.7	51.7
30–39	6.0	10.6
40–49	5.1	4.7
50+	1.4	1.0
Total cases	431	407

On the reasonableness of the assumption that girls under ten were not working in the mills see Robinson, *Loom and Spindle*, p. 30; Lucy Larcom, *A New England Girlhood* [(Boston: James R. Osgood, 1875)], p. 153. For a discussion of census schedules and instructions to enumerators see Carroll D. Wright, *The History and Growth of the United States Census* [(Washington, D.C.: Government Printing Office, 1900)], pp. 28–52, 138–55. For corroborating findings see William Scoresby, *American Factories and Their Female Operatives* [(London: Longman, Brown, Green and Longmans, 1845)], p. 53; Mass. House Document No. 50 (1845), in Commons et al., *Documentary History*, 8:146; Edith Abbott, *Women in Industry: [A Study in American Economic History* (New York: D. Appleton, 1913)], p. 124.

[10] Children's jobs included doffers in spinning and lap boys in carding. Register books recorded children who brought with them certificates of school attendance and noted only 24, about 2 percent of the work force. Lowell School Committee, *26th Annual Report* (Lowell, 1852), noted that 2,000 school certificates

Most workers at Hamilton resided in company-owned housing. Almost three fourths, 73.7 percent, lived in housing provided by the Hamilton or the adjacent Appleton Company. Males and females resided in company housing in similar proportions, 70 and 74 percent respectively, but there remained important differences in housing patterns for the two groups. Male workers living in company housing were divided almost evenly between single, adult men in boardinghouses and married men with families in company tenements. In contrast, about 95 percent of women workers in Hamilton Company housing were single residents of female boardinghouses.[11]

More than a fourth of the women employed at Hamilton resided in private housing, but considerably fewer lived with their own families. Only 11.5 percent—about one in nine—of the females at Hamilton lived at home with their families; the remainder, 88.5 percent, resided in either company-owned or private boardinghouses.[12] This separation of women workers from their immediate families heightened the importance of the peer group among Lowell operatives, . . .

These data on the composition of the mill work force at the Hamilton Company in the mid-1830s are crucial to an understanding of the nature of community and the growth of labor protest in Lowell in this period. To limit the analysis to Lowell, however, is to gloss over the fact that the work force was the product of a rural-urban migration that linked the factory town to numerous villages in the surrounding countryside. Tracing women workers back to the families and communities from which they came will more clearly place the Lowell work force in a broader context and contribute to a fuller understanding of the meaning of the mill experience in the lives of women workers.[13]

---

had been issued in the previous fourteen years, making an average of about 150 per year, consistent with the findings for Hamilton alone. On school attendance legislation see Charles Persons, "The Early History of Factory Legislation in Massachusetts [From 1825 to the Passage of the Ten Hour Law in 1874," in Susan M. Kingsbury, ed., *Labor Laws and Their Enforcement, With Special Reference to Massachusetts* (New York: Longmans, Green, 1911)], pp. 19, 21.

[11] Hamilton Co., vols. 506–508, BL [Baker Library, Harvard Graduate School of Business Administration, Boston, Mass.], lists all tenants of company houses and from the rental figures one can determine whether a given unit was a boardinghouse or a tenement.

[12] The Boott Manufacturing Company agent in 1841 analyzed his company's register book and found that only 9 percent of operatives had permanent homes in Lowell, a finding comparable to the Hamilton data. Mass. House Document, No. 50 (1845), Appendix A, p. 19, as quoted in Ware, *Early New England Cotton Manufacture*, p. 219.

[13] This study will be at once an examination of rural-urban migration and of the place of mill employment in the female life cycle. Earlier works that have influenced the approach taken here include Michael Anderson, *Family Structure in Nineteenth-Century Lancashire* [(Cambridge, Eng.: Cambridge University Press, 1971)], chs. 4, 5, 7; Peter R. Uhlenberg, "A Study of Cohort Life Cycles: [Cohorts of Native-Born Massachusetts Women, 1830–1920," *Population Studies* (1969), 23]; Laurence Glasco, "The Life Cycles and Household Structure of

Here again the register volumes of the Hamilton Company provide a starting point for the analysis. These volumes recorded the entrances and departures of operatives, noting their nativity as well. Seven hundred workers entered the Hamilton mills in the first six months of 1836, and New Hampshire towns predominated among those sending large numbers into the company's employ. Excluding Lowell itself, twelve of the fourteen towns that sent the largest numbers of workers to Hamilton were found in New Hampshire, five of these in central Merrimack County. From the communities in Merrimack County that supplied so many workers to Hamilton, I selected three towns with particularly complete published vital records—Boscawen, Canterbury, and Sutton—for detailed examination.[14]

These towns were long-settled agricultural communities by the second third of the nineteenth century. The initial land grants for all three towns had been made by 1750; first settlement and incorporation of the towns were complete by 1784. They moved rapidly beyond the frontier stage and reached relative population peaks before 1830. Their populations held steady between 1830 and 1850, ranging from about 1,400 for Sutton to a bit more than 2,000 for Boscawen. The steady growth of previous decades halted at the good lands were absorbed and the local economies stagnated.[15] Unable to fulfull their ambitions at home, the young people departed to more fertile western lands or to the growing cities of New England. In this respect the three sample communities shared an experience common to a majority of the hill-country towns of central Vermont and New Hampshire in the period: rapid growth followed by decline and outmigration.[16]

American Ethnic Groups: [Irish, Germans, and Native-born Whites in Buffalo, New York, 1855," *Journal of Urban History* (1975), 1]; Tamara Hareven, "The Family as Process: The Historical Study of the Family Cycle," *Journal of Social History* (1974), 7.322-29; Hareven, "The Dynamics of Kin in an Industrial Community: [A Historical Perspective," (Davis Center Seminar, April 1977. Unpublished manuscript)].

[14] . . . Published sources included Charles Coffin, *The History of Boscawen and Webster*, [*From 1773 to 1878* (Concord: Republican Press Association, 1878)]; James Otis Lyford, *History of the Town of Canterbury, New Hampshire, 1727–1912*, [2 vols. (Concord: Rumford Press, 1912)]; Augusta Harvey Worthen, *The History of Sutton, New Hampshire: [Consisting of the Historical Collections of Erastus Wadleigh, Esp., and A. H. Worthen*, 2 parts (Concord: Republican Press Association, 1890)]; Willis Burton, *History: Boscawen-Webster, Fifty Years, 1883–1933* [(Penacook, N.H.: W. B. Ranney, n.d.)].

[15] D. Hamilton Hurd, ed., *History of Merrimack and Belknap Counties, New Hampshire* [(Philadelphia: D. L. Lewis, 1885)], pp. 181, 229, 627; Alonzo J. Fogg, *The Statistics and Gazeteer of New Hampshire* [(Concord: D. L. Guernsey, 1874)], pp. 69–73, 83–86, 345–46; Bryn E. Evans, "Sutton, New Hampshire, and The Kearsarge Valley: [Life and Wealth in Rural New England, 1810–1870" (M.A. Thesis, Salem (Mass.) State College, 1975)].

[16] For overviews of the general difficulties confronting the majority of towns in New Hampshire in the period see Harold Fisher Wilson, *The Hill Country of Northern New England* [(New York: Columbia University Press, 1936)], chs. 1–4; Norman W. Smith, "A Mature Frontier—The New Hampshire Economy,

In economic as in demographic terms, Boscawen, Canterbury, and Sutton had much in common. All three were overwhelmingly agricultural communities. The vast majority of adult men worked in farm occupations, the proportions in 1840 varying from 82 percent for Boscawen to 87 percent for Canterbury. All three had, however, a small number of artisans—blacksmiths, shoemakers, carpenters, and furniture makers were most numerous—providing needed services for the local community. A number of grist and saw mills, carding and fulling mills, and tanneries dotted the banks of local streams, but they were invariably small affairs and generated few jobs. In fact the most significant "industry" reported in an 1833 census of manufactures was sheepraising. Boscawen counted some 5,000 sheep, Sutton another 4,000, and both communities derived considerable cash income from the sale of wool in Lowell and Boston. The 1830s saw a rapid growth in the size of herds in central New Hampshire as the price of wool rose substantially. By 1836 the number of sheep in Boscawen, Canterbury, and Sutton was reliably reported to be greater than 18,000. Increasingly, the communities looked toward urban markets for their wool. Treading the same paths were the many young women who sought employment in the Lowell mills.[17]

While all three towns were primarily farming communities, there were differences among them. Boscawen and Canterbury were river valley settlements, located just across the Merrimack River from one another. They had lush, flat farm land periodically enriched by deposits from spring flooding, while in sharp contrast, Sutton was a hill town, marred by steep hills that minimized the prime farmlands. As a result sheep and dairy farming were more important in the Sutton economy than in the other two towns.[18] Sutton was also a far poorer community,

---

1790–1850," *Historical New Hampshire* (1969), 24:3–19; Stewart Holbrook, *The Yankee Exodus,* [*an Account of Migration from New England* (New York: Macmillan, 1950)]; Lois Kimball Mathews, *The Expansion of New England:* [*The Spread of New England Settlement and Institutions to the Mississippi River, 1620–1865.* (New York: Russell and Russell, 1962)]; Lewis Stilwell, *Migration From Vermont* [(Montpelier: Vermont Historical Society, 1848)].

[17] U.S. Department of State, *Compendium of the Enumeration . . . From the Returns of the Sixth Census,* pp. 106–17; 1840 Manuscript Census of Merrimack County, M704, Roll 240; Worthen, *History of Sutton,* pp. 285–91; Lyford, *History of Canterbury,* ch. 8; U.S. Department of Treasury, *Documents Relative to the Manufactures of the United States,* Document 5, Nos. 2, 6, 9, 20, 21; C. Benton and S. F. Barry, *A Statistical View of the Number of Sheep . . . in 1836* (Cambridge: Folsom, Willson and Thurston, 1837), pp. 13, 122. In terms of industry, Canterbury stood out somewhat from the other two towns as it included a thriving Shaker community with strong traditions of craft production. There is no evidence however that any Shakers were included in the Lowell migration, and in the analysis of tax inventories and census occupations Shakers have been excluded from consideration.

[18] Fogg, *Statistics and Gazetteer,* pp. 69, 83, 345; Evans, "Sutton, New Hampshire," p. 8. The 1850 Agricultural Census for Merrimack County (manuscript volume in State Library, Concord, N.H.) provides the first breakdown at the town level of principal agricultural commodities for these three communities. Boscawen

TABLE 2.
First Entrances of New Hampshire Women
at Hamilton, 1827–1850

ENTRANCE DATE	PROPORTION (%)
1827–1834	47.7
1835–1839	30.8
1840–1844	12.8
1845–1850	8.7
Total cases	172
Missing cases	3

NOTE: Although the sample consisted of women recorded in register volumes between 1830 and 1850, a few actually entered earlier, necessitating the 1827 beginning date for the table.

as evidenced in the low property valuations of taxpayers in 1830. The mean valuation of individual taxed property in that year for Sutton was $362, well below the comparable figures of $518 and $685 for Boscawen and Canterbury respectively.[19]

Despite these differences among the towns, large numbers of young women from all three set out for Lowell and found employment in the Hamilton Company. Between 1830 and 1850 at least 75 women left Boscawen to work in the mills of the Hamilton Company, while 55 and 45 came from Canterbury and Sutton respectively. In contrast to the total of 175 women recorded in company register volumes, only 9 men from these communities came to work at Hamilton, although larger numbers worked elsewhere in Lowell as city directory and marriage records make clear.[20]

The women began employment at the Hamilton Company primarily in the 1830s, particularly in the first half of that decade. Table 2 indicates

and Canterbury per capita yields of oats and Indian corn were substantially above those of Sutton, while the latter had relatively larger herds of sheep than the other two.

[19] Based on analysis of 1830 tax inventories for Boscawen, Canterbury, and Sutton. Means are for resident taxpayers only, and exclude property held in the names of heirs of estates. . . .

[20] Figures based on counting the number of individuals who entered or departed the company with nativity recorded in the appropriate register volume as Boscawen, Canterbury, or Sutton. Undoubtedly, a certain proportion of those for whom nativity was left blank came from these towns. Furthermore, one volume had faded so thoroughly that names and nativity could not be determined. Finally, register volumes are not extant for a period in the first half of the 1830s. Taken together, the difficulties suggest that the figure of 175 understates the actual number of women from these towns who worked at Hamilton.

the distribution of their first entrances into the mill work force at Hamilton.

Women from these three New Hampshire towns were a representative cross section of the female work force at Hamilton. Since almost 80 percent of the women entered employment before 1840, it is reasonable to compare the group with women employed at Hamilton in July 1836. In terms of the rooms they worked in, their age and marital status, and the length of their careers, they did not deviate significantly from the work force as a whole.

The New Hampshire women were distributed throughout the major rooms of the Hamilton Company in proportions quite similar to those for the overall female work force. Table 3 makes this point clear.

There were slightly more weavers and proportionately fewer carders and spinners among the New Hampshire sample members than in the female work force as a whole. This occupational distribution suggests that sample members were probably earning wages somewhat higher than those of the female work force as a whole. These differences were not great enough, however, to indicate that they were a privileged stratum within the mills.

The ages of the New Hampshire operatives are consistent with the findings presented earlier for residents of Hamilton Company boardinghouses. Few children or older women came to the mills from these three rural communities. The mean age for beginning work at the company was 19.8, and women on the average completed their careers at Hamilton when they were 22.4 years old. Table 4 provides data on the age distribution of New Hampshire women at the beginning of their employment at Hamilton.

As with the boardinghouse residents enumerated in the 1830 and 1840 censuses of Lowell, about 80 percent of the women were between the ages of 15 and 29 when they began work at Hamilton. The proportion under 15, 14.3 percent, seems on the high side, but this age distribution catches the group at first entrance into the mills. By the time of their departures, only 4.5 percent of the women were under 15 years of age.

The data on age suggest that mill work attracted young women seek-

TABLE 3.
Room Distribution of New Hampshire Women at
First Entrance at Hamilton, Compared to
Overall Female Work Force, July 1836

	PROPORTION	
ROOM	NH WOMEN	FEMALE WORK FORCE
Carding	10.9%	14.3%
Spinning	20.0	26.1
Weaving	51.4	43.0
Dressing and others	17.7	16.5
Total cases	175	880

TABLE 4.
Age Distribution of New Hampshire Women
at First Entrance at Hamilton

AGE GROUP	PROPORTION[a] (%)
Under 15	14.3
15.0–19.9	46.2
20.0–24.9	25.2
25.0–29.9	9.2
30.0 and over	5.0
Total cases	119
Missing cases	56

[a] Column may not add up to 100.0% due to rounding.

ing employment for a brief period before marriage, and the evidence on marital status confirms this supposition. Almost 97 percent—124 of the 128 with usable marriage linkage—were single, never married at the beginning of their careers at Hamilton. At the end of their employment, fully 93 percent remained single. In terms of actual numbers, only 5 married women and 3 widows were included in this group of mill workers.

The married women in the sample group present a special and interesting case, and although their absolute numbers are small, they deserve some additional consideration. Their careers reveal a number of striking elements. As a group they tended to have very brief stays in the mills. Mary Morrill worked for three months at Hamilton in 1835. Later she married George Chase, a housewright in Lowell, and returned to Hamilton for four months during the depression months of the winter of 1839–40. Similarly, Naomi Herriman, wife of an overseer at the carpet factory in Lowell, worked two months in 1831–32. Other evidence makes it clear that these married women worked before the birth of children. The living situation of the married working women was also unusual. Two of the women, Mary Morrill Chase and Lydia Currier Bickford, lived with sisters in Lowell during their stints in the mill. Perhaps their husbands' work, or the search for work, had taken them out of the city for a period. Also, the married couples may have been separated, as in the case of Mary Morrill Chase whose earnings were "trusteed"—that is, garnished—by a grocery firm. This practice was common in dealing with men who absconded leaving bad debts behind. All in all, the little that is known about married women workers at Hamilton suggests that such employment was infrequent, that the work periods were brief, that women with children did not work, and that unusual family circumstances were often associated with employment.

Mill employment represented a stage in a woman's life cycle before marriage; this was demonstrated by the fact that the vast majority of operatives did marry after their sojourn in Lowell. Of the 115 women for whom adequate data survive, 98 married. About 15 percent—17 of 115—definitely did not marry, either because they died at a relatively young age —one while working at Hamilton, for instance—or because they chose to remain single. Despite the claims of some contemporary critics of the mills, it is clear that mill employment did not disqualify young women for marriage.[21]

These women came to the mills, of course, as individuals, but they also brought along with them a social position and cultural outlook from their home towns. Nominal record linkage, which provides evidence on the age and marital status of women workers, also enables the historian to place them and their families within the economic and social structure of their home towns. What kinds of generalizations may be made about the families of women operatives? What sort of place did they occupy in their rural communities? And how did millhand daughters fit within their families? It is possible to move beyond the solely individual focus and examine the women and their families within a broader context.

The vast majority of women came from farming families. Almost two thirds of their fathers traced in the 1850 manuscript censuses of these three towns—21 of 32—were listed as farmers by census enumerators. This proportion was slightly higher than that for all male household heads in the three communities. The remainder of the fathers of millhands filled a variety of skilled occupations—blacksmith, stonemason, and wheelwright among others. The occupations of the fathers suggest that the women came from rather typical rural families.[22]

Tax inventories reinforce this conclusion. In all, the parents of 62 women workers were successfully linked to tax inventories for Boscawen, Canterbury, or Sutton for 1830. The composition of this group of linked parents and their property holdings indicates that the women were drawn from almost the entire range of families in these town. Five of the 62 linked parents were widows, 8 percent of the group as a whole. Looking at the data in another way permits a somewhat different perspective. For the three towns taken together, 11 percent of tax-paying female heads of households had a daughter working at Hamilton; among males the com-

---

[21] *Boston Quarterly Review* (1840), 3:369–70. Whether the 15 percent figure for never married is high or low is difficult to judge without comparable studies for this time period. Robert V. Wells, "Quaker Marriage Patterns in a Colonial Perspective," *William and Mary Quarterly*, (1972), 3d ser., 29:415–42, found 15.9 percent of females in two Quaker meetings living to 50 without marrying. Uhlenberg, "A Study in Cohort Life Cycles," p. 411, found 12.9 percent of an 1830 cohort never marrying. Yasukichi Yasuba, *Birth Rates of the White Population in the United States, 1800–1860* [An Economic Study (Baltimore: Johns Hopkins University Press, 1962)], p. 109, found less than 10 percent of women born in cohorts after 1835 single between the ages of 45 and 54. The figures here suggest that millhands did not differ significantly from other rural women.

[22] An earlier linkage would have been preferred, but the 1850 census provides the first enumeration of occupations. Unfortunately death and migration limited the number of fathers who could be traced at that date. The combination of census occupations and tax inventories gives some assurance, however, that fathers of millhands were primarily farmers.

TABLE 5.
Assessed Property Valuations of Fathers of Hamilton
Operatives, Compared to Male Household Heads,
Boscawen, Canterbury, and Sutton, 1830

ASSESSED VALUE OF PROPERTY	PROPORTIONS[a]	
	MILLHAND FATHERS	MALE HOUSE-HOLD HEADS
$0	0.0%	5.1%
1–99	14.0	15.3
100–499	43.9	32.8
500–999	26.3	27.8
1000–1999	15.8	13.7
2000+	0.0	5.1
Total cases	57	746

a Columns may not add up to 100.0% due to rounding.

parable figure was 7.7 percent. Even though female-headed families were somewhat more likely to have a daughter working in the mills, more than 90 percent of linked operatives came from typical male-headed households. The female millhand supporting her widowed mother is hardly as common in actuality as contemporary sources suggest.

Property valuations of the fathers of operatives place them in the broad middle ranges of wealth in their home towns. None of the linked fathers was propertyless in 1830 or among the very richest in their communities. Table 5 compares the distribution of taxable property among linked fathers with that of all male household heads.[23]

If those fathers linked in tax inventories are representative, then it is evident that women workers did not come from families near destitution. Fully 86 percent of linked fathers had property valued at $100 or more; for all male household heads in these towns the comparable proportion was less than 80 percent. On the whole, however, the typical millhand

[23] Since the fathers of millhands were all household heads it seemed important to find a similar group for purposes of comparison. Therefore the tax inventories were linked with the enumeration of household heads in the manuscript census for the same year. All taxpayers were then recorded either as household heads or nonheads and the comparison made accordingly. . . .

The findings here undoubtedly are subject to a certain amount of bias from the nature of the linkage process. Only parents of millhands linked in genealogies or local vital records could be traced in tax inventories. This process necessarily excludes millhands who lived in the three towns but were born and married elsewhere. The tendency would be to exclude millhands who were rather transient and to include those who persisted for relatively long periods of time. Given what we know from studies of geographical mobility, it is likely that the linkage process overstates somewhat the property holdings of the families of millhands. Unfortunately it is impossible to estimate the magnitude of any error resulting from this bias.

father was less wealthy than other taxpayers around him. The median property holding of millhand fathers in 1830 was only $338, compared to $459 for all male household heads taxed in the three towns.[24] Even if the typical sample father was somewhat below this town median, he remained a propertied member of the community. That only three parents were ever traced to Lowell is indicative of the fact that absolute poverty did not drive these families into the factory town.

Tax inventories list not only the total amount of property owned by families sending daughters into the mills but also reveal what kind of property it was. Benjamin Kendrick of Sutton, a rather typical father as far as his 1830 tax assessment was concerned, had three daughters, Mary, Judith, and Sarah, who worked at Hamilton between 1835 and 1840. The family also had four sons who undoubtedly helped their father with the work of the farm. Included in the Kendrick property assessed in 1830 were two horses, two oxen, four cows and three "stock," undifferentiated. In all, 15.5 acres were under cultivation, while another 50 unimproved acres rounded out the farm. The Kendrick family, like so many others with daughters employed at Hamilton, was thus tied to a system of mixed agriculture common in New Hampshire.

The fathers of millhands in 1830 did not comprise a depressed group within the towns; nor is there any evidence that over time their economic conditions were worsening. For those who could be traced after 1830, property holdings increased steadily. The median value of their property increased more rapidly than did that of other male household heads in these three towns.[25] As table 6 shows, in 1830 their median property holdings were $120 less than those of all male household heads; by 1860 they were almost $400 above those of other male household heads of similar ages.

There is some possibility that the findings here are an artifact of the linkage process, and I would not want to make too much of the apparent improvement of millhand fathers relative to other male household heads. Those fathers successfully linked in the 1850 and 1860 censuses had persisted in their home towns for two and three decades respectively, a fact

[24] In order to insure that aggregate patterns did not mask significant variations among the three towns, I analyzed the data initially at the town level. The individual town results did vary, but in a manner that seemed to reinforce rather than contradict the main argument. In Boscawen and Sutton the median property holdings of fathers of millhands were below those for all male household heads. In Canterbury, the reverse was true. In all three towns, property holdings of millhand fathers were distributed in the middle tiers of assessed valuations. On the comparability of assessment practices over the 1830–1860 period see *Laws of the State of New Hampshire . . . Published by Authority* (Hopkinton: Isaac Long, Jr., 1830), pp. 551–59; *General Statutes of the State of New Hampshire* (Concord: B. W. Sanborn, 1867), pp. 115–23.

[25] Persistent fathers obviously aged over this period and an attempt was made to compare them each census year with an appropriate control group. In 1850, 97 percent of linked fathers were 50 or over, and their property holdings were compared with those of male household heads of that age. Similarly, for 1860, millhand fathers were compared with household heads 60 and over.

TABLE 6.
Median Property Holdings of Linked Millhand Fathers,
1830–1860, Compared to Male
Household Heads of Similar Ages

	MEDIAN PROPERTY HOLDINGS	
	MILLHAND FATHERS	MALE HOUSEHOLD HEADS OF SIMILAR AGES[a]
1830	$338 (57)	$459 (746)
1850	960 (33)	998 (386)
1860	1600 (14)	1203 (346)

SOURCES: 1830 tax inventories and 1850, 1860 Manuscript
Censuses. Data for 1830 refer to all taxed property and for
1850 and 1860 to real property only.
[a] For 1830 all male household heads listed in tax inventories
have been included; for 1850 and 1860 only those in the same
age group as millhand fathers, those over 50 and 60 years of
age respectively.

that immediately sets them apart from all household heads of the same ages. If possible one would want to compare millhand fathers only to other persistent household heads within this age group, but this comparison would require extensive nominal record linkage of the manuscript censuses between 1830 and 1860, a task beyond the scope of this study.

Still the evidence undermines any argument that sheer economic need drove large numbers of women into the Lowell mills in the period 1830–1850. At least the economic needs of the families of operatives could not have been a compelling force. Some women, perhaps the 8 percent whose fathers had died, may well have worked in the mills in order to contribute to the support of their families. The evidence strongly suggests that most young women themselves decided to work in the mills. They were generally not *sent* to the mills by their parents to supplement low family incomes but went of their own accord for other reasons. When we also consider the distance separating mill operatives from their families, the probability is strong that it was the women themselves who decided how to spend their earnings.[26]

The correspondence of a number of operatives supports this view. Mary Paul, of Barnard, Vermont, began work in the Lowell mills at 15 or 16, in November 1845. Before going to the mills she had worked briefly as a domestic servant and then lived with relatives a short distance from her home; at that time she wrote seeking her father's permission to go to Lowell. In this letter she revealed the basic motivation that prompted her request: "I think it would be much better for me [in Lowell] than to stay

[26] This pattern contrasts with evidence on European working women presented in Joan W. Scott and Louise A. Tilly, "Women's Work and The Family in Nineteenth-Century Europe," [*Comparative Studies in Society and History* (1975), 17]; [Louise] Tilly, [Joan] Scott, and [Miriam] Cohen, "Women's Work and European Fertility Patterns," [*Journal of Interdisciplinary History* (1976), 6]. Unfortunately Scott and Tilly's recent book, *Women, Work, and Family* (New York: Holt, Rinehart and Winston, 1978), was not available at the time of this writing.

about here. . . . I am in need of clothes which I cannot get about here and for that reason I want to go to Lowell or some other place." After getting permission, Mary Paul worked in Lowell off and on for at least four years. In 1850 she lived briefly with her father, but then went on her own again, this time working as a seamstress in Brattleboro, Vermont. She evidently felt some guilt at not contributing to her father's support. In an 1853 letter she wrote "I hope sometime to be able to do something for you and sometimes feel ashamed that I have not before this." But there were obstacles which she noted:

> I am not one of the *smart* kind, and never had a passion for laying up money, probably never shall have, can find enough ways to spend it though (but I do not wish to be extravagant). Putting all these things together I think explains the reason that I do not lay up anything.

She expressed the wish that sometime she could live with her father and provide for him but always fell back on the argument that sent her to Lowell in the first place: "I . . . must work where I can get more pay."[27]

Sally Rice of Somerset, Vermont, left her home in 1838 at the age of 17 to take her first job "working out." Her work and her travels took her to Union Village, New York, where she supported herself on farm work, and led eventually to Thompson, Connecticut, where she found employment in a textile factory. That she was working for her own personal support and not to assist her family is evident in a poignant letter she wrote to her parents from Union Village in 1839 rejecting her familial home:

> I can never be happy there in among so many mountains. . . . I feel as though I have worn out shoes and strength enough riding and walking over the mountains. I think it would be more consistent to save my strength to raise my boys. I shall need all I have got and as for marrying and settling in that wilderness, I wont. If a person ever expects to take comfort it is while they are young. I feel so. . . . I have got so that by next summer if I could stay I could begin to lay up something. . . . I am most 19 years old. I must of course have something of my own before many more years have passed over my head. And where is that something coming from if I go home and earn nothing. . . . You may think me unkind but how can you blame me for wanting to stay here. I have but one life to live and I want to enjoy myself as well as I can while I live.[28]

Sally Rice left home to earn "something of my own," which was obviously not possible in the family economy of her father's farm. The more

[27] Mary Paul to Bela Paul, Sept. 13, 1845, Nov. 27, 1853, Dec. 18, 1853, VHS. Mary Paul, 21, and her father, 60, were recorded living in dwelling 533 in Claremont, New Hampshire. Manuscript Census (1850), M432, Roll 441.

[28] Nell Kull, ed., " 'I Can Never Be Happy There In Among So Many Mountains'— The Letters of Sally Rice," [*Vermont History* (1970), 38], pp. 49–57; quote, p. 52.

fertile farm lands of neighborning New York created a demand for agricultural labor and offered wages high enough to attract Sally Rice away
from the "wilderness" about Somerset. The wages in the textile mills of
central and southern New England soon proved an even greater lure for
this farmer's daughter eager to earn her own money.

Earning wages to provide for a dowry seems to have been Sally Rice's
primary motivation for leaving home in 1838. Mill employment appealed
to her principally because its wages were higher than those for farm
laborers or domestic servants. She did not consider mill work a long-term
prospect but intended to remain there only briefly: "I should not want to
spend my days in a mill unless they are short because I like a farm too
well for that." Finally, in 1847, probably with a sufficient dowry laid up,
Sally Rice married the brother of a fellow operative and settled in
Worcester, Massachusetts.[29]

If clothes and a dowry provided the motivation for Mary Paul and
Sally Rice to leave home and work in textile factories, a desire for education stimulated the efforts of one mill worker in Clinton, Massachusetts,
in 1851. One Lucy Ann had her sights set on using her wages to attend
Oberlin College. In a letter to a cousin she wrote: "I have earned enough
to school me awhile, & have not I a right to do so, or must I go home,
like a dutiful girl, place the money in father's hands, & then there goes
all my hard earnings." If she had to turn her wages over to her family
she would consider them a "dead loss" and all her efforts would have
been "spent in vain." Clearly mill employment could be turned to individualistic purposes. As Lucy Ann summed up her thinking: "I merely
wish to go [to Oberlin] because I think it is the best way of spending the
money I have worked so hard to earn."[30]

Lucy Ann wrote in a belligerent, but defensive, tone which seemed
to say, "Others may find fault with me, and call me selfish, but I think I
should spend my earnings as I please." Her need to justify her conduct
suggests that others had not risen in her defense. One senses, however,
that she would spend her money as she chose, regardless of what others
had to say. Other letters reveal that it was often taken for granted, by
operatives and their parents alike, that women's earnings were their own
to spend as they pleased. Consider an 1840 letter from Elizabeth Hodgdon, of Rochester, New Hampshire, to her sister, Sarah, working in the
mills in nearby Great Falls:

> You say you want to come home when we all think you have staid
> long enough, but we do not know better than you or so well either
> when you have earned as much as you will want to spend. Yet it is
> Mothers opinion & mine that you have already as much as you will
> probably want to spend if you lay it out to good advantage which
> we doubt not but you will.[31]

[29] Kull, "The Letters of Sally Rice," pp. 54, 57.
[30] Loriman Brigham, ed., "An Independent Voice: A Mill Girl from Vermont
Speaks Her Mind," [*Vermont History* (1973), 41], pp. 142–46; quote, p. 144.
[31] Elizabeth H. Hodgdon to Sarah D. Hodgdon, March 29, 1840, Rochester, N.H.,
Hodgdon Letters, NHHS.

Elizabeth suggests, and her mother evidently concurs, that Sarah should work as long as necessary to earn as much as she felt she needed. When Sarah returned to Rochester it is likely that she would not turn her savings over to her parents, but would spend them as she chose. The earnings would undoubtedly relieve her parents of certain expenses they might have incurred had she simply lived at home, and in this way her income was a help to them. The letter reinforces the distinct impression that emerges from the correspondence as a whole that when daughters left home and entered the mills they ceased to be "dependents" in the traditional sense. They supported themselves while at work and used their savings to maintain a certain independence even during the periods they lived at home.

The Hodgdon correspondence is important because it suggests that there was no great conflict between familial and individual interests for most women workers. Parents gave their approval to daughters' plans to work in the mills and were glad to see them earning money for themselves. Times were often hard in rural northern New England after 1830, and even in prosperous years there were few opportunities for women to earn anything while living at home. Whether or not working women actually contributed to support their families back home, each departure did mean one less mouth to feed. And with the growth of factory textile production, the contributions of farmers' daughters to the family economy declined significantly. Eben Jennison of Charleston, Maine, may have reflected the changing calculus of the family economy when, in 1849, he wrote to his daughter Elizabeth who was employed at the Merrimack Company in Lowell: "The season with us has been verry Dry and the Drough[t] verry severe. The crops are very light indeed and business verry Dull. If you should be blessed with your health and are contented I think you will do better where you are than you could do here." For Jennison, the decade of the 1850s appears to have been a difficult one, and by 1858 he had two daughters, Elizabeth and Amelia, working in the mills. In one of his letters to them he acknowledges the receipt of five dollars and expressed his hope that "some day or other" he would be able to repay them *with interest*. He needed the money but felt shame accepting it. Throughout his correspondence to his daughters, it is clear that he felt they should be in Lowell, but not because he expected them to contribute to his support as a matter of course. In fact his pride and sense of self-respect made it difficult for him to accept their apparently unsolicited aid, although need won out in the end. Still, even as he accepted their money, he viewed it as a loan to be repaid when his economic fortunes had improved.[32]

The view of women's motivations that emerges from analysis of their social origins and correspondence with their families stands in sharp contrast to contemporary writings, especially to the *Lowell Offering*, an

[32] Eben Jennison to Elizabeth Jennison, Charleston, Maine, Sept. 2, 1849; Eben Jennison to Elizabeth and Amelia Jennison, July 13, 1858. Jennison Letters, Private, in possession of Mary A. Dinmore, of Lowell, Mass. My thanks to Harry and Mary Dinmore for sharing these letters and permitting their use here.

operatives' literary magazine of the period.[33] In the repeated "factory tales" published in the *Offering*, writers stressed the selfless motivations that sent women into the mills. Characters in the stories were invariably orphans supporting themselves and younger brothers and sisters, or young women helping to pay off the mortgage on a family homestead or to send a brother to college, or widows arising and supporting families. Never, in the fiction at least, did an operative work in the mills in order to buy "new clothes" or to get away from a domineering father, though in real life these motivations must have been common enough. The more idealistic themes of the *Offering* presented the best possible case against those who argued that women should not work in the mills at all. The data on the social origins of workers, together with their letters, tell a rather different story.

Mill work should not be viewed as simply an extension of the traditional family economy as work for women moved outside the home. Work in the mills functioned for women rather like migration did for young men who could see that their chances of setting up on a farm in an established rural community were rather slim. The mills offered individual self-support, enabled women to enjoy urban amenities not available in their rural communities, and gave them a measure of economic and social independence from their families. These factors made Lowell attractive to rural women and led them to choose to work in the mills. The steady movement of the family farm from a subsistence to a commercial basis made daughters relatively "expendable" and gave fathers who otherwise might have guarded the family labor supply reason to allow them a chance on their own.

The work patterns in Lowell are strikingly different from those evident for young, single European women in this period. Joan Scott and Louise Tilly have argued convincingly that women's work outside the home in nineteenth-century Europe should be viewed primarily as an extension of the traditional family economy within a changed economic setting. They argue that parents *sent* their daughters out to work and that daughters routinely turned over all or large portions of their earnings directly to their parents.[34] Such practices may have prevailed earlier in those spinning mills of southern New England that hired entire families, but there is little evidence of this sort of pattern in mill towns of the Waltham-Lowell variety. For the New Hampshire women traced here, only 3 of 175 parents were linked to Lowell. Furthermore, operatives' correspondence suggests that most women spent and saved their earnings as they chose with little pressure to contribute to their family's support.

Several factors are relevant in explaining the differences in the Amer-

---

[33] *Lowell Offering*, 1:161–71, 263–66; 2:145–55, 246–250. Here I differ also with [Nancy F.] Cott, [*The*] *Bonds of Womanhood*: ["*Women's Sphere*" *in New England, 1780–1835* (New Haven: Yale University Press, 1977)], p. 55, who argues that women operatives "usually engaged in wage earning in order to help sustain their families." This is certainly the conventional wisdom, but the evidence marshalled here calls this view into question.

[34] Scott and Tilly, "Women's Work and the Family," pp. 42, 50–55.

ican setting. First, the nature of the traditional family economy in rural New England differed from its counterpart among European peasants. Diaries of American women suggest that daughters living at home often kept a portion of their earnings, indicating that they were not totally subordinated within the family economy even when living at home.[35] Secondly, as New England daughters sought mill employment they generally left home and accepted a considerable separation from their families, in terms of both distance and time. The physical separation of women and their residence in a peer-group community of other young, single women further encouraged their economic and social independence. Finally, their correspondence suggests they did not have to buck very strong parental counterpressures in this regard. Parents encouraged their daughters, or at least appear to have given their approval, and do not seem to have demanded that they place their earnings in the family till. Scott and Tilly point out that over time "more individualistic and instrumental" attitudes did develop among European working women, but these attitudes appear to have developed more rapidly and with less resistance in northern New England than in the European context.[36]

While Lowell women do not appear to have been working to support their families, analysis of family patterns among operatives reveals that family factors did influence entry into the mills. The families of women workers at Hamilton were large ones, but daughters did not enter the mills at random. On the average there were 7.2 children in completed families, 3.7 of whom were daughters. Employed daughters tended to be first or second daughters rather than younger ones. Among the families of millhands, 63 had two or more daughters who can be placed in their proper birth order.[37] In all, these 63 families had 244 daughters. From among these daughters, 90, or 36.9 percent, worked for the Hamilton Company at some point between 1830 and 1850, but as table 7 shows very clearly, firstborn daughters were much more likely to be employed at Hamilton than were their younger sisters.

Almost half of firstborn daughters, 46 percent, worked at the Hamilton Company in this period. The proportion declined steadily, though, for younger siblings, until fifth or later-born daughters, of whom only 15.6 percent went to Hamilton. Among these families oldest daughters were about three times as likely as the youngest to work away from home. This pattern may reflect a greater adventuresomeness among older girls in the family or a somewhat more protective attitude on the part of parents toward their younger daughters. Or perhaps a daughter's departure for the mills may have been tied in with the family cycle. Oldest daughters may have responded to a kind of population pressure within the fam-

35 [Blanche Brown] Bryant and [Gertrude Elaine] Baker, eds., [The] Diaries of Sally and Pamela Brown [Springfield, VT.: William L. Bryant Foundation, 1970)], Feb. 11, 1832, May 31, Oct. 30, Nov. 7, Dec. 2, 7, 1833, Nov. 3, Dec. 5, 1837.

36 Scott and Tilly, "Women's Work and the Family," pp. 61–62.

37 In determining the proportion of first-, second-born (and so on) children working at Hamilton, I excluded five operatives who were only daughters in their families.

TABLE 7.
Rank Birth Order of New Hampshire Women
Employed at the Hamilton Company, 1830–1850

RANK ORDER AMONG DAUGHTERS	NUMBER OF DAUGHTERS IN RANK	NUMBER OF DAUGHTERS AT HAMILTON	PROPORTION (%)
1st	63	29	46.0
2d	63	27	42.9
3d	51	18	35.3
4th	35	11	31.4
5th or higher	32	5	15.6
Overall	244	90	36.9

NOTE: Includes only women drawn from families with two or more daughters for whom rank birth order is known.

ily. The families may have been particularly crowded in small farmhouses, or the farm simply may have been unable to produce enough for such a large family. Their departures to the mills, and their subsequent marriages, would have relieved this pressure, thus enabling younger daughters to remain in the household. Since the millhands tended to come of age in the 1830s and younger sisters a decade later, the figures may reflect the declining attraction of the Lowell mills for Yankee women. While the explanations offered here must remain conjectures, the pattern of recruitment into the mills is clear.

An additional finding that emerges from the study of the families of operatives is evidence that women came to Lowell not as isolated individuals but as members of broader kin networks.[38] Almost two thirds—71 of 111 for whom family reconstitution is possible—had other relatives employed at Hamilton at some time or other in the period 1830–1850. Sister pairs predominated among operatives, as is evident from the figures in table 7 that indicate that 90 daughters from 63 families worked in the Hamilton mills. But at least 13 operatives had cousins employed at Hamilton as well. Even these figures must be seen as minimum estimates, since vital records and genealogies shed little light on broader kin relations. For the most part it is only possible to trace networks on the father's side of the families.

Illustrations drawn from a number of individual cases illuminate the importance of kin networks for women workers. Lucinda and Abigail White of Sutton came to Lowell in June 1835 and worked together in Carding Room A at Hamilton. Abigail remained only 6 months, but her

[38] Tamara Hareven, "Dynamics of Kin," describes a similar phenomenon among French Canadians in the Manchester (N.H.) mills at the turn of the twentieth century. For the classic sociological statement of this pattern of chain migration see John S. MacDonald and Leatrice MacDonald, "Chain Migration, Ethnic Neighborhood Formation, and Social Networks," *Milbank Memorial Fund Quarterly* (1964), 42:82–97; see also Anderson, *Family Structure*, pp. 62, 152–60.

sister worked on and off until at least March 1840. Her entire family may have moved to Lowell, for her father died there in May 1841. Both sisters married Lowell men and continued to reside there after marriage. Thus the Whites as a family made the move from the countryside to the city, and for at least several family members the move proved to be a permanent one.[39]

Two other families came to Lowell from their rural homes; in each case the father's death appears to have been the precipitating event. Mary Woodward came from one of the poorer Sutton families. Her father, David Woodward, was assessed in 1830 for two cows, eight acres of "wild" lands, and one building worth $25. He had no other livestock and no cultivated land whatsoever. The exact date of his death is uncertain, but in June 1845, Mary Woodward began work at the Hamilton Company and lived with her mother, Ruth, on Cady Street in Lowell. Two brothers, Dana and David, married and died in Lowell. Mary herself died in Lowell in the cholera epidemic of 1849.

The Sawyer family, of Canterbury, also moved to Lowell. Apphia Sawyer, almost certainly a widow, kept a boardinghouse at the Appleton Company in 1830 and at the adjacent Hamilton Company between 1832 and 1836. Two daughters, Nancy and Mary, worked briefly at the Hamilton Company, living at their "Mom's" according to company registers.[40]

Apphia Sawyer, Ruth Woodward, and Henry White were the only parents of women operatives from Boscawen, Canterbury, and Sutton known to have lived in Lowell. They were unusual, as intergenerational kinship ties among workers in Lowell were rare. More frequently, sisters worked together in the mills. Eunice and Mary Austin, of Boscawen, for instance, worked in Upper Weaving Room C at Hamilton in 1830. They lived together in a company boardinghouse, and both left in July of that year. Two Canterbury sisters, Lucy Jane and Caroline Ames, began work together in April 1835 and resided in the same boardinghouse. They did not, however, work in the same room in the mills. Fourteen-year-old Caroline worked as a weaver, while her 18-year-old sister was employed in the dressing room. Usually dressing room hands were experienced operatives, suggesting that Lucy Jane Ames may have worked elsewhere before coming to Hamilton. In any event, Lucy remained at the company only a year, while Caroline worked off and on over the course of the next five years.

Kinship ties among mill operatives played a number of important roles for women workers in early Lowell. The existence of these bonds must have eased the shock of adjustment both to work in the factories

---

[39] The description of the White family experience and other examples for operatives from Boscawen, Canterbury, and Sutton are based on the record linkage carried out in the social origins study. For each woman worker I prepared a separate index card and with each successive linkage I added new data to the card. Finally, I coded the data and prepared it in machine-readable form for statistical analysis. The index cards provide a rich source for the biographical information presented here.

[40] For literary evidence on boardinghouse families in early Lowell, see Robinson, *Loom and Spindle*, chs. 2, 4, 5; Larcom, *New England Girlhood*, ch. 7.

and to the novel urban setting. The fact that so many pairs of sisters at Hamilton resided together in company boardinghouses and often worked in the same rooms at the mill strongly suggests the importance of a familial support network for newcomers. Experienced operatives probably arranged for housing accommodations ahead of time and may have been able to speak to the overseer on their sisters' behalf. Julia A. Dutton, of Clintonville, Massachusetts, described such arrangements in an 1847 letter to her mother in Vermont:

> I have engaged a place for Martha Coffren the first of Nov[ember]. The overseer sayed she might come at that [date] and if she is large enough for a weaver he will take her if not she can go into some other room. There is no doubt but she will work a plenty. She will have [$]1.25 [a week above board] while she is learning to weave.[41]

The presence of an older, more knowledgeable family member in Lowell must have comforted parents thinking about allowing a second child to make the journey. An 1849 letter from Eben Jennison of Charleston, Maine, to his daughter, Elizabeth, in Lowell, makes this point explicitly. Referring to a younger daughter, Emily, then sixteen, he noted:

> A few words in relation to Emily. She has got about ready to come to Lowel. Martha A. Marshall expects to return to Lowel in the course of some two or three weeks and if Emily comes she will come with hir. I should not consent to hir coming at any rate if you was not there. She is young and needs a mothers care and a mothers advise. You must se to hir and give hir such council as you thinks she needs. She may be Homesick for a spell but if you comfort hir up she will soon get the better of it.[42]

Since most of the women were in their teens when they first set off for the mills, family ties must have been a comfort for both the operatives and their parents.

Sisters or cousins working together constituted only the simplest of kin networks at the Hamilton Company. Groupings of this sort could in fact become quite intricate. The Danforth family of Boscawen was at the heart of one such network. Jedidiah and Rachel Danforth had eight children between 1803 and 1827, four boys and four girls. Twin oldest daughters, Rachel and Sarah, worked together in Weaving Room A at Hamilton between March 1830 and July 1832. Both resided at Number 6, Hamilton Company. A bother, Nathan, worked in Lowell as a stonemason and boarded at the Lawrence Corporation in 1834. The next year found him employed by the Tremont Company in Lowell.

---

[41] Julia A. Dutton to Lucretia Dutton, Sept. 26, 1847, Clintonville, Massachusetts, Dutton Family Letters, Private. Martha Coffren may have been a sister. Earlier, another sister, Jane Dutton Witherby, had written to her sister Martha encouraging her to come work in the mills. Jane Witherby to Martha Dutton, Feb. 28, 1847, Grafton, Massachusetts.

[42] Eben Jennison to Elizabeth Jennison, Sept. 2, 1849, Jennison Letters, Private.

Although Sophia Brown of Boscawen had no immediate kin at the Hamilton Company, she was not alone there. She worked in Weaving Room A alongside Rachel Danforth and lived in the same boardinghouse. In July 1833 she married Nathan Danforth, and thus the Brown and Danforth families of Boscawen were linked in Lowell. The young couple resided in Lowell for two years and then returned to Boscawen, where they raised five children.

Marriage also linked the Danforth and Fowler families of Boscawen and Lowell. Four Fowler sisters worked at Hamilton, sometimes together and sometimes sequentially between 1831 and 1842. Harriet and Sarah Fowler both worked in Weaving Room A in 1831, overlapping for a period with Sarah and Rachel Danforth. The eldest sister, Mary, came to Lowell in March 1836 and worked with her sister Harriet. Finally, a fourth sister, Elizabeth, came to Lowell in 1842, and after a stretch at the Lawrence Company, she too worked in Weaving Room A at Hamilton. Mary Fowler united the two mill families when she married Jedidiah Danforth, another brother of Rachel and Sarah, in Lowell in 1838.

The kin networks described here and traced through Hamilton Company records reveal only part of a dense thicket of relationships. First, they trace only blood relatives for the most part. Rachel and Sarah Danforth, for instance, had two future sisters-in-law working beside them at Hamilton, as did Mary Fowler and Sophia Brown. Furthermore, these operatives had additional relatives in Lowell, though they may never have worked at Hamilton. Only the marriages of Mary Fowler and Sophia Brown revealed that two Danforth brothers resided in Lowell.

Moreover, similar kin networks extending beyond the bounds of the Hamilton Company can be traced. Martha, Mary, and Nancy Emery of Canterbury all worked at Hamilton; one even lived in Mrs. Sawyer's boardinghouse for a time. In addition, four Emery brothers worked and married in Lowell, though none seems to have found his way to the Hamilton Company. Mary Morrill Chase had no relatives employed with her in the mills, but a sister, Sarah Morrill, married in Lowell and raised three children there between 1840 and 1849. Mary Woodward of Sutton had two cousins in Lowell, one a carpenter for many years, the other a "popular" teacher in Lowell, or at least so the compiler of Sutton's genealogies thought. Many more examples might be cited, but the point is clear. Rich kinship networks—along blood and marriage lines—joined women workers to one another while living and working in Lowell. They came to Lowell not as isolated individuals but as members of larger supportive groups. Those who did not come as part of a group seem to have been able to recreate such a network once arrived in Lowell.

From the vital records and local genealogies one can reconstruct the dimensions of the kinship network among women workers in early Lowell. But the support system extended beyond blood ties and included unrelated friends from the home towns as well. These sorts of bonds are not so easily traced through the kinds of records cited thus far, but literary sources can be particularly useful in this regard. Although none of the women in this sample left letters, diaries, or reminiscences describing their lives in Lowell, other New England women did. These sources confirm the importance of a support system based on kinship and friendship among rural women in urban, industrial Lowell.

Two sisters, Sarah and Elizabeth Hodgdon, worked in the textile mills of Lowell and Great Falls, New Hampshire, between 1830 and 1840. They came to Lowell together, and a family friend, Wealthy Page, took them in hand and aided them in the difficulties of their first months. The sisters lived together and worked in the same weaving room. They felt ill-treated by members of the Freewill Baptist Church, apparently because they could not afford to rent a pew. Wealthy Page stood by them during this crisis and assured mutual Rochester friends: "I am just the same friend to Sarah that I was when I promised to befriend her."[43]

Similarly, Mary Paul of Barnard, Vermont, went to Lowell in November 1845 and worked there periodically until at least July 1849. She went by stage to Lowell, the first time accompanied by a friend, Mercy Griffith. When in Lowell, Luthera Griffith took her to the mills and helped her find her first job. Here again, in the absence of kin in Lowell, friends from the rural home town played a supportive role for a newcomer.[44]

Surviving letters reveal the importance of continuing family ties for women in the mills. Family members often visited Lowell even when they did not reside there. Louisa Sawyer wrote a cousin that her brother had come to Lowell with her from her home in East Andover, New Hampshire, and that she expected he would come again soon. Her brother later lived in Lowell, himself, for she noted in a subsequent letter written from her rural home: "Brother Daniel came Home yesterday and is well and left the Lowell friends all well." While Louisa and Daniel were home in New Hampshire one winter, their sister, Emeline, went to work in Lowell.[45]

Obviously, visits of relatives reinforced links between kin networks in Lowell and those back in the countryside. Mary Hall's diary, cited earlier, is remarkable for the repeated accounts it contains of visiting relatives. Two weeks after Mary began work, brother Learned visited briefly. Another brother, Robert, called at the countinghouse two weeks later and stayed for five weeks. Learned returned for a second visit while his brother was still there. Mary left the mills after seven months, and when she returned to Lowell, a year and a half later, two cousins accompanied her. An aunt resided in Lowell at this time, but Mary continued to board in company housing. Family visits quickly resumed. Mary's father and brother Robert appeared just two days after she started work, with her brother staying for two months. A third brother, Isaac, stopped in Lowell en route to Boston shortly thereafter. Learned visited one more time before Mary left Lowell, accompanied appropriately enough by brother

---

[43] Wealthy Page to "Respected friends," June 6, 1830; Sarah Hodgdon to "Sister and mother," June ——; Wealthy Page to "Dear friends," n.d., Hodgdon Letters, NHHS.

[44] Mary Paul to Bela Paul, Sept. 13, Nov. 20, 1845, April 12, 1846, Mary Paul Letters, VHS.

[45] Louisa A. Sawyer to Sabrina Bennett, Dec. 30, ——, Bennett Family Letters, HPL.

Isaac. The visits came so often that one almost wonders whether the Hall family felt a need to keep a watch on Mary.[46]

Frequent visits kept Mary Hall in close touch with her family. Others, however, had to bridge the gap that separated them from their families with correspondence. The letters they wrote indicate that even when work in the mills took women away from family and friends, they continued to feel strong affection and concern for those at home. They felt distant but by no means estranged from loved ones.

Sarah Hodgdon's first letter home poignantly expresses the continuing bond that tied women to their families. It closed: "Give my love to farther. Tell him not to forget me and to my dear sister and to my brothers and to my grammother. Tell her I do not forget her. And to my Aunts and to all my enquiring friends." Her feelings welled into homesickness in a poem she quoted in closing a subsequent letter:

> I want to se you more I think
> Than I can write with pen and ink.
> But when I shall I cannot tell
> But from my heart I wish you well.
> I wish you well from all my heart
> Although we are so far apart.
> If you die there and I die here,
> Before one God we shall apeare.[47]

Taken together, the family reconstitution data, the reconstruction of individual women's careers in Lowell, and the operatives' correspondence all indicate that women workers in the early mills were part of a social network of family and friends which had its roots in the countryside and which played an important role in their lives in Lowell. While women may not have been working expressly to contribute to their families back home, they were still operating within a familial context that is best viewed as a part of their traditional rural culture. Mill employment had not recast women within a completely individualistic mold. In Lowell women continued to provide crucial support to one another, as neighbors and family members had done for years in the countryside. They recruited one another into the mills, secured jobs for each other, and helped newcomers make the numerous adjustments called for in a very new and different setting. Here we see clear evidence of the maintenance of traditional kinds of social relationships in a new setting and serving new purposes.[48]

[46] Mary Hall Diary, *passim*, NHHS.

[47] Sarah Hodgdon to Mary Hodgdon, June ——, Hodgdon Letters, NHHS. See also *Lowell Offering*, 1:245.

[48] Visiting, care of sick neighbors, and the exchange of work were common elements in women's rural lives and provided bases for close same-sex relations among rural women. See Bryant and Baker, eds., *Diaries of Sally and Pamela Brown*, May 31, 1833, May 19, July 27, 1836, and Feb. 10, 1837. For an urban, middle-class variant, see Carroll Smith Rosenberg, "The Female World of Love

TABLE 8.
Initial Room Assignment of New Hampshire Women
at the Hamilton Company

INITIAL ROOM ASSIGNMENT	PROPORTIONS[a]	
	WITH RELATIVES	WITHOUT RELATIVES
Carding	9.9%	17.5%
Spinning, winding	19.7	30.0
Weaving	54.9	42.5
Dressing	15.5	10.0
Total cases	71	40

[a] Columns may not add up to 100.0% due to rounding.

These kinship networks helped operatives adjust to urban life, but they also made a more direct contribution to women's success in the mills. Women operatives whose kin were also employed at Hamilton were able, on the whole, to secure better jobs in the mill. Table 8 contrasts the initial room assignment of those sample members who had relatives at Hamilton with the experience of those who did not.

More than 70 percent of women with relatives in the work force were hired initially to work in the high-paying weaving and dressing rooms, while only 52.5 percent of those without relatives began their mill careers there. These figures reinforce what Julia Dutton's letter quoted earlier pointed out: knowing someone already employed in the mills helped in securing one of the better-paying jobs.[49]

One of the consequences of better job placement of newcomers with kin was that they remained longer at the company. Those with relatives worked at Hamilton an average of 3.66 years; those without kin remained only 2.21 years.[50] Having other members of the family at Hamilton

and Ritual: [Relations Between Women in Nineteenth-Century America," *Signs* (1976), 1]. In this pioneering piece, Smith-Rosenberg argues for that centrality of intimate same-sex relationships in the lives of women in the nineteenth century. Although she bases her argument on letters and diaries of upper- and middle-class women, the evidence presented in this chapter suggests that support networks of female friends and kin may have played as important a role in the lives of working-class women.

[49] For similar findings among mill operatives in other communities see Anderson, *Family Structure*, pp. 118–20; Hareven, "Dynamics of Kin," p. 17–21. Both these cases, however, examine kin networks in which parents played a significant role. In early Lowell, parents were conspicuously absent from the mills.

[50] The difference in means reported here was paralleled by the actual distributions of the lengths of careers. More than 45 percent of those without relatives worked less than a year for the company, while only 24 percent were so transient among those with relatives. At the other end of the spectrum, 19.4 percent of those with relatives stayed six years or longer at Hamilton, compared to only 8.6 percent among those who came alone.

clearly opened up opportunities for women and led them to stay longer in the mills. It also aided the companies. Because mill managers often complained that no sooner had they trained newcomers than they quit, encouraging family ties among workers made good business sense. Family networks reduced labor turnover and resulted in a more experienced and more productive labor force, which in turn contributed to greater profits. In the end, both workers and corporations benefited from the growth of kinship networks in the mill work force.

Clearly, then, the rural backgrounds as well as the kinship and friendship networks of these women were important factors in their entry into Lowell and their careers in the mills. It remains to examine the lives of these operatives after their years in the mills to ask how important the mill experience was to them. Did Lowell make any difference in their later lives, or was their experience there simply a brief and rather inconsequential episode? To answer this question it is necessary to look at the married lives of women in the sample group after they left the Hamilton Company.

Two contrasting illustrations may clarify the relevant issues. The marriages of Judith Kendrick and Agibail Hale provide the polar extremes for the marital experience of women workers in Lowell. Judith Kendrick of Sutton worked for two years at the Hamilton Company in the late 1830s. Two sisters worked at Hamilton as well. In April 1840 Judith Kendrick married James Peaslee of Sutton and the two settled in their home town. They followed a life much like that of their parents. By 1850 the census noted James's occupation as laborer and set the value of his real property at $600. Tax inventories for the same year agree with the census but indicate that he owned five cows and four sheep as well. He may in fact have inherited his father's farm, since his widowed mother resided with the family. The Peaslees prospered over the decade of the 1850s, and by 1860 James owned $2000 worth of real property and another $465 in personal property. His occupation, or rather his status, was that of yeoman farmer. Clearly, James and Judith Peaslee had a secure place in their rural community.

Abigail Hale of Boscawen took a somewhat different route after leaving the mills. She also worked two years at Hamilton in the early 1830s, but she evidently did not leave for good when she married Ebenezer Calef in Lowell in January 1837. Calef worked at the neighboring Appleton Company and boarded nearby. Upon marriage, the Calef family lived in a house on High Street. They continued to reside in Lowell at least until 1851, and Abigail Hale Calef gave birth to a son and a daughter during this period. Abigail had clearly forsaken her rural roots. It is unlikely that the Calefs, after fourteen years of married life in Lowell, returned to a rural home.

These two sketches raise an obvious question: which was more typical of the experience of women workers in early Lowell? Did most women return to their home towns, marry, and settle into the rural patterns of their childhood, or did they remain in Lowell or some similar urban setting? Clearly, their lives touched two worlds—that of the countryside and that of the city. Which one had the greater attraction?

TABLE 9.
Occupations of Husbands of Former Hamilton
Operatives in New Hampshire Sample

OCCUPATION	PROPORTION (%)
Skilled trades	33.3
Farmers, farm laborers	31.1
Textile mills	20.0
Others	**15.6**
Total cases	45

The occupations of the husbands of millhands are instructive on this score. I have been able to determine the occupations of almost half of the known husbands—45 of 98—through linkage in the *Lowell Directory* or in the federal manuscript censuses of Boscawen, Canterbury, and Sutton. Whereas two thirds of the fathers of these operatives had held agricultural occupations, less than a third of their husbands did so, either at the time of marriage or at any time thereafter (see table 9). Skilled trades—carpenters, masons, and machinists among others—made up the largest single occupational group, accounting for fully a third of the jobs held by husbands of former millhands. Overall, more than two thirds of these men worked in nonagricultural occupations.[51]

Husbands' occupations reflect in part the simple fact that a large proportion of them resided in Lowell and that they could hardly have been farmers in that setting. However, a majority of even those husbands who lived in Boscawen, Canterbury, and Sutton after their marriages chose nonagricultural occupations. Of the 24 husbands living in these three towns in 1850, only 10—or 41.7 percent—were farmers. Nine were skilled artisans, and the remaining 5 were unskilled workers. Ten years later the proportion principally engaged in agriculture had increased, but still it reached only 50 percent—9 of 18.

One might argue that the difference between the fathers and the spouses of millhands was basically a generational one. Perhaps the occupational patterns of fathers and husbands simply reflected the fact that the fathers were 20 years older and more likely to have owned land upon which they could earn their living. However, if one compares husbands to male household heads of roughly the same age—between 30 and 50

[51] Occupational data on husbands came from disparate sources: marriage records, Lowell city directories, and the 1850 and 1860 federal manuscript censuses. For numerous individuals, more than one occupation was found. Since some of the men worked in Lowell briefly before settling in Boscawen, Sutton, and Canterbury, the latest occupational linkage (in point of time) was taken as the husband's occupation. Thus a Lowell machinist who returned to a Sutton farm was coded a farmer. This procedure attempted to make husbands of millhands as comparable to fathers as sources would permit.

TABLE 10.
Age at First Marriage of Millhands and Husbands

	MILLHANDS (1)	HUSBANDS (2)	AGE DIFFERENCE[a] (1) — (2)
Mean	26.3	25.3	+0.83
Median	25.2	24.5	+0.58
Total cases	80	36	35

NOTE: Table excludes ages at second marriages.
[a] Age differences calculated only for marriages for which ages of both millhand and husband are known.

years old in 1850—one finds that they were much less likely to be farmers than their peers. In 1850, for instance, 59.5 percent of male household heads in this age group were farmers, compared to only 41.7 percent of husbands of former millhands. Even controlling for age, these men were more likely to be working in artisan or unskilled manual occupations than were all males in their home towns.[52]

In yet another way the marriage patterns of women in the sample differed significantly from those of their parents—and of other rural women in their own generation. Former operatives tended to marry rather later than usual and to marry men who were on average the same age or slightly younger than themselves. Table 10 presents findings for the ages at first marriage for sample members and for their spouses. On average, these women workers married when they were 26 years old and tended to marry men who were ten months younger than themselves.

These figures stand in sharp contrast to data on age at first marriage for men and women throughout New England at this time. Vital registration data for Massachusetts between 1845 and 1860, for instance, indicate that on average men married 2.5 years later than did women. Vermont state figures for 1858 show men marrying at 24.6 years of age on average and women at 21.4, a difference of more than three years. Local community studies based on family reconstitution confirm these state-level findings. In Sturbridge, Massachusetts, between 1820 and 1849, women married for the first time at a mean age of 25.5; for men the comparable figure was 27.8. For Concord, Massachusetts, between 1831 and 1850 mean ages at first marriage for men and women were 26.5 and 23.4 respectively. Finally, for Hingham, Massachusetts, in a roughly comparable period, male and female figures came to 26.0 and 23.3 respectively. In every study *except* that of mill operatives in the Hamilton sample, the

[52] Of the 24 husbands found in the 1850 census heading their own households, 75 percent were between the ages of 30 and 49, providing the basis for choosing this control group. The gap between husbands and their age peers continued through 1860, when 50.0 percent of husbands—9 of 18—were listed as farmers, compared to 63.1 percent of all male household heads between 40 and 59.

mean age at first marriage for men exceeded that for women by more than two years.[53]

The difference between the New Hampshire millhands and the other groups probably stems from the fact that in the years before marriage these women were separated from their families, living away from home and supporting themselves. It is likely that the economic and social independence that they achieved was reflected in their choice of spouse. Their parents probably had only a limited voice in the final selection, especially for those who met their husbands in Lowell. Furthermore, marrying a bit later than was typical for rural women in this period, the pool of men they chose from would have been younger (at least relative to themselves). The savings women brought with them and the similarity of ages of husband and wife in these couples may have placed the marriage partners on a more equal footing than would have been true in marriages for most rural women. In all, the data on marriage age of mill women suggest that the mill experience may have set them apart from others and prepared them for marriages that represented something of a departure from traditional patterns.

The evidence on the age of millhands at marriage suggests one important way in which early industrial capitalism changed the lives of women who worked in the early mills. It seems to have led women to marry considerably later than was general for rural women in this period. This pattern contradicts the conclusion that David Levine reached on examining similar data for the village of Shepshed, an industrial outwork community in Leicestershire, England. With increasing industrialization, Levine found a decline in the mean age at first marriage for both men and women. The growth of opportunities in framework knitting, according to Levine, led couples to marry earlier and begin having children immediately. Apparently children were viewed as an economic asset, and framework knitters sought to enjoy their contributions to the family economy as soon as possible.[54]

---

[53] Thomas Monahan, *The Pattern of Age at First Marriage in the United States* [(Philadelphia, published by the author, 1951)], pp. 161, 174–76, 316–18; Nancy Osterud and J. Fulton, "Family Limitation and Age at Marriage [Fertility Decline in Sturbridge, Massachusetts, 1730–1850," *Population Studies* (1976), 30]; Marc Harris, "A Demographic Study of Concord, Massachusetts, 1750–1850," [(Undergraduate honors thesis, Brandeis University, 1973)], p. 42; Daniel Scott Smith, "Parental Power and Marriage Patterns: An Analysis of Historical Trends in Hingham, Massachusetts," *Journal of Marriage and the Family* (1973), 35: 419–28.

I have to acknowledge at this point that the strongest test of age at marriage data for millhands in the sample would be to compare millhands with non-millhands from the same three towns, or perhaps even with non-millhand sisters in the same families. This comparison, however, would require additional nominal record linkage far beyond the scope of this study. The uniformity of all the other studies of age at first marriage, and their contrast to the findings for women operatives, provide assurance of the distinctiveness of the patterns described here.

[54] David Levine, *Family Formation in an Age of Nascent Capitalism* [(New York: Academic Press, 1977)], pp. 51, 61–62.

The New England social and economic setting varied on several counts from the English outwork environment, and these differences help explain the contrasting impact of industrial capitalism on marriage patterns. Industrial capitalism never seriously penetrated the local economies of Boscawen, Canterbury, and Sutton, which remained almost totally agricultural before 1850. Thus women had to migrate to find mill employment, in contrast to the scene at Shepshed, where framework knitters worked in their own homes. Because of its location, mill employment was never so totally integrated into the household economy of these New Hampshire towns as was framework knitting in Shepshed. With increasing economic opportunity, young men and women in Shepshed could marry and establish their own households much more easily than earlier. In Boscawen, Canterbury, and Sutton, in contrast, industrialization gave women a degree of economic and social independence that led them to postpone marriage. They put off marriage and by virtue of residence in Lowell and other mill towns had a wider range of men to choose among than women who remained at home. This greater choice is reflected in the varied occupations of the men they married. The different forms industrial capitalism took in New England and Leicestershire account for its contrasting impact on marriage patterns in the two regions.

As industrialization progressed, job opportunities within Shepshed increased, leading to a decline in outmigration and an increase in the proportion of young people marrying and settling in the village. In Boscawen, Canterbury, and Sutton, industrialization created job opportunities beyond the confines of the towns, luring increasing numbers of young people into the growing mill towns. With this migration we begin to see a widening gulf between the experiences of millhands and those of their parents. Residence patterns of women workers after marriage reflect their growing independence from parental dominance. They suggest that the Lowell experience was not just a passing moment, at least not in the lives of a fair proportion of the women. More than a third of the women married Lowell men and the same proportion continued to reside there after their marriages. For them life in Lowell was more than a brief sojourn in the years before marriage; work constituted an entry into the urban industrial world and signaled a permanent departure from the one in which they had grown up.[55]

For many of the women in the early mills, the world of their parents was not their world. The Lowell experience may have made them restless, made them unfit for the slower, more traditional life they had known. Or perhaps women who went to Lowell in the first place were particularly open and receptive to the urban, industrial world growing up nearby. In any event, the letters of women workers and the writings of New Englanders critical of the movement into the mills provide numerous indications that contemporaries were conscious of the tension between the two

[55] Marriage records, genealogies, and city directories were utilized to determine spouse's place of residence before marriage. These sources plus the federal manuscript censuses of Boscawen, Canterbury, and Sutton were used to trace couples' residences after their marriage. Families were followed until the birth of their

worlds and cultures—the urban world of Lowell and the rural world of the surrounding countryside.

One Sutton historian, herself the sister of two Lowell operatives, captured an element of this tension in a brief description of the experience of going to the mills for women of her town:

> The girls began to go to work in the cotton factories of Nashua and Lowell. It was an all-day ride, but that was nothing to be dreaded. It gave them a chance to behold other towns and places, and see more of the world than most of the generation had ever been able to see. They went in their plain, country-made clothes, and after working several months, would come home for a visit, or perhaps to be married, in their tasteful city dresses, and with more money in their pockets than they had ever owned before.[56]

Augusta Worthen wrote these lines in 1890, looking back on the mill experience with an appropriate sense of distance. Other contemporaries, however, did not look so calmly upon their daughters returning with "tasteful city dresses, and more money . . . than they had ever owned before." Zadock Thompson, in his 1842 *History of Vermont,* described much the same phenomenon in a more judgmental tone: "It is too common for farmers' daughters to grow up young ladies, play the piano . . . and spend their father's surplus funds for fine clothing."[57] Perhaps the daughters Thompson decried had picked up their tastes in mill towns or

---

first child but attrition in the sample introduced considerable bias at this point. Table N.2 presents data on the overall marriage residence patterns of women workers.

TABLE N.2.
Marriage Residence Patterns of New Hampshire
Women Workers

PLACE	HUSBAND'S RESIDENCE BEFORE MARRIAGE[a]	COUPLE'S RESIDENCE AFTER MARRIAGE[b]
Millhand's home town	35.5%	45.0%
Lowell	35.5	33.3
Other rural	22.8	13.3
Other urban	10.1	8.3
Total cases	79	60

[a] Proportions in this column add to more than 100.0% because a few men resided before marriage in both the millhand's home town and Lowell.
[b] Taken to be the first residence found after the marriage date through linkage in city directories, manuscript censuses, and local genealogies.

---

[56] Worthen, *History of Sutton,* p. 192.
[57] Zadock Thompson, *The History of Vermont,* p. 39, as quoted in Nicholas Hayes Ward, "Pianos, Parasols, and Poppa: [The Migration of Vermont Farm Girls to the Massachusetts Mill Towns," (M.A. Thesis, Brown University, 1974)], p. 44.

from sisters who worked there. Whatever the causes, or whether such difficulties actually existed in fact is really beside the point; what is important is that contemporaries felt them to be matters of real concern.

The problem was not simply that some rural spokesmen observed their wayward daughters and found them wanting. Others felt that the judgment was mutual, that these young women rejected the values of their parents. An 1858 article, "Farming in New England," made just this point:

> The most intelligent and enterprising of the farmer's daughters become school-teachers, or tenders of shops, or factory girls. They contemn the calling of their father, and will nine times out of ten, marry a mechanic in preference to a farmer. They know that marrying a farmer is a serious business. They remember their worn-out mothers.[58]

The lines recall the marriage patterns of the women workers from the Hamilton Company. They were farmers' daughters, all right, but, seven times out of ten, they married a mechanic "in preference to a farmer." They chose not to follow in the footsteps of their "worn-out mothers."

The last example is particularly pointed because it shifts the emphasis away from the reaction of others and focuses on the attitudes of the women themselves. Passages in the letters of a number of mill women reveal that they did in fact make just these sorts of negative judgments about rural life. Maria and Lura Currier, two sisters from Wentworth, New Hampshire, worked in Lowell in the 1840s. In the winter of 1845–46 they wrote a number of letters to a friend and fellow operative in Lowell, Harriet Hanson. The sisters were most discontented. Their parents would not allow them to go to Lowell that winter and they felt penned up in the wilderness. As Lura wrote: "I cannot as you anticipated tell you of any pleasant sleigh rides . . . of the nice supper, and *turnovers* for they have no ambition for anything of that kind, up here in these *diggins*." Social life in Wentworth seemed barren indeed after all the excitement and bustle of city life: "It is extremely dull here now, there is nothing at all interesting going on here, save the orthodox have a singing school, but *that*, *we* do not attend." To the Currier sisters all the lively and interesting people in Wentworth seemed to be going to the mill towns. Wrote Maria: "A great many of our young people are leaving this Spring for Manchester and Lowell. Blaisdell will be about the only gentleman there will be left here and he is just about the same as a married man so we do not place any dependence upon him." It was indeed a long winter and spring for the two sisters who had their hearts set on returning to Lowell.[59]

---

[58] "Farming Life in New England," *Atlantic Monthly* (August 1858), 2:341; also quoted in Joseph Kett, *Rites of Passage: Adolescence in America, 1790 to the Present* (New York: Basic Books, 1977), p. 96, and Wilson, *Hill Country*, p. 72.

[59] Lura Currier to Harriet Hanson, Dec. 14, 1845; Maria Currier to Harriet Hanson, April 5, 1846, in Harriet Hanson Robinson Collection, SL. For published, but occasionally inaccurate typescripts of these letters, see Allis Rosenberg Wolfe,

Mary Paul, whose letters have been quoted earlier, also developed a degree of sophistication that led her to look down upon certain aspects of rural life and culture. Several years after she left Lowell, she moved to a utopian cooperative community in New Jersey. While working there she was surprised to meet a couple from her home town in Vermont, who were on something of a sightseeing tour that included this community. As Mary wrote to her father: "They are travelling for pleasure I expect and came here to *see* people go to Niagara [Falls] to see." Mary expressed the distance between herself and her visitors when she noted: "They are real nice folks but seem rather countryfied in their ideas."[60]

The complaints of Zadock Thompson and the comments of the Currier sisters and Mary Paul provide contrasting views of the same basic dilemma. Women workers in the early mills were caught between two worlds. Born and raised in rural New England, they identified with the pride and independence of their yeoman farmer parents. At the same time, however, they experienced a new life in Lowell and enjoyed the social and economic independence it provided. They returned home with new clothes and with periodicals and more modern ideas picked up in the fluid urban setting. They also came back with money in their pockets and spending habits that surprised some of their rural neighbors. For many, work in Lowell proved to be a first, and an irreversible, step away from the rural, agricultural lives of their parents. Fully a third found the urban world and culture of Lowell and other cities too alluring to return to rural villages. And those who remained in their home towns tended to marry nonfarmers and thus did not follow in the footsteps of their mothers either. For both groups, for those who remained at home and those who settled in Lowell, the mill experience signaled the beginning of a new life. The world of their parents was the world of their past; they had moved beyond.

"Letters of a Lowell Mill Girl and Friends, 1845–1846," [*Labor History* (1976), 17], pp. 96–102; for corrections and a successful attempt to place these letters in context see Lise Vogel, "Humorous Incidents and Sound Common Sense." My thanks to Lise Vogel for sharing her work in manuscript.

[60] Mary Paul to Bela Paul, June 11, 1855, Mary Paul Letters, VHS.

Religious Conflict

in

Ante-Bellum Boston

Religious conflict in early American history involved not merely discrimination against the non-Christian Indians and Africans but also
hostility among competing Christian sects. Puritan intolerance in
New England and Anglican establishment in the Southern colonies
worked against the unification of the several Christian denominations.
Although the Bill of Rights established a legal basis for religious
toleration—at least at the federal level—as early as 1789, religious
discrimination has been a persistent problem in American society.

One of the most virulent outbreaks of religious prejudice in
American history occurred in the 1840s and 1850s, when tens of
thousands of Irish Catholic immigrants arrived on the Eastern seaboard. Fleeing the horrors of famine in Ireland, many came to America destitute and deeply antagonistic toward all things English, including the Protestant religion. There had been Irish immigrants to
America before—those deported in the civil wars of the seventeenth
century and the United Irishmen refugees from the attempted republican rebellion of 1798. But never before had the Irish come in
such numbers, and never had America been so ill prepared to receive
them.

Many German Catholics also emigrated to America in these
years, but the majority of the Germans avoided religious conflict by
moving to the West, where they formed homogeneous farming communities and settled in cities such as St. Louis and Milwaukee. The
Irish, in contrast, tended to gather in the older cities and in the new
factory towns of the East, where they competed with the established
residents for unskilled and industrial labor, thus intensifying negative
feelings toward them. The United States economy had just begun
to recover from the depression of 1837, which had closed thousands
of businesses and manufacturing plants and caused widespread un-
employment. Now, suddenly, there was a great flood of cheap labor,
creating the first real labor surplus in American history. Industrialists
responded by cutting wages drastically in the mills and other Eastern

manufacturing enterprises. The laboring classes tended to blame the Irish for the worsening economic conditions. Religious bigotry and nativism added to the discontent, and violence of major proportions erupted in several Eastern cities. In Philadelphia, for example, a request that Catholic children be allowed to use the Catholic version of the Bible in public schools and that they be excused from Protestant religious exercises led to riots in which houses and churches were burned and at least thirty people were killed and over a hundred wounded.

The following selection is reprinted from a chapter in **Boston's Immigrants,** a study of Irish immigrants to Boston by Oscar Handlin, of Harvard University. In it, Handlin examines the rise of nativism and anti-Catholicism in Boston toward the middle of the nineteenth century.

We still drive out of Society the Ishmaels and Esaus. This we do not so much from ill-will as want of thought, but thereby we lose the strength of these outcasts. So much water runs over the dam— wasted and wasting![1]

Consciousness of identity particularized groups; but mere pluralism evoked no conflict in Boston society. Those coherently welded by circumstances of origin, economic status, cultural variations, or color differences often moved in distinct orbits, but were part of a harmonious system. In some instances, native Bostonians adopted newcomers; in others, they adapted themselves to the existence of aliens in their community. But whatever friction arose out of the necessity for making adjustments produced no conflict, until the old social order and the values upon which it rested were endangered.

Thus, while prejudice against color and servile economic origin confined the Negroes to restricted residential areas, distinct churches, special jobs, separate schools, and undesirable places in theaters until the 1850s, the relationships between Negroes and other Bostonians were stable and

[1] Theodore Parker, *A Sermon of the Dangerous Classes in Society* . . . (Boston, 1847), 12.

"Religious Conflict in Ante-Bellum Boston." Reprinted by permission of the publishers. From Oscar Handlin, *Boston's Immigrants*, Cambridge, Mass.: The Belknap Press of Harvard University Press, pp. 178–206. Copyright, 1941, 1959, by the President and Fellows of Harvard College.

peaceful.[2] Social and legal discriminations still limited Negro privileges in the Park Street Church in 1830, and incited protests when Alcott included a Negro child in his infant school.[3] But the stigmata and penalties for being different were slowly vanishing. Those who urged equality for the South were perforce obliged to apply their convictions at home. An attempt in 1822 to restrict the immigration of Negro paupers failed and repeated petitions after 1839 finally secured the repeal of laws against intermarriage, thus legalizing a process already in existence.[4] In 1855 separate schools were abolished and colored children unconditionally admitted to the public schools, so that by 1866 some 150 Negroes attended the primary, 103 the grammar, and five the high schools of Boston—in all, a high percentage of the Negro children of the city.[5] The state actively defended and protected Negroes' rights, even establishing missions for that purpose in Charleston and New Orleans where Boston colored seamen were often seized as fugitive slaves.[6] Public pressure forced the Eastern and New Bedford Railroads to admit colored people to their cars in the forties; and former slaves began to move to the same streets as whites.[7] In 1863, they were permitted to fight in the Union Army when Governor Andrew, with the aid of Lewis Hayden, recruited the Fifty-fourth Massachusetts Regiment, which included 300 fugitive slaves. In the same year, the militia was opened to them, and a colored company in Ward Six received a grant from the city. Negro regiments were segregated, but many prominent Bostonians "taking life and honor in their hands cast in their lot with" them.[8] By 1865, the Negroes, though still a separate part of Boston society, participated in its advantages without conflict. And most Bostonians agreed that "the theory of a natural antagonism and in-

[2] Cf., e.g., the sober editorial on Negro problems in *Daily Evening Transcript*, September 28, 1830; cf. also Mary Caroline Crawford, *Romantic Days in Old Boston* . . . (Boston, 1910), 249; Helen T. Catterall, *Judicial Cases Concerning American Slavery and the Negro* . . . (Washington, 1936), IV, 524.

[3] Cf. E. S. Abdy, *Journal of a Residence and Tour in the United States* . . . (London, 1835), I, 133 ff.; Odell Shepard, *Journals of Bronson Alcott* (Boston, 1938), 110.

[4] Cf. [Theodore Lyman, Jr.], *Free Negroes and Mulattoes, House of Representatives, January 16, 1822 . . . Report* . . . (Boston, n.d.); Henry Wilson, *History of the Rise and Fall of the Slave Power in America* (Boston, 1872), I, 489–92.

[5] 316 between the ages of 10 and 15 ("Report of the School Committee, 1866," *Boston City Documents, 1866*, no. 137, p. 188). Cf. also *Boston Pilot*, September 15, October 6, 1855.

[6] Cf. the letters of Edward Everett to John P. Bigelow, dated July 23, 1839, September 30, 1839 (Bigelow Papers [MSS., H. C. L.], Box V, VI); Arthur B. Darling, *Political Changes in Massachusetts* . . . (New Haven, 1925), 320; Catterall, *op. cit.*, IV, 511, 524; Edward Channing, *History of the United States* (New York, 1925), VI, 93 ff.

[7] Cf. Wilson, *op. cit.*, I, 492–95; Lady Emmeline S. Wortley, *Travels in the United States* . . . (New York, 1851), 60; Edward Dicey, *Six Months in the Federal States* (London, 1863), II, 215.

[8] *Exercises at the Dedication of the Monument to Colonel Robert Gould Shaw . . . May 31, 1897* . . . (Boston, 1897), 10; Henry Greenleaf Pearson, *Life of John A. Andrew* . . . (Boston, 1904), II, 70 ff.; William S. Robinson, *"Warrington" Pen-Portraits* . . . (Boston, 1877), 107, 274, 406; A. B. Hart, *Commonwealth History of Massachusetts* . . . (New York, 1930), IV, 535; *Boston City Documents, 1863*, no. 100, pp. 11, 18.

superable prejudice on the part of the white man against the black is a pure fiction. Ignorant men are always full of prejudices and antagonisms; and color has nothing to do with it."[9]

Group consciousness based upon religious differences was likewise not conducive to conflict. The Puritan dislike of Catholics had subsided during the eighteenth century,[10] and had disappeared in the early nineteenth as a result of the good feelings produced by revolutionary collaboration with the French and the growth of the latitudinarian belief that "inside of Christianity reason was free."[11] Governor Hancock had early abolished Pope's Day, and the Constitution of 1780 had eliminated the legal restrictions against Catholics. Catholics established a church in the city in 1789 "without the smallest opposition, for persecution in Boston had wholly ceased," and "all violent prejudices against the good bishop of Rome and the Church . . . he governs" had vanished, along with hostility towards hierarchical institutions in general.[12] Bishop Carroll, visit-

---

[9] Robinson, *op. cit.*, 298; cf. also Dicey, *op. cit.*, I, 70, 74; *Massachusetts Senate Documents, 1841*, no. 51; *Massachusetts House Documents, 1841*, no. 17.

[10] Thus with few exceptions there was a "general absence of anti-Catholic references" in eighteenth-century textbooks, and the Dudleian lectures were founded to counteract "the rapid rise of liberalism" (Rev. Arthur J. Riley, *Catholicism in New England* . . . [Washington, 1936], 23, 31, 225, 307). The only exception was the hostility, primarily political, to Jesuit activities in Maine (*ibid.*, 6, 193 ff.; Channing, *op. cit.*, II, 131 ff., 531, 545 ff.). Puritan intolerance sprang from the desire to found a "bible commonwealth" and was therefore directed against Baptists, Quakers, and Arminians as well (cf. Channing, *op. cit.*, II, 68; Ray Allen Billington, *Protestant Crusade, 1800–1860, A Study of the Origins of American Nativism* [New York, 1938], 7, 15, 18; Riley, *op. cit.*, 45 ff., 217 ff.). When priests visited Boston under circumstances that did not endanger the "Standing Order" they "received a cordial welcome befitting the social amenities exchanged between educated persons" (Riley, *op. cit.*, 190, 184 ff., 206, 207).

[11] Octavius B. Frothingham, *Boston Unitarianism, 1820–1850* . . . (New York, 1890), 23; Archibald H. Grimké, *Life of Charles Sumner* . . . (New York, 1892), 38. For the popularity of the French in Boston, cf. H. M. Jones, *America and French Culture* . . . (Chapel Hill, 1927), 126; for the effect of the Revolution, cf. John G. Shea, "Catholic Church in American History," *American Catholic Quarterly Review*, January, 1876, I, 155; Billington, *op. cit.*, 19.

Those who regard anti-Catholicism as inherent in the nature of Protestant society and define "the Protestant milieu" as "nothing else than opposition to Catholicism" (Riley, *op. cit.*, vii, 1; "Anti-Catholic Movements in the United States," *Catholic World*, XXII [1876], 810; Billington, *op. cit.*, 1) have been hard put to explain the tolerance of the early nineteenth century. The simplest escape has been to mark it a period of subsidence arising from absorption in other problems (cf. Billington, *op. cit.*, 32; Humphrey J. Desmond, *Know-Nothing Party* [Washington, 1904], 12), with the anti-Catholicism of the forties and fifties simply a recrudescence of forces always present, thus missing completely the significance of the special factors that produced it in those two decades.

[12] Samuel Breck, "Catholic Recollections," *American Catholic Historical Researches*, XII (1895), 146, 148; E. Percival Merritt, "Sketches of the Three Earliest Roman Catholic Priests in Boston," *Publications of the Colonial Society of Massachusetts*, XXV, 218 ff.; William Wilson Manross, *Episcopal Church in the United States, 1800–1840, A Study in Church Life* (New York, 1938), 59; Samuel Eliot Morison, *History of the Constitution of Massachusetts* . . . (Boston, 1917), 24.

ing Boston in 1791, preached before the Governor, pronounced the blessing at the annual election of the Ancient and Honorables, and was amazed
at the good treatment accorded him. Bishop Cheverus commanded the
respect and affection of all Protestants.

Thereafter the government was no longer hostile. The City Council
frequently gave Catholics special privileges to insure freedom of worship,
closing the streets near Holy Cross Church to exclude the noise of passing
trucks.[13] It never took advantage of the laws that permitted it to tax all
residents for sectarian purposes; on the contrary, Boston Protestants often
contributed to Catholic churches and institutions. After 1799 no tithes
were collected, by 1820 religious tests were abolished, and in 1833 Church
and State completely separated.[14] The anti-Catholic activities of the *New
York Protestant* and of the New York Protestant Association in the early
thirties had no counterpart in Boston where an attempt to found an anti-
Catholic paper (*Anti-Jesuit*) in 1829 failed.[15] Accepted as loyal members
of the community, Catholics could easily partake of its opportunities.[16]
Their right to be different was consistently defended by natives who
urged that the particular sect each person chose was a private matter.

> In individual instances where our friends and acquaintances join
> the Romish Church, there may be reason either to be glad of it or
> to grieve. If they join the Church . . . because they need its peculiar
> influence for their own good, if never having found peace in Christ
> elsewhere they do find it there, ought we not to rejoice in such a
> result? Why should we doubt that some minds are better fitted
> to find a personal union with God by the methods of the Catholic
> Church than by any other?[17]

There were of course differences between the sects, expressed in
theological disputations. As early as 1791 Thayer offered to debate any

---

13 Cf. Merritt, *loc. cit.*, 205–07; Billington, *op. cit.*, 20; Josiah Quincy, *Figures of the
    Past from the Leaves of Old Journals* (Boston, 1883), 311, 312; *Minutes of the
    Selectmen's Meetings, 1811 to 1817* . . . (*Volume of Records Relating to the
    Early History of Boston,* XXXVIII), *Boston City Documents, 1908,* no. 60, p. 69;
    James Bernard Cullen, *Story of the Irish in Boston* . . . (Boston, 1890), 125; Leo
    F. Ruskowski, *French Emigré Priests in the United States* . . . (Washington,
    1940), 85.

14 Cf. Morison, *op. cit.*, 24, 32; *Boston Catholic Observer,* April 17, 1847; Rev. James
    Fitton, *Sketches of the Establishment of the Church in New England* (Boston,
    1872), 141; Darling, *op. cit.*, 23; Hart, *op. cit.*, IV, 12.

15 Cf. Billington, *op. cit.*, 53 ff., 76. The Boston Irish Protestant Association which
    Billington claimed was anti-Catholic (*ibid.*, 78, n. 48) specifically disavowed such
    activities (cf. the correspondence in *Boston Pilot,* June 25, July 2, 1842; also *Boston
    Catholic Observer,* August 2, 1848).

16 Cf., e.g., *Jesuit or Catholic Sentinel,* July 23, 1831; Marcus Lee Hansen, *Immigrant
    in American History* . . . (Cambridge, 1940), 107.

17 James Freeman Clarke, *The Church . . . as It Was, as It Is, as It Ought to Be, a
    Discourse at the . . . Chapel . . . Church of the Disciples . . . 1848* (Boston,
    1848), 13; Arthur M. Schlesinger, Jr., *Orestes A. Brownson* . . . (Boston, 1939),
    175.

Protestant in a "controversial lecture."[18] Beecher and Bishop Fenwick, assisted by Father O'Flaherty, engaged in a series of debates in 1830–34, the most prominent of the period. And the religious press and sermons occasionally attacked Catholicism, sometimes violently, in the spirit of all contemporary disputes, while Protestant denominations urged their ministers to resist the spread of "Popery."[19]

But the expression of theological differences did not imply intolerance. Thus the Congregationalists urged their ministers to labor "in the spirit of prayer and Christian love . . . ," and even the *Christian Alliance and Family Visitor*, founded "to promote the union of Christians against Popery," failed to print "a single article or paragraph of any description against . . . Catholics."[20] Arguments were aimed against Catholicism, not against Catholics, just as they were against Methodism, or by the Orthodox against Unitarianism and by "Christians" against transcendentalists.[21] When Beecher became too violent, the *Boston Courier* and the Boston Debating Society, both non-Catholic, denounced him. For though some preferred one sect to another, the predominant feeling among Bostonians of this period was that "wherever holiness reigns, whether in the Protestant or Catholic communion . . . wherever there is a pious heart . . . there is a member of the true church."[22] Indeed, such men as Channing cared little for the particular sect in which they ministered. Their "whole concern was with religion, not even with Christianity otherwise than as it was, in . . . [their] estimation, the highest form of religion. . . ."[23]

Those who recognized distinctions between the sects generally felt that more important were

> the grand facts of Christianity, which *Calvinists* and *Arminians*, *Trinitarians* and *Unitarians*, *Papists* and *Protestants*, *Churchmen* and *Dissenters* all equally believe. . . . We all equally hold that he came . . . to save us from sin and death, and to publish a covenant of grace, by which all sincere penitents and good men are assured of favour and complete happiness in his future everlasting kingdom.[24]

In that vein, Holmes' "Cheerful Parson" affirmed,

[18] Cf. *Columbian Centinel* (Boston), January 26, 1791; *ibid.*, February 2, 1791; *American Catholic Historical Researches*, V (1888), 51.

[19] Cf. Dissertation Copy, 347, 348; Billington, *op. cit.*, 43 ff., 69 ff., 79. For the religious press in general, cf. Frank Luther Mott, *History of American Magazines* . . . (Cambridge, 1938), II, 60.

[20] Cf. the complaints on this score in *Boston Catholic Observer*, March 1, 1848; also Billington, *op. cit.*, 86, 177.

[21] Cf., e.g., Darling, *op. cit.*, 29; Clarence Hotson, "Christian Critics and Mr. Emerson," *New England Quarterly*, March, 1938, XI, 29 ff.

[22] R. C. Waterston, "*The Keys of the Kingdom of Heaven*," a Sermon . . . (Boston, 1844), 13; cf. also Frothingham, *op. cit.*, 48; *Jesuit or Catholic Sentinel*, December 29, 1830; *ibid.*, February 26, 1831.

[23] Frothingham, *op. cit.*, 6.

[24] Richard Price, *Sermons on the Christian Doctrine as Received by the Different Denominations of Christians* . . . (Boston, 1815), 8.

> Not damning a man for a different opinion,
> I'd mix with the Calvinist, Baptist, Arminian,
> Greet each like a man, like a Christian and brother,
> Preach love to our Maker, ourselves and each other.[25]

And even the more conservative Baptists granted that "the various erring sects which constitute the body of Antichrist, have among them those who are beloved of God. . . ." "Wherein we think others err, they claim our pity; wherein they are right, our affection and concurrence."[26] In this roseate scheme of salvation there was room even for Jews, and from Bunker Hill, a poet proclaimed:

> Christian and Jew, they carry out one plan,
>   For though of different faith, each in heart a man.[27]

Government action reflected the community's attitude towards immigrants. They were still welcome. The state had no desire to exclude foreigners or to limit their civic rights; on the contrary, during this period it relaxed some surviving restrictions.[28] Since the care of aliens was charged to the Commonwealth, the problem of poor relief aroused less hostility within Boston than outside it.[29] Yet nowhere was pauperism transmuted into a pretext for discrimination against the Irish. Legislation aimed only at barring the dependent, the insane, and the unfit, and shifted to newcomers part of the cost of those who could not support themselves. The function of the municipal Superintendent of Alien Passengers, under the act of 1837, was merely to prevent the landing of persons incompetent to maintain themselves, unless a bond be given that no such individual become a public charge within ten years, and to collect the sum of two dollars each from all other alien passengers as a commutation for such a bond.[30] All the subsequent changes in the law only modified it to conform with a decision of the Supreme Court.[31] Attempts to extend these

---

[25] Cf. M. A. DeWolfe Howe, *Holmes of the Breakfast Table* . . . (New York, 1939), 17.

[26] *Minutes of the Boston Baptist Association . . . 1812* (Boston, n.d.), 13.

[27] Cf. Morris A. Gutstein, *Aaron Lopez and Judah Touro* . . . (New York, 1939), 98.

[28] Cf. Massachusetts Commissioners of Alien Passengers and Foreign Paupers, *Report . . . 1851* (Boston, 1852), 14; also Edith Abbott, *Historical Aspects of the Immigration Problem* . . . (Chicago, 1926), 622, 739 ff.; *Cork Examiner*, July 6, 1853; *Massachusetts House Documents, 1828–29*, no. 25; *ibid., 1829–30*, no. 8; *Massachusetts Senate Documents, 1852*, no. 11.

[29] Cf. the source of petitions for repeal of the state pauper laws, *Massachusetts Senate Documents, 1847*, no. 109.

[30] *Ordinances of the City of Boston Passed Since the Year 1834* . . . (Boston, 1843), 3, 4; Hart, *op. cit.*, IV, 143 ff.; Edith Abbott, *Immigration, Select Documents* . . . (Chicago, 1924), 105 ff., 148.

[31] Cf. Norris v. City of Boston (7 *Howard's U.S. Reports*, 283, XVII, 139 ff.); *Massachusetts Senate Documents, 1847*, no. 109; *ibid., 1848*, no. 46; Peleg W. Chandler, *Charter and Ordinances of the City of Boston Together with Acts of the Legislature Relating to the City* . . . (Boston, 1850), 25 ff.; *Charter and Ordinances of the City of Boston Together with the Acts of the Legislature* . . . (Boston, 1856), 34 ff.

restrictive provisions failed, partly because of the pressure of shipping firms which profited by the immigrant traffic, but primarily because successive administrations recognized that, "The evils of foreign pauperism we cannot avoid," and it is "wise to avail ourselves of the advantages of direct emigration which increases the business of the State."[32]

In the two decades after 1830, however, the differences so tolerantly accepted impinged ever more prominently upon the Bostonians' consciousness. The economic, physical, and intellectual development of the town accentuated the division between the Irish and the rest of the population and engendered fear of a foreign group whose appalling slums had already destroyed the beauty of a fine city and whose appalling ideas threatened the fondest conceptions of universal progress, of grand reform, and a regenerated mankind. The vague discomforts and the latent distrusts produced by the problems of these strangers festered in the unconscious mind of the community for many years. Though its overt manifestations were comparatively rare, the social uneasiness was none the less real.

Thus pauperism aroused some resentment among those who saw Massachusetts overwhelmed by a rising tax bill;[33] and indigent artisans continually complained that Irishmen displaced "the honest and respectable laborers of the State; and . . . from their manner of living . . . work for much less per day . . . being satisfied with food to support the animal existence alone . . . while the latter not only labor for the body but for the mind, the soul, and the State."[34] Above all, as the newcomers developed consciousness of group identity and sponsored institutions that were its concrete expression, they drove home upon other Bostonians a mounting awareness of their differences, and provoked complaints that

> instead of assimilating at once with the customs of the country of their adoption, our foreign population are too much in the habit of retaining their own national usages, of *associating too exclusively with each other*, and living in groups together. These practices serve no good purpose, and tend merely to alienate those among whom they have chosen to reside. *It would be the part of wisdom, to* ABANDON AT ONCE ALL USAGES AND ASSOCIATIONS WHICH MARK THEM AS FOREIGNERS, *and to become in feeling and custom, as well as in privileges and rights, citizens of the United States.*[35]

The inability of the native-born to understand the ideas of their new neighbors perpetuated this gap between them, rousing the vivid fear that

---

[32] *Massachusetts Senate Documents, 1852*, no. 7, p. 7. For the influence of shipping firms, cf. *Massachusetts Senate Documents, 1847*, no. 109, p. 5; Boston Board of Trade, *Second Annual Report of the Government . . . 1856* (Boston, 1856), 3.

[33] For evidence of this complaint, cf. *American Traveller* (Boston), August 5, 1834; *American*, October 21, 1837; Abbott, *Immigration*, 112 ff.; Edith Abbott, *Historical Aspects of the Immigration Problem . . .* (Chicago, 1926), 572 ff., 758 ff.; *Massachusetts House Documents, 1836*, no. 30, pp. 9 ff.

[34] Cf. *Massachusetts Senate Documents, 1847*, no. 109, p. 4.

[35] *American* (Boston), October 21, 1837.

the Irish were "a race that will never be infused into our own, but on the contrary will always remain distinct and hostile."[36]

That fear was the more pronounced because the Catholic Church in these years was a church militant, conscious of its mission in the United States, vigorous and active in proselytization and the search for converts. In the strategy of the hierarchy, and in their own minds, immigrants played a clear role in this process of redemption: they had been carried across the waters by a Divine Providence to present an irrefutable example of fortitude and faith to their unbelieving neighbors, to leaven the dull mass of Protestant America and ultimately to bring the United States into the ranks of Catholic powers.[37] No figure was more insistently, clearly, and admiringly drawn in immigrant literature than that of the humble Irishman in every walk of life who succeeded in converting his employer, friend, or patron.[38] Though Bostonians could not do without the Irish servant girl, distrust of her mounted steadily; natives began to regard her as a spy of the Pope who revealed their secrets regularly to priests at confession.[39] The growth of Catholicism in England warned them that a staunchly Protestant country might be subverted. Meanwhile, close at home, the mounting power of the Oxford movement in the Episcopal Church, reflected in the estrangement of Bishop Eastburn and the Church of the Advent (1844 ff.), and a growing list of widely publicized conversions lent reality to the warning of Beecher and Morse that Catholics plotted to assume control of the West.[40]

Before 1850, the potential friction inherent in these fears broke out only infrequently and sporadically. Incepted by irresponsible elements, these spontaneous brawls were always severely criticized by the community. Indeed, they were only occasionally directed against aliens, more often involving neighborhoods or fire companies. The rowdies singled out no special group. In 1814 West Enders rioted against Spanish sailors, in 1829 against Negroes and Irishmen, and in 1846 against some drunken Irishmen in Roxbury; but these were no more significant than the count-

---

36 Mayor Lyman (*Inaugural Addresses of the Mayors of Boston* . . . [Boston, 1894], I, 195).

37 Cf., e.g., *Boston Catholic Observer*, February 16, 1848; Thomas D'Arcy McGee, *History of the Irish Settlers in North America* . . . (Boston, 1852), 71; Billington, *op. cit.*, 291.

38 Cf. e.g., Ellie in Agnes E. St. John, "Ellie Moore or the Pilgrim's Crown," *Boston Pilot*, June 30–September 1, 1860.

39 Cf. James O'Connor, "Anti-Catholic Prejudice," *American Catholic Quarterly Review*, I (1876), 13.

40 Cf. Billington, *op. cit.*, 118 ff., 263; William Wilson Manross, *History of the American Episcopal Church* (New York, 1935), 283 ff.; *Boston Catholic Observer*, July 24, 1847; S. F. B. Morse, *Foreign Conspiracy Against the United States* (s.l., n.d.) 3, 26, 29, [186–], S. F. B. Morse, *Imminent Dangers to the Free Institutions of the United States* . . . (New York, 1854), *passim;* Louis Dow Scisco, *Political Nativism in New York State* (New York, 1901), 21.

less feuds between North Enders and South Enders, or between truckmen and sailors, details of which enlivened many a police dossier.[41]

The Broad Street riot was exceptional only in size. On June 11, 1837, a collision between a volunteer fire company and an Irish funeral procession led to an outbreak, quelled after an hour or so by the militia. Caused by hotheaded, unruly firemen, proverbially a disruptive factor, it in no way reflected the feeling of the community. The firemen were immediately repudiated, and partly as a result of the affair, Mayor Lyman took the first steps towards replacing the volunteer system with a paid fire department.[42] A less permanent result was the establishment by the disbanded firemen of the *American*, the first anti-Catholic paper in Boston which for somewhat less than a year attacked alternately the Irish and the "*paid patriots*" who replaced them.[43]

Because it served for many years as an argument throughout the country in the propaganda for and against Catholics, the Charlestown Convent fire received a greater degree of notoriety than any other riot.[44] This disturbance grew primarily out of the failure of the school and the rural community in which it was located to adjust themselves to each other. To the laborers who lived nearby, the convent was a strange and unfamiliar institution, with which it was difficult to be neighborly or to follow the customary social forms. In addition, Catholicism meant Irishmen and for non-Irish laborers the convent was a symbol of the new competition they daily encountered. Rebecca Reed's lurid stories of life in the convent and the bickering of the Bishop and the Charlestown Selectman over a cemetery on Bunker Hill provoked a sense of irritation that came to a head with the appearance and disappearance of Elizabeth Harrison, a demented nun.[45] The refusal of the Mother Superior to admit the Charlestown Selectmen to investigate the purported existence of dungeons and torture chambers until the very day of the fire inflamed

---

[41] Cf. "Boston as It Appeared to a Foreigner at the Beginning of the Nineteenth Century," *Bostonian Society Publications*, Series I, IV, 117, 118; Joseph E. Chamberlin, *Boston Transcript* . . . (Boston, 1930), 37 ff.; *Minutes of the Selectmen's Meetings, 1811 to 1817* . . . (*Volume of Records* . . . , XXXVIII), *Boston City Documents, 1908*, no. 60, p. 113; *Boston Pilot*, September 12, 1846; Arthur Wellington Brayley, *Complete History of the Boston Fire Department* . . . (Boston, 1889), 185, 186; Edward H. Savage, *Police Records and Recollections* . . . (Boston, 1873), 65, 66, 110, 257.

[42] Chamberlin, *op. cit.*, 48 ff.; Brayley, *Complete History*, 197 ff.; State Street Trust Company, *Mayors of Boston* . . . (Boston, [1914]), 15.

[43] Cf. *American*, October 21, 1837, March 17, 1838.

[44] There are numerous short accounts of this affair; but the best, though differing in interpretation from that offered here, is in Billington, *op. cit.*, 68 ff.

[45] Billington, *op. cit.*, 71 ff.; Shea, *op. cit.*, III, 462, 463; Charles Greely Loring, *Report of the Committee Relating to the Destruction of the Ursuline Convent* . . . (Boston, 1834), 8. Miss Harrison's disappearance was probably not important. In 1830 a rumor spread by the *New England Herald* (Vol. I, no. 28) that "a young lady, an orphan, has lately been inveigled into the Ursuline Convent . . . after having been cajoled to transfer a large fortune to the Popish massmen" was ridiculed and had no repercussions (cf. *United States Catholic Intelligencer*, April 24, 1830).

the forty or fifty Charlestown truckmen and New Hampshire Scotch-Irish brickmakers who led the curious mob; and her threat that, unless they withdrew, she would call upon the Bishop for a defense contingent of 20,000 Irishmen precipitated the holocaust.[46]

After the initial excitement, every section of public opinion in Boston greeted the fire with horror and surprise. Bostonians had not disliked the school; many had actually sent their children there. There is no evidence that the residents of the city had any connection with the plot; not a voice was raised in its support. The press condemned the absence of adequate protection, and deplored the "high-handed outrage." Bostonians asserted that "The Catholics . . . are as . . . loyal citizens as their brethren of any other denomination." A mass meeting at Faneuil Hall expressed sympathy with the unfortunate victims of mob action and, resolving "to unite with our Catholic brethren in protecting their persons, their property, and their civil and religious rights," recommended a reward for the capture of the criminals and compensation to the convent, as did similar meetings under John Cotton in Ward Eight, under Everett at Charlestown, and under Story at Cambridge.[47] A reward of $500 offered by Governor Davis resulted in the arrest of thirteen men, the trial of eight, and the conviction of one. The life imprisonment sentence for the one of whose guilt there seemed to be no doubt was far more significant than failure to convict those who might have been innocent.[48]

The convent, reestablished in Roxbury, failed "because of lack of harmony among the Sisters."[49] But the legislature was petitioned for compensation repeatedly in the next twenty years. Despite persistent reluctance to grant public funds for religious purposes, $10,000 was voted in 1846, but rejected by the Ursulines.[50] The rise of Know-Nothing sentiments thwarted further overtures, while anti-Catholic activities of city rowdies and the circulation of *Six Months in a Convent* somewhat balanced expressions of sympathy. But these antagonisms were more marked outside than within the city. None of the anti-Catholic papers founded after the publication of that scurrilous book were published in Boston.[51]

Occasional manifestations of hostility in the next few years were restricted in scope. The Montgomery Guards, the first Irish military

[46] Billington, *op. cit.*, 81, n. 85; Benj. F. Butler, *Autobiography and Personal Reminiscences* . . . (Boston, 1892), 111; Darling, *op. cit.*, 165, n. 79.

[47] Cf. Billington, *op. cit.*, 69, 81–85, 86, 108; Loring, *op. cit.*, 2, 6, 16; *American Traveller*, August 15, 19, 1834; [H. Ware, Jr.], *An Account of the Conflagration of the Ursuline Convent . . . by a Friend of Religious Toleration* (Boston, 1834), 3; Chamberlin, *op. cit.*, 44 ff.; *Jesuit or Catholic Sentinel*, August 16, 1834; *ibid.*, August 23, 1834; Crawford, *Romantic Days*, 22.

[48] Cf. Ware, *op. cit.*, 10; *Jesuit or Catholic Sentinel*, August 23, 1834; Billington, *op. cit.*, 86, 87; Loring, *op. cit.*, 4.

[49] Robert H. Lord, "Organizer of the Church in New England," *Catholic Historical Review*, XXII (1936), 182.

[50] Cf. Billington, *op. cit.*, 89, 110, n. 27; *Documents Relating to the Ursuline Convent in Charlestown* (Boston, 1842), 21, 22, 31; "Anti-Catholic Movements in the United States," *Catholic World*, XXII (1876), 814; *Boston Pilot*, February 18, 1854.

[51] Cf. *Boston Pilot*, April 16, 1853; Billington, *op. cit.*, 92 ff.

company, were attacked in 1837 by the rank and file of the Boston City Guards who refused to parade with an Irish company to uphold "the broad principle . . . that *in all institutions springing from our own laws, we all mingle in the same undisguised mass, whether native or naturalized.*" Although the native militiamen complained that "the press . . . condemned our conduct with . . . openmouthed language of wholesale reprehension . . . ," the very next year the same newspapers severely criticized the Irish soldiers who were finally disbanded in 1839.[52] In 1844 the reaction to the school quarrels in New York, to the riots in Philadelphia, and to the defeat of the national Whig ticket by the Irish vote produced a short-lived nativist branch of the Whig Party. Although the American Republicans under T. A. Davis gained the mayoralty in 1845, it was only on the eighth ballot, in an election fought primarily on the issue of the local water supply.[53] Nativism declined steadily thereafter. An attempt to revive it in 1847 failed so disastrously, that the *Boston Catholic Observer* could triumphantly proclaim nativism dying.[54]

Nativist fears failed to develop more significantly because the Irish before 1845 presented no danger to the stability of the old society. They were in a distinct minority and, above all, were politically impotent. In 1843 the Irish claimed no more than 200 voters in all Suffolk County, and in 1839, no more than 500, while in 1845 less than one-sixth of the adult male foreigners in Boston were citizens.[55] Only a few had secured the right to vote, or took an interest in politics; their opinions were still a matter of private judgment, with no influence upon the policies of the community. The old inhabitants, as individuals, might look down upon their new neighbors as unabsorbable incubi, but the still powerful tradition of tolerance stifled their accumulated resentments. The dominant group took no step to limit social and political rights or privileges until the ideals of the newcomers threatened to replace those of the old society. At that moment the tradition of tolerance was breached and long repressed hostilities found highly inflammable expression.

The crisis came when, after a decade of efforts in that direction, the Irish acquired a position of political importance. After 1840 their press insisted upon the duty "to themselves as well as to their families" of naturalization and a role in the government. Politicians sponsored societies which aided the unknowing and stimulated the indifferent to become citizens, and professional agents drew up papers, filled out forms, and rapidly turned out new voters for the sake of fees and political power.[56] Between 1841 and 1845, the number of qualified voters increased by 50

---

[52] Cf. *American*, October 21, 1837; *Boston Pilot*, February 3, 17, 1838, October 12, 1839.

[53] Cf. State Street Trust Company, *Mayors of Boston*, 17; Darling, *op. cit.*, 327–29; William G. Bean, Party Transformation in Massachusetts . . . (MS. H. C. L.), 228 ff.

[54] *Boston Catholic Observer*, August 28, June 19, July 24, 1847; Bean, *op. cit.*, 232 ff.

[55] Cf. *Jesuit or Catholic Sentinel*, January 18, 1834; *Boston Pilot*, November 9, 1839; George H. Haynes, "Causes of Know-Nothing Success in Massachusetts," *American Historical Review*, III (1897), 74, n. 1.

[56] Cf. *Boston Pilot*, February 19, 1853; Dissertation Copy, 367.

percent, then remained stable until 1852, when it grew by almost 15 percent in two years, while in the five years after 1850, the number of naturalized voters increased from 1,549 to 4,564. In the same period, the number of native voters grew only 14 percent.[57] Perennial political organizations flourished with every campaign and further mobilized the Irish vote.[58]

The coherence and isolation of Irish ideas facilitated political organization. And Irish leaders, consciously or unconsciously, encouraged group solidarity and the maintenance of a virtual Irish party. Though the Irish vote was not yet used to serve corrupt personal interest,[59] both those who aspired to gain public office in America through the support of a large bloc of voters and those who hoped to return as liberators to the Emerald Isle directed their energies towards activizing their countrymen. These efforts were so widespread that one of the most far-sighted Irish leaders complained that Irish political influence was being "fatally misused" and warned that "keeping up an Irish party in America is a fatal mistake, and . . . I will seek to induce them rather to blend and fuse their interests with American parties, than cause jealousy and distrust by acting as an exclusive and independent faction . . . a man has no right to interfere in American politics unless he thinks as an American. . . ."[60] But such views were rare.

With the political mobilization of the Irish in Boston, tolerance finally disappeared. The possibilities of Irish domination were the more startling because the political situation in Massachusetts, 1845–55, permitted a coherent, independent group to exercise inordinate influence. The unity of the old parties was crumbling as dissatisfied elements demanded new policies to meet the problems of reform, particularly those posed by slavery.[61] Although all, including the most conservative Abbott Lawrence, agreed on the ultimate desirability of reform, they were divided as to the methods of attaining it. Within each political party a restless group contended that the forces of good must prevail immediately, even at the expense of failure in national politics. Their insistence upon immediate, unequivocal action destroyed the coherence of the old alignments and yielded to the unified Irish the balance of power. For four years the reformers found these foreigners square in their path, defeating their most valued measures. In the critical year of 1854 this opposition drove them into a violent xenophobic movement that embodied all the hatreds stored up in the previous two decades.

Rantoul and Morton had blasted the stability of the Democrats, but

---

57 Cf. Josiah Curtis, *Report of the Joint Special Committee . . . 1855 . . .* (Boston, 1856), 11; "Report and Tabular Statement of the Censors," *Boston City Documents, 1850*, no. 42, p. 12; Billington, *op. cit.*, 325, 326.

58 Cf., e.g., *Boston Pilot*, July 8, 1860.

59 The only instance of devious Irish politics in this period came in the election of John C. Tucker to the legislature in 1860 (cf. E. P. Loring and C. T. Russell, Jr., *Reports of Controverted Elections . . . 1853 to 1885 . . .* [Boston, 1886], 89 ff.).

60 Richard O'Gorman to W. S. O'Brien, May 24, 1849, W. S. O'Brien Papers and Letters, 1819–1854 (MSS., N. L. I.), XVIII, no. 2, p. 547.

61 Cf. Darling, *op. cit.*, 312 ff.

the Whig party was the first torn asunder by the anti-slavery men. In the early forties, some members had already deserted to the Liberty party, but until 1846 most anti-slavery Whigs continued to believe in "reform within the Party." Even in that year the magic personality of Webster nullified the damage done by Southern aggressions and the turbulent Texas and Mexico questions, and held in rein such conscientious rebels as Stephen C. Phillips, Charles Allen, and Sumner. But the Whig nomination of a slaveholder to the presidency and the rejection of the Wilmot Proviso by their National Convention in 1848 opened an unbridgeable gap between the two factions, though the Whigs remained strong enough to win the gubernatorial election that year and again in 1849.[62]

A similar development among the Democrats led a few to support Van Buren, the Free-Soil nominee in 1848, but the party quickly united to profit from the more serious division of its rivals. In addition, hoping for a coalition, it offered the Whig dissidents an anti-slavery plank in 1849. But these overtures failed; Free-Soilers still preferred cooperation with the Whigs to alliance with the Democrats who, nationally, were the most prominent supporters of the South's peculiar institution. But while Webster squinted at the federal scene and dreamed of the White House, the Whigs would have no meddling with reform. Though controlling the legislature of 1849, they failed to pass a single Free-Soil measure. Finally, their support of the Fugitive Slave Law, and particularly Webster's role in its enactment, completed the cleavage and consolidated the Free-Soil party in Massachusetts.[63]

When the gubernatorial election of 1850 gave no candidate a majority, Democratic ambitions, after seven years of famine, approached fulfillment. The constitution provided for the choice of a governor by an absolute majority, in the absence of which the election was thrown into the legislature—a situation susceptible to a great deal of political maneuvering. In this election the Democratic state platform had endorsed the Free-Soil program, though without a formal coalition. A trade between the two parties, which together had a majority in the legislature that convened in January, 1851, was inevitable. The Free-Soilers, anxious to be heard in Washington, were impatient with the Whig demand that the designation of a senator wait eleven months for a new legislature, and threw their votes for a Democratic governor. In return, the Democrats supported a radical policy and handed the United States senatorship and the organization of the legislature to the Free-Soilers. Banks became speaker of the House, and Henry Wilson, president of the Senate; although the former was nominally a Democrat, both were actually Free-Soilers. The reformers got the better of the bargain, passing a series of radical measures,

[62] Cf. Robinson, op. cit., 28–38, 416, 513; Bean, op. cit., 8–38; Darling, op. cit., 245 ff., 317, 334, 290, n. 67, 326; Wilson, op. cit., I, 545 ff., II, 145 ff.; George S. Merriam, Life and Times of Samuel Bowles (New York, 1885), I, 45 ff.; Reunion of the Free-Soilers of 1848–1852 . . . June 28, 1888 (Cambridge, 1888), 15, 17; Hart, op. cit., IV, 97; Grimké, op. cit., 182 ff., 190 ff.

[63] Bean, op. cit., 17, 28, 35 ff., 53 ff.; Darling, op. cit., 340, 349–54; Grimké, op. cit., 205; Haynes, loc. cit., 80; Wilson, op. cit., II, 247 ff.

including a general incorporation law to break the power of monopolies, a law for more democratic control of Harvard College, a homestead and mechanics' lien law, and measures ensuring the secret ballot and plurality voting in national elections.[64]

The coalition held through the election of 1851. But though the Free-Soilers managed to push through the Maine Law over Governor Boutwell's veto, they were dissatisfied. They disliked the governor, who had obstructed many reform measures, and they distrusted their Democratic allies, who had bolted in considerable numbers on Sumner's election to the United States Senate and had contrived to defeat a personal liberty law, acts to liberalize divorce, to protect the property rights of women, and to extend the powers of juries. Whittier voiced the apprehension of the Free-Soilers when he wrote, after seeing the governor's first message, "It is . . . monstrous and insulting. May God forgive us for permitting his election."[65]

The Free-Soilers now recognized the need of a reform in government to gain complete control of the state—a reform impossible under the existing conditions of amending the constitution, which called for a two-thirds vote in the House of Representatives of two successive legislatures on each clause.[66] With parties divided as they were, a simple majority was difficult enough, two-thirds almost impossible, and two-thirds in two successive legislatures out of the question. One solution was to change the basis of representation to reduce the influence of the conservative elements opposing them in Boston. But an attempt to do so in 1851 failed, leaving the reformers no alternative but a complete revamping of the constitution by a convention.[67]

In 1851 the Free-Soilers forced through the legislature a resolution for a constitutional convention. But when the question was presented to the voters, Democratic support was weak. The Irish, theretofore consistently Democrats, failed to follow their representatives who had indorsed revision. In the election several thousand who had voted for coalition candidates turned against the constitutional convention.[68] Of

[64] Cf. Bean, *op. cit.*, 54, 57, 64–87; Wilson, *op. cit.*, II, 347 ff.; *Address to the People of Massachusetts* (s.l., n.d., [Boston, 1852]), 3, 6, 7, 10 ff.; Robinson, *op. cit.*, 47, 433; Hart, *op. cit.*, IV, 99, 475.

[65] Alfred S. Roe, "Governors of Massachusetts . . . ," *New England Magazine*, XXV (1902), 547; Bean, *op. cit.*, 90–92, 113–20; Robinson, *op. cit.*, 433; *Address*, 5 ff.; Grimké, *op. cit.*, 209.

[66] A simple majority sufficed in the Senate (Bean, *op. cit.*, 116; Morison, *op. cit.*, 38).

[67] Bean, *op. cit.*, 88, 89. Legislators from Boston were elected on a general ticket which usually denied representation to minorities and gave the whole delegation to the Whigs (cf. Morison, *op. cit.*, 41).

[68] The election of 1851:

	GOVERNOR			CONVENTION	
	State	Boston		State	Boston
Winthrop (W)	64,611	7,388	no	65,846	7,135
Boutwell (D)	43,992	3,632			
Palfrey (FS)	28,599	1,294	yes	60,972	3,813

(*Boston Semi-Weekly Advertiser*, November 12, 1851; Bean, *op. cit.*, 109, 111.) Cf. also Morison, *op. cit.*, 42.

these, more than 1,100 were in Boston, and they were predominantly Irish Democrats bolting the party.[69]

When the Democratic State Convention again supported coalition and revision the following year, the Irish, under J. W. James, the Repeal leader, finally seceded from the party. Though opposing the Democrats in the state election of 1852, they supported the national Democratic party, which had repudiated Rantoul and coalition and whose presidential candidate, Pierce, was most acceptable as a conservative. Following the advice of Brownson and the *Pilot*, the Boston Irish became national Democrats and state Whigs. As a result of the confusion, the coalition ticket lost, but the project for a convention won.[70]

Impressed with the opportunity the convention presented for strengthening the party and consolidating its position, the Free-Soilers made special exertions in the March election and gained control. Their imprint upon the constitution that resulted was unmistakable. Single-unit senatorial districts and plurality elections by secret ballots were proposed. To decrease the power of the executive, many appointive offices, including the Council, became elective; the judiciary was controlled by limiting the term of office and extending the powers of jurors; and the use of public funds for religious education was prohibited. While these measures would render government more responsive to the voice of the people, the proposed constitution was undemocratic in its most important provision. By changing the system of representation to favor country towns at the expense of large cities, bailiwicks of conservatism, the reformers unquestionably compromised their principles.[71]

With one important exception party lines held in the vote on the adoption of the constitution. The opposition of the few conscientious Free-Soilers who would not support the unfair system of representation was trivial compared with the force of conservative Irish Catholic opinion clamoring for defeat.[72] At the Democratic Convention which indorsed the constitution, James again led a seceding group of Boston Irishmen who formed a party of their own. Pressure for recruitment and organization of voters increased. In September the Calvert Naturalization Society in the South End joined the Ward Three Association of the North End. The *Pilot* repeatedly warned that "no Catholic . . . can possibly vote for this . . . Constitution without giving up rights for which he has been all along contending," and Brownson pointed out its revolutionary implications.[73]

[69] Bean's claim that the Free-Soilers bolted (*op. cit.*, 111) is wholly illogical since they wanted the convention and the Irish did not (for the Free-Soilers' attitude on constitutional change, cf. Robinson, *op. cit.*, 401 ff.).

[70] Cf. in general, Bean, *op. cit.*, 127 ff., 217–20. For the new attempt to revise the constitution, cf. *Massachusetts Senate Documents, 1852*, no. 36, pp. 6 ff.

[71] Cf. J. B. Mann, *Life of Henry Wilson* . . . (Boston, 1872), 36 ff.; Hon. Charles Allen, *Speech . . . at Worcester, Nov. 5, 1853* (s.l., n.d.), 1–3; Bean, *op. cit.*, 147–66; Morison, *op. cit.*, 49–60; Henry F. Brownson, *Orestes A. Brownson's Middle Life* . . . (Detroit, 1899), II, 465, 466; Mann, *op. cit.*, 43.

[72] For Free-Soil opposition, cf. Bean, *op. cit.*, 168, 177.

[73] Cf. Brownson, *Brownson's Middle Life*, II, 455 ff.; Dissertation Copy, 377–78; Bean, *op. cit.*, 221.

In their campaign, the Irish joined the die-hard Whigs under Abbott Lawrence, who led "hundreds of honest men gulled by their sophistry" in opposing a constitution which seriously curtailed the influences of State Street in politics. Lawrence conferred with Bishop Fitzpatrick on the problem, and Whig newspapers appealed particularly to the Irish. Against this alliance the reformers' contention that the *Boston Pilot* was "trying to lead Irishmen into the jaws of a Boston aristocracy as remorseless as the one they had left Ireland to get rid of" counted little. The combination of Irish votes and cotton money in Boston defeated the constitution and elected a Whig ticket.[74]

In this crisis the reformers inveighed against the lords of the counting house and bemoaned the slowness of rank-and-file Whigs to recognize their true interests, but concluded that while the former could never be redeemed, and the latter would have to be educated, the main obstacle to reform was Catholic opposition. And by this time they had learned that differences with the Irish were too deep to be easily eradicated; they could only be fought. Butler, sensitive to every shift in popular opinion, realized that the "performance, which struck down the Constitution, invoked a bitterness among the people against the Catholic religion, such as had never before been, to any considerable degree, either felt or foreshadowed in the State of Massachusetts."[75]

Through the early months of 1854 a series of unconnected events heightened resentment against Catholics and evoked many antipathies developed since 1830. In December, 1853, Father Gavazzi, a rebellious priest, lectured in Boston on the reactionary role of the Church.[76] A few months later, the visit of the papal nuncio Bedini, who had been connected with the massacre of revolutionaries in Bologna, though not provoking the expected riot, did refresh memories of Irish opposition to liberalism.[77] Meanwhile, events at home confirmed that impression. Failure of the enforcement of the prohibition laws was laid at the door of the Irish, and the State Temperance Committee announced it would fight Catholicism as part of its struggle for human freedom.[78] The Burns case

---

[74] Robinson, *op. cit.,* 204; Bean, *op. cit.,* 162, 166, 174–79; Butler, *op. cit.,* 119. The analysis of the vote from which Morison concludes that "the wards where most of the Irish-born population then lived did not poll so heavy a negative vote as the fashionable residential districts" (*op. cit.,* 63) is not valid because the wards were gerrymandered in the redistricting of 1850 to split the Irish vote (cf. Dissertation Copy, 383). Even in 1854 votes against the Know-Nothings showed no special concentration in any area (cf. *Boston Atlas,* November 14, 1854). Bean has shown that votes to defeat the constitution came from Boston: the 5,915 negative balance of Suffolk County more than offset the 997 positive balance elsewhere in the state (*op. cit.,* 173).

[75] Butler, *op. cit.,* 120.

[76] Cf. *Boston Semi-Weekly Advertiser,* November 30, December 3, 1853; Billington, *op. cit.,* 301.

[77] *Boston Pilot,* October 8, 1853, February 11, 1854; Billington, *op. cit.,* 300–02; Desmond, *op. cit.,* 72; Shea, *op. cit.,* IV, 360 ff.

[78] *Massachusetts Life Boat,* September 19, 1854; cf. also *Address of the State Temperance Committee to the Citizens of Massachusetts on the Operation of the Anti-Liquor Law* (Boston, 1853), 2; Billington, *op. cit.,* 323.

clearly linked the immigrants to pro-slavery forces and man-hunters. The *Pilot* supported the rendition of the fugitive slave; and the selection of the Columbian Artillery and Sarsfield Guards to protect him against indignant mobs seeking his freedom incited an inflammatory handbill:

AMERICANS TO THE RESCUE!
AMERICANS! SONS OF THE REVOLUTION!!
A body of seventy-five Irishmen, known as the
"Columbian Artillery"
have volunteered their services to shoot down the
citizens of Boston! and are now under arms to defend
Virginia in kidnapping a Citizen of Massachusetts!
Americans! These Irishmen have called us
"Cowards and Sons of Cowards"!
Shall we submit to have our Citizens shot
down by a set of Vagabond Irishmen?

that turned many reformers against the Irish.[79] Finally, their defense of the Kansas-Nebraska Act connected them with the slave power, and drew criticism from such respectable sources as the *Commonwealth*, the *Worcester Spy*, and Theodore Parker.[80]

Distrust of the Irish at once encouraged and was stimulated by attacks upon Catholics. Hatred and violence marched arm in arm, sustaining and strengthening each other. Early in 1853, the purported kidnapping of Hannah Corcoran, a Baptist convert, almost led to a riot. In the same year the city government entered into a long-drawn-out controversy with the Catholics over their right to build a church on the "Jail lands." In May, 1854, John S. Orr, the Angel Gabriel, led a mob that carried away a cross from the Catholic Church in Chelsea, and in July a church was blown up in Dorchester. *The Wide Awake: and the Spirit of Washington*, a vituperative sheet, appeared in October, 1854, to combat the "swarms of lazaroni from abroad"; and a venomous stream of anti-Papist literature reached Boston, particularly in the form of Frothingham's convent novels (1854).[81]

Meanwhile, as slavery absorbed the attention of Congress and the country, excited Free-Soilers found "every indication that the people are awakening from their unaccountable stupor on the . . . question."[82] The Kansas-Nebraska Bill infuriated even Everett and the conservative

[79] Cf. *Boston Pilot*, June 3, 1854; *Irish-American*, September 23, 1854; Billington, *op. cit.*, 435, n. 81; Bean, *op. cit.*, 187, 239, 241.

[80] Cf. Bean, *loc. cit.*, 239 ff.; Carl Wittke, *We Who Built America* . . . (New York, 1939), 168.

[81] *Boston Pilot*, April 9, December 10, 1853, May 13, 1854, January 20, 1855; *Wide Awake: and the Spirit of Washington* (Boston), October 7, 1854; Billington, *op. cit.*, 305–13, 348 ff., 368; Bean, *op. cit.*, 207, 209; Shea, *op. cit.*, IV, 509; Charles W. Frothingham, *Six Hours in a Convent:—or—The Stolen Nuns!* . . . (Boston, 1855).

[82] Albert G. Browne to Sumner, July 28, 1854, Sumner Correspondence (MSS., H. C. L.), XXV, no. 109.

Webster Whigs. Sumner's correspondents informed him that "all parties seem to be approaching that happy state of . . . dissolution, for which we have sighed so long."[83] A Freedom party tentatively formed in Boston, a "Republican" convention adopted a radical program, and a host of excited energies eagerly sought an outlet. Precisely where the immense anti-slavery impulse would be exerted was uncertain, however.[84]

But the Boston municipal elections of December, 1853, had already revealed the ultimate outlet. Only one month after their decisive defeat on the constitution, the reformers rallied to resist the reelection of Nathaniel Seaver, a Whig supported by the liquor interests. As the "Citizens Union party," they appealed to nativist feelings and drew 2,000 Whig votes, the entire Free-Soil vote, and 500 voters who had not troubled to go to the polls a month earlier.[85] These 500 voters came from a tremendous fund of non-voting citizens, many of them Whigs disgusted with their party's vacillation.[86] The lesson to the reformers was obvious and was confirmed by simultaneous elections in Charlestown and Roxbury:[87] the Irish stood in the way of reform; reform forces could best be augmented and galvanized on an anti-Irish basis; the dormant voters must be awakened by an anti-alien alarm.

By 1853 the Order of the Star-Spangled Banner, a nativist secret organization popularly known as the Know-Nothings, had emerged in New York State.[88] Early in 1854 it spread into Massachusetts, swiftly, though quietly and unobtrusively, drawing "into its lodges tens of thousand of . . . anti-Nebraska men, ripe for Republicanism. . . ."[89] These recruits, inwardly ashamed of adopting means incompatible with the principles they professed, wrapped themselves in mantles of secrecy which served as a "spiritual fist-law" for gaining ascendancy without the use of force, and pursued their "purposes with the same disregard of the purposes of the structure external to . . . [themselves] which in the case of the individual is called egoism."[90]

In July, Henry Wilson, already a member, began to harness Know-

[83] Seth Webb, Jr., July 14, 1854, *ibid.*, XXV, no. 72; also Bean, *op. cit.*, 188 ff.

[84] Cf. Amasa Walker to Sumner, Sumner Correspondence, July 2, 1854, XXV, no. 15; Bean, *op. cit.*, 193; Merriam, *op. cit.*, I, 122.

[85] Cf. *Boston Semi-Weekly Advertiser*, December 10, 1853.

BOSTON ELECTIONS, 1853

GOVERNOR	(Nov.)	MAYOR	(Dec.)
Whig	7,730	Whig	5,651
Free-Soil	1,403	Citizens Union	4,691
Coalition Democrat	2,455	Young Men's League	2,010
Hunker Democrat	821	Democrat	596
Total	12,409	Total	12,948

(*Boston Semi-Weekly Advertiser*, November 16, December 14, 1853.)

[86] Cf. Darling, *op. cit.*, 290.

[87] Cf. Bean, *op. cit.*, 246.

[88] Cf. Billington, *op. cit.*, 380; Bean, *op. cit.*, 226; Desmond, *op. cit.*, 66; Scisco, *op. cit.*, 63 ff., 71 ff.

[89] Pearson, *op. cit.*, I, 65.

[90] Cf. Georg Simmel, "Sociology of Secrecy and of Secret Societies," *American Journal of Sociology*, XI (1906), 446 ff., 489.

Nothingism to the anti-slavery cause, and Seth Webb, Jr., decided, "Know-Nothingism is to be an important, perhaps the controlling, element in our state election; it will probably take us out of the hands of the Whigs. Into whose hands it will put us, nobody can tell."[91] The Know-Nothings presented the clearest platform in the next election. Without the support of the intellectual fronts of reform—Adams, Phillips, and Sumner—who felt no ends justified nativist methods, they elected Henry J. Gardner, formerly president of the Boston Common Council, to the governorship by the unprecedented majority of 33,000, and gained complete control of the legislature in November. Until 1857, they ruled the state.[92]

Everywhere the success of the party rested upon thousands of new men drawn into politics by nativism.[93] The complexion of the new legislators reflected the ranks from which they rose. Among them were no politicians, and few lawyers. They were true representatives of those for whom they spoke. They included a few rascals and self-seekers; but by and large they were honest men, convinced that they were acting in the best interests of the community. Even the Democratic editor of the *Post* had to admit later that "the moral tone of the party was unquestioned. . . ."[94] Many did not even feel a personal antagonism to the Irish; J. V. C. Smith, an amateur sculptor, and Know-Nothing mayor in 1854, associated with them in business and executed a fine bust of Bishop Fitzpatrick.[95]

Although the Know-Nothings made numerous mistakes, their administration was progressive and fruitful. They relaid the basis for the school system, abolished imprisonment for debt, established the first insurance commission, took the first steps to eliminate danger from railroad

---

[91] Webb to Sumner, July 14, 1854, Sumner Correspondence, XXV, no. 72; cf. also Wilson to Sumner, July 2, 1854, *ibid.*, XXV, no. 12; Bean, *op. cit.*, 192; Harry J. Carman and R. H. Luthin, "Some Aspects of the Know-Nothing Movement Reconsidered," *South Atlantic Quarterly*, XXXIX (1940), 221.

[92] Roe, *loc. cit.*, 653; Haynes, *loc. cit.*, 68; Bean, *op. cit.*, 259 ff.; George H. Haynes, "Know-Nothing Legislature," *New England Magazine*, XVI (1897), 21, 22.

[93] Robinson, *op. cit.*, 219. In Boston, 1,101 voters who had not gone to the polls in 1853 cast their ballots for the Know-Nothings together with the whole coalition reform vote, and almost half the Whig vote.

GUBERNATORIAL VOTES IN BOSTON

	1853	1854
Whig	7,730	4,196
Know-Nothing	...	7,661
Free-Soil	1,403	401
Democrat	2,455	1,252
Hunker Democrat	821	...
	12,409	13,510

(*Boston Atlas*, November 14, 1854; *Boston Semi-Weekly Advertiser*, November 16, 1853.)

[94] Benjamin P. Shillaber, "Experiences During Many Years," *New England Magazine*, VIII (1893), 722; George H. Haynes, "Know-Nothing Legislature," *Annual Report of the American Historical Association . . . 1896* (Washington, 1897), I, 178 ff.; Roe, *loc. cit.*, 654.

[95] State Street Trust Company, *Mayors of Boston*, 23.

crossings, extended the power of juries, strengthened the temperance, homestead and women's rights laws, made vaccination compulsory, and assumed a firm anti-slavery position by passing a personal liberty law and petitioning for the removal of Judge Loring, who had presided at the fugitive slave cases. In general, they embodied in their legislation the program of the party of reform. By 1855, they had sent Wilson to the United States Senate, amended the constitution so that a plurality sufficed in the gubernatorial election, and introduced many other innovations vetoed by the more conservative governor.[96]

The party's anti-foreign accomplishments were quite insignificant. To begin with, they disclaimed any intention of excluding immigrants, but stressed the necessity of making them "be as we are."[97] The most prominent achievement was the disbanding of the Irish military companies which annoyed natives particularly because they carried off prizes at drills. They served no useful purpose and in 1853 the *Boston Pilot* had itself suggested their dissolution. A breach of military discipline provided the pretext for the abolition of the Bay State Artillery in September, followed early the next year by the elimination of the remaining companies. Foreigners on the police force and in state agencies were discharged, and a number of cruel deportations displayed an ugly animus against helpless aliens. Finally, the misdeeds of individual members, notably of the Hiss Nunnery Committee, were exploited by the opposition and did much to discredit the party and obscure its constructive achievements.[98]

Ostensibly the party had acquired power to restrict the influence of immigrants in politics. Yet, though it had absolute control of the government, it failed to pass a single measure to that effect. In 1854, a bill to exclude paupers was not considered until the end of the session, and then referred to committee where it died. A literacy amendment to the constitution was rejected, and an amendment requiring a twenty-one-year residence for citizenship, which passed, was defeated at the second vote by the next Know-Nothing legislature.[99] Once reform, the essential feature of Know-Nothingism in Massachusetts, was assured, the party

[96] Cf. Billington, *op. cit.*, 425; Robinson, *op. cit.*, 62, 209, 210; Bean, *op. cit.*, 166, 268, 272–77, 284, 286–88; Merriam, *op. cit.*, I, 126, 132 ff., 164; Haynes, "Know-Nothing Legislature," *Annual Report of the American Historical Association . . . 1896*, I, 180–84; Bean, *loc. cit.*, 322.

[97] Bean, *op. cit.*, 261.

[98] Cf. Dissertation Copy, 389; Desmond, *op. cit.*, 77; *Boston Pilot*, May 13, 1854, April 7, May 12, 1855; Abbott, *Immigration*, 160, 161; Billington, *op. cit.*, 414 ff.; Bean, *op. cit.*, 291 ff.; Shea, *op. cit.*, IV, 510.

[99] Cf. *Debates and Proceedings in the Massachusetts Legislature . . . 1856, Reported for the Boston Daily Advertiser* (Boston, 1856), 141, 343, 348; Bean, *loc. cit.*, 322; Billington, *op. cit.*, 413. Most of these measures were sponsored by the purely nativist branch of the party, which declined in importance after 1854 and left the reformers in complete control (cf. Bean, *op. cit.*, 248). To those overlooking the concrete accomplishments of the 1854 legislature, the Free-Soilers under Wilson seemed to have "captured" the Know-Nothing organization in 1855 (cf., e.g., Haynes, "Causes of Know-Nothing Success," *loc. cit.*, III, 81). In fact, true nativists like Morse had so little sympathy for Massachusetts Know-Nothingism that they charged it was "a Jesuitical ruse, gotten up for the purpose of creating a sympathy in favor of the church" (Morse, *Foreign Conspiracy*, 31).

leaders attempted to jettison the anti-Catholic program. But the intolerance they had evoked could not readily be dispelled. Its influence persisted long after the death of the party it had served.

The Know-Nothings dissolved over the question of slavery, for the national party drew its strength from incompatible sources. In Massachusetts it was anti-slavery; elsewhere in the North it was unionist; in Virginia and throughout the South, it was pro-slavery.[100] Lack of a unified program inevitably split the party. Despite their strategic position in Congress, they could unite on few measures. Finally, when the national convention adopted a pro-slavery plank in June, 1855, the Northerners under Henry Wilson bolted and the Massachusetts Council on August 7 adopted an uncompromising liberal position. At the same time a section of the party broke away and met at Worcester in June, called itself the Know-Somethings or American Freemen, and advocated an abolition platform and an end to secrecy.

The nomination of Fillmore, a pro-slavery man, in 1856, completed the break between the state and national parties and a *de facto* coalition with the rising Republican party spontaneously formed. The latter nominated no candidate to oppose Gardner for the governorship, and most Know-Nothings voted for Frémont.[101] Thereafter the Know-Nothings in the state were absorbed in the tremendous growth of the new party, and Banks led the remnants to the Republicans in 1857–58 on his election to the governorship.[102]

[100] Cf. Bean, *loc. cit.*, 324 ff.; E. Merton Coulter, *William Brownlow* . . . (Chapel Hill, 1937), 124 ff.; Scisco, *op. cit.*, 137; Carman and Luthin, *loc. cit.*, 223.

[101] Cf. Billington, *op. cit.*, 407 ff., 426; James Ford Rhodes, *History of the United States* . . . (New York, 1893), II, 89 ff.; Bean, *op. cit.*, 295–322, 339 ff.; Mann, *op. cit.*, 50; Scisco, *op. cit.*, 146 ff.; Wilson, *op. cit.*, II, 423 ff.; Merriam, *op. cit.*, I, 165, 173 ff.; cf. also Fred H. Harrington, "Frémont and the North Americans," *American Historical Review*, XLIV (1939), 842 ff.

VOTE IN BOSTON, 1856

PRESIDENTIAL		GUBERNATORIAL	
Frémont (R)	7,646	Gardner (KN)	7,513
Fillmore (KN)	4,320	Gordon (Fillmore KN)	7,511
Buchanan (D)	5,458	Bell (Whig)	1,449
	17,424	Beach (D)	5,392
			16,865

(*Boston Semi-Weekly Advertiser*, November 5, 1856.)

[102] Cf. Fred H. Harrington, "Nathaniel Prentiss Banks . . . ," *New England Quarterly*, IX (1936), 645 ff. The "straight" American party nominated candidates in 1857 and 1858 but received a meager vote and then expired (Bean, *op. cit.*, 362–65). Gardner's personal popularity helped them in the former year but in the latter they received less than 2,000 votes.

VOTES FOR GOVERNOR IN BOSTON

	1857	1858
Republicans	4,224	6,298
Know-Nothings	4,130	1,899
Democrats	5,171	6,369
	13,525	14,566

(*Boston Semi-Weekly Advertiser*, November 4, 1857; *Boston Daily Courier*, November 3, 1858.)

Produced by the same reform impulse that fathered Know-Nothing-ism, the Republican party continued to express animosity towards the Irish, "their declared and uncompromising foe." The defeat of Frémont in 1856 was laid at the door of the Irish Catholics, and confirmed the party's hostility to them. In retaliation, it helped pass an amendment in 1857 making ability to read the state constitution in English and to write prerequisites to the right to vote; and in 1859, another, preventing foreigners from voting for two years after naturalization.[103]

Though the restrictive legislation affected all foreigners, the venom of intolerance was directed primarily against the Irish. Waning group consciousness among the non-Irish gave promise of quick acculturation, and similarities in economic condition, physical settlement, and intellectual outlook had left little room for disagreement. In fact, the Irish found all others united with the natives against them. A Negro was as reluctant to have an Irishman move into his street as any Yankee,[104] and though the Germans distrusted the Know-Nothings and resented the two-year amendment, liberal principles led them into the Republican party.[105]

Indirectly, the Know-Nothing movement revived Irish nationalism. In Boston, nationalist activities first assumed the guise of the Irish Emigrant Aid Society, whose innocuous title concealed a secret revolutionary club, ostensibly aimed at organizing a liberating invasion of Ireland. Though some hotheads spoke of chartering ships to transport an army of Irish-Americans across the Atlantic, most recognized the obvious futility of such efforts. By and large, they hoped to organize politically, to support anti-English parties in America, to prepare for the Anglo-American war that would free Ireland, and to mobilize support against Know-Nothingism.[106] That the last motive, presumably incidental, was in fact primary, was clear from the movement's exclusively American character: it had no counterpart in Ireland. While expanding rapidly throughout 1855, the organization had little ultimate success. The clergy opposed it, cautious prosecution of would-be liberators in Cincinnati checked its growth, and internal quarrels finally dissipated its strength.[107]

But failure did not end the quest for a fatherland. So long as the Irish were unaccepted in Boston, they looked back across the ocean. There was "always . . . some . . . machination to draw money from the pockets of the deluded lower order of Irish. . . ."[108] The Fenian

---

[103] Cf. Bean, *op. cit.*, 367–72; Bean, *loc. cit.*, 323; Charles Theo. Russell, *Disfranchisement of Paupers* . . . (Boston, 1878), 8; *Massachusetts House Documents, 1857,* no. 114; *ibid., 1859,* no. 34.

[104] Cf., e.g., the petition of the residents of Elm Street (Bean, *op. cit.*, 206).

[105] Cf. Ernest Bruncken, *German Political Refugees in the United States* . . . (s.l., 1904), 45 ff.

[106] Cf. the illuminating report of Consul Grattan to Crampton, Boston, November 23, 1855, British Embassy Archives, F.O. 115/160; also Rowcroft to Crampton, November 12, 1855, *ibid.,* F.O. 115/160.

[107] Cf. Grattan to Crampton, January 21, 1856, *ibid.,* F.O. 115/172; Grattan to Crampton, March 4, 1856, *ibid.,* F.O. 115/172; Abbott, *Historical Aspects,* 475, 476; *Citizen* (New York), August 25, 1855, February 9, 1856.

[108] Lousada to Russell, September 8, 1864, British Consular Correspondence, F.O. 5/973.

Brotherhood emerged after 1859 and despite ecclesiastical disapproval grew in secret until it held its first national convention in Chicago in 1863. Its "centres" in Boston were numerous and active.[109]

Moreover, the Irish persisted in their opposition to reform. With Brownson, they believed Know-Nothingism "an imported combination of Irish Orangism, German radicalism, French Socialism and Italian . . . hate" and regarded Republicanism as its pernicious successor.[110] After 1856 they consistently supported the conservative Democratic party, voting for Buchanan and Douglas.[111] Although the violent phase had passed, the bitterness of conflict and antagonism remained. Out of it had grown a confirmed definition of racial particularism: the Irish were a different group, Celtic by origin, as distinguished from the "true" Americans, who were Anglo-Saxon, of course.[112] Once aroused, hatred could not be turned off at the will of those who had provoked it. The *Springfield Republican* sanely pointed out that "the American party, starting upon a basis of truth . . . has gone on, until [it] . . . denies to an Irishman . . . any position but that of a nuisance. . . ."[113] Group conflict left a permanent scar that disfigured the complexion of Boston social life even after the malignant growth producing it had disappeared.

[109] Cf. Jeremiah O'Donovan-Rossa, *Rossa's Recollections* . . . (Mariner's Harbor, N.Y., 1898), 271, 272, 381; "Proceedings . . . ," British Consular Correspondence, F.O. 5/973; E. Wells to Lousada, *ibid.*, F.O. 5/973; *Boston Pilot*, November 21, 1863.

[110] Cf. Bean, *op. cit.*, 257.

[111] Cf. references to *Irish-American* and *Boston Pilot*, 1856–1860, Dissertation Copy, 397, ns. 301–03; *Boston Pilot*, November 3, 1860; *Boston Post*, November 7, 1860.

[112] Cf., e.g., "The Anglo-Saxon Race," *North American Review*, LXXIII (1851), 34 ff., 53.

[113] *Springfield Daily Republican*, July 10, 1857.

The Quest for Certainty: Slave Spirituals

LAWRENCE W. LEVINE

After slavery was well established in the New World, attempts were made by the masters to weaken the remaining elements of African culture in the slave community. Members of the same tribal groups were often separated, use of African languages was forbidden, and blacks were discouraged from continuing their religious practices. Since most African religions were linked with specific land areas where the ancestors of the people were buried, these religions would not have traveled well in any case. Unlike blacks in the Caribbean and in Brazil, who were able to preserve certain aspects of African culture because of the enormous concentrations of slaves from the same African regions as well as continuous massive imports of slaves directly from Africa, blacks in the United States were increasingly cut off from their African past as successive generations of slaves born here participated in the acculturative process.

It does not necessarily follow, however, that American blacks were left with no cultural and intellectual resources with which to form a new culture. Nor does the fact that the slaves left few written records of their past imply that their inner lives suffered from lack of substance. Until recent years, historians, sociologists, and anthropologists have vehemently disagreed over the extent to which distinctive African cultural traits have carried over into the culture of American blacks and over the impact of African culture on the United States, especially the South. In addition, the prior emphasis of some historians on the passivity and childlike qualities often attributed to the slaves has given rise to an impassioned controversy over the slave personality. These and other debates centering on the experience of slavery have aroused a greater interest than ever before in exploring the cultural and intellectual lives of the slaves, and historians are now drawing on the substantial body of source material that was previously utilized almost exclusively by anthropologists and folklorists. Apart from the descriptions of slave life provided by white observers, both sympathetic and hostile, the slaves themselves left a mass of illuminating material, including several hundred narratives composed by fugitive slaves, the religious and secular slave songs (primarily spirituals and work songs), and a large body of folktales.

The spirituals, particularly, provide significant insights into the developing intellectual life of the American bondsmen. After the beginning of the Second Great Awakening at the turn of the nineteenth century, revivalist churches, chiefly Baptist and Methodist, began to seek actively the conversion of the slaves. In this they sometimes had the support of slaveowners who were genuinely concerned for the spiritual welfare of their slaves or who were convinced that Christianity would increase the slaves' passivity. Other, perhaps more perceptive masters recognized the revolutionary potential of a religion that proclaimed all men equal before God, and they prohibited their slaves from participating in religious services of any kind. During the nineteenth century, what has been called the "invisible church" grew up among the slaves, who were taking the ideas of Christianity but altering them in subtle ways to make them their own. It was this church that produced many of the spirituals and that inspired such rebels as Nat Turner, who drew his imagery of wrath and judgment from the Bible.

In his book on the oral tradition of American blacks, Lawrence Levine, of the University of California at Berkeley, has drawn on the vast array of available folk materials to produce a remarkable study of the Afro-American subculture. The selection from that work reprinted below deals with the role the spirituals played in creating a world view among the slaves that gave them confidence in the face of an otherwise apparently hostile universe.

It is significant that the most common form of slave music we know of is sacred song. I use the term "sacred" not in its present usage as something antithetical to the secular world; neither the slaves nor their African forebears ever drew modernity's clear line between the sacred and the secular. The uses to which spirituals were put are an unmistakable indication of this. They were not sung solely or even primarily in churches or praise houses but were used as rowing songs, field songs, work songs, and social songs. Seated in a long cypress bark canoe on the Altamaha River in Georgia in 1845, Sir Charles Lyell listened to the six slave rowers improvise songs complimenting their master's family and celebrating a

"The Quest for Certainty: Slave Spirituals." From *Black Culture and Black Consciousness: Afro-American Folk Thought from Slavery to Freedom* by Lawrence W. Levine. Copyright © 1977 by Oxford University Press, Inc. Reprinted by permission. Pp. 30–55.

black woman of the neighborhood by comparing her beauty to that of the red bird. "Occasionally they struck up a hymn, taught them by the Methodists, in which the most sacred subjects were handled with strange familiarity, and which, though nothing irreverent was meant, sounded oddly to our ears, and, when following a love ditty, almost profane."[1] Mary Dickson Arrowood recalled slave boatmen in the late 1850s singing the following spirituals which, characteristically, were as congenial to the work situation as to the praise house:

> Breddren, don' git weary,
> Breddren, don' git weary,
> Breddren, don' git weary,
> Fo' de work is most done.
>
> De ship is in de harbor, harbor, harbor,
> De ship is in de harbor,
> To wait upon de Lord. . . .
>
> 'E got 'e ca'go raidy, raidy, raidy,
> 'E got 'e ca'go raidy,
> Fo' to wait upon de Lord.[2]

On the Sea Islands during the Civil War, Lucy McKim heard the spiritual *Poor Rosy* sung in a wide variety of contexts and tempos:

> On the water, the oars dip "Poor Rosy" to an even andante; a stout boy and girl at the hominy-mill will make the same "Poor Rosy" fly, to keep up with the whirling stone; and in the evening, after the day's work is done, "Heab'n shall-a be my home" [the final line of each stanza] peals up slowly and mournfully from the distant quarters.[3]

For the slaves, then, songs of God and the mythic heroes of their religion were not confined to a specific time or place, but were appropriate to almost every situation. It is in this sense that I use the concept sacred—not to signify a rejection of the present world but to describe the process of incorporating within this world all the elements of the divine. The religious historian Mircea Eliade, whose definition of sacred has shaped my own, maintains that for people in traditional societies religion is a means of extending the world spatially upward so that communication with the other world becomes ritually possible, and extending it temporally backward so that the paradigmatic acts of the gods and mythical

---

[1] [Sir Charles] Lyell, [*A Second Visit to the United States of North America* (New York, 1849)], I, 244–45.

[2] Mary Dickson Arrowood and Thomas Hoffman Hamilton, "Nine Negro Spirituals, 1850–61," *JAF* [*Journal of American Folklore*], 41 (1928), 582, 584.

[3] Lucy McKim, *Dwight's Journal of Music*, 21 (1862), 255.

ancestors can be continually re-enacted and indefinitely recoverable. By creating sacred time and space, Man can perpetually live in the presence of his gods, can hold on to the certainty that within one's own lifetime "rebirth" is continually possible, and can impose order on the chaos of the universe. "Life," as Eliade puts it, "is lived on a twofold plane; it takes its course as human existence and, at the same time, shares in a trans-human life, that of the cosmos or the gods."[4]

Claude Lévi-Strauss, who found these same cosmological outlooks in South America and Asia, has eloquently expressed the difficulties modern Westerners have in relating to them. As a boy he lived with his grandfather, the rabbi of Versailles, in a house which was linked to the synagogue by a long inner corridor. To the young Lévi-Strauss that long passage was appropriately symbolic: "Even to set foot in that corridor was an awesome experience; it formed an impassable frontier between the profane world and that other world from which was lacking precisely that human warmth which was the indispensable condition to my recognizing it as sacred."[5] For men and women of traditional societies, such as those the slaves had originally come from, such corridors were absent. This is not to deny that the slaves were capable of making distinctions between this world and the next. Of course they were, and some of their songs do reflect a desire to release their hold upon the temporal present. "Why don't you give up de world?" they sang at times. "We must leave de world behind." Or, again:

> This world is not my home.
> This world is not my home.
> This world's a howling wilderness,
> This world is not my home.[6]

But for the most part when they looked upon the cosmos they saw Man, Nature, and God as a unity; distinct but inseparable aspects of a sacred whole.

This notion of sacredness gets at the essence of the spirituals, and through them at the essence of the slave's world view. Denied the possibility of achieving an adjustment to the external world of the antebellum South which involved meaningful forms of personal integration, attainment of status, and feelings of individual worth that all human beings crave and need, the slaves created a new world by transcending the nar-

---

[4] Mircea Eliade, *The Sacred and the Profane* (New York, 1961), Chaps. 2, 4, and *passim*. For the similarity of Eliade's concept to the world view of West Africa, see W. E. Abraham, *The Mind of Africa* (London, 1962), Chap. 2; R. S. Rattray, *Religion and Art in Ashanti* (Oxford, 1927); and John S. Mbiti, *African Religions and Philosophies* (Garden City, N.Y., 1969), especially Chap. 3.

[5] Claude Lévi-Strauss, *Triste Tropiques* (New York, 1964), 215.

[6] William Francis Allen, Charles Pickard Ware, and Lucy McKim Garrison, *Slave Songs of the United States* (1867; reprint ed., New York, 1951), 27–28; William E. Barton, *Old Plantation Hymns: A Collection of Hitherto Unpublished Melodies of the Slave and the Freedmen* (Boston, 1899), 9.

row confines of the one in which they were forced to live. They extended the boundaries of their restrictive universe backward until it fused with the world of the Old Testament, and upward until it became one with the world beyond. The spirituals are the record of a people who found the status, the harmony, the values, the order they needed to survive by internally creating an expanded universe, by literally willing themselves reborn. In this respect I agree with the anthropologist Paul Radin that

> The ante-bellum Negro was not converted to God. He converted God to himself. In the Christian God he found a fixed point and he needed a fixed point, for both within and outside of himself, he could see only vacillation and endless shifting. . . . There was no other safety for people faced on all sides by doubt and the threat of personal distintegration, by the thwarting of instincts and the annihilation of values.[7]

The spirituals are a testament not only to the perpetuation of significant elements of an older world view among the slaves but also to the continuation of a strong sense of community. Just as the process by which the spirituals were created allowed for simultaneous individual and communal creativity, so their very structure provided simultaneous outlets for individual and communal expression. The overriding antiphonal structure of the spirituals—the call and response pattern which Negroes brought with them from Africa and which was reinforced in America by the practice of lining out hymns—placed the individual in continual dialogue with his community, allowing him at one and the same time to preserve his voice as a distinct entity and to blend it with those of his fellows. Here again slave music confronts us with evidence which indicates that, however seriously the slave system may have diminished the central communality that had bound African societies together, it was never able to destroy it totally or to leave the individual atomized and psychically defenseless before his white masters. In fact, the form and structure of slave music presented the slave with a potential outlet for his individual feelings even while it continually drew him back into the communal presence and permitted him the comfort of basking in the warmth of the shared assumptions of those around him. Those shared assumptions can be further examined by an analysis of the content of slave songs.

The most persistent single image the slave songs contain is that of the chosen people. The vast majority of the spirituals identify the singers as "de people dat is born of God," "We are the people of God," "we are de people of de Lord," "I really do believe I'm a child of God," "I'm a child ob God, wid my soul sot free," "I'm born of God, I know I am."

[7] Paul Radin, "Status, Phantasy, and the Christian Dogma," in Fisk University, *God Struck Me Dead: Religious Conversion Experiences and Autobiographies of Negro Ex-Slaves,* A. P. Watson, Paul Radin, and Charles S. Johnson, eds. (Nashville, 1945, unpublished typescript).

Nor is there ever any doubt that "To the promised land I'm bound to go," "I walk de heavenly road," "Heav'n shall-a be my home," "I gwine to meet my Saviour," "I seek my Lord and I find Him," "I'll hear the trumpet sound / In that morning."[8]

The force of this image cannot be diminished by the observation that similar images were present in the religious singing of white evangelical churches during the first half of the nineteenth century. White Americans could be expected to sing of triumph and salvation, given their long-standing heritage of the idea of a chosen people which was reinforced in this era by the belief in inevitable progress and manifest destiny, the spread-eagle oratory, the bombastic folklore, and, paradoxically, the deep insecurities concomitant with the tasks of taming a continent and developing an identity. But for this same message to be expressed by Negro slaves who were told endlessly that they were members of the lowliest of races *is* significant. It offers an insight into the kinds of barriers the slaves had available to them against the internalization of the stereotyped images their masters held and attempted consciously and unconsciously to foist upon them.

Not only did slaves believe that they would be chosen by the Lord, there is evidence that many of them felt their owners would be denied salvation. On a trip through the South, Harriet Martineau recorded the instance of a mistress being told by one of her slaves, "You no holy. We be holy. You in no state of salvation."[9] "Slaves knew enough of the orthodox theology of the time to consign all bad slaveholders to hell," Frederick Douglass wrote in his autobiography.[10] Some went even further than this. "No white people went to Heaven," a correspondent in the *Southern Workman* noted in 1897, summing up the attitude of his fellow slaves before the Civil War and added, "Many believe the same until this day."[11] The fugitive slave Charles Ball insisted that his fellow slaves refused to picture Heaven as a place where whites and blacks lived in perfect equality and boundless affection. "The idea of a revolution in the conditions of the whites and the blacks, is the corner-stone of the religion of the latter," he maintained. "Heaven will be no heaven to him [the slave], if he is not to be avenged of his enemies."[12] One hundred years later a former slave bore witness to Ball's assertion: "This is one reason why I believe in a hell. I don't believe a just God is going to take no such man as that [her master] into His Kingdom."[13] Martha Harrison re-

[8] Lines like these could be quoted endlessly. For the specific ones cited, see [Thomas Wentworth] Higginson, *Army Life [in a Black Regiment* (1869; Beacon Press ed., Boston, 1962)], 206, 216–17; Allen *et al.*, *Slave Songs*, 7, 13, 58, 77, 104; Thomas P. Fenner, *Religious Folk Songs of the Negro as Sung on the Plantations* (1874; revised ed., Hampton, Va., 1909), 10–11, 48; J. B. T. Marsh, *The Story of the Jubilee Singers: With Their Songs* (Boston, 1880), 136, 167, 178.

[9] Quoted in J. L. Dillard, *Black English* (New York, 1972), 103.

[10] [Frederick] Douglass, *Life and Times [of Frederick Douglass* (revised ed., 1892; Collier reprint ed., New York, 1962)], 41.

[11] *SW [Southern Workman]*, 26 (1897), 210.

[12] Charles Ball, *Fifty Years in Chains* (1837; reprint ed., New York, 1970), 220–22.

[13] Fisk University, *God Struck Me Dead*, 215.

counted how her master, "Old Bufford," who beat her mother savagely for refusing to sleep with him, offered on his death bed to spend seven thousand dollars to pay his way out of hell, "but he couldn'ta got out of hell, the way he beat my mammy."[14] Another former slave recalled that when her mistress died the slaves filed into the house "just a hollering and crying and holding their hands over their eyes, just hollering for all they could. Soon as they got outside of the house they would say, 'Old God damn son-of-a-bitch, she gone on down to hell.' "[15] Mary Reynolds described the brutality of Solomon, the white overseer on the Louisiana plantation where she had been a slave, and concluded simply, "I know that Solomon is burning in hell today, and it pleasures me to know it."[16]

Whether or not these reactions were typical, it is clear that a great many slaves agreed with H. B. Holloway that "It's going to be an awful thing up yonder when they hold a judgment over the way that things was done down here."[17] The prospect pleased slaves enough to become part of their repertory of jokes. The fugitive slave Lewis Clarke recounted two anecdotes with which the slaves on his Kentucky plantation used to delight each other. The first described the final conversation between a dying master and his slave: "Good-by, Jack; I have a long journey to go; farewell." "Farewell, massa! pleasant journey: you soon be dere, massa— *all de way down hill.*" The second told of a slave's reaction to the news that he would be rewarded by being buried in the same vault with his master: "Well, massa, one way I am satisfied, and one way I am not. I like to have good coffin when I die [but] I fraid, massa, when the debbil come take you body, he make mistake, and get mine."[18]

The confinement of much of the slave's new world to dreams and fantasies does not free us from the historical obligation of examining its contours, weighing its implications for the development of the slave's psychic and emotional structure, and eschewing the kind of reasoning that has led one historian to imply that, since the slaves had no alternatives open to them, their fantasy life was "limited to catfish and watermelons."[19] Their spirituals indicate clearly that there *were* alternatives open to them—alternatives which they themselves fashioned out of the fusion of their African heritage and their new religion—and that their fantasy life was so rich and so important to them that it demands understanding if we are even to begin to comprehend their inner world.

The God the slaves sang of was neither remote nor abstract, but as intimate, personal, and immediate as the gods of Africa had been. "O when I talk I talk wid God," "Mass Jesus is my bosom friend," "I'm

[14] Fisk University, *Unwritten History [of Slavery,* O. S. Egypt, J. Masuoka, and C. S. Johnson, eds. (Nashville, 1945, unpublished typescript)], 118.

[15] *Ibid.,* 134, 136.

[16] B. A. Botkin, ed., *Lay My Burden Down: A Folk History of Slavery* (Chicago, 1945), 121.

[17] *Ibid.,* 18.

[18] *Narrative of Lewis Clarke,* in *Interesting Memoirs and Documents Relating to American Slavery* (London, 1846), 87, 91.

[19] Stanley Elkins, *Slavery* (Chicago, 1959), 136.

goin' to walk with [talk with, live with, see] King Jesus by myself, by myself," were refrains that echoed through the spirituals.

> In de mornin' when I rise,
>   Tell my Jesus huddy [howdy] oh,
> I wash my hands in de mornin' glory,
>   Tell my Jesus huddy oh.

> Gwine to argue wid de Father and chatter wid de son,
> The last trumpet shall sound, I'll be there.
> Gwine talk 'bout de bright world dey des' come from.
> The last trumpet shall sound, I'll be there.

> Gwine to write to Massa Jesus,
> To send some Valiant soldier
> To turn back Pharaoh's army, Hallelu!

"Good news, member, good news member," the slaves sang jubilantly, "And I heard-e from Heav'n today."[20]

The images of these songs were carried over into slave religious experiences. In a small South Carolina town in the 1850s, a white visitor questioned a young slave about his recent conversion experience:

> "An den I went to hebben."
> "What!" said I.
> "An' den I went to hebben."
> "Stop, Julius. You mean you had a dream, and thought you went to heaven."
> "No, Sah: an' den I went to hebben, and dere I see de Lord Jesus, *a sittin' behind de door an' a reading his Bible.*"

There was no question, the white interrogator concluded, of the slave's "unmistakable sincerity" or of the fact that his fellow slave parishioners believed him implicitly.[21] "We must see, feel and hear something," an ex-slave exclaimed, "for our God talks to his children."[22] During a slave service in New Orleans in January of 1851, Fredrika Bremer witnessed the conversion of a black woman who, transported by religious enthusiasm, lept up and down with outstretched arms crying out "Hallelujah! Hallelujah!" and then, falling prostrate on the floor, lapsed into rigid quiescence. Gradually she recovered consciousness: "she talked to herself in a low voice, and such a beautiful, blissful expression was portrayed in

---

[20] Allen *et al.*, *Slave Songs*, 2, 7, 15, 97–98; Barton, *Old Plantation Hymns*, 19, 30; Marsh, *Jubilee Singers*, 132.

[21] "The Religious Life of the Negro Slave [Second Paper]," *Harper's New Monthly Magazine*, 27 (1863), 681.

[22] Fisk University, *God Struck Me Dead*, 61.

her countenance that I would willingly experience that which she then experienced, saw, or perceived. It was no ordinary, no earthly scene. Her countenance was, as it were, transfigured."[23]

In these states of transfiguration slave converts commonly saw and conversed with God or Christ: "I looked to the east and there was . . . God. He looked neither to the right nor to the left. I was afraid and fell on my face. . . . I heard a voice from God saying, 'My little one, be not afraid for lo! I am with you always.'" "I looked away to the east and saw Jesus. . . . I saw God sitting in a big arm-chair." "I first came to know of God when I was a little child. He started talking to me when I was no more than nine years old." "I seen Christ with His hair parted in the center." "I saw Him when he freed my soul from hell." "I saw in a vision a snow-white train once and it moved like lightning. Jesus was on board and He told me that He was the Conductor." "I saw the Lord in the east part of the world. . . . His hair was parted in the middle and he looked like he had been dipped in snow and he was talking to me."[24] For the slave, Heaven and Hell were not concepts but places which could well be experienced during one's lifetime; God and Christ and Satan were not symbols but personages with whom meetings or confrontations were quite possible.

The heroes of the Scriptures—"Sister Mary," "Brudder Jonah," "Brudder Moses," "Brudder Daniel"—were greeted with similar intimacy and immediacy. In the world of the spirituals, it was not the masters and mistresses but God and Jesus and the entire pantheon of Old Testament figures who set the standards, established the precedents, and defined the values; who, in short, constituted the "significant others." The world described by the slave songs was a black world in which no reference was ever made to any white contemporaries. The slave's positive reference group was composed entirely of his own peers: his mother, father, sister, brother, uncles, aunts, preacher, fellow "sinners" and "mourners" of whom he sang endlessly, to whom he sent messages via the dying, and with whom he was reunited joyfully in the next world.

The same sense of sacred time and space which shaped the slave's portraits of his gods and heroes also made his visions of the past and future immediate and compelling. Descriptions of the Crucifixion communicate a sense of the actual presence of the singers: "Dey pierced Him in the side . . . Dey nail Him to de cross . . . Dey rivet His feet . . . Dey hanged him high . . . Dey stretch Him wide. . . ."

> Oh sometimes it causes me to tremble,—tremble,—tremble.
> Were you there when they crucified my Lord?[25]

[23] [Fredrika] Bremer, *America of the Fifties,* [Adolph B. Benson, ed. (New York, 1924)], 277–79.

[24] Fisk University, *God Struck Me Dead,* 4, 20, 30, 96, 101, 102, 154.

[25] Fenner, *Religious Folk Songs,* 162; E. A. McIlhenny, *Befo' De War Spirituals* (Boston, 1933), 39.

In 1818 a group of white Quaker students observed a Negro camp meeting. They watched in fascination and bewilderment as the black worshippers moved slowly around and around in a circle chanting:

> We're traveling to Immanuel's land,
> Glory! Halle-lu-jah.

Occasionally the dancers paused to blow a tin horn. The meaning of the ceremony gradually dawned upon one of the white youths: he was watching "Joshua's chosen men marching around the walls of Jericho, blowing the rams' horns and shouting, until the walls fell."[26] The students were witnessing the slaves' "ring shout"—that counterclockwise, shuffling dance which frequently lasted long into the night. The shout often became a medium through which the ecstatic dancers were transformed into actual participants in historic actions: Joshua's army marching around the walls of Jericho, the children of Israel following Moses out of Egypt. The shout, as Sir Charles Lyell perceived in 1845, frequently served as a substitute for the secular dance. It was allowed even where dancing was proscribed—"Hit ain't railly dancin' 'less de feets is crossed," "dancin' ain't sinful iffen de foots ain't crossed," two participants explained—and constituted still one more compelling feature of black religion. "Those who have witnessed these shouts can never forget them," Abigail Christensen has written. "The fascination of the music and the swaying motion of the dance is so great that one can hardly refrain from joining the magic circle in response to the invitation of the enthusiastic clappers, 'Now, brudder!' 'Shout, sister!' 'Come, belieber!' 'Mauma Rosa kin shout!' 'Uncle Danyel!' 'Join, shouters!' "[27]

The thin line between time dimensions is nowhere better illustrated than in the slave's visions of the future, which were, of course, a direct negation of his present. Among the most striking spirituals are those which pile detail upon detail in describing the Day of Judgment: "You'll see de world on fire . . . see de element a meltin', . . . see the stars a fallin' . . . see the moon a bleedin' . . . see the forked lightning, . . . Hear the rumblin' thunder . . . see the righteous marching, . . . see my Jesus coming . . . ," and the world to come where "Dere's no sun to burn you . . . no hard trials . . . no whips a crackin' . . . no stormy weather . . . no tribulation . . . no evil-doers . . . All is gladness in de

---

[26] [Don] Yoder, *Pennsylvania Spirituals* [Lancaster, Pa., 1961)], 54–55.

[27] There are numerous descriptions of the ring shout in the WPA [Works Progress Administration] Slave Narratives. Contemporary white descriptions include Lyell, *Second Visit*, I, 269–70; Bremer, *America of the Fifties*, 119; [John D.] Long, *Pictures of Slavery* [*in Church and State* (1857; reprint ed., New York, 1969)], 383; H. G. Spaulding, "Under the Palmetto," *Continental Monthly*, 4 (1863), 196–200; Abigail M. Holmes Christensen, "Spirituals and 'Shouts' of Southern Negroes," *JAF*, 7 (1894), 154–55; *The Nation*, May 30, 1867, 432–33. The Library of Congress recorded a superb example of the shout in 1934 which may be heard on its record, AAFS L3, *Afro-American Spirituals, Work Songs, and Ballads.*

Kingdom."[28] This vividness was matched by the slave's certainty that he would partake of the triumph of judgment and the joys of the new world:

> Dere's room enough, room enough, room enough in de heaven, my Lord
> Room enough, room enough, I can't stay behind.[29]

Continually, the slaves sang of reaching out beyond the world that confined them, of seeing Jesus "in de wilderness," of praying "in de lonesome valley," of breathing in the freedom of the mountain peaks:

> Did yo' ever
> Stan' on mountun
> Wash yo' han's
> In a cloud?[30]

Continually, they held out the possibility of imminent rebirth: "I look at de worl' an' de worl' look new, . . . I look at my hands an' they look so too . . . I looked at my feet, my feet was too."[31]

These possibilities, these certainties were not surprising. The religious revivals which swept large numbers of slaves into the Christian fold in the late eighteenth and early nineteenth centuries were increasingly based upon notions of individual, volitional conversion and, in the words of one southern minister, "a free salvation to all men thro' the blood of the Lamb." They were based on a practical and implied, if not invariably theological or overt, Arminianism: God would save all who believed in Him; Salvation was there for all to take hold of if they would. This doctrine more and more came to characterize the revivals of the Presbyterians and Baptists as well as those of the more openly Arminian Methodists.[32] The effects of this message upon the slaves who were exposed to and converted by it are illustrated graphically in the spirituals which were the products of these revivals and which continued to spread the evangelical word long after the revivals had passed into history. "What kind o' shoes is dem-a you wear? . . . Dat you can walk upon de air?" slaves asked in one of their spirituals, and answered by emphasizing the element of choice: "Dem shoes I wear am de gospel shoes; . . . An' you can wear

---

[28] Fenner, *Religious Folk Songs*, 8, 63–65; Marsh, *Jubilee Singers*, 240–41; Higginson, *Army Life*, 205; Allen *et al.*, *Slave Songs*, 46, 53; Natalie Curtis Burlin, *Negro Folk-Songs* (New York, 1918–19), I, 37–42.

[29] Allen *et al.*, *Slave Songs*, 6.

[30] *Ibid.*, 5; Burlin, *Negro Folk-Songs*, II, 8–9; Fenner, *Religious Folk Songs*, 12.

[31] Allen *et al.*, *Slave Songs*, 75; Fenner, *Religious Folk Songs*, 127; Barton, *Old Plantation Hymns*, 26. The deep internalization of many of these spirituals is illustrated in the slaves' conversion experiences in which such lines as those above were incorporated verbatim into the slaves' own accounts of their conversions. See Fisk University, *God Struck Me Dead*, 24, 54, 87.

[32] [John] Boles, *The Great Revival*, [1787–1805 (Lexington, Ky., 1972)], Chap. 9; Charles Johnson, *The Frontier Camp Meeting* [(Dallas, 1955)], Chap. 9; William G. McLoughlin, Jr., *Modern Revivalism* (New York, 1959), Chaps. 1–2.

dem ef-a you choose." "You got a right, I got a right," they sang, "We all got a right to de tree ob life."[33]

The religious music of the slaves is almost devoid of feelings of depravity or unworthiness, but is rather, as I have tried to show, pervaded by a sense of change, transcendence, ultimate justice, and personal worth. The spirituals have been referred to as "sorrow songs," and in some respects they were. The slaves sang of "rollin' thro' an unfriendly world," of being "a-trouble in de mind," of living in a world which was a "howling wilderness," "a hell to me," of feeling like a "motherless child," "a po' little orphan chile in de worl'," a "home-e-less child," of fearing that "Trouble will bury me down."[34]

But these feelings were rarely pervasive or permanent; almost always they were overshadowed by a triumphant note of affirmation. Even so despairing a wail as *Nobody Knows The Trouble I've Had* could suddenly have its mood transformed by lines like: "One morning I was a-walking down, . . . Saw some berries a-hanging down, . . . I pick de berry and I suck de juice, . . . Just as sweet as de honey in de comb." Similarly, amid the deep sorrow of *Sometimes I Feel Like a Motherless Chile*, sudden release could come with the lines: "Sometimes I feel like / A eagle in de air. . . . Spread my wings an' / Fly, fly, fly."[35] Slaves spent little time singing of the horrors of hell or damnation. Their songs of the Devil pictured a harsh but almost semicomic figure (often, one suspects, a surrogate for the white man), over whom they triumphed with reassuring regularity:

> The Devil's mad and I'm glad,
> He lost the soul he thought he had.[36]

> Ole Satan toss a ball at me.
> O me no weary yet . . .

> Him tink de ball would hit my soul.
> O me no weary yet . . .

> De ball for hell and I for heaven.
> O me no weary yet . . .[37]

> Ole Satan thought he had a mighty aim;
> He missed my soul and caught my sins.
> Cry Amen, cry Amen, cry Amen to God!

[33] Fenner, *Religious Folk Songs*, 10; Theodore F. Seward, *Jubilee Songs* (New York, 1872), 48; Emily Hallowell, *Calhoun Plantation Songs* (Boston, 1901), 40.

[34] Allen *et al., Slave Songs*, 30–31, 55, 94; Barton, *Old Plantation Hymns*, 9, 17–18, 24; Marsh, *Jubilee Singers*, 133, 167.

[35] Allen *et al., Slave Songs*, 55; Mary Allen Grissom, *The Negro Sings a New Heaven* (Chapel Hill, 1930), 73.

[36] Allen *et al., Slave Songs*, 107–08.

[37] *Ibid.*, 12.

He took my sins upon his back;
Went muttering and grumbling down to hell.
Cry Amen, cry Amen, cry Amen to God!

Ole Satan's church is here below.
Up to God's free church I hope to go.
Cry Amen, cry Amen, cry Amen to God![38]

For all their inevitable sadness, slave songs were characterized more by a feeling of confidence than of despair. There was confidence that contemporary power relationships were not immutable: "Did not old Pharaoh get lost, get lost, get lost, . . . get lost in the Red Sea?"; confidence in the possibilities of instantaneous change: "Jesus make de dumb to speak. . . . Jesus make de cripple walk. . . . Jesus give de blind his sight. . . . Jesus do most anything"; confidence in the rewards of persistence: "Keep a' inching along like a poor inchworm, / Jesus will come by'nd bye"; confidence that nothing could stand in the way of the justice they would receive: "You kin hender me here, but you can't do it dah," "O no man, no man, no man can hinder me"; confidence in the prospects of the future: "We'll walk de golden streets / Of de New Jerusalem." Religion, the slaves sang, "is good for anything, . . . Religion make you happy, . . . Religion gib me patience . . . O member, get Religion . . . Religion is so sweet."[39]

The slaves often pursued the "sweetness" of their religion in the face of many obstacles. Becky Ilsey, who was sixteen when she was emancipated, recalled many years later:

'Fo' de war when we'd have a meetin' at night, wuz mos' always 'way in de woods or de bushes some whar so de white folks couldn't hear, an' when dey'd sing a spiritual an' de spirit 'gin to shout some de elders would go 'mongst de folks an' put dey han' over dey mouf an' some times put a clof in dey mouf an' say: "Spirit don talk so loud or de patterol break us up." You know dey had white patterols what went 'roun' at night to see de niggers didn't cut up no devilment, an' den de meetin' would break up an' some would go to one house an' some to er nudder an' dey would groan er w'ile, den go home.[40]

Elizabeth Ross Hite testified that although she and her fellow slaves on a Louisiana plantation were Catholics, "lots didn't like that 'ligion."

[38] [Harriet Brent] Jacobs, *Incidents in the Life of a Slave Girl* [(1861; reprint ed., New York, 1973)], 73.
[39] Marsh, *Jubilee Singers*, 179, 186; Allen *et al.*, *Slave Songs*, 10–11, 13, 93; Barton, *Old Plantation Hymns*, 30.
[40] McIlhenny, *Befo' De War Spirituals*, 31.

We used to hide behind some bricks and hold church ourselves. You see, the Catholic preachers from France wouldn't let us shout, and the Lawd done said you gotta shout if you want to be saved. That's in the Bible.

Sometimes we held church all night long, 'til way in the mornin'. We burned some grease in a can for the preacher to see the Bible by. . . .

See, our master didn't like us to have much 'ligion, said it made us lag in our work. He jest wanted us to be Catholicses on Sundays and go to mass and not study 'bout nothin' like that on week days. He didn't want us shoutin' and moanin' all day 'long, but you gotta shout and you gotta moan if you wants to be saved.[41]

Slaves broke the proscription against unsupervised or unauthorized meetings by holding their services in secret, well-hidden areas, usually referred to as "hush-harbors." Amanda McCray testified that on her Florida plantation there was a praying ground where "the grass never had a chance ter grow fer the troubled knees that kept it crushed down," and Andrew Moss remembered that on the Georgia plantation where he grew up all the slaves had their private prayer grounds: "My Mammy's was a ole twisted thick-rooted muscadine bush. She'd go in dar and pray for deliverance of de slaves."[42] Even here the slaves were often discovered by the white patrols. "Den dey would rush in an' start whippin' an' beatin' de slaves unmerciful," West Turner of Virginia reported. ". . . an' do you know some o' dem devils was mean an' sinful 'nough to say, 'If I ketch you here servin' God, I'll beat you. You ain't got no time to serve God. We bought you to serve us.' "[43] Slaves found many ways to continue to speak with their gods. Patsy Larkin recalled that on her plantation the slaves would steal away into the cane thickets and pray in a prostrate position with their faces close to the ground so that no sound would escape. Kalvin Woods, a slave preacher, described how slave women would take old quilts and rags and soak them before hanging them up in the shape of a small room, "and the slaves who were interested about it would huddle up behind these quilts to do their praying, preaching and singing. These wet rags were used to keep the sound of their voices from penetrating the air." On a Louisiana plantation the slaves would gather in the woods at night, form a circle on their knees, and pray over a vessel of water to drown the sound.[44] The most commonly used method, in which the slaves had great confidence, was simply to turn a large pot upside down. "All the noise would go into that kettle,"

[41] *Gumbo Ya-Ya: A Collection of Louisiana Folk Tales,* compiled by Lyle Saxon, Edward Dreyer, and Robert Tallant from materials gathered by workers of the WPA, Louisiana Writers' Project (Boston, 1945), 242.

[42] WPA Slave Narratives, interviews with Amanda McCray (Fla.) and Andrew Moss (Tenn.).

[43] WPA, [The] *Negro in Virginia* [(New York, 1940)], 110, 146.

[44] John B. Cade, "Out of the Mouths of Ex-Slaves," JNH [*Journal of Negro History*], 20 (1935), 330–31.

an ex-slave explained. "They could shout and sing all they wanted to and the noise wouldn't go outside."[45]

Religious services were not confined to formal meetings, open or secret, but were often informal and spontaneous. One former slave remembered how religious enthusiasm could begin simply with a group of slaves sitting in front of their cabins after supper on a summer evening. Someone might start humming an old hymn; the humming would spread from house to house and would be transformed into song. "It wouldn't be long before some of them got happy and started to shouting. Many of them got converted at just such meetings."[46] Wherever the slaves practiced their religion—in formal church settings, in their own praise houses, in camp meetings, in their secret hush-harbors—it was characterized by physical and spiritual enthusiasm and involvement. A white visitor observing a slave religious gathering on a Georgia plantation noted that they sang "with all their souls and with all their bodies in unison; for their bodies rocked, their heads nodded, their feet stamped, their knees shook, their elbows and their hands beat time to the tune and the words which they sang with evident delight. One must see these people singing if one is rightly to understand their life."[47] Attempting to explain why the slaves shouted, an old slave preacher testified, "There is a joy on the inside and it wells up so strong that we can't keep still. It is fire in the bones. Any time that fire touches a man, he will jump."[48]

The slaves were no more passive receptors of sermons than they were of hymns and spirituals; they became participants in both forms of worship. Attending a slave service in New Orleans in the 1850s, Frederick Olmsted carefully recorded a single passage of the black preacher's sermon which was punctuated every few sentences with cries from the parishioners of "yes, glory!" "that's it, hit him again! hit him again! oh, glory! hi! hi! glory!" "glory, glory, glory,!" "Glory!—oh, yes! yes!— sweet Lord! sweet Lord!" "yes, sir! oh, Lord, yes!" "yes! yes!" "oh! Lord! help us!" "Ha! ha! HA!" "Glory to the Lord!" The responses were not confined to ejaculations of this kind, "but shouts, and groans, terrific shrieks, and indescribable expressions of ecstacy—of pleasure or agony—and even stamping, jumping, and clapping of hands, were added. The tumult often resembled that of an excited political meeting."[49] For many slaves shouting was both a compelling personal need and a religious requirement. A well-known joke told of a master who was so embarrassed by the uproar his slave made every Sunday at church that he promised

[45] Descriptions of the turned-down pot can be found in all the testimony of ex-slaves. See, for instance, Fisk University, *Unwritten History*, 35, 44, 53, 98, 173, 193, 222, 300; Fisk University, *God Struck Me Dead*, 147, 156; WPA Slave Narratives, interviews with Oliver Bell (Ala.), Henry Bobbitt (N.C.), Mary Gladdy (Ga.), Anne Matthews (Tenn.), Charles Hinton (Ark.).

[46] Fisk University, *God Struck Me Dead*, 171–72.

[47] Bremer, *America of the Fifties*, 150.

[48] Fisk University, *God Struck Me Dead*, 153.

[49] [Frederick Law] Olmsted, [*A Journey in the*] *Back Country* [(New York, 1863)], 187–96.

him a new pair of boots if he would stop making so much noise. The slave agreed to try, and at the next meeting he did his best to keep quiet so that he might win his prize, but the "spirit" proved too great a force to contain. "Glory to God!" he finally cried out. "Boots or no boots, glory to God!"[50]

The slaves clearly craved the affirmation and promise of their religion. It would be a mistake, however, to see this urge as exclusively other-worldly. When Thomas Wentworth Higginson observed that the spirituals exhibited "nothing but patience for this life—nothing but triumph in the next," he, and later observers who elaborated upon this judgment, were indulging in hyperbole. Although Jesus was ubiquitous in the spirituals, it was not invariably the Jesus of the New Testament of whom the slaves sang, but frequently a Jesus transformed into an Old Testament warrior whose victories were temporal as well as spiritual: "Mass Jesus" who engaged in personal combat with the Devil; "King Jesus" seated on a milk-white horse with sword and shield in hand. "Ride on, King Jesus," "Ride on, conquering King," "The God I serve is a man of war," the slaves sang.[51] This transformation of Jesus is symptomatic of the slaves' selectivity in choosing those parts of the Bible which were to serve as the basis of their religious consciousness. Howard Thurman, a Negro minister who as a boy had the duty of reading the Bible to his grandmother, was perplexed by her refusal to allow him to read from the Epistles of Paul.

> When at length I asked the reason, she told me that during the days of slavery, the minister (white) on the plantation was always preaching from the Pauline letters—"Slaves, be obedient to your masters," etc. "I vowed to myself," she said, "that if freedom ever came and I learned to read, I would never read that part of the Bible!"[52]

This experience and reaction were typical. Slaves simply refused to be uncritical recipients of a religion defined and controlled by white intermediaries and interpreters. No matter how respectfully and attentively they might listen to the white preachers, no matter how well they might sing the traditional hymns, it was their own preachers and their own songs that stirred them the most. Observing his black soldiers at religious services, Colonel Higginson wrote: "they sang reluctantly, even on Sunday, the long and short metres of the hymn-books, always gladly yielding to the more potent excitement of their own 'spirituals.' "[53] In Alabama, Ella Storrs Christian noted in her diary: "When Baptist Negroes attended the church of their masters, or when their mistress sang with them, they used

[50] WPA, *Negro in Virginia*, 108.
[51] Allen *et al.*, *Slave Songs*, 10–11, 40, 51; Marsh, *Jubilee Singers*, 168, 203; Burlin, *Negro Folk-Songs*, II, 8–9.
[52] Howard Thurman, *Deep River* (New York, 1945), 16–17.
[53] Higginson, *Army Life*, 221.

hymn books, but in their own meetings they often made up their own words and tunes. They said their songs had 'more religion than those in the books.' "[54] "Dat ole white preachin' wasn't nothin'," Nancy Williams observed. "Ole white preachers used to talk wid dey tongues widdout sayin' nothin' but Jesus told us slaves to talk wid our hearts." "White folks can't pray right to de black man's God," Henrietta Perry agreed. "Cain't nobody do it for you. You got to call on God yourself when de spirit tell you."[55]

Of course there were many white preachers who were able to reach the slaves they preached to and who affected them in important ways. But even the most talented and devoted among them faced certain grave obstacles resulting from the tension between their desire to spread the Gospel and their need to use Christianity as a form of social control. In his autobiographical *Sketches from Slave Life*, published in 1855, the black minister Peter Randolph wrote that when he was a slave in Prince George County, Virginia, he and his fellow slaves had the rather uninspiring choice of listening to the white Reverend G. Harrison who taught them: "Servants obey your masters. Do not *steal* or *lie*, for this is very wrong. Such conduct is sinning against the Holy Ghost, *and is base ingratitude to your kind masters, who feed, clothe and protect you*," or the white Reverend James L. Goltney who warned: "It is the devil who tells you to try and be free."[56] The Reverend A. F. Dickson, whose Charleston congregation included over four hundred blacks and whose published sermons served as a model for other whites ministering to the slaves, reduced the Judeo-Christian ethic to a triad stressing humility, patience, and fear of sin.[57] The Reverend Charles C. Jones, who devoted so much of his life to propagating the Gospel among slaves, illustrated exactly what it was that limited his influence with them in the *Catechism* he published in 1844:

> Q. What command has God given to Servants, concerning obedience to their Masters?
>
> A. "Servants obey in all things your Masters . . . fearing God."
>
> Q. How are they to try to please their Masters?
>
> A. "With good will, doing service as unto the Lord and not unto men." . . .
>
> Q. But suppose the Master is hard to please, and threatens and punishes more than he ought, what is the Slave to do?
>
> A. Do his best to please him.

---

[54] Quoted in Dena J. Epstein, "Slave Music in the United States Before 1860: A Survey of Sources," *Music Library Association Notes*, 20 (1963), 205.

[55] WPA, *Negro in Virginia*, 108–09.

[56] Peter Randolph, *From Slave Cabin to the Pulpit: The Autobiography of Rev. Peter Randolph* (Boston, 1893), 196–97, 200–01. Pages 145–220 of this volume contain Randolph's earlier autobiography.

[57] A. F. Dickson, *Plantation Sermons, or Plain and Familiar Discourses for the Instruction of the Unlearned* (Philadelphia, 1856).

Q. When the Slave suffers *wrongfully*, at the hands of his
Master, and to please God, takes it patiently, will God reward him
for it?

A. Yes.

Q. Is it right for the Slave *to run away*, or is it right to har-
bour a runaway?

A. No. . . .

Q. Will Servants have to account to God for the manner in
which they serve their Masters on earth?

A. Yes.[58]

In a catechistic exchange between a Methodist minister and a slave in
Alabama, the message was even less subtle:

Q. What did God make you for?
A. To make a crop.[59]

This attempt to reduce Christianity to an ethic of pure submission
was rejected and resented by the slaves. After listening to the white
minister counsel obedience to whites, an old black worshipper in the
African Church in Richmond declared: "He be d——d! God am not sich
a fool!"[60] Slaves generally suffered these sermons in silence, but there
were exceptions. Victoria McMullen reported that her grandmother in
Arkansas was punished for not going to church on the Sabbath but still
she refused, insisting: "No, I don't want to hear that same old sermon:
'Stay out of your missus' and master's henhouse. Don't steal your missus'
and master's chickens. Stay out of your missus' and master's smokehouse.
Don't steal your missus' and master's hams.' I don't steal nothing. Don't
need to tell me not to."[61] In the midst of a white minister's sermon,
Uncle Silas, an elderly slave in Virginia, cried out: "Is us slaves gonna be
free in Heaven?" The preacher looked up in surprise and anger, paused
a moment, and then continued his sermon, but the old man persisted: "Is
God gonna free us slaves when we git to Heaven?" A slave who was
present described the rest of the encounter:

Old white preacher pult out his handkerchief an' wiped de sweat
fum his face. "Jesus says come unto Me ye who are free fum sin
an' I will give you salvation." "Gonna give us freedom 'long wid
salvation?" ask Uncle Silas. "De Lawd gives an' de Lawd takes
away, and he dat is widdout sin is gonna have life everlasin',"

---

58 Ralph Thomas Parkinson, *The Religious Instruction of Slaves, 1820–1860* (un-
published M.A. thesis, University of North Carolina, 1948), 81; C. C. Jones, [The]
Religious Instruction [of the Negroes in the United States (1842; reprint ed., New
York, 1969)], 198–201.

59 Donald Matthews, *Slavery and Methodism* (Princeton, 1965), 87.

60 James Redpath, *The Roving Editor: or, Talks with Slaves in the Southern States*
(1859; reprint ed., New York, 1968), 19.

61 Botkin, ed., *Lay My Burden Down*, 25–26.

preached de preacher. Den he went ahead preachin', fast-like, wid-dout payin' no 'tention to Uncle Silas.[62]

The dilemma that white ministers faced was simple to grasp but not to resolve: the doctrine they were attempting to inculcate could easily subvert the institution of slavery—and both they and the slaves realized it. Thus tensions and contradictions were inevitable. William Meade, Episcopal Bishop of Virginia, could teach slaves in one sermon that "what faults you are guilty of towards your masters and mistresses are faults done against God Himself . . . I tell you that your masters and mistresses are God's overseers, and that, if you are faulty towards them, God Himself will punish you severely for it in the next world," while in another sermon he assured the slaves that "God is no respector of per-sons" and specifically applied the case of the rich man who went to Hell while the beggar at his gate went to Heaven to the life of the black slave.[63] The Methodist minister John Dixon Long, who preached in Maryland from 1839 to 1856, was continually disturbed by the "elemen-tary and abstract preaching" he was forced to engage in and the "adulterated Gospel" he was forced to embrace because of slavery. "When you want to denounce sin," he wrote, "you must go to Adam and Eve, and to the Jews in the wilderness. You must be careful, how-ever, when slaves are present, how you talk about Pharaoh making slaves of the Hebrews, and refusing to let the people leave Egypt. At any rate, you must make no direct application of the subject." During one of his sermons on the conduct of Cain toward Abel, a slave asked him if he thought it was right for one brother to sell another. Long was at first confused and finally could do no better than to counsel: "Colored friends, it is best for you not to discuss such questions here." "What preachers in the South," he complained, "can say with Paul that they have not shunned to declare the whole counsel of God?"[64] During a debate in the South Carolina legislature over a bill (ultimately passed in 1834) pro-hibiting slaves from learning to read and write, Whitemarsh B. Seabrook put it more succinctly: anyone who wanted slaves to read the *entire* Bible was fit for a "room in the Lunatic Asylum."[65]

Until such recent studies as Eugene Genovese's,[66] the important role of the Negro preacher in slavery was largely ignored by scholars, though the historical record is clear enough. In 1790 John Leland of Virginia noted that in their religious services the slaves "seem in general to put more confidence in their own colour, than they do in whites; when they

---

[62] WPA, *Negro in Virginia*, 109.

[63] Frederick Law Olmsted, *A Journey in the Seaboard Slave States* (1856; reprint ed., New York, 1969), 118–19; Parkinson, *Religious Instruction of Slaves*, 78.

[64] Long, *Pictures of Slavery*, 227–29, 269–70.

[65] William W. Freehling, *Prelude to Civil War: The Nullification Controversy in South Carolina* (New York, 1966), 335.

[66] Eugene D. Genovese, *Roll, Jordan, Roll: The World the Slaves Made* (New York, 1974), 255–79; Henry Mitchell, *Black Preaching* (Philadelphia, 1970), Chap. 3; Charles V. Hamilton, *The Black Preacher in America* (New York, 1972), Chap. 2.

attempt to preach, they seldom fail of being very zealous; their language is broken, but they understand each other, and the whites may gain their ideas."[67] Traveling in Alabama some fifty years later, Sir Charles Lyell observed, "the negroes like a preacher of their own race."[68] Touring the slave states of the eastern seaboard, Frederick Olmsted noted that black preachers were common: "On almost every large plantation, and in every neighborhood of small ones, there is one man who has come to be considered the head or pastor of the local church. The office among the negroes, as among all other people, confers a certain importance and power."[69] Henry Ravenel of South Carolina wrote that the slaves on his plantation "had local preachers of their own who conducted their services in the absence of the other [the white preacher]. This colored preacher was always one of great influence. . . ."[70] Amanda McCray, who had been a slave in Florida, recalled that the slave minister on her plantation was not obliged to engage in hard labor, went about the plantation "all dressed up" in a frock coat and store bought shoes, and was held in awe by the other slaves.[71] Northern whites who went South to work with the freedmen during and directly after the Civil War often commented upon the "great power which the chief elders of their churches possess over the rest of the negroes." Referring to an old slave preacher, a federal official in Alexandria, Virginia, exclaimed, "this old negro has more influence over the blacks, and does more good among them, than all the missionaries and chaplains who have been sent here."[72] "Mostly we had white preachers," Anthony Dawson of North Carolina remembered, "but when we had a black preacher that was heaven."[73]

Given the precariousness and delicacy of their position, it is not surprising that black preachers often repeated the message of their white counterparts. "We had some nigger preachers," an ex-slave in Tennessee recalled, "but they would say, 'Obey your mistress and marster.' They didn't know nothing else to say."[74] Frank Roberson described a typical service on the plantation where he was a slave. First the white minister rose and preached variations on the theme "Obey your master"; then his black colleague, Parson Tom, would get up and repeat everything that the white preacher had said, "because he was afraid to say anything different."[75] Nevertheless, the evidence indicates that the behavior of black preachers would vary radically with altered circumstances. William Parker, a Methodist minister in Virginia, told Helen Ludlow shortly after

---

[67] Quoted in Herbert S. Klein, "Anglicanism, Catholicism, and the Negro Slave," in Anne Lane, ed., *The Debate Over Slavery* (Urbana, Ill., 1971), 179–80.

[68] Lyell, *Second Visit*, II, 72.

[69] Olmsted, *Seaboard*, 450.

[70] [Henry William] Ravenal, ["Recollections of Southern Plantation Life"], *Yale Review*, 25 (1936), 766.

[71] WPA Slave Narratives (Fla.).

[72] [H. G.] Spaulding ["Under the Palmetto"], *Continental Monthly*, 4 (1863), 195–97.

[73] [Norman R.] Yetman, ed., *Life Under the "Peculiar Institution"* [New York, 1970)], 95.

[74] Fisk University, *Unwritten History*, 259–60.

[75] Cade, *JNH*, 20 (1935), 329.

the Civil War that in the 1820s he had been made a preacher when the white parson on his plantation discovered he could read. His duties consisted of assisting in the singing, leading the prayer meetings, and preaching when his white superior was absent, which was often. "You know de cullered people was obleege to hab white ministers in slavery times. He usc' to come down onst in a while and preach up 'Sarvants, obey your marssas,' an' den I'd preach de gospil in between times 'cep' when he was to hear me; den I'd hab to take his tex'."[76] Parker's distinction between the "Gospel" and the message generally promulgated by the whites was commonly held among the slaves who knew the Scriptures had more to teach them than obedience. Anderson Edwards, a black preacher in Texas, was forced to preach what his master told him to: "he say tell them niggers iffen they obeys the master they goes to Heaven; but I knowed there's something better for them, but daren't tell them 'cept on the sly. That I done lots. I tells 'em iffen they keep praying, the Lord will set 'em free."[77]

Occasionally it was possible for a slave minister to disagree openly with his white colleague and to insist upon his own interpretation of the Scriptures. In 1847 an observer at a slave service in New Orleans wrote that as soon as the white minister had finished his sermon the black minister rose and corrected him:

> My brudder call your 'tention to de fact dat God did temp Abra'am; and den he go on to tell you 'bout Abra'am's temptation. Now I don't like dat word "temp-tation." "God can not be tempted wid evil; neither temptest he any man." Suppose we read that word temp *try*. Ah, my brudder (turning to the white preacher), why you no say *try?*—"After dese things God did *try* Abra'am." He try his people *now*. Who hasn't trials and triberlations from God? But I don't like dat word *temp*. I—*tell-you* (to the congregation) *God—don't—temp—any-body!*

Several years later this same white observer lived in a South Carolina courthouse town and found that week after week the slaves, tired from a hard day's work, would sleep through the white sermon at the Saturday evening services. "But let the congregation be surprised by the unexpected visit of some colored preacher, or let the exercises consist wholly of prayer, exhortation, and singing, and the fervor, vivacity, and life of the meeting would continue for the hour without diminishing." "None can move the negro," he concluded, "but a negro."[78]

There was great exaggeration in the last remark, of course. White preachers often moved the slaves, especially at the camp meetings. But it is true that slaves preferred black preachers who, all things considered,

---

[76] Mrs. M. F. Armstrong and Helen W. Ludlow, *Hampton and Its Students* (New York, 1874), 102.

[77] Botkin, ed., *Lay My Burden Down*, 26.

[78] "The Religious Life of the Negro Slave," *Harper's New Monthly Magazine*, 27 (1863), 482–83, 677.

were in a better position to understand the kind of message the slaves wanted to hear, as in this sermon delivered by a Negro Baptist minister named Bentley to a congregation of Georgia slaves in 1851:

> I remember on one occasion, when the President of the United States came to Georgia and to our town of Savannah. I remember what an ado the people made, and how they went out in big carriages to meet him. The clouds of dust were terrible, and the great cannon pealed forth one salute after another. Then the president came in a grand, beautiful carriage and drove to the best house in the whole town, and that was Mrs. Scarborough's! And when he came there he seated himself in the window. But a cord was drawn around the house to keep us negroes and other poor folks from coming too near. We had to stand outside and only get a sight of the president as he sat at the window. But the great gentlemen and the rich folks went freely up the steps and in through the door and shook hands with him. Now, did Christ come in this way? Did He come only to the rich? Did He shake hands only with them? No! Blessed be the Lord! He came to the poor! He came to us, and for our sakes, my brothers and sisters!

It is not surprising that the same slaves who would sit silently through sermons admonishing them to treat their masters and mistresses as they would treat the Lord, greeted Bentley's offering with several minutes of laughter, tears, stamping feet, and cries of "yes, yes! Amen! He came to us! Blessed be His name! Amen! Hallelujah!"[79]

Like other forms of Christianity, that preached to the slaves contained elements of what Karl Mannheim has identified as *ideology* and *utopia*.[80] The former, conducive to order and stability, and the latter, conducive to transcending and shattering the existing order, were so intermeshed that it is difficult to separate them into totally antithetical forms of slave religion. The teachings of white sermons and songs contained the seeds not merely of submission and docility but of egalitarianism and fundamental change, while those of black sermons and songs certainly can be seen as fostering the promulgation of stability as well as of discontent and the urge toward a different order of things. In spite of this important overlap, distinctions can be made: the religion the masters attempted to inculcate was laced with an emphasis upon morality, obedience, and right conduct as defined by the master class, while that which filled the sermons of black preachers and the songs of black folk was characterized by the apocalyptic visions and heroic exploits of the Scriptures. This was particularly true of slave spirituals, which were informed not by the Epistles of Paul but by the history of the Hebrew Children.

Judging from the songs of his black soldiers, Colonel Higginson concluded that their Bible was constructed primarily from the books of

---

[79] Bremer, *America of the Fifties*, 132–33.
[80] Karl Mannheim, *Ideology and Utopia* (New York, 1936).

Moses in the Old Testament and of Revelations in the New: "all that lay between, even the life of Jesus, they hardly cared to read or to hear." "Their memories," he noted at another point, "are a vast bewildered chaos of Jewish history and biography; and most of the great events of the past, down to the period of the American Revolution, they instinctively attribute to Moses."[81] Many of those northerners who came to the South to "uplift" the freedmen were deeply disturbed at the Old Testament emphasis of their religion. H. G. Spaulding complained that the ex-slaves needed to be introduced to "the light and warmth of the Gospel," and reported that a Union army officer told him: "Those people had enough of the Old Testament thrown at their heads under slavery. Now give them the glorious utterances and practical teachings of the Great Master."[82] Shortly after his arrival in Alabama in 1865, a northern army chaplain wrote of the slaves, "Moses is their *ideal* of all that is high, and noble, and perfect, in man," while Christ was regarded "not so much in the light of a *spiritual* Deliverer, as that of a second Moses."[83]

The essence of slave religion cannot be fully grasped without understanding this Old Testament bias. It is important that Daniel and David and Joshua and Jonah and Moses and Noah, all of whom fill the lines of the spirituals, were delivered in *this* world and delivered in ways which struck the imagination of the slaves. Over and over their songs dwelt upon the spectacle of the Red Sea opening to allow the Hebrew slaves past before inundating the mighty armies of the Pharaoh. They lingered delightedly upon the image of little David humbling the great Goliath with a stone—a pretechnological victory which postbellum Negroes were to expand upon in their songs of John Henry. They retold in endless variation the stories of the blind and humbled Samson bringing down the mansions of his conquerors; of the ridiculed Noah patiently building the ark which would deliver him from the doom of a mocking world; of the timid Jonah attaining freedom from his confinement through faith. The similarity of these tales to the situation of the slaves was too clear for them not to see it; too clear for us to believe that the songs had no worldly content for blacks in bondage. "O my Lord delivered Daniel," the slaves observed, and responded logically: "O why not deliver me, too?"

> He delivered Daniel from de lion's den,
> Jonah from de belly ob de whale,
> And de Hebrew children from de fiery furnace,
> And why not every man?[84]

[81] Higginson, *Army Life*, 27, 205.
[82] Spaulding, *Continental Monthly*, 4 (1863), 195–96.
[83] Quoted in Peter Kolchin, *First Freedom: The Responses of Alabama's Blacks to Emancipation and Reconstruction* (Westport, Conn., 1972), 118.
[84] Allen *et al.*, *Slave Songs*, 94; Fenner, *Religious Folk Songs*, 21; Marsh, *Jubilee Singers*, 134–35; McIlhenny, *Befo' De War Spirituals*, 248–49; *SW*, 41 (1912), 241.

In another spiritual the slaves rehearsed the triumphs of the Hebrew Children in verse after verse, concluding each with the comforting thought: "And the God dat lived in Moses' [Dan'el's, David's] time is jus' de same today." The "mighty rocky road" that "I must travel," another of the slaves' songs insisted, is "De rough, rocky road what Moses done travel."[85]

These songs state as clearly as anything can the manner in which the sacred world of the slaves was able to fuse the precedents of the past, the conditions of the present, and the promise of the future into one connected reality. In this respect there was always a latent and symbolic element of protest in the slave's religious songs which frequently became overt and explicit. Frederick Douglass asserted that for him and many of his fellow slaves the song, "O Canaan, sweet Canaan, / I am bound for the land of Canaan," symbolized "something more than a hope of reaching heaven. We meant to reach the *North,* and the North was our Canaan," and he wrote that the lines of another spiritual, "Run to Jesus, shun the danger, / I don't expect to stay much longer here," had a double meaning which first suggested to him the thought of escaping from slavery.[86] Similarly, when the black troops in Higginson's regiment sang:

> We'll soon be free,
> We'll soon be free,
> We'll soon be free,
>   When de Lord will call us home.

a young drummer boy explained to him, "Dey tink *de Lord* mean for say *de Yankees.*"[87] These veiled meanings by no means invariably eluded the whites. At the outbreak of the Civil War slaves in Georgetown, South Carolina, were jailed for singing this song, and Joseph Farley, who had been a slave in Virginia and Kentucky, testified that white patrols would often visit the slaves' religious services and stop them if they said or sang anything considered offensive: "One time when they were singing, 'Ride on King Jesus, No man can hinder Thee,' the padderollers told them to stop or they would show him whether they could be hindered or not."[88]

There is no reason to doubt that slaves may have used their songs as a means of secret communication. An ex-slave told Lydia Parrish that when he and his fellow slaves "suspicioned" that one of their number was telling tales to the driver, they would sing lines like the following while working in the field:

> O Judyas he wuz a 'ceitful man
>   He went an' betray a mos' innocen' man.

---

[85] Hallowell, *Calhoun Plantation Songs,* 30; Yetman, ed., *Life Under the "Peculiar Institution,"* 112.

[86] Douglass, *Life and Times,* 159–60.

[87] Higginson, *Army Life,* 217.

[88] *Ibid.;* Fisk University, *Unwritten History,* 124–25.

Fo' thirty pieces a silver dat it wuz done
He went in de woods an' 'e self he hung.[89]

As many writers have argued and as some former slaves have testified, such spirituals as the commonly heard "Steal away, steal away, steal away to Jesus!" could be used as explicit calls to secret meetings. Miles Mark Fisher was correct in seeing the slaves' songs as being filled with innuendo and hidden meaning. But it is not necessary to invest the spirituals with a secular function only at the price of divesting them of their religious content, as Fisher has done.[90] While we may make such clear-cut distinctions, I have tried to show that the slaves did not. For them religion never constituted a simple escape from this world, because their conception of the world was more expansive than modern man's.

Nowhere is this better illustrated than during the Civil War itself. While the war gave rise to such new spirituals as "Before I'd be a slave / I'd be buried in my grave, / And go home to my Lord and be saved!" or the popular *Many Thousand Go*, with its jubilant rejection of all the facets of slave life—"No more peck o'corn for me, . . . No more driver's lash for me, . . . No more pint o'salt for me, . . . No more hundred lash for me, . . . No more mistress' call for me"[91]—the important thing was not that large numbers of slaves now could create new songs which openly expressed their views of slavery; that was to be expected. More significant was the ease with which their old songs fit their new situation. With so much of their inspiration drawn from the events of the Old Testament and the Book of Revelation, the slaves had long sung of wars, of battles, of the Army of the Lord, of Soldiers of the Cross, of trumpets summoning the faithful, of vanquishing the hosts of evil. These songs especially were, as Higginson put it, "available for camp purposes with very little strain upon their symbolism." "We'll cross de mighty river," his troops sang while marching or rowing,

We'll cross de danger water, . . .
O Pharaoh's army drownded!
My army cross over.

"O blow your trumpet, Gabriel," they sang,

Blow your trumpet louder,
And I want dat trumpet to blow me home
To my new Jerusalem.

[89] [Lydia] Parrish, *Slave Songs [of the Georgia Sea Islands* (1942; reprint ed., Hatboro, Pa., 1965)], 247.
[90] "Actually, not one spiritual in its primary form reflected interest in anything other than a full life here and now" [(Miles Mark] Fisher, *Negro Slave Songs in the United States*, New York, 1963, 137).
[91] Barton, *Old Plantation Hymns*, 25; Allen *et al.*, *Slave Songs*, 48; James McKim, *Dwight's Journal of Music*, 21 (1862), 149.

But they also found their less overtly militant songs quite as appropriate to warfare. Their most popular and effective marching song was:

> Jesus call you. Go in de wilderness,
>   Go in de wilderness, go in de wilderness,
> Jesus call you. Go in de wilderness
>   To wait upon de Lord.[92]

Black Union soldiers found it no more incongruous to accompany their fight for freedom with the sacred songs of their bondage than they had found it inappropriate as slaves to sing their spirituals while picking cotton or shucking corn. Their religious songs, like their religion itself, was of this world as well as the next.

Slave songs present us with abundant evidence that in the structure of their music and dance, in the uses to which music was put, in the survival of the oral tradition, in the retention of such practices as spirit possession which often accompanied the creation of spirituals, and in the ways in which the slaves expressed their new religion, important elements of their shared African heritage remained alive not just as quaint cultural vestiges but as vitally creative elements of slave culture. This could never have happened if slavery had so completely closed in around the slave, so totally penetrated his personality structure as to reduce him to a kind of *tabula rasa* upon which the white man could write what he chose.

Slave songs provide us with the beginnings of a very different kind of hypothesis: that the preliterate, premodern Africans, with their sacred world view, were so imperfectly acculturated into the secular American society into which they were thrust, were so completely denied access to the ideology and dreams which formed the core of the consciousness of other Americans, that they were forced to fall back upon the only cultural frames of reference that made any sense to them and gave them any feeling of security. I use the word "forced" advisedly. Even if the slaves had had the opportunity to enter fully into the life of the larger society, they might still have chosen to retain and perpetuate certain elements of their African heritage. But the point is that they really had no choice. True acculturation was denied to most slaves. The alternatives were either to remain in a state of cultural limbo, divested of the old cultural patterns but not allowed to adopt those of their new homeland—which in the long run is no alternative at all—or to cling to as many as possible of the old ways of thinking and acting. The slaves' oral tradition, their music, and their religious outlook served this latter function and constituted a cultural refuge at least potentially capable of protecting their personalities from some of the worst ravages of the slave system.

The argument of Professors Tannenbaum and Elkins that the Protestant churches in the United States did not act as a buffer between the slave and his master is persuasive enough, but it betrays a modern pre-

---

[92] Higginson, *Army Life*, 201–02, 211–12.

occupation with purely institutional arrangements.[93] Religion is more than an institution, and because Protestant churches failed to protect the slave's inner being from the incursions of the slave system, it does not follow that the spiritual message of Protestantism failed as well. Certainly the slaves themselves perceived the distinction. Referring to the white patrols which frequently and brutally interfered with the religious services of the slaves on his plantation, West Turner exclaimed: "Dey law us out of church, but dey couldn't law 'way Christ."[94] Slave songs are a testament to the way in which Christianity provided slaves with the precedents, heroes, and future promise that allowed them to transcend the purely temporal bonds of the Peculiar Institution.

Historians have frequently failed to perceive the full importance of this because they have not taken the slave's religiosity seriously enough. A people cannot create a music as forceful and striking as slave music out of a mere uninternalized anodyne. Those who have argued that Negroes did not oppose slavery in any meaningful way are writing from a modern, political context. What they really mean is that the slaves found no *political* means to oppose slavery. But slaves, to borrow Professor Hobsbawm's term, were prepolitical beings in a prepolitical situation.[95] Within their frame of reference there were other—and from the point of view of personality development, not necessarily less effective—means of escape and opposition. If mid-twentieth-century historians have difficulty perceiving the sacred universe created by slaves as a serious alternative to the societal system created by southern slaveholders, the problem may be the historians' and not the slaves'.

Above all, the study of slave songs forces the historian to move out of his own culture, in which music plays a peripheral role, and offers him the opportunity to understand the ways in which black slaves were able to perpetuate much of the centrality and functional importance that music had for their African ancestors. In the concluding lines of his perceptive study of primitive song, C. M. Bowra has written:

> Primitive song is indispensable to those who practice it. . . . they cannot do without song, which both formulates and answers their nagging questions, enables them to pursue action with zest and confidence, brings them into touch with gods and spirits, and makes them feel less strange in the natural world. . . . it gives to them a solid centre in what otherwise would be almost chaos, and a continuity in their being, which would too easily dissolve before the calls of the implacable present. . . . through its words men, who might otherwise give in to the malice of circumstances, find their old powers revived or new powers stirring in them, and through these life itself is sustained and renewed and fulfilled.[96]

---

[93] Elkins, *Slavery*, Chap. 2; Frank Tannenbaum, *Slave and Citizen* (New York, 1946).

[94] WPA, *Negro in Virginia*, 110, 146.

[95] E. J. Hobsbawm, *Primitive Rebels* (New York, 1959), Chap. I.

[96] C. M. Bowra, *Primitive Song* (London, 1962), 285–86.

This, I think, sums up concisely the function of song for the slave. Without a general understanding of that function, without a specific understanding of the content and meaning of slave song, there can be no full comprehension of the effects of slavery upon the slave or the meaning of the society from which slaves emerged at emancipation.

Suggestions for Further Reading

A number of studies of violence in American history have appeared in recent years, but most have been superficial and lacking in perspective. A rather good collection of essays, many of them prepared for the President's Commission on the Causes and Prevention of Violence, is High Davis Graham and Ted Robert Gurr (eds.), *Violence in America: Historical and Comparative Perspectives** (2 vols.: U.S. Government Printing Office, 1969), also available in one-volume editions from New American Library and Bantam. A useful collection of primary sources is Richard Hofstadter and Michael Wallace (eds.), *American Violence: A Documentary History** (Knopf, 1970), which includes a long introductory essay by Hofstadter. Leonard L. Richards, *"Gentlemen of Property and Standing": Anti-Abolition Mobs in Jacksonian America** (Oxford University Press, 1971) surveys one aspect of violence in this period. A recent study is Michael Feldberg, *The Turbulent Era: Riot and Disorder in Jacksonian America* (Oxford University Press, 1980).

General introductions to the history of immigration in the United States are M. A. Jones, *American Immigration** (University of Chicago Press, 1960) and Leonard Dinnerstein and David M. Reimers, *Ethnic Americans: A History of Immigration and Assimilation** (Harper and Row, 1975). On ante-bellum immigration in particular, the standard work is Marcus L. Hansen, *The Atlantic Migration, 1607–1860** (Harvard University Press, 1940). John Cogley has provided us with an introduction to the Roman Catholic Church in the United States in his *Catholic America** (Dial, 1973). See also Jay P. Dolan, *The Immigrant Church: New York's Irish and German Catholics, 1815–1865** (Johns Hopkins Press, 1975). The conflict between established settlers and Irish immigrants in Boston is discussed in Barbara Miller Solomon, *Ancestors and Immigrants** (Harvard University Press, 1956). Ray A. Billington, in *The Protestant Crusade, 1800–1860** (Macmillan, 1938), deals more generally with religious conflict in the first half of the nineteenth century. The story of the Irish community in the United States is told by Carl Wittke in *The Irish in America** (Louisiana State University Press, 1956), while Terry Coleman's *Going to America** (Pantheon, 1972) describes, among other things, the Irish migration in the years 1846–1855. John Higham's *Strangers in the Land: Patterns of American Nativism, 1860–1925** (Rutgers University Press, 1955) provides useful insights into nativist sentiment during the ante-bellum years, although it is primarily concerned with a later period.

On nineteenth-century feminism there is useful information in the relevant portions of several general studies of American women. See, for example, Andrew Sinclair, *The Emancipation of the Amer-*

* Available in paperback edition.

*ican Woman** (Harper and Row, 1965), first published under the title *The Better Half;* Eleanor Flexner, *Century of Struggle: The Women's Rights Movement in the United States** (Harvard University Press, 1959); and Robert Riegel, *American Feminists** (University of Kansas Press, 1963). A useful collection of documents is Aileen S. Kraditor (ed.), *Up from the Pedestal: Selected Writings in the History of American Feminism** (Quadrangle, 1968). Hannah Josephson examines the plight of women textile workers in *The Golden Threads: New England's Mill Girls and Magnates* (Duell, Sloan and Pearce, 1949). Impressive biographies of leading feminists in the ante-bellum period are Gerda Learner, *The Grimke Sisters from South Carolina: Rebels Against Slavery** (Houghton Mifflin, 1967), and *Created Equal: A Biography of Elizabeth Cady Stanton* (Day, 1940) and *Susan B. Anthony: Rebel, Crusader, Humanitarian* (Beacon, 1959), both by Alma Lutz. A study related to the role of women in American society is Bernard Wishy, *The Child and the Republic: The Dawn of Modern American Child Nurture** (University of Pennsylvania Press, 1967). On the origins of the feminist movement see Miriam Gurko, *The Ladies of Seneca Falls: The Birth of the Women's Rights Movement** (Schocken Books, 1976). Two valuable new studies of this period are Nancy F. Cott, *The Bonds of Womanhood: "Woman's Sphere" in New England, 1780–1835** (Yale University Press, 1977) and Susan P. Conrad, *Perish the Thought: Intellectual Women in Romantic America, 1830–1860** (Oxford University Press, 1976). Two general surveys of working women are Roslyn Baxandall, Linda Gordon, and Susan Reverby (eds.), *America's Working Women: A Documentary History—1600 to the Present** (Random House, 1976) and Barbara Meyer Wertheimer, *We Were There: The Story of Working Women in America** (Pantheon, 1977). Thomas Dublin has employed documentary material in *Farm and Factory: The Mill Experience and Women's Lives in New England, 1830–1860* (Columbia University Press, 1981).

A number of good books have appeared on slavery in the United States. Some of these are noted in the suggestions for further reading at the close of Section 1 (see pp. 125–26). Excellent recent books on the life of the slaves include John W. Blassingame, *The Slave Community: Plantation Life in the Antebellum South** (Oxford University Press, 1972); Eugene Genovese, *Roll, Jordan, Roll: The World the Slaves Made** (Pantheon Books, 1974); and Herbert G. Gutman, *The Black Family in Slavery and Freedom, 1750–1925** (Pantheon Books, 1976). Recent works dealing with aspects of black culture during slavery include Dena J. Epstein, *Sinful Tunes and Spirituals: Black Folk Music to the Civil War* (University of Illinois Press, 1977); Albert Raboteau, *Slave Religion: The "Invisible Institution" in the American South** (Oxford University Press, 1978); and Thomas Webber, *Deep Like the Rivers: Education in the Slave Quarter Community, 1831–1865** (Norton, 1978). Of particular i~   here are works pertaining to the slaves' formulations of their own experience—the folktales, songs, and narratives that make up the distinctive oral tradition of black America. A brief presentation of the variety of primary source materials available to historians is William F. Cheek (ed.), *Black Resistance Before the Civil War** (Glencoe, 1970). Spirituals are collected in James Weldon Johnson and J. Rosamond Johnson (eds.), *The Books of American Negro Spirituals** (Viking, 1925, 1926). See also Harold Courlander, *Negro Folk Music U.S.A.** (Columbia University Press, 1963). On the relationship between African and New World religion, see Melville J. Herskovits, *The Myth of the Negro Past** (Harper & Row, 1941). Folktales are collected in Langston Hughes and Arna Bontemps (eds.), *The Book of Negro Folklore** (Dodd, Mead, 1958); Richard Dorson (ed.), *American Negro Folktales** (Fawcett, 1967); and J. Mason Brewer (ed.), *American Negro Folklore** (Quadrangle, 1968). For analyses of black folklore see Alan Dundes (ed.), *Mother Wit from the Laughing Barrel: Readings in the Interpretation of Afro-American Folklore** (Prentice-Hall, 1973). Charles H. Nichols has surveyed and analyzed narratives composed by fugitive slaves in *Many Thousands Gone: The Ex-Slaves' Account of Their Bondage and Freedom** (Brill, 1963). Perhaps the most important of these narratives is the *Narrative of the Life of Frederick Douglass, an American Slave, Written by Himself** (Anti-Slavery Office, 1845). Readily available collections of narratives by former slaves are Gilbert Osofsky (ed.), *Puttin' On Ole Massa: The Slave Narratives of Henry Bibb, William Wells Brown, and Solomon Northup** (Harper & Row, 1969), and Arna Bontempts (ed.), *Great Slave Narratives** (Beacon, 1969), which presents the narratives of Olaudah Equiano, W. C. Pennington, and William and Ellen Craft. B. A. Botkin (ed.), *Lay My Burden Down: A Folk History of Slavery** (University of Chicago Press, 1945), and Norman R. Yetman (ed.), *Life Under the Peculiar Institution: Selections from the Slave Narrative Collection** (Holt, Rinehart and Winston, 1970), are samplings of narratives collected from former slaves under the auspices of the Federal Writers' Project in the 1930s. George P. Rawick describes slave life using the above collection as source material in *From Sundown to Sunup: The Making of the Black Community** (Greenwood 1972). Three novels that expertly explore slave attitudes are Arna Bontemps' *Black Thunder** (Macmillan 1936), the story of Gabriel's rebellion in 1800; Harold Courland's *The African** (Crown, 1967), the tale of an African boy who is captured and sold into slavery in the Caribbean and the United States South; and Alex Haley's *Roots: The Story of an American Family** (Doubleday, 1976).

Westward Expansion

4

Legacy of Hate:
The Conquest of the Southwest

RODOLFO ACUÑA

By the middle of the nineteenth century, three nonwhite ethnic minorities had become inhabitants of the United States against their will—Afro-Americans, American Indians, and Mexican-Americans. The last of these groups has traditionally received the least attention by historians. Their story and place in American history has been seen as less dramatic and less consequential than that of either blacks or Indians. But they are here. And in rather large numbers. While Chicanos—as Mexican-Americans have recently begun calling themselves—make up less than three percent of the total American population, they contribute over ten percent of the population in the Southwest. And in many areas of the United States from Texas to California, they are a majority in small towns and rural counties.

From the beginning they have been discriminated against on several counts: they are not considered white, they are of mixed (Spanish-Indian) ancestry, and they are predominantly Roman Catholic in religion. Any one of these characteristics would have led them to be victimized by the dominant ideology of Anglo-Saxon expansionists. The attitude of many Americans was expressed by a famous Texas gunman who, when asked how many notches he had in his gun, replied: "Thirty-seven—not counting Mexicans."

As the theory of manifest destiny and the rigorous drive for national expansion thrust the United States government westward, it was clear that the American leadership was not concerned with "counting Mexicans." Once the conquest was complete, however, and the vast and potentially rich Southwestern area was a part of the United States, there were the Mexicans, now residents on American soil, with many of them claiming hereditary property rights to land granted their families and communities by the Spanish and Mexican governments. These property rights were not recognized by the laws of the United States or by the individual states that the Mexican-Americans found themselves subject to, and much of the political activity of Chicanos in recent years—particularly the **Alianza**

351

movement in New Mexico—has called for a restoration of those
rights or for reparations of some kind.

The existence of large numbers of these "alien" peoples in the
territories of New Mexico and Arizona delayed statehood for those
areas for decades even after they had qualified constitutionally for
admission to the Union. As the editor of **Harper's Weekly** wrote in
1876 after the Senate had passed a statehood bill: "New Mexico is
virtually an ignorant foreign community under the influence of the
Roman Church, and neither for the advantage of the Union nor for
its own benefit can such an addition to the family of American States
be urged."

In the second edition of his history of Mexican-Americans, Chi-
cano historian Rodolfo Acuña, of the University of California at
Northridge, has drawn on much recent scholarship to tell his story.
In the selection from his work printed below, Acuña describes the
conquest of Northern Mexico by the United States in the second
quarter of the nineteenth century. He properly points out the role
of slavery and racism in this struggle and indicates the way some
American historians have sought to justify the conquest in terms that
show the continuing legacy of the racial and nationalistic attitudes of
the nineteenth century.

The tragedy of the Mexican cession is that most Anglo-Americans have
not accepted the fact that the United States committed an act of violence
against the Mexican people when it took Mexico's northwestern territory.
Violence was not limited to the taking of the land; Mexico's territory was
invaded, her people murdered, her land raped, and her possessions plundered. Memory of this destruction generated a distrust and dislike that is
still vivid in the minds of many Mexicans, for the violence of the United
States left deep scars. And for Chicanos—Mexicans remaining within the
boundaries of the new United States territories—aggression was even
more insidious, for the outcome of the Texas and Mexican-American wars
made them a conquered people. Anglo-Americans were the conquerors,
and they evinced all the arrogance of military victors.[1]

[1] Robert A. Divine, ed., *American Foreign Policy* (New York: World Publishing,
1966), pp. 11–18.

BACKGROUND TO THE INVASION OF TEXAS

An integral part of Anglo rationalizations for the conquest has been either to ignore or to distort events that led up to the initial clash in 1836. To Anglo-Americans, the Texas War resulted because of a tyrannical or, at best, an incompetent Mexican government that was antithetical to the ideals of democracy and justice. The truth is that the roots of the conflict extended back to as early as 1767 when Benjamin Franklin marked Mexico and Cuba for future expansion. Filibusters* from the United States planned expeditions into Texas in the 1790s. The Louisiana Purchase in 1803 stimulated U.S. ambitions in the Southwest and six years later Thomas Jefferson predicted that the Spanish borderlands "are ours the first moment war is forced upon us."[2] The war with Great Britain in 1812 heightened Anglo-American designs on the Spanish territory.

The U.S. experience in Florida set the pattern for expansionist activities in Texas. In 1818 several posts in East Florida were seized in unauthorized, but never officially condemned U.S. military expeditions. Negotiations then in progress with Spain finally terminated in the Adams-Onis or Transcontinental Treaty (1819) whereby Spain ceded Florida to the United States and the United States renounced its claim to Texas. The treaty set the U.S. boundary at the Sabine River, thereby excluding Texas. When the treaty was ratified in February 1821 Texas was part of Coahuila, a state in the independent Republic of Mexico. Many North Americans claimed that Texas belonged to the United States, pointing to Jefferson's contention that Texas's boundary extended to the Rio Grande and that it was part of the Louisiana Purchase. They condemned the Adams-Onis Treaty. The expanded boundary would have "put several key Mexican posts, notably San Antonio, Albuquerque and Santa Fe inside the United States." Therefore, Anglo-Americans made forays into Texas similar to those they had made into Florida. In 1819 James Long led an abortive invasion to establish the "Republic of Texas." Long, like many Anglos, believed that Texas belonged to the United States and that "Congress had no right or power to sell, exchange, or relinquish an 'American possession.'"[3]

The Mexican government opened Texas, provided settlers agreed to certain conditions and for a time filibustering subsided. Moses Austin was given permission to settle in Texas. He died shortly afterwards, and

---

* A *filibuster* is an adventurer who engages in insurrectionist or revolutionary activity in a foreign country.

[2] Manual Medina Castro, *El Gran Despojo: Texas, Nuevo México, California* (México. D.F.: Editorial Diogenes, 1971), p. 9; Carlos E. Castañeda, *Our Catholic Heritage in Texas, 1519–1933,* vol. 6, *Transition Period: The Fight for Freedom, 1810–1836* (New York: Arno Press, 1976), p. 86.

[3] Richard W. Van Alstyne, *The Rising American Empire* (New York: Norton, 1974), p. 101; T. R. Fehrenbach, *Lone Star: A History of Texas and the Texans* (New York: Macmillan, 1968), p. 128; Castañeda, vol. 6, pp. 160–162.

his son continued his venture. In December 1821 Stephen Austin founded the settlement of San Felipe de Austin. Large numbers followed, many coming to Texas in the 1820s as refugees from the depression of 1819 and in the 1830s as entrepreneurs seeking to profit from the availability of cheap land. By 1830 there were about 20,000 settlers, along with about 2,000 slaves.

Settlers agreed to obey the conditions set by the Mexican government —that all immigrants be Catholics and that they take an oath of allegiance to Mexico. However, Anglo-Americans became resentful when Mexico tried to enforce the agreements and Mexico became increasingly alarmed at the flood of immigrants from the U.S., most of whom retained their Protestant religion.[4]

It soon became apparent that the Anglo-Texans had no intention of obeying Mexican laws. Many settlers considered the native Mexicans to be the intruders in the territory and encroached upon their lands. In a dispute with Mexicans and Indians, as well as Anglo-American settlers, Hayden Edwards arbitrarily attempted to evict settlers from the land before the conflicting claims could be sorted out by the Mexican authorities. As a result the authorities nullified his settlement contract and ordered him to leave the territory. He and his followers seized the town of Nacogdoches and on December 21, 1826, proclaimed the Republic of Fredonia. Mexican officials, who were supported by some Anglo-Americans (such as Stephen Austin), suffocated the Edwards revolt. However, many U.S. newspapers played up the rebellion as "200 Men Against a Nation!" and described Edwards and his followers as "apostles of democracy crushed by an alien civilization."[5]

In 1824 President John Quincy Adams "began putting pressure on Mexico in the hope of persuading her to rectify the frontier. Any of the Texan rivers west of the Sabine—the Brazos, the Colorado, the Nueces— was preferable to the Sabine, though the Rio Grande was the one desired."[6] In 1826 Adams offered to buy Texas for the sum of $1 million. Mexican authorities refused the offer. The United States launched an aggressive foreign policy, attempting to coerce Mexico into selling Texas.

Mexico tried to consolidate its control over Texas, but the number of Anglo-American settlers and the vastness of the territory made it an almost impossible task. Anglo-Americans in Texas had already created a privileged caste, which depended in great part on the economic advantage given to them by their slaves. When Mexico abolished slavery on September 15, 1829, Texans circumvented the law by "freeing" their slaves and then signing them to lifelong contracts as indentured servants. Anglos resented the Mexican order and considered it an invasion of their personal liberties. In 1830 Mexico prohibited further Anglo-American immigration to Texas. Anglos were outraged at the restrictions. Meanwhile, Andrew

---

[4] Walter Prescott Webb, *The Texas Rangers: A Century of Frontier Defense* (Austin: University of Texas Press, 1965), pp. 21–22.

[5] Fehrenbach, pp. 163–164.

[6] Van Alstyne, p. 101.

Jackson increased tensions by attempting to purchase Texas for as much as $5 million.

Mexican authorities grew more nervous as the Anglo-Americans' dominance of Texas increased; they resented the Anglo-Americans' refusal to submit to Mexican laws. Mexico moved reinforcements into Coahuila, and readied them in case of trouble. Anglos viewed this move as a Mexican invasion.

Anglo-Texas colonists grew more defiant and refused to pay customs and actively supported smuggling activities. Armed clashes broke out. When the "war party" rioted at Anahuac in December 1831 it had the popular support of Anglo-Texans. One of its leaders was Sam Houston, who "was a known protégé of Andrew Jackson, now president of the United States. . . . Houston's motivation was to bring Texas into the United States."[7]

In the summer of 1832 a group of Anglos attacked a Mexican garrison and were routed. A state of insurrection existed and Mexican authorities were forced to defend the territory. Matters worsened when the Anglo settlers met at San Félipe in October 1832. At this convention Anglos drafted resolutions sent to the Mexican government and to the state of Coahuila which called for more autonomy for Texas. A second convention was held in January 1833. Significantly, not one Mexican pueblo in Texas participated in either convention, many clearly branding the act sedition. Increasingly it became evident that the war party under Sam Houston was winning out.[8] Sam Houston was elected to direct the course of events and Austin was appointed to submit the grievances and resolutions to Mexico City.

Austin left for Mexico City to press for lifting of restrictions on Anglo-American immigration and separate statehood. The slave issue also burned in his mind. Austin, anything but conciliatory, wrote to a friend from Mexico City, "If our application is refused . . . I shall be in favor of organizing *without it*. I see no other way of saving the country from total anarchy and ruin. I am totally done with conciliatory measures and, for the future, shall be uncompromising as to Texas."[9]

On October 2, 1833, he wrote a letter to the *ayuntamiento* at San Antonio encouraging it to declare Texas a separate state. He later stated that he had done so "in a moment of irritation and impatience"; nevertheless, his actions were not those of a moderate. Contents of the note fell into the hands of Mexican authorities, who had begun to question Austin's good faith. Subsequently, they imprisoned him, and much of what Austin had accomplished in the way of compromise was undone.

Contributing to the general distrust were actions of U.S. Minister to

[7] Eugene C. Barker, *Mexico and Texas, 1821–1835* (New York: Russell & Russell, (1965), pp. 52, 74–80, 80–82; David J. Weber, ed., *Foreigners in Their Native Land* (Albuquerque: University of New Mexico Press, 1973), p. 89, quoted in Fehrenbach, p. 182.

[8] Castañeda, vol. 6, pp. 252–253; Fehrenbach, p. 181.

[9] Nathaniel W. Stephenson, *Texas and the Mexican War: A Chronicle of the Winning of the Southwest* (New York: United States Publishing, 1921), p. 51.

Mexico Anthony Butler, whose crude attempts to bribe Mexican officials to sell Texas infuriated Mexicans. He offered one official $200,000 to "play ball."[10]

In the autumn of 1834 Henry Smith published a pamphlet entitled *Security for Texas* in which he advocated open defiance of Mexican authority. The agents of Anglo land companies added to the polarization by lobbying in Washington, D.C., and within Texas for a change in governments. The Galveston Bay and Texas Land Company of New York, acting to protect its investments, worked through its agent Anthony Butler, the U.S. Minister to Mexico to bring about the cooperation of the U.S.[11]

According to Dr. Carlos Castañeda:

> The activities of the "Land Companies" after 1834 cannot be ignored. Their widespread advertisement and indiscriminate sale of "landscrip" sent hundreds, perhaps thousands, to Texas under the impression that they had legitimate title to lands equal to the amount of scrip bought. The Galveston Bay and Texas Land Company, which bought the contracts of David S. Burnet, Joseph Vahlein, and Lorenzo de Zavala, and the Nashville Company, which acquired the contract of Robert Leftwitch, are the two best known. They first sold scrip at from one to ten cents an acre, calling for a total of seven and one-half million acres. The company was selling only its permit to acquire a given amount of land in Texas, but since an empresario contract was nontransferable, the scrip was, in fact, worthless. . . .[12]

The scrip would be worthless as long as Texas belonged to Mexico.

On July 13, 1835, a general amnesty released Austin from prison. While enroute to Texas, he wrote a letter from New Orleans to a cousin expressing the view that Texas should be Americanized even though it was still a state of Mexico, and indicating that it should one day come under the American flag. In this letter he called for a massive immigration of Anglo-Americans, "*each man with his rifle*," whom he hoped would come "passports or no passports, *anyhow*." He continued: "For fourteen years I have had a hard time of it, but nothing shall daunt my courage or abate my . . . object . . . to *Americanize* Texans."[13]

---

[10] Stephenson, p. 52; Barker, p. 128. Carlos Castañeda, in vol. 6, on p. 234 refers to Col. Anthony Butler, Jackson's minister to Mexico, as "an unscrupulous, passionate and scheming character . . . ." The new proposal provided final confirmation of the United States' intentions. Gene M. Brack, *Mexico Views Manifest Destiny, 1821–1846: An Essay on the Origins of the Mexican War* (Albuquerque: University of New Mexico Press, 1975) pp. 67–68, states that Jackson told the minister to do anything to get Texas.

[11] Stephenson, p. 52.

[12] Castañeda, vol. 6, 217–218.

[13] Fehrenbach, p. 188. Hutchinson, p. 6, quotes a letter from Austin to Mrs. Mary Austin Holly: "The fact is, we must and ought to become a part of the United States. Money should be no consideration . . . . The more the American popula-

Anglos in Texas saw separation from Mexico and eventual union with the United States as the most profitable political arrangement. Texas-Mexican historian Castañeda notes:

> Trade with New Orleans and other American ports had increased steadily. This development was naturally distasteful to Mexico, for the colonists fostered strong economic ties with . . . the United States rather than with Mexico. Juan H. Almonte in his 1834 report, estimated the total foreign trade of Texas—chiefly with the United States—at more than 1,000,000 pesos, of which imports constituted 630,000 and exports, 500,000. He calculated the exportation of cotton by the settlers in 1833, as approximately 2,000 bales.[14]

Colonel Almonte recognized the fundamental economic conflict reflected in these figures and his report recommended many concessions to the *Tejanos*, but also urged that "the province be well stocked with Mexican troops."[15]

THE INVASION OF TEXAS

Not all the Anglo-Texan settlers favored the conflict. Austin belonged to the peace party, which at first opposed a confrontation with Mexicans. Ultimately, this faction joined the "hawks." Eugene C. Barker states that the immediate cause of the war was "the overthrow of the nominal republic [by Santa Anna] and the substitution of centralized oligarchy," which allegedly would have placed the Texans more strictly under the control of Mexico. Barker admits that "Earnest patriots like Benjamin Lundy, William Ellery Channing, and John Quincy Adams saw in the Texas revolution a disgraceful affair promoted by the sordid slaveholders and land speculators."

Barker draws a parallel between the Texas revolt and the American Revolution, stating: "In each, the general cause of revolt was the same—a sudden effort to extend imperial authority at the expense of local privilege." In fact, in both instances the central governments attempted to enforce existing laws that conflicted with illegal activities of some very articulate men. Barker further attempts to justify the Anglo-Texans' actions by observing: "At the close of summer in 1835 the Texans saw themselves in danger of becoming the alien subjects of a people to whom they deliberately believed themselves morally, intellectually, and politically superior. The racial feeling, indeed, underlay and colored Texan-

tion is increased the more readily will the Mexican government give it up . . . . For fourteen years I have had a hard time of it, but nothing shall daunt my courage or abate my exertions to complete the main object of my labors, to *Americanize* Texas."

[14] Castañeda, vol. 6, pp. 240–241.
[15] Fehrenbach, p. 180.

Mexican relations from the establishment of the first Anglo-American colony in 1821." Therefore, the conflict, according to Barker, was inevitable and, consequently, justified.

Texas history is elusive—a mixture of selected fact and generalized myth. Many historians admit that racism played a leading role in the causes for revolt, that smugglers were upset with Mexico's enforcement of her import laws, that Texans were upset about emancipation laws, and that an increasing number of the new arrivals from the United States actively agitated for independence. But despite these admissions, many historians like Barker refuse to assign guilt to their countrymen. Instead, Barker blamed it on the racial and cultural mistrust between Mexicans and the colonists.[16]

The antipathies of the Texans escalated into a full-scale rebellion. Austin gave the call to arms on September 19, 1835, stating, "War is our only recourse. There is no other remedy."[17] Anglo-Americans enjoyed very real advantages in 1835. They were "defending" terrain with which they were familiar. The 5,000 Mexicans living in the territory did not join them, but the Anglo population had swelled to almost 30,000. The Mexican nation was divided, and the centers of power were thousands of miles away from Texas. From the interior of Mexico Santa Anna led an army of about 6,000 conscripts, many of whom had been forced into the army and then marched hundreds of miles over hot, arid desert land. Many were Mayan and did not speak Spanish. In February 1836 the majority arrived in San Antonio, Texas, sick and ill-prepared to fight. Although the Mexican army outnumbered the Anglo contingent, the latter were much better armed and enjoyed the position of being the defenders. (Until World War I, this was a decided advantage during wartime.) Santa Anna, on the other hand, had overextended his supply lines and was many miles from his base of power.

The defenders of San Antonio took refuge in a former mission, the Alamo. In the days that followed, Texans inflicted heavy casualties on the Mexican forces, but eventually the Mexicans' sheer superiority in numbers won out. Much has been written about Mexican cruelty in relation to the Alamo and about the heroics of the doomed men. The result was the creation of the Alamo myth. Within the broad framework of what actually happened—187 Texans barricading themselves in the Alamo in defiance of Santa Anna's force and the eventual triumph of the Mexicans—there has been much distortion.

Walter Lord, in an article entitled "Myths and Realities of the Alamo," sets much of the record straight. Texas mythology portrays the Alamo heroes as freedom-loving defenders of their homes; they were supposedly all good Texans. Actually, two-thirds of the defenders had recently arrived from the United States, and only a half dozen had been in Texas for more than six years. The men in the Alamo were adventurers. William Barret Travis had fled to Texas after killing a man, abandoning his wife and two children. James Bowie, an infamous brawler, made a

---

[16] Barker, pp. 146, 147, 148–149, 162.
[17] Fehrenbach, p. 189.

fortune running slaves and had wandered into Texas searching for lost mines and more money. The fading Davey Crockett, a legend in his own time, fought for the sake of fighting. Many others in the Alamo were men who had come to Texas for riches and glory. These defenders were hardly the sort of men who could be classified as peaceful settlers fighting for their homes.

The folklore of the Alamo goes beyond the legendary names of the defenders. According to Lord, it is riddled with dramatic half-truths that have been accepted as history. Defenders at the Alamo are portrayed as selfless heroes who sacrificed their lives to buy more time for their comrades-in-arms. As the story is told, William Barret Travis told his men that they were doomed; he drew a line in the sand with his sword, saying that all who crossed it would elect to remain and fight to the last. Supposedly all the men there valiantly stepped across the line, with a man in a cot begging to be carried across it. The bravery of the defenders has been *dramatized* in countless Hollywood movies.

In reality the Alamo had little strategic value, it was the best fortified fort west of the Mississippi, and the men fully expected help. The defenders had twenty-one cannons to the Mexicans' eight or ten. They were expert marksmen equipped with rifles with a range of 200 yards, while the Mexicans were inadequately trained and armed with smooth-bore muskets with a range of only 70 yards. The Anglos were protected by the walls and had clear shots, while the Mexicans advanced in the open and fired at concealed targets. In short, ill-prepared, ill-equipped, and ill-fed Mexicans attacked well-armed and professional soldiers. In addition, from all reliable sources, it is doubtful whether Travis ever drew a line in the sand. San Antonio survivors, females and noncombatants, did not tell the story until many years later, when the tale had become well circulated and the myth was a legend. Probably the most widely circulated story was that of the last stand of the aging Davey Crockett who fell "fighting like a tiger," killing Mexicans with his bare hands. This is a myth; seven of the defenders surrendered, and Crockett was among them. They were executed. And, finally, one man, Louis Rose, did escape.[18]

Travis's stand delayed Santa Anna's timetable by only four days, as the Mexicans took San Antonio on March 6, 1836. At first, the stand at the Alamo did not even have propaganda value. Afterwards, Houston's army dwindled, with many volunteers rushing home to help their families flee from the advancing Mexican army. Most Anglo-Texans realized that they had been badly beaten. It did, nevertheless, result in massive aid from the United States in the form of volunteers, arms, and money. The cry of "Remember the Alamo" became a call to arms for Anglo-Americans in both Texas and the United States.[19]

After the Alamo and the defeat of another garrison at Goliad, southeast of San Antonio, Santa Anna was in full control. He ran Sam Houston out of the territory northwest of the San Jacinto River and then camped

[18] Walter Lord, "Myths and Realities of the Alamo," *The American West* 5, no. 3 (May 1968): 18, 22, 24.
[19] Lord, p. 25.

an army of about 1,100 men near San Jacinto. There, he skirmished with Houston on April 20, 1836, but did not follow up his advantage. Predicting that Houston would attack on April 22, Santa Anna and his men settled down and rested for the anticipated battle. Texans, however, attacked during the *siesta* hour on April 21. Santa Anna had made an incredible blunder. He knew that Houston had an army of 1,000, yet he was lax in his precautionary defenses. The surprise attack caught him totally off guard. Shouts of "Remember the Alamo! Remember Goliad!" filled the air. Houston's successful surprise attack ended the war. He captured Santa Anna, who had no choice and signed the territory away. Although the Mexican Congress repudiated the treaty, Houston was elected president of the Republic of Texas.

The battle of San Jacinto was literally a slaughter of the Mexican forces. Few prisoners were taken. Those who surrendered "were clubbed and stabbed," some on their knees. The slaughter . . . became methodical: the Texan riflemen knelt and poured a steady fire into the packed, jostling ranks. . . .[20] They shot the "Meskins" down as they fled. The final count showed 630 Mexicans dead versus 2 Texans.

It is commonly believed that after the surrender Texan authorities let Santa Anna off lightly, but, according to Dr. Castañeda, Santa Anna "was mercilessly dragged from the ship he had boarded, subjected to more than six months' mental torture and indignities in Texas prison camps."

The Texas victory paved the way for the Mexican-American War, feeding the growing nationalism of the young Anglo-American nation. Officially the United States had not taken sides, but men, money, and supplies poured in to aid fellow Anglo-Americans. U.S. citizens participated in the invasion of Texas with the open support of their government. Mexico's minister to the United States, Manuel Eduardo Gorostiza, vehemently protested the "arming and shipment of troops and supplies to territory which was part of Mexico, and the dispatch of United States troops into territory clearly defined by treaty as Mexican territory."[21] General Edmund P. Gaines, Southwest Commander, had been sent into Western Louisiana on January 23, 1836; shortly thereafter, he crossed into Texas in an action that was interpreted to be in support of the Anglo-American filibusters in Texas: "The Jackson Administration made it plain to the Mexican minister that it mattered little whether Mexico approved, that the important thing was to protect the border against Indians and Mexicans."[22] U.S. citizens in and out of Texas loudly applauded Jackson's actions. The Mexican minister resigned his post in protest. "The success of the Texas Revolution thrust the Anglo-American frontier up against

---

[20] Carlos Castañeda, *Our Catholic Heritage in Texas, 1519–1933.* vol. 7, *The Church in Texas Since Independence, 1863–1950* (New York: Arno Press, 1976), p. 5.

[21] Lota M. Spell, "Gorostiza and Texas," *Hispanic American Historical Review,* no. 4 (November 1957): 446.

[22] Brack, pp. 74–75.

the Far Southwest, and the region came at once into the scope of Anglo ambition."[23]

THE INVASION OF MEXICO

The United States during the nineteenth century moved its boundaries westward. In the mid-1840s, Mexico was again the target. Expansion and capitalist development moved together. The two Mexican wars gave U.S. commerce, industry, mining, agriculture, and stockraising a tremendous stimulus. "The truth is that [by the 1840's] the Pacific Coast belonged to the commercial empire that the United States was already building in that ocean."[24]

The United States's population of 17 million people of European extraction and 3 million slaves was considerably larger than Mexico's 7 million, of which 4 million were Indian, and 3 million Mestizo and European. The United States acted arrogantly in foreign affairs, partly because its citizens believed in their inherent cultural and racial superiority. Mexico was plagued with financial problems, internal ethnic conflicts, and poor leadership. General anarchy within the nation conspired against its cohesive development.[25]

By 1844 war with Mexico over Texas and the Southwest was only a matter of time. James K. Polk, who strongly advocated the annexation of Texas and expansionism in general, won the presidency by only a small margin, but his election was interpreted as a mandate for national expansion. Outgoing President Tyler decided to act and called upon Congress to annex Texas by joint resolution; the measure was passed a few days before the inauguration of Polk, who accepted the arrangement. In December 1845, Texas became a state.[26]

Mexico promptly broke off diplomatic relations with the United States, and Polk ordered General Zachary Taylor into Texas to "protect" the border. The location of the border was in doubt. Texas contended it

[23] Burl Noggle, "Anglo Observers of the Southwest Borderlands, 1825–1890: The Rise of a Concept," *Arizona and the West* (Summer 1959): 122.

[24] Van Alstyne, p. 106.

[25] Medina Castro, p. 74, Charles A. Hale, *Mexican Liberalism in the Age of Mora, 1821–1853* (New Haven, Conn.: Yale University Press, 1968), pp. 11–12, 16.

[26] On March 1, 1845, Congress passed the joint resolution, but it was not until July 1845 that a convention in Texas voted to accept annexation to the United States. The political maneuverings behind annexation in the U.S. Congress document the economic motive underlying it. Van Alstyne, p. 104, writes: "The pro-annexationists, some of whom like Senator Robert J. Walker of Mississippi had speculated heavily in Texas real estate, managed to influence public opinion in both North and South to the point where, on March 1, 1845, sufficient votes were mustered in Congress to authorize admission to the Union. There was a small margin of votes in each house in favor of annexation: in the House of Representatives, 22; in the Senate, only two."

was at the Rio Grande, but based on historical precedent, Mexico claimed it was 150 miles farther north, at the Nueces River.[27] Taylor took his forces across the Nueces into the disputed territory, wanting to provoke an attack.

In November 1845, Polk sent John Slidell on a secret mission to Mexico to negotiate for the disputed area. The presence of Anglo-American troops between the Nueces and the Rio Grande and the annexation of Texas made negotiations an absurdity. They refused to accept Polk's minister's credentials, although they did offer to grant him an ad hoc status.[28] Slidell refused anything less than full acceptance and returned to Washington in March 1846, convinced that Mexico would have to be "chastised" before it would negotiate. By March 28, Taylor had advanced to the Rio Grande with an army of 4,000.

Polk, incensed at Mexico's refusal to meet with Slidell on his terms and at General Mairano Paredes' reaffirmation of his country's claims to all of Texas, began to draft his declaration of war when he learned of a Mexican attack on U.S. troops in the disputed territory. He immediately declared that the United States had been provoked into war, that Mexico had "shed American blood upon the American soil." On May 13, 1846, Congress declared war and authorized the recruitment and supplying of 50,000 troops.[29]

Years later, Ulysses S. Grant said that he believed Polk wanted and planned for war to be provoked and that the annexation of Texas was, in fact, an act of aggression. He added: "I had a horror of the Mexican War . . . only I had not moral courage enough to resign. . . . I considered my supreme duty was to my flag."[30]

[27] José María Roa Barcena, *Recuerdos de la Invasión Norte Americana (1846–1848)*, ed. I. Antonio Castro Leal (México, D.F.: Editorial Porrua, 1947), pp. 25–27.

[28] Albert C. Ramsey, ed. and trans., *The Old Side or Notes for the History of the War Between Mexico and the United States* (reprint ed., New York: Burt Franklin, 1970), pp. 28–29; Ramón Alcaraz et al., *Apuntes para la Historia de la Guerra Entre México y los Estados Unidos* (México, D.F.: Tipografía de Manuel Payno, Hiho, 1848), pp. 27–28. For an excellent account of Slidell's mission set Dennis Eugene Berge, "Mexican Response to United States Expansion, 1841–1848" (Ph.D. dissertation, University of California, 1965). Berge fully documents Slidell's arrogance, stating that at one point he even threatened war.

[29] J. D. Richardson, *A Compilation of the Messages and Papers of the Presidents*, 10 vols. (Washington, D.C., 1905), 4:428–442, quoted in Arvin Rappaport, ed., *The War with Mexico: Why Did It Happen?* (Skokie, Ill: Rand McNally 1964), p. 16. Mexican authorities had been requested by Taylor to leave the area; most impartial sources consider his refusal a hostile act, especially since he accompanied it by a naval blockade of Mexican supply ships servicing Matamoros. Troops clashed initially on April 26, 1846; but the first major confrontation did not take place until May 8, 1846, 12 miles north of Matamoros (Berge, pp. 196–297. In short, the movement of U.S. troops forced the war on Mexico (Brack, p. 146).

[30] Grady McWhiney and Sue McWhiney, eds., *To Mexico with Taylor and Scott, 1845–1847* (Waltham, Mass.: Praisell, 1969), p. 3.

The poorly equipped and poorly led Mexican army stood little chance against the thrust of expansion-minded Anglos. Even before the war Polk planned a campaign of three stages: (1) Mexicans would be cleared out of Texas; (2) Anglos would occupy California and New Mexico; and (3) U.S. forces would march to Mexico City to force the beaten government to make peace on Polk's terms. And that was the way the campaign basically went. In the end, at a relatively small cost in men and money, the war netted the United States huge territorial gains. In all, the United States took over 1 million square miles of Mexican lands.[31]

THE RATIONALE FOR CONQUEST

In his *Origins of the War with Mexico: The Polk-Stockton Intrigue*, Glenn W. Price states: "Americans have found it rather more difficult than other peoples to deal rationally with their wars. We have thought of ourselves as unique, and of this society as specially planned and created to avoid the errors of all other nations."[32] In this vein, many Anglo-American historians attempt to dismiss the Mexican-American War by simply stating that it was a "bad war," which took place during the United States' era of Manifest Destiny.

Manifest Destiny had its roots in Puritan ideas, which continue to influence Anglo-American thought to this day. According to the Puritan ethic, salvation is determined by God. The establishment of the City of God on earth is not only the duty of those chosen people predestined for salvation, but is also the proof of their state of grace. This belief carried over to the Anglo-American conviction that God had made them custodians of democracy and that they had a mission, that is, that they were predestined to spread its principles. As the young nation survived its infancy, established its power in the defeat of the British in the War of 1812, expanded westward, and enjoyed both commercial and industrial success, its sense of destiny heightened. Many citizens believed that God had destined them to own and occupy all of the land from ocean to ocean and pole to pole. Their mission, their destiny made manifest, was to spread the principles of democracy and Christianity to the unfortunates of the hemisphere. By dismissing the war simply as part of the era of Manifest Destiny the apologists for the war ignore the consequences of the doctrine.

The Monroe Doctrine of the 1820s told the world that the Americas were no longer open for colonization or conquest; however, it did not say anything about that limitation applying to the United States. Uppermost in the minds of the U.S. government, the military, and much of the public was the acquisition of territory. No one ever intended to leave Mexico without extracting territory. Land was the main motivation.

Further obscuring the issue of planned Anglo-American aggression

---

[31] Brack, p. 2.

[32] Glenn W. Price, *Origins of the War with Mexico: The Polk-Stockton Intrigue* (Austin: University of Texas Press, 1967), p. 7.

is what Professor Price exposes as the rhetoric of peace, which the United States has traditionally used to justify its aggressions. The Mexican-American War is a study in the use of this rhetoric.

Consider, for example, Polk's war message of May 11, 1846, in which he gave his reasons for going to war:

> The strong desire to establish peace with Mexico on liberal and honorable terms, and the readiness of this Government to regulate and adjust our boundary and other causes of difference with that power on such fair and equitable principles as would lead to permanent relations of the most friendly nature, induced me in September last to seek reopening of diplomatic relations between the two countries.[33]

He went on to state that the United States had made every effort not to inflame Mexicans, but that the Mexican government had refused to receive an Anglo-American minister. Polk reviewed the events leading to the war and concluded:

> As war exists, and notwithstanding all our efforts to avoid it, exists by the act of Mexico herself, we are called upon by every consideration of duty and patriotism to indicate with decision the honor, the rights, and the interests of our country.[34]

Historical distance from the events has not reduced the prevalence of this rhetoric. The need to justify has continued. In 1920 Justin F. Smith received a Pulitzer prize in history for a work that blamed the war on Mexico. What is amazing is that Smith allegedly examined more than 100,000 manuscripts, 120,000 books and pamphlets, and 200 or more periodicals to come to this conclusion. It is fair to speculate that he was rewarded for relieving the Anglo-American conscience. His two-volume "study," entitled *The War with Mexico*, used analyses such as the following to support its thesis:

> At the beginning of her independent existence, our people felt earnestly and enthusiastically anxious to maintain cordial relations with our sister republic, and many crossed the line of absurd sentimentality in the cause. Friction was inevitable, however. The Americans were direct, positive, brusque, angular and pushing; and they would not understand their neighbors in the south. The Mexicans were equally unable to fathom our goodwill, sincerity, patriotism, resoluteness and courage; and certain features of their character and national condition made it far from easy to get on with them.[35]

---

[33] Rappaport, p. 16.
[34] Rappaport, p. 16.
[35] Justin H. Smith, *The War with Mexico*, vol. 2, (Gloucester, Mass.: Peter Smith, Publisher, 1963), p. 310.

This attitude of righteousness on the part of government officials and historians toward their aggressions spills over to the relationships between the majority society and minority groups. Anglo-Americans believe that the war was advantageous to the Southwest and to the Mexicans who remained or later migrated there. They now had the benefits of democracy and were liberated from their tyrannical past. In other words, Mexicans should be grateful to the Anglo-Americans. If Mexicans and the Anglo-Americans clash, the rationale runs, naturally it is because Mexicans cannot understand or appreciate the merits of a free society, which must be defended against ingrates. Therefore, domestic war, or repression, is justified by the same kind of rhetoric that justifies international aggression.[36]

Professor Gene M. Brack, in the most recent of these works, attacks those who base their research on Justin Smith's outdated work: "American historians have consistently praised Justin Smith's influential and outrageously ethnocentric account."[37]

THE MYTH OF A NONVIOLENT NATION

Most works on the Mexican-American War have dwelt on the causes and results of the war, sometimes dealing with war strategy.[38] It is necessary, however, to go beyond this point, since the war left bitterness, and since Anglo-American actions in Mexico are vividly remembered. Mexicans' attitude toward Anglo-Americans has been influenced by the war just as the United States' easy victory conditioned Anglo-American behavior toward Mexicans. Fortunately, many Anglo-Americans condemned this aggression and flatly accused their leaders of being insolent, land hungry, and of having manufactured the war. Abiel Abbott Livermore in *The War with Mexico Reviewed* accused his country, writing:

> Again, the pride of race has swollen to still greater insolence the pride of country, always quite active enough for the due observance of the claims of universal brotherhood. The Anglo-Saxons have been apparently persuaded to think themselves the chosen people, annointed race of the Lord, commissioned to drive out the heathen, and plant their religion and institutions in every Canaan they could subjugate. . . . Our treatment both of the red man and

---

[36] Recently it has become fashionable for political theorists to oversimplify the war by reducing it to the victory of one system of production and land tenure over a less progressive one. This kind of extreme economic determinism results in the same conclusions that Justin Smith arrives at. See Raúl A. Fernández, *The United States-Mexico Border: A Politico-Economic Profile* (Notre Dame, Ind.: University of Notre Dame Press, 1977), p. 7. Seymour V. Connor and Odie B. Faulk, *North America Divided: The Mexican War, 1846–1848* (New York: Oxford University Press, 1971).

[37] Brack, p. 185.

[38] Brack, p. 10, states that the general view has been that Mexico erred because it chose to fight rather than "negotiate."

the black man has habituated us to feel our power and forget right. . . . The passion for land, also, is a leading characteristic of the American people. . . . The god Terminus is an unknown deity in America. Like the hunger of the pauper boy of fiction, the cry had been, 'more, more, give us more.'[39]

Livermore's work, published in 1850, was awarded the American Peace Society prize for "the best review of the Mexican War and the principles of Christianity, and an enlightened statesmanship."

The United States provoked the war and then conducted it violently and brutally. Zachary Taylor's artillery leveled the Mexican city of Matamoros, killing hundreds of innocent civilians with *la bomba* (the bomb). Many Mexicans jumped into the Rio Grande, relieved of their pain by a watery grave.[40] The occupation that followed was even more terrorizing. Taylor's regular army was kept in control, but the volunteers presented another matter:

> The regulars regarded the volunteers, of whom about two thousand had reached Matamoros by the end of May, with impatience and contempt. . . . They robbed Mexicans of their cattle and corn, stole their fences for firewood, got drunk, and killed several inoffensive inhabitants of the town in the streets.[41]

There were numerous eyewitnesses to these incidents. For example, on July 25, 1846, Grant wrote to Julia Dent:

> Since we have been in Matamoros a great many murders have been committed, and what is strange there seemes [sic] to be very week [sic] means made use of to prevent frequent repetitions. Some of the volunteers and about all the Texans seem to think it perfectly right to impose on the people of a conquered city to any extent, and even to murder them where the act can be covered by dark. And how much they seem to enjoy acts of violence too! I would not pretend to guess the number of murders that have been committed upon the persons of poor Mexicans and our soldiers, since we have been here, but the number would startle you.[42]

On July 9, 1846, George Gordon Meade, who like Grant later became a general during the U.S. Civil War, wrote:

> They [the volunteers] have killed five or six innocent people walking in the street, for no other object than their own amusement.

[39] Abiel Abbott Livermore, *The War with Mexico Reviewed* (Boston: American Peace Society, 1850), pp. 8, 11, 12.

[40] T. B. Thorpe, *Our Army on the Rio Grande*, quoted in Livermore, p. 126.

[41] Alfred Hoyt Bill, *Rehearsal for Conflict* (New York: Knopf, 1947), p. 122.

[42] John Y. Simon, *The Papers of Ulysses S. Grant*, vol. 1 (London, England and Amsterdam: Feffer & Simons, 1967), p. 102.

... They rob and steal the cattle and corn of the poor farmers, and in fact act more like a body of hostile Indians than civilized Whites. Their officers have no command or control over them. ... [43]

Taylor knew about the atrocities, but Grant observed that Taylor did not restrain his men. In a letter to his superiors, Taylor admitted that "There is scarcely a form of crime that has not been reported to me as committed by them."[44] Taylor requested that they send no further troops from the state of Texas to him. These marauding acts were not limited to Taylor's men. The cannons from U.S. naval ships destroyed much of the civilian sector of Vera Cruz, leveling a hospital, churches, and homes. The bomb did not discriminate as to age or sex. Anglo-American troops destroyed almost every city they invaded; first it was put to the test of fire and then plundered. *Gringo* volunteers had little respect for anything, desecrating churches and abusing priests and nuns.

Military executions were common. Captured soldiers and civilians were hanged for cooperating with the guerillas. Many Irish immigrants, as well as some other Anglos, deserted to the Mexican side, forming the San Patricio Corps.[45] Many of the Irish were Catholics, and they resented treatment of Catholic priests and nuns by the invading Protestants. As many as 260 Anglo-Americans fought with the Mexicans at Churubusco in 1847:

> Some eighty appear to have been captured. ... A number were found not guilty of deserting and were released. About fifteen, who had deserted before the declaration of war, were merely branded with a "D," and fifty of those taken at Churubusco were executed.[46]

Others received two hundred lashes and were forced to dig graves for their executed comrades.[47]

These acts were similar to those in Monterey when George Meade wrote on December 2, 1846:

> They plunder the poor inhabitants of everything they can lay their hands on, and shoot them when they remonstrate; and if one of their number happens to get into a drunken brawl and is killed, they run over the country, killing all the poor innocent people they find in their way to avenge, as they say, the murder of their brother. ... [48]

[43] William Starr Meyers, ed., *The Mexican War Diary of General B. Clellan*, vol. 1 (Princeton: Princeton University Press, 1917), pp. 109–110.

[44] Quoted in Livermore, pp. 148–149.

[45] Smith, vol. 1, p. 550, n. 6.

[46] Smith, vol. 2, p. 385, n. 18.

[47] Livermore, p. 160.

[48] Meyers, vol. 1, pp. 161–162.

As Scott's army left Monterey, they shot Mexican prisoners of war.[49]

Memoirs, diaries, and news articles written by Anglo-Americans document the reign of terror. Samuel F. Chamberlain's *My Confessions* is a record of Anglo racism and destruction. He was only 17 when he enlisted in the army to fight the "greasers." At the Mexican city of Parras, he wrote:

> We found the patrol had been guilty of many outrages. . . . They had ridden into the church of San José during Mass, the place crowded with kneeling women and children, and with oaths and ribald jest had arrested soldiers who had permission to be present.[50]

On another occasion, he described a massacre by volunteers, mostly from Yell's Cavalry, at a cave:

> On reaching the place we found a "greaser" shot and *scalped*, but still breathing; the poor fellow held in his hands a Rosary and a medal of the "Virgin of Guadalupe," only his feeble motions kept the fierce harpies from falling on him while yet alive. A Sabre thrust was given him in mercy, and on we went at a run. Soon shouts and curses, cries of women and children reached our ears, coming apparently from a cave at the end of the ravine. Climbing over the rocks we reached the entrance, and as soon as we could see in the comparative darkness a horrid sight was before us. The cave was full of our volunteers yelling like fiends, while on the rocky floor lay over twenty Mexicans, dead and dying in pools of blood. Women and children were clinging to the knees of the murderers shrieking for mercy. . . . Most of the butchered Mexicans had been scalped; only three men were found unharmed. A rough crucifix was fastened to a rock, and some irreverent wretch had crowned the image with a bloody scalp. A sickening smell filled the place. The surviving women and children sent up loud screams on seeing us, thinking we had returned to finish the work! . . . No one was punished for this outrage.[51]

Near Satillo, Chamberlain reported the actions of Texas Rangers. His descriptions were graphic:

> [A drunken Anglo] entered the church and tore down a large wooden figure of our Saviour, and making his lariat fast around its neck, he mounted his horse and galloped up and down the *plazuela*, dragging the statue behind. The venerable white-haired Priest, in attempting to rescue it, was thrown down and trampled under the feet of the Ranger's horse.[52]

[49] Winfield Scott, *Memoirs of Lieut.-General Scott*, vol. 2 (New York: Sheldon, 1864), p. 392.

[50] Samuel E. Chamberlain, *My Confessions* (New York: Harper & Row, 1956), p. 75.

[51] Chamberlain, pp. 87, 88.

[52] Chamberlain, p. 174.

Mexicans were enraged and attacked the Texan. Meanwhile, the Rangers returned:

> As they charged into the square, they saw their miserable comrade hanging to his cross, his skin hanging in strips, surrounded by crowds of Mexicans. With yells of horror, the Rangers charged on the mass with Bowie Knife and revolver, sparing neither age or sex in their terrible fury.[53]

Chamberlain blamed General Taylor not only for collecting over $1 million (from the Mexican people) by force of arms, but also for letting "loose on the country packs of human bloodhounds called Texas Rangers." He goes on to describe the Rangers' brutality at the Rancho de San Francisco on the Camargo road near Agua Fria:

> The place was surrounded, the doors forced in, and all the males capable of bearing arms were dragged out, tied to a post and shot! . . . Thirty-six Mexicans were shot at this place, a half hour given for the horrified survivors, women and children, to remove their little household goods, then the torch was applied to the houses, and by the light of the conflagration the ferocious *Tejanos* rode off to fresh scenes of blood.[54]

These wanton acts of cruelty, witnessed by one man, augmented by the reports of other chroniclers, add to the evidence that the United States, through the deeds of its soldiers, left a legacy of hate in Mexico.[55]

THE TREATY OF GUADALUPE HIDALGO

By late August 1847 the war was almost at an end. General Winfield Scott's defeat of Santa Anna in a hard-fought battle at Churubusco put Anglo-Americans at the gates of Mexico City. Santa Anna made overtures for an armistice, and for two weeks negotiations were conducted. Santa Anna reorganized his defenses and, in turn, the Anglo-Americans renewed their offensives. On September 13, 1847, Scott drove into the city. Although Mexicans fought valiantly, the battle left 4,000 of their men dead with another 3,000 taken prisoner. On September 13, before the occupation of Mexico City began, *Los Niños Héroes* (The Boy Heroes) fought off the conquerors and leapt to their deaths rather than surrender. These teenage cadets were Francisco Márquez, Agustín Melgar, Juan Escutia, Fernando Montes Oca, Vicente Suárez, and Juan de la Berrera. They became "a symbol and image of this unrighteous war."[56]

[53] Chamberlain, p. 174.

[54] Chamberlain, pp. 176–177.

[55] Stephen B. Oates, *"Los Diablos Tejanos:* The Texas Rangers," in Odie B. Faulk and Joseph A. Stout, Jr., eds., *The Mexican War: Changing Interpretations* (Chicago: Sage, 1973), p. 121.

[56] Alonso Zabre, *Guide to the History of Mexico: A Modern Interpretation* (Austin, Tex.: Pemberton Press, 1969), p. 300.

Although beaten, the Mexicans continued fighting. The presidency devolved to the presiding justice of the Supreme Court, Manuel de la Peña y Peña. He knew that Mexico had lost and that he had to salvage as much as possible. Pressure mounted, with U.S. troops in control of much of present-day Mexico.

Nicholas Trist, sent to Mexico to act as peace commissioner, had arrived in Vera Cruz on May 6, 1847, but controversy with Scott over Trist's authority and illness delayed arrangements for an armistice and hostilities continued. After the fall of Mexico City, Secretary of State James Buchanan wanted to revise Trist's instructions. He ordered Trist to break off negotiations and come home.[57] Polk apparently wanted more territory from Mexico while paying less for it. Trist, however, with the support of Winfield Scott, decided to ignore Polk's order, and began negotiations on January 2, 1848, on the original terms. Mexico, badly beaten, her government in a state of turmoil, had no choice but to agree to the Anglo-Americans' proposals.

On February 2, 1848, the Mexicans agreed to the Treaty of Guadalupe Hidalgo, in which Mexico accepted the Rio Grande as the Texas border and ceded the Southwest (which incorporated the present-day states of California, New Mexico, Nevada, and parts of Colorado, Arizona, and to the Anglo-Americans' proposals.

Polk was furious about the treaty; he considered Trist "contemptibly base" for having ignored his orders. Yet he had no choice but to submit the treaty to the Senate. With the exception of article X, which concerned the rights of Mexicans in the ceded territory, the Senate ratified the treaty on March 10, 1848, by a vote of 28 to 14. To insist on more territory would have meant more fighting, and both Polk and the Senate realized that the war was already unpopular in many sections. The treaty was sent to the Mexican Congress for ratification; although the Congress had difficulty forming a quorum, the agreement was ratified on May 19 by a 52 to 35 vote.[58] Hostilities between the two nations were now officially ended. Trist, however, was branded as a "scoundrel," because Polk was disappointed in the settlement. There was considerable support and fervor in the United States for acquisition of all Mexico.[59]

During the treaty talks Mexican negotiators were concerned about Mexicans left behind and expressed great reservations about these people's being forced to "merge or blend" into Anglo-American culture. They protested the exclusion of provisions that protected Mexican citizens' rights, land titles, and religion.[60] They wanted to know the Mexicans' status, and protect their rights by treaty.

---

[57] Dexter Perkins and Glyndon G. Van Deusen, *The American Democracy: Its Rise to Power* (New York: Macmillan, 1964), p. 273.

[58] Robert Self Henry, *The Story of the Mexican War* (New York: Ungar, 1950), p. 390.

[59] See John D. P. Fuller, *The Movement for the Acquisition of All Mexico* (New York: DaCapo Press, 1969).

[60] Letter from Commissioner Trist to Secretary Buchanan, Mexico, January 25, 1848, *Senate Executive Documents*, no. 52, p. 283.

Articles VIII, IX, and X specifically referred to the rights of Mexicans. Under the treaty Mexicans left behind had one year to choose whether to return to Mexico or remain in "occupied Mexico." About 2,000 elected to leave; most remained in what they considered *their* land.

Article IX of the treaty guaranteed Mexicans "the enjoyment of all the rights of citizens of the United States according to the principles of the Constitution; and in the meantime shall be maintained and protected in the free enjoyment of their liberty and property, and secured in the free exercise of their religion without restriction."[61] While Anglo-Americans have respected the Chicanos' religion, their rights of cultural integrity and rights of citizenship have been constantly violated. Lynn I. Perrigo in *The American Southwest* summarizes the guarantees of articles VIII and IX: "In other words, besides the rights and duties of American citizenship, they [the Mexicans] would have some special privileges derived from their previous customs in language, law, and religion."[62]

The omitted article X had comprehensive guarantees protecting "all prior and pending titles to property of every description."[63] When this provision was deleted by the U.S. Senate, Mexican officials protested. Anglo-American emissaries reassured them by drafting a Statement of Protocol on May 26, 1848, which read:

> The American government by suppressing the Xth article of the Treaty of Guadalupe Hidalgo did not in any way intend to annul the grants of lands made by Mexico in the ceded territories. These grants . . . preserve the legal value which they may possess, and the grantees may cause their legitimate (titles) to be acknowledged before the American tribunals.
>
> Conformable to the law of the United States, legitimate titles to every description of property, personal and real, existing in the ceded territories, are those which were legitimate titles under the Mexican law of California and New Mexico up to the 13th of May, 1846, and in Texas up to the 2nd of March, 1836.[64]

Considering the Mexican opposition to the treaty, it is doubtful whether the Mexican Congress would have ratified the treaty without this clarification. The vote was close.

The Statement of Protocol was reinforced by articles VIII and IX, which guaranteed Mexicans rights of property and protection under the law. In addition, court decisions have generally interpreted the treaty as protecting land titles and water rights. Generally, the treaty was ignored

[61] Wayne Moquin et al., eds., *A Documentary History of the Mexican American* (New York: Praeger, 1971), p. 185.

[62] Lynn I. Perrigo, *The American Southwest* (New York: Holt, Rinehart and Winston, 1971), p. 176.

[63] Perrigo, p. 176.

[64] *Compilation of Treaties in Force* (Washington, D.C.: U.S. Government Printing Office, 1899), p. 402, quoted in Perrigo, p. 176.

and during the nineteenth century most Mexicans in the United States were considered as a class apart from the dominant race.[65] Nearly every one of the obligations discussed above was violated, confirming the prophecy of Mexican diplomat Manuel Crescion Rejón who, at the time the treaty was signed, commented:

> Our race, our unfortunate people will have to wander in search of hospitality in a strange land, only to be ejected later. Descendants of the Indians that we are, the North Americans hate us, their spokesmen depreciate us, even if they recognize the justice of our cause, and they consider us unworthy to form with them one nation and one society, they clearly manifest that their future expansion begins with the territory that they take from us and pushing [sic] aside our citizens who inhabit the land.[66]

CONCLUSION

As a result of the Texas War and the Anglo-American aggressions of 1845–1848, the occupation of conquered territory began. The attitude of the Anglo, during the period of subjugation following the wars, is reflected in the conclusions of the past-president of the American Historical Association, Walter Prescott Webb:

> A homogenous European society adaptable to new conditions was necessary. This Spain did not have to offer in Arizona, New Mexico, and Texas. Its frontier, as it advanced, depended more and more on an Indian population. . . . This mixture of races meant in time that common soldiers in the Spanish service came largely from pueblo or sedentary Indian stock, whose blood, when compared to that of the plain Indians, was as ditch water. It took more than a little mixture of Spanish blood and mantle of Spanish service to make valiant soldiers of the timid Pueblo Indians.[67]

In material terms in exchange for 12,000 lives and more than $100,000,000 the United States acquired a colony two and a half times as large as France, containing rich farm lands and natural resources such as gold, silver, zinc, copper, oil, and uranium which would make possible its

---

[65] Weber, p. 14, states that the Supreme Court in *McKinney v. Saviego*, 1855, found that the treaty did not apply to Texas.

[66] Antonio de la Peña y Reyes, *Algunos Documentos Sobre el Tratado de Guadalupe-Hidalgo* (México, D.F.: Sec de Rel. Ext. 1930), p. 159, quoted in Richard Gonzales, "Commentary on the Treaty of Guadalupe Hidalgo," in Feliciano Rivera, *A Mexican American Source Book* (Menlo Park, Calif.: Educational Consulting Associates, 1970), p. 185.

[67] Walter Prescott Webb, *The Great Plains* (New York: Grosset & Dunlap, 1931), pp. 125–126.

unprecedented industrial boom.[68] It acquired ports on the Pacific which generated further economic expansion across that ocean. Mexico was left with its shrunken resources to face the continued advances of the expanding capitalist force on its border.

[68] Leroy B. Hafen and Carl Coke Rister, *Western America*, 2nd ed. (Englewood Cliffs, N.J.: Prentice-Hall, 1950), p. 312.

The Overland Emigrants

JOHN MACK FARAGHER

The image of a train of covered wagons moving slowly but surely over the Great Plains toward California or Oregon is familiar to all Americans who have watched Western movies or television shows. Under the leadership of a skillful captain, the wagons and their occupants managed to surmount innumerable obstacles as they pursued their vision of the American dream. Except for the fact that the caravans were rarely attacked by hostile Indians, the fictional portrayal of this migration is often close to the truth, at least for those aspects of the journey it chooses to describe.

The very existence of this migration points out a major difference between American agricultural life and that of most of the world's farmers. The white farmers of ante-bellum America were not peasants as were most of the rest of the world's agriculturalists. Peasants were virtually fixed on the soil they worked. There was very little mobility, either social or geographical, in peasant societies. In the United States, on the other hand, mobility tended to be the rule rather than the exception. The apparent availability of an unlimited amount of land to be put to the plow undoubtedly contributed to this movement.

Another factor encouraging movement of farmers was the belief that money could be made from farming. From the very beginning of settlement in America, there was a desire on the part of the farmers to turn a profit. Subsistence farming, though widespread, was not satisfactory to those engaged in it. This attitude fueled the restless seeking for new lands and new opportunities for profit making.

The overland migration to the newly opened settlements on the West Coast took place between 1840 and 1870. Prior to that time, only a few hardy explorers, miners, or fur traders set out on the trail. After 1870, the transcontinental railroad provided the means for westward movement. The wagon train adventure in American history, then, is limited to three decades. But the romance of that venture causes it to loom large in the American imagination.

It is noteworthy that in recent years two prizewinning studies of this migration have been published. One, *The Plains Across* (University of Illinois, 1979), by John Unruh, Jr., deals in detail with the entire process, The other, *Women and Men on the Overland Trail* (Yale University Press, 1979), by John Mack Faragher, of Mt. Holyoke College, focuses on the families who undertook the journey. This emphasis on family history leads the author to an extensive study of sex-role differentiation in midwestern agriculture generally, as well as along the trail.

The selection from Faragher's work reprinted below presents a general description of the way the migration was organized, first in large and cumbersome trains and later in smaller, more congenial units composed primarily of kin or friendship-related groups. It is important to note that the westward migrants were not poor people. A certain amount of capital was required in order to outfit one's family for the journey. The only people without capital to make the trip tended to be single, young men who would attach themselves to families and supply labor in exchange for board on the journey.

We have no way of knowing how many of the families who migrated to the West Coast during this period actually bettered themselves economically. It is likely that, because of the newly developing settlements of the Far West, the children of these families found economic opportunities not available to their parents. As the railroad contributed to the rapid expansion of commercial and industrial firms, more opportunities were made available to the migrants. Surely some of the overland migrants of the ante-bellum years benefited substantially as the entrepreneurial spirit encouraged economic diversification and supplied goods and services in rapidly increasing amounts to the growing population of the area. But, whether or not the migrants bettered themselves, it is clear that they looked back upon their journey over the trail as the most significant experience of their lives.

The written record of the overland emigration was left by all kinds of people: city and country folk, college graduates and the barely literate, old and young, rich and poor. Nonetheless, there was a social homogeneity among the writers that reflected the common background of the emigrants, most of whom were poor farmers from the Mississippi Valley. As Francis Parkman observed in 1846, the overland emigrants came from "the extreme Western states."[1] Three-quarters of the writers left homes

---

[1] Francis Parkman, *The Oregon Trail* (New York: New American Library Signet Classics, 1950), p. 419. . . .

in Indiana, Illinois, Iowa, and Missouri, and most of the rest came from closely bordering areas. In 1850 the Midwest was overwhelmingly agricultural. No northern states were more totally devoted to agriculture than these; almost 90 pecent of the adult male workers of the Midwest were farmers, compared to only about two-thirds in the Atlantic and New England states.[2] Within this region the emigrants came from solidly agricultural, nonurban counties.

Emigrant occupations correspond with this profile. Six out of ten male heads of household were farmers. The other men worked at jobs common to a rural or small-town setting: carpenter, blacksmith, cooper, county teacher, doctor, editor, and especially itinerant or parish preacher. Judging from the way almost everyone took up the farmer's calling in Oregon and California, farming must have been a general skill known to most of these men.[3]

Most of the emigrants took up the move with a farmer's motives; they wanted to claim new and better farmlands. Over a quarter of the writers of the diaries and recollections stated unequivocally that new agricultural land was *the* motive in their decision to emigrate. Clarence Dan has put it well: "The impulse toward removal to the West did not arise from a desire to recreate the pattern of the eastern farm left behind, but came from a vision of a rich soil producing an abundant surplus of products, readily salable for cash upon markets which, if not immediately available, would certainly develop and could somehow be reached."[4] Many were leaving a bad economic situation: unable to find cheap but productive lands, unhappy with the out-of-the-way location of the lands they owned, burdened with debt.

John and Cornelia Sharp are examples of these land-hungry emigrants, willing to undergo extreme hardship for new opportunities. A couple in their late thirties with a growing family of children, they had struggled unsuccessfully for years to make their poor farm in Washingon County,

---

[2] Of the adult male work force of these four states, 85.9 percent were in agricultural occupations, 82.3 percent in the north-central census districts (including these four states plus Ohio, Michigan, and Wisconsin). This compares with 67.9 percent in the mid-Atlantic district and 61.6 in New England. Richard Easterlin, "Inter-regional Differences in Per Capita Income, Population and Total Income, 1840–1950," in National Bureau of Economic Research, *Trends in the American Economy in the Nineteenth Century*, Studies in Income and Wealth, vol. 24 (Princeton: Princeton University Press, 1960), pp. 97–98.

[3] Of the 25 Oregon male heads of households who contributed either a diary or a recollection to this study, 22 appear in the federal population schedules for the 1850 census, and 18 of these, or 82 percent, also appear in the agricultural schedules as farm operators. Of the nonfarmer emigrants, 7 out of 10 had taken up farms in Oregon. See Oregon State Archives, *Pioneer Families of the Oregon Territory, 1850*, Bulletin no. 3, Publication no. 17 (Eugene, Ore., 1951). Although I have not collected systematice postemigration data for the rest of the heads of household in this study, these findings correspond with the data I have randomly accumulated.

[4] Clarence H. Danhof, *Change in Agriculture: The Northern United States, 1820–1870* (Cambridge, Mass.: Harvard University Press, 1969), p. 150.

Ohio, pay. In 1848 John decided that they could do better in Oregon. After a strenuous ride of over 900 miles on their homemade Ohio River flatboat, the couple and their seven children disembarked in Independence, Missouri. The Sharps rented two one-room cabins and scratched out a mostly corn diet from the poor soil, all the while working for wages to accumulate the necessary cash for the trip. It took four years, and even then John had to borrow $500 from a nearby brother-in-law for the outfit. All these were acceptable sacrifices for new land to farm.[5]

Oregon and California offered cheap, abundant, and rich lands. Phoebe Judson, who traveled there in 1853, remembered their reason for emigrating quite distinctly: "The motive that induced us to part with the pleasant associations and the dear friends of our childhood days, was to obtain from the government of the United States a grant of land that 'Uncle Sam' had promised to give to the head of each family who settled in this new country."[6] A year earlier this motive had inspired the refrain of a popular camp song:

> Come along, come along—don't be alarmed,
> Uncle Sam is rich enough to give us all a farm.[7]

Certainly other reasons were important: milder winters, a healthier climate, an escape especially from malarial chills and fever. Reasons of health motivated nearly all the emigrants, as Parkman noted.[8] Indeed, a large number decided to emigrate specifically for a change in climate and, they hoped, an improvement in their health.[9] Others went to join family members who had gone earlier. Most left for these and a combination of other, more idiosyncratic reasons. But in general, the promise of free land and changed economic circumstances was the primary attraction for the Judsons, the Sharps, and their midwestern peers. These farmers were motivated by a desire to transform the material conditions around them;

---

[5] The Sharp family left three documents: Cornelia A. Sharp, "Diary: Crossing the Plains from Missouri to Oregon in 1852"; Joseph A. Sharp, "Crossing the Plains"; and James M. Sharp, *Brief Account of the Experiences of James Meikle Sharp.* James Sharp's account is the most complete in background detail.

[6] Phoebe Goodell Judson, *A Pioneer's Search for an Ideal Home,* p. 9. By the 1840s the preemption principle was fully established. Any squatter on unclaimed land could, when the land was surveyed and came up for auction, exercise the first right to buy at a minimum price, usually $2 an acre. In Oregon the Donation Land Act of 1850 provided for grants of 320 acres to single men, 640 to married men; provisions extended until 1855. In California the complexities of Mexican titles left much attractive land vulnerable to squatters.

[7] Camilla Thomson Donnell, "The Oregon Pilgrimage," [in Origin Thomson, *Crossing the Plains* (Greenburg, Ind.: O Thomson, 1896)], p. 8.

[8] Francis Parkman, "The Overland Trail Journal," vol. 2 of *The Journals of Francis Parkman,* ed. Mason Wade (New York: Harper, 1947), p. 442.

[9] See, for example, Margaret M. Hecox, *California Caravan: The 1846 Overland Trail Memoir of Margaret M. Hecox,* and Nancy A. Hunt, "By Ox-Team to California," [*Overland Monthly,* 67 (April 1916)].

the emigration was the most obvious consequence of their willingness to change.[10]

Historians have commonly judged the emigrants to have been "perennial movers," and indeed, most emigrants had moved before.[11] All but 10 percent of the male heads of household had been born in areas outside the Midwest. An examination of the mobility histories of families who made the trek shows that only 22 percent of the male heads of household had made no moves as adults.[12] The majority had moved at least once, many twice, some three or more times. As one would expect, the number of moves increased with age.

But more interesting, most men made their moves at the same general points in their lives. Nearly all had moved westward from their parents' homes in their early twenties (46 percent) or had made a similar move westward within the first two years of marriage (38 percent). Many men moved a second time in their middle thirties; among the men who had been married at least fifteen years by the time of their overland emigration, 80 percent followed their initial move west with a second move, again westward, some ten years later. The combination of these two moves typically took a man from his birthplace on the east coast first to the Appalachian or Ohio River region and finally to the western frontiers of Illinois, Iowa, or Missouri.

[10] The willingness to move and change has long been noted as a characteristic of North American—as opposed to European peasant—farmers. Paul Gates, representing the consensus of opinion in agricultural history, takes this factor to be the essential component in characterizing American farmers. "American farmers regarded their land as the means of quickly making a fortune through the rising land values which the progress of the community and their own individual improvement would give it. Meanwhile they mined the land by cropping it continuously to its most promising staple. They did not look upon it as a lifetime investment, a precious possession whose resources were to be carefully husbanded, whose soil they could enrich and would ultimately pass on to their children more valuable and more productive than when they acquired it." Gates thus emphasizes the element of change in the structure of farming. Paul W. Gates, *The Farmer's Age: Agriculture, 1815–1860* (New York: Holt, Rinehart, and Winston, 1960), pp. 399–400. Clearly a study of migration would support this emphasis. As will become clear . . . , however, I think a more complicated change/tradition structure describes farming more adequately. For a suggestive use of this mixed structure, see James Henretta, *The Evolution of American Society, 1700–1815: An Interdisciplinary Analysis* (Lexington, Mass: D. C. Heath, 1973).

[11] Ray Allen Billington, *Westward Expansion: A History of the American Frontier*, 3d ed. (New York: Macmillan, 1967), p. 5. . . .

[12] Out of the 122 reconstituted families, I was able to complete mobility histories for 58 male heads of household and 21 women. These histories were drawn from diaries and journals, supplemented by family histories, genealogies, local histories, and other sources. I considered a history completed when I could locate an individual residentially for each year up to the year of emigration. By movement I mean such movemnet as would be noted in the sources; generally I have not counted moves within a county.

The association of westward moves with particular points in men's lives suggests that the life cycle of families was influential in the nature and timing of emigration. Families, like institutions and individuals, have their own unique histories. These histories, however, are punctuated by epochal events common to all—marriage, the birth of children, their departure at majority, death. Family sociologists conventionally divide families into four types corresponding to all these stages: newly married couples, still childless; families with all children under fifteen years; families in which the oldest child has reached fifteen; and couples whose children have grown and left to establish families of their own.[13]

Families of each stage are represented in the group of reconstituted emigrant families. Unfortunately the only comparable set of data I have found are drawn from rural North Carolina society in 1934,[14] but if one assumes a similarity between the two populations, it becomes apparent that young families were traveling in proportion to their numbers in the society, while mid-stage families were underrepresented and newlyweds more preponderant. In both populations there were very few independent mature families.[15]

A reexamination of the mobility histories by these structural family types shows a strong association between family stages and movement. On the average, families moved once for each stage of the life cycle they passed through. Mobility, then, was correlated with the first three stages of the family life cycle.

Few newlywed men had previously moved as adults; for them the move to the coast would mean setting up their first homes and farms. Honeymoon emigrations were a tradition. Second-stage couples—those with young children—had also first moved at the time of their marriages, from Pennsylvania to Indiana or from Kentucky to Missouri. Now these young families were making their second major move. After eight or ten years of marriage, six to eight years farming the same ground, perhaps setting aside a few savings, these families felt secure enough to try improving their situation with a move to the coast.

The men of the third family type had come to the agricultural frontier in just such a move, as husbands in young families. The move to the coast was to be their third major move. We are on safe ground when we speculate that families in each stage undertook their moves to the coast

---

[13] This model is not meant to include all types of family structure but merely to provide a general model. I find the concepts of life cycle and family types ably summarized in Lowry Nelson, *Rural Sociology* (New York: American Book Company, 1948), pp. 307–12.

[14] North Carolina, circa 1930, is, of course, a good distance from the Midwest, circa 1850. The two do have the advantage of probably sharing a basic rural social composition. See Nelson, *Rural Sociology*, pp. 310–11.

[15] There were elderly couples on the trail, usually grandparents in kin parties, but I have found only one journal of an older married person—John Udell, *John Udell's Journal*. Because the Udells were the only family in the last stage, I will confine myself to the first three family types in the discussion to follow. In North Carolina, elderly couples were residing with grown children (Nelson, *Rural Sociology*, p. 310); hence, by accident, both mature categories appear the same. . . .

with differing perspectives, perhaps even differing motives. For the couples of the third stage, with near-grown children soon to set out on their own, the move was perhaps a last chance to find the kind of home and farm suitable for their later years, perhaps in a region of abundant good land where their children would not be tempted so far afield in their own search for a place to settle.[16]

The emigration to the coast was, of course, made possible by a variety of objective social developments: large-scale economic and diplomatic trends, the discovery of gold in California, and changing technologies, to name a few. Social events and trends opened possibilities and framed the context for choices by individual men and women. The actual decision to emigrate, however, was made within the personal logic of each family, a subjective process controlled by the movement of the family life cycle. The willingness to pick up and leave the old farming life for a better one —the willingness to change—was so strong that it seemed almost institutionalized. The overland emigration was fundamentally bound up with family life. Because of the traditions that the mobility histories reveal, we can be reasonably certain that emigration at these points was culturally sanctioned; the only question was where they would go.

The emigrants were willing to move, certainly. But relocating was also a question of resources. Unfortunately there is no way to make an objective determination of the emigrants' economic condition from their written documents. We do know that they came from a region with the lowest per capita wealth in the nation.[17] According to their own testi-

[16] This typology has not been simply imposed on the data but has a validity based on the clustering of age-values. Since I have grouped the families into three sequential stages, it is to be expected that the median ages of the husband and wife would increase in each successive stage. More significantly, the ages of the wives are not distributed randomly within each age range but tend to cluster around the median for each age. Thus the semi-interquartile range (defined as half the difference of the range of values for the mid 50 prcent of the cases of a stage) is less than the difference between the medians for two stages in all cases but one. In other words, this is a positive indication that people did not emigrate at just any time but at particular points in the family life cycle. . . .

The median and the quartile deviation are preferable as measures here because they are uninfluenced by extreme, atypical values, unlike the mean and standard deviation. Roderick Floud, *An Introduction to Quantitative Methods for Historians* (Princeton: Princeton University Press, 1975), recommends this approach in demographic work. Because men tend to marry and remarry at a greater variety of ages than women, the age of the wife is a better index to the family life cycle. For a similar assessment, see Crandall A. Shifflett, "The Household Composition of Rural Black Families: Louisa County Virginia, 1880," *Journal of Interdisciplinary History* 6 (1975): 235–60.

[17] In 1850 per capita wealth in the north-central census districts was $249, in the mid-Atlantic district, $358, in New England, $417; calculated from tables in Joseph C. G. Kennedy, *Preliminary Report of the Eighth Census, 1860* (Washington, D.C.: Government Printing Office, 1862), pp. 130, 195. Per capita annual income was similarly distributed: $47 in the north central districts, $77 in the mid-Atlantic, $83 in New England; Easterlin, "Interregional Differences," pp. 97–98.

mony, they were an unprosperous lot. Almost two-thirds of the emigrant writers were silent about their economic status, but of those who did write about it, nearly half the emigrants thought of themselves as poor and another third as middling. Considering their ages, of course, the newlywed and young families had not yet had the time to acquire much wealth.

At any rate, few emigrants had much financial flexibility. Peter Burnett, emigrant of 1843, knew his audience when he wrote that "the trip to Oregon is not a costly or expensive one. An individual can move here as cheap if not cheaper than he can from Tennessee or Kentucky to Missouri."[18] Agricultural historians, however, point out that the initial costs of farming were not insubstantial. The preparations for a trip across the continent and investment in new farmlands in the valleys of the Willamette or the Sacramento required some personal capital.[19] Emigrants had to have some means, but how much?

Contemporary estimates as well as historians' hindsight both suggest that farmers would have been safe to start with from $500 to $1,000 in cash or property.[20] Few emigrants could come up with funds like those; each farmer would need carefully to assess his needs, hoping to meet them with ingenuity and sagacity in lieu of funds. He could count first of all on his own and his family's labor, and very possibly the help of neighbors, in clearing fields, fencing, constructing a first rude shelter and outbuilding, and digging his well. He could hope to meet subsistence costs of the first year by temporary employment with the Hudson's Bay Company or at Sutter's Fort in the 1840s, or in the stable Oregon or heady California economies of the 1850s. Farm animals and seed could also be purchased with this income. Draft animals and a wagon would come with the family over the trail.

The essential costs, then, were those of the trip itself. The trail's special conditions required a new set of goods, although some household and farm goods could be converted for trail use. The means of transportation—a wagon, oxen, and running gear—were the most expensive, coming close to $400. The wagon had to be constructed with care for the journey:

[18] Peter H. Burnett, "Letters," p. 421. Burnett had considerable knowledge on this point; he made the move from Tennessee to Missouri in 1817, and after two moves within Missouri returned to Tennessee in 1826, finally moving back to Missouri again in 1830.

[19] Clarence Danhof, "Farm Making Costs and the Safety Valve," *Journal of Political Economy* 44 (1941): 317–59.

[20] Danhof, *Change in Agriculture*, pp. 114–15. Merrill E. Jarchow, *The Earth Brought Forth: A History of Minnesota Agriculture to 1865* (St. Paul: Minnesota Historical Society, 1949), p. 6, cites the Minnesota commissioner of statistics' estimate (1860) of $795 to start a farm; William Oliver, *Eight Months in Illinois* [(Chicago: W. M. Hill, 1924; original edition, 1834)], pp. 240–46, suggested a range of $500 to $1,000, depending on the availability of labor; Robert E. Ankli, "Farm-Making Costs in the 1850s," *Agricultural History* 48 (1974): 51–74, reviewing recent work with census data, revises Danhof's estimate of $1,000 down to $500.

strong enough to transport provisions for six months, but light enough for a reasonable team. Emigrants commonly employed a 2,000 to 2,500-pound farm wagon with a flat bed about ten feet long with two-foot sides. It had to be made of well-seasoned hardwood to stand the trip's great extremes of temperature and moisture; an ordinary farm wagon would not do. Emigrants were particularly careful in the purchase of a wagon. Other skilled farmers, to economize and be sure, took the time to make their own. Benjamin Bonney remembered that his father "put in his spare time for months making a strong sturdy wagon in which to cross the plains."[21] A wagon of this size loaded with some 2,500 pounds required a team of six mules or more commonly four yoke of oxen. Since emigrants were completely dependent upon these animals, keeping weight down to conserve the animals' strength was all-important. The provisions for the entire trip and all the baggage would have to conform to the weight limitations of the team.

The limitation on weight showed most obviously in the emigrants' diet. People prepared to exist on the staples of bread, bacon, and coffee, but these were not sufficient. The list of supplemental foodstuffs mentioned by emigrants is long, but reducible to an essential ten or fifteen. Some of these could be brought from home, but most of the trail fare was special and had to be purchased in quantity. A family of four would be lucky to spend less than $120 for food stores. Cooking utensils too were purchased specially for the trip, and contemporary estimates suggest a minimum of $20 for a four-person mess.

Each family would already possess firearms, but the Indian presence was sufficient inducement for many to trade up in quality or add to their store. There was also a healthy supply of powder, lead, and shot to buy: $60 or $70 for arms.[22]

With these minimums, and emigrant family could count on spending an initial $125 to $150 per person before crossing the Missouri. If the oxen, rifle, and foodstuffs such as bacon, lard, and dried fruit could be brought from the family farm, the cost could be cut down to $70 per person. To this had to be added cash for toll ferries (established on the trail as early as 1847), emergency provisions along the way, and cash for the first few weeks on the coast while the men were looking for work.[23] For some, raising this kind of money was no problem. Wealthy farmers like James Frazier Reed of Sangamon County, Illinois, purchased his stores with savings. But for most, the investment required liquidating their property holdings, and many emigrants sold their household goods as well as their farms to finance the move. Here again is evidence of the

[21] Benjamin F. Bonney, *Across the Plains by Prairie Schooner* [(Eugene, Ore.: Kohe-Tiffany, 1923)], p. 1.

[22] R. Carlyle Buley, *The Old Northwest: Pioneer Period, 1815–1840* (Indianapolis: Indiana Historical Society, 1950), 1:153.

[23] "If you want to come you must start by the first of April with six or seven yoke of oxen to the wagon and as much as one or two hundred dollars in cash." Lafayette Spencer to William Spencer, Oregon Territory, December 27, 1852, in Lafayette Spencer, "Journal of the Oregon Trail," *Annals of Iowa* 8 (1908): 309.

willingness to change: most left with all their worldly goods loaded in the wagons.

Purchased goods, plus other necessary items brought from home—candles, towels, soap, articles of personal hygiene, sewing supplies, changes of clothing, and essential tools—must have weighed in at around 550 pounds per person. For one quarter of the families, weight presented no problems, since they took extra wagons over and above the minimum required and enjoyed considerable cargo space (2,500 to 3,500 pounds was the general range). Most emigrants, however, were pressed to economize and tried to carry their weight in the fewest possible number of wagons. Economic pressures pushed another quarter of the families beyond the weight limits and forced them to overload at the outset of the trip. In 1852 Eliza Brooks answered her husband's call to join him in California and packed her five children and goods into a single four-yoke wagon. She brought along two laying hens and drove two cows, so the fresh eggs and milk along the way may have allowed her to cut the weight of her foodstuffs; nonetheless, the wagon must have been loaded with well over 2,500 pounds of provisions alone.[24]

Most families, however, conformed to the minimum requirements set by their size and took the necessary number of wagons. A family of four could make the trip in a single wagon, although in such a move there was very little capacity for cargo, perhaps space enough for an additional 300 pounds. Ezra and Eliza Meeker, their son, and Ezra's brother Oliver traveled to Oregon in a single wagon in 1852, James and Lavinia Porter, their infant son, and her brother in 1860.[25] But because of their size, the majority of families were compelled to take more than one wagon. A single vehicle simply could not be crammed with enough provisions for all. Since each wagon could be loaded with 2,500 pounds, emigrants generally had a little extra space; on the average families should have been able to pack in cargo weighing 1,000 to 1,200 pounds.

Within these limits, without overloading, what could a family take? With an eye to a farmer's priorities, we can surmise that the means of production were at the top of the list. The farm tools were the first items packed after the essentials. The writer of an advice circular for the 1843 emigration suggested that "each man should have the necessary implements of husbandry to go right to work and each mechanic should take his tools with him." This counsel was nearly universal. Joel Palmer warned against taking "useless trumpery" but urged farmers and craftsmen to take a long list of tools "as it is difficult getting such articles" on the coast.[26] Any room left over was probably allocated according to the

24 Elisha Brooks, *Pioneer Mother of California* [(San Francisco: Herr Wagner, 1922)], p. 5.

25 Ezra Meeker, *Covered Wagon Centennial and Ox Team Days* [(Yonkers-on-Hudson, N.Y.: World Book Company, 1922)], Lavinia Honeyman Porter, *By Ox Team to California: A Narrative of Crossing the Plains in 1860* [(Oakland, Calif.: Oakland Enquirer Publishing Company, 1910)].

26 "Advice to Prospective Emigrants to Oregon," *Iowa Capitol Reporter*, March 25, 1843, reprinted in *Oregon Historical Quarterly* 15 (1914): 297; Joel Palmer, *Journal of Travels*, in Early Western Travels, 1748–1846, ed. R. G. Thwaites

priorities of individual families. Some took books, others household articles, extra clothing, perhaps a camp oven, or some items of furniture.
To be sure, these last were the first items to go overboard when the going
got rough.

This emigrant outfit—wagon and team, provisions, arms, and other
essentials—was designed as a mobile household for one family. Most
emigrants outfitted mainly at home, in family groups, buying their goods
at local establishments. Planning for the trip as a family set the pattern
and the material basis for the entire journey. Except for the collective
planning of some single men during the Gold Rush there was little experi-
mentation with larger-than-family economies. Each family expected to
be mainly self-supporting and most work would be performed in the
context of the family economy.

Outfitted and packed up, emigrant families headed out sometime in
the late winter or early spring for the Missouri River towns known as
the jumping-off places. Nearly three-quarters of the families traveled to
the Missouri in their family wagons.[27] For many this first section of the
trip was a lark; roads were generally good, accommodations readily available at inns or friendly farmhouses. Often the route was set so the travelers
could visit friends or relatives on the way. For others the early parts of
the trip were more of a shakedown cruise. Late winter storms and the
thaw frequently flooded roads, making them temporarily impassable and
the going slow. Perhaps most difficult was the pain of leaving home and
loved ones; the sadness slowly ebbed away as the wagons rolled west.

Before 1849 nearly everyone headed toward Independence, the starting point for the Santa Fe trade and the fur caravans. In these early years
most came by wagon across the settled hills of central Missouri, a third
by steamboat up the Missouri River. The local economy of what would
later be known as Kansas City boomed with the emigrant trade throughout the forties.[28] But Independence was south of the juncture of the
Platte and the Missouri and necessitated a long trek north to the main

---

(Cleveland: Arthur H. Clark, 1906), 30:258, 259, 262. See also Burnett, "Letters,"
p. 417, and Joseph E. Ware, *The Emigrants Guide to California* (Princeton:
Princeton University Press, 1932), p. 5. Overton Johnson and William Winter,
on the other hand, recognized the need but feared the added weight and suggested that the wise farmer-traveler send his tools by ship around the Horn; *Route
across the Rocky Mountains* (Princeton: Princeton University Press, 1932), p.
182. By the late 1850s, when the availability of tools on the coast had brought
down the price, guidebooks advised leaving tools behind; see Randolph B.
Marcy, *The Prairie Traveler: A Hand-Book for Overland Expeditions* (London:
Tribune, 1863), p. 13.

[27] There was a significant difference here between farmers and others. A full 45
percent of men with occupations other than farmer traveled to the Missouri
crossings by boat or train, but only 17 percent of the farmers.

[28] At the beginning of the 1847 season there were over a hundred retail establishments catering to the emigrant trade in Independence. George W. Buchanan,
"Oregon and California" (a circular written for the *Western Expositor*), *Oregon Historical Quarterly* 11 (1910): 310–11.

highway. By 1850 Independence had relinquished its preeminence to other towns upriver; only local emigrants continued to use it as a jumping-off place.

The extension of steamboat service upriver to St. Joseph had drawn most of the emigrant crowd north, closer to the mouth of the Platte.[29] St. Joe was the center for the Gold Rush traffic in 1849 and 1850. With effective steamboat service, and in 1859 the first rail connection from the frontier to the east, St. Joe, of all the crossings, attracted emigrants from the greatest variety of states. From 1846 to 1863 over half the families who crossed at St. Joe arrived by steamboat or train, and of these 60 percent were from states east of Indiana. The river traffic drew wagoneers from the lower Mississippi and Ohio River valleys to the St. Joe crossings.

Council Bluffs, another 160 miles up the Missouri, was not connected by regular steamboat lines until the late fifties, and rail lines creeping across Iowa did not link it with the east until after the Civil War. But the Mormon base camp and ferries established there in 1846 attracted many gentiles. The settlement at Kanesville (permanently renamed Council Bluffs after the last Mormon exodus in 1853) was primitive and rough until commercial lines came through. Nevertheless, nearly six out of every ten emigrants jumped off from Council Bluffs after 1851. Nearly 80 percent of the Council Bluffs emigrant families came from the northern Midwest; it was simply the most convenient crossing for the mass of emigrants with homes in Iowa, Illinois, Indiana, and Wisconsin. In addition many emigrants thought the north side of the Platte a better road and headed for the northern ferries. The rudeness of Council Bluffs could not compare with the Mexican color of Independence, the diversity of St. Joseph, or the commercial prosperity of either of those crossings, but this shabby outpost served the most typical of the overland travelers throughout the fifties: run-of-the-mill midwestern farmers, too poor for steamboats, who traveled across Iowa by wagons provisioned, for the most part, at home. If we were to pick one most characteristic jumping-off place we would do best to remember Council Bluffs; its outward drabness was a reflection of the plain and sturdy character of the farmer-emigrants.

Families drove to the Missouri in small groups, but few families, especially in the forties, thought of setting out for Oregon or California alone. Later, when the road was better known and there were more trading posts and forts along the route, some individual families ventured out, but in the first year emigrants looked to large assemblages of people for support and protection. Over the whole period about half the families traveled without trains, but from 1843 to 1848 almost everyone traveled

---

[29] Louis Hunter, *Steamboats on the Western Rivers* (Cambridge, Mass: Harvard University Press, 1949), pp. 48–49, 488. For railroad connections with the Missouri, see Robert E. Riegel, "Trans-Mississippi Railroads during the Fifties," *Mississippi Valley Historical Review* 10 (1923): 165–68. For a lengthier discussion of the jumping-off points, see Mattes, *Great Platte River Road*, chap. 4, and Unruh, "The Plains Across: [The Overland Emigrants and the Trans-Mississippi West, 1840–1860" (Ph.D. diss., University of Kansas, 1975)], chap. 5.

in organized wagon trains that set out to journey together to either
Oregon or California.

The great trains of the forties were in the tradition of the caravans
of the American Fur Company and the Sante Fe traders. Trans-Mississippi
wagon travel had begun with the trade between Missouri and Sante Fe,
New Mexico, in the 1820s. As we have seen, in the early thirties wagons
began also crossing the continent to the north, carrying furs and goods
up and down the Platte River plain. To maximize efficiency and safety,
these commercial trains organized militarily. The leadership set a line of
march, reconnoitered for water and camp, watched for Indian signs, and
generally kept the train together with a code of discipline.[30]

The first emigrants followed in this tradition. Independence, the
home of the commercial trade, was a natural starting point for their
journey. During April, emigrants gradually assembled in spring camp, a
few miles into Indian territory, waiting for the sprouting grass to ripen
into forage. Usually in early May they set out, following the well-defined
wagon tracks across Indian country to the Platte and beyond, guided by
the experience and the scouts of the commercial trains. Likewise in the
tradition of the earliest trains, emigrants usually settled on a semimilitary
form of organization. An election among the male heads of household
was held for a slate of officers, often from general right down through
colonels, captains, lieutenants, and sergeants.[31] The ranking officers then
divided the train into platoons or companies of armed men to apportion
responsibility and set a rotation for defensive duties.[32] Unlike the commercial trains, however, the emigrant trains were composed of family units,
each of which assumed nearly all responsibility for routine work. Emigrant
trains rarely attempted to collectivize any more than purely defensive
obligations. Some early trains placed minimum requirements on the size of
a family's provisions, but the regulation was intended to guarantee, not
undermine, the essential self-sufficiency of each unit.

The trains were more than simply functional affairs, however, for the
emigrants' concern about Indians and accidents was equaled and in many
cases overpowered by their anxiety about the absence of civil authority.
How would they handle themselves when the constraints of civilization
were loosened? Mary Medley Ackley, remembering her trip of 1852,
wrote; "When we set foot on the right bank of the Missouri River we
were outside the pale of civil law. We were in Indian country, where no

---

[30] Stanley Vestal, *The Old Sante Fe Trail* (Boston: Houghton Mifflin, 1939), pp.
55–75, passim; David Lavender, *Westward Vision: The Story of the Oregon Trail*
(New York: McGraw-Hill, 1963), chap. 12.

[31] See George Wilkes, *A History of Oregon* (New York: n.p., 1945), 2:70; Ed-
ward E. Parrish, "Crossing the Plains," [*Transactions of the Oregon Pioneer
Association* (1888)], p. 95; Joel Palmer, *Journal of Travels*, p. 42; and Samuel
Tetherow, *Captain Sol Tetherow, Wagon Master*, [edited by Fred Lockley
(Portland, Ore., 1923)], p. 23.

[32] In general this picture fits nearly all the organized trains from 1843 through 1848.
See Harrison C. Dale, "The Organization of the Oregon Emigrating Companies," *Oregon Historical Quarterly* 16 (1915): 205:27.

organized civil government existed."[33] Randall Hemitt, traveling to Washington Territory with his uncle's family ten years later, echoed her: "To the westward civil authority practically ceased; everything was in an unsettled condition, and where emigrant parties had joined for security and combined for their own protection each company was a law unto itself. In a region without law are apt to be lawless and troublesome characters."[34]

The wagon train had to be a surrogate society, "a fully equipped American community," in John Minto's description, "with all the incidents of orderly community life."[35] Full societies necessitate a complex organization, and in spring camp the emigrants turned their attention to the form of their temporary society. The earlier the emigration, the more complicated the organization. The huge trains of 1843, '44, '45, and '46 drew up constitutions and bylaws, elected officers, and tried to enforce an overall train discipline.[36] Their adopted rules and regulations specified flat punishments for specific crimes, but more importantly their codes tried to plot a moral direction for the organization: "Every man to carry with him a Bible and other religious books, as we hope not to degenerate into a state of barbarism."[37]

We have been left a view of these trains shaped more by what emigrants wanted them to be than what they actually were. Jesse Applegate's classic, "A Day with the Cow Column," which depicted daily life in a portion of the 1843 emigration, was colorful and picturesque, but in its portrayal of harmony and efficiency Applegate's was an inaccurate account of trail operation. Even at the time, the image of the train was highly romantic, the facade hard to penetrate. James Henry Carleton, on the trail as second lieutenant of the U.S. Dragoons, was beguiled by this image as he observed an 1845 train from a distance: "It was really a beautiful sight to see this company while on the march. The white topped wagons—the long line of cattle—the horsemen upon each flank, with their long rifles—the drivers with their big whips—all moving so regularly forward, that when viewed from a distance it seemed as if they were united and propelled by the same power."[38]

But upon closer inspection the picture of unity dissolved. At their best these little communities stumbled along. Once the fears of Indian attack had been dispelled, for example, the military posture became burdensome. With experience, Carleton shed his earlier illusions; he later

33 Mary E. Ackley, *Crossing the Plains and the Early Days in California* [(San Francisco: privately printed, 1928)], p. 19.

34 Randall H. Hewitt, *Across the Plains and over the Divide* [(New York: Argosy Antiquarian, 1964)], p. 102.

35 John Minto, "Reminiscences," p. 133.

36 See, for example, Burnett, "Letters," p. 407; Tetherow, *Captain Sol Tetherow*; George L. Curry, Letter of May 1, 1846, in Dale Morgan, ed., *Overland in 1846: Diaries and Letters of the California-Oregon Trail* (Georgetown, Calif.: Talisman Press, 1963), pp. 520–23.

37 "Oregon Meeting," reprinted from the *Ohio Statesman*, April 26, 1843, *Oregon Historical Quarterly* 3 (1902): 392.

38 J. Henry Carleton, *The Prairie Logbooks*, ed. Louis Pelzer (Chicago: Caxton Club, 1943), p. 182.

complained about a train captain who "made not a few pretenses of having all manner of duties performed with a method; and where ever there was an opportunity for the introduction of military discipline, and military command, he was sure to improve it. He was . . . what in the army would be called a martinet. Hardly a yoke of oxen could be permitted to drink without a command."[39]

Anxious about the wilderness, emigrants empowered a leadership which soon conflicted with their inherent individualism. Samuel Tetherow recalled the work of his father Solomon as captain of one of those 1845 trains Carleton had observed: "My dad was a pretty good man. He was capable as well as popular. . . . But if you think it's any snap to run a wagon train of 66 wagons with every man in the train having a different idea of what is the best thing to do, all I can say is that some day you ought to try it."[40] Men argued about how fast or slow to move, where to camp, how many guards to post, whether or not to hunt. Any difference was a potential cause of heated argument during the frustrating journey. All these trivial conflicts and more became pretexts for splitting the unmanageable trains into smaller companies.

Parkman provided a glimpse into this disintegration:

> It was easy to see that fear and dissension prevailed among them; some of the men—but these, with one exception were bachelors—looked wistfully upon us as we rode lightly and swiftly by, and then impatiently at their own lumbering wagons and heavy gated oxen. Others were unwilling to advance at all, until the party they had left behind should rejoin them. Many murmuring against the leader they had chosen, and wished to depose him; and this discontent was fomented by some ambitious spirits, who had hopes of succeeding in his place. The women were divided between regrets for the homes they had left and fear of the deserts and savages before them.[41]

The splintering could not be stopped, for the trains were never able to effect any meaningful discipline. The inherent discipline of the company—worker relationship stabilized the fur caravans; in these groups disobedience on the plains was tantamount to mutiny. The Santa Fe traders were tied together by the expedient of protecting their goods; even so, each proprietor was likely to counteract the orders of the elected captain, especially as the train neared Santa Fe and the premium shifted from safety to competition for the best stall at market.[42] Emigrants were even less successful. In the early trains there were some attempts to enforce the collective regulations, and discussions of punishments for infrac-

[39] Ibid., p. 233.
[40] Tetherow, *Captain Sol Tetherow*, p. 8.
[41] Parkman, *The Oregon Trail*, p. 50.
[42] Vestal, *Old Santa Fe Trail*, pp. 57–75, passim; Everett N. Dick, *Vanguards of the Frontier* (New York: D. Appleton-Century, 1941), pp. 187–204; Bernard DeVoto, *Across the Wide Missouri* (Boston: Little, Brown, 1947), p. 34.

tions of the rules can be found in the record.[43] But there is a striking gap between the elaborate sets of regulations and punishments and their actual enforcement. Even for serious crimes, the most common punishment was banishment. This tacit admission of the inability of the trains to govern themselves reflected their lack of unity, a situation that made the elaborate formal organization meaningless.[44]

Emigrants would have had more incentive for maintaining a developed, albeit temporary, society if they had not soon discovered that there were few trail tasks which required efforts beyond the ability of a single family. The family could meet even unexpected exigencies with ad hoc arrangements. Written evidence of the spontaneous cooperation of many people is abundant. Fording rivers, for example, was a task that required great effort and much manpower. "In case of difficulty all helped," wrote Edward Allen on his way to Oregon in 1852 without a train; "in fording the rivers and creeks no sooner was one team over than all went to the aid of the remainder."[45] Unacquainted emigrants worked together for as long as it took to complete a task: "The emigrants that are here, all join and make a bridge," Henry Allyn noted in his 1853 diary.[46] Noah Brooks, also of 1853, remembered that "the cheerfulness with which these emigrants, total strangers to one another buckled to the work, never leaving it until all were safely over, was beautiful to behold."[47] Such cooperative behavior was typical in scores of different areas of work.[48]

Another reason the emigrants soon found trail organization somewhat irrelevant was the dissipation of their concerns about civil authority. There were no sudden outbursts of incivility once established law had been left behind, and in general the emigrants found that society as they knew it pretty much continued in the simple company of other travelers. The big trains nearly all splintered and many dissolved completely after South Pass, not because people decided to go it alone, but because circumstances did not require train organization. By the early fifties travel seemed so much more possible that most people were content simply to fall in and out with each other along the way; indeed, at times the trail was so crowded that they longed for a little family privacy. During the late fifties and sixties parties formed loose trains because of the perceived

---

[43] See, for example, James W. Nesmith, "Diary of the Emigration," pp. 339–40.

[44] For a good discussion of these points in more detail, see David J. Langum, "Pioneer Justice on the Overland Trails," *Wyoming Historical Quarterly* 5 (1974): 421–39.

[45] Edward Jay Allen, "Oregon Trail," n.p.

[46] Henry Allyn, "Journal of 1853," p. 381.

[47] Noah Brooks, "The Plains Across," p. 807.

[48] See, for example, Mrs. Velina A. Williams, "Diary of a Trip across the Plains in 1853," p. 196; Sarah Royce, *A Frontier Lady; Recollections of the Gold Rush and Early California*, [edited by Ralph Henry Gabriel (New Haven: Yale University Press, 1932)], p. 21; Mrs. Lee Whipple-Haslam, *Early Days in California: Scenes and Events of the '50s As I Remember Them* [(Jamestown, Calif., 1923)], p. 10; and Hewitt, *Across the Plains*, pp. 130–31. See also Unruh, "The Plains Across," pp. 197–214.

Indian threat on the Plains, but with some exceptions these later trains were much more limited affairs.

During the forties most emigrants traveled as members of trains, but within the caravans nearly half of all the emigrants traveled with only their conjugal families, including parents and children (with perhaps a hired man or two) but no other companions. Households simply packed up and headed for the spring rendezvous, expecting to take their place in an organized wagon train.

Peter and Harriet Burnett traveled that way. Burnett was an up-and-coming lawyer-politician from the raw western Missouri country. He had stumped all the winter of 1842–43 to organize the first substantial emigration to Oregon. In the spring the Burnetts and their six children moved to the rendezvous some distance outside Independence where Peter continued to pour his considerable energies into the organization of the train. His reward was election on May twentieth as captain of a most unwieldy train of at least 1,000 people, organized into perhaps as many as a hundred distinct parties, along with some 3,000 cattle and other livestock. The inevitable tensions of the march, exacerbated by the diversity of the group, soon made the well-planned organization a mockery, and Burnett resigned after only two weeks. The train divided, ostensibly into two administrative units but actually into a long meandering line of march in which the real solidarities were among kinship and neighborhood groupings. The Burnetts were without permanent associates, and although there were always people close enough with whom to share their extraordinary burdens, it was a lonely trip for Harriet, solely responsible, as she was, for the six children.[49] The same thing must have happened to hundreds of other families who found themselves alone, without kith or kin, on the trail.

Throughout the history of the trail some families—about a third of them—continued to embark on the trip without any company. The instability of train organization could have proved disastrous for them if casual associations had not made up for train failures, although later generations have exaggerated the dangers they faced. There were many accidents, but serious injuries were probably no more common on the trail than on the farm. Cholera was a terrible problem during the epidemics of 1849, '50, '52, and '53, but the complaints of most years were certainly no more fearful than the Mississippi malaria which many were fleeing.

Indians presented few real problems for the emigrants; the toll was great in incessant worry and anxiety, but even this was partially overcome by the exotic and colorful presence they lent to the experience of those emigrants who encountered them. The majority of emigrants, in fact, saw very few Indians along the route. In the 1840s and early fifties the ones they did encounter were a trial but not a serious danger, demanding

[49] Peter H. Burnett, *Recollections and Opinions of an Old Pioneer* [(New York: D. Appleton, 1880)]. This conclusion is based on my own reading and cannot be documented precisely.

tribute in sugar, coffee, or whiskey in exchange for free passage through Indian territory, or simply begging. Through the forties and early fifties there were no war parties directed at emigrants, although occasionally a group of braves might steal stock, a kind of plundering that resulted in a few killings on both sides.

It was when settlers began seriously to encroach on the plains and mountains after 1854 that Indian resettlement, broken treaties, and finally the growing Indian awareness that white farmers would soon lay claim to all the western lands resulted in a more hostile and aggressive attitude on all sides. In the late fifties and sixties the emigrants had to be more vigilant, especially in the regions beyond South Pass, on the routes to southern Oregon and northern California, where 90 percent of all armed conflict took place. But even in those years and regions most people got through with little or no difficulty. Over the whole history of the trail, emigrants undoubtedly killed and injured more Indians than Indians did emigrants, although there were provocation and aggression on both sides. More important at the time was the assistance Indians provided to emigrants down on their luck, by ferrying wagons, guiding lost parties, and sharing food and drink. In general families traveling alone fared reasonably well.[50]

Nonetheless, most emigrants were not content to travel with only the company of their immediate families. Emigrants of the fifties were less likely to travel in large wagon trains but more likely to make arrangements before the trip to travel as a member of a party—a group of individuals and families bound together by agreement, prior acquaintance, or kinship for the duration of the trip. While the emigrants themselves used the terms "train," "party," or "company" imprecisely and interchangeably, "party" as it is used here refers to larger-than-family traveling associations based on personal connections, distinguished from the usually larger and more formal "trains."[51] Parties were mobile and efficient and did not suffer the structural weaknesses of the lumbering trains. Most importantly, parties guaranteed people the company of other travelers. Because the trains broke apart easily and quickly, families like the Burnetts were thrown upon their own resources for social contact; for many this was an isolating and lonely experience. The social needs of the emigrants —a companion for the long walks, company outside the conjugal circle, a place to share a smoke or enjoy a bit of crocheting—could be met in the day-to-day associations of the trail party.

A quarter of the parties were voluntary associations, sometimes composed of acquaintances of the road or spring camps, but more commonly friends and neighbors from back home. In 1846, for example, Charles Imus,

---

[50] My own conclusions on these points are corroborated by Jean Webster, "The Myth of Pioneer Hardship on the Oregon Trail," *Reed College Bulletin* 24 (January 1946): 27–46. For discussion of emigrants and Indians, see Robert L. Munkres, "The Plains Indian Threat on the Oregon Trail before 1860," *Annals of Wyoming* 40 (1968): 193–221, and Unruh, "The Plains Across," chap. 7, where emigrant-Indian cooperation is stressed.

[51] I have reconstructed the traveling arrangements as a part of reconstituting 122 emigrant families. Because a few of these families traveled together, the 122 families constituted 118 parties. . . .

an early settler along the Apple River in northwestern Illinois, organized a party of neighbors to emigrate to California. Included in the company were Imus's nephew, the families of Joseph Aram, Adna Hecox, Charles Isbell, his brother James Isbell, the Savage family, and several single men. All twenty-two members had lived within a few miles of each other and knew each other before the trip.[52] Isaac G. Foster, a prosperous farmer of Plainfield, Illinois, a township thirty miles southwest of Chicago, organized a similar company in 1854. In addition to Foster's family the party included the Burrell clan—Edward and Louisa Burrell, his mother and sister Mary, Mary's fiancé Wesley Tonner, Louisa's parents the Hannibals, and a cousin—the Silas Wrightman family, and five hired men, twenty-two in all.[53]

The most common organizing principle for the party, however, was kinship. Close to half of all the emigrant families traveled in larger-than-family parties based on kin. In a few cases, kinship parties were composed of distant relatives—an uncle with a nephew and niece, a conjugal family with a couple of cousins.[54] But most often the kinship party was a version of an extended family: an association of direct descendants and siblings. Frequently a full three-generation family would make the trip together. The Belshaw clan, for example, left their homes in Lake County, Indiana, for Oregon in 1853. Five of George and Elizabeth's seven grown children, two with families of their own, accompanied their parents. The Parsons and three of the McCarty brothers, all in-laws, also took up with them for Oregon. Counting the cook and three unrelated travelers, there were twenty-six people in the party.[55] The Barber party of 1845 was smaller: Samuel and Susannah with their teenaged and older children, married daughter and her husband, and grandchildren.[56]

Sometimes the first generation was too old, too ill, or too settled to make a move of such consequence; sometimes grandparents were no longer living. But many families were held together by strong sibling unity. Kinship parties were often groups of siblings with their spouses, children, and sometimes in-laws: Jesse, Charles, and Lindsey Applegate together with their families moved from the Osage River country of

---

[52] Joseph Aram, "Reminiscences"; Hecox, *California Caravan; The History of Jo Daviess County, Illinois* (Chicago: H. F. Kett, 1878), pp. 550, 575–76, 610.

[53] Roxanna C. Foster, "The Third Trip across the Continent"; Mary Burrell, "Mary Burrell's Book"; *The History of Will County, Illinois* (Chicago: William LeBaron, Jr., 1878), p. 858.

[54] Hewitt, *Across the Plains;* Mrs. Francis H. Sawyer, "Overland to California."

[55] George Belshaw, "Journey from Indiana to Oregon"; Maria Parsons Belshaw, "Diary"; T. H. Ball, *Lake County Indiana* (Chicago: J. W. Goodspeed, 1873), pp. 101, 147–48, 319–20; T. H. Ball, ed., *Lake County, Indiana, 1884* (Crown Point, Ind.: Lake County Star, 1884), p. 400.

[56] William Barlow, "Reminiscences of 70 Years." In three-generational families norms of residential association are at issue: does the second-generation married couple associate mainly with the parents of the husband (patrilocal) or the wife (matrilocal)? Among these 27 extended family parties there were 17 instances of patrilocal, 19 matrilocal, and 5 bilocal associations. Here parental associations would seem to have been a preferential rather than a customary matter.

Missouri to Oregon in 1843;[57] Gustavus, Jeddadiah, and Harvey Hines left for Oregon from Oswego, New York, with their families ten years later.[58] Usually these sibling parties included sisters as well as brothers. In 1852 Harmon Davis of Mahaska County, Iowa, headed a party for California which included his family and those of his brother and two sisters.[59] That same year, sixty miles to the southeast, Stuart, Eliza, and Caleb Richey, their spouses, and ten children left for Oregon after burying their father.[60]

Both the voluntary and kinship parties afforded the emigrants the security and comfort of numbers, even in the almost inevitable event of a train's collapse. Extended family groups, indeed, could be quite large. The Zumwalt clan, the brothers Jacob and Joseph with their wives, children, children's spouses, and grandchildren, for example, totaled thirty-seven persons.[61] On the road to Oregon in the same year (1853) was the Stearns family: the Reverend John Sterns, an elderly widower, his three married sons, two married daughters, nineteen grandchildren, plus ten more unrelated people, the forty of them occupying ten wagons.[62]

Although the wagon train has been the most enduring image of the overland experience, in fact the most salient social feature of overland emigration and its predominant family cast. The emigration was for many a final severing of family ties and the liberation, for better or worse, of the conjugal family from the bonds of parents. But for nearly half of the family emigrants, the move was undertaken by and with a large network of close kin, with the effect of pulling kin together even though they might previously have lived quite some distance apart. The quest for something new would take place in the context of the very familiar.

In the days of the fur trade, the cross-continental traffic had been predominantly male. The beginning of family emigration in the 1840s completely changed the sexual composition of trail travel. Until 1849 (judging from the available figures for 1843, 1844, and 1846) women constituted 15 to 20 percent of all emigrants. Probably only a few women

[57] Jesse Applegate, "A Day with the Cow Column in 1843"; Jesse A. Applegate, *Recollections of My Boyhood* (Rosebud, Ore.: Review Publishing Company, 1914).

[58] Celinda E. Hines, "Diary of Celinda E. Hines." The party was later joined by the Judsons; see Judson, *Pioneer's Search.*

[59] Mrs. Mary Jane Long, *A True Story: Crossing the Plains in the Year of 1852 with Ox Teams* [(McMinnville, Ore., 1915)].

[60] Stuart and Caleb Richey, "Letters." James Akin, Jr., *Journal* [edited by Edward Everett Dale, *University of Oklahoma Bulletin*, no. 9 (Norman, 1919)], is the record of Eliza Richey Akin's son.

[61] Hunt, "By Ox-Team."

[62] We have three records of the Stearns emigration: Orson A. Stearns, "Appendix [to Mrs. Williams' Diary: Recollections]"; Charlotte Emily Pengra, *Diary of Mrs. Bynon J. Pengra* [(Eugene, Ore.: Lane County Pioneer-Historical Society, n.d.)]; and Velina A. Williams, "Diary." Parties of this size were as large as small trains.

traveled outside families; in fact, there is only one extant diary of a woman traveling without either husband or kin, that of Rebecca Ketcham who traveled along the trail in 1853.[63] Family parties sometimes employed female cooks and servants, but hired hands were integrated as part of the working family unit, and if children are counted as well, we see that the 1840s were years of farm family emigration.[64]

The Gold Rush marked a second fundamental shift in the character of the western emigration. The Army command at Fort Laramie kept a register of passing emigrants in the early 1850s; while some people must have shunned stopping to record their names on the ledger, the emigrants' penchant for leaving their names carved on rocks and cliffs suggests that people might well have been eager to sign up for posterity. Unfortunately the register was lost in a fire in the late fifties, but luckily some cumulative figures were noted and recorded by passing journalists, giving us some figures on the sexual and age composition of the 1850, 1852, and 1853 emigrations.[65] Not surprisingly, the Gold Rushers were overwhelmingly male. Yet in spite of the tens of thousands of single men the absolute number of families on the trail was probably not significantly lower than in previous years. The estimated number of children in 1850, for instance, is in the same range as previous years.

Thus the steady flow of farm families continued through the Gold Rush. In fact it increased dramatically from 1850 to 1852, by a factor of ten judging by the number of children on the trail. A correspondent for the *Daily Missouri Republican* noted the change from previous seasons: "A marked feature of the emigration this year is the number of women who are going out by the land route."[66] It was probably the opening of California as a region of wide economic opportunity that was responsible for the increase in family emigration in these years, along with the liberal provisions of the Donation Land Act of 1850, which granted families twice the land of single men in Oregon.

By the early fifties, then, two groups were moving along the trail together, miners and farmers, single men and families, respectively.[67]

---

[63] Rebecca Ketcham, "From Ithaca to Clatsop Plains."

[64] Thomas Holt, in his journal record of efforts to assist the stranded 1846 emigrants on the southern (Applegate) route to Oregon, described nearly all the emigrants he encountered as members of families. Indeed, when he distributed rations, he divided it among "the families." Thomas Holt, "Journal," in Morgan, *Overland in 1846*, 1:317.

[65] For a discussion of the register, see Julia Cooley Altrocchi, *The Old California Trail* (Caldwell, Idaho: Caxton Printers, 1945), p. 18. Cumulative figures reported in Albert Watkins, ed., *Publications of the Nebraska State Historical Society*, vol. 20 (Lincoln, 1922), pp. 230, 239, 252. LeRoy Hafen and Francis [Marion] Young, *Fort Laramie [and the Pageant of the West, 1834–1890* (Glendale, Calif.: Author H. Clark, 1938)], p. 164, claim that 80 percent of the passing emigrants signed up.

[66] *Missouri Daily Republican*, April 15, 1852, quoted in Watkins, *Publications*, p. 238.

[67] Jack D. Eblen has shown the difference between the social and sexual composition of mining and farming populations in his demographic survey, "An Analysis of Nineteenth Century Frontier Populations," *Demography* 2 (1965): 405.

There are no direct statistical data on the relative size of these unattached male and married populations. For our purposes, however, we can assume that nearly all adult women were married and accompanied by their husbands, and take the percentage of women as a rough index to the number of married couples; consequently the excess of men over women would be a rough estimate of the percentage of unattached men in the emigration.[68] By that standard, the percentage of married people in the total adult population must have fallen from around 50 percent in the 1840s to 20 or 30 percent in the 1850s, while the percentage of single men had doubled as a consequence of the mining boom. For 1853 the statistics have the added dimension of distinguishing between Oregon- and California-bound emigrants, showing that over 85 percent of the single men on the trail were on their way to California, but only 66 percent of the families. The composition of the 1853 Oregon emigration was more nearly like the movements of the 1840s.[69]

Nonetheless, in contrast with the forties, there was a strong and at times predominant male character to the emigrations of the fifties and sixties. Many of these otherwise unattached men, however, traveled within the family system. While the majority of families who left written accounts traveled without hired help, some employed two or three men, so that on the average there were about nine family-hired men working for every ten families on the trail. If this ratio was typical for the emigration as a whole, a fifth of all the unattached men traveled with family parties.[70] The diaries and recollections of men who emigrated to the Pacific Coast without wives, parents, or other kin provide a second perspective.[71] Of 115 accounts by single men, over a third of the writers (37.3 percent) hired into family parties. These rough statistics, meant only to indicate the broad boundaries of the situation, suggest that between 20 and 40 percent of all single men traveled with families if the male-dominated Gold Rush is excluded.[72]

Forty parties, over a third of those reconstructed, employed single

---

[68] Eblen, "Frontier Populations," p. 412, also found that adult women were nearly all married. There were of course some single women on the trail; for mentions see C. B. Glasscock, *Lucky Baldwin* [(Indianapolis, 1933)]; Theodore Edgar Potter, *Autobiography* [(Concord, N.H.: Rumford Press, 1913)]; and William H. Knight, "An Emigrant's Trip." But the numbers of single women were so small as not to seriously affect the assumption I make here.

[69] . . . The Oregon and California statistics are given in the *Missouri Daily Republican*, November 4, 1853, quoted in Watkins, *Publications*, p. 252.

[70] There were .86 hired men per family. Assuming again that most women were married and traveling with families, we can consider .86 times the percentage of women to be an approximation of the percentage of single men traveling in families; . . . Overall, then, it is likely that about 11.6 percent of the emigration were single men in families, or 20.2 percent of all single men.

[71] For the years 1843–48 and 1852–66, excluding the Gold Rush years to avoid biasing the sample in favor of all-male parties.

[72] Adding the hired male and married percentages . . . gives an idea of the percentage of emigrants moving within the family system.

men to drive the wagon, the cattle, or generally to help out with the daily labor of the march. They worked in exchange for board, transportation for their personal outfit, and mutual assistance over the long haul. Essentially this same situation prevailed on the farms at home. In all agricultural areas young men, frequently new arrivals without property, were employed by farm families as occasional or seasonal workers. Probably about 20 percent of the mid-century agricultural work force were wage-earning farm laborers. While the percentage would rise dramatically during the next three decades as midwestern farming shifted to a solid commercial basis, farm labor itself remained within a continuing tradition.[73] Nearly all hired hands lived with individual farm families for the duration of the working season, April to November, and many resided with the families in the crude and cramped frontier accommodations year-round.[74] As recent studies of household composition indicate, boarding among families was a common, even normative situation in nineteenth-century North America.

Some farm workers may have chosen to accompany a family when a decision was made to emigrate. The four hired hands of the Burrell family, for example, seem to have worked for Mrs. Burrell on her Will County, Illinois, farm. Samuel and Jasquay Hall, who traveled the southern route to California with their children in 1853, brought along four hired men from their ranch in addition to their former female slave Delia. Traveling with the Reeds of Sangamon were three hired men, Milt Elliot, James Smith, and Walter Herron—each of whom had worked for Reed in one capacity or another before the trip—the family cook, Eliza Williams, and her brother Baylis. Other men hired on especially for the trip. Reed's friends, Jacob and George Donner of Springfield, placed a help-wanted ad in the *Sangamon Journal* just a few weeks before their departure:

> Who wants to go to California without costing them anything? As many as eight young men, of good character, who can drive an ox

[73] Farm laborers constituted a minimum of 25 percent of the midwestern work force in 1860; calculated from statistics in *Eighth Census of the United States, 1860: Population,* pp. 662–63. All authorities agree that hired hands were under-enumerated in the census, the main evidence for these conclusions. The published census reports do not distinguish between farm workers and farmers until 1860, and even then the latter category includes sharecroppers, tenants, and renters as well as proprietors. The manuscript population schedules, indexed by county, could be employed to develop a more accurate picture, as Curti demonstrates; see Merle Curti, *The Making of an American Community* (Stanford: Stanford University Press, 1959), pp. 449–58. For an extended treatment of agricultural workers, see David Schob, *Hired Hands and Plowboys: Farm Labor in the Midwest, 1815–1860* (Urbana: University of Illinois Press, 1975), especially pp. 250–72. See also [Paul W.] Gates, *Farmer's Age: [Agriculture, 1815–1860* (New York: Holt, Rinehart and Winston, 1960)], pp. 196–99, 272–75, and Curti, *American Community,* pp. 140 ff., 146, 459. See chap. 2 for a discussion of the shift to commercialism.

[74] Schob, *Hired Hands,* pp. 228–30.

team, will be accommodated by gentlemen who will leave this vicinity about the first of April. Come, boys![75]

More typically, however, single men would approach a family or party leader with an offer of assistance in exchange for board. In 1844, for example, John Minto and Willard Rees were hired on by Robert Morrison of Andrew County, Missouri. Early that year twenty-two-year-old Minto had left his coal-mining family in Pittsburgh and headed west for adventure and fortune. On the steamboat to St. Louis he was attracted by the Oregon talk, but having spent his meager savings for transportation to the frontier and an outlandish set of weapons, he was unable, like so many others, to finance his own trip. A friend, however, introduced him to the means of getting passage: "There are men with families and means who need help, and will furnish board to single men for their work."

Morrison and Minto agreed to a simple, direct contract: "I can furnish you," Minto remembered his employer saying, "bed and board, and have your washing and mending done; and you shall give me your help as I require, to get my family and effects to Oregon. I have four guns, and two wagons, and after we are fairly started my oldest children will be able to keep up the loose stock; so that one of us can be spared to hunt every day if we choose, and you shall have your turn at that." Minto was, in other words, accepted as a male family member, almost as a son. By midpoint in the journey Minto's feelings for the family had developed significantly: "The old and the young of the family seemed already something like father and mother and brothers and sisters to me"; he called his party "our traveling family of ten."[76]

Hired men commonly became quite attached to and loved by others in the party. Virginia Ivins was a young wife of twenty with a small child and an infant in arms (born on the trail) in a family party that included her husband, guardian aunt, and uncle traveling to California in 1853. Mr. Ivins was a sober and silent husband, and Virginia came to depend on the five young hired men for conversation and companionship during the trip. The boys, in their turn, each became attached to the small group, to the children and especially to Virginia. Finally, outside Sacramento, came the time to part ways. "Then men seemed loathe to say goodbye," Virginia recalled later, "but by nine oclock next morning all were gone except Louis, who lingered to go into the city with us and say goodbye there. At ten oclock we were again on the road. Louis driving my wagon

---

[75] Burrell, "Mary Burrell's Book"; Margaret Hall Walker, ["Crossing the Plains,"] *The Hall Family Crossing the Plains* [(San Francisco: Wallace Kibbee, 1952)]. The best background on the Donner–Reed party is George R. Stewart, *Ordeal by Hunger: The Story of the Donner Party* (New York: Henry Holt, 1936), especially chap. 2. The Donner literature is enormous, but one can be content with Stewart supplemented by C. F. McGlashan, *History of the Donner Party. A Tragedy of the Sierras* (Truckee, Calif.; Crowley & McGlashan, 1879). The advertisement is reprinted in Morgan, ed., *Overland in 1846*, 2:491.

[76] Minto, "Recollections," pp. 125, 127, 159. See also John Minto, "Biography of Robert Wilson Morrison," *Transactions of the Oregon Pioneer Association* (1894): 53–57. On worker-family contracts generally, see Schob, *Hired Hands*, pp. 209–33.

to be with me a while longer, to tell me all his hopes and fears, and how much he loved us. My tears would come for I had learned to look upon the noble boy almost as a brother. When we reached the city he left us with a sorrowful face, and I never saw him again."[77]

The hired men were largely accepted and trusted as members of the household circle. Years after the trip, Mrs. J. T. Gowdy, a nine-year-old girl when she emigrated with her father and mother, Riley and Mary Kemp, remembered that "our family consisted of my father, mother, eight children and three hired men, 13 in all."[78] Of course there were also instances of argument, of hired men deserting or quitting mid-route. Jessy Quinn Thornton's driver, Albert, without whom the patrician Thornton was quite helpless, tried unsuccessfully to abscond with a yoke of his employer's oxen at Fort Bridger. But examples of such petty contractual relations can be matched with displays of heroic loyalty. Charles Stanton, a bachelor traveling with the George Donners, was one of the few in the Donner party to make it safely over the Sierra pass and into Sutter's Fort when the majority remained stranded in the early snows. But despite his lack of family ties to the emigrants, Stanton returned twice through Sierra blizzards to assist the Donner rescue, finally perishing on his third trip out.[79]

The affective relations between single men and the emigrant families remind us that single men hired on not only for economic but for social reasons as well. Unattached men could and did group themselves into all-male companies, but many men preferred the well-understood and accepted divisions and unities of the family. These men, like John Minto, were attracted to a place where they could find "bed and board" and have their "washing and mending done" in exchange for masculine contributions to the family economy. This was a family, a place of hunting and sewing, a meeting place for men and women. In a move where so much would change, elements of stability were at a premium. The family was the most accessible unit of social organization.

[77] Virginia Wilcox Ivins, *Pen Pictures of Early Western Days* [(n.p., 1905)], p. 121.

[78] Mrs. John T. Gowdy, *Crossing the Plains: Personal Recollections of the Journey to Oregon in 1852* [(n.p., 1906)], p. 1. Cf. Schob's comments on farm family-worker relations: "Farm hands in pre-Civil War America were usually considered members of the family, or at least treated on a fairly equal basis." Schob, *Hired Hands*, p. 228.

[79] Jessy Quinn Thornton, *Oregon and California in 1848* [(New York: Harper & Brothers, 1849)]. For Stanton's story in detail, see Stewart, *Ordeal by Hunger*, pp. 22–23, 55, 77–86, 113, 116, 120–25.

Work Camp and Chinatown

GUNTHER BARTH

Too often the study of immigration in American history deals only with the Atlantic migration, overlooking the fact that there were several waves of immigration from East Asia. The first major wave was a large-scale migration from the Pearl River Delta area of China into California and the West during the gold rush, beginning in 1848. The second was an influx of Japanese settlers on the West Coast around the turn of the twentieth century.

Toward the middle of the nineteenth century, political unrest in China displaced many peasants and urban poor. Many of the latter migrated to Latin America and the American tropics under a system of contract labor that was much like indentured servitude. There they sometimes replaced African‑slaves, whose numbers were dwindling because of the abolition or suppression of the Atlantic slave trade. These Oriental laborers were called "coolies," which in China meant merely unskilled laborers but which in the Western Hemisphere soon acquired the connotation of bound, or involuntary, laborers. In this sense of the word, very few of the Chinese immigrants to the United States were technically coolies, although they were under the strict control of those Chinese organizations who had arranged for their passage, most notoriously, the Six Companies. Most of these immigrants had belonged to the free peasantry in China and thus had roots in the same class that produced the Irish and German immigrants of the period.

If it was difficult for white European immigrants to find a place in the relatively stable Eastern society at mid-century, it was even more difficult for East Asians to move into the highly fluid, rapidly changing, rambunctious society of California. Next to the blacks, the Chinese were the immigrant group most different from the dominant whites. Their physical appearance was distinctive, and they tended to preserve their own language, religion, customs, and culture. Over half of these immigrants were married men who had left their families in China and who found it necessary to work hard and live extremely frugally in order to send money home, to visit their families in China, or to return to China permanently. All these factors tended to set the Chinese apart from white America, though by 1852 the Chinese in California alone numbered 25,000 and made up 10 percent of the state's total population.

Although the Chinese were at first fairly well received because of a desperate shortage of unskilled labor in California, they found themselves less and less welcome as more white laborers became available. They soon came to dominate the restaurant and laundry businesses in San Francisco and in the northern part of the state. Furthermore, they demonstrated an ability to take over apparently worthless mining claims and make them pay by working harder and longer than the white miners. This phenomenon produced so much hostility in the mining camps that the Chinese were frequently barred from owning or working claims. The willingness of the Celestials (as they were often called) to work long hours at low pay, which had originally worked in their favor, came to be seen by white migrants from the East and the South as unfair competition.

As early as 1852 attempts were made to bar the Chinese from admission to the West Coast. Anti-Chinese sentiment culminated in the passage of the Chinese Exclusion Act of 1882. Although this law was intended to halt immigration for only a ten-year period, it virtually put a stop to Chinese migration to the United States. Ironically, it had the effect of opening the West Coast to Japanese immigration, which was stimulated by the need to fill various jobs in the expanding economy that would earlier have been filled by the Chinese.

In his book on the Chinese in the United States in the middle of the nineteenth century, Gunther Barth, of the University of California at Berkeley, has included a chapter on the working and recreational life of the sojourners. That chapter is reprinted below. One can see there the isolation of the Chinese workers and understand clearly the necessity for the development of the Chinatowns which provided the illusion of community and a taste of the familiar for those so far from home.

An invisible control system based on district loyalty, filial piety, and fear circumscribed the realm of Chinese California and re-enforced the basic allegiances of traders and miners in isolated mountain camps. These

"Work Camp and Chinatown." Reprinted by permission of the author and publishers from *Bitter Strength: A History of the Chinese in the United States, 1850–1870*, by Gunther Barth, Cambridge, Mass.: Harvard University Press, Copyright © 1964 by the President and Fellows of Harvard College.

sentiments formed a stronger and more effective confine than the bricks and mortar of the walls of the visible world, or the chains of daily drudgery that bound the indentured emigrants. Consequently, the Chinese quarters of the cities needed merely to symbolize the presence of control without duplicating the whole system. They permitted a release for emotions checked by restraint and oppression, and provided a brief retreat from work in an alien environment into a world resembling home.

Long before large numbers of Chinese withdrew from California's countryside in the 1870s and crowded into settlements in urban centers, Chinatowns acquired a vital role as safety valves of the control system.[1] In these quarters, islands of freedom and license within the reach of the lowliest bordered on centers of authority and oppression. In a crude mixture of order and chaos, the headquarters of district companies and tongs neighbored the theaters and gambling halls. The Chinatowns fleetingly admitted indentured emigrants to a life of affluence. Visions of that leisure once had stimulated the sojourners' dreams of success and had prompted them to leave home and risk years of certain hardship in a strange country in the struggle for an uncertain fortune. The Chinese quarter liberated the indentured emigrants briefly from the shackles of work which debt bondage placed on their shoulders. For hours the excitement of a gambling table or the air of abundance pervading one of the great public festivals elevated them above their lowly status. These brighter interludes added color and brought relief from the gray monotony and strict discipline of an austere world of work.

Descriptions of San Francisco's Chinese quarters in official reports and newspaper accounts of the 1850s and 1860s furnish more useful information than the political, sociological, and missionary polemics, or the fantastic tales of succeeding decades.[2] The Chinatown of popular fancy, if it ever existed at all, flourished between 1882 and 1906. Some of the later belletristic sources also give a broader perspective of the extraordinary life in Chinatown.[3]

The 1850s and 1860s labeled the Chinese quarters in San Francisco

---

[1] A few accounts, such as Arnold Genthe and Will Irwin, *Pictures of* [San Francisco's] *Old Chinatown* (New York, 1908), and Edgar M. Kahn, "Chinatown and the Cable Cars," *Cable Car Days in San Francisco* (Stanford, [1940]), 77–84, in passing touch on this function of Chinatown.

[2] [Alfred Trumble], *The 'Heathen Chinee' at Home and Abroad. Who He Is; What He Looks Like; How He Works and Lives; His Virtues, Vices and Crimes. A Complete Panorama of the Chinese in America. By an Old Californian* (New York, [1882]), and Walter J. Raymond, *Horrors of the Mongolian Settlement, San Francisco, Cal. An Enslaved and Degraded Race of Paupers, Opium Eaters and Leepers* (Boston, [1886?]), combine several aspects.

[3] William Purviance Fenn, *Ah Sin and His Brethren in American Literature* (Peking, [1933]), and John Burt Foster, "China and the Chinese in American Literature, 1850–1950," unpub. diss. University of Illinois, 1952, looked into the literary merits of the writings on Chinatown. Chester B. Fernald, *The Cat and the Cherub and Other Stories* (New York, 1896), and William Norr, *Stories of Chinatown. Sketches from Life in the Chinese Colony of Mott, Pell and Doyers Streets* (New York, [1892]), proved to be helpful.

variously. Little Canton and Little China were two of the appellations in use. However, the name "China Town" appeared as early as 1853 in newspaper reports.[4] Sacramento Street, where Chinese had first located canvas houses in 1849 between Kearny and Dupont Streets, was called by the sojourners T'ang Yen Gai, *t'ang-jen chieh*—the Street of the Men of T'ang, Chinese (Cantonese) Street.[5] The early Chinese occupied scattered localities in San Francisco which were yet a far cry from the later strictly confined area of Chinatown, roughly encircled by California, Stockton, Broadway, and Kearny Streets, and depicted in the "Official Map of Chinatown in San Francisco" published under the supervision of the Special Committee of the Board of Supervisors in July, 1885.[6] In these pages the term Chinatown has been applied indiscriminately to all Chinese settlements in the United States, without regard for *the* Chinatown. Chinese quarters in urban areas, isolated fishing villages, or stores in distant mining camps, irrespective of size or location, all harbored the world of freedom, license, and escape which sanctioned their existence.

In mountain villages and mining towns Chinese stores were the focus of life. As soon as several Chinese moved into a settlement, one of them sent to Marysville, Sacramento, Stockton, or some other supply center for the groceries and other wares needed by the colony.[7] These he sold to his comrades without at first discontinuing his regular work. If the colony increased in numbers, he rented a small store and formed a trading company with the assistance of friends, clan association, or district company. Often, a Chinese physician began to dispense medicines from a supply of drugs ranged along one side of the store, and an itinerant barber made it a place of call. In a short time, an auspicious name, goods from San Francisco, and news from the Pearl River Delta made the store the resort of all Chinese in the vicinity.[8]

In time the aspiring merchant hired a cook who at first was available only for banquets but later ran a small restaurant in an annex. Another

[4] *Alta*, November 21, 1853, October 15, 1857, February 8 (quoting Oroville *Record*), 18, 1858, February 17, 1859; *Herald*, April 12, July 10, 1852, January 17, June 23, 1853; William H. Goetzmann, *Army Exploration in the American West, 1803–1863* (New Haven, 1959), 401. Foster, "China and the Chinese in American Literature, 1850–1950," p. 141, dates the application of the name Chinatown "only after 1860."

[5] William J. Hoy, "Chinatown Devises Its Own Street Names," *California Folklore Quarterly* (Berkeley), 2:72 (April 1943); Hoy, (trans.), "Gold Mountain, Big City, Chinese Map," *California Historical Society Quarterly*, 27:256–58 (September 1948).

[6] "San Francisco As It Is. Chinese Population," *Herald*, April 12, 1852; *Herald*, December 8, 1853, August 22, 1854, June 12, 1857; *Alta*, October 30, 1851, April 25, November 15, 1853, February 15, September 2, 3, 4, 1854, October 15, 1857, May 7, 23, 1858. Willard B. Farwell, *The Chinese at Home and Abroad* (San Francisco, 1885), also has the map, originally part of the Appendix of the San Francisco *Municipal Reports for 1884–85*.

[7] Loomis to Lowrie, December 10, 1860, April 17, 1862, CPBFM.

[8] J. D[ouglas]. Borthwick, *Three Years in California* (Edinburgh, 1857), 266–67, describes briefly the interior of a store.

room housed a couch for opium smokers or a table for gamblers; once a slave girl found her way into the store, another island of freedom and license sprang into existence.[9] On the mining frontier old timers remembered hearing at dusk the call "mei hanna [probably *mo k'un na*]," and took it as a signal for all Chinese who wanted to gamble.[10] Their hunch, essentially correct, did slight injustice to the precise meaning of the invitation, "Not yet to bed." Frequently sojourners from isolated settlements, craving greater diversions than the country store offered, visited larger Chinatowns. In September California farmers came from far and near to Sacramento for the state fair, in October Chinese from the countryside flocked to the capital for their religious festivals.[11] Hardly any of the pictorial advertisements of early California stage lines failed to depict a couple of Chinese traveling on top of the coach.[12] Entire mining companies left their tents, huts, and claims with the beginning of the rainy season to winter in Chinatown.

San Francisco's Chinatown was similar to those of other California settlements.[13] Its Chinese population in the 1850s and 1860s was hardly larger than that of some of the half-forgotten mining towns, where no traces of Chinese life have been preserved save the remnants of a general store, the skeleton of a gambling hall, a dilapidated joss house, or simply the words China or Chinese which were among the most popular of California place names derived from nationalities.[14]

Few indentured emigrants ever shook off the shackles of work for periods longer than a New Year's celebration, a day in the theater, or a night at the fan-tan table. With the explosion of the last firecracker, an actor's closing line, and the loss of the last copper cash, the pressure of the control system brought the sojourners back to their life of service.

[9] *Herald*, August 8, 1853, quoting the Mokelumne *Calaveras Chronicle*, about Chinese gambling and women at Mokelumne Hill.

[10] Fern Coble Trull, "The History of the Chinese in Idaho from 1864 to 1910," unpub. diss., University of Oregon, 1946, p. 30.

[11] Demas Barnes, *From the Atlantic to the Pacific, Overland. A Series of Letters, Describing a Trip from New York, via Chicago, Atchison, the Great Plains, Denver, the Rocky Mountains, Central City, Colorado, Dakota, Pike's Peak, Laramie Park, Bridger's Pass, Salt Lake City, Utah, Nevada, Austin, Washoe, Virginia City, the Sierras and California to San Francisco, Thence Home, by Acapulco, and the Isthmus of Panama* (New York, 1866), 93–95; [Hemmann] Hoffmann, *California, Nevada und Mexico* [(Basel, 1871)], 282–83.

[12] For examples see Harry T. Peters, *California on Stone* (Garden City, New York, 1935), plates 44, 108.

[13] In 1860 Chinese California numbered 34,919 inhabitants. They concentrated in the following counties: El Dorado (4,762), Calaveras (3,657), San Francisco (2,719), Amador (2,568), Placer (2,392), Sierra (2,208), Butte (2,177), Nevada (2,147). "The Indians and Chinese in California," *Alta*, January 13, 1863; [Elmer Clarence] Sandmeyer, *Anti-Chinese Movement in California* [(Urbana, 1939)], 19; Rose Hum Lee, "The Decline of Chinatowns in the United States," *American Journal of Sociology* (Chicago), 54:424 (March 1949).

[14] Erwin Gudde (comp.), *California Place Names; The Origin and Etymology of Current Geographical Names* (2nd rev. ed., Berkeley, 1960), 59.

For a few hours, the atmosphere of Chinatown had alleviated their home-sickness. Their dreams of freedom, dignity, and grandeur released by the visit, vanished rapidly in the ordinary air of Chinese California. Incessant toil and drudgery, rigid regimentation, and strict supervision again filled their ordinary world of labor and debt bondage. Less colorful and exotic than Chinatown, this world of labor has never been adequately depicted, although it harbored the majority of Chinese sojourners and formed the setting which gave Chinatown meaning and value.

Mining and railroad construction work absorbed the masses of in-dentured emigrants. In both occupations large groups of laborers could be easily employed, regimented, and controlled. In mining companies and construction gangs agents of the merchant-creditors applied Chinese Cali-fornia's invisible controls to the world of work. The indentured emi-grants' constant drudgery sustained debt bondage in Chinese California. In the 1850s and 1860s the Chinese drifted also into other pursuits. They found employment as fishermen, freighters, wood choppers, washermen, gardeners, farm hands, and cooks. The world of control also dominated these occupations, although they attracted far fewer laborers than mining and railroad construction.[15]

The life of service in early Chinese California centered around min-ing. Various sources frequently registered the number of Chinese miners during the 1850s and 1860s. The Sacramento *Daily Union* estimated on October 10, 1855, that 20,000 out of 36,557 Chinese on the Pacific Coast mined in the California gold region. Thirty thousand out of 48,391 Chi-nese worked the mines in 1862, according to the calculations of Chinese merchants in San Francisco.[16] By 1873 the Chinese formed the largest single ethnic or national group of of miners, Americans included.[17] How-ever, contemporary writers and chroniclers failed almost completely to record the habits of the Chinese miners. The world of regimented

---

[15] Loomis to Lowrie, March 5, 1864, CPBFM; *Alta*, September 20, October 1, 1849, May 11, 1850, March 31, 1851, March 1, August 28, October 1, 18, 1852, March 24, 28, April 25, May 20, September 28, 1853, February 2, March 25, 1854, August 26, September 16, 1856, October 15, 1857, May 30, July 17, 23, August 13, 1858, June 16, October 29, November 2, 3, December 13, 1859, February 9, 26, May 24, July 7, October 20, 1860, January 14, 28, March 1, 5, 16, 17, 19, April 16, August 22, 1861, March 12, May 7, October 17, November 14, 1862, May 5, July 28, December 9, 1864, March 2, June 6, 1865, January 14, April 1, 5, July 26, Septem-ber 16, 1866, May 12, June 9, September 29, 1867, May 9, 1868; *Herald*, April 12, August 29, 1852, May 16, 23, 1853, January 11, 1854, October 27, 1855, July 2, 18, 24, August 13, 1858, June 6, 1859, May 12, June 16, 1860; [Augustus W. Loomis], "How Our Chinamen Are Employed," *Overland Monthly*, 2:231–240 (March 1869). For data on Orientals in specific industries turn to Ping Chiu, *Chinese Labor in California, 1850–1880; An Economic Study* (Madison, 1963).

[16] "Report of the Joint Select Committee Relative to the Chinese Population of the State of California," Appendix B, Brooks, *Appendix to the Opening Statement*, 73.

[17] John S. Hittell, *The Resources of California, Comprising the Society, Climate, Salubrity, Scenery, Commerce and Industry of the State* (6th rev. ed., San Fran-cisco, 1874), 40–41; Rodman W. Paul, *California Gold, The Beginning of Mining in the Far West* (Cambridge, 1947), 320.

drudgery in the mountain camps has to be pieced together from incidental remarks of travelers, the reminiscences of pioneers, newspaper accounts, and scenes preserved in lithographs and on letter sheets.

Missionary reports and news items depict the arrival of Chinese newcomers at San Francisco, their lodging in company houses, and their subsequent dispatch to the mining region. These accounts form the border
stones of the mosaic delineating the life of service in California.[18] The
Chinese on landing in San Francisco usually remained there but a few
days. They "then proceeded by the steamers to Sacramento, Stockton,
Marysville, and other points on the Sacramento and San Joaquin Rivers."[19]
In these supply centers and in other outfitting posts agents directed the
companies of indentured emigrants into the Mother Lode Country, distributing the miners into camps between Mariposa in the South and
Downieville in the North. The "portly Chinese Agent, Si Mong, one of
our merchant princes," stated the Stockton *Republican* in describing a
supervisor, "is a stout important looking personage, apparently about
thirty-five years of age." He is "quite wealthy and dressed in the most
approved American fashion . . . , has dispensed with his tail appendage,
. . . and has taken unto himself a Mexican lady for a wife, . . . by whom
he has one or two children."[20]

The Chinese miner in the foothills of the Sierra retained his blue
cotton blouse and his "broad trowsers, his wooden shoes," and "his broad
brimmed hat." He wore "his hair close cropped before with a long jet
black queue hanging down behind."[21] His concession to Western civilization consisted of working in American-made boots that were always too

[18] Speer to Lowrie, December 18, 1852, Loomis to Lowrie, March 1, 9, June 25,
September 19, 1860, April 17, 1862, June 29, 1863, CPBFM; *Alta,* May 2, 18, July
29, 1851, February 26, March 28, May 2, 5, June 8, 1852, May 14, October 14,
1854, May 6, 1857, June 8, August 3, 1860, October 17, 1861; *Herald,* May 17,
August 20, December 29, 1851, April 11, 1852, March 2, 1853, July 2, 6, 1857, May
10, 1859; *Daily Evening News,* February 16, 1854; Robert Glass Cleland, ed., *Apron
Full of Gold; Letters of Mary Jane Megquier from San Francisco, 1849–1856*
(San Marino, 1949), 58.

[19] [William] Speer, *Humble Plea* [(San Francisco, 1856)], 18; *Alta,* June 15, 1853,
June 16, 1855 (quoting Georgetown *News*), May 24, July 31 (Stockton *Argus*),
1857, February 18, September 23, 1860; *Herald,* April 21, 1852 (Sacramento
Union), October 28, November 24, 1854; John Russell Bartlett, *Personal Narrative of Explorations and Incidents in Texas, New Mexico, California, Sonora,
and Chihuahua; Connected with the United States and Mexican Boundary Commission, During the Years 1850, '51, '52, and '53,* 2 vols. (New York, 1854), II, 12;
"Mining Life in California," *Harper's Weekly,* 1:632 (October 3, 1857).

[20] *Herald,* June 5, 1858 (quoting Stockton *Republican*). For a brief description of
the Sacramento agency see Speer to Lowrie, December 18, 1852; for Placerville,
Marks to Solis-Cohen, January 13, 1854, Solis-Cohen, "A California Pioneer; The
Letters of Bernhard Marks to Jacob Solis-Cohen (1853–1857)." *Publications of the
American Jewish Historical Society,* 44:22–23 (September 1954).

[21] Edward Eberstadt, ed. *Way Sketches; Containing Incidents of Travel Across the
Plains, From St. Joseph to California in 1850, With Letters Describing Life and
Conditions in the Gold Region By Lorenzo Sawyer, Later Chief Justice of the
Supreme Court of California* (New York, 1926), 124.

large for him. As some observers speculated, he probably delighted in gaining a maximum return from his purchase money. The isolation in which he and his countrymen labored in strictly controlled companies strengthened their adherence to their customary way of life. While "traveling in a desolate mountain region" in 1868, Charles Loring Brace "was much impressed by the sad, lonely form of a Chinaman, walking pensively toward a solitary grave, and scattering little papers as he went, . . . his prayers to the spirit of his ancestors and to the departed."[22]

On the banks of the rivers and in ravines, a correspondent of the San Francisco *Herald* found companies of twenty or thirty Chinese "inhabiting close cabins, so small that one . . . would not be of sufficient size to allow a couple of Americans to breathe in it. Chinamen, stools, tables, cooking utensils, bunks, etc., all huddled up together in indiscriminate confusion, and enwreathed with dense smoke, present a spectacle which is . . . suggestive of anything but health and comfort."[23] The Chinese miners enjoyed little ease. If not crowded into abandoned cabins they dwelt in tents and brush huts. In groups of a hundred they banded together in short-lived villages which studded the Mother Lode or occupied camps deserted by white miners. Rice, dried fish, and tea formed the staples of their diet. Pork and chicken represented the luxuries in the life of service in Chinese California.[24]

Ordinarily the Chinese worked only placers with rockers, long toms, and river dams in companies of ten to thirty men who were supervised by bosses.[25] Occasionally the reports of the United States Commissioner noted Chinese hired for quartz operations or employed in several quartz mills "for certain inferior purposes, such as dumping cars, surface excavation, etc."[26] At times the superstitions of the workers prevented the bosses from engaging their companies in types of mining which disturbed the multitude of gods inhabiting mountains, meadows, and rivers. Apart from this limitation, drawings and photos show headmen and crews in any place where other miners left the Chinese undisturbed.[27] The head-

[22] Charles Loring Brace, *The New West: Or, California in 1867–1868* (New York, 1869), 227.

[23] *Herald*, November 28, 1857.

[24] *Alta*, August 24, 1858 (quoting Mariposa *Gazette*), describes such a Chinese village in the vicinity of Coulterville, Mariposa County. Additional details appear in "Chinese Coulterville Burned Down," *Alta*, July 22, 1859 (Mariposa *Star*), which reports the complete destruction of the village by fire. Rebuilt, fire destroyed Chinese Coulterville again on August 8, 1862; *Alta*, August 22, 1862. Borthwick, *Three Years in California*, 143; [Frank] Marryat, *Mountains*, [*and Molehills* (New York, 1855)], 295–96.

[25] "Chinamen in Rich Diggings," *Alta*, October 9, 1858 (quoting Sacramento *Union*), depicts the operation of a successful Chinese company on the junction of the North and Middle forks of the American River.

[26] Rossiter W. Raymond, *Statistics of the Mines and Mining in the States and Territories West of the Rocky Mountains* (Washington, 1872), 4. This report was also published as *House Ex. Doc. 10*, 42 Cong., 1 Sess.

[27] For pictures of Chinese miners and camps see "A Series of Interesting Sketches and Scenes in California," *Gleason's Pictorial Drawing Room Companion* (Boston), 3:277 (October 30, 1852); Borthwick, *Three Years in California*, facing 264; "The

men bought the claims and directed the reworking of the deserted diggings, the "scratching," as American miners labeled the desolate placers.
"Long files of Chinamen alone break the monotony of the landscape as
they scrape and wash the sands in the nearly dry beds of the torrents,"
Ludovic de Beauvoir observed on his tour through the Sierra Nevada.[28]

The Chinese quickly took to the rocker method of placer mining,
Charles Peters noted, and "a line of sluice boxes appeared to be especially
adapted to their use." They introduced the Chinese water wheel and the
bailing bucket, attached to ropes and manipulated by two men, to clear
holes of water. Given a choice, the Orientals continued to use their familiar tools in their own way.[29] Their working methods endeared the
Chinese miners to the numerous water companies which found in them
faithful customers.

Among the miners "were Chinamen of the better class," J. Douglas
Borthwick noted, "who no doubt directed the work, and paid the common men very poor wages—poor at least in California."[30] Charles Peters
recorded several colorful episodes in the life of Ah Sam, a Chinese boss,
who in 1856 "had a large company of coolies working on Auburn Ra-
vine," near Ophir in Placer County. For twenty-five dollars Ah Sam acquired a log cabin from six Americans who had mined the ground and
dissolved their partnership. Some of his men, under his personal supervision, washed three thousand dollars out of the dirt floor of the cabin,
thus justifying his speculation that the American miners' practice of clearing their gold dust nightly in a blower before the fire had left the floor
covered with particles of gold. However, Ah Sam never admitted to
more than three hundred dollars profit. That, he felt, was all he had

---

Cradle and the Manner of Using It," in "Mining for Gold in California," *Hutch-
ings' Magazine*, 2:5 (July 1857); J. Ross Browne, "Washoe Revisited [Third
Paper]," *Harper's Monthly* (New York), 31:160 (July 1865); [Charles Peters], *The
Autobiography of Charles Peters, In 1915 the Oldest Pioneer Living in California
Who Mined in 'The Days of Old, The Days of Gold, The Days of '49'. Also
Historical Happenings, Interesting Incidents and Illustrations of The Old Mining
Towns in The Good Luck Era, The Placer Mining Days of the '50s* (Sacramento,
[1915]), 142; Carl I. Wheat, ed. " 'California's Bantam Cock,' The Journals of
Charles E. DeLong, 1854–1863," *California Historical Society Quarterly*, 9: facing
348 (December 1930); [Harry T.] Peters, *California on Stone* [(Garden City,
N.Y., 1909)], plates 22, 28; Newell D. Chamberlain, *The Call of Gold; True
Tales on the Gold Road to Yosemite* ([Mariposa, 1936]), facing 26; Mae Hélène
Bacon Boggs, (comp.), *My Playhouse Was A Concord Coach; An Anthology
of Newspaper Clippings and Documents Relating to Those Who made California
History During the Years 1822–1888* ([Oakland, 1942]), 119.

[28] Agnes and Helen Stephenson, (trans.), *Pekin, Jeddo, and San Francisco. The
Conclusion of a Voyage Round the World. By the Marquis* [Ludovic] *de Beauvoir*
(London, 1872), 252.

[29] *Autobiography of Charles Peters*, 141–42; James W. Bartlett, "Annotations to Cox's
Annals of Trinity County," Isaac Cox, *The Annals of Trinity County* (Eugene,
Oregon, 1940), 210; Robert F. G. Spier, "Tool Acculturation Among 19th-Century
California Chinese," *Ethnohistory* (Bloomington), 5:111 (Spring 1958).

[30] Borthwick, *Three Years in California*, 263.

realized with his scheme, since he subtracted from his gain the twenty-seven hundred dollars that two of his men had cheated him out of. These two members of his company, while Ah Sam was busily looking after the cabin floor, discovered, unknown to him, a nugget worth a little less than three thousand dollars as they were shoveling dirt into his sluice box line a short distance from the cabin. They concealed their find, left at night, and sold the nugget in San Francisco.[31]

The ordinary life of Chinese miners with its regimentation and supervision by headmen precluded such escapades. Extreme cases depicting disciplinary measures were most likely to find their way into the newspapers. At Drytown in Amador County a Chinese miner who had stolen four hundred dollars received twenty-five lashes and lost his queue. When he was returned to his mining company his countrymen whipped him again, cut off his left ear, marched him to San Francisco, and shot him by the road.[32] However, the long chain of uneventful days, filled with drudgery and toil, was more typical of the life of Chinese miners.

The working discipline of the mining companies, enforced by constant supervision, accounted for the mass of conflicting reports about the miners' diligence. At times the authors of these accounts marveled at the laborers' incessant toil, "burrowing like ants in the depths" of river beds and ravines; at other times they criticized the miners' lengthy siestas and gay nights. Now and then the workers openly fought the bosses' discipline because there was " 'too muchee workee and too little payee.' "[33] Outside the reach of the headmen's control the Orientals quickly adjusted the rate of their drudgery to their own standards of industry. Cut off from an alien environment by customs and habits, with the bosses controlling contacts with the settlements, the miners eagerly relied on such diversions as the company of their comrades or the nearby Chinese store provided after the working hours.[34]

[31] *Autobiography of Charles Peters*, 143–45. "A Chinaman in Luck," *Herald*, March 24, 1856, records the discovery of a hidden purse in an abandoned cabin by a Chinese miner. See also C. B. Glancock, *A Golden Highway; Scenes of History's Greatest Gold Rush Yesterday and Today* (Indianapolis, [1934]), 122.

[32] *Herald*, June 6, 1853.

[33] Eduard Vischer, "A Trip to the Mining Regions in the Spring of 1859. 'Californischer Staats-Kalender' in the Leap Year A. D. 1860," *California Historical Society Quarterly*, 11:230 (September 1932); Brace, *New West*, 218.

[34] The general picture of Chinese miners is chiefly based on: *Alta*, May 2, 18, July 29, 1851, May 2, 5, 14, 15, June 26, 1852, February 16, June 15, October 12, 13, December 29, 1853, March 4 (quoting Jackson *Sentinel*), 14 (Nevada *Journal*), 29 (Mokelumne *Calaveras Chronicle*), July 6, August 23 (Marysville *Express*), September 11 (Grass Valley *Telegraph*), 1854, May 21 (Mokelumne *Calaveras Chronicle*), June 11 (Sacramento *Union*), June 16, October 26 (Nevada *Democrat*), 1855, October 13, 1856 (Shasta *Republican*), May 19 (Auburn *Press*), July 13 (Auburn *Placer Herald*), 21 (Mariposa *Gazette*), 23 (Mariposa *Democrat*), August 8, October 8, December 2 (Marysville *Express*), 1857, February 1, 13 (Hornitas *Democrat*), 15, March 1 (Sacramento *Bee*), 14 (Placerville *Index*), August 5, 24, October 9, November 11 (Shasta *Courier*), December 5, 6, 1858, January 19 (Auburn *Placer Herald*), 31 (Sonora *Democrat*), February 16 (Coloma

Companies of docile Chinese laborers slowly but surely found their way into the "great army laying siege to Nature in her strongest citadel," the construction crews of the Central Pacific building the Western section of the Transcontinental Railroad.[35] Smaller projects prepared the way for and accompanied the ultimate employment of ten thousand Chinese in the completion of the Pacific Railway.[36] In the late 1850s one hundred and fifty of the five hundred hands working on the San Francisco and Marysville Railroad were Chinese, "employed by a Chinese subcontractor."[37] Other early California railroads, such as the Sacramento and Vallejo Railroad, also used Chinese in grading and track-laying. In 1869 one thousand "obedient Chinese toiled like ants from morning to night" on the construction of the Virginia and Truckee Railroad in the

---

Times), May 21, October 9 (Sacramento Standard), 1859, September 23, December 8 (Mariposa Gazette), 1860, April 3 (Sacramento Union), August 10 (Stockton Independent), October 8 (Mariposa Gazette), 1861, March 12, 1862, January 13, May 3 (North San Juan Hydraulic Press), 1863, July 26, August 6, 1866, November 10, 1867, June 17, 1869; Herald, October 27 (Mokelumne Calaveras Chronicle), December 29, 1851, March 6, April 25, May 9 (Sacramento Union), 10 (Mokelumne Calaveras Chronicle), 12 (Marysville Express), June 9 (Sacramento State Journal), November 26, 1852, March 18, May 24, June 6 ,8, 9, July 4, November 9, 26, December 8, 1853, March 27, 1854, July 31 (Butte Record), August 6 (Mokelumne Calaveras Chronicle), November 12, 1855, March 24 (Auburn Press), April 21 (Mariposa Gazette, Jackson Ledger), May 4, 11, 1856, March 15, 23 (Mariposa Gazette), June 12, November 10 (Shasta Courier), 1858, March 16, April 2, 1861; [John] Carr, Pioneer Days [(Eureka, Calif., 1891)], 69–70; William Shaw, Golden Dreams and Waking Realities; Being the Adventures of a Gold-Seeker in California and the Pacific Islands (London, 1851), 50, 56, 64, 65–66, 81–82, 86, 94–95, 122; Franklin Langworthy, Scenery of the Plains, Mountains and Mines: A Diary Kept upon the Overland Route to California, By Way of the Great Salt Lake: Travels in the Cities, Mines, and Agricultural Districts— Embracing the Return by the Pacific Ocean and Central America, In the Years 1850, '51, '52 and '53 (Ogdensburg, New York, 1855), 184; Marryat, Mountains, 295–97; Speer, Humble Plea, 19–26; "Mining for Gold in California," Hutchings' Magazine, 2:5 (July 1857); "Mining Life in California," Harper's Weekly, 1:632–33 (October 3, 1857); Borthwick, Three Years in California, 51, 55, 143–45, 262–67, 319; Holbrook, "Chinadom in California. In Two Papers.—Paper the Second," Hutchings' Magazine, 4:173 (October 1859); Horace Greeley, An Overland Journey, from New York to San Francisco, in the Summer of 1859 (New York, 1860), 288–89; Francis P. Farquhar, ed. Up and Down California in 1860–1864. The Journal of William H. Brewer, Professor of Agriculture in the Sheffield Scientific School from 1864 to 1903 (Berkeley, 1949), 330, 481; Browne, "Washoe Revisited," Harper's Monthly, 31:159–61 (July 1865); Bowles, Our New West, 400; [Russell H.] Conwell, Why and How [(Boston, 1871)], 126–27; de Beauvoir, San Francisco, 250–53.

[35] Albert D. Richardson, Beyond the Mississippi: From the Great River to the Great Ocean. Life and Adventure on the Prairies, Mountains, and Pacific Coast, 1857– 1867 (Hartford, 1867), 462.

[36] Senate Rept. 689, 44 Cong., 2 Sess., 667, 723; "How Our Chinamen Are Employed," Overland, II (March 1869), 232.

[37] "Monthly Record of Current Events," Hutchings' Magazine, 4:238 (November 1859).

Washoe and Comstock mines of Nevada, "spurred on continually by urgent supervisors."[38]

The steady demand for laborers on the Central Pacific Railroad attracted increasing numbers of Chinese. Between 1863 and 1868 many left the mines, and a large portion of them ended up in the construction force. In the mid-1860s Chinese merchants and American firms at San Francisco, such as Koopmanschap & Co. and Sisson, Wallace, & Co., also began to supply groups of laborers directly from China.[39] Agents of the Central Pacific recruited men in the mountain districts of the Pearl River Delta. They paid for outfit and passage, and received in return from each Chinese a promissory note for $75 in United States gold coin, secured by endorsement of family and friends. The contract provided for regular installments, to complete repayment of the debt within seven months from the time the newcomers commenced labor on the railroad.[40] These shipments tripled the figures of Chinese arriving at the San Francisco Custom House in 1868 and 1869 as compared with the four preceding years. Soon the "rugged mountains . . . swarmed with Celestials, shoveling, wheeling, carting, drilling and blasting rocks and earth."[41]

The use of indentured emigrants and contract laborers on the Pacific section of the Transcontinental Railway provided ammunition for the political warfare following the completion of the road. However, the hearings of congressional investigation committees, the arguments of lawyers, and the explanations of company executives and engineers throw little light on the daily drudgeries of the construction crews. The amassed material leaves the impression that politicians, financiers, lawyers, accountants, and engineers alone built the road.[42] The San Francisco earthquake and fire of 1906 destroyed all existing records of the Southern Pacific Company, including those of the Central Pacific Company. Later attempts to restore the files met with little success.[43] There are incidental remarks of travelers, the information in early railroad guides, and the jottings of itinerant newspaper editors, but these sources fall short of the observations of Hemmann Hoffmann, a Swiss student, who worked as Chinese overseer on the Central Pacific near Dutch Flat in Placer County in 1864 and 1865 and whose notes furnish the outline for the following sketch of the life and work of the Chinese construction companies.[44]

[38] Eliot Lord, *Comstock Mining and Miners. A Reprint of the 1883 Edition* (Berkeley, 1959), 253, 355.

[39] *Senate Rept. 689*, 44 Cong., 2 Sess., 724.

[40] *Alta,* June 24, 1869, contains a statement by a foreman of the Central Pacific about the contract of Chinese laborers.

[41] "Chinese Arrivals at San Francisco Custom House," [Mary Roberts] Coolidge, *Chinese Immigration* [(New York, 1909)], 498; Richardson, *Beyond the Mississippi,* 462.

[42] [F. S. Hickman, publisher], *The Pacific Rail Road, Congressional Proceedings in the Thirty-seventh, Thirty-eighth, and Forty-first Congresses* (West Chester, Pennsylvania, 1875); *Senate Ex. Doc. 51,* 50 Cong., 1 Sess.

[43] Robert Hancocks, Assistant Editor, Bureau of News, Southern Pacific Company, to G. Barth, September 2, 1959; Irene Authier Keeffe, Director, Union Pacific Historical Museum, to G. Barth, September 17, 1959.

[44] Hoffmann, *Californien, Nevada und Mexico,* 210–25. See also Effie Mona Mack,

Along the projected line of work between Dutch Flat and the Nevada boundary, numerous small huts crowded the camps of Chinese workers. The laborers slept and ate on simple wooden cots. Chinese bosses, working with the overseers, effectively kept discipline in the companies. The extra workers in the compounds enabled the headmen to live up to their contracts and to report a complete company of toilers for work every morning. The extras substituted for those workers who on the previous evening had succumbed to the attractions of Chinese stores in the nearby settlements, but who would doubtless show up again for work in a few days. The replacements also filled the gaps left by comrades unable to shake off the effects of a dissolute night. The headmen received wages for the number of men which they regularly reported, and divided the money among all members of their gang. Groups of twelve to twenty men formed a mess and kept a cook who obtained his provisions from the nearest Chinese merchant. At times the kitchen of the white workers furnished meat for the Chinese rice bowls.

During the long working day of grading and track-laying, the sheer number of Chinese workers compensated for the delay caused by the running conversation which accompanied the laborers' drudgery. The multitude of his comrades enabled the individual worker to interrupt his toil frequently for a sip of tea or the forbidden taste of a small pipe of tobacco. At the mercy of his bosses and headmen, disciplined on the job and in the camp, the worker took every opportunity to minimize the effect of the control. Whenever the slightest obstacle interrupted the routine curious laborers crowded together for a brief dispute over the event.

The masses of laborers on the Pacific Railroad appeared to occasional observers as well regimented gangs and smoothly running working machines. Chinese formed part of the celebrated construction crew which on April 28, 1869, laid ten miles of track in a single day. To one of the editors of the *Alta*, the Chinese railroad workers often seemed "in these dreary solitudes . . . the presiding genius." Regimentation and discipline, however, vanished completely when basic differences between district companies broke into the open. The final days of the construction of the Pacific Railroad brought not only the track-laying feast but also the "Grand Chinese Battle in the Salt Lake Valley" between members of the Sze Yap Company and the Yeong Wo Company.[45]

Annual festivals, celebrated with public spectacles and tradition-honored ceremonies, provided a regular outlet from the rigid controls of the

---

Nevada, *A History of the State from the Earliest Times through the Civil War* (Glendale, California, 1936), 374–75; Wesley S. Griswold, *A Work of Giants; Building the First Transcontinental Railroad* (New York, [1962]), 108–25; and Robert West Howard, *The Great Iron Trail; The Story of the First Trans-Continental Railroad* (New York, [1962]), 224–36.

[45] *Alta*, April 25, 30, May 1, 8, 12, 1869; J. N. Bowman, "Driving the Last Spike at Promontory, 1869," *California Historical Society Quarterly*, 36:265–66 (September 1957).

work camp.[46] The atmosphere of the gambling halls, theaters, and other
centers of entertainment and diversion quickly released the indentured
emigrants from the confines of constant toil and loneliness and gave them
a substitute for the missing home. Since the ordinary life of Chinese
workers resembled a succession of days of reckoning, their religious festivals furnished a string of holidays. Like their system of control or their
methods of work, most of their temporary escapes followed forms familiar from the homeland. Scenes of freedom and license gained significance from the work and drudgery which filled the ordinary days of the
sojourners.

The observance of the traditional holidays interrupted the routine.
During these celebrations, employers of Chinese mining companies in
Mariposa County informed the United States Commissioner of Mining
Statistics, the laborers "leave the mines *en masse*, and cannot be induced
to work, for sometimes a week altogether."[47] These festivities momentarily linked the world of Chinese sojourners in California with the familiar scenes of the Pearl River Delta. The impressive ceremonies which
formed part of the popular cycle of the three festivals of the living and
the three festivals of the dead, though Californian in their setting, gave
even on-lookers the illusion of glimpsing life in villages and towns along
the course of the Chu Kiang.[48] Of these six traditional holidays the
Dragon-boat festival never took deep roots in Chinese California, while
New Year's from the beginning occupied a dominant position as the
greatest and gayest occasion of the year.

The first recorded Chinese New Year celebration in the United States
on February 1, 1851, only incidentally served the needs of Chinese California. Primarily it enhanced the status of a single individual. Norman
Assing entertained as his guests "a number of policemen . . . , many ladies and 'China Boys.' " Within two years, however, the celebration lost
its private character and assumed the traits of a "grand holiday . . . ,
with the moving multitude of Celestials rigged out in their finest tog-
gery."[49] Step by step distinctive features of the holiday emerged until the
festival became a California ritual at the beginning of the 1860s.

The blaze and the noise of firecrackers signaled the beginning of the
New Year's Festival. For as many as six days the din of the squibs filled
the air, except during "quiet hours" established in negotiations between the
chief of police and the headmen of the district companies. Gay workers
who crowded the roofs of the brick stores with hundreds of packages of
explosives at their side, abandoned yearlong restraints and pitched ignited
bombs into the crowded alleys. Huge strings of firecrackers, suspended
from the balconies of restaurants, temples, and company houses, emitted
noise and fumes over the multitude of Chinese dressed in new blue cot-

46 [G. B.] Densmore, *Chinese in California* [(San Francisco, 1880)], 64–66, lists the
main festivals of the Chinese in San Francisco.
47 Raymond, *Statistics of Mines and Mining*, 4.
48 *Alta*, October 30, 1853, February 17, 1855, February 16, May 7, 1858, January 23,
1860, February 18, 1863; *Herald*, April 4, 1852.
49 *Alta*, February 3, 1851, February 8, 1853.

ton suits. "The Chinese throughout the State have been celebrating their New Year's Day with an energy which does them credit," the *Alta* observed in 1858. "The number of firecrackers burned and the quantity of noise and smoke let loose are beyond calculation," the paper marveled.[50]

The narrow streets presented the appearance of a small-scale bombardment. A pall of smoke covered the freshly cleaned quarter. The aristocracy of Chinatown donned their "costly fur and silk robes," with "black satin pants fitting tightly at the ankles," and "snow-white stockings and heavy sandals, lined or covered with silk or satin," and made their rounds of New Year's calls. Tables laden with the choicest fruits and conserves greeted these special guests. The multitudes flocked into the brilliantly lighted temples, the festively decorated theater, or the cook shops "where swarms were feasting in the highest apparent bliss." In this pandemonium, filled with the explosions of firecrackers, the din of gongs, the music of countless orchestras, and the elated ejaculations of a thousand voices, the mass of Chinese forgot the grey monotony of their work-filled days.[51]

In the spring the Ch'ing-ming, one of the three festivals of the dead, provided an outlet for pent-up emotions. In early Chinese California, the district companies, clan associations, or groups of men on this day visited the tombs of their members and friends to sweep the graves clean. In the course of two decades this "Chinese Feast of the Dead" developed an elaborate ritual. Covering a period of three or four days, the festival centered around a ceremony in the open brick enclosure, or temple, of San Francisco's Lone Mountain Cemetery.[52]

Nearly every party of Chinese visitors announced its arrival with a fusillade of firecrackers before they arranged around each grave roast pigs, oranges, bananas, pieces of fresh sugar cane, and tiny porcelain cups filled with brandy. After the worshippers had burned baskets of vari-colored papers and conducted other rites, they collected the offerings again. Exchanging congratulations and laughs with their living friends, each group of visitors traveled back to a sumptuous banquet in Chinatown, the rich merchants in the courtliest hacks, followed by an "express wagon loaded with common laborers . . . while a third would be filled

---

[50] *Alta*, February 14, 1858.

[51] *Alta*, February 8, 1853, January 29, 30, 1854, February 8, 17, 1855, January 25, 26, 1857, February 14, 16, 1858, February 2, 4, 1859, January 21, 22, 23, 31, 1862, February 18, 19, 1863, January 14, February 6, 9, 1864, January 2, 26, 27, 28, 1865, January 1, February 12, 14, 15, 1866, February 3, 1867, February 9, 10, 1869; *Herald*, February 15, 20, 1855, February 5, 6, 1856, January 25, 26, 1857, February 13, 14, 1858, February 3, 5, 1859, January 23, 1860, February 11, 12, 1861, January 29, 31, 1862; Huggins, (comp.), *Continuation of the Annals of San Francisco*, 36. For additional descriptions of the New Year's festivities see Farquhar, ed. *Journal of William H. Brewer*, 243, 360–70; Hoffmann, *Californien, Nevada und Mexico*, 316; [James F.] Rusling, *Across America* [(New York, 1875)], 311–12; J. W. Ames, "Day in Chinatown," *Lippincott's Magazine* (Philadelphia) 16:496–97 (October 1875); Mary Cone, *Two Years in California* (Chicago, 1876), 188–90.

[52] "Chinese Temple at Lone Mountain," *Alta*, January 10, 1864. See also *Alta*, November 25, 1863.

with women of the public class only." In the fall, the Feast of Souls and the Midautumn or Moon Festival marked similar ceremonies.[53]

In addition to these and other fixed holidays, Chinese California relied on a multitude of festivities to disrupt temporarily the monotony and restraint of work-filled days. "Where the purse will admit," Augustus W. Loomis observed in 1868, "but few legitimate occasions for feasting are allowed to pass unimproved."[54] The headman's recovery from a dangerous illness, the safe arrival of travelers, or the opening of a temple occasioned elaborate pageants. Universal gaiety and jollity surrounded weddings as well as funerals. The pompous entombment of wealthy Chinese, formally bewailed by groups of official mourners, Buddhist priests, and honored with an impressive procession, or conducted in American style with a richly trimmed mahogany coffin, first class hearse, and thirty carriages of attendants, contrasted with the feasting and mirth which followed. During fashionable nuptial ceremonies, such as the marriage between Cum Chum of the house of Lun Wo & Co. and Ah Too, or the wedding of Tom Quan of the firm of Hong Yuen & Co. to Lai Nyne, banquets, musical performances, and fireworks for one day excited Chinatown. Smaller weddings bridged the interludes between the great affairs.[55]

The pageants of holidays and ceremonies relied for staging on the available settings. They centered around temples, but included restaurants, theaters, gambling houses, opium dens, and brothels in the less ceremonious yet more popular pursuits of the holidays. In the summer of 1853 the Sze Yap Company constructed the first joss house in San Francisco. It dominated all other temples in Chinese California until the Ning Yeong Company opened a larger temple in August 1864, on Dupont Alley, on a lot in the center of the block formed by Pacific, Dupont, Broadway, and Kearny Streets, paying $4,000 for the lot, $12,000 for the construction, and the enormous sum of $16,000 for furniture and decoration. These two temples maintained their leading position among the eight joss houses existing in 1875 and the thirteen located on the Official Map of Chinatown

53 *Herald*, April 3, 4, 5, 12, 1852, October 11, 1853, April 3, 4, 21, 1856, April 19, 1858 (quoting Butte *Record*), April 5, 1860 ("The Chinese Festival Tsing Ming," from Sacramento *Standard*), April 5, October 12, 1861; *Alta*, April 4, 5, September 30, October 22, 1852, April 11, October 11, 1853, February 25, 1854, October 20, 1855, April 27, 1856, March 28, 1861, April 6, 1862, August 23, 1866, April 4, 1868; Caroline C. Leighton, "Chinese Feast of the Dead," *Life at Puget Sound with Sketches of Travel in Washington Territory, British Columbia, Oregon and California, 1865–1881* (Boston, 1884), 215–17.

54 [Augustus W. Loomis], "The Old East in the New West," *Overland Monthly*, 1:363 (October 1868).

55 *Alta*, July 27, August 21, 1851, March 28, 1852, February 25, 1854, November 14, 1855, December 10, 1856, October 10, 1857, February 18, 19, 21, April 23, June 9, 1858, May 9, June 19, July 9, August 24, 1859, January 9, June 7, August 5, 16, December 2, 17, 1860, March 28, 1861, June 22, October 6, 24, 1862, February 19, June 3, October 28, 1863, February 28, November 2, 1864, September 14, 1866, April 5, 8, 27, May 26, November 4, 1867; *Herald*, April 8, November 15, 16, 1855, December 20, 22, 1857, February 20, June 26, 1858, April 25, 1859, March 28, 1861; Huggins, (comp.), *Continuation of the Annals of San Francisco*, 80.

in 1885. The California Supreme Court preserved the public character of the Buddhist rites in the spring of 1859. The justices decided in their review of John Eldridge *v.* See Yup Company that the court had no power to determine whether " 'this or that form of religious or superstitious worship—unaccompanied by acts prohibited by law—is against public policy or morals.' "[56]

Tucked away in ordinary dingy business blocks of Chinatown, the joss houses suggested only to the Chinese sojourners the splendor and magnificence of the Honam Temple or other edifices in the Pearl River Delta.[57] Several flights of narrow stairs led up to the chambers of the enthroned deities located in the top stories of the buildings to guard the idols against thieves and to insure that nothing used by human hands came above the gods. The first "Chinese church," the Sze Yap's temple, was designed by the San Francisco architect Lewis R. Townsend. Except for the "great" Chinese architect who allegedly supervised the construction of John Parrott's Granite Block in 1852, there is no record of any significant activity by oriental designers in early Chinese California.[58]

The sojourners adapted existing American structures to their cultural needs by adding elaborate balconies, paper or bronze lanterns, richly colored inscriptions, and rows of porcelain pots. Similarly, they substituted their own colorful names for the official designations of Chinatown's thoroughfares.[59] A crude brick building with a tin roof formed the joss house in Fiddletown, Amador County, an ugly adobe box constructed in the Spanish-Mexican manner housed the temple at Dutch Flat, Placer County. Wooden frame structures or log buildings served in other settlements, such as San Andreas in Calaveras County or Weaverville in Trinity County. Only the elaborate interior decoration fostered the illusion of ornate Chinese temples.[60]

[56] *Alta,* July 10, 15, 16, 1853, April 5, 1856, May 11, June 19, 1859, January 24, August 16, 1860, January 28, 1861, August 23, 1864, January 27, 1865, August 17, 1867; Eldridge *v.* See Yup Company, 17 Cal. 45; Williams, "City of the Golden Gate," *Scribner's Monthly,* 10:285 (July 1875); [Benjamin E.] Lloyd, *Lights and Shades in San Francisco* [(San Francisco, 1876)], 272–75.

[57] Loomis to Lowrie, November 18, 1859, CPBFM.

[58] *Alta,* July 10, 15, 16, 1853; Harold Kirker, "Eldorado Gothic, Gold Rush Architects and Architecture," *California Historical Society Quarterly,* 38:33–34 (March 1959). Lewis R. Townsend is listed in the San Francisco *City Directory,* 1854, 134, as architect and in the *Directory,* 1858, 271, as architect and civil engineer; he is briefly mentioned in Harold Kirker, *California's Architectural Frontier; Style and Tradition in the Nineteenth Century* (San Marino, 1960), 76, 215.

[59] "The Chinese Quarter," *Herald,* July 25, 1853; "Chinese Houses on Jackson Street," *Herald,* January 7, 1858; [I. J.] Benjamin, *Three Years in America,* [*1859–1862,* 2 vols. (Philadelphia, 1956)], I, 281; Hoy, "Chinatown Devises Its Own Street Names," *California Folklore Quarterly,* 2:71–75 (April 1943).

[60] *Alta,* April 5, 1856, July 24, 1860, August 23, 1864, January 27, 1865; *Herald,* April 21, 1856; Holbrook, "Chinadom in California. In Two Papers—Paper the First," *Hutchings' Magazine,* IV (September, 1859), 131–32; Todd, *Sunset Land,* 275–77; Robert von Schlagintweit, *Californien, Land und Leute* (Köln, 1871), 332–34; Cone, *Two Years in California,* 191–95; Densmore, *Chinese in California,* 61–62; Theodor Kirchhoff, *Californische Kulturbilder* (Kassel, 1886), 99–100.

Restaurants and theaters furnished the extraordinary life of Chinese California with other focal points during the hours when the religious ceremonies turned into feast days. Every restaurant, from the lowliest soup kitchen to the famous cafés of the rich and the dissolute, held its banquets. Musicians and entertainers, in ravishing, dainty garments, lent excitement to a life void of ordinary diversions. To the accompaniment of brass gong, moon guitar, Tartar fiddle, drums, and cymbals they sang operatic ballads, frequently celebrating the past glory of ancient dynasties. At the stage in which food meant less to the guests than liquor and games, the feasters drank and played and played and drank, and their expressions showed a fierceness usually hidden beneath the mask of placid docility that they assumed under regimentation.[61]

On holidays festive multitudes thronged boxes, pit, and balcony of Chinatown's theaters. Following the actors' lines, the singing, the jugglers' feats, and the music of the orchestra, visitors lost themselves in an illusionary world which their imagination built despite the contrast between the barren stage and the actors' dazzling finery. Long historical dramas seemed as endless as the audience's craving for the extension of the illusion. In such plays as "The Return of Sit Ping Quai [Hsieh P'ing-kuei]" the Chinese sojourners suffered for days the warrior's anguish, endured his hardships, basked in his fame, and finally found their way home with the hero to his virtuous wife.

The familiarity of the onlookers with the content of romances, dramas, and ballads, told and retold by storytellers, facilitated the process. The participants in the eagerly solicited world of fancy squatted on crowded benches in a plain hall. On stage Sit Ping Quai balanced on one table protected by a mighty and impassable torrent from the pursuing Princess Liufa three feet away on another. The spectators' freed imagination, however, conveniently dissolved the reality of their world which lacked similar ready escapes from a daily routine of hardship and oppression.[62]

61 *Alta*, October 4, 25, 1849, January 11, September 18, 1850, May 15, 1862; *Herald*, September 30, 1858, May 2, 1860; E[lisha]. S[mith]. Capron, *History of California, From Its Discovery to the Present Time; Comprising Also a Full Description of Its Climate, Surface, Soil, Rivers, Towns, Beasts, Birds, Fishes, State of Its Society, Agriculture, Commerce, Mines, Mining, etc. With a Journal of the Voyage from New York to San Francisco, and Back, via Panama* (Boston, 1854), 154–56; C. J. W. R., "A Dinner with the Chinese," *Hutchings' Magazine*, 1:512–13 (May 1857); Ames, "Day in Chinatown," *Lippincott's Magazine*, 16:497–500 (October 1875); "A Chinese Reception," *Harper's Weekly*, 21:466 (June 9, 1877); F. Taylor, *Between the Gates* (Chicago, 1878), 107–10; Densmore, *Chinese in California*, 47–48; William Henry Bishop, *Old Mexico and Her Lost Provinces; A Journey in Mexico, Southern California, and Arizona by Way of Cuba* (New York, 1883), 338; Daniel Knower, *The Adventures of a Forty-Niner. An Historic Description of California, with Events and Ideas of San Francisco and its People in those Early Days* (Albany, 1894), 49, 81; [Arnold] Genthe and [Will] Irwin, *Pictures of Old Chinatown* [(New York, 1908)], 26–32.

62 *Alta*, October 6, 7, 18, 20, December 20, 25, 1852, April 1, September 2, December 19, 1853, December 14, 1856, May 11, August 12, 15, 1857, February 23, 1859, January 6, May 10, 11, 12, 14, 15, 16, 17, 1860, February 17, 1865, November 21,

Year in, year out, regardless of the occasion, Chinatown provided respite from daily drudgeries. Since the set of holidays barely furnished a legitimate excuse for the enjoyment of these escapes, their pursuit lay outside of the accepted cycles of diversion. The visit to a gambling hall, a brothel, or an opium den added precious hours of freedom to the life of indentured emigrants who lacked the means for these entertainments in their homeland. In Chinese California they saw themselves momentarily admitted to that life of leisure which in part had motivated them to leave their native village in search for a fortune overseas. The dreams of an opium smoker or the dissipations waiting in a house of prostitution ranked second in attraction to the fascination which a gambling table radiated.[63] Here, desperate daring could change the course of a gambler's life with one single stroke of luck.

Games of chance particularly attracted the men who existed at the point of no return. Hunting for escapes from their daily hardships, they readily took solace in a set of simple games which combined a maximum of thrill with a constant chance of sudden gain. With the fate of gamesters continually hanging upon a breath, they fatalistically accepted an adverse verdict of chance. Accustomed to attribute almost every phenomenon of nature to the intervention of supernatural powers, the sojourners hardly questioned the outcome of a gambling game in which chance played a slightly greater role than it appeared to in the daily course of their lives. Only a short step separated divination from gambling, and the circulation of a handbook for calculating the prices of chances and

---

1867, January 28, June 18, September 20, 1868; *Herald*, August 16, October 6, 8, 10, 17, 18, 19, 20, 21, 22, 23, 24, December 22, 1852, March 10, 27, 31, April 1, November 27, 1853, April 26, 1858, May 11, August 11, 1860; "The Royal Theatre, A Popular Performance," in "Character Sketches in San Francisco: An Evening in the Chinese Quarter," *Frank Leslie's Illustrated Newspaper* (New York), 46:422 (August 24, 1878); Densmore, "Chinese Theatres," *Chinese in California*, 54–58; George Augustus Sala, "The Drama in China Town," *America Revisited: From the Bay of New York to the Gulf of Mexico, and From Lake Michigan to the Pacific*, 2 volumes (3rd ed., London, 1883), II, 238–52; [George R.] MacMinn, "Celestial Entertainments," *Theater of the Golden Era in California* [(Caldwell, 1941)], 493–508; Lois Rodecape, "Celestial Drama in the Golden Hills; The Chinese Theatre in California, 1849–1869," *California Historical Society Quarterly*, 23:97–116 (June 1944), Alice Henson Ernst, "The Chinese Theatre," *Trouping in Oregon Country; A History of Frontier Theatre* (Portland, [1961]), 96–102.

[63] Loomis to Lowrie, November 18, 1859, CPBFM; *Herald*, December 22, 1852, July 15, 1853, September 22, December 29, 1854, April 14, July 28, August 17, 1855, March 22, 26, 27, October 31, November 1, 1857, January 16, November 28, 1858; *Alta*, September 18, 1853, September 22, 1854, August 28, 1863, January 11, 1864, February 15, 1866; Bowles, *Our New West*, 406; Williams, "City of the Golden Gate," *Scribner's Monthly*, 10:283–84 (July 1875); Ames, "Day in Chinatown," *Lippincott's Magazine*, 16:500 (October 1875); Vogel, *Vom Indischen Ocean bis zum Goldlande*, 421; "Elysium of the Opium Smoker," in "Character Sketches in San Francisco: An Evening in the Chinese Quarter," *Leslie's Illustrated*, 46:422 (August 24, 1878); Taylor, *Between the Gates*, 115–16; Densmore, *Chinese in California*, 99–101; Iza Duffus Hardy, "In China Town," *Belgravia* (London), 43:218–19 (December 1880).

the prizes for the literary lottery called "White Pigeon Ticket" suggested an application of the art.[64]

Lithographs, letter sheets, and broadsides depict scenes in Chinese gambling houses in early California. Reminiscences, travelogues, news accounts, and official reports add color to these contours.[65] Great numbers of silent spectators motionlessly observed the gamblers' moves. The voice of a richly dressed singer, the music of an accompanying orchestra, and a view of the exciting scenes compensated these onlookers for their lack of Chinese copper cash to participate in a round of fan-tan, the most popular game.[66] The tension produced by various games served one end: they furnished a sudden escape from confines and anxieties. Between two quickened heartbeats gambling offered an abrupt breath of the diluted air of freedom.

The type of game was unimportant. If somebody took the fan-tan counters away or destroyed the pie-gow [p'ai-chiu] blocks, the sojourners would bet on the number of seeds in an uncut orange. While merchants

[64] Stewart Culin, "Popular Literature of the Chinese Laborers in the United States," *Oriental Studies, A Selection of Papers Read Before the Oriental Club of Philadelphia, 1888–1894* (Boston, 1894), 54–55.

[65] Speer to Lowrie, December 18, 1852, CPBFM; *Alta,* November 12, 1852, May 18, 1855, March 2, September 2, 4, 5, 11, 12, 1857, November 13, 17, December 17, 18, 22, 1858, October 2, 1860; *Herald,* October 29, 1852, March 21, July 23, 25, 1853, February 11, 22, June 30, 1854, March 30, 1856, September 6, 12, December 12, 1857, December 3, 16, 17, 1858, February 25, March 13, November 2, 1859, September 29, October 2, 1860; California State Senate, *Chinese Immigration 1876,* 44, 47, 60, 89, 100, 110, 116, 124, 152; *Senate Rept. 689,* 44 Cong., 2 Sess., 10, 151, 191. 192, 196, 222, 224, 240, 309, 829; California State Senate, *Chinese Immigration 1878,* 109, 112, 125, 165, 175, 187, 189, 217; Capron, *History of California,* 150–51; [Frank] Soulé [et al.], [*The*] *Annals* [*of San Francisco* (New York, 1855)], 382–83; Balduin Möllhausen, *Wanderungen durch die Prairien und Wüsten des westlichen Nordamerika vom Mississippi nach den Küsten der Südsee im Gefolge der von der Regierung der Vereinigten Staaten unter Lieutenant* [Amiel Weeks] *Whipple ausgesandten Expedition* (2nd ed., Leipzig, 1860), 461–62; [John] Todd, *Sunset Land* [(Boston, 1870)], 277–80; Charles Nordhoff, *California* (New York, 1872), 87–89; Albert S. Evans, *A la California. Sketches of Life in the Golden State* (San Francisco, 1873), 287–90; Rusling, *Across America,* 310–11; Densmore, *Chinese in California,* 97–98; Chamberlain, *Call of Gold,* 145. For scenes in Chinese gambling houses see Peters, *California on Stone,* 57, 62, 69, 121, plates 3, 61; Soulé, *Annals,* 383 (also reproduced in Henry Evans, *Curious Lore of San Francisco's Chinatown* [San Francisco, 1955], 7); Sala, *America Revisited,* II, 272; Bishop, *Old Mexico and Her Lost Provinces,* 339; Wheat, ed. "Journals of Charles E. DeLong," *California Historical Society Quarterly,* 9:facing 348 (December 1930); Boggs, (comp.), *Anthology of Newspaper Clippings and Documents,* 119.

[66] For a description of the games among the Chinese in the United States see Stewart Culin, *The Gambling Games of the Chinese in America. Fán t'án: the Game of Repeatedly Spreading Out. And Pák kòp piú or, the Game of White Pigeon Ticket* (Philadelphia, 1891), and "Chinese Games [in America] with Dice and Dominoes," *Report of the U.S. National Museum, under the Direction of the Smithsonian Institution, For the Year Ending June 30, 1893* (Washington, 1895), 491–537, based on a preliminary study, *Chinese Games with Dice—Read Before the Oriental Club of Philadelphia, March 14, 1889* (Philadelphia, 1889).

and professional gamblers grew steadily richer from the profits which these means of escape in Chinatown produced, the picture of the losing indentured emigrant appeared again and again. Having paid off his debts and saved for years to return to his family in China, on the eve of his departure the free man might drop into a gambling house, lose his savings in one night, and turn back, with great surface indifference, to begin a life of service again.

In the scheme of control and work Chinatown ensured the drudgery of mining company and railroad construction crews. With major commodities and supplies under their management, the merchant-creditors profited from the sojourners' very existence at a time when the debtors' labor furnished a constant return on the initial investment in indentured emigrants. The mass of lowly workers earned just enough to keep alive their hopes and guarantee their acquiescence to the system, but not enough to free themselves from it. Chinatown also gave these workers in an alien environment the illusion of home.

Chinatown and work camp fulfilled an essential role in Chinese California. However, their significance went beyond the confines of the regimented world in which the small realm of diversion provided only the background for the large domain of work. Chinatown and work camp also furnished the major contacts with the alien world that encompassed Chinese California. The vast variety of reactions to the newcomers crystallized around these vital institutions. Chinatown and work camp provoked incidents of strife and stimulated humanitarian attempts at acculturation as the Americans became aware of the sojourners in their midst.

The Birth and Death

of the

Plains Indians

PETER FARB

After the appearance of the white man in the Western Hemisphere, different Indian groups went through various cultural changes as they struggled to preserve their identity and their lands. Perhaps the most impressive product of the Indians' adaptations to the white presence on the American continent was the elaborate culture that evolved among the nomadic tribes of the Great Plains once they acquired the white man's animal—the horse.

When the Indians of Latin America first saw the conquistadors astride the horses they had brought from Spain to the Western world, they thought the two were a single animal (a mistake that may also account for the mythical centaur). The Indians soon learned, however, that man and horse were separate creatures and that the latter could be domesticated to great advantage. The Spaniards introduced horses in Mexico in the sixteenth century, and herds of the animals spread northward over the plains. Late in the seventeenth century, North American Indians began to breed Spanish horses. When white settlers reached the Great Plains over a century later, they met the first mounted Indians ever to be seen—the prototypes of the fierce, proud Indians encountered today in Western movies.

By the time of their first real contacts with whites, the Indians were well on their way to developing a complex culture that centered on the horse and the buffalo, the great native of the plains on which they relied for food, shelter, and clothing. The horse had literally transformed their lives by dramatically increasing their mobility and giving them greater effectiveness in waging war and in hunting the all-important buffalo. By the time of the Civil War, more than two-thirds of the Indians that remained in the United States belonged to the Great Plains civilization.

In his book **Man's Rise to Civilization as Shown by the Indians of North America from Primeval Times to the Coming of the Industrial State,** Peter Farb, an anthropologist previously on the staff of the

New York Museum of Natural History, examines the life and history
of the American Indians and traces their cultural evolution. Although
many scholars have quarreled with Farb's perspectives and have accused him of oversimplifying cultural and historical elements to
accommodate his theory, the book stands as a valuable and beauti-
fully written introduction to the varieties of American Indian life. The
following selection, taken from this book, is a chapter in which Farb
discusses the impact of the horse on the various Indian cultures that
coalesced into the Plains group.

The tragic end of the Plains Indian culture at the close of the
nineteenth century was marked by the massacre of Indians' at
Wounded Knee, South Dakota. Wovoka, the last of the great Indian
messiahs, had dreamed of a resurgence of the declining Indian culture, but the greater powers of the United States government held
sway.

THE GREAT AMERICAN EPIC

To many people, the typical Indian was the Plains Indian, a painted
brave in full regalia, trailing a war bonnet, astride a horse which he rode
bareback, sweeping down upon a wagon train, in glorious technicolor. In
actual fact, the picturesque culture of the Plains Indian was artificial, not
aboriginal, and it did not last very long. The amalgam known as the Plains
culture was not fully accomplished until the early 1800's—and like the
spring grass of the high plains, it withered quickly.

This culture emerged almost inconspicuously in the middle of the
eighteenth century as its catalytic agent, the horse, spread northward from
Spanish settlements in New Mexico. Within only a few generations, the
horse was found throughout the central heartland of the continent, and
Indians from all directions spilled onto the plains. They originally spoke
many different languages and had various customs, but they all found in
the horse a new tool to kill greater numbers of bison than they had ever
believed possible. They became inconceivably rich in material goods, far
beyond their wildest dreams, and like a dream it all faded. By about 1850,
the Plains culture was already on the wane as the "manifest destiny" of a
vigorous United States to push westward shoved them aside. The fate of
the Plains Indians had been sealed with the arrival of the first miners and
the first prairie schooner. The battles of extermination between Plains

"The Birth and Death of the Plains Indians." From *Man's Rise to Civilization as
Shown by the Indians of North America from Primeval Times to the Coming of the
Industrial State* by Peter Farb, pp. 112–32. Copyright © 1968 by Peter Farb. Re-
printed by permission of the publishers, E. P. Dutton.

Indians and United States cavalry represent America's own great epic—its *Iliad*, its *Aeneid*, its Norse saga—but this epic was no more true than any other.

Despite the surrounded forts, the saving of the last bullet for oneself, the occasional acts of heroism, and the frequent acts of bestiality on both sides—despite this picture portrayed in the Great American Epic, there was remarkably little formal combat. Deaths and hardship there were in plenty as the Plains Indians met their catastrophic end, but most deaths were due to starvation, exposure, disease, brutality, and alcoholism, and not to bullets. In all the actual battles between White soldiers and Indian braves, only several thousand deaths on both sides were due to bullets and arrows. The wars of the plains were not epics but mopping-up operations. In the process, the millions of bison very nearly vanished without leaving any survivors, the plains were turned into a dust bowl, and the once-proud Indian horsemen were broken in body and spirit.

The famed Plains Indian culture did not exist in all its glory when Coronado first explored the plains. Lured on by tales of rich lands, where kings were supposed to be lulled to sleep by the chimes of golden bells, Coronado eventually reached Kansas in 1541. Here the Spaniards saw the beast they had been hearing so much about: the remarkable "cow," actually a bison, as large as a Spanish bull, but with an enormous mane and small curved horns. They also met some impoverished Indians who lived in conical tipis "built like pavilions," according to the chronicler of the expedition. He was particularly impressed by the way the bison seemed to provide most of the materials needed by the Indians:

> With the skins they build their houses; with the skins they clothe and show themselves; from the skins they make ropes and also obtain wool. With the sinews they make threads, with which they sew their clothes and also their tents. From the bones they shape awls. The dung they use for firewood, since there is no other fuel in that land. The bladders they use as jugs and drinking containers.[1]

Hunting bison on foot was not productive, and it certainly could not support large numbers of Indians. Such hunting was practiced largely by the wretched nomads who moved around in small groups and who lived off the occasional weakened bison they could kill or those they could stampede over bluffs. Most of the aboriginal cultures on the plains and prairies were based on the cultivation of maize, beans, and squash. Agriculture had spread westward from the eastern Woodlands, and it followed the fingerlike extensions of rivers throughout the arid Dakotas, Texas, and virtually to the foothills of the Rockies. Hunting bison, for these people, was only incidental to the primary subsistence based on agriculture. They went on a hunt about once a year to supplement their vegetable diet and to obtain hides, sinew, bone, and other raw materials.

Once the horse arrived on the plains, that way of life changed. The

[1] This quote and subsequent ones from the Coronado expedition are from *Eyes of Discovery* by John Bakeless, New York: Dover, 1961, pp. 92–93.

nomadic bison hunters became ascendant over the farmers, who either were driven off their lands or abandoned agriculture to become bison hunters themselves. Indians had never seen the horse until the Spaniards brought it to the New World, for sometime during the great glacial melt it had become extinct in North America. The Indians obtained the first horses after the Spaniards settled New Mexico in 1598. (Contrary to previous belief, the Indians captured no horses from de Soto, Coronado, or other early explorers, for these horses either died or were taken home again.) The Spaniards prohibited the sale of horses to Indians, but the revolt of the Pueblo Indians between 1680 and 1692 threw some of the animals on the Indian markets of North America. The Spaniards restocked their herds, which proliferated, but they were unable to prevent further horse stealing by Indians. Horses were bartered—or stolen—from Indian group to group. Soon a whole new Indian profession of horse merchant grew up, and the animals—as well as the knowledge of how to break and train them—spread northward from New Mexico. In addition, some Spanish horses had gone wild and roamed the plains in herds. The Spaniards called them *mesteños* ("wild"), from which the English word "mustangs" is derived.

By the first half of the eighteenth century, enterprising Indian merchants had already sold the horse to Indians as far north as the Northern Shoshone of Wyoming and taught them its management. The Shoshone slowly built up their herds and learned to ride as if they had been born to the saddle. No longer did they have to remain impoverished and secretive inhabitants of the Rocky Mountains, at the mercy of more powerful Indian groups. They swooped down the eastern flanks of the mountains and onto the high plains, where they found a bonanza in bison and a way to even the score with their traditional persecutors, the Blackfoot. From all over, other Indian groups converged on the plains and quickly adapted themselves to an economy based on the bison. The lands of the agriculturists were usurped, and the plains became a maelstrom of varied and often conflicting cultures.

A LIVING EXPERIMENT IN CULTURE CHANGE

The stolen, bartered, bought, or captured horse was a new cultural element in the heartland of North America, and it changed the entire way of life there.[2] The whole of the plains, from Alberta to Texas, became peopled by groups of great diversity who had come from all directions and often from great distances. There were Athabaskans from the north (Kiowa-Apache), Algonkians (Cree, Cheyenne, Blackfoot) and Siouans (Mandan, Crow, Dakota) from the east, Uto-Aztecans (Comanche, Ute) from the west, Caddoans (Pawnee, Arikara) from the south. The plains

---

[2] An excellent summary of the effect of the horse on many Indian cultures is [F. G.] Roe [*The Indian and the Horse*, Norman: University of Oklahoma Press, 1955]. See also [J. C.] Ewers ["The Horse in Blackfoot Indian Culture," *Bureau of American Ethnology Bulletin*, 1955].

became a melting pot for more than thirty different peoples, belonging to at least five language stocks. It has given anthropologists a living laboratory of culture change. Culture change is the way in which a group alters because of new circumstances, or the way it borrows traits from other cultures and fits them into the configurations of its own.

By about 1800 the gross differences in culture among all these peoples had disappeared; the Sun Dance ceremony, for example, was eventually observed by virtually every tribe. Of course differences apparent to the trained eye of the anthropologist still existed; yet it is remarkable that a people from the eastern forests and another from the Great Basin of the West, two thousand miles away, should within only a few generations have become so nearly identical. Even more remarkable, this homogeneity was achieved with great speed, was not imposed on unwilling people by a more powerful group, and was done in the absence of a common tongue—save for "sign language," the lingua franca of the Plains tribes.

The Plains Cree demonstrate how a people originally distant from the plains in both culture and geography eventually could become so typical of it. The Cree were first recorded in the *Jesuit Relations* of 1640, but at that time they had nothing to do with the plains at all. They inhabited the forests between Hudson Bay and Lake Superior, and they were roving hunters and gatherers of wild rice. Their culture was typical of the Northern Algonkian bands, and after the Hudson's Bay Company was founded they turned to trapping. The demand by Whites for more beaver pelts led them to push westward; because they had obtained guns from White traders, they were able to dispossess the previous inhabitants. By about the middle of the eighteenth century, some of the Cree had already penetrated to the west of Lake Winnipeg. Their culture had changed considerably. It was now parasitic on the White trader for weapons, clothing, and cooking utensils—and sometimes even food, because the Cree spent his time trapping rather than hunting. Then the Cree living farthest west discovered the resource of the bison. Historical records reveal that as early as 1772 they had developed primitive ways of hunting bison, although they still did not possess the horse. Within only a generation, though, the Plains Cree had emerged—a typical equestrian Plains tribe, very different in customs and outlook from the Cree that still inhabited the forests, although both groups continued to speak the same language.

And all this was due to the horse. No longer were just stray or stampeded bison taken, but the herds were pursued on swift horses and the choicest animals killed. No longer was the whole animal utilized for raw materials, which had so impressed the chronicler of the Coronado expedition, but the Indians could now afford the luxury of waste. They stocked the tipi with supplies for the future: meat dried in the sun (jerkee), or else pounded and mixed with fat and berries to become pemmican. Even though most of the Plains Indians never saw a White close up until their swift decline, his influence was felt profoundly as his goods and trade articles flowed westward across the plains by barter from one tribe to another. Tipis almost twenty-five feet in diameter were filled to overflowing with new-found riches. An economic revolution, for which the Indians' traditions had not prepared them, took place. The women no longer toiled in the fields—for gardening was not as profitable as hunting, nor could it be practiced in the presence of nomadic horsemen —and they stopped making pottery because brass kettles were obtained from Whites. Permanent villages disappeared, and with them went the elaborate customs and crafts, rules for marriage and residence.

After the Indians discovered the effectiveness of rifles, an armaments race began on the plains. Just as Indians earlier had realized the value of horses, and those lacking them were driven to obtain them by any means, the acquisition of rifles upset the entire balance of power. As soon as one tribe acquired firepower, the competition for others to obtain equal armaments became fierce. Not only the rifles had to be acquired, but there was also a continuing need for powder and for lead. The Indians were driven to take ever greater chances in raids to steal horses which they might barter for guns and ammunition. For a period of nearly fifty years, the plains became an arena of turmoil in which the status quo changed from year to year, as successive groups became supreme in supplies of horses or guns, or in the powerful allies they could muster.

THE MAKE-BELIEVE INDIANS

The Plains Indians in their heyday were a study in hyperbole, and as make-believe as the set for a western movie. They sprang from greatly differing traditions, from farmers and from hunters and from collectors of wild plants. Each contributed something of its own that created almost overnight a flamboyant culture whose vigor was for a time unequaled. In this world of hyperbole, many traditions that existed in non–Plains Indian societies became wildly exaggerated. Other Indians also possessed clubs and associations, but none were so extravagant in ritual and insignia as the Plains warrior societies. Indians elsewhere also believed in the reality of visions, but none so relentlessly pursued the vision quest and were so caught up in the emotional excesses of religion as the Plains tribes. Other Indians tortured captives, but none evoked pain so exquisitely in their own bodies.

A special kind of social organization developed on the plains that is known as the composite tribe. Wherever the composite tribe is found, it always signifies a breakdown in culture with a subsequent readaptation. Sometimes the breakdown is due to population loss through migration or increased warfare, as occurred to the Pueblo Indians around the Rio Grande River of New Mexico. Sometimes it is due to the disturbance of the resource base through economic exploitation by outsiders, as has been characteristic of primitive African societies. Occasionally, as happened on the North American plains, it is due to the loss of old culture traits and the borrowing of new ones. Whatever the cause, composite tribes usually arise after an alien culture appears; and almost everywhere Whites have penetrated around the world their presence has resulted in the formation of the composite tribe.

A distinguishing characteristic of the composite tribe is that descent reckoning is unspecific: It can be through either the father's or the mother's line, or both. Marital residence rules also are unspecific, and the newly married couple lives with whichever relatives expediency suggests. The composite tribe of the Plains Indians was much more a collection of bands than were the Zuni or the Iroquois lineal tribes. During most of the year the bison lived scattered in small herds, but during the late summer rutting season they came together in huge herds that blackened the plains. The Indians responded with a parallel social cycle. Most of the year a number of Plains Indian families lived together as a band, uniting only at the time of the summer encampment with other bands for tribal ceremonies and a communal hunt. Furthermore, band membership tended to change, and many Plains Indians belonged to several bands during their lifetimes. One cause of the changing membership within bands was the constant feuding, which often became so oppressive that the only way to preserve any peace at all was by fragmentation of the original band. The Plains Indians appear to have been no more complex in their social organization than the Eskimo and the Great Basin Shoshone bands, but that is not really true. They became functioning tribes at least during their summer encampments, and they managed to maintain that identity the rest of the year, even though they broke up into small bands.

The primary way in which identity was achieved was not through clans but through nonkinship sodalities. The word "sodality" is derived from the Latin *sodalis*, which means "comrade" or "associate," and in a modern society it is equivalent to fraternities and sororities, political parties, service clubs like the Rotary or the Lions, and religious organizations. It is an association that binds people together around a single interest. It may be the burial association of the Irish-American immigrants in the last century, credit associations in medieval Europe, even the crop-watching societies in Chinese villages. When the Plains tribes united in the summer, they were crosscut by a bewildering variety of sodalities with ceremonial, social, and military functions. There were dance societies and feasting societies, and even societies based on a common supernatural experience. Some societies were only for women, like the craft guilds of the Cheyenne. Others were open to both men and women, like the tobacco societies of the Crow, which revolved around the raising of special kinds of tobacco for ceremonial use.

The Cheyenne, as just one example, had six military societies that somewhat resembled the dueling societies of German students. A youth was permitted to join any one of them if he could demonstrate his courage, but he usually chose to go into the one his father belonged to. These societies served not only as the tribe's military force but as its police as well. And each of the six had a particular area of responsibility, such as protecting the movement of the encampment from one place to another, or enforcing the rules against individual hunting that might scare away the bison. Only the bravest of the brave warriors could belong to the elite military society known as the Contraries. Somewhat like the Zuni Mudheads, they were privileged clowns. They did the opposite of everything:

They said *no* when they meant *yes;* went away when called and came near when told to go away; called left *right;* and sat shivering on the hottest day.

A special development in the warrior societies was found among the Mandan, Hidatsa, Arapaho, and Blackfoot, which had a hierarchy of societies. The societies were arranged in order of the age of their members, and as the members grew older they moved up a step. In this way a warrior society existed for every male from the youngest to the oldest, with the exception of the effeminate male known as a berdache. No scorn was attached to his position; he was regarded with pity and with a degree of sacred awe for being the victim of a condition that was not of his own doing. Even the berdache found his place in Plains Indian society. He permanently adopted woman's clothing and woman's role; he became skilled in the female tasks of beadwork or skin-tanning, and he was eligible to join the women's societies.

The richness and diversity of the Plains sodalities is explained by the lack of lineal residential groups. The need for non-kin sodalities was so great on the plains because they filled the social void caused by the absence of clans. Had these non-kin sodalities failed to develop, with their complexity of rules and regulations that often seem so ridiculous to us today, the tribes would have been reduced to mere collections of bands. The sodalities brought unity to one of the most diverse collections of people on earth.

COUPS AND SCALPING

Almost all the sodalities had religious aspects, and almost all were concerned with war in one way or another. The various cultures had engaged in warfare even before they migrated onto the plains and obtained horses, but with the emergence of the Plains Indian culture during the nineteenth century, warfare became as ritualized as medieval knighthood. Only during the very twilight of the Plains culture did large battles take place that pitted Indian against Indian or Indian against the United States Army, with each group seeking to exterminate the other. Previous to that, tactics consisted of forays and raids by small war parties; the conflicts were brief and usually indecisive.

The Plains Indians fought not to win territory or to enslave other tribes, but for a variety of different reasons. One was the capture of horses, which had a high economic value. Another reason . . . was that external strife served to unify the tribe internally. A tribe, especially one as fragile as the composite tribe unified only by non-kin sodalities, needed a common enemy as a rationale for its existence. A third reason was that war was regarded as a game in which the players might win status. In this game, exploits were graded according to the dangers involved. The exploit itself was known as the *coup*, from the French trapper's word for "blow," because originally it signified that the brave had struck the enemy's body with a special stick that was often striped like a barber pole. Later, "counting coups" referred to the recital by the brave of all his war deeds; as he immodestly proclaimed each one he gave a blow against a pole with his ax. These recitals went on endlessly. Each time a young man accumulated a new honor, he used it as an excuse to recount his old exploits. If he lied about his exploits, though, or even shaded the truth a bit, he was challenged immediately by someone who had been along on the same war party.

Each Plains tribe had its own ranking for coups. Among the Blackfoot, stealing an enemy's weapons was looked upon as the highest exploit. Among some other tribes, the bravest deed was to touch an enemy without hurting him. The least important exploit usually was killing an enemy, but even that deed was ranked according to the way it was done and the weapons that were used. The whole business of counting coups often became extremely involved. Among the Cheyenne, for example, coups could be counted by several warriors on a single enemy, but the coups were ranked in the strict order in which the enemy was touched by the participants; it was immaterial who actually killed or wounded him. Like a sort of heraldry, these deeds were recorded in picture writing on tipis and on bison robes. They gave the warrior the right to hold public office. Among many tribes, each coup earned an eagle's feather, and the achieving of many coups accounts for the elaborate headdresses of some of the Plains war leaders.

Scalps taken from dead or wounded enemies sometimes served as trophies, but they were insignificant when compared with counting coups. Many Plains tribes did not take scalps at all until the period of their swift decline, which began in the middle of the last century. Most people believe that all Indians took scalps, and that scalp-hunting was exclusively a New World custom. Neither idea is true. Herodotus, the ancient Greek historian, mentioned the taking of scalps by the Scythians, for example. In South America scalp-taking as a custom was practically unknown; in North America it *may* have existed before the arrival of Whites, but only in a few areas in the eastern Woodlands. Many historians still question whether scalp-taking was an aboriginal Indian practice or rather one learned quite early from the White settlers.

Whatever its exact origins, there is no doubt that scalp-taking quickly spread over all of North America, except in the Eskimo areas; nor is there any doubt that its spread was due to the barbarity of White men rather than to the barbarity of Red men. White settlers early offered to pay bounties on dead Indians, and scalps were actual proof of the deed. Governor Kieft of New Netherland is usually credited with originating the idea of paying for Indian scalps, as they were more convenient to handle than whole heads, and they offered the same proof that an Indian had been killed. By liberal payments for scalps, the Dutch virtually cleared southern New York and New Jersey of Indians before the English supplanted them.[3] By 1703 the colony of Massachusetts was paying the equivalent of about $60 for every Indian scalp. In the mid-eighteenth

---

[3] [W. T.] Hagan [*American Indians*, Chicago: University of Chicago Press, 1961], p. 15, is the source for the origin of scalping.

century, Pennsylvania fixed the bounty for a male Indian scalp at $134; a female's was worth only $50. Some White entrepreneurs simply hatcheted any old Indians that still survived in their towns. The French also used scalp-taking as an instrument of geopolitics. In the competition over the Canadian fur trade, they offered the Micmac Indians a bounty for every scalp they took from the Beothuk of Newfoundland. By 1827 an expedition to Newfoundland failed to find a single survivor of this once numerous and proud people.[4]

Among the Plains tribes, apparently only the Dakota and the Cree placed any value on scalps; both tribes were late immigrants to the Plains from the East, where they probably learned the practice from Whites. Nor was there as much torturing of captives by Plains tribes as was once believed. The tradition of the White settler's saving his last bullet for himself to avoid a horrible death was a needless precaution. Unlike the Indians of the eastern Woodlands, the Plains Indians killed swiftly. They looked upon the White custom of hanging, for example, as cruel and barbaric.

CAUSES OF WARFARE

The Great American Epic has traditionally regarded the Plains Indians as the most "warlike" on the continent. Indeed, history does confirm that the heartland of the continent was an arena for continual strife. Yet, stating that a Blackfoot, for example, was "warlike" reveals nothing. The entire Blackfoot tribe did not habitually engage in war because individual members possessed "warlike" personalities. Individual men go to war for individual reasons: for social prestige, for economic rewards and for booty, because of religious convictions—even to escape from frustrations at home. Entire societies, though, do not go to war for such personal reasons. The fact is that the individual Blackfoot was warlike simply because his whole cultural system obliged him to be that way.

All the various theories as to why groups of people go to war fall into four general categories. The first states that it is the very physical nature of man to be pugnacious and aggressive. Such a view of man holds that a warlike urge is biologically inherent in him. This is an old theory, and it keeps popping up from time to time in new presentations, most recently in Konrad Lorenz' On Aggression (1966). But there is no evidence in the physical makeup of man to suggest that he has been fashioned as a warlike animal. Man, in truth, is a puny creation, lacking fangs, claws, thick skin, speed, or other adaptations for combat. The whole idea of the innate belligerency of man is laid to rest by evidence that warfare is virtually absent among the most primitive of men, those whose "true" biological nature might appear to be closest to the surface. The Great

---

[4] The extinction of the Beothuk is described in [F. W.] Hodge ["Handbook of American Indians North of Mexico," Bureau of American Ethnology Bulletin, 1906 (reprinted New York: Pageant Books, 1960)], p. 142.

Basin Shoshone, for example, never waged war, nor did most other very simple societies before the arrival of Whites.

The second explanation is an affront to logic: Men are warlike because they are warlike. Such an explanation is ridiculous, but even so noted an anthropologist as Ralph Linton wrote that the Plains Indians would not have been so interested in war if "they had not been warlike."[5] Similar statements exist in Ruth Benedict's *Patterns of Culture*. Obviously, such logic is akin to explaining obesity in middle-aged males by saying that many middle-aged males are obese.

The third explanation is a psychological one, and it probably boasts the most adherents—which is understandable, for these people can bolster their case by surveys, personality tests, statistical analyses, and other impressive tools of modern scholarship. Even before the widespread use of such tests and surveys, Freud, in an exchange of correspondence with Einstein in 1932 about the causes of war, agreed that "there is an instinct for hatred and destruction . . . which goes halfway to meet the efforts of the warmongers."[6] All of these psychological studies, though, can explain only the motivations behind why *individuals* go to war. The real point is that although individuals slug each other in a barroom brawl or drop napalm from airplanes over Vietnam, individuals do not go to war. Only societies do that.

That leaves the fourth explanation, which states simply that the causes for war are to be found within the cultures of the contending groups. This explanation avoids confusing the issue with related problems, such as individual motivations or the kinds of warfare practiced. The Plains Indians confirm this cultural explanation. For one thing, the composite tribes of the Plains Indians could not have survived without external enemies, real or imagined, against whom their warrior associations could unite. For another, the Plains culture was artificial, brought into being by the reverberations sent across the continent by the arrival of the Whites. The Whites upset delicate adjustments the Indians had made to each other over very long periods of time. As just one example, the French encouraged warfare between the Ojibway and surrounding groups; the Ojibway spread westward and displaced Siouan tribes, which migrated westward and southward to the plains; there the Sioux displaced Hidatsa and Mandan, who in turn stirred up the Cheyenne and others. The whole unreal situation was very much like a series of balls caroming off one another and resulting in new rebounds.

Most important, once all these groups were on the plains and had altered their cultures by acquiring horses and guns, their whole make-believe world had to be kept in motion or it would collapse. Horses had to be stolen so they could be bartered for more guns to aid in the stealing of more horses. Many White traders encouraged the strife to capitalize on it by selling guns, liquor, and kitchenware. The herds of bison, once

[5] *The Study of Man* by Ralph Linton, New York: Appleton-Century, 1936, p. 463.
[6] Freud's letter on the causes of war is in *Character and Culture*, Vol. 9 in *The Collected Papers of Sigmund Freud*, New York: Collier Books, 1963, p. 141.

thought limitless, dwindled, and as they did there was additional cause for strife over hunting territories. In any event, there were good cultural—that is, social, political, economic, and technological—reasons why the Plains Indians were warlike. They were that way not because of their biology or their psychology, but because their new White-induced culture demanded it.[7]

THE NEW RICH

Among the Mandan, Hidatsa, Arapaho, and Blackfoot, a member of a war society purchased his way up the ladder of age-grades until he arrived at the topmost grade and was thereupon entitled to wear the famous feathered bonnet. At each step, he selected a seller from the next older brotherhood, and then purchased his rights. A buyer was free to select any seller he wanted, but he usually chose someone from his father's family. Often, as part of the payment, the purchaser had to relinquish his wife to the seller for a time; if the purchaser was unmarried, he had to borrow a wife from a relative. The whole business of joining an age-grade brotherhood was accompanied by an elaborate etiquette that was also somewhat sophomoric and not unlike the mock seriousness of today's Masonic initiation.

Membership in other kinds of societies was also often purchased, and in fact many things were for sale among the Plains tribes: sacred objects, religious songs, and even the description of a particularly good vision. The right to paint a particular design on the face during a religious ceremony might cost as much as a horse. Permission just to look inside someone's sacred bundle of fetishes and feathers was often worth the equivalent of a hundred dollars. A Crow is known to have paid two horses to his sponsor to get himself invited into a tobacco society, and the candidate's family contributed an additional twenty-three horses. A prudent Blackfoot was well advised to put his money into a sacred bundle, an investment that paid him continued dividends. The investment was as safe as today's government bond is; and it was readily negotiable at a price usually higher than the purchase price. By permitting the bundle to be used in rituals, its owner received fees that were like dividends. As the Plains tribes became richer, the price of sacred bundles continued to rise, much as the price of a stock-exchange seat goes up during prosperous times.

[7] Two excellent papers on Plains warfare are by [W. W.] Newcomb ["A Re-examination of the Causes of Plains Warfare," *American Anthropologist*, 1950, pp. 317–29; and "Toward an Understanding of War," in G. L. Dole and R. L. Carneiro, eds., *Essays in the Science of Culture in Honor of Leslie A. White*, New York: Thomas Y. Crowell, 1960, pp. 317–36]. See also [B.] Mishkin ["Rank and Warfare Among Plains Indians," *American Ethnological Society Monograph*, 1940] for the importance of economic factors. Various theories of primitive warfare in general can be found in [H. H.] Turney-High [*Primitive Warfare: Its Practices and Concepts*, Columbia: University of South Carolina Press, 1949].

Until they became horsemen, almost none of these tribes had ever known wealth. The Comanche, for example, had been an impoverished Shoshonean people from the Great Basin before the nineteenth century. Most of the other tribes only a few decades before had been marginal hunters, all of whose possessions could be dragged along by a single dog. But the Plains tribes learned the laws of the marketplace rapidly, both from each other and from the White trader. The accumulation of wealth became important, but it was not incorporated into the societies in any meaningful way. Perhaps it would have been in time, and the Plains tribes might have served economic theorists as the very models of the steps by which societies become capitalistic.

Anthropologists can do no more than guess what might have happened to the concept of wealth had the Plains culture endured for another century, or even for a few more decades. Some indication is given by tribes such as the Kiowa, who learned how to use wealth to create more wealth. A Kiowa warrior was forced by custom to give away some of his wealth, but he also learned to hoard it, not only for himself but also to keep it in his family through inheritance. Classes based on wealth arose in what had once been an egalitarian society. The wealthiest classes could afford to give their sons certain benefits. They equipped them with the best horses and guns and sent them down the road to military glory at an early age. And when the son of a wealthy Kiowa achieved an exploit, everyone heard about it, for the wealthy controlled the channels of publicity through their ability to give gifts. Such publicity paid further economic benefits: The scion of a wealthy Kiowa, with his well-publicized exploits, could increase his wealth even more because he easily obtained followers for a raiding party.

Not knowing what to do with the new-found wealth that crammed their tipis, the Plains Indians regarded it as materially unimportant, but valued it as a status symbol. It became another way to count coups, to get one up on a neighbor. And since the primary way to acquire wealth was to steal horses from someone else, wealth became a validation of bravery. The warrior also could be sure that no one forgot his prowess by the constant reminder of gifts. Gift-giving emphasized that the giver was brave enough to go out and steal more wealth anytime he felt like it.

The sudden wealth achieved by the mass slaughter of bison changed customs in other ways also. It took only a moment for a man on horseback to kill a bison with a bullet, but it still remained a long and arduous task for his wife to dress the hide for sale to the White trader. As a result, a shortage of women arose and a premium was placed on them to the extent that eventually "bride price" was paid. Men always needed the hands of extra women to dress the skins, and the parents of a healthy girl could negotiate her marriage from a position of strength. At the same time, polygyny, which probably had existed in some tribes to a limited extent, became widespread, for a good hunter needed as many wives as he could afford. There are even instances known of berdaches being taken on as second wives, not for any sexual variety they might offer, but merely because they performed women's tasks.

VISION QUESTS

Most North American Indians greatly respected visions, but few immersed themselves so deeply in them as did the Plains tribes. Sometimes a spirit might come of its own accord in a vision, just to befriend a mortal, but usually the Plains Indian had to go in active pursuit of his vision. He did this by isolating himself, fasting and thirsting, and practicing self-torture, at the same time imploring the spirits to take pity on his suffering. The youth gashed his arms and legs, and among the Crow it was the custom to cut off a joint from a finger of the left hand. Cheyenne vision-seekers thrust skewers of wood under pinches of skin in the breast; these skewers were attached to ropes, which in turn were tied to a pole. All day the youth leaned his full weight away from the pole, pulling and tugging at his own flesh while he implored the spirits to give him a vision.

Mortification of the flesh has always held a fascination for religious fanatics everywhere, for it is the most obvious way that this too, too human flesh can break its link with the world of men and approach the threshold of the gods. Among those who have groped toward deities in this way are the Jewish Essenes around the Dead Sea, the many ascetic orders of Christian monks, the Whirling Dervishes of Islam, and the hermits of Buddhism.

The spirit might at last take pity on the Plains Indian youth—actually it was dehydration, pain, and delirium taking their effects—and give him supernatural guidance. A successful vision supported the youth for the rest of his life. He always had a guardian spirit on whom he could call for help and guidance, although from time to time he had to repeat the self-torture to renew his familiarity with the spirit. During his vision, the youth usually learned what items—such as feathers, a stone pipe, a piece of skin, maize kernels—he should collect for a sacred medicine bundle and put in a small pouch. A particularly lucky youth might also receive his own songs, which when sung served as a call to supernatural aid; that they sounded like gibberish to everyone else only reinforced the belief that he had received a unique vision. A few youths failed to receive any visions at all, even though they tried repeatedly. Those who could not obtain a vision on their own could sometimes purchase one, as well as a replica of the successful visionary's sacred medicine bundle.

What is remarkable about such visions is that they were not invariably experienced, since the entire Plains culture worked toward producing them. Every Plains youth grew up believing firmly in the reality of the vision, so no resistance to the idea had to be overcome. Secondly, the youth worked himself into an intense emotional state by starvation, thirst, self-torture, exposure to the sun, and isolation—all of which are known to produce hallucinations. Thirdly, the shape in which the vision came to him was predetermined by the structure of the myths and visions he had heard about since childhood. Finally, in retelling his vision, he unconsciously reconstructed it and filled in gaps, adapting it to the norms of behavior of his culture—much as we do in reporting an incoherent dream, no matter how sincerely we believe we are not distorting it.

Plains Indian visions were clearly recognized as differing from person to person and from tribe to tribe. Some of the individual differences were biological and psychological. An Indian with an auditory personality might hear loud calls of birds or gibberish songs, whereas a visual type would be apt to see a horse with strange markings. Probably some individual fears and anxieties went into the vision. Despite the Plains warrior's attitude of fearlessness, a common vision was the sudden transformation of rocks and trees into enemies; but the youth was made invulnerable to their arrows by his guardian spirit. Often the vision involved the visit of some animal. An eagle might fly by, the flapping of its wings sounding like crashes of thunder; and bison, elk, bears, and hawks appeared quite often among the nobler beasts. Among the Pawnee (who, alone of the Plains tribes, had worked out an orderly system of religious beliefs, including a supreme being), the stars and other heavenly bodies entered quite freely into visions.

The desire for a vision existed among most of the Indians of North America, and it seems to have developed in two different directions. Among some Indians, it led directly to shamanism, for shamans were believed to be recipients of particularly intense visions and to have the power to summon up new visions at will. The other line of development led to visions of more limited power that had to be sought after. In this second category, there was a great range of variation, from the Plains youth, who suffered ordeals, to the Great Basin Shoshone, who passively waited for the spirit to find him.

Before the contrasting attitudes of the Plains tribes and the Great Basin Shoshone can be explained, the vision must first be recognized for what it is: a resort to supernatural aid in a dangerous undertaking, in which individual skill alone is not enough to guarantee success. The Plains culture provided numerous such dangerous undertakings, such as riding among a herd of stampeding bison or stealthily entering an enemy camp. For the Plains warrior, the rewards of such undertakings were certainly great enough to compensate for the few days of self-torture and fasting required to obtain a guardian spirit. The arid country of the Great Basin Shoshone, however, provided no such rewards. There the land yielded a bare minimum, and the rewards went not to the man who showed courage and daring, but to the one who simply exerted industry in collecting seeds or grasshoppers. Any yearning for visions that existed among the Great Basin Shoshone was not for protection in the dangers of the hunt or in warfare, but for the cure of snake bites or sickness.[8]

The various responses of different cultures toward visions partly explains why some Indians took enthusiastically to the White man's alcohol and others did not. The use of firewater was particularly intense among the Plains, as well as among the nearby forest Indians, who were the ancestors of many Plains Indians. Alcohol was promptly recognized by the Plains Indians as a short-cut method of producing derangement of the senses and hallucinations. In primeval North America the Plains tribes had

---

[8] For a discussion of the vision quest in several cultures, see [R.] Underhill ["Ceremonial Patterns in the Greater Southwest," *American Ethnological Society Memoir,* 1948].

been remarkably free from the use of hallucinogenic plants such as peyote and mushrooms. The Plains vision-seekers were not even fortunate enough to have *Datura* or Jimsonweed, for its original range in the West was probably in only portions of the Southwest and southern California. Nor had the Plains tribes learned that tobacco, which they smoked in a few ritual puffs, could be swallowed to produce considerable discomfort and emotional upset, the way many Central and South American Indians used it.

Only when the Plains culture was disintegrating rapidly after about 1850 did a hallucinogenic cactus known as peyote take hold. Peyote is native to northern Mexico, but it spread like a grass fire from tribe to tribe as far north as the Canadian plains. Although peyote is used elsewhere in North America to a limited extent, it was most widely and promptly accepted by the Plains tribes. Peyote afforded a way to seek visions; it also provided an escape from the humiliation of the complete defeat by Whites in the latter part of the last century.

THE END OF A CULTURE

After the Civil War, a tide of White settlers streamed westward, and they sealed the fate of the Plains tribes. Treaty after treaty was broken by Whites as the Indian lands were crisscrossed by easterners covetous of acreage and precious metals. At first the Whites tried to restrict the Plains Indians to valueless territories, but that policy soon changed to a war of extermination. Said General William Tecumseh Sherman in 1867: "The more I see of these Indians, the more convinced I am that they all have to be killed or be maintained as a species of paupers." To help clear the Indians from the plains, the Whites struck at their food base, the bison. They themselves not only destroyed the animals, but they also contrived to get the Indians to collaborate with them by offering to buy vast quantities of such delicacies as bison tongue.

Tensions between the Whites and the Plains Indians increased during the 1870's. On July 5, 1876, newspapers reporting celebrations of the young nation's Centennial reported also the news of a humiliating defeat. The elite Seventh Cavalry, a tough outfit of 260 men, which was organized specifically for killing Plains Indians—and led by Lieutenant Colonel Custer—had been annihilated on June 25 by a combined force of Sioux and Cheyenne in the battle of Little Bighorn. But for Sitting Bull and Crazy Horse, the victory over Custer had been empty, and only marked the beginning of the end for the Plains Indians. From that time on troops pursued them mercilessly from waterhole to waterhole; their women and children were slaughtered before their eyes, their encampments and their riches burned. The glory and the poetry had gone out of the Plains Indians. Mighty chiefs emerged from hiding as miserable fugitives, hungry and without bullets for their guns. The survivors, like so many cattle, were herded onto reservations, where rough handling, cheap whiskey, starvation, exposure, and disease severely depleted their numbers.

The very end of the Plains culture can be dated exactly. In 1890 the surviving Plains Indians enthusiastically listened to a native messiah who foretold the return of dead Indians and the magical disappearance of the Whites. Alarmed, the United States government sent out cavalry to suppress this Ghost Dance, as it was called. While being placed under arrest, Sitting Bull was accidentally killed; and some three hundred Sioux, mostly women and children waiting to surrender at Wounded Knee Creek, South Dakota, were massacred by trigger-happy troops. Wounded Knee marked the end of any hopes the Plains Indians still cherished. The Ghost Dance had proven as make-believe as the rest of their improbable culture.

Suggestions for Further Reading

Several books deal in general fashion with the westward movement of settlers in North America. The standard work is Ray A. Billington, *Westward Expansion* (rev. ed.; Macmillan, 1967), but more relevant here is his *The Far Western Frontier, 1830–1860** (Harper & Row, 1956). See also *The New Country: A Social History of the American Frontier, 1776–1890** (Oxford University Press, 1974) by Richard A. Bartlett. The basic studies of the doctrine of Manifest Destiny are A. K. Weinberg, *Manifest Destiny** (Johns Hopkins Press, 1935) and Frederick Merk, *Manifest Destiny and Mission in American History: A Reinterpretation** (Knopf, 1963).

The standard survey of Mexican-American history is Carey McWilliams, *North from Mexico: The Spanish-Speaking People of the United States** (Lippincott, 1949). See also Matthew S. Meier and Feliciano Rivera, *The Chicanos: A History of Mexican Americans** (Hill and Wang, 1972). Regional history is stressed in Ernesto Galarza, Herman Gallegos, and Julian Samora, *Mexican Americans in the Southwest** (McNally and Loftin, 1969).

The overland migration is treated exhaustively in John D. Unruh, Jr., *The Plains Across: The Overland Emigrants and the Trans-Mississippi West, 1840–1860* (University of Illinois Press, 1979). Two studies of women on the frontier are Joanna L. Stratton, *Pioneer Women: Voices from the Kansas Frontier* (Simon and Schuster, 1981) and Julie Roy Jeffrey, *Frontier Women** (Hill and Wang, 1979).

The Chinese immigration to the West Coast of the United States has received very little attention from historians. Virtually the only works on the subject are Mary Coolidge, *Chinese Immigration* (Henry Holt, 1909), which was written with the hope of reopening immigration after it was brought to a halt by the Chinese Exclusion Act of 1882, and Gunther Barth, *Bitter Strength: A History of the Chinese in the United States, 1850–1870* (Harvard University Press, 1964). A recent study of the reception met by Chinese immigrants in America is Stuart C. Miller, *The Unwelcome Immigrant: The American Image of the Chinese, 1785–1882** (University of California Press, 1969). The conflict between the Chinese immigrants and Americans is described in Alexander Saxton, *The Indispensable Enemy: Labor and the Anti-Chinese Movement in California** (University of California Press, 1971) and Elmer Sandmeyer, *The Anti-Chinese Movement in California** (University of Illinois Press, 1939). In *The Challenge of the American Dream: The Chinese in the United States** (Wadsworth, 1971), Francis L. K. Hsu provides a general introduction to the entire Chinese experience here. For an account of some of the problems that the Chinese faced in the United States, see Herbert

* Available in paperback edition.

Asbury, *The Barbary Coast: An Informal History of the San Francisco Underworld* (Knopf, 1933) and Victor Nee and Brett de Bar Nee, *Longtime Californ': A Documentary History of an American Chinatown* (Pantheon Books, 1973).

Two basic anthropological studies of the Plains Indians are E. A. Hoebel, *The Cheyennes: Indians of the Great Plains* (Holt, Rinehart and Winston, 19603), and R. H. Lowie, *Indians of the Plains* (McGraw-Hill, 1954). For the impact of the horse on Indian culture, see F. G. Roe, *The Indian and the Horse* (University of Oklahoma Press, 1955). Mari Sandoz movingly recounts the breakup of the Plains Indian culture in *Cheyenne Autumn* (Hastings House, 1953). The defeat of the Sioux is described in Robert Utley, *Last Days of the Sioux Nation* (Yale University Press, 1963). United States Government policy is described in M. Thomas Bailey, *Reconstruction in Indian Territory: A Story of Avarice, Discrimination, and Opportunism* (Kennikat Press, 1972). Thomas Berger's novel *Little Big Man* (Dial, 1964) presents an authentic picture of elements of Plains Indian culture.

A 1
B 2
C 3
D 4
E 5
F 6
G 7
H 8
I 9
J 0